STUDIES IN
EARLY
CHRISTIANITY

A Collection of Scholarly Essays

edited by
Everett Ferguson
ABILENE CHRISTIAN UNIVERSITY

with
David M. Scholer
NORTH PARK COLLEGE AND THEOLOGICAL SEMINARY

and
Paul Corby Finney
CENTER OF THEOLOGICAL INQUIRY

A Garland Series

CONTENTS OF SERIES

VOLUME XI

Conversion, Catechumenate, and Baptism in the Early Church

edited with introductions by

Everett Ferguson

Garland Publishing, Inc.
New York & London
1993

Library of Congress Cataloging-in-Publication Data

Conversion, catechumenate, and baptism in the early church / edited
by Everett Ferguson.
    p.   cm. — (Studies in early Christianity ; v. 11)
    English, French, and German.
    Includes bibliographical references.
    ISBN 0–8153–1071–4 (alk. paper)
    1. Evangelistic work—History—Early church, ca. 30–600.
2. Conversion—History of doctrines—Early church, ca. 30–600.
3. Catechumens—History—Early church, ca. 30–600. 4. Baptism—History—Early church, ca. 30–600. 5. Church history—
Primitive and early church, ca. 30–600. I. Ferguson, Everett,
1933–   . II. Series.
BR195.E9C66   1993
270.1—dc20
                                 92–40951
                                 CIP

Printed on acid-free, 250-year-life paper
Manufactured in the United States of America

Contents

Series Introduction

Christianity has been the formative influence on Western civilization and has maintained a significant presence as well in the Near East and, through its missions, in Africa and Asia. No one can understand Western civilization and the world today, much less religious history, without an understanding of the early history of Christianity.

The first six hundred years after the birth of Jesus were the formative period of Christian history. The theology, liturgy, and organization of the church assumed their definitive shape during this period. Since biblical studies form a separate, distinctive discipline, this series confines itself to sources outside the biblical canon, except as these sources were concerned with the interpretation and use of the biblical books. During the period covered in this series the distinctive characteristics of the Roman Catholic and Eastern Orthodox Churches emerged.

The study of early Christian literature, traditionally known as Patristics (for the church fathers), has experienced a resurgence in the late twentieth century. Evidences of this are the flourishing of a new professional society, the North American Patristics Society, a little over twenty years old; the growing number of teachers and course offerings at major universities and seminaries; the number of graduate students studying and choosing to write their dissertations in this area; the volume of books published in the field; and attendance at the quadrennial International Conferences on Patristic Studies at Oxford as well as at many smaller specialized conferences. This collection of articles reflects this recent growing interest and is intended to encourage further study. The papers at the International Conferences on Patristic Studies from the first conference in 1951 to the present have been published in the series *Studia Patristica,* and interested readers are referred to these volumes for more extensive treatment of the topics considered in this series of reprints and many other matters as well.

The volumes in this series are arranged topically to cover biography, literature, doctrines, practices, institutions, worship, missions, and daily life. Archaeology and art as well as writings are drawn on in order to give reality to the Christian movement in its early centuries. Ample attention is also given to the relation of Christianity to pagan thought and life, to the Roman state, to Judaism, and to doctrines and practices that came to be judged as heretical or schismatic. Introductions to each volume will attempt to tie the articles together so that an integrated understanding of the history will result.

The aim of the collection is to give balanced and comprehensive coverage. Early on I had to give up the idealism and admit the arrogance of attempting to select the "best" article on each topic. Criteria applied in the selection included the following: original and excellent research and writing, subject matter of use to teachers and students, groundbreaking importance for the history of research, foundational information for introducing issues and options. Preference was given to articles in English where available. Occasional French and German titles are included as a reminder of the international nature of scholarship.

The *Encyclopedia of Early Christianity* (New York: Garland, 1990) provides a comprehensive survey of the field written in a manner accessible to the average reader, yet containing information useful to the specialist. This series of reprints of Studies in Early Christianity is designed to supplement the encyclopedia and to be used with it.

The articles were chosen with the needs of teachers and students of early church history in mind with the hope that teachers will send students to these volumes to acquaint them with issues and scholarship in early Christian history. The volumes will fill the need of many libraries that do not have all the journals in the field or do not have complete holdings of those to which they subscribe. The series will provide an overview of the issues in the study of early Christianity and the resources for that study.

Understanding the development of early Christianity and its impact on Western history and thought provides indispensable insight into the modern world and the present situation of Christianity. It also provides perspective on comparable developments in other periods of history and insight into human nature in its religious dimension. Christians of all denominations may continue to learn from the preaching, writing, thinking, and working of the early church.

Introduction

What was the appeal of Christianity? Why did people become Christians? Why did Christianity win the religious and philosophical competition for the loyalty, or at least adherence, of people in the Roman empire? How did one become a Christian? These are among the questions explored in this volume.

The motives of converts varied. The testimonies of certain individuals, for instance an intellectual such as Justin, may not be representative of others and especially not of the ordinary people. The experience of such a notable convert as Augustine, although influential in modern times as in some ways normative for a conversion experience, appears unique. The conversion, if that is the right way to describe it, of Constantine had profound consequences for Christian faith and practice as well as for the Roman state.

A. D. Nock's classic book on *Conversion* defined the difference between conversion and adhesion and set the phenomenon of Christian conversion in the context of the religious history of the time.[1] The chapter from that book reprinted here sets the stage for the rest of the volume by examining the social circumstances involved in the spread of Christianity.

Ramsay MacMullen identifies two types of conversion to Christianity, that of the educated elite and that of the uneducated masses. Justin Martyr (on whom see further in Volumes I and VIII) and Augustine (Volumes I and frequently in this series) represent the conversion of intellectuals to Christianity. They were selected as two of the case studies in Nock's book. Justin identifies some of the factors, as he saw them in his conversion (Skarsaune); Augustine's conversion invites the consideration of psychological factors (Daly). MacMullen has been especially concerned about the conversion of the common people to Christianity. He has emphasized the place of the miraculous in demonstrating the power of the Christian God and in appealing to the masses.[2]

W. H. C. Frend takes a different look at the process by which Christianity eventually spread from the cities into rural areas. Christianity also won out with the imperial house, as a result of which Christianity became the official religion of the Roman empire (Case, a pioneer in the social history of Christianity, and Ehrhardt, trained in Roman law before turning to ecclesiastical history) and received acceptance and support.

Constantine was the most famous convert to Christianity.[3] Also, his conversion had the greatest consequences for Christianity. Hence, several articles relevant to him are here, even if their theme might belong elsewhere in this series, for it seemed desirable to have the studies on Constantine grouped together.[4] Our principal source for the life of Constantine is Eusebius of Caesarea, and Storch discusses the image of Constantine projected by Eusebius, an image harmonious with that expected from a panegyrist of an emperor[5]. Eusebius was not an impartial source, so there have been various efforts to get behind or go around Eusebius's portrait.[6] MacMullen treats the conversion of Constanine in relation to the motif of the miraculous that his other writings stressed.[7] The contemporary Christian ideological and theological interpretations of Constantine are the subject of studies by Gillman and Azkoul (see also the articles in Volume VII). The definitive change of the church in the Roman Empire from a persecuted to a tolerated people came in 313. The "Edict of Milan" is often considered a misnomer, on the grounds that an agreement between Constantine and Licinius at Milan was issued by the latter only later, and from elsewhere. Anastos goes against the tide of scholarly opinion in defending the traditional designation.

The process of becoming a Christian became standardized quite early. The training for church membership (the catechumenate) aimed to preserve the distinctiveness of the church by a period of moral testing, psychological preparation, and doctrinal instruction. The catechumenate was the principal tool for inculcating Christian perspectives and values to new converts. E. Glenn Hinson has even argued that it was the principal tool in the missions of the early church.[8] Folkemer gives a helpful general survey of this training. There has been more work done in French than in English on the catechumenate, especially by J. Daniélou and A. Turck.[9] An important structure and content of the catechetical instruction was provided by the biblical story of the history of salvation.[10]

Baptism was closely connected with the imparting of the essentials of the faith and was a profession of faith by the candidate. The baptismal formula was itself influential in doctrinal developments. The process of teaching, confession, and baptism followed by the eucharist is, according to L. DeBruyne, reflected in early Christian art. For the confession of faith made at baptism in response to the teaching given in the catechumenate, the reader is referred to Volume IV and its article on the

Apostles' Creed as well as the article by Carpenter in this volume, which emphasizes that there were no early fixed creedal formulas. An early and widespread practice was for the candidate to confess his/her faith in response to questions (an interrogatory creed), but it became common, especially after the rise of infant baptism, for the Trinitarian faith to be expressed in the words spoken by the officiant (Whitaker).

Baptism was the dividing line between the church and the world. It was the climax of conversion and the entrance into the church. Much mischief in the history of Christian thought has come from the practice of treating baptism in connection with the "sacraments" or as part of other categories to which it did not belong in the life of the church. Hence, baptism and related topics are treated here as part of the context in which it was experienced in early Christianity, namely in relation to conversion and incorporation into the body of Christ. As with baptism, the other "sacraments" are discussed in these volumes in their natural context in the life of early Christianity, instead of being grouped together according to an artificial category from later Christian thought.

Although modern Christianity displays a variety of theologies of baptism, the early church had a fairly uniform doctrine of baptism (Ferguson, "Baptismal Motifs"). As the boundary between the church and the world, baptism was given great ceremonial development in order to emphasize its importance. There was also a tendency to emphasize the water itself more than the act of obedience, some would say at the expense of the Spirit and faith, and so there developed the practice of consecrating the water.[11] The calling of the Spirit on the baptismal waters arose when baptism was no longer normally administered in running water (in Greek, "living water").[12]

Modern scholars debate the origins of infant baptism. The interpretation based on inscriptional evidence that the practice arose with the "emergency baptisms" of children with serious illnesses (Ferguson, "Inscriptions") is supported not only by Tertullian (*On Baptism* 18, cited in the article) but also by Gregory of Nazianzus, *Oration* 40.28.[13] The liturgical evidence is decisive that the baptismal ceremonies were designed with adults in mind and had to be adapted when infant baptism became common (Didier). There were debates in the ancient church over the validity of baptism administered by heretics and schismatics (Kirchner). Eventually the view of the objective validity of baptism regardless of the person performing the act came to prevail, because one's salvation could not be left dependent on the (uncertain) standing of the administrator.

Notes

1. Oxford: Clarendon, 1933. Evangelism as viewed from inside the church is presented by Michael Green, *Evangelism in the Early Church* (Grand Rapids: Eerdmans, 1970).

2. Ramsay MacMullen, *Christianizing the Roman Empire, A.D. 100–400* (New Haven: Yale, 1984); see also his "Conversion: A Historian's View," *The Second Century* 5 (1985/86):67–81 and in the same issue the responses by W. S. Babcock (pp. 82–89) and M. D. Jordan (pp. 90–96) and the independent paper by L. Michael White, "Adolf Harnack and the 'Expansion' of Early Christianity: A Reappraisal of Social History" (pp. 97–127), evaluating Harnack's *The Mission and Expansion of Christianity in the First Three Centuries* (tr. of 2nd German ed.; New York, 1908). For more on missions see Volume XII.

3. Note especially Henry Chadwick, "Conversion in Constantine the Great," in *Studies in Church History* 15, ed. Derek Baker (Oxford: Basil Blackwell, 1978), 1–13.

4. One exception is Gregory T. Armstrong, "Church and State Relations: The Changes Wrought by Constantine," *Journal of Bible and Religion* 32 (1964):1–7, reprinted in Volume VII. Cf. also his "Constantine's Churches: Symbol and Structure," *Journal of the Society of Architectural Historians* 33 (1974):5–16, reprinted in Volume XVIII.

5. N. H. Baynes, "Eusebius and the Christian Empire," *Mélanges Bidez* (Brussels: Secrétariat de l'Institut, 1934), 13–18, reprinted in *Byzantine Studies and Other Essays*, pp. 168–172, parallels the Hellenistic philosophy of kingship and the Christian theory of Eusebius.

6. E.g., N. H. Baynes, *Constantine the Great and the Christian Church* (London: British Academy, 1932); T. D. Barnes, *Constantine and Eusebius* (Cambridge: Harvard UP, 1981). A modern rave notice for Constantine is P. Keresztes, *Constantine: A Great Christian Monarch and Apostle* (Amsterdam: J. C. Gieben, 1981).

7. See also his book on *Constantine* (New York: Dial, 1969).

8. *The Evangelization of the Roman Empire: Identity and Adaptability* (Macon, Ga.: Mercer UP, 1981).

9. J. Daniélou and R. du Charlat, *La Catéchèse aux premiers siècles* (Paris: Fayard-Mame, 1968); A. Turck, *Evangélisation et catéchèse aux deux premiers siècles* (Paris: Cerf, 1962);

10. J. Daniélou, "L'Histoire de salut dans la Catéchèse," *La Maison-Dieu* 30 (1952):19–35, who exaggerates the difference between Irenaeus and Augustine in their approaches; E. Ferguson, "Irenaeus' *Proof of the Apostolic Preaching* and Early Catechetical Instruction," *Studia Patristica* 18.3 (1989):119–140.

11. J. D. C. Fisher, "The Consecration of Water in the Early Rite of Baptism," *Studia Patristica* 2 (1957): 41–46.

12. Th. Klauser, "'Taufet in Lebendigem Wasser!' Zum religions-und kulturgeschichtlichen Verständnis von Didache 7,1/3," *Pisciculi . . . F. J. Dölger* (Münster: Aschendorff, 1939), pp. 157–164.

13. This passage is used by David F. Wright, "The Origins of Infant Baptism—Child Believers' Baptism?" *Scottish Journal of Theology* 40 (1987):1–23 to suggest the extension of children's baptism to baby baptism.

XII

THE SPREAD OF CHRISTIANITY AS A
SOCIAL PHENOMENON

THE frame of mind in which a man interested in Christianity approached it was in the first place determined largely by the impressions of it generally current in society as a whole. We must here endeavour to form some idea of the nature of these impressions and to see Christianity not as Irenaeus or Eusebius saw it but as the John Doe and Richard Roe of the second century did. First, however, we must briefly review the early evolution of the Church. The Christian movement started as a ferment within Judaism and was at Jerusalem so placed as to be able to influence other Jews who came up for festivals and visiting Jews from the Dispersion in all its extent. Such personal contacts and carryings explain the presence of disciples of John the Baptist at Ephesus, and the origin of the Christian communities at Rome and Alexandria. There was much coming and going; a rescript of Claudius in 41 refers to the fact that the Alexandrian Jews were in the habit of bringing in their brethren from Syria or Egypt and forbids the practice.

It is not likely that the Apostles in Jerusalem had a missionary aim in the full sense. Difficult as it is to disentangle the threads of our tradition, such sayings as Matt. x. 5–6, '*Go not into the way of the Gentiles, and into any city of the Samaritans: but go rather to the lost sheep of the house of Israel*'; x. 23, '*Ye shall not have gone over the cities of Israel, till the Son of Man be come*'; and xv. 24, '*I am not sent but unto the lost sheep of the house of Israel*', ring true as indications of the character of this first period. The task of the followers of Jesus was ideally to prepare the chosen people for the impending coming of the kingdom and the end of the present world-order; in fact, to prepare as large a proportion as they could. They did this not by an attempt primarily at persuasiveness but by a statement of certain facts which Israel ought to know: *kerygma*, heralding, implies an activity like that of the town-crier. Like the town-crier they made known the resurrection of Jesus as proving his divine mission, the duty of repentance, and the future coming of the Kingdom and the Judgement of God. From their point of view they were a movement within Judaism destined by God to proclaim to it God's summons to fulfil its vocation. This purpose was radical, but in a sense comparable with that of the Pharisees in their beginning, and with that of the people of the New Covenant at Damascus, known to us from the so-called Zadokite work (in which, be it remembered, the official caste at Jerusalem is stigmatized very much as in the Synoptic Gospels). Of necessity the failure of the main body of Jews to respond to their announcement made them, like the Covenanters of Damascus or the Wesleyans in the Church of England, into a community within the community. Their interest in the reception of foreign proselytes was probably no greater than that of normal Judaism: perhaps it was less, for they had a special and pressing duty with their own folk.

There was, however, in this movement, even from the earliest stage, an element which had in it the seeds of development in a further direction. It was the belief that the Spirit of God had been poured out upon the community. It is not necessary here to discuss the

2

precise origins of that belief: what is relevant is that we should observe that the Jewish prophets ascribed this possession to the future Messiah and (later) to the people of Israel, that a general outpouring of Spirit was expected to come in the days of the Messiah, that the belief is very firmly fixed in our tradition, and that this fixation is manifested by the variety of concepts current both as to the possession itself and as to the way in which it was communicated to each individual who adhered to the movement. The consciousness of spirit-possession carried with it the consciousness of authority. The Synoptic Gospels give us an uncertain answer on the nature of this Spirit experience: but in effect the truth is that John the Baptist had appeared in the guise of a prophet and had opened the long-closed flood-gates of the tide of prophecy, and Jesus had thrown them wide. The Synoptists ascribe this consciousness of authority to Jesus personally and represent him as giving it to the Twelve and to the Seventy. This means that individual Jews of the larger world with a wider perspective and freer views would be liable to feel empowered to take a bolder line. Acts preserves the memory of the emergence of such men in its account (ch. vi), of the appointment of the Seven, all men with Greek names and one a proselyte of Antioch: their appointment is expressly described as resulting from complaints of the 'Hellenists', Greek-speaking disciples, against the Jews in the Christian community.

One of the Seven, Stephen, incurred a charge of blasphemy and was put to death after uttering a passionate protest against the behaviour of official Judaism. This incident quickened the pace of events. It made the movement as a whole suspect to Jewish

3

conservatism, which did not shrink from coercive measures: there was a dispersion.

> 'Those who were scattered after the tribulation in Stephen's time went as far as Phoenicia and Cyprus and Antioch, speaking to none save Jews alone. Now there were some of them from Cyprus and Cyrenaica who came to Antioch and talked to Greeks also, preaching the Lord Jesus. And the hand of the Lord was with them and a large number believed and turned to the Lord. And word concerning them reached the ears of the Church in Jerusalem, and they sent Barnabas to Antioch.' (Acts xi. 19–22.)

There first the disciples were called Christians.

This means that in the life of that city, where Greek and Semitic elements blended freely, and where there were many Gentiles who had been drawn to Judaism, there grew up a full self-consciousness in the new movement. While there may be an accentuated conservatism in a group living under these conditions, the inward pressure of Jewish loyalty on reformers was weaker here. To break with tradition in Jerusalem was a hard thing; it was like starting the Protestant Reformation in Rome. In Antioch Judaism and this new sect within it had their being in a community the external culture of which was pagan, in spite of the presence of many Jews.

This community was joined by Paul, who had earlier attached himself to the Christian movement under circumstances which gave him a new attitude. The Twelve in Jerusalem, and no doubt most of their early adherents, had found in the Gospel of Jesus and the Gospel which took shape around Jesus the integration and completion of the religious traditions in which they had always lived. For them he came to fulfil, and not to destroy. Paul, on the other hand, had regarded them and theirs as apostates and had thrown himself heart and soul into the struggle to suppress them. For him to become a Christian meant in the first instance a complete change of face. It is the first conversion to Christianity of which we have knowledge. He brought to it not merely a fresh enthusiasm but also an imperious inner need to discover an interpretation and reconciliation of the old and the new in his religious life.

From Antioch Paul and Barnabas set out to Cyprus, no doubt because it was Barnabas's home: there they operated in synagogues. What induced Paul and Barnabas to go farther afield, whether for instance the puzzling story of the encounter with Elymas before Sergius Paulus covers some real success in the wider world, we do not know. Movements go ahead on their impetus and belief in the Spirit gave an authoritative if disciplined sanction to the sudden impulses of the mind.

According to Acts, this missionary journey and those which succeeded it observed the principle that the message must be preached first in synagogues. It reached in this way the public of Hellenistic Jews, proselytes, sympathizers who would not go the whole way, and others who were drawn to the synagogue by the rumour that an interesting visitor was in the city: gossip travelled fast in an ancient town. From the point of view of the last class the coming of Paul was of the order of the arrival of Dion of Prusa or any other wandering sophist. He talked also to individuals in the market-place at Athens and by special invitation before the Areopagus, but normally he used the synagogue until that was made impossible for him, as at Corinth.

5

where he taught for eighteen months in the house of Justus (xviii. 7), and at Ephesus, where he used the lecture hall of Tyrannus (xix. 9); even so at the next town he went to the synagogue; at Rome of necessity he taught in his own quarters (xxviii. 16 ff.). At Lystra he spoke perforce to the multitude (xiv. 15 ff.), but otherwise he did not, like a wandering Cynic, address popular audiences at random.

This is no doubt characteristic of the early spread of the movement. The world as a whole did not know much of Christians as distinct from Jews till the fire of Rome in 64, when Nero seized on them as scapegoats to satisfy popular resentment and made the admission of Christianity proof of guilt. Thereafter they were in the public mind, rather than in the public eye, as the object of the general odium directed against the Jews for being an anti-social and highly cohesive body, and of the special odium incurred by their reputation as incendiaries, revolutionaries, and generally abominable. But they were not conspicuous. The works directed against Christianity do not allude to out-of-door preaching. In the second century literary works were written in defence of the new faith, but there is no indication that they were read by any save Christians or men on the way to be such or professed students of the movement such as Celsus. There was a school of religious education at Alexandria at the end of the second century, but it did not advertise its existence, and presumably people were brought to it or came to it as a result of incidental knowledge of it. There were no visible out-of-door ceremonials, no temples recognizable as such till much later, and no priesthood displaying its character by its dress or its tonsure, or (in the early stages) its abstinence from secular employments. I mean that the man in the street did not know this as a type like the priests of Cybele or Isis. The magistrate did, as we see from the singling out of Ignatius for punishment. The one Christian type known to the populace was that of the martyr.

We must seek to make clear to ourselves what a martyr was from a non-Christian point of view. Law has been defined as the interference of the State in the actions and passions of humanity. The martyr is the man who resists this interference, who claims that his resistance is based on other and higher sanctions, and who will not concede a point even if compliance would save him from the consequences of his previous disobedience. Often he welcomes the opportunity of bearing witness to the faith which is in him. For the Christian there was no doubt how he must act. 'Whosoever therefore shall confess me before men, him will I confess also before my Father which is in heaven. But whosoever shall deny me before men, him will I also deny before my Father which is in heaven' (Matt. x. 32–3). To fail at this point was the supreme betrayal and damnation; to succeed, the supreme proof of love and assurance of Heaven. Herein Christianity follows a Jewish tradition which crystallized in the time of the Maccabees and appeared again under Caligula: to die rather than break the law was the ideal way of hallowing God's name.

We have to see this as did pagan spectators. They knew similar situations. Dionysus in the *Bacchae*, appearing as one of his priests and standing before Pentheus, is a perfect type: he cannot yield to the king, having received his commission from the god in person and he knows that the god will deliver him when he wills. Four centuries later this scene comes into Horace's mind as an illustration of the front which the wise man can present to hostile circumstances (*Epistles*, i. 16.73). Socrates again, in Plato's *Apology*, p. 29 c, makes the explicit statement :

'If you should say to me, *O Socrates, at the moment we will not hearken to Anytus, but we release you on this condition, that you no longer abide in this inquiry or practise philosophy—and if you are caught still doing this, you will be put to death*, if then you would release me on these conditions, I should say to you, *You have my thanks and affection, men of Athens, but I will obey the god rather than you and, while I have breath and power, I will not desist from practising philosophy.*'

Further, in *Crito* we are taught that he respected the laws of the city and would not run away. For him safety was not enough: he had to witness, not indeed to a dogma (for he had none) but to the imperious validity of his vocation.

The blood of martyrs is the seed of the Church: the death of Socrates created the type of wisdom and virtue standing in heroic opposition to a world which can kill but which does not have the last word. We have seen that philosophic martyrs were not lacking later. Epictetus, in a discourse *On Firmness*, thus sets forth the lesson that we must fulfil the duties to which we are called (i. 29. 45). If a man is told to lay aside his purple-striped robe and go forth in rags, how will he do it? As a witness called by God. '*Come and bear witness to me: for you are worthy to be brought forward as a witness by me.*' Elsewhere he remarks (iii. 24. 112):

'Zeus wished to make me obtain from myself the proof of this and himself to know whether he has in me such a soldier, such a citizen as he should and to produce me before the rest of men as a witness to what things are unworthy of choice. Behold, all of you, your fears are false, your desires are vain. . . . Zeus shows me to men in poverty, out of office, in sickness: he sends me to Gyara, he carries me off to prison, not in hatred nor in neglect . . . but by way of training me and using me as a witness to others.'

Again Epictetus tells of the answer which Helvidius gave to Vespasian's message forbidding him to attend the meeting of the Senate (i. 2. 19):

'It is in your power to forbid me to be a senator: but while I am I must attend.' 'Well, but when you attend keep silence.' 'Do not ask my opinion and I will be silent.' 'But I must ask it.' 'And I must say what seems right to me.' 'If you do I will put you to death.' 'Well, did I say to you that I was immortal? You will do your part and I mine. It is your part to put me to death, mine to die without a quiver, yours to send me into exile, mine to go without repining.'

So in a passage from Porphyry's *Letter to Marcella* quoted earlier (p. 185) the word *martys* is used of the constant witnessing to one's tenets by one's actions. Of course the word *martys* is not a title; it is a predicate describing the role of individuals who by their conduct testify to the goodness of the scheme of the universe; so Seneca says of the Cynic Demetrius, 'He is not a teacher of the truth but a witness to it' (*Epistles*, 20. 9).

We have spoken earlier of the life of Apollonius by Philostratus. It tells how Apollonius was brought before Tigellinus (iv. 44); there was a miracle, and Apollonius expressed his utter indifference. 'The God who allows him to be terrifying allows me to be unterrified.' The judge feared that he might be fighting

against God. Later, Domitian was said to desire him
to stand his trial for treason. Apollonius went volun-
tarily to Rome, holding on the way at Cicero's villa
a discourse in which he maintained that the wise man
ought to lay down his life for his tenets (vii. 14): 'he
will cleave to all he knows no less than to the sacred
rites in which he was initiated.' When summoned
before Domitian he was ready to trust the inspiration
of the moment (vii. 30): in prison he lifted his leg out
of the fetters and put it back again (vii. 38). He looked
forward to his trial as a dialectical discussion rather
than as a race to be run for his life (viii. 2). The final
charges were (1) Apollonius's peculiar dress, (2) his
being called a god, (3) his prophecy of the plague at
Ephesus, (4) the sacrifice of a boy. Domitian acquitted
him in the open court, which was attended by all the
notables, but kept him for private discussion. Apollonius uttered a few words and vanished from sight.
This type of the philosopher martyr is very notable;
in stories of persecution, Christians are represented as
referring to the condemnation of Socrates as typical
of the evil things done by paganism.

The Neronian persecution may well have suggested
to the onlooker no such analogy. It is not clear that
recantation availed then as it did later: the victims
were socially inferior to the class whose sufferings were
glorified; the charge was in substance incendiarism; and
the proceedings (like the measures against magicians
and astrologers at various times, or Jews and Isiac worshippers under Tiberius, or Jews under Claudius after
tumults) were police measures to secure public order.
Trajan wrote very pertinently to Pliny: 'We cannot
establish any universal ordinance which should have,

so to speak, a fixed form' (x. 97). Some popular emotion of sympathy might of course be aroused (Tacitus says it was, *Annals*, xv. 44), such as occurred in A.D. 61 when it was proposed to put to death the whole household of Pedanius Secundus, who had been murdered by one of his slaves: the execution had to be carried out under strong military protection. But from the time of Domitian probably, Trajan certainly, it was clear that 'obstinacy' was punished and that a Christian on trial for being such could save his life by recantation. To a calm person like Pliny this seemed a blameworthy quality: 'I did not doubt that, whatever it was they admitted, their pertinacity and unbending obstinacy ought to be punished'; and in like manner Marcus Aurelius says (xi. 3):

'What a fine thing is the soul which is ready if it must here and now be freed from the body and either extinguished or scattered or survive. But let this readiness come from a personal judgement and not out of a mere spirit of opposition, like that of the Christians; let it be in a reasoned and grave temper, capable of convincing another, and without theatricality.'

Now this word *theatricality* deserves careful consideration, for there was a certain fascination about self-chosen death. We see this not only in the Stoic cult of suicide in the first century of our era (it is then the Stoic form of martyrdom *par excellence*), but also in the constantly recurrent literary commonplace of the Gymnosophistae (Brahmins) who threw themselves into the fire and thereby made a demonstration against Alexander, and again in the frequent tendency of Christians in times of persecutions to force themselves on the notice of the magistrates by tearing down images

11

or by other demonstrations, with which we may compare the offer of Rusticus Arulenus to veto the decree of the Senate against Thrasea. Clement of Alexandria says:

> 'We ourselves blame those who have leapt on death: for there are some who are not really ours but share only the name, who are eager to deliver themselves over in hatred against the Creator, poor wretches, passionate for death. We say that these men commit suicide and are not martyrs, even if they are officially executed.'

This popular attitude has various causes—a sort of fascination of death, the aura surrounding voluntary death in legend and life, a desire for theatrical prominence, the very widespread idea of the body as a prison for the soul, and pessimism. In Christianity there is the special conviction that it was the way to life, as in Ignatius, who begs the Roman community not to make interest to save him. *Amor mortis conturbat me.*

We must linger a little longer on these considerations, for they bear materially on our understanding of the ethos of the time. The Hellenistic period saw the birth of the novel. The earliest complete specimen, that of Chariton, is not later than the second century of our era, and the genre is certainly earlier. It is an imaginary narrative based on romantic history: the specimens preserved have plots which conform closely to a type. A young married couple (in later forms a pair of lovers) are separated by circumstances, pass through a series of tragic and violent misfortunes, and are finally reunited. The misfortunes generally include some very close approximation to death, often something which to the one member of the pair appears to be in truth the other's death, and generally the flogging of one or

both parties, sometimes other tortures. Throughout
there is an accent of theatrical pose. One incident may
suffice. In the romance of Achilles Tatius (vi. 20–1)
Thersandros has in his power the heroine Leucippe.
She refuses to accept his advances and he begins to
threaten. Leucippe says: 'If you wish to exercise
tyranny, then I wish to suffer it, only you shall not take
my virtue.' And she looks at Sosthenes and says: 'Bear
witness how I face evil treatment: for you wronged me
even more.' Sosthenes is ashamed at having been caught
out and says: 'She should be scourged with whips,
master, and subjected to countless tortures, that she
may learn not to despise her master.' 'Do as Sosthenes
bids,' says Leucippe, 'for he gives excellent advice.
Produce your tortures. Bring a wheel: here are my
hands, let him stretch them. Bring whips: here is my
back, let him beat it. Bring fire: here is my body, let
him burn it. Bring a sword: here is my neck, let him
cut it. Behold a novel contest: one woman contends
against all tortures and conquers everything. . . . Tell
me, are you not afraid of your Artemis, but do you
force a maiden in the Maiden's city? O Mistress, where
is thy bow?' A little later she says, 'Arm yourself
therefore: now take against me your whips, wheel,
fire, sword: let your counsellor Sosthenes enter battle
with you. I naked, alone, a woman, have one weapon,
freedom, which is neither crushed by blows nor cut by
the sword nor burnt by fire.' Earlier (v. 18) she writes
to her lover Clitopho: 'For you have I left my mother
and entered on wanderings. For you I have suffered
shipwreck and robbers, for you I have become a victim
and scapegoat and died twice already, for you I have
been sold and bound with iron and carried a hoe and

dug the earth and been scourged; and all that I may be to another man what you have been to another woman? Heaven forbid!' Such episodes are recurrent in these novels.

This is popular writing of a type hardly mentioned by superior persons—except by the Emperor Julian, when in his account of what pagan priests should read he says, 'It would be suitable for us to handle histories composed about real events: but we must avoid all the fictions written of old in the style of history, love subjects and everything in fact of that type.' The Greek novel bears witness to the fascination exercised by the thought of invincible chastity and beautiful young persons facing pain with reckless readiness, features which we find again in hagiographic romance. Leucippe's utterance is the popular equivalent of Seneca's: 'Here is a contest worthy of God, a wise man at grip with Fortune.' The same attitude appears in the school exercises in declamation of the period, for instance in one speech in the collection passing under Quintilian's name (*Declamationes maiores*, vii) in which a poor man offers to be tortured, taunts his rich adversary with fears as to what he might then say, and enlarges on the sufferings which he is prepared to face.

Lucan's epic on the civil war is written in this tone: one episode which may be mentioned is that of the cutting off of a detachment of Caesar's men under Vulteius in the Adriatic. Before the last conflict against overwhelming odds Vulteius says to his men (iv. 492): 'The gods have set us on a boat which allies and foes can both see: the waters, the land, the island with its soaring rocks will all give witnesses; the two opposing forces will watch from different shores. You, Fortune,

14

are preparing some great and memorable example by what happens to us.' That is it: they have the spotlight on them, and they will go into the *examples*, the collections of instances of valour and other virtues compiled

> To point a moral or adorn a tale.

In all this there is a certain stridency of self-expression. Man struts his hour upon the stage: he must not fail to make an impression on the audience of the present and future. He will in any event die, but let him, like a Homeric hero, die 'having done something great to come to the ears of those who are to be'. To most of us it is obvious that our portion after death will very soon be oblivion. The men of the ancient world lived in more limited circles, which clung to memories and preserved them. The prospect of being forgotten was to them very terrible, and to avoid that a man would do and suffer much.

It is some distance from words to deeds, but Lucian gives us an extraordinary story of how a Cynic Peregrinus, who had been a Christian, burnt himself to death on a pyre at Olympia as a way of apotheosis. Cassius Dio (liv. 9. 10), in commenting on the self-immolation of an Indian at Athens in 20 B.C., says:

> 'Wishing to die either because he was of the caste of sophists (i.e. Brahmins) and was therefore moved by ambition, or because of old age, in accordance with ancestral custom, *or because he wished to make a display for the benefit of Augustus (who had come there) and of the Athenians*, he was initiated into the mysteries of the goddess . . . and cast himself alive into the fire.

It is important to realize that the common metaphor

4039   D d

15

of life as a stage on which Fortune casts us for different roles is no superficial metaphor.

To return to methods: the definite rejection of the new ideas by conservative Judaism and the withering of Jewish Christianity after the disaster of 70 and its sequel in 135 cut the connexion with the synagogue, though its members and the fringe of interested Gentiles remained a source of individual converts. Christianity had by now its own unobtrusive places of meeting. Pliny's Christians met before dawn, but the place is unspecified although, as Pliny tells us, the numbers involved were considerable. Celsus taunts them with privately doing and teaching the things which seem good to them, and speaks of Christian rites as performed in cobblers' shops or fullers' shops.

We do not hear of open-air preaching to large audiences. For one thing, the early movement probably included few people of sufficient rhetorical skill to be an attraction; for another, at any time from the Flavian period onwards, even when there was no direct persecution, there was the possibility: it was wiser not to be provocative, except perhaps in Anatolia, where the numerical strength of the movement early became considerable. We find mass conversion in Pontus in the third century. There Gregory the Thaumaturge, when he came, was a man far superior in culture to the *milieu* in which he preached.

It has been remarked earlier that Christianity had no outdoor ceremonies capable of catching the eye. Their own private worship was not likely to excite interest. Those on the way to baptism were excluded from the Eucharist proper; so were outsiders. The group which met for these purposes in any place would

16

be composed of people who knew one another, and while there would be visitors from other communities they would have letters of introduction. Of course in the larger bodies, as for instance at Rome, it would no doubt have been possible for an inquisitive person to find his way in, as Burton did to Mecca. If he did, he was probably very disappointed. He saw no orgies, and he saw little which would suggest to him worship as he knew it. He certainly witnessed nothing so moving as the rite described by Walter Pater in *Marius the Epicurean*. He heard scriptural readings, a little wearisome, perhaps, by reason of their length, an exhortation like those of the synagogue, and his impression here also may well have been that this was of the nature of a philosophical school. If he was able to stay for the central ceremony, he would have difficulty in recognizing it as cultus in any ordinary sense. The officiants did not use a fixed form of words, followed as in Roman prayers through fear that the supernatural powers invoked would not give what was desired if one syllable or gesture was varied.

The impression made on an educated pagan would probably be that this was of the nature of superstition, that is ungentlemanly popular religion. It might seem to him as extemporary prayer in public worship does to a man brought up in the tradition of the Roman liturgy. The prayer was unusual also in its absence of careful invocation by name—except for the prayers which in certain churches were probably addressed to Jesus—and with reference to favourite seats of worship. The culminating point was but the distribution of bread and wine with a formula, after a long recital of God's mercies. In pagan worship of a mystery

17

type what theology there was grew out of the rite; in
this the rite was till the fourth century a very simple
expression of a theology, with no deeper sense that
would be apparent unless you were in the know. Even
in the fourth century, when the Eucharist acquired
a dignity of ceremonial appropriate to the solemn
worship of the now dominant church, it is not to me
clear either that there was a deliberate copying of the
ceremonial of the mystery dramas or that any special
appeal was made by the ritual to the new mass of
converts. It is surely not without significance that at
Antioch, where there had indeed been substantial
Jewish influence in the Christian community, there
was a tendency in the fourth century for churchmen
to attend merely that part of the service which was
concerned with the reading of scripture and not to join
in the prayers and assist in the celebration of the
Eucharist proper. The elaboration of ceremonial
would appear to be in fact due to the new standing of
Christianity and to the influence of Old Testament
ritual, and perhaps in some measure of the Apocalypse
and its account of the worship performed in Heaven,
certainly to the idea of the union of human and
angelic worship. The one piece of straight copying
is the screen, or *iconostasis*, and that came from the
theatre and not from cultus.

The *True Word* of Celsus which we know from
Origen's refutation and the liberal excerpts therein
contained gives the view taken by a highly educated
pagan of the movement in the latter part of the second
century of our era. To him, as to other onlookers,
Christianity has or is a new rite: to him, writing as he

did from a detached speculative standpoint and maintaining the distinction of superstition and piety (formulated in the Academy and maintained in different ways by Epicureans and Stoics but involving throughout a cultural distinction), in so far as Christianity is or offers a rite it may be compared with other Oriental or popular forms of worship.

> 'The Christians act like folk who put an illogical faith in those who collect alms for the Great Mother and in examiners of portents, and in figures like Mithras and Sabadios or whoever it is on whom a man has chanced, or in visions of Hecate or of some other daemon or daemones. Just as there wicked men often impose on the simplicity of the gullible and lead them where they will, so it is among the Christians. Some will not give or hear reason about their faith, but stick to *Ask no question but believe* and *Thy faith shall save thee* and *The wisdom in the world is a bad thing and the foolishness a good.*'

Later he compares Christianity with Egyptian religion, with its combination of brilliant temples and animal-worship, remarking that the Christians mock at Egyptian piety (which suggests that Celsus has read some of the Christian apologetic writings: in them, as in earlier Jewish apologia, attacks on Egyptian animal-worship are *de rigueur*) although that piety has a symbolic meaning. Again, before describing Christian hole-and-corner preaching, he says, 'We see those in the market-places who make the most infamous demonstrations and beg (i.e. the priests of Dea Suria or Cybele or Isis) would never come into a concourse of men of intelligence or dare to show their tricks there, but are sought after and glorified wherever they see striplings or a crowd of slaves and fools'. He says later,

'They do these things to excite the admiration of the ignorant like those who in Bacchic rites bring forward visions and terrors'. Further, he compares the Mithraic ladder as a symbol of the soul's passage through the spheres with the diagram of a Christian sect (the Ophites) and draws a parallel between Christian thaumaturgy with its foreign names and the names of power in Egyptian magical books.

From the standpoint of morality Celsus makes a contrast between Christianity and its rivals:

> 'Those who invite people to other *teletai* make these preliminary announcements: *Whosoever is pure of hand and wise of tongue*—or again others, *Whosoever is pure from every defilement and has no evil on his conscience and has lived well and justly.* These are the preliminary announcements made by those who provide means of cleaning away sin. But let us hear whom these people invite: *Whosoever*, they say, *is a sinner, whosoever is unwise, whosoever is foolish*—in a word, *whosoever is a wretch—he will be received into the Kingdom of God.'*

He again draws a parallel between Christianity and other religions of salvation when he asks:

> 'If they introduce this one (Christ), and others another, and all have the common formula ready to hand, *Believe if you would be saved, or go away*, what will be done by those who really wish to be saved? Will they cast dice and so get an omen for the path which they are to take and the people whom they are to join?'

Celsus thus far puts Christianity on a level with popular mysteries and immigrant Oriental cults in general. He is not a rationalist and his theism is not purely theoretical. But like most serious thinkers of antiquity he objects to what he regards as the piety of the ignorant and gullible, and he has a genuine moral indignation against ideas which seem incompatible with his high concept of the supernatural.

Yet to Celsus there is a vital distinction between Christianity and these parallel phenomena. To him and to his like Christianity is primarily a mass movement of falling away from tradition, as earlier Suetonius says of the Neronian persecution, which he reckons among the acts of Nero which were not blameworthy (*Nero*, 16. 2), 'There were punished the Christians, a race (*or*, kind; *genus*) of men characterized by a novel and maleficent superstition.' Both the Christians and their opponents came to think of themselves as a new people: and it is clear in the work of Celsus that his real aim was to persuade the Christians not to forget loyalty to the State in their devotion to this new state within the State. Other Oriental incomers were to Celsus mildly contemptible: this was a social phenomenon fraught with danger. It is to be noted that, though the test before Pliny was invocation of the gods in a form prescribed by him, the offering of incense and wine to the Emperor's image and cursing Christ, Trajan's reply indicates that 'prayer to our gods' would be a sufficient indication of conformity to give immunity, and in the serious persecution of Decius only a document recording past piety, the performance of sacrifice and libation, and tasting of the victims in the presence of a commissioner was required. That is to say, there was no formal and explicit abjuration of Christian cultus.

The average man in antiquity has left little record of his thoughts. We know his epitaphs, his dedications, his proverbs, but ancient literature is aristocratic and little interested in the ordinary citizen except as a foil or as the material for a *genre* study. So far as we can infer his attitude to Christianity, it was not altogether unlike that of Celsus. To him, as we saw, it was at first something indistinguishable from Judaism, and then a subdivision which bore the odium of the. fire in Rome and under Domitian was perhaps particularly liable to incur the official wrath with which Jewish proselytism was then visited. In time it became apparent that this was a separate movement of godlessness, with peculiar cohesion and special charities.

He might turn in passionate hatred against this anti-social organization. Persecution was in many cases forced on the magistrates by the crowds, who clamoured, *The Christians to the lions.* We have a very interesting petition from the people of Lycia and Pamphylia to Maximinus in 311–12 (in an inscription at Arycanda) asking him 'that the Christians, who have long been mad, and still continue in their diseased state, be made to stop and not by any foolish new worship to transgress against that which is due to the gods'. The petition is probably inspired and due to men who knew that the Emperor desired to be thus entreated, but it crystallizes a popular attitude.

There was much in ancient feeling to explain this: notably the idea that the welfare of the Roman State hung together with the due performance of the traditional Roman rites (we find an emphasis on the cult of Vesta at the very time of the Decian persecution); the belief in Jonahs—I mean the belief that the misfortunes of the Empire might be due to this widespread apostasy; a general willingness to accept additional rites which made the Christian refusal seem cantankerous and unreasonable; and also a widespread readiness to believe the strange stories of sexual excesses and ritual murder and cannibalism which always attach themselves to a sect which is under the ban of social disapproval. All this was powerful and gave strength to the resistance of paganism. Our concern in the remaining chapters is with the analysis of the attitude of those who heard the word gladly.

Pure curiosity and casual contacts, sometimes due to a wife, might bring a man within its periphery. If he had Judaizing tastes he came naturally; here were the merits of that which had attracted him and he was not treated as one of the lesser breeds without the law. Again, if people died rather than perform a sacrifice which could be as much a matter of convention as standing for a national anthem, the divine name on which they relied might have its effectiveness, and the use of this same name of Jesus in exorcisms and cures by the Christians had its effect. At least it was worth adding to the Egyptian, Babylonian, and Greek names used in magic: 'I adjure you by the god of the Hebrews, Jesus' occurs in the great Paris magical papyrus. But a man's curiosity might lead him further and cause him to hear the preaching. What would he know of it from the outside? Certainly that it would mean his forsaking polytheism: that he must believe in a certain Jesus who had died for man's sins and risen, fulfilling thereby ancient Jewish prophecies; that he must repent and obtain forgiveness of sins and rebirth by a sacrament; that he must live by an ethic of love in a society of like-minded men. The sacrament of rebirth would not bother him: he knew of such, if he had not used them (they were, as we have seen, expensive), and, if he had, there was no objection to one more; in any case

the new content ascribed to rebirth was attractive
(p. 220 below). So much (with the possible exception
of baptism) he would know: what more he might know,
and what he would learn in the community when being
prepared for baptism we shall consider next. Before
we pass to this, one word of caution is perhaps necessary.

We are sometimes told that the unique attractiveness
of the central figure of Christianity as presented in the
Synoptic Gospels was a primary factor in the success
of Christianity. I believe this idea to be a product
of nineteenth-century idealism and humanitarianism.
In early Christian literature those aspects of the Gospel
picture which are now most prominent in homiletic
writing are not stressed, and all the emphasis is on
the superhuman qualities of Jesus, as foreshadowed by
prophecy and shown by miracle and Resurrection and
teaching, and not on his winning humanity. He is
a saviour rather than a pattern, and the Christian way
of life is something made possible by Christ the Lord
through the community rather than something arising
from the imitation of Jesus. The central idea is that of
divinity brought into humanity to complete the plan
of salvation, not that of perfect humanity manifested
as an inspiration; it is *Deus de deo* rather than *Ecce homo*.
The personal attractiveness of Jesus had done much to
gather the first disciples, though even then the impression of power was probably more important than the
impression of love: thereafter the only human qualities
which proved effective were those of individual Christian teachers and disciples.

The success of Christianity is the success of an institution which united the sacramentalism and the philo-

sophy of the time. It satisfied the inquiring turn of mind, the desire for escape from Fate, the desire for security in the hereafter; like Stoicism, it gave a way of life and made man at home in the universe, but unlike Stoicism it did this for the ignorant as well as for the lettered. It satisfied also social needs and it secured men against loneliness. Its way was not easy; it made uncompromising demands on those who would enter and would continue to live in the brotherhood, but to those who did not fail it offered an equally uncompromising assurance.

Vigiliae Christianae 37 (1983) 174-192, E. J. Brill, Leiden

TWO TYPES OF CONVERSION TO EARLY CHRISTIANITY

BY

RAMSAY MACMULLEN

What pagans saw *in* Christianity (in the sense of being drawn to it) depended greatly on what they saw *of* it. Self-evidently, their first allegiance could be inspired only by those parts and aspects of the faith that were openly displayed. So there is one topic to explore: exactly what *was* displayed, undeniably and demonstrably?

And displayed at the moment of conversion, so as to account for it—not when the process was well begun. I therefore exclude consideration of the converts made in Judaea or in or around Jewish communities in Greek cities.

But further: conversion depended greatly on the fit between Christianity and prevailing expectations regarding the world above us. No challenge on all fronts, nor a faith centered in some practice perfectly unacceptable (such as human sacrifice, let us say, or ritual prostitution), could have prevailed. There is a second topic to explore—relatively accessible, at least if we limit our exploration to our surviving texts, their writers, and their readers.

They immediately confine us within a circle constituting less than a tenth of the population. A cultural elite: even St. Paul almost a member, or on the fringes, since he like the pagan Celsus or the convert Justin had added years of further study to a training in mere literacy. The basic elements of their education are well known. In one part of the Greek-speaking world, Egypt, they are known through the whole accumulation of literary papyrus-fragments, in which the Iliad emerges as favorite, the Odyssey a good second; Demosthenes a poor third; Euripides next; then Callimachus, Hesiod, and Plato (and students who were aiming for law explain the popularity of the orator; but Plato's works, like the tenets of Stoicism and other chief doctrines, would circulate mostly in excerpts and condensations, and these would be commonly memorized if not discussed in advanced schools). The whole list makes specific the pair of words, "poets and philosophers," continually

26

used by the Christian Apologists to define the written basis of their opponents' beliefs. Tertullian (*Apol.* 14) in his attack on them looks at the Trojans and Achaeans, at Venus and Mars; moves on to Euripides; next to one of the lyric poets; and so to Plato—Tertullian, a *Latin* Apologist, exactly duplicating the list from Egypt. It was very much one world, that cultural élite we are considering.

Its theology (for pagans who ventured on such speculation) supposed a world above Olympus; at the top, some version, relation, or descendant of Plato's Supreme Being. Pagans could therefore be said, like Christians, to believe in one god, maker of heaven and earth.[1] Visions so abstract, like Immanuel Kant's 'categorical imperative' or Sartre's existentialism today, were more often mentioned, and nodded to in passing, than really understood. Yet the philosophers' notion of one god, perfection complete, above all things, needing nothing, not to be touched by Achilles' spear, Eros' arrows, or the worshipper's prayers, provided a theoretical base for very widespread ideas about the nature of divinity. It precluded whatever was capricious or trivial, deceitful, harmful, or vengeful, foul, wicked, or cruel. No divine being could be anything but beneficent.

The divine *dramatis personae* of literature and myth, however —where did they fit? They stood in sharp opposition to the ideas just outlined. Christian Apologists exploited the opposition between "poets and philosophers" to the full. The philosophers, as Tertullian says (*Apol.* 46.4) "openly destroy your gods and attack your superstitions with their treatises, while you cheer them on, forsooth!" He was quite right. There was Seneca in the Latin West, in a work *Against Superstition* (now largely lost); in the Greek East, there was Heraclitus, not the famous philosopher but a figure belonging to the generation or two before Seneca, writing on myths from a very rationalistic point of view; and both of these writers only summed up and gave greater circulation to convictions long common among the educated, convictions quite incompatible with a literal belief in the stories about the gods; and should not Christians join in the debate? As one of their tormentors sourly remarks, "This is the Christians' custom, to invent many foul calumnies against our gods."[2]

In trying to determine, however, what expectations or presuppositions about religion might await evangelists of Christianity, we should not assume that people's general ideas of godhead had made no broad advances since the days of Homer and Hesiod. Not at all: in the days of Seneca or Tertullian, we do not find them expressing the belief that Apollo takes sides with one mortal against another, or that Zeus might defenestrate some second Hephaestus. The gods had grown up, in company with more advanced moral, and intellectual standards than prevailed in the eighth century B.C. Attacks by Christian polemicists indeed made more public but they did not create the gulf that had long opened between literature and philosophy. They only struck at a bookish vulnerability, not at a living faith.

That living faith, if it had little room for a Supreme Being in its daily concerns, did commonly acknowledge some sort of supremacy of a more familiar, less remote figure, whether Zeus (or Jupiter) as king of all gods, directing them, or presiding over them in looser fashion in the way that Agamemnon had presided among the Achaean chiefs. Either view permitted the very widespread interpretation of local gods as no more than reflections, under various names, of some single one: Zeus was Sarapis was Jupiter was Helios,[3] and similarly Selene was Astarte was Artemis was Diana.

To repeat: none of these beings was harmful, all were kindly to each other—if they were thought to have any interrelationship at all—and kindly toward their worshippers. Prayers went up to them seeking benefits only, not to avert their wrath. We do not find in the non-Christian (and non-Jewish) world much evidence even of punishment by the gods for wicked behavior. It is attested, as we will see below, but not very commonly.

Which raises the question not easily solved by anyone, Christian or not: πόθεν τὸ κακόν; for if divinity is beneficent, where can afflictions and evil deeds originate? If there is any broadly shared view in the Roman world about this matter, it is that the gods, like ourselves though not in the same degree, inhabit a universe they cannot control. They can modify but not entirely direct events like death, disaster at sea, or drought. Sometimes only Chance, Tyche, Fortuna is to blame, sometimes the picture is a little sharper: we find a plague caused by a particular evil power.[4] It can be driven away, then. It is not a god but some lowlier being.

For underneath the gods lie *daimones*. It is best to leave the word in its Greek and, by adoption, its Latin form so as not to confuse it with our word 'demons'. No one asked a *daimon* for a favor (and if that is what is meant by prayer, then no one prayed to one), nor does any *daimon* have his temple or priest. From having been, in Homer and certain later writers, a word applied to the familiar Olympians, *daimon* had sunk down below Olympus to an intermediate though still superhuman and supernatural realm, denoting powers that fill the heavens, fill the air. They are beings without name or dignity but not without capacities that set them above us. Some are beneficent, some the reverse. It is the latter that are invoked or coerced by spells for purposes alien to divinity.[5]

Such, in loose outline, are the views that Christianity must fit or challenge. But in trying to understand in what light it might appear to the holders of those views, two difficulties arise. First, the new faith could only be judged by its visible, audible parts. Yet, as Tertullian says, "no one turns to our literature who is not already Christian"[6]— meaning that, in his opinion, the New Testament and apparently the Apologists like Tertullian himself, Justin, Origen, Minucius Felix and the rest should not be counted as either visible or audible to a pagan audience. Perhaps we should not take Tertullian's remark quite literally. The pagan Celsus in the later second century had read the Bible, if only to refute it. On the other hand, he himself was so instantly forgotten that one of the best-read men of a somewhat later day, Origen, could find no trace of him. Celsus appears to have been a quite minor oddity, then. A few generations later, a governor of Egypt, a man evidently unusually interested in religion, nevertheless shows that he knows almost nothing about Christianity—the judge of the martyr Phileas.[7] Other bits of evidence could be cited to the same effect. So when we speak of people observing and becoming acquainted with Christianity, we should be careful not to draw into our discussion too much detail regarding doctrine or practice. As a parallel, the widespread ignorance about Judaism is instructive.

And if we exclude from our discussion St. Paul's letters, the *Didache*, Clement's letter from Rome, in sum, the bulk of pre-Nicene Christian writings because they are not likely to have been read outside the Church, then as our second difficulty we confront a very puzzling poverty of sources. Just how *can* we discover what that outer face was, that the new religion showed to the unconverted?

The sources that can be used, I think, include three sorts. There are those parts of the Acts of the Apostles in which, at some moment around A.D. 90, the writer described how an earlier evangelist might have been expected to speak (we do not know, of course, what the evangelist really did say). We also have some early apocryphal acts.[8]

29

Second, from about the same period as these last—that is, from the last half of the second century—we have the bulk of the Apologists, to the extent that they really reached non-converts. Third, we have exchanges between the martyrs and their tormentors. As strictly as possible we should try to limit ourselves to things that were specifically and express-ly said to non-believers. We should not use what was written for eastern pagans by Lucian or Galen or what was spoken to an audience in Rome by Fronto and Crescens: they are looking at Christians (at behavior, that is), not at Christianity (that is, at belief).[9]

In the canonical Acts, it may be recalled, there are from the very start some tell-tale mis-perceptions of Christianity, revealing both what people expected in the way of religion and what they were being actually shown. They supposed Peter, Barnabas, and Paul at various junctures to be gods come down to earth,[10] just as they thought Simon Magus the literal embodiment of divine force.[11] They would have better understood the reaction of Peter when he saw Moses and Elijah before him: Should he, he wondered, set up a tabernacle for each of the two on the spot?[12] Pagans also expected the apostles to offer their supernatural gifts for a price, because cures, exorcisms, and prophecies by itinerant wonder-workers evidently were for sale here and there from time to time.[13] These incidents takes us over a great span of the Greek-speaking world, incidentally, from Samaria to the coast, up into Anatolia, and beyond to northeastern Greece. It is in these same lands that we can best become acquainted with non-Christian circles and sources, too, to con-firm in other ways the truth of the glimpses given us by the Acts.

In Philippi, the apostles are by error taken for servants of the All-High God, as a woman of the crowd terms him.[14] Some dominant male deity generally stands out in the worships of both Semitic and Asianic Greek-speaking lands. At Lystra they are taken for gods again. On this occasion, Zeus is thought to have his younger, lesser agent with him, Hermes,[15] just as would be expected—and just as God had Jesus, it might be said: for ditheistic confusion occasionally invades the relation between Father and Son, and would have to be cleared away.[16]

Ordinarily, however, pagans are presented by Christians with a God new but one they can understand: Creator, Lord, Ruler over all things.[17] They betray no uneasiness about the implied picture of a divine monarchy. To be sure, it does not resemble the picture of paganism that is seen from a distance, embracing many worshippers, cities, and regions. Rather, it resembles what could be discovered in the mind of

most single individuals. The distinction is important. In the daily practice of religion, they acknowledged some local deity as supreme without
bothering about other people's preferences in the next county. It is this
as much as the shadow of Plato's Supreme Being in their minds that
allows Tertullian to say, "Do you not grant, from general acceptance,
that there is some being higher and more powerful, like an emperor of
the world, of infinite power and majesty?—for that is how most men
settle divinity: with the enjoyment of the top command in the hands of
one, subordinate tasks distributed among many."[18] So non-Christians
in the world of St. Paul, Justin, or Origen were in reality both polytheist
and monotheist.[19]

But those terms are in fact only a source of extraneous confusion
when they are applied to the centuries and developments we are looking
at. They did not exist in the ancient lexicon of debate.[20] What modern
interpretation conceals and what ancient sources abundantly reveal is a
struggle over the meaning of the word 'god', *theos, deus.*

Christians and non-Christians alike supposed there was a multitude
of supernatural beings above them. Non-Christians acknowledged
Supreme Gods, each one illogically *hypsistos* or *kratistos* or *invictus*;
next, gods of the familiar order (Venus or Hermes) with *daimones* and
lesser spirits beneath them. As to Christians, they proclaimed their own
particular Supreme God; His ministers, angels; what non-believers
probably saw as divinized heroes, Moses and Elijah; with hordes of
daimones or more often little *daimonia* under *their* Supreme God the
Devil, μέγας δαίμων as Origen calls him (*C. Cels.* 1.31) or Prince
(ἀρχηγέτης, I *Apol.* 28) in Justin's term. A pagan governor need find
nothing disturbing, then, in the picture a martyr explains to him, of
"'Adonai the All-High seated above cherubs and seraphs.' Marcianus
says, 'What are cherubs and seraphs?' Acacius answers, 'The agent of
the All-High God and attendant on His lofty seat.'"[21]

There was thus no basis for conflict between the two structures of
belief so long as the nature of 'god' remained undefined. But of course
Christians could not tolerate *that.* In the first place, they must re-define
other people's 'gods'. They called them mere objects, that is, idols. Very
offensive, no doubt, but more for the manner of the accusation than its
matter.[22] Pagan writers in the educated circles they moved in had been
making the same accusation for centuries. There remained the deeds
wrought through forces which pagans called by the name Apollo or
Poseidon or Zeus—miracles beyond denial by Christians, wrought even

31

in their own day, but which they attributed to mere *daimones*;[23] for *theoi* were no more than gods so-called and in quotation-marks.[24] Tertullian asserts and makes use of the terminological argument: "If angels and *daemones* perform the very same feats as your gods, where then lies the superiority of their godhead? ... Is it not better to think, when they do what makes us believe in the gods, that they have *made themselves* gods, rather than that gods should be on a level with angels and *daemones*?"[25] Clearly the word *deus* was to be reserved for a being or beings of commanding power, truly sovereign, independent, superior. As Simon Magus proclaims to a crowd in Rome, " 'He that has a master is not a god.' And when he said this, many said, 'You put it well.' "[26]

But how can superiority which thus defines the word be demonstrated save by measurement against every alternative? How can Christian 'monotheism' in the peculiar meaning of the term we have discovered be asserted save through proving the inferiority of everyone else's 'god'? Here, too, and in a second respect, Christians presented a new definition of divinity—but of their own God, not the pagan ones. Unlike the latter which had for centuries been hymned, acclaimed, portrayed in sculpture or praised in oratorical performances without ever a hint of hostility among them—in this respect as in others entirely departing from Homeric tradition—the focus of worship for Christians was a being perpetually in arms, a jealous God always to be feared.

It is in this light that we ought to understand the exceptional prominence accorded by Christians to their success in overcoming demons through Jesus' name. It could only be seen as a test of strength. The winner was the 'true' god; for truth in that regard must be established precisely through the demonstration of commands given by one and obedience yielded by another. Stories of Jesus' casting out of devils no doubt were among those parts of the faith first to be shown and talked about before unbelievers; exorcism was enjoined by Jesus upon his disciples when He sent them out to the Gentiles,[27] and was performed often by the apostles in their travels, too. Beyond all tales of such confrontations and triumphs, or others like them, found in the apocryphal second-century Acts of John and Peter, there were the boasts of the Apologists. One of them, Tertullian, makes clear what is at stake: through Christian exorcism "that spirit will own himself in truth a *daemon* just as he will elsewhere call himself a 'god', falsely."[28] Exorcism and mastery of spirits—not unknown among pagans but much more practiced and proclaimed before them by Christians—exorcism thus was a demonstration of a theological position and thereby a missionary instrument. It made converts.[29]

Truly divine power also displayed itself in acts of dramatic punishment. That was common knowledge. But the Christian perception was far more dreadful than the pagan, so far at least as we can generalize about the latter. There was certainly no pagan match for the declaration with which Paul introduced his God to a pagan crowd: "The living God, the God of vengeance, the jealous God who has need of nothing ..." had sent him, Paul, to preach repentance from sin.[30] Non-Christians of course knew what they might expect if they defied a deity head-on, by breaking an oath taken in his name or by violating some tabu right in his sacred precinct.[31] They could have found the match for their own stories within the Christian community: the story of Ananias and his wife, for example, who were struck dead for cheating the poor-box. But there was a great deal more to it than that. What Christianity put forward was the fearful novelty of a God who would burn them alive in perpetuity for their very manner of life, spying out their transgressions wherever committed, as He would correspondingly reward the virtuous. Beginning with John the Baptist's and Jesus' preaching, on through Paul's acknowledgement of "the wrath to come," the flames of hell illuminated the lessons of Christianity quite as much as the light of Grace.[32] Actual scenes of speeches delivered to non-believing crowds show that the message was made plain, for example, by Paul at Iconium very much as Jesus had told His desciples to do;[33] and we know that it got through, at least to Celsus. He remarks that Christians "believe in eternal punishments" and "threaten others with these punishments."[34] Clearest of all is the scene in the amphitheater at Carthage where the martyrs, referring to their coming torment, tell the crowd by sign-language. "You, us; but God, you;" but Pionius had elaborated on similar comparisons and warnings of condemnation and suffering, in the city-square of Smyrna.[35] It is likely that this particular article of faith was as widely known as any outside the Church. Despite the Apologists' attempts, however, to make eternal hell-fire credible by reference to Tartarus or to Stoic predictions of universal conflagration, non-believers found it novel and hard to accept. That much we can tell from the way the Apologists handle the subject.

No source indicates that the unconverted saw a necessary connection between eternal torture and an eventual existence after death *in the flesh*. Perhaps the connection was seen, but forgotten in the surprise and controversy roused by the latter proposition itself. "This very flesh will rise?" asks the judge of Phileas martyr, "astonished."[36] His astonishment reminds us once more of the gap that had opened between the poets and philosophers over the course of centuries: an after-life peopled with forms that were recognizably what they had been before death was indeed to be found in primitive Greek religion—for that matter, in Etruscan and therefore early Roman religion. But outside of literature, in the real Roman empire, and among real convictions throughout our period of study, there is hardly a trace of Tartarus, the Elysian Fields, or any such world beyond death. Even a belief in the immortality of the soul alone is hard to find—a fact reflected in the second-century Lucian's saying about Christians: "The poor devils have utterly persuaded themselves that they will be immortal and live forever."[37]

Christian certainty of a heavenly reward for the virtuous was known to pagans, though that knowledge is just barely attested.[38] It made a pair with eternal punishment, and was to be attained, so a non-believer might have heard, through acts of denial of the flesh.[39] This was a teaching often discussed by the Apologists, and the call to repentance had been earlier raised by St. Paul before crowds in Iconium and Athens.[40] Celsus declares all this to be familiar: pagans likewise, so he says, believed in divine retribution for wicked acts, because they were so taught by their initiators into certain cultic mysteries. He himself seems to espouse the view,[41] but it cannot be found anywhere else nor can we be sure what mysteries he is talking about.

Of course what we call paganism was an immensely rich, variform, criscrossed and, above all, a randomly reported world of beliefs, in which no doubt you could find almost anything somewhere. But when allowance has been made for the danger in any attempt at generalizing, there still remain some conclusions to be summed up at this point.

To begin with, we *can* determine what things most educated pagans thought they knew about their own gods, and what other things they were likely to know about the God of the Christians; and we can compare the two credos and find the novelty of the latter to lie in *the dramatic polarities it presented*. This is perceived by a pagan, charging that the Christian "impiously divides the kingdom of god and makes two opposing forces, as if there was one party on one side and another one at variance with it." He means, naturally, Satan and *daimones* that are falsely called 'gods', versus the real deity and His angels.[42] And a

34

Christian for his part points to "a certain rational agency, rival in its operations"[43]—again meaning the Satanic kingdom. Apologists echo such words very often. The dualism, the resulting warfare in supernatural realms, and the implied necessity that you should choose up sides and hate the one and love the other just as you were in turn loved or hated by the divine powers, was absolutely new and strange outside the Judaeo-Christian community; and it was perceived as such.

Moreover, the polarity expressed itself in the most savage terms, terms almost if not entirely novel: in an eternity of torture for the soldiers in the wrong camp, with corresponding bliss for those in the right. Right and wrong took on the starkest outlines. There was no escaping the choice between them, for neutrality counted against you; and this novelty, by which religious preference was for the first time demanded, then itself demanded a corresponding way of life. That, too—the moral implication in religious preference—was all but unheard-of among pagans. Cult and philosophy had been kept quite separate: prayer for benefits was one thing, a Stoic chaplain in one's house was another. But now the two came together. As Apollonius martyr said to his tormentor, it was through belief in "judgement after death, a reward for virtue in the resurrection, with God as judge ... through this above all we have learned how to live a fair life, in the expectation of the hope to come."[44]

Two warring camps above and all around us, life resumed after death in eternal bliss or agony; and a choice in conduct here on earth that was at every moment scrutinized and borne in mind against the day of judgement—these remarkable images in the harshest black and white were all entirely strange. They were presented to an audience that was conservative, perhaps no more than any other people in history, yet deeply and expressly conservative in matters of religious allegiance. That we know from countless proofs and testimonies of pagans addressing other pagans; we know it also from pagans addressing Christians, and from various Christian passages in reply.[45] By what possible means, then, could such aggressively novel novelties win any adherents?

The specific moments and details of conversion seem not to have been much studied. Perhaps it is assumed that the job of winning adherents would have been a rather easy one, given the intrinsic attractions of the new faith—if only it had been fully and fairly understood. However, persecutions intervened and thus the spread of Christianity was impeded unnaturally. The horrific crucifixions of A.D. 64 were only the first in a series. From then on, even if thinly spread out in time and space, renewed attacks drove the evangelists off the streets of most cities.[46] All the more difficult to understand how the faith they preached could be communicated and diffused!

In addressing the difficulty, no doubt the first step must be to assemble some body of evidence. We may begin by excluding consideration of any rewards that awaited new recruits—rewards spiritual, social, emotional, and financial[47]—which came only *after* conversion; for it seems fair to define our topic, conversion, as that experience by which non-believers first became convinced that the Christian God was almighty, and that they must please Him.

The evidence includes a very limited number of persons who speak to us as Christians but were not always such.[48] "I came," says one, "to my faith [in the Scriptures] through the unpretentious style, the artlessness of the speakers, the clear explaining of Creation, the foreknowledge of what was to happen, the excellence of the precepts, and the single ruler over the whole universe. And my soul being taught of God, I have learned that [Greek] writings lead to our being judged and condemned, but that these others put an end to our slavery." Herein, the level of internal dialogue is obviously high, high enough to place the speaker in that uppermost tenth of the population or less that we have so far been dealing with. It is an eastern immigrant to Rome, Tatian, who is quoted. His remarks, except in their length and explicitness, may stand for the group as a whole. What *they* saw in Christianity that led them to adopt it is about what we might have predicted. Its style of thought we can easily understand.

We are also familiar with the view that martyrs made converts; but with this, we take leave of the élite and enter among the masses, who supply our second type of convert.

"The blood of the martyrs is the seed of the Church"—famous epigram, long afterward endorsed by the policy of the apostate emperor Julian. The fourth-century biography of the Egyptian monk Pachomius declares, "after Diocletian's and Maximian's persecutions, conversion of pagans increased greatly for the Church."[49] Why did this happen? Just how did pagan witnesses reason, when they saw martyrdoms and became converts? There are several plausible explanations but only one bit of evidence that I know of. In Carthage in A.D. 203, Christians were incarcerated, they behaved with splendid cheer and spirit, and the jailer "began to make much of us, realizing that there was a great power in us," a great *virtus*. Shortly afterward he appears a convert.[50] His reasoning can only have been: their conduct is beyond nature, a real god must be at work—in short, they constitute a miracle.

To revert to the monk Pachomius: he himself was won over through a bargain he struck when he was held in close custody against draft-dodging. "If you set me free from this affliction," he prayed to God, "I will serve your will all the days of my life."[51] On a vastly more important scale, such was the basis for Constantine's conversion, a sort of *do ut des*, or perhaps *credo quia vinces*; and so on into the first of those early medieval conversions of entire nations for the same cause, that they might engage in war with better prospects of victory. The Burgundians in A.D. 430 decided that the God of the Romans must be a very superior one. They applied to a convenient bishop, fasted, were instructed, and within a week were all baptized.[52]

With these reports from the empire's jails, barracks, and frontiers, we have entered on calculations quite different from those of the schools, quite different from Tatian's that were quoted a little earlier. Tatian puts fear of damnation at the end of his list of considerations. By contrast, we know of a woman, also of Rome but a little earlier (the 140s) and of a lower class, who put it first: for, "coming to know the lessons of Christ" and thus being won over herself, subsequently she "recalled the teachings of Christ and warned [her husband] of punishment in the eternal flames for those who do not live modestly and according to right reason."[53] We do not know, and it is inconsequential, just who she was; but she does provide one of our very rare glimpses into someone's thought-processes. We have seen that pagans were informed of Gehenna and damnation; here we see those horrors used as the chief, perhaps the only, argument for conversion.

We also have a few scenes where the thoughts of persons not among the elite are anticipated by speakers trying to bring over whole crowds to belief. The fullest are naturally the speeches given by Paul and Stephen to Jews in Jerusalem. The setting is not comparable to those involving a pagan audience, but it is worth noting the emphasis in one of the speeches that is laid on the miracle on the road to Damascus. Since Paul often refers to it in his letters as something instantly familiar to his readers, it seems likely to have been a prominent feature also in his preaching generally.[54] He had seen God with his own eyes, and his being blinded was the proof. Very similarly, when Peter preaches in Rome, he recounts how he too thought he had been blinded by the revelation granted of God, for a moment, visible in His true form.[55]

37

But there is another scene of Paul addressing non-believers. He is in Ephesus. He tells his listeners how, in that same period when he had been in the Damascus area, he encountered and spoke with a lion, and won it over, and baptized it in a river. After that, the lion departed in peace, thereafter even eschewing lady-lions. It had become an ascetic. "And as Paul told this," our source declares, "a great crowd was added to the faith."[56] They were converted—why? Surely because the story, which audiences of the time could be credibly portrayed as believing, demonstrated *virtus* working through the man who was at that very moment addressing them.

If this scene may be taken as really written before A.D. 200 and really circulated among various churches in an interested and reverential fashion, as seems clear, then it matters not whether it transmits words actually spoken or behavior actually observed; for our concern is with the mentality of the audience—how they thought, how contemporaries who wanted to be believed would depict that thought, in short, what generally seemed familiar and credible. There is confirmation in just the same period from Tertullian's saying, "When were even droughts not ended by our going down on our knees, and fasting? At those times, too, the populace, hailing 'The God of Gods, who alone prevails!' have been witnesses to our God."[57] He is reminding his own living audience of moments of mass conversions upon the working of wonders by prayer, even if the conversions are along quite unreconstructedly pagan, "Great-is-God" lines. And there is confirmation, too, in the account Eusebius gives of the successors to the Apostles, evidently toward the turn of the first century in the Aegean area: addressing audiences who "had heard nothing at all of the word of faith, they moved about with God's favor and help, since in that time, too, many wonderful miracles of the divine spirit were wrought by them, with the result that whole crowds, every man of them upon the first hearing, eagerly espoused piety toward the Maker of all things" (*H. E.* 3.37.3).

The most precious scenes prior to the triumph of the Church under Constantine are to be found in the *Life of St. Gregory Thaumaturgus*, strangely enough, never translated into a modern tongue and therefore relatively little known. Its author Gregory of Nyssa makes clear that he had been in the region of Gregory's mission and had heard, passed down orally over the span of some hundred and thirty years, a wealth of stories which he transmits to us.[58] Through them all runs the theme of supernatural force displayed and, for no other reason and without need of any further word, conversions wrought.[59] The Wonder-worker puts an end to an outbreak of plague, for example, and the pagans thereupon turn to his God, "whom they acclaimed the One True God and ruler of all things." We can almost hear them shouting, like those around Carthage in Tertullian's day at the end of a drought, "The God of Gods!", or in Rome, beholding Peter's miracles, "One is the God, One God of Peter!"[60] The *Acta Petri* develops the same theme repeatedly and at length: a miracle is wrought and thereby the onlookers are made Christians on the spot.[61]

That this is how it really happened, and the Church really grew in historically significant numbers through demonstrations, or the report of demonstrations, that seemed beyond all but divine *virtus*, I do not doubt. In evaluating the evidence, we must of course bear in mind all that has been said about the religious habits and expectations of the world evangelized. For other explanation of that great growth, there is no evidence—no mass meetings, no great sermons, no speaking in tongues or dramatic inner spiritual crisis. But our view can be confirmed from two further sorts of information: first, information about conversions to belief in pagan deities, in just the same ways that availed to make Christians, in the same period and regions, that is, through proofs of power;[62] and second, information about conversions to Christianity post-Constantine. There is a small corpus of sketches giving us the specific moment and reason that belief was inspired.[63] What they reveal is just what is found also in earlier parallels, that is, religious allegiance following upon displays of divine efficacy.

Words and logic unassisted by wonderful deeds did sometimes have the same effect among ordinary folk as we have seen them having among the élite, and they are so reported;[64] but the surviving evidence does not show them to be any considerable factor, whatever rationalists might prefer. Celsus, representing that latter view, tries to discountenance the Church by his ridicule of the supernatural element in Christian expansion; but Origen defends it head-on as operating and absolutely essential in the time of Jesus, of the Apostles, and down into his own day near the mid-third century.[65] Both he and his opponent are at one in assuming that it is an element at work only among simple folk. Both writers, like the Apologists generally, distinguish between what should be shown to the educated and the uneducated.[66]

What is shown naturally determines what is seen, and seen to be good. So we return to our subject and starting-point. The devotees of

39

other gods saw in Christianity what could be accommodated in their level of perception. Among them, among the most highly articulate and intellectual, we ourselves feel not too ill at ease. They both produce and tend to occupy the pages of our sources. We can see how they think, we can generally understand them, and we are inclined instinctively to explain the rise of the Church in terms of these elite figures. But if we are rather to estimate Christianity as an historical force, that drew in scores of thousands, we must take account (even if we cannot quite enter the thoughts) of Everyman as well.

NOTES

[1]   See *Acta Pionii* 19.11 p. 162 of the edition of H. Musurillo, *Acts of the Martyrs* (1972), by which I cite most of the martyr-acts from here on; also see my *Paganism in the Roman Empire* (1981) 83, adding from later times Aug., *Ep.* 16.1: a pagan's doubts about Olympus, while believing in *salutaria numina* (but also in "the one god all-high, without beginning or offspring, a grand and magnificent father").

[2]   See my *Paganism* 76 and P. A. Brunt in *Studies in Latin Literature*, ed. C. Deroux (1979) 512, on pagan skeptics; on the Christians' involvement, see *Acta Acacii* 2.7 p. 58 of the edition of R. Knopf, *Ausgewählte Märtyrerakten*, ed. 3 by G. Krüger (1929).

[3]   *POxy.* 1382 (mid/late 2nd cent.), in an aretalogy; on a 3rd cent. gem, A. Dimitrova-Milceva in *Vorträge des 10. int. Limeskongresses* (1977) 285; more examples in my *Paganism* 186; and the interesting scene in the *Acta Petri* 26 p. 73 of the edition of R. A. Lipsius, *Acta Apostolorum apocrypha* 1 (1891), where the crowd in Rome shouts *unus deus, unus deus Petri*.

[4]   Plin., *Nat. Hist.* 2.5.22, *Fortuna, toto mundo et omnibus locis ... Fortuna sola invocatur ... et cum conviciis colitur.* For demons causing plague etc., cf. Philostr., *Vita Apoll.* 4.10, the same view being Origen's at *C. Cels.* 1.31 and 8.31, and in Just., II *Apol.* 5 or Tert., *Apol.* 22.4.

[5]   See sources cited in my *Paganism* 185.

[6]   *Test. animae* 1, cf. A. D. Nock, *Conversion* (1933) 192.

[7]   Orig., *C. Cels.* 1.8; *PBodmer* 20 cols. IV-V, cf. Just., II *Apol.* 3.

[8]   Caution dictates the use of only a few. See W. Schneemelcher in E. Hennecke, *Neutestamentliche Apokryphen*[3], Eng. trans. (1965) 2.275, dating the *Acta Petri* to the 180s and, pp. 261ff., showing its use by the *Didascalia* and Origen; ibid. 351, the *Acta Pauli (et Theclae)* dated to ca. 185-195; and texts in Lipsius, *op. cit.*

[9]   Lucian, *Peregrinus* 11-13; Galen, in R. Walzer, *Galen on Jews and Christians* (1949) 15; Min. Fel., *Octavius* 9.6, given maximum proportions by P. Frassinetti, *Giornale ital. di filol.* 2 (1949) 238-54; and Just., II *Apol.* 3.1.

[10]   Acts 10.25 (Peter) and 14.11-12 (Barnabas and Paul) and 28.6, cf. Musurillo 348 and *Acta Petri* 28 p. 78 Lipsius (Peter worshipped). For a wholly pagan parallel, see Philostr., *op. cit.* 4.44 and 7.32, Apollonius saluted as a god.

[11]   Acts 8.11.

[12]   Lk 9.33.

[13]   Acts 8.19 and 16.16.

[14] *Hypsistos* in Acts 16.17.

[15] Acts 14.12.

[16] E.g. Musurillo 148 and 158 (*Acta Pionii* 9.9 and 16.4), cf. Celsus supposing Jesus would be an angel, in a Jew's eyes, or anyone else's, *C. Cels*. 2.9.1 and 2.44, and pointing out the flaw in Christian monotheism, 8.12. Further, pagans could only have understood θεοῦ παῖς as "God's slave", at Musurillo 42, cf. Acts 3.26 and elsewhere.

[17] E.g. Musurillo 162, Zeus *basileus* compared with Christ *basileus*, *ibid.* 8 and 188, or Paul to the Areopagus, Acts 17.24, Christ *kyrios*.

[18] *Apol.* 24.3ff., cf. Min. Fel., *Octavius* 20.1, and Athenagoras, *Leg.* 6, attributing a widespread belief in One God to pagans generally, or to "the philosophers" (as does Clement, *Protrepticus* 5, PG 8.164ff., and meaning especially Plato, *Protr.* 6, PG 8.172ff.). Further, see my *Paganism* 86ff. and above, n. 1.

[19] As H. Chadwick says in his translation of the *Contra Celsum* (1965) p. xvii: for subscribers to a sort of Platonism, "monotheism and polytheism are not mutually exclusive". But my own interpretation includes not only philosophers.

[20] Eusebius (*H. E.* 2.3.2) says the disciples induced people to reject δαιμονικὴ πολυθεία, but I find no other uses of the term in Christian sources before A.D. 337 (nor the word *monotheia*).

[21] *Acta Acacii* 1.9ff. p. 58 Knopf-Krüger.

[22] E.g. Acts 17.29 and 19.26 and Musurillo 24, 94, and 296; often in the Apologists, e.g. Theophilus, *Ad Autolycum* 1.1 and 2.2 and Athenag., *Leg.* 15.

[23] *Daimones* = pagan "gods" in Tert., *Apol.* 23.11, Just., I *Apol.* 56, 58, and 62-4, *Acta Claudii* et al. 1.4 and 8 p. 107 Knopf-Krüger, or Musurillo 22 (or in Jewish sources like Jos., *A. J.* 8.2.5), more often *daimonia* (regularly in NT, also Musurillo 306 and *Acta Claudii* et al. 5.2 p. 108 Knopf-Krüger); demons, not gods, in idols do miracles, cf. Athenag., *Leg.* 23 and 26; Orig., *C. Cels.* 8.62; Tert., *Apol.* 22.8ff.; and pagan predecessors in these views, in my *Paganism* 82. For *daimonia* as a derogatory term, see Acts 17.18 and Jn 10.21.

[24] I Cor. 8.5: εἴπερ εἰσὶν λεγόμενοι θεοὶ ... ὥσπερ εἰσὶν θεοὶ πολλοὶ καὶ κύριοι πολλοί, ἀλλ᾽ ἡμῖν εἷς θεός, cf. Gal. 4.8, and perhaps some reflection of the point of dispute in Celsus' calling Hecate along with other powers "*daimones*", *C. Cels.* 1.9, or angels, "gods", 5.4.

[25] *Apol.* 23.2.

[26] *Acta Petri* 23 p. 71 Lipsius.

[27] Mt 10.8.

[28] *Apol.* 23.4, trans. T. R. Glover (Loeb ed.), where *dominus* = "god" like Gr. *Kyrios*.

[29] See passages quoted in my *Paganism* 168 n. 4, and conversions wrought upon seeing exorcisms, in Euseb., *H. E.* 5.7.4 = Iren., *C. haer.* 2.32.4 (Gaul in the 180s). They continued to exert their power later, e.g. in Augustine's world, *Civ. dei* 22.8 CSEL 40, 2, pp. 602ff.

[30] *Acta Pauli* (*et Theclae*) 17 p. 246 Lipsius, Paul addressing the throng at Iconium.

[31] Tert., *Apol.* 17.6; Orig., *C. Cels.* 8.45; and more evidence in my *Paganism* 32. For Christian stories of divine punishment, cf. for example Acts 4.5-10 and 13.10-11 (compare I Tim. 1.20); Tert., *Ad Scap.* 4.3; *Acta Petri* 15 p. 62 Lipsius (the wicked are stricken dumb); *Acta Andreae* narr. 36 (Ep. Gr. 15) (the wicked a suicide); Euseb., *H. E.* 6.9.5, comparing Acts 12.23 and more famous victims among the persecutors, e.g. in Lactantius. For God as spyer-out of wickedness, see Min. Fel., *Octavius* 10.5: Christians "would have Him a hostile figure, restless, shameless and inquisitive", etc., repeated at 23.9.

41

³² Lk 3.9 and 17; 10.12 and 12.5; 1 Thess. 1.10; and, as general impression, A. von Harnack, *The Mission and Expansion of Christianity* (1961) 90.

³³ Above, n. 30, and Mt 10.7 and 15 (cf. Lk 3.7-9; 10.12; 12.5; 19.27; and elsewhere); at Thessalonica, warning of God's wrath, *Acta Andreae* 12; but not at Lystra, Acts 14.15ff., and barely at Athens, 17.31.

³⁴ C. Cels. 8.48, trans. Chadwick; cf. Just., 1 *Apol.* 8 and 68, offering the parallel of Rhadamanthus and Minos (as do Theoph., *Ad Autol.* 37, and less clearly Min. Fel., *Octavius* 35) which he expects to be told is incredible. On divine retribution threatened in martyr-scenes, see Musurillo 10, 22 and 32 (bare mentions only, by Polycarp, Carpus and Pamphilus) and the *Acta Acacii* 1.8 p. 107 Knopf-Krüger.

³⁵ Musurillo 126, cf. the preaching to the populace on the night before, p. 124, and 14-44 (Pionius, at length and explicitly), and implied at lines 8ff. of the *Passion of Phileas, ibid.* p. 332.

³⁶ Musurillo 332, similar to the pagan's challenge, *ipso corpore*? etc., in Min. Fel., *Octavius* 11.7; cf. also Acts 17.32, the Athenians hearing of the raising of the dead "jeered"; and among the Apologists conscious of the difficulty of the doctrine, notice Theoph., *Ad Autol.* 1.8; Tat., *Ad Graecos* 6; Origen meeting Celsus' protests, *C. Cels.* 4.56ff., 5.14, 5.18 (Celsus' ridicule), and 8.49; and special treatises on the resurrection by Athenagoras, Justin, Tertullian and others.

³⁷ *Peregrinus* 13; and, for the rarity of beliefs in immortality, my *Paganism* 53-57. C. B. Welles in *Excavations at Dura-Europus, Prelimin. Report* IX (1944) 179, reports the Durene epitaph containing the wish, "may the ψυχαί θεαί receive him", but can find no parallel to this thought. I am also struck by the evidence in W. Peek, *Griechische Vers-Inschriften* 1 (1955), where, among many hundreds of epitaphs of the Roman period, only a handful (among nos. 1755-1777, passim) offer the distinction, "the earth holds the body but the Aether (or Heaven, the Gods, the Muses, etc.) hold the soul." All the rest are silent about eternity, or they urge the reader to "drink up, you see what you will come to" (e.g. no. 378), or they refer to the soul in its earthly existence (no. 540).

³⁸ Origen, *C. Cels.* 2.5 and 6.11, knowledge less stated than hinted at by Celsus; knowledge declared, by Justin to his tormentors, Musurillo 52; and indicated, by imagined pagans, ibid. 206 (the *Passio SS Mariani et Iacobi* 8.7) and Min. Fel., *Octavius* 11.5; preached to the unconverted only by Apollonius martyr (not a source to be pressed), Musurillo 100.

³⁹ *Acta Pauli (et Theclae)* 11 p. 243 Lipsius.

⁴⁰ Ibid. 17 p. 246 Lipsius; Acts 17.30-31; and taught by Peter in Judea, *Acta Petri* 17 p. 64 Lipsius.

⁴¹ C. Cels. 3.59 and 8.48-49, cf. 4.10; above, n. 31. As to punishment after death, I find almost nothing. F. Cumont in *Afterlife in Roman Paganism* (1923) cites outright denials of it (p. 83), discounts the unusable (pp. 84f.), and is left with only the Syrian novel, Heliod., *Aeth.* 8.9, and the *Apocalypse of Peter.* The pictures they present claim no generality and their origin is unknown. S. G. F. Brandon, *The Judgement of the Dead* (1967), Chap. 4, adds nothing from the centuries A.D. except (p. 93) Lucian's *Menippus*, which is surely a *jeu d'esprit* and nothing more (like the *Catabasis*, e.g. § 3 and 13). In Plutarch's *De sera num. vind.* a company of the widely learned, including a high Roman, discuss divine punishment of the wicked after death; they enjoy the idea as a novelty (566f.); but it seems to me decisive (cf. esp. 555D) that they know no such living faith anywhere.

⁴² *C. Cels.* 8.11, trans. Chadwick.

³⁶ Tert., *Apol.* 2.18, trans. Glover—cf. "our fight is not against human foes but against Cosmic Powers, against the authorities and princes of the dark world", etc. (Ephes. 6.12).

⁴⁴ Musurillo 102.

⁴⁵ On the overwhelming respectability (to say no more) of worshipping in the way of one's fathers, see my *Paganism* 3ff.; on Christians' consciousness of their innovating predicament, see e.g. Clem. Alex., *Protrepticus* 10, or Just., I *Apol.* 12.

⁴⁶ Though without any thorough search, I find only one possible active evangelist attested in post-Biblical times, outside of Asia: a certain Alexander in Gaul, Euseb., *H. E.* 5.1.49. I discount another possibility, see my *Paganism* 98 and J. Reynolds et al., *JRS* 71 (1981) 136; I also discount teachers one-to-one, inside private homes, such as Origen's (Euseb., *H. E.* 6.3.1 and 5) or such as Celsus describes, *C. Cels.* 3.55, and teachers against heresies in public but only a Christian public, in Euseb., *H. E.* 5.16.4, 6.37, and 7.24.7; and I discount Justin in a public setting at Ephesus, *Dial.* 122.4, since the interested bystanders are apparently Jews or *sebomenoi*, and in Rome as well, where Eusebius (*H. E.* 4.16.1: Justin "in debates with listeners present often refuted him", i.e. Crescens) seems only to draw out the implications of Just., II *Apol.* 3, δημοσίᾳ, and 5, προθέντα με καὶ ἐρωτήσαντα αὐτὸν ἐρωτήσεις τινάς. But the mob in Smyrna does know Polycarp as "the teacher of Asia ... teaching many not to offer sacrifice nor venerate the gods," Musurillo 10; and see further below, p. 186.

⁴⁷ It was not cynical in Julian the Apostate to stress the importance of the eleemosynary factor: notice the consternation in the Roman Christian community when its chief patron withdrew support, *Acta Petri* 8 p. 55 Lipsius.

⁴⁸ For example, Just., *Dial.* 8 (but so elaborate in setting—a dialogue within a dialogue—and so indebted to Plato, e.g. *Symp.* 201ff., that I cannot take it as truly autobiographical); Tat., *Ad Graecos* 29 (quoted); Theoph., *Ad Autol.* 1.14 (brief mention of prophecies); Tert., *De paenit.* 1.1 (conversion unexplained); Greg. Thaumat., *Paneg. to Origen* (hints hidden in the verbiage, esp. chaps. 5, 13, and 15). From the fourth century I can add, besides Augustine, only two cases: of Victorinus briefly described by him, *Conf.* 8.2.3f., cf. C. Monceaux, *Hist. littéraire de l'Afrique chrétienne* 3 (1905), pp. 377f., and Synesius, cf. J. Bregman, *Synesius of Cyrene* (1982), Chap. 1 and passim—both coming to Christianity through Neoplatonism, and doing so as philosophers.

⁴⁹ *Vita Pachomii* 2 p. 4 Athanassakis, cf. Just. II *Apol.* 12, observation of martyrs discredits slanders about their vices (but here there is no connection with conversion).

⁵⁰ Musurillo 116 and 124 (*Passio S. Perpetuae* 9.1 and 16.4), recalling the terrified jailer's conversion through the miracle at Philippi, Acts 16.25-34, and a disciple's deepening of belief in his teacher's divinity, Philostr., *Vita Apoll.* 7.38.

⁵¹ *Vita Pachomii* 5 p. 6 Athanassakis.

⁵² Soc., *H. E.* 7.30 (they promptly won the battle, destroying three times their weight in enemies).

⁵³ Musurillo 38 (*Passio SS Ptolemaei et Lucii* 2), cf. the *Acta S Dasii* 4.2 p. 93 Knopf-Krüger.

⁵⁴ Acts 22.3-21, esp. 6-13; and in letters, Gal. 1.16, I Cor. 9.1 and 15.8, and Phil. 3.12.

⁵⁵ *Acta Petri* 20 p. 67 Lipsius.

⁵⁶ Schneemelcher in Hennecke 2.389.

⁵⁷ *Apol.* 4.6.

⁵⁸ Notice φασί, PG 46.916B, λέγεται at 917B, etc., and caution at 957D.

⁵⁹ *Ibid.* 917Aff. (of the *neokoros*), 920Cff. (of the Neocaesarian crowds), 924D (the same, plus countryfolk), and 957B (relief of plague). Compare above, n. 29; and the last pre-Constantinian scene I find, of Agapetus (s.v., in Suidas) making conversions "through miracles", e.g. raising the dead and moving mountains, and so, ca. 300 A.D., "won over many pagans to enroll themselves in Christianity" (Philostorgius, *Hist. eccl.* pp. 19f. Bidez).

⁶⁰ Above, nn. 3 and 58, and Marc. Diac., *Vita Porphyrii* 21 and 31, the pagans exclaim at the miracle, ὁ Χριστὸς μόνος θεός, and μέγας ὁ θεὸς τῶν χριστιανῶν.

⁶¹ *Acta Petri* 10 p. 57 Lipsius; 12 p. 60 (the call, *alium signum nobis ostende ut credamus*); 13 p. 61 (*secuti sunt plurimi hoc viso et crediderunt in domino*); 17 p. 63 (*propter hoc enim factum credent*).

⁶² Tert., *Apol.* 21 and 31, paganism wins devotees: *quibusdam signis et miraculis et oraculis fidem divinitatis operatur.* Also material in my *Paganism* 95ff.

⁶³ I know of no collection of the evidence. As a beginning, notice Soz., *H. E.* 5.15 (in Gaza ca. A.D. 350, instantly upon seeing a devil exorcized); Soc., *H. E.* 1.20 (PG 67.129ff. = Theodoret, *H. E.* 1.23, PG 82.971ff. = *H. E.* 1.24 in GCS ed. 2, 1954), in the reign of Constantine; *ibid.* 5.21.7 (PG 82.1244), in A.D. 388, pagans burst into hymns to God at a miraculous temple-destruction; Jerome, *Vita Hilarionis* 25 (PL 23.41), of the A.D. 380s near Gaza; Rufinus, *H. E.* 2.4 (PL 21.512Cff.) of A.D. 373 or a little later, near Nitria in Egypt (cf. Soc., *H. E.* 4.24); and, of date ca. A.D. 400, Marc. Diac., *Vita Porphyrii, locc. citt.* and elsewhere. For the nature of that work, likely to be least distorted in its descriptions of miracle scenes, see the Introduction in H. Grégoire and M. A. Kugener's edition (1930). Miracles often change the minds of persons already Christian, of course, e.g. Soz., *H. E.* 6.27 (PG 67.1369B) and 8.1 (1509B).

⁶⁴ On the simple folk, see *C. Cels.* 3.44 and 55, and *Acta Petri* 1 p. 44 Lipsius; on the highly educated, see Min. Fel., *Octavius* 40.1.

⁶⁵ *C. Cels.* 1.46, "even if Celsus, or the Jew that he introduces, ridicule what I am about to say ..." (trans. Chadwick); cf. also 8.47, and compare Augustine's views: the foundations of Christian faith were laid through miracles, for we find in Scripture *quae facta sunt, et propter quod credendum facta sunt,* etc. (*Civ. dei* 22.8, CSEL 40, 2, p. 596).

⁶⁶ *C. Cels.* 1.9 and 18; 5.15, 19, and 29; and elsewhere; also among Apologists, e.g. Min. Fel., *Octavius* 19.15, or *Jnl. Theol. Stud.* 17 (1966) 111, and cf. Clem. Alex., *Stromat.* 1.12, PG 8.753, care taken to avoid guffaws of the masses, like the warning by Menander Rhetor, p. 14 Russell-Wilson, not to "look unconvincing and ridiculous to the masses" through subtlety of theological argument.

New Haven, Yale University, Ct. 06520   R. MacMullen

Studia Theologica 30 (1976) pp. 53–73

The Conversion of Justin Martyr

OSKAR SKARSAUNE

I

'In welcher Weise Justins Übertritt zum Christentum stattgefunden hat, weiss man nicht'. This terse statement by N. Hyldahl in his recent monograph on Justin[1] may at first glance seem a little surprising. Apparently, we should be well informed as to the conversion of this second century apologist. He seems to give us the whole story in the first chapters of his *Dialogue with Trypho* (Chs 1–8).[2] However, there are two facts which complicate our use of this source.

First, there is the question of historicity. The use of these chapters as an – at least essentially – correct autobiography, was challenged by E. R. Goodenough, who pointed out the conventional character of this type of *curriculum vitae*.[3] Later, Hyldahl has maintained the view that these chapters are a literary fiction, the intention of which is kerygmatic, not autobiographical.[4]

Secondly, there is the twelfth chapter of the *Second Apology,* where Justin seems to tell a different story, at variance with his words in the *Dialogue*. According to the *Second Apology,* the reason for Justin's conversion was the profound impression made on him by the Christian martyrs. In the *Dialogue*, on the other hand, the process of conversion seems to be one of rational argumentation, leading step by step from Platonism to Christianity.

---

[1] N. Hyldahl: Philosophie und Christentum. Eine Interpretation der Einleitung zum Dialog Justins (*Acta Theologica Danica, IX*), Copenhagen 1966, p. 173.

[2] The *Dialogue* and Justin's *Apologies* are cited according to E. J. Goodspeed's edition: *Die ältesten Apologeten. Texte mit kurzen Einleitungen,* Göttingen 1914. The translations of texts from the *Dialogue* are taken from A. Lukyn Williams: *The Dialogue with Trypho, transl. introd. and notes,* London 1930, while texts from the *Apologies* are rendered according to the translation in A. Roberts & S. J. Donaldson (ed.) *The Ante-Nicene Fathers,* Vol I, Grand Rapids 1967, unless otherwise indicated.

[3] E. R. Goodenough: *The Theology af Justin Martyr. An Investigation into the Conception of Early Christian Literature and its Hellenistic and Judaistic Influences,* Jena 1923, repr. Amsterdam 1968, pp. 58ss.

[4] Hyldahl, op.cit., passim.

Many commentators have found the two accounts more or less difficult to reconcile.[5] According to Hyldahl, they are contradictory, and this evaluation is part of his argument against the historicity of the opening chapters of the *Dialogue*.[6] Others have tried to harmonize the two motives of conversion psychologically. This is done by Goodenough: 'It may well have been that just at the time when his attention was called to the Christians by some remarkable instance of Christian fortitude during a persecution, he was in a state of discouragement at the discovery of new teachings in Platonism which he had found difficult to understand.'[7] M. von Engelhardt advanced a similar point of view: 'Ein Ausgleich zwischen den Aussagen der Apologien und denen des Dialogs ist nur dann möglich, wenn man annimmt, dass Justin auf die staunenerregenden Wirkungen der neuen Lehre im Leben der Christen erst aufmerksam geworden ist, nachdem er bereits durch jenen alten Mann in seinem Glauben an die Philosophie wankend gemacht und auf das Christenthum hingewiesen worden war.'[8]

Now, while this may seem a plausible psychological explanation, it certainly strengthens the impression that the two motives for Justin's conversion belong to quite different categories. From the impression made by the Christian martyrs to the philosophical argument of the *Dialogue*, there appears to be a *metabasis eis allo genos*. Is this really so?

II

We have regarded Justin's conversion as a problem as far as his biography is concerned. It may be a fascinating problem, but it is after all a question of only limited relevance. There is, however, another aspect of these Justinian texts. After all, the way a man describes his own conversion may reveal some very essential ideas of his concerning conversion in general, indeed, it may tell us something important about his conception of Christianity.

Justin relates his own conversion in a context where he is writing to convert others, especially in the *Dialogue*. Of course, the very aspects of Christianity which a man is emphasizing as valid reasons for the conversion of others, are not necessarily the reasons behind his own conversion. We should, however, expect some kind of connexion at this point. Even if we regard the autobiographical form as a mere literary fiction, the autobio-

---

[5] M. von Engelhardt found the two texts to be 'scheinbar im Widerspruch', *Das Christenthum Justins des Märtyrers. Eine Untersuchung über die Anfänge der katholischen Glaubenslehre,* Erlangen 1878, p. 83.

[6] Op.cit. p. 49.

[7] Goodenough, op.cit. p. 72.

[8] Von Engelhardt, op.cit. p. 83.

graphical texts are obviously meant to have a *paradigmatic* significance. And this paradigm must not be too far from the actual experience of the apologist, or it will prove a complete failure.[9] In this sense I would agree with Goodenough when he says that Justin's conversion story in the *Dialogue*, 'while probably not autobiographical in detail, is thoroughly autobiographical in spirit'.[10]

In defending his conversion, Justin is defending Christianity, and vice versa. What A. D. Nock says of the apologists generally is very true of Justin: they 'were without exception men who were not the sons of Christians but had been converted to Christianity themselves. The *apologia* of each of them was therefore in a measure an *apologia pro vita sua*.'[11] This close connexion in Justin between apology on behalf of Christianity and apology on behalf of his conversion, is the reason why his conversion story has more than biographical interest. It may indeed give us some precious pointers to essentials in his whole conception of Christianity.

III

Let us briefly summarize the contents of *Dial* 1–8. Justin, wearing a philosopher's cloak, becomes engaged in a conversation with the Jew Trypho, who shows himself interested in philosophical enquiry. This interest is surprising to Justin, since a Jew should have the Scriptures to answer his questions about God. Trypho retorts that philosophy, to his knowledge, is occupied with the very same questions (1:1–3). Yes, says Justin, it ought to be so, but most philosophers have taught these matters in the wrong way, or not at all. Trypho then asks what Justin's own philosophy is (1:4–6). The answer falls into five parts: 1) Praise of the true philosophy as opposed to the doctrines of the philosophical schools (2:1). 2) An outline of the history of philosophy (2:2). 3) Justin's philosophical itinerary (2:3–6). 4) The dialogue with the Old Man (3:1–7:3). 5) Justin's conversion to Christianity as the True Philosophy (8:1–2).

[9] This is well brought out by E. F. Osborn: Justin Martyr (*Beiträge zur hist. Theologie, 47*), Tübingen 1973, p. 67: 'He wanted to show why he had become a Christian by explaining how it had happened. He remembered with advantages, used literary devices and followed the conventions of conversion stories. He did all this because he wanted others to follow him to the only safe and useful philosophy. Without general accuracy and verisimilitude his plea would have been ineffective.'

[10] Op.cit. p. 72. Cf. a similar point of view in von Engelhardt, op.cit. p. 84: 'Seine Schriften . . sind durchzogen von Hinweisen auf *die* Seiten des Christenthums, welche die grosse Wandelung in seinem Leben veranlasst und zum Abschluss gebracht hat.'

[11] A. D. Nock: *Conversion. The Old and the New in Religion from Alexander the Great to Augustine of Hippo,* Oxford 1933, repr. 1969, p. 250.

The literary and logical interplay between these units has been analysed
in great detail by Hyldahl, T. Christensen, J. C. M. van Winden and R.
Joly.[12] The discussion is unfinished, and I shall only mention some relevant
points here.

The first is that the actual conversion to Christianity does not take place
until *Dial* 8:1. The philosophic itinerary does not lead to Christianity, it
ends in *Platonism*. Nor does the anti-Platonic argument of the Old Man
lead Justin to Christ (3:1–6:1).[13] These two elements balance each other:
The itinerary leads up to Platonism, the dialogue with the old Man destroys
Platonism. The combined effect is to give Platonism a prominent position
among the schools of Greek philosophy, but not as a 'bridge' to or a 'preparation' for Christianity. There is no smooth passage from Plato to Christ
in Justin's story. Instead there is a complete break, marked by a literary
break in the *Dialogue* between Chapters 6 and 7. The prominent place of
Platonic philosophy is not that of a 'bridge', it is that of the only serious
rival to True Philosophy (i.e. Christianity). It is not Platonism itself but its
destruction that prepares Justin for conversion.[14]

The positive reason for conversion is given in *Dial* 7:1–8:2. Since I am
going to analyse this text in some detail, I shall reproduce it here in full, according to A. Lukyn Williams's translation:[15]

7:1 'Whom else, then, I reply, could one take as teacher, or from what
     quarter might one derive advantage, if the truth is not even in these
     philosophers?'
     'There were a long time ago men of greater antiquity than all these
     reputed philosophers, men blessed and righteous and beloved of God
     who spake by the Divine Spirit, and foretold those things of the

---

[12] Hyldahl, op.cit., and Bemærkninger til Torben Christensens analyse af indled-
ningen til Justins Dialog, *Dansk Teol. Tidsskr. 30* (1967), pp. 129–146; T. Christensen:
Bemærkninger og overvejelser til Niels Hyldahl: 'Philosophie und Christentum...'
Dansk Teol. Tidsskr. 29 (1966), pp. 193–232; J.C.M van Winden: *An Early Christian
Philosopher. A Commentary to Justin Martyr, The Dialogue with Trypho,* Chap. 1–9,
Leiden 1971; R. Joly: *Christianisme et Philosophie. Études sur Justin et les Apologistes
grecs du deuxième siècle,* Brussels 1973, pp. 9–83.
[13] It is not quite correct of R. M. Grant to say: 'They (i.e. the anti-Platonic arguments) produced Justin's conversion', in: Aristotle and the Conversion of Justin,
J. Theol. Stud., New Series VII (1956), pp. 246–48, quotation p. 247. The anti-Platonic
argument *prepared* Justin's conversion, it did not produce it.
[14] This interpretation of the content and function of the dialogue with the Old Man
has been elaborated in great detail by Hyldahl and van Winden in their respective
monographs. R. Joly tries to minimize the anti-Platonic tendency of Justin's text, partly
by assuming that the Old Man is more anti-Platonic than Justin himself (op.cit. p. 67).
[15] Lukyn-Williams, op.cit. pp. 14–16.

future, which indeed have come to pass. Prophets do men call them. They, and they only, saw the truth and declared it to mankind, without fear or shame of any, not dominated by ambition, but saying only what they had heard and seen, filled as they were with the Holy Spirit.

7:2   Now their writings still remain with us even to the present time, and it is open to anyone to consult these, and to gain most valuable knowledge both about the origin of things and their end, and all else that a philosopher ought to know, if he believes what they say. For they have not made their discourses, when they wrote, with logical proof, inasmuch as being trustworthy witnesses of truth they are superior to all such proof, but the things that did take place and are taking place now compel agreement with what they have spoken.

7:3   And yet even on account of the miracles which they wrought they were entitled to belief, for they both glorified the Maker of all things as God and Father, and proclaimed the Christ sent from Him, as His Son, a thing which the false prophets who are filled with the seducing and unclean spirit never did nor ever do, but dare to work miracles of a sort to amaze men, and give glory to the spirits of error and daemons. But pray that before all else the gates of light may be opened to thee. For things are not seen nor comprehended by all, save of him to whom God and His Christ shall have given understanding.'

8:1   After saying this and many other things besides, which it is not now a fitting time to tell, he went away, bidding me follow his advice, and I saw him no more. But as for me, straightway a fire was kindled in my soul, and a passionate desire possessed me for the prophets, and for those great men who are the friends of Christ. And as I weighed his words within me I found that this alone was philosophy, and philosophy safe and serviceable.

8:2   In this way then and for these reasons am I a philosopher. And, further, I could wish that all should form a desire as strong as mine, not to stand aloof from the Saviour's words. For these have in themselves a something of dreadful majesty, and are enough to put to shame those that turn out of the right way; while rest most delightful comes to those who carry them out in practice. If therefore you have any regard for yourself, and are in earnest after salvation, and are trusting on God, you may, forasmuch as you are no stranger to the subject, know the Christ of God and be initiated, and then live a prosperous and happy life.

This account offers some difficulties. It certainly exhibits a high degree of condensation. Indeed, Justin himself indicates this: The Old Man said 'many other things besides, which it is not now a fitting time to tell' (8:1). This brevity makes it difficult to grasp exactly *what* Justin found to be the only 'safe and serviceable philosophy', and *how* he found it.

There is a remarkable shift between *Dial* 8:1 and 8:2. In *Dial* 7 the Old Man has been speaking of the prophets, their words and their books. Christ is only mentioned indirectly, as an object of prophetic teaching and originator of Christian understanding, but not as an historical person. In *Dial* 8:1, Justin says that he acquired a strong love for the prophets and the 'friends of Christ'.[16] Here, too, Christ is only mentioned indirectly. Then, in 8:2, the prophets suddenly disappear, and Justin goes on to speak of 'the Saviour's words', as if these, not the words of the prophets, were the content of True Philosophy.[17]

This would seem to imply that the content of True Philosophy is a timeless doctrine, taught by the prophets *and* by Christ. The prophets taught the same philosophy as Christ, therefore Justin can change from one source of doctrine to the other. They are interchangeable.

This is in principle the classic interpretation of Justin advanced by von Engelhardt and von Harnack.[18] The contents of Christian doctrine for Justin are, according to these scholars, 'jene einfachen und grosse Sätze von dem geistigen Gott, der Tugend und der Unsterblichkeit'. The prophets and Christ are the teachers of this doctrine.

What, then, about the prophecies concerning Christ? They cannot be part of a timeless doctrine, since they are concerned neither with the spiritual God, nor with virtue, nor eternal life. According to von Engelhardt and von Harnack the answer is this: The prophecies about Christ and their fulfilment are not, strictly speaking, *part* of the Christian message, but they *authenticate* the message. The prophecies are proved to be true by their fulfilment, and Christ is shown to come from God because of the prophecies. Christ and the prophets authenticate each other.

In this way the conversion of Justin from philosophy to Christianity is shown to be only a semi-conversion. Justin abandoned philosophy to become

---

[16] To whom does this expression refer? Van Winden (op.cit. pp. 118f) says that the Christians in Justin's own time, and especially in their capacity as martyrs, were what Justin had in mind. This suggestion is supported if we examine the New Testament use of the expression 'my friends' in the mouth of Christ. In the two places in which this use occurs: Luke 12:4 and John 15:13–15, the context is clearly martyrological. This interpretation of the term 'friends of Christ' is in excellent harmony with *II Apol* 12:1, where Justin is speaking of the impression made on him by the Christian martyrs. This would mean that the conversion motive in *II Apol* 12 is not altogether absent from *Dial* 8.

[17] This expression is not found *verbatim* in Justin, but I use it as a shorthand for what Justin calls 'the only safe and profitable philosophy' (*Dial* 8:1). The expression was coined by Goodenough. Hyldahl speaks of 'Die Urphilosophie' in consequence of his interpretation of *Dial* 2:1–2.

[18] Von Engelhardt, op.cit., passim, esp. pp. 223–41, A. von Harnack: *Lehrbuch der Dogmengeschichte*, I. Band: Die Entstehung des kirchlichen Dogmas. Here cited according to the 5th ed., Tübingen 1931. On the apologists, see pp. 496–550.

a Christian, but at the same time brought philosophy with him, making Christianity another philosophy. With this, Justin contributes his share to what von Harnack calls 'der Weltgeschichtliche Bund zwischen kirchlichem Christenthum und griechischer Philosophie', or simply 'die Hellenisirung des Christenthums'.[19]

There are some features in Justin's text that can be cited in support of this interpretation of his conversion. Justin (in the character of the Old Man) says that by reading the prophetic books one 'can gain most valuable knowledge both about the origin of things and their end, and all else that a philosopher ought to know' (7:2). The prophetic doctrine about the 'beginnings' is certainly to be taken as a reference to the first chapters of Genesis, and by implication, to Old Testament monotheism. This would correspond to the 'doctrine of God' in the Harnack interpretation. 'The end of things' would correspond to 'eternal life', and 'the Saviour's words' in 8:2 would correspond to 'virtue' – and so we have the Harnack triad! In 7:2 we have the authentication: 'The things that did take place and are taking place now compel agreement with what they (i.e. the prophets) have spoken.' That is, the fulfilment of prophecy authenticates the prophets (and Christ) as reliable and inspired teachers of True Philosophy concerning God, virtue and eternal life.

There is, however, one serious objection to this interpretation, as far as *Dial* 7–8 is concerned. The shift from 'the words of the prophets' to 'the Saviour's words' in 8:2 can be explained by a shift in the polemical front, and does not therefore imply that for Justin the two entities were equal.

In *Dial* 7 Justin is mainly concerned with the superiority of the prophets over the Greek philosophers. This superiority is due to their greater antiquity. This argument is valid for the *prophets* only, not for the words of Jesus recorded in the Gospel. Futher, in *Dial* 7 Justin's argument is not addressed to Trypho, the Jew, but to the gentile readers of the *Dialogue*. Trypho had no need to be convinced of the superiority of the prophetic books, but the pagan readers of the *Dialogue* had. Justin brings this out by putting the words in the mouth of the Old Man addressing Justin, the Platonist. *Dial* 8:1 is Justin's epilogue and conclusion to this section, while 8:2 marks a new start. 8:2 is the prelude to the dialogue proper between Christianity and Judaism, beginning in 8:3. In 8:2, therefore, Justin is for the first time addressing Trypho in his capacity as a *Jew*. The dividing line between Trypho and Justin was not the belief in the divine origin of the prophetic books, but Justin's belief in Jesus as the Messiah. What is at stake

---

[19] Von Harnack, op.cit. p. 498 and 496.

here is not the books or the words of the prophets, but precisely 'the words of the Saviour'.

This, I think, is a sufficient explanation of the change from 8:1 to 8:2, and this change does not imply that for Justin the words of the prophets and those of the Saviour were identical. We are thus forced once more to ask the question of what the *content* of True Philosophy is. I shall start with a preliminary study.

In *Dial* 8:2: 'I could wish that all should form a desire as strong as mine, *not to fall away* (ἀφίστασθαι) from the Saviour's words', the italicized words are a little surprising. One expects Justin to urge his readers, all of them, to *come to* Christ, *listen* to his words and so on. But Justin's use of the term ἀφίστασθαι creates the impression that he is urging them *not to become apostates,* and that even before they have become Christians! In fact, ἀφίστασθαι in Justin is a *terminus technicus* for apostasy: *Dial* 76:3 and 79:1: apostasy of men and angels; *Dial* 20:1: apostasy of the Jews; *Dial* 106:1 and *I Apol* 50:12: apostasy of the disciples at the arrest of Jesus; *Dial* 78:6 and *I Apol* 14:1: Christians falling away from demons; *Dial* 111:2: Jesus saving those who do not fall away from him.[20] The two remaining occurrences are of special interest, since they contain further parallels to *Dial* 8:2[21]:

Dial 8:2	Dial 121:3	Dial 110:4
I could wish that all should form a desire... *not to fall away* (ἀφίστασθαι) from the Saviour's words... (which) are enough *to put to shame* those that *turn out of the right way*...	Will He not then most assuredly at His coming in glory *destroy* all them that have *hated him,* and them that have unjustly *fallen away from* Him (ἀποστάντας)...	Though we are be-headed, and crucified... it is plain that we *do not fall away* (ἀφιστάμεθα) from the confession of our faith...
while *rest* ἀνάπαυσις most delightfull comes	and *give rest* (ἀνναπαυσει)	and there is *none that maketh afraid,* and *leadeth into captivity*
to *those who carry them out.*	to *His own (people),* rendering to them all that they are expecting	*us who... have set our faith on Jesus.* For the vine that has been planted by God, and Christ the Saviour, is *His people.*

[20] Cf. also ἀποστάτης as a *terminus technicus* for Satan in *Dial* 103:5 and 125:4.
[21] To bring out the points more clearly, I have slightly altered the Lukyn Williams translation.

The apostasy Justin has in mind in *Dial* 121:3 and 110:4 is the apostasy in face of persecution and martyrdom. This is a frequent theme in Justin, and so is the contrast between the Jews and the Christians in this respect, as shown by these two texts: The Jews do not carry on the tradition of the prophets, who suffered martyrdom, but the Christians do (*Dial* 11:4; 16:4; 34:8; 93:4; 96:2; 110:4–6; 112:5; 120:6; 130:4; 131:2; 132:1; 133:1–6; 136:2–3). The Jews, by contrast, have created for themselves what might be called a tradition of *apostasy*. To Justin, apostasy is always falling away from God. In rejecting Christ the Jews reject God himself. This was pre-figured in the Old Testament: The Jews, showing disbelief with regard to the types of Jesus, became *idolators*, committing the *gentile sin kath' exochen*: 'You are convicted by the prophets . . . of having gone so far as to sacrifice your own children to the demons' (*Dial* 133:1). *Christ* is the powerful weapon of God against the Devil and the demons. It is Christ who is turn-ing the elect ones of all nations from idolatry to the worship of the only true God. The demons cannot tolerate this, and so the true believers in God have been persecuted at all times and even slain. This was the case with the prophets. And you cannot understand the prophets unless you have the same willingness to be martyred as they had: 'Except, therefore, you despise the precepts of them that exalt themselves and desire to be called Rabbi, Rabbi, and you approach the words of the prophets with such a mind and purpose that you suffer at the hands of your fellows what also the prophets themselves suffered, you cannot get anything at all useful from the prophetic writers' (*Dial* 112:5).

What provoked these considerations was the fact that Justin is urging his readers not to become apostates, even before they have become Christians. Yes, indeed, this is exactly what Justin is saying: Do not become apostates, in other words: *Do not become Jews*. This further explains the change from *Dial* 8:1 to 8:2. Justin has been exhorting his readers to turn from Greek philosophy to the prophetic books of the Old Testament (8:1). He does not, however, want them to become Jews, i.e. apostates. Therefore he urges them 'not to fall away from the Saviour's words' as the Jews do. This gives inner coherence and meaning to Justin's statements. The only way to understand the prophets is to become a Christian. This is also intimated in the last words of the Old Man in *Dial* 7: 'Pray that before all else the gates of light may be opened to thee. For (these) things are not seen nor com-prehended of all, save of him to whom God, and His Christ, shall have given understanding'.

Now, concerning Justin's notion of True Philosophy, two questions must be discussed:

1) What is the relation between the prophets and Christ, and 2) What is the *content* of True Philosophy?

1) We have seen that the battle between God and the demons is the great cosmic framework of Justin's sayings about the prophets and Christ. The martyr-prophets, 'they, and they only, saw the truth and declared it to mankind, without fear or shame of any' (*Dial* 7:1). Justin gives several hints about the content of their preaching in *Dial* 7, but most of these are rather formal: 'those things of the future, which indeed have come to pass' (7:1) 'what they had heard and seen' (ibid.), 'the origin of things and their end, and all else a philosopher ought to know' (7:2).[22] In 7.3, however, Justin is a little more specific, as (in the character of the Old Man) he contrasts the true prophets with the false ones. Both groups worked miracles, but only the true prophets are thereby entitled to belief, since they, and they only, 'both glorified the Maker of all things as God and Father, and proclaimed the Christ sent from Him, as His Son'. This the false prophets never do; on the contrary, they glorify the *spirits of error* (τὰ τῆς πλάνης πνεύματα) and the demons. This criterion is very characteristic of Justin. His whole soteriology operates mainly within this framework: The demons lead men away from the true God, and deceive men to honour the demons as gods instead. Further, they lead men to all kinds of moral depravity, and finally: they instigate persecution of all those who will not submit to their tyranny.

God's great combatant against the demons is His own Son, Christ, the Logos. He was already shown to be their conqueror at birth, *Dial* 78:9. The final victory was won on the cross (*Dial* 31:1; 49:8; 91:4; 111:2 et al. (cf. Col. 2:15)). The central term in this context is Christ's power, His δύναμις. This power is directed against the demons as a terrifying weapon, and at his ascension Christ is enthroned as their conqueror, so that all demons may be exorcised and driven away by the mention of his name (*Dial* 76:6; 85:2–3).

The victory over the demons – and thereby the possibility for man to get rid of their tyranny and turn to God – is in this way intimately connected with the historical work of Christ. It is not primarily as a *teacher* that Christ conquers the demons – in fact Justin calls Christ διδάσκαλος only twice in the *Dialogue* (76:3; 108:2). It is by his birth, passion and ascension that Christ subdues all the powers that are against God. The prophets *proclaimed* in advance this victory of Christ. That is the central content of their message (e. g. *Dial* 78:9). The prophets did not teach mono-

---

[22] For the philosophical connotations of these terms, see Hyldahl, op.cit. p. 228.

theism, virtue and eternal life in an abstract way. They proclaimed these truths by announcing the approaching defeat of the demons in the history of Jesus. In this way they 'foretold those things of the future, which indeed have come to pass' (*Dial* 7:1). The fulfilment of the prophecies is therefore precisely the centre and heart of the Christian message. In the prophets God by his Logos (or Spirit) announces that he is going to create himself a people of worshippers in Spirit and Truth, purged of idolatry and all moral wickedness instigated by the evil powers (*Dial* 130–31). God says he will do so by sending his own Son. In Christ he has done so, and he is still doing so in the ongoing gathering of the Christian Church. This is not an authentication of the Christian message, this *is* the message! The relation between Christ and the prophets is not that of different teachers teaching the same, timeless doctrine.[23] The prophets *announce*, Christ *acts*; that is the relation.

2) What does Justin mean by calling himself a philosopher and Christianity a philosophy? What is the meaning of this designation? Hyldahl has maintained that Justin has a very specific conception in mind: Christianity is 'die wiedergefundene Urphilosophie'. Hyldahl connects *Dial* 7 with *Dial* 2:1–2, and interprets these texts in the light of a conception found in Poseidonius. According to Poseidonius (in Hyldahl's somewhat hypothetical reconstruction), philosophy was sent down to men in primordial times, but later became degenerate and split up into philosophical schools. Justin sharpens the negative aspect of the theory: The primordial philosophy has not only degenerated, it has actually been lost, and is now only to be found in the books of the prophets. This is the conception Justin has in mind when he calls Christianity a philosophy.[24] Justin does not mean to say that Christianity is *one* or even *the best* philosophy among other philosophies. He is saying that Christianity is the only philosophy worthy of this name, since Christianity is the primordial, true philosophy recovered. This interpretation is thought-provoking indeed, and Hyldahl has rightly been acclaimed for this important step forward in understanding the concept of philosophy in Justin.[25] But I do not think this clarification takes us very far towards answering the question of whether Justin is 'Hellenizing' Christian-

[23] As in the interpretation of von Engelhardt and von Harnack referred to above. It is a gross misrepresentation of the importance of Christ's historical work in Justin when von Engelhardt goes so far as to say: '. . es (hätte) der Menschwerdung des Sohnes Gottes nicht bedurft. . .wenn das Christenthum in Wirklichkeit nur das wäre, wofür Justin es hält: eine Philosophie höherer Ordnung. . .', op.cit. p. 453.

[24] Hyldahl, op.cit., esp. pp. 112–140 and 227–255.

[25] See van Winden, op.cit. pp. 2f, and Osborn, op.cit. p. 8 n. 40. But cf. also the severe criticism in R. Joly, op.cit. pp. 23–26.

ity by calling it a philosophy. Primordial philosophy is an empty designation as long as its *content* is not defined. The definition given by Hyldahl is not very helpful in this respect: Philosophy is *de divinis humanisque verum invenire* (Seneca, *Ep.* 90:3).[26] Yes, but what *is* the truth about God and man?

Here a very stimulating study by E. Benz can take us further.[27] Benz has called attention to the role played by Socrates in early Christian apologetics. The standard accusation against the Christians was *atheism* (ἀσέβεια). They were martyred as atheists. But so was Socrates! He was a very welcome ally and spokesman as far as the accusations of atheism (and destruction of the ancient tradition) were concerned. In fact, Socrates became something of a model martyr for the Christians. This is especially true of Justin: 'When Socrates endeavoured, by true reason and examination, to bring these things to light [i.e. the false divine pretensions of the demons!], and deliver men from the demons, then the demons themselves, by means of men who rejoiced in iniquity, compassed his death, as an atheist and profane person, on the charge that "he was introducing new divinities", and in our case they display a similar activity. For not only among the Greeks did reason (Logos) prevail to condemn these things through Socrates, but also among the Barbarians were they condemned by the Logos Himself, who took shape and became man, and was called Jesus Christ. . .' (*I Apol* 5:3–4, cf. *I Apol* 46).

I think this passage is essential for grasping Justin's concept of philosophy and the philosopher's task. *The proper task of philosophy is to reveal the true nature of the demons (pretending to be gods) and to bring men to the only true God.* This thesis can not only be confirmed by a study of this and parallel passages in the *Apologies*, it is indicated by Justin's definitions of philosophy in the *Dialogue* itself: 'Do not the philosophers turn every discourse on God? And do they not always probe into His μοναρχία and πρόνοια? Is not this truly the duty of philosophy, to investigate the Deity?' (*Dial* 1:3). In *Dial* 2:1 it is said that 'it (philosophy) alone brings us to and unites us with God'. The meaning of these statements is surely not only that the task of philosophy is theology, but that it is *qualified* theology, so to speak: A theology that takes a stand in the great battle between the Logos and his enemies, the demons. Therefore the true philosopher is a potential martyr, a potential Socrates. In *I Apol* 46:3 there is a noteworthy enumeration of such philosopher-martyrs: 'among the Greeks, Socrates and Heraclitus and

---

[26] Hyldahl, op.cit. p. 135.

[27] E. Benz: Christus und Socrates in der alten Kirche, *Zeitschr. für die Neutest. Wissenschaft, 43* (1950/51), pp. 195–224. This important study has not received its due attention in recent studies on Justin.

men like them; and among the barbarians, Abraham, and Ananias, and Azarias, and Misael and Elias. . .' The uniting feature of all these men is obvious: They all – in Justin's eyes – *denounced idolatry,* they were 'atheists', and were persecuted or even martyred by the demons and pseudo-gods (and their worshippers).[28]

This, I think, explains why Justin can call Christianity the True Philosophy, or conversely the philosopher-martyrs 'Christians'. In order to decide whether Justin is thereby Hellenizing Christianity, a second question must be answered: Is this conception of philosophy mainly Greek (i.e. middle-Platonic), or mainly Jewish/Christian? One way to answer this question is to consider the *demonology* that is so dominant in Justin's definition of philosophy.

This demonology has been studied in great detail by H. Wey.[29] I think his main results are beyond dispute: Justin's demonology is *not* to be explained against the background of Greek philosophical demonology (the most relevant being that of the Platonic tradition). To the Platonists, e.g. Xenocrates and Plutarch, the demons have a mainly *positive* function, filling the gap between God and man.[30] They are never thought of as rivals or imitators of God, or leading men away from God. This idea is not Greek in origin, but originates from Jewish and Christian sources. Its main sources are to be found in the apocalyptic literature of Judaism (e.g. *1.Henoch* and *XII Patr. Test.*) and the LXX.

It follows from this that Justin's conception of philosophy cannot be called typically Greek. Many Greek philosophers were in some sense monotheists, but theirs was not a monotheism involved in a fight to the death with the demons. If they were aware of this battle motive at all, they would not have defined it as *the* task of philosophy. Justin does so, and thereby shows himself deeply rooted in Jewish/Christian soil. What is striking in Justin is not a supposedly 'philosophical' conception of Christianity, but a very un-philosophical conception of philosophy!

---

[28] For the belief that even Heraclitus was accused of atheism, see Benz, op.cit. pp. 202 and 209. Abraham abandoned polytheism, Ananias, Azarias and Misael were the three men thrown into the furnace because they would not fall down before the idol of Nebuchadnezzar (Dan. 3), Elias was the great fighter against Baal, and was also persecuted.

[29] H. Wey: *Die Funktionen der bösen Geister bei den griechischen Apologeten des zweiten Jahrhunderts nach Christus,* Winterthur 1957. This very careful and diligent study refines and corrects many observations already made by F. Andres: Die Engellehre der griechischen Apologeten des zweiten Jahrhunderts und ihr Verhältnis zur griechisch-römischen Dämonologie (*Forsch. zur christl. Lit. und Dogmengeschichte, XII, 3*), Paderborn 1914.

[30] Cf. Andres, op.cit. pp. 121–146.

IV

After this analysis of *Dial* 7–8, my comments on *II Apol* 12:1 can be rather short.

In this text Justin says that while he was still rejoicing in the doctrines of Plato, he understood that the accusations of hedonism brought against the Christians could not be true. No hedonist despises death as the Christians do. The apologetic intention is obvious: You do not have to be a Christian to detect the falseness of the popular accusations against the Christians. Proof: Justin himself did so while still a Platonist.

There is undeniably an element of autobiography here. And yet the intention is not to tell the story of Justin's conversion, not even to indicate a motive for his conversion. According to the context, the point at stake is Justin's behaviour *before* his conversion, as an unconverted Platonist.

This text, then, should not be put in immediate juxtaposition to *Dial* 1–8. On the other hand, *II Apol* 12:1 may indicate that the idea of martyrdom, so prominent in the Christian Justin, meant something even to the Platonist Justin.

In Justin's philosophical milieu there was a deep reverence for the philosopher martyred to death, the great model of course being Socrates.[31] This 'populär-philosophisches Märtyrerideal' (von Campenhausen) may have been part of Justin's philosophical ideals before his conversion, and if so, may have made him puzzled by and interested in the Christian martyrs. A similar reaction is to be seen in *Galen*, who compares the Christians with the philosophers because of their behaviour in the face of torture and death.[32]

In this sense Justin's philosophical ideals before his conversion may indeed have been a 'bridge'. They may have created a sympathy that helped Justin on his way to Christianity. In this sense he could be called a fruit of the *semen sanguinis Christianorum*.

We are now once more touching on the autobiographical question proper, and before terminating my study, I shall treat this question separately.

V

There was in Justin's time an already conventionalized picture of Christian conversion (from paganism). These stereotyped descriptions are often met with, especially in baptismal contexts, and are surely in the last resort taken over

---

[31] Cf. H. von Campenhausen: *Die Idee des Martyriums in der alten Kirche*, 2. Aufl., Göttingen 1964, pp. 152–155.

[32] Cf. G. Bardy: *La Conversion au christianisme durant les premiers siècles*, Paris 1947, p. 72.

from Jewish proselytizing practises. The first lines in this picture are already drawn in the New Testament: '. . . how you turned to God from idols, to serve a living and true God' (1.Thess. 1:9, cf. Col. 1:13–14, 21–23; 2:13; 3:7–8; Eph. 2:1–10 et al.). In *Barnabas* we read: 'Before we believed in God the habitation of our heart was corrupt and weak, like a temple really built with hands, because it was *full of idolatry,* and was *the house of demons* through doing things which were contrary to God. . . When we received the remission of sins, and put our hope on the Name, we became new. . .' (XVI, 8). The typical convert turns from idolatry and the coarse sins of paganism to belief in the one true God, and to the high ethics of Christianity. We find this same picture in Justin: *I Apol* 16:4; 49:5, *II Apol* 2:1–2. In *I Apol* 14 he even includes himself in this scheme: 'We who former-ly delighted in fornication, but now embrace chastity alone; we who for-merly used magical arts, dedicate ourselves to the good and unbegotten God. . .', likewise in *I Apol* 25 and 39, *Dial* 110:3 and 116:1.

This, to Justin, is the conventional picture of a Christian conversion. And Justin's own conversion story does not correspond to it at all! Justin does not depict himself as an idolator practising the vulgar sins of paganism before his conversion. On the contrary – he was a Platonic monotheist and occupied with the contemplation of the divine. This is an undeniable autobiographical element in Justin's account. And to my knowledge it is not questioned as such by anyone. Even Hyldahl concedes that Justin was a Platonist before his conversion, although he strives to minimize the importance of this fact, and denies that Justin had received an education in the middle-Platonic school (as maintained by C. Andresen).[33]

The next point in Justin's account to be considered here is his philosoph-ical itinerary leading up to Platonism. This itinerary is admittedly a literary convention of the time, as pointed out by many commentators. But this fact in itself does not decide the question of historicity. This kind of itinerary may very well have become a commonplace in literature because such experiences were frequent in real life.

And as a matter of fact the itinerary is not quite as smoothly integrated in the logical sequence of the opening chapters of the *Dialogue* as Hyldahl and Christensen have tried to show in their analyses of the text.[34] Instead of supposing the insertion or adaptation of a pre-existing literary source or scheme, I should opt for the possibility that the reason for the roughness of the literary composition is to be found in the actual experience of the apolo-

---

[33] C. Andresen: Justin und der mittlere Platonismus, *Zeitschr. für die neutest. Wis-sensch. 44* (1952/53); Hyldahl, op.cit. pp. 156s, 175.
[34] Cf. note 12.

gist, which breaks through his literary framework.[35] This is not to say that
the itinerary is a precise, factual record; it seems reasonable to think
that Justin stylized his account to make it palatable to his educated readers.
In the words of H. Chadwick: 'It is much more probable than not that we
are being given an essentially veracious autobiography, even if Justin's
memory, looking back after twenty years, is likely to have shortened and
compressed the story. Like the rest of us, Justin is remembering the past in
a way that the present requires.'[36]

We then turn to the Old Man. There can be no doubt that this figure is
to a great extent a spokesman for Justin himself. The Old Man's *reductio
ad absurdum* of the Platonic theory of God and the soul is perhaps the most
important part of the prelude (Chapters 1–8) of the *Dialogue,* and its literary
function is excellent in the context. Justin certainly did not want his readers
to think that – after perhaps 30 years – he is giving a word-by-word report
of the dialogue with the Old Man. The Old Man is saying what Justin himself at this point in his work wanted to say his readers.[37]

This does not decide the question of the historicity of the Old Man. Here
two questions arise. First: What kind of figure is the Old Man? Second:
Can the picture of Justin's conversion implied in the report of the dialogue
with the Old Man be regarded as historically true?

Hyldahl has drawn attention to a lot of more or less striking parallels to
the figure of the Old Man in Hellenistic literature.[38] He thinks he recognizes
in the Old Man the 'barbaric stranger', representing the wisdom of the
barbarians as against Greek philosophy. This was a frequent topic in Greek
literature, though no exact parallel to Justin is to be found.

Perhaps Justin's readers would be reminded of such a character, but in
the main I hold Hyldahl's thesis to be wrong (and suffering from inner

---

[35] Hyldahl thinks there is a discrepancy between the inherent criticism of the philosophical schools in the itinerary itself, and the criticism Justin puts forward in the context (Hyldahl op.cit. pp. 140–159). The criticism in the itinerary is of Cynic origin and
different from Justin's own. Granted that this discrepancy exists – it is completely
denied by van Winden, (op.cit. pp. 49–53) – it seems easier to explain it by the fact
that some recollections of the apologist's actual experiences break through his literary
scheme. If he were using a literary source, we should have expected him to adjust it
to the context.

[36] H. Chadwick: Justin Martyr's Defence of Christianity, *Bulletin of the John
Rylands Library 47* (1965), pp. 275–297, quotation p. 280.

[37] This is true even if the Old Man preaches a doctrine on the mortality of the soul
that isi ncompatible with Justin's own view (see Hyldahl's analysis pp. 182–227). This
doctrine is not important here, since the function of the Old Man's words is mainly
negative: the destruction of Platonic epistemology, cf. Hyldahl, p. 201.

[38] Hyldahl, op.cit. pp. 162–172.

inconsistency).[39] As Hyldahl admits, Justin does not represent the Old Man as a barbarian,[40] and the opposition between Greek and barbaric wisdom is not prominent anywhere else in the writings of Justin.[41] What has led Hyldahl to introduce the concept 'barbaric' at all, is perhaps the apparent *ignorance* shown by the Old Man at the beginning of the dialogue with Justin. Hyldahl takes this ignorance to be real: The Old Man does not even know the meaning of 'philology' or 'philosophy' (*Dial* 3:3–4).[42] Van Winden, on the other hand, takes the ignorance of the Old Man to be only *apparent*, its purpose being to provoke Justin to define his concepts. In other words: The ignorance of the Old Man is Socratic. 'The raising of a question in this context does not necessarily mean that the interrogator has no idea about the answer.'[43]

This seems to me a very valuable observation. Every reader perceives that the picture of the Old Man is drawn *con amore*. He compares favourably in every respect with the philosophers in *Dial* 2:3–6. He is not a professional, he is not a representative of a philosophical school, handing on a traditional body of doctrine. He is asking maieutic questions – he is something of a *Christian Socrates*. And that, I think, is precisely what Justin wanted his readers to recognize in him. This Socratic aspect of the Old Man may represent a literary idealization of a person Justin had really met with, or the whole figure may be fictitious. I shall return to this question below.

Another possible literary idealization can be seen in the *angel-like* appearance of the Old Man. He meets Justin, delivers a message, and then suddenly disappears, 'and I saw him no more' (*Dial* 8:1). The Old Man in this way takes the role of the messenger of the Lord, the *malak Jahve* of

---

[39] Cf. the criticism of Hyldahl's thesis in R. Joly, op.cit. pp. 42s.

[40] Hyldahl, op.cit. p. 169.

[41] Ibid. pp. 170–72. This leads Hyldahl to the rather remarkable hypothesis that Justin is here dependent on a literary model 'the barbaric stranger', while he is *silent* about the true character of his model, since barbaric wisdom meant nothing to him!

[42] Ibid. p. 183.

[43] Van Winden, op.cit. p. 56. The Socratic and maieutic character of the Old Man's questions is also observed by M. Hoffmann: Der Dialog bei den christlichen Schriftstellern der ersten vier Jahrhunderte (*Texte u. Unters. z. Gesch. d. Altchr. Lit., 96*), Berlin 1966, pp. 21–24. 'Offensichtlich bedingt hier die sokratische Methode die Dialogform: Justin wird mittels der Fragen des alten Mannes den Erkenntnisweg bis an Grenze des platonischen Apriorismus geführt. . .' (ibid. p. 23). B. R. Voss gives a similar judgement, Der Dialog in der frühchristlichen Literatur (*Studia et test. antiqua, IX*), Munich 1970, p. 30.

the Old Testament.[44] In the New Testament one is reminded of the evangelist Philip in Acts 8:26–39. Philip is led to an encounter with the Ethiopian eunuch, and a dialogue ensues that ends with the conversion and baptism of the eunuch. And immediately Philip disappears, 'and the eunuch saw him no more' (Acts 8:39).

The first mention of the Old Man deserves notice. Justin underlines his venerable old age by a strangely pleonastic expression: παλαιός τις πρεσβύτης. Justin obviously connected old age with authority and wisdom.[45]

And now the 'historicity'. This is a difficult question to decide, but I should like to present the following considerations: What would the literary technique of the *Dialogue* as a whole lead Justin's *contemporary readers* to think about his report on the dialogue with the Old Man? As far as I can see, they would have to think about the historicity of this report in exactly the same way as they would do concerning the greater dialogue with Trypho. In the latter case they would probably think in a way not very different from the modern commentators: They would not take Justin's rendering, after more than twenty years, to be a stenographic report of the dialogue with Trypho. They would grant Justin his share of literary freedom. But they would probably believe the encounter with Trypho to be an historical fact, and Trypho to be an historical person. And would they not think in the same way about the Old Man – and must not Justin have known they would?

I think *Dial* 23:3 is an important argument in favour of a positive answer to these questions. Here Justin – quite casually – is quoting 'a Divine word' he 'heard from that man': κηρύξω ἐγὼ θεῖον λόγον ὃν παρ' ἐκείνου ἤκουσα τοῦ ἀνδρός. There is no literary motive for introducing the Old Man again at this point, and it is precisely this casual introduction of him that serves to give it an authentic ring.

Now, what kind of person can be discerned behind the ideal picture of the Old Man? And what kind of conversion is implied in Justin's account? The following proposals are admittedly somewhat speculative, but might nevertheless be worth considering.

The two main components in the Old Man's presentation of Christianity were a critical evaluation of Greek philosophy, and an extensive use of the argument from prophecy. These are obviously also the main elements

---

[44] Cf. Hoffmann's observation op.cit. p. 12: 'So wirkt die ganze Szene mit dem "Alten" unwircklich und wunderhaft, sein Auftreten fast wie eine überirdische Erscheinung'. Similar judgements among older commentators are recorded in Hyldahl, pp. 160s.

[45] I owe this suggestion to Professor E. Molland. Cf. also van Winden, op.cit. pp. 53s.

in Justin's own presentation of Christianity. Justin himself claims to be the Old Man's successor: 'I proclaim the Divine message which I heard from that (old) man.' Justin is handing on the word received from the Old Man, and this word is addressed to potential Christian proselytes: ὅτι βουλόμενοι προσήλυτοι γενέσθαι.

Justin was a Christian teacher of the same type as Clement of Alexandria. Was the Old Man also a Christian teacher, philosophically trained, presenting Christianity mainly by means of the argument from prophecy? Behind Clement of Alexandria there is a teacher – the shadowy figure of Pantaenus. Justin became the teacher of Tatian. But who was Justin's teacher? Of course, there could have been more than one; there certainly was. In the case of Clement, there were at least three. But Clement says that it was while listening to *one* of them, 'the true, the Sicilian bee' (i.e. Pantaenus), that he finally 'found rest'.[46] May not in a similar way one of Justin's Christian teachers have been the man who made him take the decisive step over to Christianity? And may not the ideal picture of the Old Man, the angel-like Socrates, be Justin's way of honouring him? In any case, the contents of Justin's writings taken into consideration, it does not seem unreasonable to think that the words of the Old Man represent the kind of Christian teaching that made Justin a convert.

VI

At the beginning of this essay I pointed out that a man's conversion story may reveal important clues to his religious outlook, his conception of Christianity. By way of summary and some additional comments I shall try to indicate what this means in Justin's case.

Justin describes himself as a convert to Christianity, but the conversion is not described in a traditional way. It is described as a conversion from pseudophilosophy to True Philosophy. The preeminent task of True Philosophy is to reveal the real nature of the demons and to lead men to the only true God. This the prophets had already done, speaking in the power of the pre-existent Logos – yes, even Socrates unveiled the pseudogods to the best of his ability. The final victory over the demons was won by the Incarnate Logos on the cross. This victory was predicted by the prophets, and so Christ and the prophets confirm each other.

In this picture of the True Philosophy to which Justin was converted, it is easy to recognize the main elements of early Christian missionary preaching and teaching (cf. I.Thess. 1:9). I have proposed the hypothesis that Justin

---

[46] *Strom.* I, 11, 2.

encounted this Christian message in the teaching of a proselytizing, philosophically trained Christian teacher, whom he idealizes in the character of the Old Man.

Now, can anything be said of the theological *profile* of this Christian teaching? What kind of 'Gemeindetheologie' is the background to Justin's own theology?

This was a very live issue in the classic period of Justinian studies in the 19th century. Some, like C. A. Credner, found that Justin was mainly dependent on *Jewish*-Christian theology. The opposite position was taken by e. g. A. Ritschl, who saw in Justin a typical representative of *gentile* Christianity, 'ein herabgekommener Paulinismus'. Von Engelhardt offers a very lively report on this debate in the opening chapter of his monograph on Justin.[47] Von Engelhardt's own position is that Justin cannot be ranged with a specific party or group within the Church. He is a representative of 'die Grosskirche, die Christenheit schlechtweg'.[48] The peculiarities of Justin's theology cannot be explained by the kind of Christianity he was converted to, but by the heathen philosophical background he was converted *from* – that is, not *fully* converted from. '... seine Ansichten...verrathen den Heiden, der Christ sein will aber sich von der gewohnten Denkweise nicht losmachen kann.'[49] Goodenough's position is the opposite one: Justin is no original thinker, the peculiarities in his theology were already present in the kind of Christianity Justin met, a Christianity already permeated with the thoughts of Hellenistic Judaism.[50] In our own time Hyldahl has reopened the issue by comparing the theology of Justin with that of St. Luke.[51] The similarities are found to be so great that Justin can be said to belong to a very definite form of Christianity, 'nämlich zu derjenigen, die sich durch die Tradition, die auch bei Lukas zu Worte kommt, auszeichnet'.[52]

Faced with these contradictory views one might be tempted to dismiss altogether the possibility of a precise definition of the theological tradition in Justin. To call it an 'average Hellenistic gentile Christianity' is not precise; this term is more a term of resignation. The relationship with Judaeo-Christian traditions is difficult to describe because of the varying and im-

---

[47] Von Engelhardt, op.cit. pp. 30–51.
[48] Ibid. p. 369.
[49] Ibid. p. 372.
[50] Goodenough, op.cit., passim, esp. pp. 292s.
[51] Thereby renewing the quest of F. Overbeck: Ueber das Verhältnis Justins des Märtyrers zur Apostelgeschichte, *Zeitschr. für wissensch. Theol. XV* (1872), pp. 305–349.
[52] Hyldahl, op.cit. p. 272.

precise definitions of what is meant by 'Judaeo-Christianity'.[53] Instead of stating the problem in terms of these wide and comprehensive entities, I suggest a more direct approach: Are there conceptions which are predominant in Justin, and which cannot have come to him from his Hellenistic surroundings, but from the Christianity he encountered? If so, in what kind of Christian (or Jewish) literature were these ideas most prominent? The preceding paragraphs afford some material for answering these questions, and I should like to terminate this essay by calling attention to this aspect again.

Justin's Christology and soteriology operate within a battle-and-victory framework in which demonology is dominant. I even found that this motive determined his concept of True Philosophy. There is a distinct branch of Jewish and Christian literature in which demonology comes to the fore, namely the *apocalyptic* books. This may point the way to further questions. There is a close connexion between apocalyptics and martyrology, apocalyptic ideas being mainly fostered when martyrdom is envisaged. We have seen the importance of martyrdom in Justin. I should mention here his very lively expectation of an earthly millennium in Jerusalem (*Dial* 80).

There is in apocalyptics a certain rationalistic tendency. And rationalism has been a stock accusation against Justin. This list could be prolonged, but I break off to ask a final question: Do some – or even most – of the characteristics of Justin's theology come from the fact that the kind of Christianity Justin was converted to was a Christianity in which apocalyptic elements were predominant?

To answer this question one would have to analyse the whole structure of Justin's theology, supplemented by a study of the theological traditions discernible behind the vast body of his exegesis, and Justin's own place within these traditions. This I plan to do in another context.

---

[53] Cf. the various definitions given by J. Daniélou: *Théologie du Judéo-Christianisme (Histoire des doctrines chrétiennes avant Nicée I)*, Tournai 1958, and H. J. Schoeps: *Theologie und Geschichte des Judenchristentums,* Tübingen 1949. A critical review of the latest discussion is given by A. F. J. Klijn: The Study of Jewish Christianity, *New Test. Stud. 20* (1974), pp. 419–31.

Psychohistory
and St. Augustine's Conversion Process

An Historiographical Critique

The classic scene in the garden is most probably what immediately comes to mind at the mention of the conversion of St. Augustine. There, in the late summer of 386, after years of much inner turmoil and conflict, Augustine finally arrived at his « moment of truth » when, responding to a child's voice, he took up and read a passage from Paul's Epistle to the Romans. Suddenly released from the ambivalence that had plagued his way and paralyzed his will for almost two decades, he made the decision to commit himself fully to Catholic Christianity. It was, of course, an intense personal experience, as any reading of the *Confessions* reveals and confirms. Although written eleven years afterwards, that autobiographical account of the turning point in his life recaptures the mood as much as it recalls the manner of its occurrence. Indeed, no less than centuries of readers since, even the author of that intimate and vivid self-analysis long remained deeply moved by his own reconstruction of the first critical passage of adulthood : « Thirteen books of my *Confessions*, which praise the just and good God in all my evil and good ways, and stir up towards Him the mind and feelings of men : as far as I am concerned, they had this effect on me when I wrote them, and they still do this, when now [twenty-nine years later] I read them » (*Retractiones* II.32).

It is just this intensity of experience and honesty of expression that make the *Confessions* such a remarkable and valuable piece of literature. For, unlike most people, Augustine is hardly reluctant in recognizing and probing the subtle relationship between emotions and actions. The emphasis he places on the affective as well as cognitive aspects of that particular incident in the garden in Milan likewise characterizes his treatment of the whole skein of events constituting the process of conversion. Emotional impact becomes the criterion of crisis :

An intellectual event, such as the reading of a new book, is registered only, as it were, from the inside, in terms of the sheer excitement of the experience, of its impact on Augustine's feelings : of the *Hortensius* of Cicero, for instance, he would never say « it changed my views» but, so characteristically, « it changed my way of feeling» — *mutavit affectum meum* [1]).

Given that capacity for relating the external and internal dimensions of his being, it is little wonder that Augustine is often seen as somehow the precursor of the modern behavioral scientist. Thus, as A. C. Outler observed, Augustine

> was far and away the best — if not the very first — psychologist in the ancient world. His observations and descriptions of human motives and emotions, his depth analyses of will and thought in their interaction, and his exploration of the inner nature of the human self — these have established one of the main traditions in European conceptions of human nature, even down to our own time. Augustine is an essential source for both depth psychology and existentialist philosophy [2]).

Despite the obvious, if not outrageous, hyperbole, such claims do point up the fact that a central feature of the *Confessions* is its psychological orientation. This is not to say that Augustine himself was in any way a professional psychologist with empirical and theoretical expertise; rather, the point is that, since he seems to have realized intuitively that feeling as much as thinking is an integral part of living and acting, his observations regularly included the emotional as well as the intellectual factors at work in his development. Therefore, because of Augustine's fascination with the complexity of human behavior and the frankness of his explicitly introspective autobiography, there is available a wealth of data from his own hand and heart for configuring the personality of a man trying to cope with a difficult environment.

The *Confessions* provides, in short, the makings of the psychological profile of Augustine. Seen from this perspective, Augustine's conversion is not a product but a process, a series of events constituting a dialectic encounter over time between self and society that was rooted in his past and reached into his future. What came to a conclusion, then,

---

[1]) Peter BROWN, *Augustine of Hippo : A Biography* (Berkeley and Los Angeles : University of California Press, 1967), 169; the citation is from Conf. III, 4, 8.

[2]) A. A. OUTLER, ed. & trans., *Augustine : Confessions and Enchiridion* (« Library of Christian Classics », Vol. VII; Philadelphia : The Westminster Press, 1955) 15.

in Augustine's thirty-second year was the integration of basic
behavioral patterns of his identity : self-image, world view, and style.
Put another way, Augustine had discovered at last, during his stay
in Milan, who he was, what his normative and existential postulates
were, and how he would accordingly function. As such, it represented
the critical transition in his life and career, something that he not
only acknowledged but also analyzed. In their handling of this
crucial phase of Augustine's biography, however, historians have
generally shied away from taking the psychological dimension into
account. Even a sensitive scholar of the calibre of Henri-Irénée
Marrou, while acknowledging « l'importance de cette crise... dans
l'évolution psychologique d'un homme », fails to include it in his
suggested mode of inquiry into that phenomenon : « Précisément à
cause de son caractère total, cette 'conversion' offre plusieurs aspects
que l'analyse peut et doit séparer, mais dont il ne faut pas oublier
la commune présence » — namely, the religious, the moral, the social,
the philosophical, and the cultural [3]). Although one cannot quarrel
with their inclusion, one may seriously question whether, given the
exclusion of the psychological aspect, any sufficient realization of
« la commune présence » of those external influences can be achieved.
For what especially ties together the forces that impinged on
Augustine from so many directions and at various degrees is, quite
simply, the man himself. His interior world engaged no less than it
encountered the exterior world. Construed in that light, Augustine's
conversion can be interpreted as a web of decisions involving the
nonconscious and non-rational as well as the conscious and rational.
Furthermore, the psychological frame-of-reference thereby opens up
another avenue of research for explaining that conversion. The
perspective is focused in the kind of question posed by the psychoanalyst James Dittes :

> How did Augustine happen to come finally to make a particular
> set of affirmations ? To answer this question, the intellectual
> historian can trace the influence of particular people, schools,
> and books. But with so many potential influences available,
> this only pushes the question a step or two back : why should
> Augustine respond to *these* influences ? Can there have been
> something about the person of Augustine... which was parti-

---

[3]) Henri-Irénée MARROU, *Saint Augustin et la fin de la culture antique* (4th ed.;
Paris : Éditions E. de Boccard, 1958) 164-165.

cipating in the process of screening and selectively responding to the range of intellectual positions available to the growing young man ? [4]).

Working from the proposition that the subjective elements are much more contributory than the objective to determining human fate, the psychoanalytic approach answers that question in terms of a basically Freudian theory of behavior. But to frame an explanation of Augustine's conversion process in those terms, it might be argued, challenges not only the ordinary conventions of history-as-story but also the very convictions about history-as-inquiry.

At first glance, the kind of investigation proposed by Dittes would not appear to be all that threatening to the canons of historical scholarship. A sampling of Augustinian historiography, for example, indicates general subscription to R. G. Collingwood's injunction that the historian « is investigating not mere events... but actions, and an action is the unity of the outside and inside of an event » [5]). The problem, however, is that the historian employs different conceptions of « inside » and « outside » from the psychoanalyst — and, consequently, a different causal scheme in relating the twin aspects of a single phenomenon. To be sure, both agree that it involves a temporal process. But where the former concentrates on the intellectual, the other probes the emotional; and what the one sees as the social and cultural, the other defines as the individual and familial. The different approaches are most evident from how Augustine's conversion is treated by historians, for theirs has been the compelling as well as prevalent interpretation. Accordingly, three reputable and representative studies will be briefly considered : A. D. Nock's *Conversion* : *The Old and the New in Religion from Alexander the Great to Augustine of Hippo* (1933), John J. O'Meara's *The Young Augustine* : *The Growth of St. Augustine's Mind up to his Conversion* (1965), and Peter Brown's *Augustine of Hippo* : *A Biography* (1967).

Although his work is premised on the idea that conversion means « the reorientation of the soul of an individual, his deliberate turning from indifference or from an earlier form of piety to another, a turning which implies a consciousness that a great change is involved, that

[4]) James E. DITTES, « Continuities between the life and thought of Augustine », *Journal for the Scientific Study of Religion* 5 (1965), 130.

[5]) R. G. COLLINGWOOD, *The Idea of History* (New York : Oxford University Press, 1965) 213.

the old was wrong and the new is right » ⁶), Nock's abbreviated case study of Augustine's experience conveys neither the intensity nor the profundity of the crisis that the convert himself remembered. Instead, it is presented as a matter of rational calculation of options, a choice made without any urgency or involving any complexity of feeling. The gist of Nock's interpretation is that what occurred in Milan was the final and logical working out of a problem that had more to do with fate than faith :

> From early manhood Augustine sought to find an adequate theistic scheme of the universe. This quest fascinated him, and he could not escape from it. The various things which interested him — Manichaeism, Neoplatonism, Christianity — did so in so far as they contributed to this problem... So his quest ran its way to an intellectual conviction [that Christianity was intellectually respectable], and this conviction gradually acquired an emotional strength sufficient to bring him to decisive action... it is like a chemical process in which the addition of a catalytic agent produces a reaction for which all the elements were already present ⁷).

O'Meara, on the other hand, maintains that what happened to Augustine was more than the recognition and adoption of some abstract world view. Conceived as « a new study of the development of Augustine's mind » ⁸), his monograph nonetheless can perceive that moral conflict was as much a part of his conversion as intellectual confusion. Discovery of the truth was only penultimate to the decision to live by it : « In point of fact conversion came... not in the assent to propositions but in the acceptance of an Authority which guaranteed the truth of mysteries which [he] could never be expected to understand... conversion ultimately was not a question of understanding, but of submission » ⁹). In that vein, O'Meara entitles the two chapters (XI and XII) concerned with the final stages of Augustine's religious evolution « Submission of Intellect » and « Submission of Will ». Yet,

---

⁶) A. D. NOCK, *Conversion : The Old and New in Religion from Alexander the Great to Augustine of Hippo* (London : Oxford University Press, 1955) 7.

⁷) *Ibid.*, 262 & 265. The alomst passive character that Nock ascribes to Augustine's conversion is summed up on p. 261 : « Augustine thus grew up 'Between two worlds, one dead, / The other powerless to be born' ».

⁸) John J. O'MEARA, *The Young Augustine : The Growth of St. Augustine's Mind up to his Conversion* (Staten Island, N.Y. : Alba House, 1965) 9.

⁹) *Ibid.*, 166.

despite some incisive references to the agitation and excitement that seized Augustine at the time of his experience in the garden and thereafter colored its recollections [10]), O'Meara's analysis remains locked in to the « history of ideas » explanation form, a mode of inquiry much more concerned with the rationality of the action than the personality of the actor. Convinced that « it is our duty to explain what we can of the change that came upon Augustine in terms of human reason alone » [11]), he has perforce limited himself to giving a constricted view of his subject's total growth and development. Peter Brown, however, has no such compunctions or constraints — and, therefore, more compassion and comprehension. Perhaps because his biography is, to quote W. H. C. Frend, « one in which the scholar's full range of skills, those of the historian, the philosopher, and human psychologist have been brought to bear » [12]), he has captured the context no less than the content of Augustine's life and world. At any rate, Brown presents a man with a mind *and* a milieu. A public as much as a private person, Augustine belonged to a generation fashioned by old patterns and faced with new pressures. In North Africa as well as the rest of the Latin West — not to mention the Greek East — the dominant culture of fourth-century society was both traditional and transitional, with the momentum clearly running with change. Given that environment, Augustine's conversion process was not at all untoward; indeed, in comparison with the radical shifts in behavior of an Ambrose, a Paulinus, and a Jerome, his experience seems, Brown notes, almost unexceptional: « A sense of purpose and continuity is the most striking feature of Augustine's 'Conversion'. Seen in his works at Cassiciacum, this 'conversion' seems to have been an astonishingly tranquil process. Augustine's life 'in Philosophy' was shot through with S. Paul; but it could still be communicated

---

[10]) *Ibid.*, 182 ff.

[11]) *Ibid.*, ix. Obviously, O'Meara is saying that he is going to use his own human reason — in contradistinction to the credulity of hagiography — to explain Augustinian behavior. Nonetheless, his treatment becomes exclusively concentrated on just the rational or intellectual aspect of his subject, as a statement on p. 208 clearly indicates : « ... he was intellectual, even if he was not primarily interested in philosophy. His constant absorption in the beginning was neither Religion nor women, but truth : he was always interested in ideas, and captivated by them ».

[12]) W. H. C. Frend, Review of *Augustine of Hippo* by Peter Brown, in *Journal of Theological Studies*, N.S. 19 (1968), 654.

in classical terms» [13]). The upshot of Brown's analysis of Augustine's reorientation — particularly when coupled to the curious fact that it is defined as conversion only within inverted commas in a chapter entitled « Philosophy » — would appear to be, in essence, intellectually centered, albeit much more situationally grounded, and consequently not substantially different from the treatments already cited. Yet, if he speaks of that experience as « the tranquil synthesis of great [classical and Biblical] traditions», Brown can also see at the same time that this impression is perhaps deceiving. « Augustine's own tranquility of mind, however, may have had deep, personal roots », he allows.

> These are only revealed ten years later in Augustine's *Confessions*, that work of deep psychological authenticity, rather than in the formal, literary works of the time of his 'conversion'. In his formal works Augustine wrote as one public figure to other public men : he is a professor in retirement, and so his illness, the reason for this retirement, is mentioned, as are the effects of his retirement on his public career, that is, his abandonment of a rich marriage and the prospects of a governmental post : but the classic scene in the garden in Milan is passed over in silence. Yet it is only in this scene that we can glimpse the depth of the reorientation which was taking place in Augustine. It affected parts of him which bore little relation to his public life as a literary man : it affected the nature of his painful involvements with women, and, of course, his even more intimate relation with his mother [14]).

Unfortunately, that insight is not elaborated. What was broached is not bridged.

The unexplicated reference to Monica is typical of historians' failure to span the false dichotomy between feeling and thinking. Although Nock insists that « This is a conversion which rests in the last resort on the permanence of an early impression and of the religious atmosphere with which his mother had invested his childhood», he completely ignores her role in what, admittedly, « was an emotional background for conversion» [15]). Even O'Meara's admission that the « *Confessions* portray her as playing a dominant part in his life and in this they doubtless only represent the truth» does not

13) Brown, *op. cit.* (n. 1 above), 113.
14) *Ibid.*, 113-114.
15) Nock, 265-366.

prompt any effort to link up Augustine's external and internal worlds by means of the mother-son relationship. Granted that Monica was a major figure, still

> her efforts were not the decisive factor in his conversion and in his life. One can rule out of account any notion that Augustine was completely dominated by his mother. In point of fact he had defied her in his whole manner of life and more than once in important issues. Naturally, however, she had considerable influence on his actions [16]).

Yet that judgment betrays the same ambivalence about the maternal role shared by Augustine himself throughout his autobiography. As Brown has correctly observed, « What Augustine remembered in the *Confessions* was his inner life; and that inner life is dominated by one figure — his mother, Monica » [17]). This is not to say that it was a unilateral bond, in which Augustine merely played a subservient and resentful role. His own anguished recognition, at the time of Monica's death, that « her life and mine had been as one » (*Conf.* IX. 12, 30) is a revealing as it is touching. Accordingly,

> The relationship between mother and son that weaves in and out of the *Confessions*, forms the thread for which the book is justly famous. Yet it takes two to make such a relationship. What Augustine says about Monica throws as much light on his own character as on that of his mother; and what he says is less important than the way in which he says it [18]).

The same insight, too, could be applied, it seems, to fleshing out the identity of Augustine's father and defining more precisely the nature of their affiliation. Though hardly as prominent and certainly not as pivotal a figure in Augustine's life as Monica was, nonetheless Patricius did contribute, positively or negatively, to the configuration of his son's personality. The commonplace observation that Augustine's almost indifferent report of his father's death (*Conf.* III. 4, 7) stands in marked contrast to the very deep hurt he expressed concerning the deaths of friends as well as of his mother may conceal but cannot cancel out the more sympathetic composite of Patricius to be gleaned from references scattered throughout the *Confessions*. To stress the impetus of the relentless Monica need not result in glossing over

[16]) O'MEARA, 205.
[17]) BROWN, 29.
[18]) *Ibid.*

Patricius' impact. In any event, they both left their imprint on his sensitive disposition and sensible character — and, to that extent, the saint's own feelings about his parents belie the claim, made to discourage psychological speculation, that « Augustine was different from his parents and greater than them » [19]).

Not surprisingly, it has been by his frank intimations of that « subterranean tension » between Monica and Patricius that « Augustine has deservedly brought down upon his own head the attentions of modern psychological interpreters » [20]). They, in turn, have incurred at least the skepticism of historians. O'Meara is particularly critical of, if not hostile toward, their claims; on several occasions he severely censures what he considers the « crudely drawn picture » psychoanalysts have constructed of Augustine's conversion process. « Some writers », he complains, « have been less than fair to Patricius and more than fair to Monica ».

> They represent Augustine as never saying anything but evil of his father, and tell us even that that father was the sole author of Augustine's lust. Contrariwise, they commend Augustine's praise for his mother and make her the human author of what was good in him. They speak of Augustine's dual heredity, of his nature harbouring both the unbridled sensuality of his father and the gentle mysticism of his mother, and of his having within him a tangle of seething, overflowing passions, yet as being also possessed of the power to raise himself to the *templa serena* of metaphysics. They see a radical division of Augustine's *ego*, due to his parents, a dualism within him which kept him stranded for nine years in the dualistic heresy of Manicheism [21]).

Viewing the complexity of traits associated with such a portrait as inherently contradictory and therefore absurd, he concludes his running criticism with a sweeping condemnation of the value and validity of the psychoanalytic treatment of Augustine's relationships with his parents : « In short, too much has been made in this matter of questionable psychological theories, too little care has been taken in their application, and not enough attention has been paid to the evidence » [22]). Brown, by contrast, is much more restrained, eschewing O'Meara's reproachful attitude. He doubts rather than dismisses the

[19]) O'MEARA, 205.
[20]) BROWN, 31.
[21]) O'MEARA, 50-51.
[22]) *Ibid.*, 207.

efficacy of the psychological perspective and approach for historical inquiry :

> It is... one thing to take due note of a blatant childhood tension, that was still very much alive in Augustine's mind as he wrote the *Confessions* in middle age; and it is quite another, to follow this tension through, from its roots in Augustine's childhood, throughout a long and varied life. The unexpected combinations, ramifications and resolutions that a properly sophisticated knowledge of modern psychology would lead us to expect, escape the historian [23]).

Yet his reservations are stronger than his reasons; the former are beyond quarrel but the latter are open to question. « The studies known to me », Brown declares in an explanatory footnote, « ... show that it is as difficult as it is desirable to combine competence as an historian with sensitivity as a psychologist » [24]). It is both a curious and an incongruous statement. Curious because, apart from the citation of three works (none of which, significantly, is by an historian), it stands without any argument and substantiation, much less any elaboration of what it is that he expects from « a properly sophisticated knowledge of modern psychology ». Thus, the conclusion can be faulted for failing to demonstrate why the very data that invite psychological speculation inhibit historical explanation. The incongruity is that Brown's own biographical study not only disproves the improbability of combining in a single scholar the competence and sensitivity he posits, but also provides how it is possible to achieve it. Quite frankly, all that prevented Brown himself from fully realizing that combination was not doing explicitly and systematically what, in fact, he was doing intuitively and implicitly. Consider, for example, his characterizations of the *Confessions*, which he has defined as « a manifesto of the inner world » : on the one hand, « The *Confessions* are a masterpiece of strictly intellectual autobiography »; on the other, « The *Confessions* are, quite succinctly, the story of Augustine's 'heart', or of his 'feelings' — his *affectus* » [25]). The point is not that

---

[23]) Brown, 31.

[24]) *Ibid.*, n. 4. The cited works are « notably B. Legewie, *Augustinus : Eine Psychographie*, 1925, E. R. Dodds, 'Augustine's Confessions : a study of spiritual maladjustment', *Hibbert Journal*, 26, 1927-1928, pp. 459-472, Rebecca West, *St. Augustine*, 1933 and C. Kligemann [*sic*], 'A psychoanalytic study of the Confessions of St. Augustine', *Journal of the American Psychoanalytic Association*, V, 1957, pp. 469-484 ».

[25]) *Ibid.*, 168, 167, 169.

Brown is being contradictory but that the cognitive and affective sides of Augustine's « inner world » are complementary; they can be distinguished but not separated from his personality. Of course, Brown knows this very well and hence employs both extrinsic and intrinsic analysis of the *Confessions* and other Augustinian literature in his composition; again, it is just that he does not « put it up front ».

At any rate, whether because of hostility or hesitancy on their part, the fact is that historians have shied away from any explicit and systematic analysis of the mental state of Augustine at the time of his conversion. Though their resistance or reluctance may not be unwarranted, what is disturbing has been the failure even to consider seriously and critically the studies available regarding the connection between internal and external reality in an individual personality. A relevant case in point, *inter alia*, is Brown's attribution of *dolor pectoris*, a physical impairment Augustine suffered only during the summer of 386, to possible psychosomatic causes [26]). But the question remains, Was that condition a function of this conversion? Nor is it sufficient to reply that an area like that lies outside the historian's expertise. Anything that elucidates the circumstances or explicates the causes of change in human behavior is within his province. Moreover, as sociologists have already been informed, « ... the body of [psychoanalytic]theory exists for *anyone* to use. Neither personal analysis nor clinical training is a guarantee of superior insight » [27]). Accordingly, both the empirical data and the theoretical constructs for a psychohistorical analysis of Augustine's conversion process are

---

[26]) *Ibid.*, 109-110 : « During the summer he had developed some illness of the chest, a *dolor pectoris*, which affected his voice, and so would have made it impossible to continue his work [*Conf.* VIII, 12, 28-30]. It would be of great importance to know the exact nature of this sudden development : such knowledge might reveal the stress under which Augustine had been living. Some, for instance, have suggested that this 'pain' was a bout of asthma, which is often a psychosomatic illness; and it more than probable that in these tense months, Augustine had come to develop the physical manifestations of a nervous breakdown. It is perhaps most revealing, that although Augustine suffered from frequent ill-health in his later life, this 'pain in the chest,' a pain which seemed to strike him just where he was most implicated in his career as a public speaker, and in just that part of the body which he later came to regard as the symbolic resting-place of a man's pride, is never again mentioned ».

[27]) Fred WEINSTEIN and Gerald M. PLATT, *Psychoanalytic Sociology : An Essay on the Interpretation of Historical Data and the Phenomena of Collective Behavior* (Baltimore and London : The Johns Hopkins University Press, 1973) 1, n. 1 (emphasis added).

at hand. But the problem is that they have yet to be used with competence and sensitivity.

One of the earliest interpretations of Augustine's conversion in terms of a psychological frame-of-reference is William James' citation of it in his treatment of « some typical cases of discordant personality, with melancholy in the form of self-condemnation and sense of sin ».

> Saint Augustine's case is a classic example. You all remember his half-pagan, half-Christian bringing up at Carthage, his emigration to Rome and Milan, his adoption of Manicheism and subsequent skepticism, and his restless search for truth and purity of life; and finally how, distracted by the struggle between the two souls in his breast, and ashamed of his own weakness of will, when so many others whom he knew and knew of had thrown off the shackles of sensuality and dedicated themselves to chastity and the higher life, he heard a voice in the garden say, « *Sume, lege* » (take and read), and opening the Bible at random, saw the text, « not in chambering and wantonness », etc., which seemed directly sent to his address, and laid the inner storm to rest forever. Augustine's psychological genius has given an account of the trouble of having a divided self which has never been surpassed [28]).

Granted that it was published in 1901 and hardly constitutes an in-depth analysis, nonetheless James' interpretation deserves extended quotation because it contains what is both desirable and difficult about the psychoanalytic approach. On the one hand, it apparently explains the phenomenon of Augustine's conversion with a theory of the discordant personality or divided self that makes it a simple and predictable thing. His behavior, otherwise so odd and bewildering to the modern mind, becomes intelligible; its cause, course, and cure are encapsulated in a single idea whose imposition reduces complexity to simplicity. Reality, on the other hand, is not so easily constrained. The perceptive reader familiar with Augustine's life and career notes discrepancies in the portrait — for example, the sloppy handling of events (adoption of Manicheism put after emigration to Italy), the vague description of his problem (« the struggle between the two souls in his breast »), and the absolute certainty of judgment (the Scripture reading « laid the inner storm to rest forever »). Worse still, Augustine's condition is presented in isolation; there is no consider-

---

[28]) William JAMES, *The Varieties of Religious Experience* (repr.; New Hyde Park, N.Y. : University Books, 1963) 171-172.

ation, much less incorporation, of such key biographical data as his social background, intellectual interests, and religious experiences. As a result, James is unable to explain how that condition came to be, how it reacted to experience, and how it changed.

Perhaps because he comes out of a Freudian paradigm that James did not belong to, E. R. Dodds is better equipped to try to answer those questions about the structure, function, and process of Augustine's psychological state at the time of his conversion. In an article published in 1927, Dodds, picking up the notion though not the term of divided self, identifies the condition as neurotic, its source as familial conflict, and the resolution as achieved in conversion [29]. The origin and definition of the saint's « spiritual maladjustment » were rooted in the circumstances of early childhood — and therefore beyond his control, though not his consciousness.

Duae voluntates meae confligebant inter se («two wills were at war within me») : this is the recurrent ground-theme of the *Confessions*, as of most of its successors in the same kind. The origins of the conflict are to be looked for in Augustine's family history. His mother, Monica, was a pious countrywoman who had been reared by an old nurse in a tradition of fervent Catholicism, at a time when paganism was still in the ascendant in Roman Africa... While still in her teens this devout and sensitive child was given in marriage to a small country squire named Patricius, a pagan by tradition and temperament if not also by conviction... Of this ill-assorted union Augustine was the fruit. It was his tragic destiny to combine in a small and sickly body the warring souls of both his parents and a fastidious intellect which served each soul in turn [30].

Thus, the strain of their incompatibility engendered the neurosis that plagued Augustine from childhood into manhood. The tensions were always at work, affecting his outlook and effecting his growth. In the end, Dodds argues, Augustine was forced, after much confusion in his personal and intellectual wanderings, to make a choice between the competing identities of the paternal and maternal presences. « The natural man — the soul inherited from his father — was now dominant in Augustine; but it was not long to remain in undisturbed

[29] E. R. Dodds, « Augustine's Confessions : A Study of Spiritual Maladjustment », *The Hibbert Journal* 26 (October 1927-July 1928), 459-473.
[30] *Ibid.*, 460-461.

possession» [31]). For Monica, «the only member of his family who counted for him» [32], succeeded because she survived her husband and stayed close to her son. Throughout his Aeneas-like travail, her pressure as well as presence was insistent. Coinciding, moreover, with the submission taking place to his mother's domination was the clarification of the search of truth that had taken him from the company of the Manichees to the coterie of the Neo-Platonists. And it was this not coincidental termination of his emotional and intellectual pursuits that set the stage for the dramatic finale which would resolve his conflicts. «Once furnished with the framework of a theology which his intellectual conscience accepted as rational», Dodds argues,

> Augustine could not long postpone the final trial of strength between the two souls which shared the tenancy of his body. Their conflict had already reduced that body almost to a ruin. The last stage of the struggle was fought out in bodily sickness and mental anguish. A decision had to be reached, but the old Adam resisted stoutly to the end; after all argument spent, *remanserat muta trepidatio*. We can sympathize with that «dumb panic», for the battle ground had by this time shifted from the intellectual to the moral field. On the one side stood arrayed his bodily pleasures, his worldly ambitions, his professional interests, his joy in free discussion with his fellows, in a word, most of the dispositions acquired in thirty years of rich intellectual and sensuous experience. On the other side stood Monica, and the monastic ideal. He had reached, as it were, the watershed between the ancient and the mediaeval world. Once and again he cried «It is decided! I will do it now»; but his own will refused to obey him. So it goes on, day after day, page after page; in all literature there is no more faithful and arresting picture of a neurotic crisis [33]).

Unlike James, however, Dodds does not think that the experience in the garden ended the conflict once and for all. Viewing the conversion more as a suppression than a resolution of Augustine's neurosis, he finds «it is difficult to believe that this man had found within the Church the true mental balance which he had failed to achieve outside it» [34]). Rather, the introspective autobiography itself is evidence of

[31]) *Ibid.*, 464.
[32]) *Ibid.*, 465.
[33]) *Ibid.*, 471.
[34]) *Ibid.*, 472.

the continuing neurotic conflict, for « no man faces the anguish of self-analysis unless there be grave trouble in his soul... its *raison d'être* is a condition of spiritual maladjustment which must be laid bare before it can be fully dealt with » [35]). In effect, there was no conversion at all. As proof of the persistence of « the old Adam » he alleges the misogyny and asceticism of Augustine's episcopal life, purportedly the permanent effects of his abnormal love for his mother [36]). « From this springs the inability to find happiness in the love of women; from this his desperate pursuit — in philosophy, in friendship, at last in religion — of an elusive substitute for that happiness » [37]).

The deleterious impact of Monica on Augustine's personality from nursery through episcopacy is the *idée fixe* of psychoanalytic interpretations of his conversion process. « One need not have studied Freud », Dodds rightly observes, « to recognise in this exceptional relationship to his mother one of the determining factors in Augustine's life-history » [38]). More to the point, given what Dodds has done implicitly and the psychoanalysts explicitly, Monica is actually treated as *the* cause, period. The mother-son relationship is emphasized alone, at the expense of any other considerations. Augustine's social environment, intellectual evolution, and religious experiences are neglected or slighted, except only insofar as they might be used to illustrate that « exceptional relationship ». This concentration on the internal to the exclusion of the external side of Augustine's crisis explains, though it does not excuse, the psychoanalysts' unfamiliarity with, much less reference to, the scholarly literature covering all aspects of his life and thought. Even granted the obviously questionable assumption that an individual's personality is permanently fixed in the early years, logic demands that serious attention be paid to the cultural context, uniquely defined by temporal and spatial dimensions, in which those alleged influences developed and operated. If, because orthodox Freudians fail to take historical factors into account in their conceptual schemes of human begavior, « no sound theory of change has ever emerged from psychoanalytic thought » [39]),

[35]) *Ibid.*, 460.
[36]) *Ibid.*, 472.
[37]) *Ibid.*, 461.
[38]) *Ibid.*, 466.
[39]) WEINSTEIN and PLATT, 57.

by the same token none has ever been incorporated into it. Divorced from external reality, Augustine's internal development is — and can be — only analyzed within the restricted confines of libidinal and narrowly familial theoretical frameworks. Ironically, as a result of their ahistorical stance, one can fault the Freudian analysts with Augustine's essential complaint against the books of the Platonists : they are too abstract and theoretical, insisting on the eternal state of being and ignoring the actual state of becoming [40]).

Typical of the failing is Charles Kligerman's analysis [41]). Terming Augustine « possibly the greatest introspective psychologist before Freud », he holds a similar high regard for his *Confesiisons* :

> the book is essentially a psychiatric personal history without the contaminating presence of an interviewer. This history is particularly suitable because Augustine is not rigid and systematic, but emotionally labile and speaks from the heart in a rhapsodic fashion. Thus, the text has the spontaneous quality of free association, and in this spirit we shall follow the continuity and be alert for clues [42]).

His key to defining and explaining that continuity is, of course, Freud's concept of the oedipal complex. Put within the psychosexual frame of reference, Augustine's neurotic behavior is rooted in the intractable (and inevitable) contrariety of having a pagan father and a Christian mother. « This religious difference », Kligerman maintains, « led to intense parental conflict which was decisive for Augustine's entire development » [43]). Because of her incompatibility with Patricius, Monica transferred her erotic needs to her son, an incestuous affection translated into frustrating demands on his divided loyalties. Thus, at the death of his father, the young Augustine's latent hostility toward his domineering mother surfaced when he went to Carthage, where he lived in concubinage and joined the Manichees. Such defiance, it is argued, had already ·manifested itself subconsciously with his preoccupation with Virgil's moving story of Dido and Aeneas.

---

[40]) See particularly *Conf.* VII, 9. It would not be remiss to indicate here that none of the authorities cited in this paper ever deals forthrightly, much less sympathetically, with Augustine's reaction to the core Christian doctrine of the Incarnation and its decisive role in his conversion.

[41]) Charles KLIGERMAN, M. D., ‹ A Psychoanalytic Study of the Confessions of St. Augustine ›, *American Psychoanalytic Association Journal* 5 (1957), 469-484.

[42]) *Ibid.*, 470-1.

[43]) *Ibid.*, 470.

« It is my thesis », Kligerman declares, « that this story contains the nuclear conflict of Augustine's infantile neurosis and played a most decisive role in his subsequent career » [44]). But the relentless Monica was not put off, and so, in desperation, « Like Aeneas, Augustine left the seductive blandishments and entreaties of his widowed African queen; ... The parallelism is too striking to be coincidental; it was the compulsive repetition of his boyhood fantasy » [45]. In Italy Augustine was introduced to Ambrose and Neoplatonism, yet, despite what historians make of their influences on his final conversion, Kligerman insists that « another fact was more significant :

> Monnica came to Milan. When Monnica failed to commit suicide like Dido, but sailed the seas to rejoin her son, it proved to him that her magic was stronger, and from that moment he began to surrender — not without periods of violent struggle, but there is never much doubt about the outcome [46]).

Accordingly, Kligerman concludes that « the end result of his conversion experience was an identification with the mother and a passive feminine attitude to the father displaced to God » [47]).

Kligerman's interpretation is both distorted and contrived. The distortion is twofold. First, the psychiatrist posits a fundamental hostility between Patricius and Monica that the *Confessions* do not substantiate. Indeed, Augustine, while candidly admitting what Peter Brown has termed « subterranean tension » within his family, specifically states nonetheless that the circumstances of his parental relations, though strained, were more harmonious than in most other homes in Thagaste [48]). Cavalierly confusing tension with trauma,

---

[44]) *Ibid.*, 472. Psychoanalytic reference to Augustine's « preoccupation » with the story of Aeneas and Dido (Virgil, *The Aeneid*, Bks. I & IV) as symbolic of his inner neurotic conflict was first made by DODDS, *art. cit.* (n. 28 above), pp. 462 & 470.

[45]) *Ibid.*, 478.

[46]) *Ibid.*, 480.

[47]) *Ibid.*, 483.

[48]) See *Conf.* IX, 9 (R. S. Pine-Coffin's trans. in Penguin ed.) : « ... my mother was brought up in modesty and temperance. It was you [the Lord] who taught her to obey her parents rather than they who taught her to obey you, and when she was old enough, they gave her in marriage to a man whom she served as lord. She never ceased to try to gain him for you as a convert, for the virtues with which you had adorned her, and for which he respected, loved, and admired her, were like so many voices constantly speaking to him of you. He was unfaithful to her, but her patience was so great that his infidelity never became a cause of quarrelling between them.

Kligerman seriously misconstrued the nature of the parental conflict and therefore its impact on the son. (Other than the misreading of the *Confessions* regarding Augustine's family situation, there is also a conspicuous absence of any informed knowledge of or reference to domestic relations — particularly the roles of parents therein — in fourth-century society.) Secondly, there is what can only be termed the gross distortion of Monica herself; indeed, the scandalous caricature of her as a castrating mother is outdone only by Kligerman's unfounded speculation that, due to Monica's wish to be buried in Italy rather than Africa, « Augustine exulted even as she lay dying. He had fulfilled the infantile oedipal fantasy of separating his parents forever, and was even able to rationalize it as an act of piety » [49]). The contrivance of Kligerman's approach is that the exclusive use of the oedipal complex permits the displacement of even legitimate conflicts within Augustine into the wider world. One instance of this is Kligerman's invention of a dichotomous culture externalized by Augustine's neurosis. « In the childish imagination of Augustine », he claims,

> Patricius represented the power and prestige of Rome, paganism, the religion of the ruling class, and masculinity. Monnica represented Africa, the mother country, whose great city was Carthage, Christianity, then more prevalent almong the ower classes, and femininity. His boyhood dreams of glory must have been associated with following in his father's footsteps leading him to Rome — magnificent center of the universe. Carthage was great, but it was not Rome; Africans were provincials [50].

Much more captivated by the Aeneas-myth than Augustine, it

For she looked to you to show him mercy, hoping that chastity would come with faith. Though he was remarkably kind, he had a hot temper, but my mother knew better than to say or do anything to resist him when he was angry. If his anger was unreasonable, she used to wait until he was calm and composed and then took the opportunity of explaining what she had done. Many women, whose faces were disfigured by blows from husbands far sweeter-tempered than her own, used to gossip together and complain of the behaviour of their men-folk. My mother would meet this complaint with another — about the women's tongues... These women knew well enough how hot-tempered a husband my mother had to cope with. They used to remark how surprising it was that they had never heard, or seen any marks to show, that Patricius had beaten his wife, or that there had been any domestic disagreement between them, even for one day ».

[49] KLIGERMAN, 483.

[50] *Ibid.*, 478.

would seem, is Kligerman himself, for he declares that, since it proved impossible for Augustine to sublimate his tensions entirely in religion, « he fought the battle all over again in his monumental work, *The City of God...* Rome was still the city of his father, and the 'City of God' the province of his mother » [51]). Finally, coupled to and complementing those two shortcomings in Kligerman's interpretation (which are likewise in evidence in his treatment of the saint's Manichean phase) is a basic ignorance about the social conditions and intellectual climate of Late Antiquity. To think, for example, that Augustine's journeys to Carthage and Rome were merely flights from a relentless mother overlooks entirely the fact that education served as a major vehicle for ambitious men to climb the social ladder. Moreover, anyone who declares that Augustine's « study of Neoplatonic philosophy... led directly into Christianity » [52]) has not only not read carefully Book VII of the *Confessions* but has also no real understanding of either Neoplatonism or Christianity. Unfortunately, such shortcomings seem endemic to the Freudian model, with its emphasis on internal reality to the neglect of its social counterpart.

The other psychoanalytic study under review here — James E. Dittes' article in a journal volume carrying several other Augustinian contributions [53]) — simply confirms the judgment, made on other grounds, that « it is not possible to render an analysis of historical and cultural problems in terms of drives and psychosexual phases » [54]). In many ways a more sophisticated and compelling conceptualization of Augustine in Freudian typology than Kligerman's, Dittes' essay still suffers from the divorce between the environmental and psychological factors. The gist of Augustine's thought, says Dittes, is that it is not only monistic but also « mom-istic » [55]). And, of course, this interpenetration of philosophical and psychosexual tendencies stemmed from the infantile configuration of personality. « Augustine shared with Joseph of Egypt and with Freud of Vienna the fate of being

[51]) *Ibid.*, 484.

[52]) *Ibid.*, 480.

[53]) James E. DITTES, « Continuities between the Life and Thought of Augustine », *Journal for the Scientific Study of Religion* 5 (1965), 130-140. Companion papers on the *Confessions* in this volume include articles by Paul W. Pruyser, Joseph Havens, Walter H. Clark, and David Bakan.

[54]) WEINSTEIN and PLATT, 47.

[55]) DITTES, 138.

the first-born son of a young woman and of an older and aloof father» [56]). The deduction, therefore, is that Monica, deprived of affection, sought gratification through her domination of Augustine. Aside from his testimony in the *Confessions*, there is also indirect evidence of the son's dependence on a strong mother in terms of what Dittes diagnoses as Augustine's oral preoccupation, supineness as «a cowering 'mama's boy'», narcissism, self-abasement, and the hint of homosexuality — all symptoms of a repressed frustration expressed in hostility and aloofness [57]). This internal conflict found expression in such behavior as Augustine's concubinage and Manichean association, both efforts to free himself from dependence on his mother and to establish his own autonomy. However, it all proved vain. « After years of the most vigorous assertion of his independence, Augustine submitted. He surrendered to his mother, and to her church and to her wishes... He abandoned, in short, the effort to be a father. Instead, he became an obedient son» [58]).

Reliance on the Freudian concept of the oedipus complex as the single explanatory principle of Augustine's lifetime behavior is, to be sure, the most characteristic feature of the psychoanalytic approach. Employing this preconveived image of Augustine as the point of reference for their orientation, the studies considered here deduce conclusions which are not fully substantiated either in fact or logic, even when couched carefully in qualifying terms like « may's » and « must's ». Dittes, however, goes further in imposing the tyranny of theory on the data. In a footnote speculating on the cause of Augustine's « conversion », he proposes, however tentatively, an interpretation that destroys the integrity of the text, the authenticity of the event, and the honesty of the author :

> The conversion may have been part of a guilt-filled reaction to his mother's death. A rebellion which goes so far as to kill the object of ambivalent feelings is sure to elicit counter-reaction. The conversion and the death of his mother are closely linked chronologically in Augustine's own account, with the conversion preceding. Is it possible that he has consciously or unconsciously reversed the sequence ? Such a reversal would not be too surprising for a man who now fervently wished that it were possible to tell her of his conversion and to fill her with « exultation and

[56]) *Ibid.*, 133.
[57]) *Ibid.*, 134-135.
[58]) *Ibid.*, 137.

triumph» and to receive her blessing (VIII, 12). The account of the conversion episode in Book VIII already appears to be something of a stylized construction — not unlike the Gospel narratives themselves — not attempting actual historical chronology, but coalescing events of different times and the significances of events all into a more unified production intended to achieve particular impact and spurpoe [59]).

This is nonsense, sheer fantasy. It is also a sobering testimony to what can happen when external controls are absent from analysis. In response, one can point out that not only did Augustine categorically report otherwise in a document read by friends and contemporaries familiar with what transpired that summer but also the epitaph of Monica's tombstone, discovered in 1945 at Ostia, substantiates his account [60]). Accordingly, nothing in the evidence calls for, much less confirms, such «demytholigization» on Dittes' part, except his own fascination with a theory in search of universal validation.

The treatment which Augustine has received at the hands of those interpreters of his conversion process adopting a psychoanalytic approach deservedly earns the very scorn which the psychiatrist Leslie Farber has directed at members of his profession for callousness toward human subjects :

Without examining these normative statements in detail, the reader can see why psychiatry is so often charged with being reductive. For while the creatures described above may bear some resemblance to animals or to steam engines or robots or electronic brains, they do not sound like people. They are in fact constructs of theory, more humanoid than human; and whether they are based on the libido theory or on one of the new interpersonal theories of relationships, it is just those qualities most distinctively human which seem to have been omitted. It is a matter of some irony, if one turns from psychology to one of Dostoyevsky's novels, to find that no matter how wretched, how puerile, or how dilapidated his characters may be, they all possess more humanity than the ideal man who lives in the pages of psychiatry [61]).

Although it is difficult to say whether it is a charade or a caricature, the format as well as substance of an essay by Paul

[59]) *Ibid.*, 138, n. 7.

[60]) Russell MEIGGS, *Roman Ostia* (Oxford : The Clarendon Press, 1960), 399-400.

[61]) Leslie FARBER, «Martin Buber and Psychiatry», *Psychiatry : A Journal for the Study of Interpersonal Processes* 19 (1956), 110.

W. Pruyser of the Menninger Foundation underscores the applicability of Farber's general criticism to Augustinian analysis [62]. Indeed, given the work done so far in this area, one is tempted to paraphrase Augustine's own famous plea : Give me psychology, Lord, but not yet! This is not to deny the inherent advantage of a psychoanalytic perspective, *viz.* its explicit and sympathetic attention to the development of personality. Rather, the complaint is that this had been done with respect to Augustine in a vacuum. Thus, a strictly orthodox Freudian frame of reference has proved much too narrow because of a fixation of its own, to wit, that internal development is determined (*not* just disposed) during infancy and early childhood and that the reality of the external world plays no significant role thereafter. What is needed for any comprehensive inquiry into Augustine's conversion process is a recognition, on the parts of traditional historians and orthodox psychoanalysts, of the dialectical experience of any human mind as it engages and encounters reality within and without. Making adjustment for the postdictive nature of their enterprise, scholars investigating the major crisis in Augustine's development ought to heed the critique registered against the deductive mode of general categorizing according to psychological types : « One cannot predict a man's opinion by knowledge of his personality alone or of his environment alone. Both must enter into any predictive formula » [63].

Despite the theoretical rigidity and historical insensitivity of the psychoanalytic studies reviewed here, a configuration of Augustine's personality still seems warranted. Without denying that « it is as difficult as it is desirable to combine competence as an historian with sensitivity as a psychologist » [64], Augustinian historiography would do well to test at least the applicability of Erik Erikson's *Young Man Luther* as a model for conceptualizing and investigating the problem of Augustine's conversion process [65]. Eschewing the psychosexual as the exclusive explanatory principle, Erikson has provided such psychosocial concepts as « identity crisis », « negative

[62] Paul W. Pruyser, « Psychological Examination : Augustine », *Journal for the Scientific Study of Religion* 5 (1965), 284-289. It is presented as a clinical report, as though Augustine himself had been interviewed.

[63] M. Brewster Smith, Jerome S. Bruner, and Robert W. White, *Opinions and Personalities* (New York : John Wiley & Sons, 1956) 39.

[64] Brown, *Augustine*, 31, n. 4.

[65] Erik Erikson, *Young Man Luther : A Study in Psychoanalysis and History* (New York : W. W. Norton & Co., 1958).

identity », and « moratorium » as well as the pattern of an eight-stage epigenetic cycle that, at first glance, appear quite appropriate for preliminarily construing a psychohistorical study of Augustine. Other than the very significant fact that Erikson's biographical studies do not assume that a subject's religiosity is *a priori* proof of neurosis indelibly fixed at childhood, the major advantage of Erikson's method over other approaches is that it extends the range of analysis beyond infancy to include the stages of adolescence and adulthood as independent foci of growth and change in the individual. « Psychoanalysis has tended to subordinate the later stages of life to those of childhood », Erikson has complained.

> It has lifted to the rank of a cosmology the undeniable fact that man's adulthood contains a persistent childishness : that vistas of the future always reflect the mirages of a missed past, that apparent progression can harbor partial regressions, and firm accomplishments, hidden childish fulfillment... In this book we will add... the historical concomitance which teaches us how, in the period between puberty and adulthood, the resources of tradition fuse with new inner resources to create something potentially new : a new person; and with this new person a new generation, and with that, a new era [66]).

Adoption of such a model for an investigation of Augustine's conversion would require, of course, some theoretical adjustment and empirical accommodation. After all, not only is the world of the fourth century quite different from that of the sixteenth, but also Erikson, for all his insistence that one's identity is the result of interaction between the individual and his social environment, remains firmly, though not slavishly, within the Freudian tradition with its narrow familial orientation and cultural devaluation. Thus, any psychohistorical inquiry into Augustine's life and career would have to incorporate other theoretical and empirical findings. The former are available in psychological studies on adult behavioral changes that, for example, have been popularized in Gail Sheehy's recent best-seller, *Passages* [67]); the latter in historical works on the society and culture of Late Antiquity, one of the foremost of which is Peter Brown's *Augustine of Hippo*. And yet such a line of inquiry

---

[66]) *Ibid.*, 18-20.

[67]) Gail SHEEHY, *Passages : Predictable Crises in Adult Life* (New York : E. P. Dutton, 1976).

promises to accomplish for Augustine and his age what Robert Bellah found most valuable about Erikson's biography of Luther (himself once an Augustinian monk) : « Erikson also contributed to the broader problem of religious change by indicating that Luther's solution, once it was embodied in communicable symbolic form, could be appropriated by others in the same society that had analogous identity problems arising from social-historical matrices similar to Luther's own » [68]).

LAWRENCE J. DALY

[68]) Robert BELLAH, *Beyond Belief: Essays on Religion in a Post-Traditional World* (New York : Harper & Row, 1970) 13.

Journal of Ecclesiastical History, Vol. XVIII, No. 1, April 1967

The Winning of the Countryside[1]

by W. H. C. FREND

University Lecturer in Divinity and Fellow of Gonville and Caius College,
Cambridge

The Christian ministry of bishops, priests and deacons is essentially an urban one. It developed in the two generations after the fall of Jerusalem when the Church, though practically destroyed in Palestine, emerged as a religious and cultural force among the synagogues of the Dispersion. These were predominantly urban communities, and their organisation had developed accordingly. Except, however, for the final phase in Jerusalem, Jesus's message had been directed almost exclusively to the inhabitants of rural Palestine. The Greek cities he had passed by: he had preached in the territory of Caesarea Philippi, but not in Caesarea itself (cf. Mk. viii. 27) and the illustrations for his parables were drawn from the daily life of the Palestinian countryside. In this paper I propose to trace briefly how this message ultimately penetrated the countryside of the Graeco-Roman world and beyond, and to suggest how its inhabitants, finding the plain words of Jesus's teaching more intelligible than the philosophic commentaries of the urban Christians, may have played their part in shaping the development of thought and doctrine in the early Church.

The fall of Jerusalem in A.D. 70 had profound repercussions on the development of the Christian mission. Whereas the Essenes had fought to the last and a fragment of a Dead Sea scroll has been unearthed among the grisly relics of Masada,[2] the Christians, so far as we know, had stood aside from the conflict, and they paid the penalty of all 'moderates' in a nationalist rising. In the succeeding generation, whatever hold they had possessed in Jesus's homeland was almost entirely lost, and with that the chance of penetrating at this early stage the Syriac and Aramaic-speaking areas astride the Roman-Parthian frontier and the Jewish settlements in Parthia itself. Instead, Christianity became a 'western religion', and its language Greek, and as such it challenged the Hellenistic-Jewish hold on the semi-proselytes and inquirers who thronged the synagogues of Syria and Asia Minor.

Its mission, however, was urban. St. Paul and his fellow apostles had journeyed from city to city. We hear nothing of any mission in rural areas.

---

[1] This paper was read at the Summer Conference of the Ecclesiastical History Society at Oxford, July 1965.
[2] Reported in *Newsweek*, 10 February 1964, to be published fully by Y. Yadin.

The 'Seven Churches of Asia' are all in large centres of population—
Ephesus, Smyrna, Thyateira, Pergamum and the like. Though in Pliny's
time we are told of both town and countryside being affected by
Christianity[1] in Bithynia, Pliny already foresaw that the combination of
firmness and lenience would see the temples full again and beasts brought
to be sacrificed at them.[2] He was right, for Bithynia has produced no less
pagan inscriptions and no more Christian ones than anywhere else in the
empire. Christianity was propagated by merchants, men like Marcion and
immigrant traders like those from Phyrgia and Asia who settled in Lyons
in the second half of the second century. Those who heard them were
also in the main Greek-speaking artisans and traders like themselves,
individuals such as the Asiatic immigrants who attended Justin Martyr's
school in Rome.[3] At the end of the second century the Church was a
federation of urban communities with a hierarchical organisation recognisably similar to those of its parent Hellenistic-Jewish body.

One can point, however, to one important exception—the population of
Phrygia. This high inland plateau of Asia Minor resembled Numidia in
North Africa geographically. Also, like their North African counterparts,
the inhabitants adhered strongly to their own native language and
traditional way of life.[4] This area, however, came under the influence of a
dissenting Christian movement by about A.D. 175, viz., Montanism.
Announcing the approaching descent of New Jerusalem near the Phrygian
villages of Tymion and Pepuza, Montanus and his prophetesses attracted
crowds of eager hearers imbued with the same apocalyptic expectancy as
themselves. Moreover, when these events did not occur, and the prophets'
message had been rejected decisively by nearly all the urban Christian
communities in Phrygia and Asia, it took root in the Phrygian countryside,
and was to retain its character there as a regional tradition of Christianity
for the next seven centuries.[5] The cause of this upsurge of enthusiastic,
Spirit-directed Christianity at this moment in Phrygia is obscure. In view
of a recognisably Judaistic bias in their dating of Easter[6] and some other
practices it might be connected with the presence of a comparatively large
number of Jewish settlers in Phrygia originally brought in by Antiochus III
of Syria c. 200 B.C., and possibly with the success of Christian missions
in the Maeander and Lycus valleys which linked Phrygia to the coast.
We know too, from Papias's surviving work that the Church's preaching
in Phrygia owed much to Jewish apocalyptic models.[7]

Montanism is often regarded as a reaction against the growing organ-

---

[1] Pliny, *Ep.*, x. 96. 9 and 10.
[2] Ibid., 10.
[3] *Acta Justini* (ed. Knopf and Krüger, Tübingen 1929), iv. In general, see the author's
article, 'A note on the influence of the Greek immigrants on the spread of Christianity in
the West', *Mullus* (=Festschrift Th. Klauser, 1964), 125–9.
[4] For instance, Socrates, *Hist. Eccl.*, iv. 28.
[5] The best account of Montanism is still to be found in P. de Labriolle, *La crise
montaniste*, Paris 1913.
[6] Epiphanius, *Panarion*, l.
[7] E.g. Papias cited in Irenaeus, *Adv. Haereses*, v. 33. 3–4; *Eusebius, H.E.*, iii. 39. 13.

2

isation and power of episcopal government. This it certainly was, and bishops who attempted to intervene against the prophetesses received short shrift from the crowds that supported them.[1] But it was also quite a different expression of Christianity itself, as different as the Graeco-Pauline gospel was from the gospel of the New Testament, as different as the *Acta Carpi* are from the Acts of Polycarp. The strongly apocalyptic tendency of the Montanists was to be repeated elsewhere and at other times in rural Christian movements, whether we are considering the African Circumcellions, the preaching of John Ball and Wat Tyler or the German peasants' reaction to Lutheranism. Christianity really did mean the humbling of the mighty and the rich being sent empty away. Compromise with existing conventions was absent. Christianity was to be proclaimed from the housetops as the religion of the Last Age.

This was to be the permanent feature of the Phrygian movement. The important group of inscriptions found in the Tembris valley (northern Phrygia) and some found elsewhere in Phrygia dating from A.D. 249 to the end of the third century, contain open professions of the faith at a time when it was imprudent to declare it. The formula: 'From Christians to Christians' is accompanied by the exaltation of the virtues of asceticism and militancy. The worshippers decorated their gravestones with symbols of their calling, such as the plough, sickle or weaver's comb.[2]

For a century, however, rural Christianity in Phrygia seems to have remained an isolated phenomenon. The first decades of the third century saw the Roman Empire as strongly pagan as it had been at any time in its existence. 'The devotion of the masses was as unchanging as the depths of the sea', wrote Cumont of the situation in the East,[3] and the excavations at Dura Europos, a site sealed on its capture by the Persians in c. A.D. 256, confirm his statement. There, the century of Roman occupation had produced a multiplication of every sort of regional and local cult. Indeed, devotion to the gods seems even to have increased as time went on. Horoscopes worked out with considerable precision were one of the obvious preoccupations of the ordinary citizen.[4] Christianity and Judaism existed, but in no great prosperity.[5] The same picture could be painted in any other Roman province. Whether one is considering the distribution of cult-centres of Saturn in Roman North Africa, shrines of Serapis in Egypt, or Romano-British or Romano-Gallic cults, the early part of the third century seems to have witnessed a climax of popular devotion. Cocidius and the Dii Veteri on the Wall are examples in Britain. In East and West alike the Graeco-Roman world meant something to those who lived in it. The emperor, as the peasants of the African Saltus

---

[1] *Eusebius, H.E.*, v. 19. 3.
[2] W. M. Calder, 'Philadelphia and Montanism', *Bull. of John Rylands Library*, vii (1923), 309 ff., and for a defence of these inscriptions as Montanist, see 'Early Christian Epitaphs in Phrygia', *Anatolian Studies*, v (1955), 27–31.
[3] F. Cumont, *Les religions orientales dans le paganisme romain*, Paris 1908, Eng. trans., 201.
[4] *Dura, Preliminary Excavation Report*, Yale University 1933–52, iv. 105–19.
[5] Ibid., v. 238 ff. and vi. 309 ff.

3

Burunitanus show, was regarded as the source of divine munificence and compassion,[1] and the 'interpretatio romana' exercised over the local cults in the provinces seems to have been accepted gladly enough. When, in 250, Decius demanded the support of the provincials, as the inscription of Aphrodisias states 'by just sacrifices and prayers', to avert impending disasters on the empire, he received full support.[2] The Christians, while gaining hearers as far afield as eastern Persia,[3] were still urbanised communities. At the moment of crisis they were overawed and apostasised in droves. Their leaders could easily be identified and either fled or were rounded up.[4] Had the empire possessed the means or the will to press home its advantage the progress of the Church might have been halted there and then.

However, in the decade before the Decian persecution there is one significant piece of evidence that the tide was beginning to turn in favour of Christianity. Origen's pupil Gregory the Wonderworker was from all accounts an exceptional man, but when he became bishop of Neo-Caesarea in 243 it was obvious that there were very few Christians either in the town or surrounding countryside. Allowing for legend-building and the exaggerations of his biographer, Gregory of Nyssa, writing more than a century later, there is no doubt that he was the cause of a considerable swing towards Christianity in the whole area of the lower Lycus valley on the borders of Pontus and Cappadocia.[5]

Gregory the Wonderworker's methods as a missionary were extremely intelligent. He combined public disputation, gifts of healing and sound commonsense with adaptability. Having shown up the cures and oracles of the local temples as swindles he began to replace traditional festivals with the celebration of the cult of the martyrs.[6] In the fifth century Theodoret of Cyrrhus shows us that the same method continued to be used to mop up the remains of paganism in eastern Syria. He writes, 'Instead of feasts in honour of Zeus, Thiasius, Dionysius and all the rest of the gods were ordered the celebration of Peter and Paul and Thomas and Sergius and Marcellus and Leontius and Panteleon and Antoninus and Maurice and other martyrs, and instead of the former disgraceful orgies there were decorous and orderly celebrations'.[7] Indeed, Theodoret gives many examples of the Syrian countryman's needs which had once

---

[1] CIL., viii. 10570. See M. P. Charlesworth, 'Providentia and Aeternitas', Harvard Theological Review, xxix (1936), 119.

[2] Monumenta Asiae Minoris Antiqua, viii. 424.

[3] For the spread of Christianity in the third century eastwards beyond the Roman frontier, see the evidence collected by A. Mingana, 'The Early Spread of Christianity in Central Asia and the Far East', Bull. of John Rylands Library, ix (1925), 297–371 (especially 300 ff.).

[4] See Eusebius, H.E., vi. 41. 9 ff. (Alexandria) and Cyprian, De Lapsis, vi ff. (Carthage).

[5] Gregory of Nyssa, De Vita Gregorii Thaumaturgi: P.G., xlvi. 909C and 954D (only 17 pagans on his death whereas there had been only 17 Christians on his arrival!).

[6] Ibid., 954C

[7] Theodoret, Graecorum affectionum curatio, viii: P.G., lxxxiii. 1033. For a similar retention of traditional rites by the Church, connected with rain-making, Acta Archelai, 2.

4

been met by supplication to the gods being satisfied by prayers to the martyrs. But already in the mid-third century faith in the traditional gods of communities was becoming brittle. Perhaps not a few would echo the alleged words of Sharbil, high priest of the planetary gods of Edessa c. 250, that he had 'consumed all his days in sacrifices and libations of imposture'.[1]

In the period between the Decian and the Diocletianic persecutions changes like that brought about by Gregory the Wonderworker were taking place in other parts of the countryside in the Mediterranean world. Indeed, it seems increasingly clear that this half century was decisive for the fortunes of Christianity in the Mediterranean. Putting miscellaneous pieces of evidence from varied sources together one can see that in some provinces, notably Egypt, North Africa and perhaps in parts of Syria and Asia Minor also, there was a marked falling off in the worship of traditional cults coupled with a rapid expansion of Christianity into the rural areas. The facts regarding this movement have been given elsewhere[2] and I will be content with one example. Egyptians, as Eusebius of Caesarea points out, had been the most superstitious of people, but, as he saw the situation himself in 311, 'it was clear to the most unobservant that the Egyptians were deserting their hereditary superstition and were greeting every form of death for their duty to Christ'.[3] He provides abundant evidence for this in his *Ecclesiastical History* and his account of the *Martyrs of Palestine*. The era of Diocletian was to remain for the Copts the era of the martyrs. If one may add the statement of the deacon Habib, arrested in his village c. 310 near Edessa in Osrhoene, that there seemed to be more persecuted than persecutors,[4] one gets the impression of a pronounced movement towards Christianity in many parts of the eastern Mediterranean provinces in these years.

In this movement the most significant figure is St. Antony (250–356). He was the son of a Coptic farmer and throughout his long life never mastered Greek. The Christian monastic movement which may justly claim him as its founder was to express the religious ideals of the new generation of rural Christians which he represented. His interpretation of Christianity had little in common with that prevailing in the churches in the Graeco-Roman cities. His appeal was to a strongly Biblical form of religion. 'The Scriptures', he is reported to have said, 'are enough for instruction'.[5] Such ideas cut across the niceties of Trinitarian and Christological discussion in which the Greek-speaking and thinking clerics in Alexandria were engaged. The Egyptian monks thought in simple and

---

[1] *Acts of Sharbil* (printed in A.N.C.L. xx. ii, Syriac Documents, 56–60). See also, F. C. Burkitt's comments in *Cambridge Ancient History*, xii. 499–500.

[2] For instance in my 'The Failure of the Persecutions in the Roman Empire', *Past and Present*, xvi (1959), 10–30 and in ch. xiv of my *Martyrdom and Persecution in the Early Church*, Oxford, 1965.

[3] *The Proof of the Gospel* (ed. and tr. W. J. Ferrar), ix. 2. 4.

[4] *Acts of Habib* (printed in A.N.C.L. xx. ii, Syriac Documents, 91).

[5] Athanasius, *Vita Antonii*, 16.

5

violent terms. Doctrine was needed to enable the demons—the old gods of Egypt—with whom they were engaged in permanent and deadly conflict to be crushed. If it did not fulfil this purpose let it be anathema. Athanasius, Cyril and Dioscorus understood this, and became Coptic national heroes. Proterius did not, and in 457 he paid for his support of Chalcedon with his life.

In Coptic monasticism there was a strong streak of the apocalyptic, perhaps delving back into an early Judaeo-Christian trend of Egyptian Christianity, and this was fed by its rejection through despair and disillusionment of the former gods. How deeply this was felt by some of the converts of this period may be shown by an incident during the Great Persecution. In 308 some native Egyptians were brought before the governor of Palestine and charged with being avowed Christians. They refused to give their names saying that these recalled the names of idols which their fathers worshipped. Instead, to the amazement of the Jews who formed the population of Diocaesarea where the trial was being held, they assigned themselves names of Old Testament prophets such as Elijah, Isaiah, Jeremiah and Daniel, and, like many other Egyptians who had been transported for forced labour in Palestine, went cheerfully to their deaths.[1]

We find the same pattern repeated elsewhere, particularly in North Africa where the Donatists drew their strength from the countryside and inspired their followers with a will towards asceticism, militancy and martyrdom long after Christianity had become the religion of the empire.[2] In Asia Minor the Novatianists of the late third and early fourth centuries were also strong among the rural populations. Significantly, like the Montanists and the African Donatists, their bishops often represented villages and not towns.[3] In the person of Eutychian, described by the historian Socrates, one sees how among them, too, monasticism was finding a ready appeal among those whose leanings towards ascetic dissent had arisen from contempt for Christians who were prepared to compromise with the pagan world.[4]

If we may trust the emperor Julian, the causes of the popular movement can be sought primarily in the tradition of service and love towards one's neighbour for which the Christians had gained a well-deserved reputation in the calamities that beset the Roman world from the mid-third century onwards. 'Why', he wrote to Arsacius, the high-priest of Galatia, 'do we not observe that it is their benevolence to strangers, their care for the graves of the dead, and the pretended holiness of their lives that have done most to increase atheism?' (i.e. Christianity).[5] Christian inscriptions from rural

---

[1] Eusebius, *Martyrs of Palestine* (ed. Lawlor and Oulton), viii. 1; cf. xi. 7.

[2] Note *inter alia* the 'Donatus miles' inscription from Henchir Bou Said illustrated in *DACL.*, s.v. 'Circumcellions', and in general, my *The Donatist Church*, Oxford 1952, 171 ff.

[3] Sozomen, *Hist. Eccl.* (ed. Bidez-Hansen, Berlin 1960), vii. 19. 2.

[4] Socrates, *Hist. Eccl.*, i. 13.

[5] Julian, *Letter* (ed. Wright) 84; cf. Socrates, *H.E.*, iv. 27, pagans convinced by acts as much as words.

6

Asia Minor tell the same story. A Christian presbyter was supposed to be an upright man, caring for the poor, the leader of his community. In Egypt, also, we see the same factors at work in the stories of individual conversions. In c. 314 Pachomius, for instance, found that the Christians were the only people who thought of bringing food to the draft of recruits to which he belonged when they had been shut up in a local prison for the night.[1] In Cirta in Numidia, *Acta* of the Great Persecution reveal that the church there was also a sort of social welfare and clothing centre.[2] This, together with a deadening formalism which was extending even to local cults seems to have lain behind the great rejection of the gods by the Mediterranean peoples in the half century either side of the Great Persecution. Constantine had the genius to take the tide in its flood.

In the fourth century the monks and holy men were the chief agents of the final rout of traditional paganism in the countryside. In the East, Sozomen for instance, narrates how in Palestine his grandfather and household were among the first Christian converts in the large and populous village of Bethelea near Gaza, where they were living c. 330. The village had a large temple sanctified by remote antiquity, but when his friend Alaphion became ill nothing that either pagans or Jews could do availed him. At this moment the monk Hilarion appeared and expelled the demon simply by calling on the name of Christ. The conversion of Alaphion and Sozomen's ancestor followed as a direct result.[3] Just as dramatic a story is told by Theodoret of events in a village in eastern Syria in the fifth century. The hermit Abram had settled near the village of Libanus with the object of converting it. He set up as a merchant in walnuts and by intervening successfully on behalf of the inhabitants in a dispute with tax-collectors won them over to Christianity. He was elected priest by the grateful people—another instance of local holy men wresting the leadership of communities from the traditional pagan priests.[4] Theodoret also tells of peasants converted by another hermit whose prayers had expelled the local god from his temple.[5] Indeed, while a few pagan centres continued to hold out, like Carrhae, by the end of the fourth century travellers recorded that the east Syrian countryside was peopled with monks and ascetics.[6]

The reverse side of this movement was the destruction of pagan shrines in the countryside by monks. Libanius, in his plea 'On behalf of the Temples' (c. 390) castigates 'the men dressed in black who eat more than elephants',[7] who committed such acts. This is confirmed by the action of

[1] *Vita Pachomii*, iv: P.L., lxxiii. 233.

[2] *Gesta apud Zenophilum* (ed. Ziwsa, *CSEL.*, xxvi), 187. Silvanus the sub-deacon who was elected bishop of Cirta in 305 was strongly supported by the country people round about Cirta (ibid., 196).

[3] Sozomen, *Hist. Eccl.*, v. 15. 14. Hilarion himself had been born in Thabatha, a village south of Gaza, of pagan parents, but converted in Egypt c. 310.

[4] Theodoret, *Historia religiosa*, xvii: P.G., lxxxii. 1421-3.

[5] Ibid., xxviii.

[6] *Pilgrimage of Etheria* (Eng. tr. McClure and Feltoe), 36-9.

[7] Libanius, *Pro Templis* (ed. R. van Loy, *Byzantion*, viii (1933), 7-39) 8.

7

John Chrysostom in selecting ascetics for destroying pagan temples in Phoenicia in 399.[1] Monks in Syria were responsible for part of the trouble at Callinicum which formed the background of the first of St. Ambrose's exchanges with the emperor Theodosius. The comment by the blunt and irritable soldier, Timasius, that 'the monks were constantly offending' in this manner was probably more than justified.[2] In Egypt, we hear that monks from Schenuti's White Monastery harried local pagans and destroyed their temples,[3] while in North Africa the overthrow of pagan shrines was one of the favourite means whereby the Circumcellions courted the martyr's crown.[4] In all these territories paganism had increasingly come to be associated with the polite but outworn Graeco-Roman society of the cities, against which the christianised peasants often felt they had old scores to repay.

Even so, there remained considerable pockets of paganism in the Byzantine empire as late as Justinian's reign. In 542, for instance, John of Ephesus, the historian of Monophysitism, was appointed official missionary to the pagans in the provinces of Asia, Caria, Lydia and Phrygia. This is a wide area about the size of the British Isles, but John found plenty to do. He records how with his priests and deacons he laboured for many years. At the end of it, he had baptised 80,000 persons, and built 99 churches and 12 monasteries.[5] This foray might resemble in some ways episcopal and archidiaconal visitations in rural areas of Europe during the Middle Ages. Paganism was not easily overcome once the immediate intensity of the apocalyptic message was past. There must have been many who, when pressed, would have echoed the reply a parishioner gave to St. Augustine, 'To be sure I visit the idols. I consult magicians and soothsayers, but I do not forsake the Church of God. I am a Catholic'.[6]

The winning of the countryside in the East had some interesting repercussions on the course of the great doctrinal controversies in the fourth and fifth centuries. The growth of the Church had led by 325 to the emergence of the great patriarchates of Rome, Alexandria and Antioch. By 381 these had been joined by Constantinople. They were not only the leading centres of great dependent territories, but were potentially capitals of great cultural and linguistic entities as well. As the fourth century wore on these factors assumed increasing importance in the debates over doctrine. Socrates states uncompromisingly, that when easterners and westerners parted at Sardica in 343, 'mount Soucis dividing the nation of the Thracians from that of the Illyrians' became the boundary between the

---

[1] Theodoret, *Hist. Eccl.*, v. 29: P.G., lxxxii., 1257.
[2] Ambrose, *Ep.*, xli. 27: P.L., xvi. 1120.
[3] J. Leipoldt, *Schenute von Atripe* (*Texte und Untersuchungen*, xxv, Leipzig 1904), 175–81.
[4] Augustine, *Contra Epistolam Parmeniani*, 1. ix. 15: P.L., xliii. 44 and *Contra Gaudentium* 1. 28. 32: ibid., 725: 'Vovebant autem Pagani iuvencs idolis suis quis quot occiderent'.
[5] John of Ephesus, *Vitae sanctorum*, *Orationes*, xl, xliii and xlvii and *Hist. Eccl.*, ii. 44. See A. H. M. Jones, *The Later Roman Empire*, Oxford 1964, 939.
[6] Augustine, *Enarratio* in Ps. 88, Sermo ii. 14: P.L., xxxvii. 1140.

8

rival theologies of East and West.[1] A language boundary had become a theological one. A generation before this, we find the Meletians, whose strength lay among the Copts, bringing pressure on bishop Alexander of Alexandria to condemn Arius as a heretic.[2] Without this pressure Arius might have preached unscathed; but his doctrines, implying the inferiority of the Son to the Father, were anathema to those Copts who demanded that Christ should be fully God in order to save from sin and guarantee victory over demonic powers. Gradually, Antioch, Rome, Constantinople and Alexandria came to represent rival christologies backed by Syriac, Latin, Greek and Coptic-speaking Christians respectively. The conversion of the countryside had introduced into religious controversy social and regional passions. 'Christianity and nationalism'[3] had become a fact by the decade which witnessed the 'Latrocinium' of Ephesus and the Council of Chalcedon.

Within this general framework, however, of regional religious allegiances one finds astonishing variations. The countryside in the eastern provinces during the fourth and fifth centuries was the refuge of many sects and heresies which reflected controversies of an earlier age. There they often took root and became the religion of an isolated community. Thus, one of the earliest dated Christian inscriptions from 'the village of the Lebaba' at Deir Ali, south of Damascus, dated 318, reveals the existence of a 'synagogue of the Marcionites' and its presbyter.[4] There were Marcionite villages in the diocese of Ancyra in Galatia in 400.[5] Half a century later we hear of Marcionite villages in eastern Syria and of a claim by Theodoret of Cyrrhus to have converted over a thousand inhabitants from eight of these.[6] He also mentions, in the same breath, an Arian and an Eunomian village. Gnostic sects also seem to have continued to exist in the villages; that of the Sethites near Nag-Hammadi is now a well-known example and Bacatha in the province of Arabia boasted a Gnostic bishop.[7] Manichaeism, too, flourished in the villages of Egypt.[8] In Asia Minor Novatianists, like the Montanists, established themselves in strength in villages, and inscriptions illustrate the loyalty of many native Christians to their Church.[9] If any conclusion may be drawn from this evidence, it would seem to be that rural Christianity in the East seldom fitted any accepted canon of orthodoxy. The bishops of the greater sees always seem to have

---

[1] Socrates, *Hist. Eccl.*, ii. 22.
[2] Ibid., i. 6, and Epiphanius. *Panarion*, lxviii. 4. 1. For the strength of the Meletian movement among the Copts, see E. R. Hardy, *Christian Egypt: Church and People*, Oxford 1952, 53.
[3] The title of E. L. Woodward's work on the character of religious dissent in the fourth and fifth centuries (London 1916).
[4] *Or. Graec. Insc. sel.*, 608. See A. Harnack, 'Die älteste Kircheninschrift', *Sitzungsberichte der Kgl. preussischen Akademie der Wissenschaften*, 28 Oct. 1915, 746–66.
[5] Theodoret, *Hist. Eccl.*, v. 31.
[6] Theodoret, *Epp.*, lxxxi, civ, cxiii: P.G., lxxxiii. 1259, 1261, 1298, 1316.
[7] Epiphanius, *Panarion*, lviii. 1. 1.
[8] As shown by the hoard of Manichaean documents found at Medinet Madi in 1931.
[9] See the Novatianist inscriptions discussed by H. Leclercq, 'Novatiens' in *DACL*, xii. 2, 1758–9, as well as the Montanist inscriptions published by W. M. Calder, loc. cit.

9

had an uphill fight to spread their views among populations who more often than not spoke a different language from them and for generations had formed subject populations. They had developed their own traditions and defences against the foreign, urban culture of their one-time conquerors. These now expressed themselves through variant traditions of Christianity. The great dissenting movements, such as Novatianism, Nestorianism or Monophysitism drew their strength and power of survival from the support they gained from the rural populations of the East.

In considering the West, outside North Africa an entirely different set of circumstances has to be taken into account. At the time of the Great Persecution the Celtic West represented a solid block of territory whither Christianity had hardly penetrated. It would seem, where the evidence can be tested, that up to this time Christianity where it existed had been brought by scattered missionaries from the East. Lyons apart, the earliest bishops of Trier and Salona, both to develop as great Christian centres, seem to have been orientals. Even at Aquileia the earliest Christian inscriptions are in Greek and the Christian church was situated (as at Dura Europos) within a stone's throw of the Jewish synagogue.[1] Here social discontent did not take on Christian-apocalyptic forms—the Bagaudae were not Christians as were the Circumcellions—and the three bishops from Britain who made their way to Arles in 314 may be compared with the 270 Africans who hastened to Carthage in 336 at the behest of Donatus.[2] The persecuting emperors of 303–12 had nothing to fear in the Celtic provinces.

Nor did the situation change rapidly with the victory of Constantine. In the last thirty years a series of thorough and painstaking excavations has revealed that over the whole cultural province bounded by the Trent, the Rhine and the Loire, the Constantinian epoch was the period in which Romano-Celtic paganism seems to have reached its climax of prosperity. Temples, such as Woodeaton, Pagan's Hill in Somerset or Pesch near Coblenz were being rebuilt and re-furbished at this time, undisturbed by any Christian buildings.[3] In Britain there is even evidence for a pagan revival in the reigns of Valentinian and Valens, instanced by the elaborate temple in Lydney Park built in 364,[4] while the reign of Theodosius (of all people) saw the repair of a temple at Maiden Castle in full view of the town of Durnovaria (Dorchester).[5] When Gildas wrote a century and a half later that the Britons had given Christianity 'a tepid reception' he was not exaggerating.[6]

[1] I have summarised the evidence in my 'Influence of Greek Immigrants on the Spread of Christianity in the West', *Mullus*, 125–9. [2] Augustine, *Ep.*, xciii, 43.
[3] See my 'Religion in Roman Britain during the Fourth Century', *Journal of the British Archaeological Association*, 3rd series, xviii (1955), 11.
[4] R. E. M. and M. V. Wheeler, *Lydney Park* (Reports of the Research Committee of the Society of Antiquaries, ix) Oxford 1932, 60 ff.
[5] R. E. M. Wheeler, *Maiden Castle* (Reports of the Research Committee of the Society of Antiquaries, xii) Oxford 1943, 75. The original temple dated to 367 or later.
[6] Gildas, *De Excidio* (ed. Th. Mommsen, *Chron. Minora*, iii), 9: 'licet ab incolis tepide suscepta sunt' (praecepta Christi).

10

As in the East, however, the conversion of rural western and northern Europe was due very largely to intrepid individuals of monastic background and training. Episcopally inspired missions there were, for instance by Vigilius of Trent in the Alpine valleys, or Victricius of Rouen along the Channel coast, but the really effective work was done by monks who often settled among the people whom they aimed at converting. Northern Gaul in the fourth century, Celtic Britain in the fifth, Anglo-Saxon England in the seventh, and Holland and Germany in the eighth centuries tell the same story. Martin, Ninian, Columba, Cedd and Boniface all have in common the monastic vocation and the ascetic's zeal. Sulpicius Severus's 'Life' of Martin of Tours gives an almost eyewitness account of the destruction of paganism in north Gaul. Martin is described as working in a territory where 'few if any had previously received the name of Christ'.[1] His methods were simple and direct. At Levroux in Normandy he attempted to destroy a large and wealthy pagan sanctuary, but was sharply discouraged by the worshippers.[2] Nonetheless the sanctuary was eventually destroyed. The same thing happened in the country of the Aedui where he was threatened with being himself sacrificed.[3] Sulpicius Severus describes the processions going through field and pasture carrying the images of the gods.[4] But despite everything the mission succeeded. Paganism lacked staying power. Perhaps the Gauls felt, like Coifi the high priest of the Northumbrians two hundred and fifty years later, that the gods did little for those who served them and it was time to change.[5] At least, on some of the Gallic temple sites the coin series stops with Magnus Maximus (383-8), an unusual point in view of the immense output of small copper coins in the West in the early years of Arcadius and Honorius.[6] That Martin's influence may have reached Britain in this twilight of the western empire is suggested by the survival of a church dedicated to him in Kent in the next century[7] and by Bede's account of Ninian. He states that the Candida Casa at Whithorn 'was named after the holy bishop Martin',[8] whom Ninian is said by his biographer Aelred to have visited. Whatever the truth or otherwise of these traditions, it seems evident that monastic Christianity inspired from Gallic models was beginning to make an impression on Celtic Britain during the last generation of Roman rule.

---

[1] Sulpicius Severus, *Vita Sancti Martini* (ed. Halm, *CSEL.* i), 13. 9: 'immo paene nulli in illis regionibus Christi nomen receperant'. See H. Leclercq, 'Paganisme', *DACL*, xiii, 1, 329-34.
[2] Ibid., 14. 3.   [3] Ibid., 15.   [4] Ibid., 12. 2.
[5] Bede, *Hist. Eccl.*, ii. 13.
[6] See L. de Vesly, *Les Fana ou les petits temples gallo-romains de la région normande*, Rouen 1909, 78 and 113.
[7] Bede, *H.E.*, i. 26.
[8] Ibid., iii. 4. On the validity of the traditions preserved in Bede and Aelred concerning the life of Ninian, see N. K. Chadwick, 'St. Ninian: a Preliminary Study of Sources', *Trans. of the Dumfriesshire and Galloway Natural History and Antiquarian Society*, xxvii (1950); E. A. Thompson, *Scottish Historical Review*, 1958; M. Anderson, *St. Ninian*, London 1964 (somewhat uncritical).

11

It must, however, be admitted that we have little if any idea of how Celtic Britain was converted. The influence of the few urban bishoprics, of the sprinkling of Christian villa-owners or even of the fanatically orthodox Magnus Maximus, the Maxen Wledig of Welsh legend, all seem to have been small. For the mid-fifth century Vortigern is recorded by Nennius as being influenced by the counsel of 'magicians'[1]—perhaps druids, but hardly bishops. Yet, a century later, the British rulers and their peoples, so roundly abused by Gildas, were Christian. In the interval the work of monastic saints, such as Ninian and his successors in south-western Scotland and in the valley of the river Irthing, and Congar, Iltyd and Teilho in Wales and Cornwall, whose respective radiuses of action have been so laboriously mapped out by Canon Doble[2] and Professor Bowen,[3] must have borne fruit. We hear, for instance, of St. Sampson baptising pagans in Pagus Tricurius, somewhere in western Britain,[4] and in Brittany the province of Dol was pagan when he began to preach there.[5] Whatever the intervening stages, Celtic Christianity at the end of the sixth century was predominantly rural in character and based on monastic settlements such as Tintagel and Iona.

In other parts of the West, the struggle with rural paganism was only gradually won. In the high valleys of the Alps, for instance, we catch a glimpse of the dangers which missions ran when in 397 Alexander, Martyrius, and Sisinnius were martyred near Trent.[6] In Piedmont Maximus of Turin describes the countryside as still strongly pagan c. 460. 'If you go through the fields', he warns, 'you will see the wooden altars and stone images'. 'If you rise early you will espy the countryman drunk with wine, and if you ask the reason you will be told that he is a fortune-teller or an augur'.[7] Even in the time of St. Benedict a shrine of Apollo existed on Monte Cassino.[8] In northern Spain, too, Christianity advanced only slowly.

All over western Europe paganism took centuries to die out. The old gods went underground—sometimes quite literally as hoards of buried statues found on some Gallic sites show. In times of stress, however, theirs was the aid to be called upon. Gregory of Tours tells how Nicetius, bishop of Trier, was once making a journey to Italy and he found himself in company with a large group of country-folk who were pagans. A storm blew

---

[1] Nennius, *Historia Brittonum*, xli (ed. Th. Mommsen, *Chronica Minora*, iii, 129).

[2] G. H. Doble, 'Saint Congar', *Antiquity*, xix (1945), 32 ff., 85 ff.

[3] E. G. Bowen, 'The Settlements of the Celtic Saints in South Wales', *Antiquity*, xix (1945), 175. See also, the same author's 'The Travels of the Celtic Saints', ibid., xviii (1944), 16 ff.

[4] R. Fawtier, 'La Vie de Saint-Sampson', *Bibl. de l'École des Hautes Études*, cxcvii (1912), 60, and *Vita* (ed. Fawtier, ibid., cc. 48–9).

[5] He got a poor reception there, especially from the local king and his consort; *Vita*, 55–8.

[6] Letters of Vigilius, bishop of Trent, to Simplicianus of Milan: P.L., xiii. 549–58. Their mission was to a 'barbarian nation' where Christian peace was 'new'.

[7] Maximus of Turin, *Sermo*, ci: P.L., lvii. 734 A.

[8] H. Leclercq, 'Paganisme', in DACL., xiii. 1. 359.

12

up. Nicetius called on the Lord and recommended prayers. The result must have surprised him for Jupiter, Mercury, Minerva and even Venus were the deities whose aid was implored. Needless to say, the story has a happy ending with everyone accepting 'the god of Nicetius', but the old gods still exercised their power.[1]

One comes finally to the problem of organisation. How did the Church organise its congregations in the countryside and consolidate its gains? The bias among the orthodox was almost always in favour of the extension of urban ecclesiastical authority. Villages would generally be placed under presbyters appointed by the bishop of the town on which they depended. Though the Donatists in Africa and the Novatianists in Asia Minor had rural bishoprics and bishops in charge of villages, or groups of villages, the Catholics were reluctant to follow their example. Thus, the Council of Serdica in 343, under the leadership of Hosius of Cordoba, laid down that 'it is not lawful to appoint a bishop in a village or a small city for which even one priest alone suffices, in order that the episcopal title and authority may not be cheapened'.[2] This canon was cited by pope Leo to the African bishops, who told them that in 'castella' presbyters would suffice,[3] and it expresses the general view in the western church. One finds, however, rural bishops in the western provinces, as in Africa in the fifth century and in the Italian peninsula, while the evangelisation of Holland and Saxony by Boniface and his fellow missionaries occasioned a reconsideration of the role of these *chorepiscopi* in the Frankish Church.[4] In the Celtic lands, whatever the formal designation of Church leaders, the monastery remained the central ecclesiastical unit. Abbots were sometimes consecrated bishops without being appointed to sees, and there were bishoprics in monasteries, such as St. David's, Bangor, St. Asaph and Llandaff in Wales. While deference might be paid to traditional ecclesiastical regularities, the abbot and his monks whether in priestly orders or not, governed the rural communities which comprised the Celtic Church in the post-Roman epoch.[5]

The East, always less legalistic and precise than the West in matters of organisation, allowed pragmatic considerations to prevail. Orthodox village bishoprics, we are told by Sozomen, were common in Cyprus,[6] and also in some of the villages in Cyrenaica in the fifth century.[7] Elsewhere, the *chorepiscopi* had a role outside the city boundaries, especially in Syria and also in Cappadocia where St. Basil ordained numbers of them.[8] It is true

---

[1] Gregory of Tours, *Liber Vitae Patrum* xvii (De Sancto Nicetio), *Mon. Germ. Hist. Scriptorum rerum Merovingicarum*, i. 732–33: 'solus eram inter illam rusticorum multitudinem christianus'.

[2] Council of Serdica, Canon 6. Discussed by H. Hess, *The Canons of the Council of Serdica*, Oxford 1958, 101 ff.

[3] Leo, *Ep.* xii. 10: P.L., liv. 654.

[4] W. Levison, *England and the Continent in the Eighth Century*, Oxford 1946, 66–8.

[5] C. J. Godfrey, *The Church in Anglo-Saxon England*, Cambridge 1962, 53–7.

[6] Sozomen, *Hist. Eccl.*, viii. 19. For eastern Syria, see Theodoret, *Ep.*, cxvi.

[7] Synesius, *Epp.*, lxvii and lxxvi. In general, A. H. M. Jones, *Later Roman Empire*, 877.

[8] See A. H. M. Jones, *The Cities of the Eastern Roman Provinces*, Oxford 1937, 184–6.

13

that their rights were viewed with a jealous eye by their urban colleagues. They were regarded as somewhat inferior beings, and compared to the Seventy whereas the bishops could trace their descent back to the Twelve,[1] and their prerogatives of ordaining clergy were circumscribed.[2] As in the West, however, they shared the administration of rural communities, which gradually, however, under the pressure of the Arab invasions came to look increasingly to the great monasteries for protection and inspiration.

The original teaching of Jesus was, as we have seen, directed to his own Aramaic-speaking people in the countryside of Palestine. It contained many absolute demands and much that was in line with contemporary Palestinian apocalyptic hopes. By the end of the second century, however, these aspects of His message were tending to be toned down and allegorised into innocuous sentiment by the dominant school of Alexandrian theologians. By contrast, in the countryside of Egypt and elsewhere they were heard as gladly as they had been in Palestine. Antony took the injunction 'sell all that thou hast' literally, and the movement that he started corresponded for centuries to the aspirations of the rural populations in the Mediterranean world and of Celtic and northern Europe. Monasticism played an extraordinary part in the conversion of these areas. The monks showed the practical value of Christianity both by their routine of prayer and work and by raising rural standards of life and education. This forms one part of the legacy of the winning of the countryside. The other part was the long survival of apocalyptic. The 'impatience populaire' of the Circumcellions and their imitators[3] rested on hopes for a reversal of personal fortunes and status through the promise of the Millennium, and was never far below the surface. Here too, the history of the Ancient World links up with the European Middle Ages. For more than a thousand years peasant movements tended to take on a religious form. The Peasants' Revolt of 1381, the Czech Adamites, the German Peasants' Revolt, or even the Cornish Rising of 1549 are only the more striking examples. Christianity provided both the evolutionary and the revolutionary elements in the countryman's creed.

[1] Canon 14 of the Council of Neocaesarea.
[2] Canon 13 of the Council of Ancyra (c. 314) and Canon 10 of the Council of Antioch (341).
[3] The phrase is J. P. Brisson's in *Autonomisme et Christianisme dans l'Afrique romaine*, Paris 1958, 325 ff.

THE ACCEPTANCE OF CHRISTIANITY BY THE ROMAN EMPERORS

By Shirley Jackson Case, Ph.D., D.D., Professor of the History of Early Christianity, University of Chicago, Chicago, Ill.

(The Presidential Address, read December 28, 1925)

FOR the church historian, there is perhaps no more baffling problem than to account for the union that was effected between Christianity and the Roman State. The acceptance of this new religion by a government bound up with the heritages and customs of a thousand years of heathenism would be an astounding phenomenon were it not already so familiar to the historian. Scarcely less perplexing is the corresponding transformation in the attitude of Christians toward the Roman government. It seems almost inconceivable that a religious movement, which began with the conviction that "all the kingdoms of the world and the glory of them" were the proper possession of Satan, should ultimately hail with approval a union of Church and State. There is no need to rehearse the course of events that marked the gradual *rapprochement* of Christianity and the Roman State. That story has been well and frequently told. But the genetic forces operating in that ancient society to bring about this remarkable result, still await further analysis. It is in this particular field of research that our present study falls.

I

In modern democracies there is a prevailing tendency to separate sharply between Church and State. Religion and

45

politics are thought to have no common ground, no identical interests, and no legitimate intercourse with one another. But this dualism represents a psychological attitude for which antiquity offers no consistent parallel. The fundamental place of religion in politics was characteristic of all the different civilizations that flourished in antiquity around the Mediterranean basin. The rule of the Pharaohs in Egypt was so closely allied with the operations of religious rites that one sometimes finds difficulty in distinguishing between the royal and the priestly functions of the prince. The laws which he promulgated, the wars which he waged, and the ceremonies of his court were all fortified by ample religious sanctions. In the Tigris-Euphrates valley King Hammurabi issued his famous legal code as a revelation from the deity, and the conquering monarchs of the Assyrian empire fought at the behest of their war-god Ashur. The same reliance upon supernatural sources of protection and authority characterized the psychology of the smaller Asiatic nations. When the Moabites were successful in their war against the Hebrews, they ascribed the victory to the favor of their local god Chemosh. On the other hand, the Hebrews were confident that their god Yahweh had handed them their laws directly out of heaven, that he had anointed their kings in the past, and that he had promised ultimately to give them a royal leader who would triumph over all their enemies.

In the matter of supernatural assurances in politics, the Greeks and the Romans did not fall behind their Asiatic and Egyptian neighbors. The Greek city states always had their patron deities; heaven was believed to have displayed its keen interest in the establishment of centers of culture through granting immortality to their founders; oracles were consulted at crucial moments in political history, and individuals who were thought to threaten faith in the gods were treated as political enemies. The famous lawgivers,

Solon and Lycurgus, were reputed by tradition to have derived their wisdom from the Delphian Apollo. And when Greek political theory became imperialistic, in the time of Alexander the Great, not only were politics a care of the gods, but the prince and his successors themselves became deities.

The relation between religion and politics in the evolution of Roman society exhibited a similar trend. To be sure, the oldest form of Roman religion was not primarily political in its emphasis. We are able to trace back to a time when the dominant interest of the people was the home, the family, and agriculture. The crucial points at which supernatural power was needed to guard the most vital interests of society were the door at which an enemy might enter the household, the hearth where the women cooked the food, the store closet where the supplies were kept, and the boundary land of the farms under cultivation. If political interests had not yet invaded the area of religion, it was because the people had not given attention to political affairs.

When the ancestors of the Romans began to form themselves into a city state, which in time grew into an aggressive, imperialistic power, religion was called upon to produce a large number of new assurances to buttress the political superstructure. Since their own religious heritages were unequal to the new demands, the Romans imported from their Eastern neighbors such cults as were needed to support their political enterprises. Ultimately they were able to affirm with full assurance that the Roman people had been chosen by heaven to rule the world, that their kings had been of divine descent, that their laws had been derived from a supernatural source, that in oracles and omens superhuman wisdom was available for the guidance of the Senate and other officials of the State, that the commonwealth was presided over by gods whose worship the State meticulously preserved, and ultimately that the rulers of the State were themselves sons of heaven.

The sophistication of twentieth century men, when applied in the sphere of modern politics, makes it very difficult for them to believe that religion ever could have been generally regarded as the cornerstone of political institutions. But it should be remembered that in a pre-scientific age, every phase of man's thinking moved much more readily in the area of the supernatural. While an Epicurean might vehemently assert that the gods did not meddle in human affairs, the masses of humanity were of a different opinion, and were very sincere in linking their political philosophy with belief in the reality of super-natural power. And, culturally, rulers were usually men of the masses. When they dedicated temples either to old gods or to new, when they sought initiation into the myster-ies, and even when they accepted the popular acclaims of their divine descent, we have no warrant for assuming that they commonly regarded the procedure as a mere formality devoid of ultimate significance, except as it produced a desirable impression upon their subjects. That there were a few who looked upon it as sham, and who at heart were sceptical about their own divinity, is of course a well known fact. But in the main they shared fully in the thinking of their own times and acted genuinely on the conviction that the government they represented was a creation and a care of the gods.

II

As the death agonies of the Roman Republic proved to be the birthpangs ushering in the new Empire, both the disasters connected with the passing of the old order and the happier state of affairs inaugurated by the new, were closely associated with the action of supernatural powers. Not-withstanding the fact that religion had figured significantly in the establishment of the Republic, in the first century before Christ, observers interested in the welfare of the State were compelled to remark upon the decline which religion had suffered. Varro was alarmed lest the Roman deities should perish from very neglect on the part of the citizens (Augustine, *City of God*, vi, 2), and Cicero warned his contemporaries that to cast off piety towards the gods would bring chaos to society. Neglect of sacred ceremonies was the inevitable forerunner of disaster, while assiduous observance of established rites was a guarantee of success (Cicero, *Nature of the Gods*, i, 2f.; ii, 3). While Varro and Cicero took a pragmatic and naturalistic view of the value of religion, many others saw in the disasters of the times clear evidences of the working of supernatural agencies.

That the fall of the Republic was really according to the will of heaven was most clearly discerned after the event, and by those who were most closely connected with the new régime. It is customary to speak of a religious revival inaugurated by Augustus. Certainly, he exhibited a very keen interest in religious affairs as related to the maintenance of the State, and the literature of this period glows with a satisfaction and confidence born of an assurance that the new political order is a superhuman creation. Ardent religionists of the Augustan age delighted to cite examples from the past showing how neglect of sacred rites had brought disaster upon the Roman people in years gone by. The violence of a Claudius, who threw the sacred chickens into the Tiber, when they refused to eat, had been attended by the destruction of his fleet, and the navy of his colleague Junius suffered a like fate because its leader had refused to heed the auspices. In contrast with these examples of perfidy stood those other leaders of Rome who, in the periods of her political success, had given scrupulous attention to religion.

An eclipse of the sun at about the time of the assassination of Julius Cæsar, and the appearance of a comet shortly afterwards, seemed clearly to indicate the interest of heaven in political events. Virgil clothed popular belief in the language of poetry, when he wrote that the very sun itself showed compassion for Rome on the day that Cæsar bled by veiling its shining face in darkness and thus causing a godless age to fear unending night. Then he went on to enumerate the portentous occurrences which had been witnessed in different parts of the Empire. Terrible voices had been heard in the depths of the silent groves. Terrifying apparitions had been seen in the early dawn. The beasts of the field had uttered human speech. Rivers had been suddenly swallowed up by terrifying cracks that had appeared in the earth. In the temples images of ivory and bronze had wept and perspired. Floods had swept away whole forests, had devastated cultivated fields, and carried away the cattle in their stalls. Wells of water had turned into blood, and wolves had appeared in the very heart of the city. Sudden electric storms had been very frequent and of great severity, and a fearful comet had appeared. These terrifying manifestations were prophetic of that climax of agony to be experienced in the terrible civil strife which brought the Republic to an end. Heaven had forecast the fact that "Thessaly and the broad plains of Hæmus should twice be glutted with Roman blood" (Virgil, *Georgic* i, 492).

The language of Pliny the Elder, as one would expect from this Epicurean naturalist, is more sober but hardly less significant. He reports that the comet, which had showed itself for seven days during the period when Augustus was celebrating games in honor of Venus, was taken by the common people to indicate that the soul of the murdered Cæsar had been admitted to a place among the immortal gods. But Augustus saw in the phenomenon an indication of heaven's favor for the new régime. While in public he expressed himself in agreement with popular opinion, in secret "he rejoiced at this auspicious omen, interpreting it as produced for himself." And even the sceptical Pliny adds "to confess the truth, it really proved a salutary omen for the whole world at large" (Pliny, *Natural History*, ii, 23). Very apparently the man in the street, the new emperor himself, and even the most noted scientist of the next century, each in his own way, coupled the political events attending the rise of the Empire with the operation of cosmic powers.

Above all others, Virgil was the prophet of the new day. In his oft-quoted Fourth Eclogue he boldly forecasts the early end of the times of agony and the dawning of a new day when the political order will embody more perfectly the kindly will of heaven. Men are to be liberated from their age-long fears, and only a few stains of the old-time sin will survive. Under the rule of a heaven-born king the earth will bring forth her fruits spontaneously, the warring elements in nature will be transformed into agencies of peace, the lion will no longer prey upon the ox, the serpent and the poisonous herbs will be exterminated, and foreign spice plants will grow spontaneously in every field. The ripening grain will no longer be smitten by blight, the grapes will hang in abundance on the bramble, and the sturdy oak will drip honey. Such are to be the divinely bestowed blessings accompanying the inauguration of the new age to be attained through the supernatural establishment of a new political order.

Virgil was more fortunate than most prophets in living to see the day when he could believe that to a considerable degree his predictions had attained fulfilment. With the institution of the new régime under Augustus, Roman history could be reread in a new light and the care of the gods for Roman politics could be discerned with new clearness and new assurances. Now the poet could say without hesitation that in the person of Augustus is to be seen the fulfilment of a divine prophecy to the effect that Ilia shall bear to the loins of Mars twin children, and that no bounds shall be set to the fortunes of the Romans, nor any term of years, for theirs is to be a never ending empire (*Æneid*, i, 272 ff.).

When we recognize the genuine interest in the super-natural which characterized the psychology of Roman imperialism, it sheds light upon a number of concurrent circumstances. It is the presence of this attitude of mind in the Roman world that makes possible, and popular, that astonishing phenomenon known as emperor worship. It ought to be apparent even to the casual observer that the Romans did not philosophize their way into this cult, by first working out a logical definition of deity as applied to the person of the ruler. Nor was emperor worship in the first instance a superimposition of the imperial court or the Senate upon the Roman world. Rather, it was the outcome of that world's effort to express its appreciation of the new, stable order of things which had been introduced into the Mediterranean basin through the elevation to power of a prince capable of maintaining peace and prosperity. Of course, the phenomenon was not wholly new. The same type of religious psychology had long existed in the East, whence the incentive for the Roman practice derived a large measure of stimulus. But, granting a situation in which people customarily credit political well-being to divine favor, it is not difficult to realize how easy it would be for them to regard the vast and powerful Roman Empire as a genuinely superhuman creation, and to think of the emperor in whom the authority centered as himself divine. Various as may have been the factors that contributed to the rise of the imperial cult, the characteristic attitude of the Romans toward religion as the foundation of political welfare, alone makes the phenomenon explicable.

The attitude in question is further illustrated by the

method of the Roman government in dealing with foreign cults. The traditions regarding formal acceptance of such cults may often be of doubtful validity, but the interpretation put upon those traditions in the imperial age is fairly clear. Livy, for example, makes it perfectly evident that the admission of a foreign god into the sacred precincts of Rome is a very serious business and a matter of fundamental significance for the welfare of the State. While it is true that in general foreign religions are to be accepted with reserve and strange rites are to be kept strictly within bounds, there is a manifest feeling that the Roman government has been able in the past to secure no small measure of benefit through the official adoption of certain foreign religions. In this way a very real supernatural increment had been added to that body of divine guarantees with which the political career of Rome began.

Hostile procedure of the government against foreign religions and philosophies is similarly motivated. It is true that practical politicians of the old school, who raised their voices from time to time in protest against the influx of those foreign cults which became more and more numerous in the imperial age, often speak as though they felt that the danger lay only in the natural realm of social well-being. They fear a perversion of Roman morals, or instigation to rebellion hatched up in secret meetings, and like social dangers. Yet these men are not unaware of the fact that the safety of Roman society rests upon the perpetuation of established customs in dealing with the divine power. The words which Cassius Dio puts into the mouth of Mæcenas as an admonition to Augustus, an address which is really meant for the benefit of the youthful Alexander Severus of Dio's own day, are typical:

Reverence the divine power yourself everywhere in every way, following our fathers' belief, and compel others to honor it. Those who introduce strange ideas about it you should both hate and punish, not only for the sake of the gods (because if a man despise them, he will esteem naught else sacred) but because such persons by bringing in new divinities, persuade many to adopt foreign principles of law. As a result, conspiracies, factions and clubs arise which are far from desirable under a monarchy. Accordingly, do not grant any atheist or charlatan the right to be at large. The art of soothsaying is a necessary one, and you should by all means appoint some men to be diviners and augurs, to whom people can resort who desire to consult them on any matter, but there ought to be no workers of magic. Such men tell partly truths but mostly lies and frequently inspire many of their followers to rebel (lii., 36).

The State's attitude of reverence toward the supernatural is still further attested by its later adoption of oriental religions, particularly the worship of the invincible sun (*sol invictus*). For a long time many Romans must have felt the inability of their own religion to provide a deity whose original magnitude was sufficient to correspond with the vastness of the Empire. Even Virgil had set the example at the very beginning of imperial times, of appealing to the sun as the true divinity who watched over the affairs of state (*Georgic* i, 463 ff.). But it was not until the third century that the oriental cult of the sun came to be fully at home in Rome and to constitute the principal religious assurance of the Empire. The motive inspiring the State in its loyalty to this new-found deity is very manifestly its desperate quest for supernatural help during the period of continued distress and frequent chaos experienced in the history of the Empire after the death of Marcus Aurelius.

A glance at the religious features of the reforms of Diocletian helps one to realize still more certainly that the late Empire had lost none of its interest in religion as basal to a well ordered government. While there had been a considerable change in the formalities of religion, as compared with the situation in the earlier days of the Empire, the same psychological attitude still prevailed.   Politics and religion were viewed as one common area of interest, and affairs of state were thought to be safe only when there was close union between the government and the gods.   While Diocletian took the title of *Jovius*, and Maximian that of *Herculius*, it was no longer the old Roman Jupiter and Hercules from whom the two Augusti thought to derive their right and power, but it was in reality the oriental *sol invictus* to whom they attached themselves in the hope of insuring restoration and permanence to the tottering Empire.   It is further significant in this connection that two years after Diocletian's retirement, when he and his old colleague met for a conference at Carnuntum to devise plans for averting the growing menace of political disintegration, their first act was to restore in that city one of the temples of this oriental deity.   By paying him this new attention they evidently thought they would secure a new increment of divine help for healing the ills of the distressed political order.

Perhaps it is unfair to generalize upon this hasty survey of examples illustrative of the religious psychology of Roman imperialism.   But as everyone doubtless knows, the number of illustrations might have been almost indefinitely multiplied.   The characteristic attitude of the Roman government toward religion throughout the whole of the imperial period was one of marked deference and very serious concern.   Interest in the old religion of the Roman people rested upon a firm and persistent conviction that the inherited religious observances were an assurance of safety to the State.   When new cults became popular, the State's attitude toward them was determined by the same criterion of value.   If they were thought to work harm to the public welfare, either by diverting the citizens into unprofitable areas of thought or action, or by angering the deities through consequent neglect, then the State was hostile toward the new cult. On the other hand, when the authorities saw a cult sufficiently powerful to attract wide attention, and when it seemed to offer new and larger guarantees of supernatural protection for the government, it was not only tolerated but by many of the princes very heartily espoused. Thus religion and politics, or, as we might say, Church and State, were never dissociated in imperial Rome, and in the thought of the people of that age religion constituted the ultimate ground of confidence in the stability and perpetuity of the political order.

III

In the light of the foregoing observations, the circumstances which brought about the Roman Empire's acceptance of Christianity, first as a tolerated religion and later as the only religion recognized by the State, become readily understandable. It must be remembered that we are not here speaking of the gradual process of historical evolution by which the Christian movement, originally an obscure oriental cult, attracted to its membership increasing numbers of adherents from Roman society at large. That would be a long story and involve the examination of a wide range of social phenomena in the Mediterranean world over a period of some three hundred years. The specific point that concerns us here is to explain the action of the Roman government itself in accepting Christianity as a favored religion of the State. Does this change represent some radical reversal of the religious psychology of the Empire? Is the policy of the government fundamentally altered by the acceptance of Christianity? Or has Christianity now come to share essentially the same sort of favor from the authorities that had always been a part of the imperial policy toward recognized areas of supernatural operation?

In the first place, the persecutions of Christianity by

the Roman government should give us some light on this problem. Such persecutions as occurred before the year 250 can scarcely be said to show any general aggressive policy of the government toward Christianity. To be sure, this new religion had fallen into disfavor in many parts of the Empire and certain officials had taken action against it, but for reasons that were in themselves mainly local. The central government had from time to time placed its approval upon the action of its representatives, but it had not itself, so far as we are aware, issued any formal declaration of policy applicable to the whole kingdom. The Christians had been roughly handled by the authorities at various points in the Empire, as occasion arose, on account of the offense which they gave either to the populace or to the local officials. The characteristic charge brought against them was in effect that they were enemies to society. They held secret meetings, they indulged in private religious rites, they refused to participate in the local, traditional religious activities. When put to the test, they would not acknowledge Cæsar as lord. They declared that the traditional gods were no gods, but were merely demons. Now in a state where religious guarantees were thought to furnish society its most genuine safeties, it is easy to perceive how Christians would incur the hostility of the authorities, and it is just here that we find the most satisfactory answer to the question, why Christianity was persecuted by the Roman government. The Roman officials never concerned themselves with specific items of Christian religious teaching, and they did not entertain any unusual measure of hostile feeling toward this new religion merely because it was a foreign cult. That was a phenomenon with which Roman society had become thoroughly familiar. But amid this mixture of religions, Christians soon became conspicuous on account of their so-called atheism, which it should be remembered is not a charge that they do not believe in any god, but rather that they do not believe in the established gods. By this attitude, they were of course threatening the very foundations of political safety as interpreted by the characteristic psychology of the imperial age.

By the middle of the third century the Christian movement had become so conspicuous in society that the emperor Decius instituted persecution of Christians as a deliberate policy of the government. His first demand was that sacrifice should be made to the gods of the State, and to the genius of the emperor. The authorities were instructed to strike particularly at the leaders of Christianity, although the requirement to sacrifice was universally applicable, and disobedience was punishable by death. Decius' own death in 251 interrupted the imperial program, but only temporarily. Valerian introduced it with vigor again in the year 258, decreeing particularly that the clergy should be put to death. But Valerian's rule ceased two years later, and it was a quarter of a century before Rome had another emperor with enough vigor, or one sufficiently interested in reorganizing the government, to give religious affairs customary attention. But under Diocletian and his colleague Galerius, religion along with other phases of social reform received proportionate consideration. In the year 303 the most severe and thoroughgoing persecution that had ever been experienced by Christians was set in motion, and when Diocletian retired in 305, his colleague Galerius still continued the policy of bringing Christians into line with the demand that all persons should worship the national gods.

It is important to note that the primary purpose of hostile action against Christians was to correct their atheism. They were dangerous to the State just because they slighted the gods who were supposed to insure the safety of the State. It is perfectly apparent that the Roman government would not have molested Christianity, merely as a foreign religious movement within the Empire, had Christians been willing to reverence the gods of the State side by side with their own special deities.   It was this exclusiveness which distinguished the Christians from the adherents of other cults who were unmolested by the authorities.   It would be just to say that the imperial government had no quarrel with Christianity as such, but only with that dangerous attitude which Christians assumed in refusing to revere those supernatural sources of authority which were supposed to guarantee the safety of the State.   And in those days, when the State was suffering from calamities of so many sorts,—the successful incursions of barbarians, the breaking down of economic prosperity, and other evidences of social disintegration,—it was thought by the best emperors to be a serious obligation on their part to restore the rites of religion as a corrective, and in the last analysis the only sure corrective, for the evils of the day.

By the year 300 Christianity had become too widely accepted in Roman society to make possible a successful persecution on the part of the government.   This fact was soon perceived by the emperors, who drew therefrom a characteristically Roman inference.   Throughout the imperial period new religious authorities had been introduced from time to time to supplement the older divinities, with the hope that these new gods would give to the State the strength needed to establish the social order in safety.   When the government became convinced that any religion had sufficient adherents to constitute a respectable body of worshipers to petition its divinities on behalf of the State, its aid might consistently be sought, provided it supplemented and did not abrogate traditional Roman religion.   Hence for the members of some new religion to worship their own gods, side by side with the gods of the State, might easily be regarded as a virtue, in that it would contribute to the common welfare that measure of supernatural help, though it might be never so small, represented by the particular deity of the cult. But the persecutors very soon discovered that Christians, when required to worship the gods of the State, either obeyed only half-heartedly or else positively refused to yield, and being no longer permitted to continue their own form of worship, they might come to constitute a rather large non-worshipping section of the population. This fact alarmed the observant emperor Galerius, who evidently was a true exponent of characteristic religious psychology of the Roman type. He very soon deplored the fact that by the persecution of the Christians the number of channels through which divine power might be drawn down from heaven into the society of the Empire was actually being reduced.

This discovery was the signal for a complete reversal of policy in dealing with Christians. The emperor's state of mind is perfectly clear from the edict of the year 311:

Among our other measures which we are always making for the use and profit of the commonwealth, we have hitherto endeavored to bring all things into conformity with the ancient laws and public order of the Romans, and to bring it about also that the Christians who have abandoned the religion of their ancestors should return to sound reason, for in some ways such wilfulness has seized the Christians and such folly possessed them that they do not follow those constitutions of the ancients which peradventure their own ancestors first established, but entirely according to their own judgment and as it pleased them they were making such [religious] laws for themselves as they would observe and in different places were assembling various sorts of people. In short, when our command was issued, that they were to betake themselves to the institutions of the ancients, many of them were subdued by danger and many also were ruined. Yet when great numbers of them held to their determination and we saw that they neither gave worship and due reverence to the gods nor yet regarded the God of the Christians, we therefore, mindful of our most mild clemency and of the unbroken custom whereby we are accustomed to grant pardon to all men, have thought that in this case also speediest indulgence ought to be granted to them, that the Christians might exist again and might establish their gatherings. Yet, so that they do nothing contrary to good order. Therefore, in accordance with this our indulgence, they ought to pray their God for our good estate, for that of the commonwealth and for their own, that the commonwealth may endure on every side unharmed and that they may be able to live securely in their own homes (Eusebius, *Church History*, viii. 17).

In this decree of toleration has the religious policy of the Roman Empire undergone any fundamental change? Or rather, have we not here simply an extension of a policy with which we are already thoroughly familiar? The controlling motive in the edict of Galerius is to secure an increment of supernatural assistance for the Empire through allowing the Christians to worship their own God unmolested. The emperor may think that this benefit will be relatively small, but nevertheless Christians constitute a sufficiently large element in society to cause him to regard their cult with respect. The charge of insincerity sometimes laid at the door of Galerius by Christian historians, or the assertion that he changed his attitude because he felt death to be near at hand, are explanations for which I find not the slightest justification. He is a perfectly good exponent to the very last of the traditional religious policy of Roman imperialism.

Constantine's attitude toward Christianity, when he and Licinius expressed their approval in what has commonly been called the first edict of toleration in 313, is almost identical with that of Galerius, and is just that of the characteristic Roman ruler, who is interested in religion because it supports the State through appeal to supernatural power. A few sentences from the document suffice to make this plain:

When I, Constantine Augustus, and I, Licinius Augustus, had happily met together at Milan and were having under consideration all things which concern the advantage and security of the State, we thought that, among other things which seemed likely to profit men generally we ought in the very first place to set in order the conditions of the reverence paid to the divinity by giving to the Christians and all others full permission to follow whatever worship any man had chosen, whereby whatever divinity there is in heaven may be benevolent and propitious to us and to all placed under our authority. . . . These things we thought it well to signify in the fullest manner to your carefulness, that you might know that we have given free and absolute permission to the said Christians to practice their worship, and when you perceive that we have granted this to the said Christians, your devotion understands that to others also a similar full and free permission for their own worship and observance is granted for the quiet of our times, so that every man may have freedom in the practice of whatever worship he has chosen. And these things were done by us that nothing be taken away from any honor or form of worship (Lactantius, *De Mortibus Persecutorum*, 48).

In this document one perceives very easily the real basis of Constantine's favor for Christianity. First, there is the characteristic attitude of an emperor who is seeking supernatural support for his government, and secondly, there is a recognition of the fact that the Christian element in the population has now become so large, and its support of Constantine and Licinius in their conflict with rivals who still opposed Christianity, is so highly esteemed, that the emperors are ready to credit the Christian God with the exercise of a measure of supernatural power on a par with that of the other gods of the State. As time went on, Constantine and his successors became more and more fully satisfied that the supernatural sources of power available to the Christians were alone adequate to meet the political situation. Constantine's ultimate victory over all his rivals seemed to be a very substantial evidence of the correctness of this position, and two generations later Theodosius was willing to risk all in the keeping of the Christian God.

If the foregoing interpretation of the historical process is correct, the acceptance of Christianity by the state authorities is after all not a strange phenomenon. It represents essentially a perpetuation of the characteristic religious psychology of all emperors. The adoption of Christianity by an emperor was not essentially different in principle from the conversion to *sol invictus*. The event was the outcome of a long process of social development. Gradually the Christian movement had won to itself larger and larger elements in society. Alarmed at its so-called atheism, some of the more vigorous rulers had attempted to whip its adherents into line and prevent their endangering the safety of the State by neglecting worship of the national gods. But, failing in this attempt, and discovering that Christians still survived and the State suffered no immediate calamity in consequence of this persistence, the emperor determined to use such help as Christians were able to give by their prayers for the State and their pledge of the favors which their God was able to bestow.

When the emperors made overtures they found the Christians ready to respond. Even as early as the second century, some Christian leaders had discovered that the real basis of imperial hostility was a fear that the Christians were dangerous to the State because their atheism was supposed to threaten its religious foundations. On learning of this, Christians rapidly changed from their original attitude of indifference toward politics, or of tacit hostility, and proceeded to affirm more and more clearly that they were ready to pray for emperors, and to assert that the adherents of this new religion constituted the most valuable element in imperial society because they themselves were in league with the God of gods, the supreme creator and master of the universe. Long before any emperor accepted their promises of help, they had been proffering their services to the State through declarations of loyalty on the part of their apologists. On one point only were they unyielding. They refused to worship any deities except those of their own cult, their Lord Jesus Christ and the God whom they had taken over from their Hebrew predecessors. But they unblushingly declared themselves to be the most honest people in the State, the most ready to pay taxes, and the most zealous and effective in their prayers on behalf of the commonwealth. As late as the end of the second century, a Tertullian could still think it impossible that any Roman emperor should ever be a Christian, but in the fourth century large numbers of Christians had attained a psychology that could pronounce the marriage between the Christian religion and Roman politics to be a perfectly legitimate and divinely authenticated union. Presently it came to be a commonly accepted opinion that Christianity and the empire were co-extensive and co-eternal. A transcendentalized imperial system furnished Augustine his model for the true city of God on earth, and the Christian Jerome, on learning of the sack of the Eternal City by Alaric, was benumbed with grief and astonishment. Evidently the eternity of the Roman State had now become as essential a belief for the Christian theologian as it had formerly been for the old Roman politician.

This was really a much more radical change in the Christian attitude as compared with earlier views, than was the change which the emperors underwent when they admitted Christianity among the recognized religions of the State, or even when they made it the only legitimate religion. If a summary statement is to be made, we should have to say that Roman emperors in adopting the new religion departed less radically from the psychology of their predecessors than Christians did in becoming Roman imperialists.

THE ADOPTION OF CHRISTIANITY IN THE ROMAN EMPIRE

By The Rev. ARNOLD EHRHARDT, Dr. jur., Ph.D., B.D.

BISHOP FRASER SENIOR LECTURER IN ECCLESIASTICAL HISTORY IN THE UNIVERSITY OF MANCHESTER.

I

ABOUT 2000 years ago a Jewish carpenter, Jesus of Nazareth, a visionary and a miracle worker, walked through Palestine. In the year A.D. 33 he decided to go, together with some of his friends, to the Jewish Passover in Jerusalem. Those friends were deeply impressed by him and regarded him as the Messiah, who had been promised to the Jews in the O.T. Since, however, the title of Messiah, " the Christ " in Greek, was dangerous in the unruly Jewish country, he was arrested—one of the friends played the unworthy part of informer in this catastrophe—and the representative of the Roman occupying power, one Pontius Pilate, a fairly brutal professional soldier, decided to let him be hanged on the gallows as a traitor. This is a fairly simple story, which happened many times in Palestine, as we can learn even from the very scanty source-material which is still at our disposal.

Now, however, the unexpected and indeed miraculous happened. The companions, who at the arrest of their master had shown anything rather than heroism, suddenly came into the open and declared that this very Jesus had appeared to them, two days after his execution, alive in his body, and that he was God, the Son of God. There are two things which are indeed astounding in this annunciation by the companions of Jesus : The first is that devout Jews, and there is no doubt that Jesus and his companions were devout Jews, could make such a statement at all. " There is no God, but God ", this watchword of Islam, comes from the most sacred prayer of Judaism, the shm'ah, " Hear O Israel, the Lord thy God is one God ", and in the ocean of polytheism, which was the Roman Empire, it was the firm foundation of Judaism that there was only one God, and that Judaism served only the Highest God. But here was a group of Jews, devout Jews, who professed that Jesus is God, the Son of God ; not a prophet, in the way in which in later time the Muslim would proclaim their Muhammed, but " the Lord ", Adonai, the name which in its deepest devotion Judaism accorded to the God of heaven and earth.

This is already sufficiently surprising ; but what is still more surprising is the second fact, that the companions of Jesus, in Jerusalem and amongst the very eye-witnesses of his execution, found a very considerable number of people who accepted their claim. Where is the man who in his right senses will honestly admit the possibility that a hanged criminal will appear alive amongst his friends two days after his execution ? This alone is already against all reason ; and it has to be added that the reports about the visitations of the disciples by the risen Lord are ambiguous and contradictory not only amongst each other, but partly even in themselves, so that the conclusion is at least near at hand that they did not agree with each other right from the beginning. At any rate it is true to say that they are so discordant that the reasonable historian should lay them aside as unsuitable for the establishing of historical truth. This would undoubtedly be done by historians, if the pleading of pious con-viction did not prevent many from doing so. For from that first Easter Sunday of A.D. 33 onwards the pious convictions first of a few, then of many, and finally of an innumerable multitude of men have found their whole happiness in the call : " The Lord is risen, he is risen indeed." However, it must not be forgotten that right from that first Easter-day the cold voice of reason has countered this enthusiastic call with the proud reply of " swindle ", so that no Christian should be allowed to refuse the trial of his belief.

II

This introduction has had to be put in front of our considera-tions because it will first of all be necessary to come to an agree-ment about what is to be understood by " Christianity ". Are we to understand by this term the teaching of Jesus Christ, or the teaching of his companions, his Apostles, even assuming that the two are identical, which would be incorrect in the case of

St. Paul, and perhaps of other N.T. authors? That might be a welcome solution provided that the teaching of that Jesus of Nazareth were indeed at our disposal. It is true that Adolf Harnack, so many years ago when I had the privilege of sitting at his feet, referred his pupils time and time again to this standard; and he makes the point also most emphatically in his great little book *The Essence of Christianity*, but it is also true to say that there will not be many nowadays who will agree with him about the content of this teaching of Jesus. And already amongst the Apostles there was the most profound disagreement about the Christian doctrine : " But if anyone, if we ourselves or an angel from heaven, should preach a gospel at variance with the gospel we preached to you, he shall be held outcast ", was what the apostle St. Paul wrote to the Galatians (Gal. i. 8), not because he wanted to prevent anyone from doing so in the future, but because the companions of James the Just, of St. Peter, and of St. Barnabas, were most zealous in doing this very thing. And it has to be remembered that this was only one case, if the most notable one, in which the Apostles were at variance with one another ; but it will be sufficient to show that it would not be quite easy for the historian to maintain that the teaching of the Apostles and " Christianity " are really one and the same thing.

Most Church historians therefore try to identify Christianity with the teaching of the Church, and for the later centuries this is indeed a convenient if not altogether commendable way out. However, it leads into grave difficulties when applied to the first century of Christianity. For who or what was this Church of the first century? Who were the men who brought the message of Jesus the Christ to Rome so successfully that St. Paul could write already c. A.D. 54 to the Christians at Rome " all over the world they are telling the story of your faith " (Rom. i. 8), a remark which presupposes not only a numerous, but at the same time, as appears from the content of the Epistle, an almost incredibly well instructed audience? Who was it who had instructed Apollos, the Jew of Alexandria, as he is called in the Acts of the Apostles (Acta xviii. 24), in the gospel, whose teaching is expressly approved by St. Paul in his first Epistle to the Corinthians (1. Cor. iii. 6)? Who were the " men of Cyprus and Cyrene " who, again according to the Acts of the Apostles (Acta xi. 20), began to preach the gospel to the Gentiles at Antioch ? Who had converted the Jews at Damascus, whom St. Paul set out to persecute, no more than at the most two years after the death and resurrection of Jesus Christ (Acta ix. 2 f.) ? We do not know any of the answers to these questions ; neither do we know the content of their teachings, apart from the fact that they all seem to have professed that Jesus Christ was the Lord, was God. There is really no more to be said about all this ; but once more we are exposed to the question : Are present-day Christians really entitled to claim that those Christians who more than 250 years later, together with the Emperor Constantine, adopted the then prevailing Christian faith, should be identified in any way with these earliest Christians ? Does it not appear from the scarce remnants of that earliest Christianity that those earliest Christians had something quite different in mind, something which did not come true at all, the immediate second coming of Jesus Christ as the Judge of all the world ? Can it be held that the Roman Empire did adopt the real, original Christianity of " Christ and His Apostles "? Or should it not be admitted plainly that the Church which took that political recognition for its foundation, as it did, actually adorned itself with false feathers ?

III

To answer these questions honestly and clearly, let us state that the continuity of Christianity was imposed upon Christianity from the outside, by the very Roman Empire which finally adopted it. It had been the Roman procurator of Judaea, Pontius Pilate, by whose decision Jesus had been crucified. It was the Roman administrative powers at Antioch which, if we may trust the witness of the Acts of the Apostles (Acta xi. 26), officially imposed upon the movement the name of " Christians ". It was the Roman Emperor Nero who first made membership of this group of Christians, the " name " of Christian, a crime worthy of the supreme penalty. It was finally the Roman pro-consul, Pliny the Younger, who, by his report to the Emperor Trajan, produced the first lasting imperial edict concerning the procedure in all the trials of the Christians. The identity of Christianity during the period from the first to the fourth centuries cannot be proved historically from inside the movement, but can indeed be amply shown by the reaction of the political power, by the reaction of the Roman Empire, to those whom it had called since the beginning " the Christians ". It was in and by their conflict with each other that Christianity and the Roman Empire grew into a community of fate, which did not end until Napoleon the First decreed that the Holy Roman Empire had seen its last day and was to be dissolved, in the year 1806.

At the same time it cannot be held that the attitude of the Emperors during those first three centuries of Christianity was altogether or at least largely consistent, neither is it true that the character of the Emperors is reflected in their attitude towards Christianity. They were not always the best Emperors who persecuted the Christians, neither were they always the most remiss and oblivious of their duty who showed them leniency. Domitian, whose memory was condemned after his death, persecuted the Christians most cruelly ; but the same is also true of that very great Emperor, Marcus Aurelius. Hadrian, on the other hand, one of the greatest Emperors Rome ever saw, promulgated in favour of the Christians his edict to the governor of Asia, Minucius Fundanus, which, however, did not find very much favour with the provincial authorities ; whereas the son of Marcus Aurelius, Commodus, again an Emperor whose memory was condemned after his death, released, under the influence of his Christian concubine Marcia, a considerable number of Christians who had been exiled—presumably under Marcus Aurelius—to the mines on the isles of Sardinia and Corsica. Nevertheless, even under these Emperors persecutions of Christians took place. Under Hadrian they were most important in the very capital, the city of Rome, whilst under Commodus, under a very slack rulership, they occurred mostly in the provinces. There are reliable reports about them from Africa, Asia Minor, and Syria. For throughout this early period of Christianity the persecution of the Christians was a permanent and stark reality, a fact which is not always taken into account by the secular, and even by the ecclesiastical historians.

And this leads us to a further consideration.   It is true to say that the constitution of the Roman Empire was that of a military dictatorship.   *Imperator*, the official title of the supreme Roman ruler, had been from of old the title of the victorious Roman military commander, and as such it had been adopted by the Emperor Augustus.   However, throughout the Empire there was a division of competence between the earlier local and the imperial administration which was by no means free from friction and rivalry, as can be seen already from St. Luke's report about the enmity between Pilate and Herod Antipas (Luke xxiii. 11).   Yet amongst those local authorities we have to count even the public assemblies, although in the great majority of cases they were no more than chance gatherings.   They served as a kind of safety valve for the democratic reminiscences especially in the Greek speaking cities of the Roman Empire, and it was policy to satisfy their demands if they involved nothing more serious than the burning of a few Christians.   Until the end of the second century it may safely be held that persecutions normally broke out by popular demand, and this was consistent with the internal policy of the imperial government, as it had been inaugurated by Trajan, and confirmed by Marcus Aurelius.   The Roman government apparently attached no great importance to the Christians, and this was obviously the reason also why no closer inspection of their doctrines and organizations took place. The government just did not care at all for the distinctions between the various heresies of the Christians.   This appears quite clearly from the, as I believe, semi-official pamphlet " A true Word ", written by a most loyal Alexandrian, Celsus.

IV

Whilst it is, therefore, true to say that the government re-garded all the varying shades of Christianity, Catholics, Gnostics of all sorts, Montanists, and Judaeo-Christians of various denominations, as nothing but Christians, and whilst the Emperor Marcus Aurelius in one of his edicts even seems to have thought that he could subsume them all under the still wider description of " new religions ", which were to be prohibited without any distinction whatsoever, one group of Christians were not so minded. They were the Catholics, presumably by that time the most numerous Christian group. From the report about the Lyonnese martyrs, preserved for us in the Ecclesiastical History of Eusebius (Euseb., E.H.,V. i. 3 f.) it appears how deeply they felt about the divergencies and schisms within Christianity, and how they succeeded in winning over the Montanist, Alcibiades, who was kept in the same prison, to partake in their Holy Supper, although he had previously made his Communion with water and bread only (Euseb., E.H.,V. iii. 3). Both the separation and the fusion of the different Christian sects were significant features of the ecclesiastical history of the second century. It was the time in which a standard for Christian orthodoxy was created, con-sisting of the three apostolic bequests, the canon of the apostolic writings of the N.T., the apostolic *regula fidei*, now usually described as the " Apostles' Creed ", and the apostolic ministry. The way in which this standard was achieved is still under dis-cussion, and it may well be true that it was different in the dif-ferent provinces of the Church ; but there can be no doubt that by the end of the century all three of them were ready to hand, and that they were immediately put into service by the great fighters against heresy who were active at the end of the century, Irenaeus, Tertullian, Hippolytus, and several others. By the end of the second century, therefore, the Catholic Church finally achieved its separation from the Christian heresies, and established itself as an universal organisation which, in intention if not in fact, covered the whole world. By doing so the Catholic Church also set itself three tasks in particular, that of worship, that of the administration of charity, and finally that of mission-arizing. It has to be remembered that of these three only the last-mentioned had been expressly commanded in the N.T. by the risen Lord (Matt. xxviii. 19 f.) ; but it cannot be denied that already then the missionary task came last on the list. This fact was to be the cause of serious embarrassment for the Catholic Church in subsequent times, especially when the great spiritual force of Gnosticism found its last vigorous expressions in Manichaeism and in Islam.

The rise of the Catholic Church was a novelty within the Roman Empire. Previously no world-wide religious organizations like the Catholic Church had existed within its boundaries. Admittedly, there were other world-religions. Above all there was the Isis religion, the religion of the Magna Mater, and— probably more important than all the others—the religion of the sun-god, Mithras, which was so dear to the Roman army. However, what seems to have been lacking particularly was not only the universal membership of the faithful, but the universality of the episcopal ministry, which already in the middle of the third century enabled Cyprian, the bishop of Carthage, for instance, to administer over a year and a half the see of Rome, which had been vacated by the martyrdom of Pope Fabianus ; or at the same time made it possible for bishop Alexander of Caesarea in a similar way to serve the Church at Jerusalem, the bishop of which, Narcissus, had for reasons which now seem obscure, taken refuge in the desert. The fact that the episcopal ministry was regarded as equal, irrespective of any local conditions causing factual differences between the more or less important sees, is borne out by the contemporary rise of the synods where all the bishops of some larger districts, normally coinciding with the provinces of the Empire, were gathered together with equal rights. In contrast to this rise of ecclesiastical administration, the Roman Empire saw in the course of that terrible third century, with its plague and barbarian invasions, an almost complete disintegration of the traditional imperial administration as established in the first century under the Julio-Claudian dynasty.

Augustus in particular had founded the position of the Roman Emperor upon the religious conception of the "mediator". He was " the last of the gods, and the first among men ". However, in order to maintain such a position it was necessary that the Emperor himself keep aloof from any established religion. Amongst men he was much rather the representative of the deity than its worshipper. During the first 150 years of the Roman Empire religion had been widely treated as the personal concern of the individual ; but in so far as it touched the influence of providence upon the political field the divine assistance was realized by and through the person of the Emperor. The turning point was reached, however, when the Emperors, since the days of Hadrian, appeared in philosophers' beards, announcing in this way that they regarded themselves as mere humans, and wished to indulge in the greater liberty assigned to mere humans. Marcus Aurelius in particular has clearly expressed this decision of his in his " Meditations ", and it was very widely heard. For in this way the Emperor resigned from his position above human religion, and thus became subject to religion ; and it was thus only natural that since the end of the second century amongst the Christians, most notably by Tertullian, the question began to be discussed whether or not the Emperor himself could become a Christian. Tertullian's answer was that he might indeed secretly do so, and that in fact the Emperor Tiberius had adhered to Christian convictions ; but it would not be possible to reconcile the Christian faith with the imperial office. As a matter of fact, the Emperors adopted, from the days of Commodus, the religion of the sun, the religion of the army. By this very decision, however, they deprived themselves of their most potent protection. For before they had taken this step they had been held sacrosanct because of their mediating position in all religious matters ; now, however, being amongst the rest of the faithful, this numinous protection was no longer at their disposal. From the days of Commodus, who was murdered in the first night of A.D. 193, I believe that it was only Septimius Severus, who amongst all the Emperors of the third century did not suffer a violent death, until first Diocletian, and more successfully Constantine, once more changed the religious position of the Emperor. After Constantine the murder of the Emperor became again the exception rather than the rule. This makes the development of the relations between the Church and the Empire in the third century so noteworthy. For it was under those Emperors, who were certain neither of their troops nor even of their personal hangers on—for example Commodus was murdered by that very concubine Marcia who had inspired his pro-Christian policy— that both the systematic persecutions and the debates between the imperial court and the leaders of the Church came to the fore.

V

Already after the first third of the second century Christian writers, the Apologists so-called, had produced pamphlets in defence of Christianity, one or the other of which had been directly addressed to an Emperor, above all to the " philosopher " Emperors, Marcus Aurelius and Lucius Verus. When the house of Septimius Severus came to the throne, a whole range of highly educated Syrian ladies, the mothers of the various succes-sors of Septimius Severus, took the lime-light. One of these at least, Julia Mammaea, the mother of Alexander Severus, who him-self was said to have placed a statue of Jesus Christ beside the various other wise men, Socrates, Zoroaster, and Moses, in his private chapel, did exchange letters with the greatest Christian scholar of her day, with Origen. Another great Christian scholar, the schismatic bishop of Rome, Hippolytus, also seems to have been ordered to court by her or one of her predecessors. However, these ladies were the last members of the Roman imperial court who still showed a lively interest in philosophical questions. After them there followed mere military simplicity, and fifty years later we see the Christian bishops of Syria on their part approach the Emperor Aurelian for his decision when the possession of the cathedral at Antioch was under dispute between the deposed Patriarch Paul of Samosata and his successor Domnus. In between there lies the obscure episode of the Emperor Philippus Arabs, of whom it is said that he and his wife actually adhered to Christianity, but were excommunicated in A.D. 248 by the Patriarch Babylas of Antioch because of the assassination of the son of his predecessor. Some grain of truth may even be contained in this anecdote.

Far more important for the relations between the Church and the Empire, however, were the systematic persecutions to which the Catholic Church in particular was exposed during the middle of the third century. After the murder of Alexander Severus in A.D. 235, whose praetorian prefect, the famous lawyer Ulpianus, had arranged a collection of all the imperial laws dealing with the treatment of the Christians, a collection which unfortunately is now lost, there followed the most brutal of all the barbarians upon the throne of the Caesars, Maximinus Thrax. However, it was hardly his brutality, but rather the effect of Ulpianus's collection, that under him the special persecution of the Christian clergy was ordered. This measure meant that now for the first time, in

A.D. 236, the Roman government at last realized that in the Catholic Church it was faced with a world-wide organization. On the negative side it meant that by this decree the old edict of Trajan that Christians should not be sought out by the police was abandoned with regard to the clergy. A new era was dawning.

It cannot be said, however, that the persecution was conducted with any exceptional energy. For such an effort the times were too troubled, and the rule of Maximinus itself was too much hated by the majority of the inhabitants of the Empire. After he had been murdered, and after a very obscure period in which no less than four Emperors and pretenders met with a violent death, there followed the episode of Philippus Arabs of which we have spoken already. The first real catastrophe for the Christians throughout the Empire occurred under his successor, the Emperor Decius.

With Decius we reach the climax of disintegration of the Augustan Empire. It was the nation of the Goths who were penetrating from the Black Sea into the apparently best protected regions in Asia Minor and the Balkans. In the East the re-established power of Persia threatened the Eastern half of the Empire. The frontiers on the rivers Danube and Rhine had also long been in serious danger. Gaul and Britain were on the verge of defection. The Roman masters saw only one way of squeezing out of those districts which had not suffered too much devastation the men and moneys for the defence. It was the appeal to patriotism. Every inhabitant of the Empire was called upon to bring sacrifices to the gods of Rome and to the Emperor. Such sacrifices had been demanded of the Christians since the days of Trajan, but only here and there, sporadically, and the Christian martyrs had refused the demand. But under Decius no distinction was made between Christians and pagans. The fairly numerous certificates on papyrus for those who had sacrificed, which have been found amongst Egyptian papyri in the course of the last seventy years, serve to make this point quite clear. They show that absolutely no religious distinction was made by the simple fact that religion is not mentioned upon them. Everyone was subjected to the performance of this religious-patriotic duty whatever his faith may have been, and it is not known that—apart from the Jews, for whom presumably special arrangements were made—any religious scruples were raised by anybody who was not a Christian. Such refusals were met with terrible punishment, for such are the demands of patriotism. Eventually the Catholic Church just managed to weather this storm, but it became evident on this occasion that the preceding—mostly local—persecutions had not prepared the Christians sufficiently for the sufferings of universal persecution. It was not patriotism which caused them to deny their faith, however, but sheer fright.

It must not be overlooked that there were numerous Christians who willingly underwent martyrdom. This fact has been neglected far too often by our modern historians, and yet it was what really mattered in the future course of history. Hundreds and thousands of Christians of all those regions where Christianity was most widely spread, as Asia Minor, Egypt, North Africa, Rome, and Syria, were arrested, tortured, and subsequently subjected to capital punishment or to work in those murderous lead and copper mines, for which free and even slave labour was practically unobtainable. There were even more who by keeping absolutely quiet or moving from their normal place of habitation managed to escape the attention of the political administration. However, there were also the others, and our sources suggest that they were even in the majority, who submitted to the demand of the state. Certainly they were much more numerous than the martyrs. There were those who, not satisfied with sacrificing, even encouraged their fellow Christians to do so, and denounced them if they refused to follow their example. There were others who only secretly, and somewhat ashamedly, put their little piece of incense upon the heathen altar, probably the vast majority of the " fallen ones " (lapsi). Christian Latin provided a special term for them, thurificati, but it is impossible to say, whether these two groups were actually distinguished in the treatment of their application for re-admission to the Church. There were finally the many who for a small bribe obtained from the officials the certificate of their having sacrificed without having actually performed the ceremony at all, the so-called libellatici. It had long, as we hear from Tertullian, been a bad tradition amongst the bishops of the Church, that they " would buy the peace of Christ with bribes "; so there were at least certain precedents for the paying of security money by the *libellatici*. However, once more it must not be forgotten that the prisons in many of the cities of the Roman Empire were indeed filled to over-flowing with faithful Christians during that terrible year of A.D. 250, that the torturers worked almost without interruption in order to convince the recusant Christians, and that the hangmen worked over-time.   Admittedly, 251 saw a certain relaxation of the zeal of the persecutors ; but it was nevertheless a surprise when the persecution was suddenly stopped in the autumn of that year, because the Emperor Decius had lost a battle and his life in the war against the invading Goths.   In Africa at least, and presumably in other provinces too, the Christians gathered together for services of thanksgiving, described most impressively by their great bishop, Cyprian, in his pamphlet *De lapsis*.

The thing which calls for an explanation is that at this juncture, even before the persecution was finally ended, the masses of the fallen streamed back to the Churches, and clamoured for re-admission.   On the one hand, it is undoubtedly an illustration of the fact that the appeal to patriotism had not found a real echo amongst these so-called *lapsi* and, so I believe, among many of the heathen population of the Empire either.   Many of those who came back must have felt genuine penitence at their lapse, and the blood of the martyrs was truly the seed of the Church.   On the other hand, it must not be forgotten that during the third century the Catholic Church developed into the greatest welfare organization ever seen in Greek and Roman time.   In many places it can be claimed to have been the only charitable organization.   Hundreds of churches of this period have been excavated by French archaeologists in North Africa, and each of them proved to have a store-house for corn and oil attached to it.   He who was separated from the Church lost not only his hope of eternal salvation, but also what may be described in modern terms as his social security.   This too should be considered as one of the reasons why the lapsed in such great numbers returned to the Church.   Their return was facilitated for many of them by the written recommendation, as we would say, or absolution, as they claimed, given them by one or the other of the martyrs, something which up to that time had never failed.   In short, what had been spared in the Christian Church by the persecution was now put in jeopardy by the return of the lapsed.   In the schism of Novatianus, which was caused by the differences about their treatment, the Catholic Church was split in two.   It may well be regarded as the grace of providence that the Emperor Valerianus decided to renew the persecution in A.D. 257, and to continue it till he was defeated in A.D. 260, and captured by the king of Persia.   For this new crisis established the institutional authority of the bishops over the spiritual author‐ ity of the martyrs, and in this way saved the Church.

These two general persecutions of the Church were followed by forty years of peaceful relations between the Empire and the Church.   We have just seen that the main burden of the conflict during the middle of the third century was borne by the Catholic Church.   Nothing, as far as I can see, is said in our sources about the attitude of the heresies during these persecutions. This does not mean that they had just quietly vanished during those ten years of crisis.   On the contrary, during the following forty years we see the beginning of a development, the effects of which were to continue right down to the middle ages.   Outside the Roman Empire, in Mesopotamia, in those regions which were under Persian rule, a Church—if it may be so called—had arisen, which was very different from the Catholic Church within the Roman Empire, so much so that one might even hesitate to call it a Christian Church.   Its fathers were some of the great Gnostic leaders of the second century, Bardesanes, Marcion, and Tatian. The latter two had seceded intentionally from the Church at Rome to which they had belonged during some period of their lives ; and it may be assumed that the differences between the Persian and the Roman Churches were not entirely accidental, caused by the political and local distance between the two, but based upon doctrinal discrepancies, as the Catholics averred.   In this Mesopotamian Church there arose at this very time, in the middle of the third century, a new prophet in the person of Mani, who between A.D. 260 and 270 sacrificed his life for his new doctrine.   His call to a life of radical asceticism was widely heard at a time which was so profoundly subjected to the miseries of wars and plagues as the third century. It presented a striking contrast to the Catholic Church which was on the way to respectability. A new world-religion, Manichaeism, made its appearance. We find its traces all over the continent of Asia, in Persia and in India as much as in Turkestan, Mongolia, and China. And they are equally wide-spread within the boundaries of the Roman Empire, in Egypt, North Africa, Spain and Gaul. At a later time there was a further invasion originating with the Bogomils in the Balkans, who received their inspiration as it seems in northern Asia Minor, and spread it amongst the Albigenses in Italy and France, in the eleventh and twelfth centuries. This illustrates the universal appeal of their ideal of a complete renunciation of the world in the face of a Christianity, which in its social life had become more or less settled.

VI

It must not be assumed, however, that the approach to respectability by the Catholic Church in the late third century had closed the door to asceticism. It does not seem probable that the new ascetic movement which started within the Church during this period, was sparked off by Manichaeism, although I cannot help feeling that it was influenced by it. I believe, however, that at the bottom of it there was a renewed and re-inforced eschatological expectation. The terrible sufferings of the time were interpreted as the travails of the new Aeon ; the coming of the Lord in judgement was eagerly expected. To the rulers of the Roman Empire hermitism and monasticism, the names by which this new movement is described, was a most unwelcome development, for by it the economy of the Empire was deprived of a very considerable portion of its labour force, which could ill be spared in view of the other losses by plague and war ; and the new eschatological movement in the Catholic Church also bore a revolutionary aspect, as all eschatological movements throughout history have done. Admittedly, the expectation was stronger in the West than in the East, where the Church in those days tended towards the doctrine that heaven and earth should be regarded as two completely separate realms. Nevertheless, even there the

Church was by and large a pacifist organization, and it has to be remembered that it was the successful generals of these forty years who succeeded in establishing the Roman Empire once more. The climax of this period of restoration was reached when a great politician came to the throne, the Illyrian, Diocletian. By appointing the outstanding generals of his time as his co-rulers, and by inspiring them by religious means with an entirely unexpected loyalty to his own person, he managed not only to secure the Roman frontiers at the Rhine, and the Danube, and the Euphrates, but also succeeded in giving the Empire a new constitution, centrally as well as regionally. With this turning of the supreme ruler of the Empire towards the problems of its internal policy, the question of its religion once more assumed supreme importance. As soon as the administrative questions were settled we see Diocletian outlaw the non-Roman form of Christianity, Manichaeism. More difficult was the problem of the Catholic Church, whose influence coincided by and large with the frontiers of the Empire. Beyond its frontiers it was only amongst the Goths that the Church could claim considerable missionary successes. Within the Empire the Christian Church had penetrated all classes of the people. There is no reason to doubt the assertion made by Eusebius that even Diocletian's own wife and daughter had been baptized, and it is also credible that one of the " Caesars ", Diocletian's subordinate Emperors, Constantius Chlorus, one of the rulers in the West, showed much sympathy for the new faith. Nevertheless, Diocletian decided to persecute Christianity. The principal reasons for this step were military. Considerable disciplinary difficulties seem to have been caused by Christian officers and other ranks ; and it seems certain that numerous Christian conscripts refused to enlist in the army. Thus the first steps taken by the government were directed towards an army purge. However, once the step had been taken towards differentiating between " true " Romans and Christians it proved impossible to limit the aim of the perse-cution. One edict against the Christians followed another in quick succession, and the years from A.D. 303 to 305 were filled with the most brutal and most thorough persecution the Church had yet experienced. However, in A.D. 305 Diocletian resigned his throne, and compelled his colleague, Maximian, to do the same. It is a plausible assumption that the failure of the persecution was one of the chief reasons for his doing so.

With the abdication of the two Emperors Diocletian and Maximian the persecution in the West came practically to an end. For the new Augustus of the East, Galerius, failed in his attempt to seize the rulership of the West for one of his creatures, and the two successful usurpers there, Constantine and Maxentius, had no heart for its continuation. In the East, however, it was cruelly and aimlessly continued, until in A.D. 311 the Emperor Galerius on his death-bed issued an edict of toleration, in order to obtain for himself the intercessions of the Christians. Diocletian's newly founded order had lost the battle for spiritual supremacy, and the Empire was once more plunged into chaos and civil wars. It seems certain that only a few Christians had offered armed resistance ; it is also true to say that considerable numbers of Christians once more lapsed under the pressure of the persecution. Very ugly scenes of mutual recrimination in the African Church are still on record ; and it is very probable that the Roman pope Marcellinus himself had betrayed his Master. However, it is true to say that the Christians in the most highly civilized provinces, Africa, Egypt, Asia Minor, and Syria, defeated Diocletian's persecution by their very numbers. For since it proved impossible to win them over at the outset of the persecution, the policy of violent destruction aimed at them recoiled on the organization and especially on the economy of the Empire. The provinces in North Africa in particular were never again fully established under the Roman rule, but remained intractable and sullen.

Diocletian's abdication was followed by nine years of usurpation and civil war. When one of these usurpers, Constantine, had defeated another of them, Maxentius, in the battle at the Milvian bridge, in October 312, he declared himself publicly in favour of Christianity. The Christians' battle for Rome, which had been begun by St. Paul, was at last won for the Church. During the remainder of the century the Roman Emperor occupied once more the position of mediator between heaven and earth, in a similar way to that in which it had been held by Augustus—and

Constantine at least was fully aware of the fact that he had to copy the first founder of the Roman Empire with regard to his religious position. In the eastern half of the Empire the Emperor continued in this position right into the middle ages, theoretically until the Turks replaced the cross on the Hagia Sophia by their half-moon. To the other fetters, says Eduard Schwartz, somewhat cynically but not without reason, with which Constantine held the Empire in bondage, he added a religious one in the form of the Nicene Creed. However, at the time when in the West the Roman Empire succumbed to the storms of the peoples' migration, St. Augustine re-stated the eternal problem of the earthly state as viewed by Christian theology : *Vacante enim iustitia, quid sunt regna nisi magna latrocinia,* without the justice of God, what else are the states than great bands of robbers ?

PRINTED IN GREAT BRITAIN AT
THE UNIVERSITY PRESS
ABERDEEN

142

The "Eusebian Constantine"

Rudolph H. Storch

Historians generally have concerned themselves with the reliability of the *Vita Constantini* of Eusebius,[1] while ignoring an important contribution of the panegyricist, namely, the *image*[2] of Constantine he projects to his readers. This image, or the "Eusebian Constantine," involves four major elements: (1) all success and benefit derive from the favor of the divinity; (2) only the pious receive divine favor; (3) the most important indication of divine favor for a pious

1. The problem of Eusebius' authorship of the *Vita* will be a continuing one. H. Grégoire argues for a Eusebian kernel with later additions: "Eusèbe n'est pas l'auteur de la 'Vita Constantini' dans sa forme actuelle et Constantin n'est pas 'converti' en 312," *Byzantion*, 13 (1938), 561-83. J. Vogt discounts Grégoire's suggestion that the faulty account of the war between Constantine and Licinius points to later interpolation: "Die Vita Constantini des Eusebius über den Konflikt Zwischen Constantin und Licinius," *Historia*, 2 (1953-4), 463-71. G. Downey in "The Builder of the Original Church of the Apostles at Constantinople: a Contribution to the Criticism of the *Vita Constantini* attributed to Eusebius," *Dumbarton Oaks Papers*, 6 (1951), 53-80, accepts the addition of later material as does J. Moreau: "Zum Problem der Vita Constantini," *Historia*, 4 (1955), 234-45. F. Vittinghoff's "Eusebius als Verfasser der 'Vita Constantini," *Rh. Mus.*, 96 (1953), 330-73 stressed Eusebian authorship as do F. W. Winkelmann's "Zur Geschichte des Authentizitätsproblem der Vita Constantini," *Klio*, 40 (1962), 187-243, and *Die Vita Constantini des Eusebius: Ihre Authentizität*, Diss. Halle (1959), at chap. 2. Most scholars accept a Eusebian kernel but also accept later redaction, the exact extent of which awaits a definitive study: N. H. Baynes, "Constantine the Great and the Christian Church," *Proc. Brit. Acad.*, 15 (1929), note 18 (i) and the earlier literature cited; Moreau, "Eusebius von Caesarea," *Real. f. Ant. u. Christ.*, 6, 1073-74. Schwartz, accepting Eusebian authorship, does not treat the problem: "Eusebius von Caesarea," *RE* 6[1], 1422-27.
   For the purpose of this essay, note that the image of Constantine attributed to Eusebius is derived from "non-controversial" passages in the *V.C.*: that is, passages which a later interpolator would have had no reason to add. For example, there is no reason to doubt that it was Eusebius, not a redactor, who made references to Constantine's closeness to the divine or to the emperor's piety, or to the benefits of his reign. There are, however, two problems, both of which relate to Eusebius' image of *Constantinus victor*: (1) There is discrepancy between Eusebius' professed purpose in the *V.C.* (I, 11) to relate only those events pertaining to Constantine's religious character and the content of the *Vita* which includes such things as military successes (I, 25, 26-40, 46; IV, 5-6: Downey, *Dum. Oaks Pap.*, 6 [1951], 62-63). These passages may have been added later, but this is not certain and two other interpretations are equally valid: perhaps Eusebius felt that Constantine's military success did pertain to his religious character in the sense that victory was an outstanding example of the close ties between God and Constantine or, Eusebius, being carried away by his panegyric, simply did not adhere to his professed purpose. (2) It has been suggested that the connection of the labarum with the victory of 312 is the work of a later redactor (on this see note 26 below). There is no conclusive evidence of this.

2. Although there has been much discussion about the purpose of the *Vita* the complete image of Constantine has not been noticed: F. J. Foakes-Jackson, *Eusebius Pamphili* (Cambridge: W. Heffer and Sons, 1933), pp. 102-14; Downey, *Dum. Oaks Pap.*, 6 (1951), 61-65; W. Telfer, "The Author's Purpose in the Vita Constantini," *Texte und Untersuchungen*, 68 (1957), 157-67; Vogt, "Constantinus der Grosse," *Real. f. Ant. u. Christ.*, 3, 371-72; Moreau "Vérité historique et propagande politique chez Lactance et dans Vita Constantini," *Annales Universitatis Saraviensis* (Philos. Lett.), 4 (1955), 89-97; Schwartz, *RE* 6[1], 1422-23 and 1426-27; but not D. S. Wallace-Hadrill, *Eusebius of Caesarea* (Westminster, Maryland, Canterbury Press, 1961). Both Schwartz (*RE* 6[1], 1423) and Moreau (*Real. f. Ant. u. Christ.*, 6, 1073), however, do refer to the famous passage in the *V.C.* (I, 3, 4) relating to the emperor's image where Eusebius remarks that, above all emperors, Constantine was a friend of God and model of Christian life to men.

Mr. Storch is assistant professor of classics and ancient history in the University of Maryland Baltimore County, Baltimore, Maryland. He first read this essay at the Fifth Biennial Conference on Medieval Studies sponsored by the Medieval Institute of Western Michigan University.

ruler is military victory; and (4) with the victory secured, divine favor will produce peace and unity for the realm. Constantine, being close to Eusebius, helped to mold his own image which is more than a representation of the first Christian emperor—it is a key to understanding the nature of Eusebius' panegyric as well as his notion of Constantine's relationship with the Christian God.

The first aspect of the "Eusebian Constantine" entails emphasis on divine participation in imperial affairs.[3] The hand of God is present in all favorable aspects of Constantine's reign, and, in the opinion of Eusebius, the emperor used God' counsel as a source of guidance.[4] Constantine is portrayed as being in intimate contact with God, who is his friend and protector.[5]

It is in the sphere of military activity that Eusebius sees his God as being closest to Constantine. It began in 312 when Constantine so earnestly sought divine aid, received it then at the Milvian Bridge and continuously thereafter against the barbarians and his adversary Licinius. Crucial to the success of Constantine as a ruler was God's help in a continuous course of conquest rendering him unsubdued and invincible, a conqueror of the race of tyrants and all mankind.[6] Eusebius' view of the final encounter with Licinius, which was the confirmation of the divine alliance formed in 312, was that Constantine had a divine ally, who fought at his side, forcing Licinius to war against God himself.[7]

Constantine was not unique in his reliance on divine aid for victory. His greatest opponents, Maxentius and Licinius, put great emphasis on their pagan ritual.[8] Maxentius, before meeting Constantine at the Milvian Bridge, consulted the Sibylline books and soothsayers, placed confidence in sorcery, and offered victims to the gods. Licinius in 313 had been favorably disposed to the God of the Christians, and had received divine aid against Maximin.[9] But when he reverted to the pagan deities before meeting Constantine,[10] he found that Constantine's God was a more formidable ally.

Once Eusebius had portrayed Constantine as being close to his God who would intervene in imperial affairs, he had to show that the emperor was pious, and thus worthy of divine favor, since God is the defender of the pious.[11]

Eusebius, through constant reference to the *pietas* of the emperor, makes the image of *Pius Constantinus* dominate the *Vita*. Constantine had every virtue of piety which guided his actions. During the Arian controversy he wept from pious concern and filled the role of a pious emperor promoting peace in the church. Godly fear and piety distinguished Constantine as he entered the assembly hall at Nicaea. The emperor's letter to the churches following the council was written so that his pure sincerity of thought and piety to God might be

---

3. Eusebius' political philosophy, perhaps deriving from Hellenistic theories of kingship, involved the view that the empire was an earthly copy of the rule of God in heaven, with the emperor being a representative of the godhead: Baynes, *Byzantine Studies and Other Essays* (London: Athlone Press, 1955), pp. 168-72.
4. *V.C.* II, 12; III, 1.
5. *H.E.* X, 9. The general view of the character of books IX and X of the *H.E.* is expressed by Schwartz (*RE* 6¹, 1423): "Die letzten Bücher der Kirchengeschichte sind eben nicht Zeitgeschichte in strengen Sinn, sondern ein kirchliches und politisches Pamphlet. . . ." Eusebius' image of Constantine appears most vivid in the *Vita* but is supported by the last two books of the *Church History*, both of which were written after Constantine's conversion.
6. *V.C.* I, 5, 6, 46.
7. *Ibid.*, II, 15.
8. Lact. *de mort. pers.* 44; Zos. II, 16; Eus. *H.E.* IX, 9 and *V.C.* I, 36.
9. Lact. *de mort. pers.* 46.
10. *V.C.* II, 4.
11. *H.E.* X, 2.

discerned. Eusebius saw Constantine continually make progress in the direction of piety and felt that others recognized the emperor as an instructor in the practice of *pietas*. It was this quality that prevented Constantine from becoming arrogant in the midst of his successes.

Important to Constantine's image was the piety of his family. Eusebius renders Helena a "pious mother of a pious emperor" or simply a "pious empress" displaying personal piety to God and discharging pious devotion. Constantius Chlorus is outstanding for his piety as are the sons of Constantine, who, having been admonished by their father to follow in this course, were instructed only by men whose piety had been approved by Constantine.

An outstanding indication of Eusebius' interest in *pietas* as a virtue of the emperor is his translation of the Edict of Milan from Latin to Greek in which here is a slight but significant addition. Lactantius' version reads: *"quibus divinitatis reverentia continebatur."*[12] The Eusebian translation: *"hois hē pros to theion aidōs te kai to sebas eneicheto."*[13]

Eusebius further emphasized Constantine's piety by stressing the impiety of others, especially the adversaries of Constantine. Licinius, earlier, as a Christian, was celebrated along with Constantine for his intelligence and piety but later he turned to impieties, emulated the wickedness of former impious tyrants, became one, and then waged an impious war against Constantine.[14] Upon his defeat, the impious one was removed. Before Licinius, Maxentius and Maximin were impious men who desolated areas of the empire by tyrannous impieties.[15] Eusebius regarded Maximin's persecution as impious fighting against God himself.[16]

Pius Constantinus is important to Eusebius, as is the next element of the "Eusebian Constantine," namely, the depiction of Constantine as victorious and triumphant. This is only logical, since Eusebius, after stressing divine intervention in imperial affairs and indicating that piety made Constantine worthy of divine favor, had to take the further step of picturing his emperor as a most successful military leader. For Eusebius victory was the deserved fruit of piety.[17]

The image of *Constantinus victor* is remarkably strong in the *Vita*, a work which ostensibly, was to overlook such things as battles, victories, and successes against the enemy and to treat only of things pertaining to the emperor's religious character and to record only his pious acts.[18] In relating the events of 325 at Nicaea, the scene of a most holy church council, Eusebius has his subject center not only as a pious participator in ecclesiastical affairs, but also as a "triumphant conqueror" possessed of "invincible strength and vigor." In old age, the most outstanding indication of Constantine's sound body and mind included his ability to make war and erect trophies.[19] Constantine is pictured as having conquered nearly the whole world[20] and as having erected many trophies. This image of victorious Constantine was an integral part of the "Eusebian Con-

12. *de mort. pers.* 48.
13. *H.E.* X, 5.
14 Licinius' impiety: *H.E.* X, 8, 9; *V.C.* II, 2, 12.
15. *H.E.* IX, 9, 11; X, 2, 8.
16. *V.C.* I, 59.
17. *H.E.* X, 9.
18. *V.C.* I, 11.
19. *Ibid.,* IV, 53.
20. *Ibid.,* 8.

stantine" because he regarded Constantine's trophies as having made him a greater ruler than ever before.[21] In this light, the title, VICTOR, is the only imperial title mention in the *Vita*.[22]

Critical to the Eusebian image of a triumphant emperor is his conviction that all imperial victories came about by the will of God who was the author of victory and whose power was with Constantine.[23] Reportedly the soldiers of Constantine were taught a prayer which acknowledged victory as coming from God's favor.[24] Eusebius includes a speech of Licinius, but composed by himself, delivered before the great battle with Constantine in which he remarks that the outcome would show who was mistaken, the followers of Christ or of the pagan gods.[25]

For Eusebius, the most outstanding indication of God's role in imperial victory is the new military standard, the labarum,[26] which plays so dynamic a role as the ever-present symbol of the "divine and mysterious" power of Constantine's ally deity. Eusebius recognizes the labarum as a true army standard,[27] innovative, yet modeled on the standards of old. It is not only a "conquering standard" or the "standard of the cross" but also a "triumphant charm,"[28] and a "sign of salvation,"[29] the symbol of Constantine's full confidence in God.[30] Then Eusebius becomes an innovator. For the first time ever, the army standard of the Romans becomes a "trophy."

Specifically, Eusebius' trophy was the Christian cross as the triumphant symbol of Christ's victory over death.[31] In describing Constantine's vision Eusebius refers to the heavenly sign as the "trophy of a cross of light."

But when the panegyricist converts the Roman army standard into a trophy, he is making a radical departure. There is no evidence, either literary or artistic, that the Roman *tropaeum* had ever been carried before an army into battle as a standard.[32] Beginning with the Augustan age, the trophy, along with the repre-

21. *Ibid.*, I, 6.
22. *Ibid.*, II, 19. This title is mentioned in the same breath with the piety of Constantine and the acknowledgement that the victories behind the title are God-given.
23. *H.E.* IX, 9; *V.C.* I, 39.
24. *V.C.* IV, 20.
25. *Ibid.*, II, 5.
26. Although the *Vita*, in its present form, connects the labarum with Constantine's vic tory at the Milvian Bridge there is a question of exactly when it was adopted as the standard of the army—A.D. 312, 324, or at some time in between: Baynes, ''Const. and the Christ. Ch.,'' note 33; Vogt, *Real. f. Ant. u. Christ.*, 3, 323-25; Grosse, ''Labarum,'' *RE* 12¹, 241. Grégoire argues that the whole account of the vision can be attributed to later interpolation but includes no specific remarks about the labarum: ''La vision de Constantin 'liquidee,'' *Byzantion*, 14 (1939), 341-51. The labarum, as described in the *Vita* (I, 31), cannot be accurate for 312 A.D. but Eusebius may have been describing it as he knew it later or the detailed description could have been added by a later redactor. It cannot be conclusively stated that the labarum, in some form, was not adopted by Constantine's army at the battle in 312. The *Vita* presents the labarum as the constant safeguard of the army from 312 (the labarum in the *V.C.*: I, 28-31, 37, 40 — here the ''salutary symbol'' is the safeguard of the government and the whole empire; II, 3-9, 16, 55; III, 2, 3; IV, 5, 21).
27. Eg. *V.C.* II, 3, 8, 9.
28. *Ibid.*, II, 7.
29. *Ibid.*, I, 31.
30. *Ibid.*, II, 3.
31. *Ibid.*, I, 32. *H.E.* IX, 9. See also Tert. *Adv. Marcion.*, IV. 20.
32. On the trophy: G. C. Picard, *Les Trophées Romaines* (Paris: E. de Boccard, 1957); A. J. Janssen, *Het Antieke Tropaion* (Lederberg-Gent: Drukkeij Erasmus, 1957), is especially valuable as a catalogue of literary and artistic references, although the study substantially ends with the close of the second century A.D.; Lammert, ''Tropaion,'' *RE* 7 A¹ 663-73; Reinach, ''Tropaeum,'' *Daremberg-Saglio*, 5, 497-518 is

sentation of Victoria, was the primary artistic symbol reflecting the universal Roman victory. It is this allusion that Eusebius is trying to convey by his careful selection of the word "trophy" to describe the new standard, the symbol of Constantine's divine alliance and his guarantee of continuing victory. By elevating the labarum to so prevalent a place in the *Vita* Eusebius makes it the physical representation of the heavenly military alliance between Constantine and his God.

The final aspect of the "Eusebian Constantine" involves the image of a kind and beneficent ruler. Here, too, Constantine was assisted by God who was present to aid him at the beginning of, during the course of, and at the end of his reign.[33] Constantine was a generous and patient ruler who united the empire and governed for its benefit. His laws brought many advantages to the provinces[34] including reduced taxes.[35] When necessary, the emperor used money from his private treasury and was liberal to the poor, even the heathen.[36] The church, too, was governed well, with the emperor building churches, opposing heretics, and promoting peace in the institution under his peculiar care. Constantine's genuine feeling for humanity dictated the tone of his legislation.[37] He so governed on principles of humanity that his rule was acceptable to all.[38] Even prisoners of war were treated humanely.[39]

Thus, the "Eusebian Constantine" emerges quite clearly from the *Vita*. Despite the emperor's background, which was taken up primarily in military training and was lacking in liberal education, Constantine was essentially a man of piety who gained the favor of God. This God was Constantine's never-failing ally who rendered Constantine always successful, first on the battlefield, then in ruling a peaceful empire as a beneficient ruler.[40]

There can be no doubt that Constantine himself helped to mold this image of Eusebius since the two men had been close for a number of years. Eusebius is proud of his contact with Constantine. On one occasion, he asked for, and received, Constantine's permission to deliver a discourse which the emperor attended.[41] Constantine was most grateful for an exposition of the mysteries of Easter written by Eusebius and requested that the bishop produce more such treatises.[42] It was Eusebius whom Constantine chose to produce fifty copies of the holy Scriptures.[43] When the people of Antioch desired to make Eusebius their bishop, Constantine was opposed but wrote to Eusebius that he had known

---

most helpful for artistic references; K. Woelcke's fundamental *Beiträge zur Geschichte des Tropaions* (Bonn: Georgi, 1911) is not useful for the imperial period.

Eusebius applied the word "trophy" to more than the labarum. For example, he referred to the remains of Peter and Paul as "trophies" (*H.E.* II, 25), On this passage see J. Carcopino, *Etudes d'histoire chretienne* (Paris: A. Michel, 1953), pp. 251-58 and E. Bernardi, "Let Mot 'tropaion' applique aux martyrs," *Vigil. Christ.*, 8 (1954), 174-75.

33. *V.C.* I, 4.
34. *Ibid.*, I, 19, 20; IV, 1.
35. *Ibid.*, IV, 2.
36. *Ibid.*, II, 22.
37. *Ibid.*, II, 20.
38. *Ibid.*, I, 9.
39. *Ibid.*, II, 13.
40. Eusebius, here, makes Constantine very little different from earlier emperors. M. P. Charlesworth, "Pietas and Victoria: The Emperor and the Citizen," *JRS*, 33 (1943), 1: ". . . the consecutive (and almost casual) connection of these adjectives: because the emperor is *pius* the gods will render him *felix* (for *felicitas* is their gift to their favorites) and his *felicitas* is best demonstrated in his being *invictus*."
41. *V.C.* IV, 33.
42. *Ibid.*, IV, 35.
43. *Ibid.*, IV, 36. Also Soc. *H.E.* I, 9 and Theod. *H.E.* I, 15.

him well for a long time, held him in high esteem, and considered him worthy to be bishop of any church.[44]

Eusebius claims that he enjoyed Constantine's acquaintance and society.[45] He is able to tell from first-hand experience[46] of foreign ambassadors being received at the court. On two occasions Eusebius includes information in the *Vita* that he claims to have received from the emperor himself,[47] and, of course, the Eusebian account of Constantine's vision is the report given to him by the emperor long after.

Eusebius' proximity to the emperor would not have been unusual since Constantine is reported to have been surrounded by Christian churchmen. After his vision, Constantine sent for those who were acquainted with the mysteries of God's doctrines and made the priests of God his counselors.[48] When he sent Hosius to deal with the Arian problem, he picked the bishop "from the bishops in his train."[49] Churchmen, who were continually about the person of the emperor,[50] were entertained by Constantine,[51] "admitted to his table,"[52] and invited to be traveling companions,[53] even on military campaigns.[54] Constantine distinguished the clergy with the highest respect and honor and showed them favor in word and deed.[55] Eusebius maintains that the entire care of the imperial household was entrusted to those in the service of God and all the attendants of Constantine's sons were Christian.[56]

Because of Eusebius' close connection with Constantine and his great admiration of the emperor, the "Eusebian Constantine," as presented in the *Vita*, must have been influenced by the subject of the panegyric himself. This suggestion becomes more certain with the understanding that Constantine's own letters and edicts[57] project the same imperial image, with the same four aspects, as is contained in Eusebius' panegyric.

To begin with, Constantine repeatedly alludes to divine intervention in affairs of state. He regarded divine providence as having been operative in the removal of Licinius[58] and hoped for divine help in his handling of the Donatist problem.[59] He believes that the general well-being of the empire was brought about by the good will of the deity whom he regards as the "author and parent

44. *V.C.* III, 61. Constantine considered Eusebius as being worthy to be bishop of the whole world—Soz. *H.E.* II, 19.
45. *V.C.* I, 10, 28.
46. *Ibid.*, IV, 7.
47. *Ibid.*, II, 8, 9.
48. *Ibid.*, I, 32.
49. *Ibid.*, II, 63.
50. *Ibid.*, II, 4.
51. *Ibid.*, IV, 24.
52. *Ibid.*, I, 42.
53. *Ibid.*
54. *Ibid.*, II, 4; IV, 56.
55. *Ibid.*, I, 42.
56. *Ibid.*, IV, 18, 52.
57. The authenticity of the Constantinian documents preserved in the *V.C.* and by Optatus and Athanasius is no longer seriously questioned: Baynes, "Const. and the Christ. Ch.," notes 18 (i), 46, 59, 64; Moreau, *Real. f. Ant. u. Christ.*, 6, 1074; Schwartz, *RE*, 61, 1423; Vogt, *Real. f. Ant. u. Christ.*, 3, 362. The strongest evidence for the genuineness of the documents in the *Vita* came with the discovery of a papyrus that guaranteed the authenticity of Constantine's letter to the provincials following his defeat of Licinius (*V.C.* II, 27-28 with the end of 26 and the beginning of 29). On this: A. H. M. Jones, "Notes on the Genuineness of the Constantinian Documents in Eusebius' Life of Constantine," *Jour. Ecc. Hist.*, 5 (1954), 196-200.
58. *V.C.* II, 46.
59. Opt. *App.* IX.

of all things."[60] Constantine considers the observance of holy laws as critical to the receipt of abundant blessings[61] and looks for the greatest benefits to accrue to the state when the clergy, being trained in the worship of the deity, show proper respect.[62] In a remarkable statement Constantine indicates his belief that he owes his life, every breath, and inmost secret thoughts to the favor of the supreme God.[63]

It is important to Constantine, in his effort to keep divine favor, that the deity not be offended or angered. Dissension is to be feared since it will cause God to move against the human race and even the emperor himself.[64] He feared that the actions of the Donatists would provoke the anger of the divinity and result in something displeasing to God and detrimental to the reputation of the emperor.[65] Constantine warns against neglecting reverence of the divinity for fear of the great dangers to follow.[66]

Divine favor is essential for Constantine because of his conviction that he was charged with the direction of all human affairs.[67] Constantine regarded himself as the administrator of God's counsel and aid and as God's instrument in ridding the world of evils.[68] He refers to himself as the servant[69] of that God with whom he believes he has a special relationship.

Pietas, too, is important to Constantine as it had been to Eusebius. He emphasizes his own piety by reference in his laws and letters to the piety of people important to himself. Constantine's father and mother-in-law are remembered for their admirable *pietas.*[70] In his letter to Sapor, Constantine says that he will commit Christians in the Persian realm to Sapor's care since his piety is outstanding.[71] Even God himself is noted for his incomprehensible piety which prevents men's weaknesses for wandering too far.[72]

But Constantine reinforces this image of his own piety primarily by reference to the impiety of others. He pictures himself as the deliverer who brought relief and remedy for the mass of impiety oppressing the human race.[73] The authors of these impieties have met bad ends, especially those who harassed the worshippers of God by impious edicts.[74] Former emperors were under the influence of impious utterances of the Pythian oracle and were led to disaster, but Constantine will shy away from profane and impious pagan superstition.[75] The church, too, had been affected by impiety. Its holy places were defiled by impious men.[76] In referring to the Donatists, Constantine, earlier, maintained that they had impious minds and should leave the church, but by 330, in the interest

60. *V.C.* IV, 11.
61. *Ibid.,* II, 24.
62. Eus. *H.E.* X, 7.
63. *V.C.* II, 29.
64. Opt. *App.* III.
65. Ibid., *App.* V; VI.
66. Eus. *H.E.* X, 7.
67. Opt. *App.* III.
68. *V.C.* II, 28, 42.
69. *Ibid.,* II, 71.
70. *Ibid.,* II, 49; III, 52.
71. *Ibid.,* IV, 13.
72. Opt. *App.* V.
73. *V.C.* II, 28.
74. *Ibid.,* II, 27; IV, 12.
75. *Ibid.,* II, 54; IV, 10.
76. *Ibid.,* II, 55; III, 52.

of peace, he is happy that the orthodox were demanding no punishment on the Donatists, impious and wicked though they be.[77]

The third element of the "Eusebian Constantine," the image of *Constantinus victor*, also appears in the laws and letters of the emperor, but not often, and not until the final defeat of Licinius when the power of God was evident in complete and dramatic form. In a letter to Alexander and Arius in 324, Constantine indicates that it was through military authority that the system of the world was restored to health and that he had won a decisive victory and unquestionable triumph.[78] A triumphant air is apparent in Constantine's edict following Licinius' defeat in which his victorious march across the empire from as far away as the Britannic Ocean is referred to.[79] Constantine acknowledged God's assistance in his victories, as had Eusebius, and, in connection with Licinius, refers to the divine help of that deity who, by 324, had given abundant proofs of his power.[80]

Finally, Constantine indicates concern with his role as a humane ruler. Here, too, he is indebted to the favor of the God through whom general prosperity had been secured and miseries removed.[81] As a beneficial ruler, Constantine is interested in obviating that which is wicked and in removing evil, harsh necessities, fear, and dissension which contribute to the destruction of mankind.[82] These dangers are to be replaced by security, which only comes about with the removal of tyrants, and with the liberty that follows.[83]

But for Constantine, peace is the greatest blessing a divinely-aided ruler can bestow upon his subjects. All men are to enjoy blessings which derive from peace.[84] He maintains that "My own desire is, for the common good of the world and the advantage of all mankind, that the people should enjoy a life of peace and undisturbed concord."[85] Constantine apparently regarded his first object as the maintenance of peace, holding this goal superior to victory itself.[86]

Perhaps the most important aspect in maintaining a peaceful empire is the preservation of unity in the church, since, in Constantine's eyes, God's wrath would be provoked if this were lost.[87] Constantine connects the prosperity of the times with tranquillity in the church[88] and indicates an intimate interest in harmony among the servants of God because of his belief that with this accomplished, the general course of events will change for the better.[89] It is well-known that in both the Donatist problem[90] and the Arian dispute, Constantine's primary object was unity and peace and not the settlement of theological questions.[91]

77. Opt. *App.* X.
78. *V.C.* II, 65; 67.
79. *Ibid.*, II, 28.
80. *Ibid.*, II, 55.
81. *Ibid.*, II, 42; III, 17.
82. *Ibid.*, II, 28, 29, 31; Opt. *App.* VIII; Athan. *Apol. c. Ar.* 86.
83. *V.C.* II, 46; IV, 9.
84. *Ibid.*, II, 59.
85. *Ibid.*, II, 56.
86. *Ibid.*, III, 60.
87. Opt. *App.* III.
88. *V.C.* III, 17; IV, 42.
89. *Ibid.*, II, 65.
90. Except for one brief reference (*V.C.* II, 66) where he makes a vague statement suggesting that Constantine settled the dispute, Eusebius ignores the Donatist problem presumably because Constantine's lack of success in solving it would blemish his image of *felicitas*.
91. Benjamin ("Constantinus der Grosse," *RE*, 4¹, 1024) correctly refers to Constantine's concern with "bad luck" as a result of disunity. It was apparently of no signi-

In summary, Constantine had precisely the same image of himself as Eusebius, his admirer. The image of the emperor Constantine, with its four facets, is more vivid in the *Vita*, a panegyric designed to magnify the religious deeds of Constantine, than in the imperial letters and edicts of his reign, the purpose of which was to treat with matters of state. Yet the similarities cannot be denied.

Lastly, and perhaps most importantly, this image is a revealing clue as to the nature of Eusebius' notion of Constantine's relationship with the Christian God. Above all, it must be recognized that the image of Constantine presented by Eusebius is not new. Rather, it is precisely the same image of Roman emperors projected by previous panegyricists,[92] with the minor substitution of the Christian God for pagan deities. Although Eusebius' *Vita* is unique in that it was the first panegyric addressed to an emperor by a Christian writer, it is not at all unique in the image it presents of a Roman ruler. The four elements of the "Eusebian Constantine," therefore, emerge very clearly from the pagan panegyric tradition even as they did from the *Vita* and from Constantine's laws and letters.

The intimate connection of the emperor with the divine is a constant theme in the panegyrics. The divinity, as creator and arbiter of earthly matters,[93] plays a role in the status of the emperor who has been honored divinely,[94] has divine power and aid,[95] and enjoys the fruits of divine power and favor.[96] The empire, being bounded not by earthly frontiers but heavenly regions,[97] has the benefit of divine intervention in a positive way, whether it be for vengeance on an enemy, successful campaigns, an imperial marriage (Constantine and Faüsta) leading to a renewal of the state, or for liberty for the city of Rome in the face of designs of men and counsels of the auspices.[98] Constantine's success in 312 against Maxentius was considered to be a victory of *divina praecepta* over *superstitiosa maleficia*.[99]

The emperor, being a gift of the gods,[100] possesses divine virtues bestowed from above. Included are his vigor, manliness, instinct, piety, judgment, dignity, swiftness, force, and providence. Divine, too, is the imperial appearance, voice, mind, plan, and glory. The medicine brought by the emperor for the healing of the state was heaven-sent.

Even the dynastic line involved things higher than human. The ruling family

ficance to Eusebius that Constantine, although lacking training in theological matters, single-handedly directed the solution of the Arian problem, again, because the perseverance of disunity would tarnish his *felicitas*.

92. Ziegler ("Panegyrikos," *RE*, 18³, 571-581) makes no attempt to discuss the content of the *XII Panegyrici Latini*, confining his remarks to problems of dating, authorship, and text. L. K. Born ("The Perfect Prince according to the Latin Panegyricists," *Amer. Jour. Phil.*," 15 [1934], 20-35 especially at 21-23) discusses only the qualities of a good ruler. *Pietas* is not mentioned, there is only one reference to the emperor *victor* (23: "The prince should be a good soldier;"), and the interest of panegyricists before Eusebius in divine forces is neglected. J. Mesk analyzes the panegyrics only in terms of rhetorical types: "Zur technik der lateinischen Panegyriker," *Rh. Mus.*, 67 (1912), 569-90.
93. Pan. IX, 26; X, 7. All references to the panegyrics are to E. Galletier, *Panégyriques latines*, 3 vols. (Paris: Societe d'Edition "Les Belles Lettres," 1949-1955).
94. *Ibid.*, II, 1; VII, 3, 9.
95. *Ibid.*, VI, 16; X, 9.
96. *Ibid.*, III, 6; Pliny, *Pan.* 5.
97. *Pan.* II, 10.
98. *Ibid.*, II, 6, 7, 11; VI, 8, 13; VII, 20; IX, 2; X, 13, 16.
99. *Ibid.*, IX, 4.
100. Pliny, *Pan.* 1.

has a divine origin[101] and ancestors.[102] After his death, Constantius was considered to be a *particeps caeli* and as having been admitted to the council of gods.[103] In like manner, Claudius, the presumed ancestor of Constantine, was a companion of the gods.[104] Finally, the panegyricists did not neglect the dynastic protector deity, whether it be Hercules, Jupiter, or Apollo.[105]

The second aspect of the "Eusbian Constantine," *pietas*, also plays a major role in the pagan panegyrics. The emperor's piety, which is perpetual and extraordinary,[106] and which, again, is held in contrast to the impiety of the adversary,[107] is related to outstanding deeds, prudence, the joy of saving humanity, and the celebration of the birth of the immortal city.[108] Subjects in the empire give thanks for the *pietas* of their emperor.[109] The panegyric itself is really a pious remembrance of a pious emperor.[110]

It was *pietas* that earned for the emperor the *fructus divinae potestatis*, especially *felicitas*,[111] and military victory with which piety is intimately connected[112] Constantine's piety was responsible for his victory over Maxentius.[113] In fact, through his *pietas*, the emperor gains what he needs most—invincibility[114]

Accordingly, the panegyricists by no means neglected the image of the emperor as *victor*. They stressed this aspect primarily by referring often to successful campaigns not only of the current emperor, as the subject of the panegyric, but also of his father or ancestor. The ruler is placed in the same light as great military heroes of the past including Scipio Africanus, Marius, Paullus Aemilius, Caesar, or even Alexander the Great. Important to his military success is the emperor's boldness (*audacia*)[115] or the quality of his army which possesses invincible courage.[116] References to the submission of foreign kings to the emperor enhance the image of a successful military leader[117] as do descriptions of the formidable circumstances under which victory was secured including unfavorable auspices or the outstanding ability of the enemy.[118]

Finally, the Eusebian emphasis on the emperor as an outstanding ruler is to be found among his pagan predecessors. The victorious emperor was able to bring important benefits to the state including liberty and eternity for Rome, joy, and security. Imperial subjects also enjoy happiness, fraternity, prosperity, and, of course, peace. The emperor is depicted as the healer of the state[119] which had been in great danger,[120] displaying many qualities of a good ruler.[121]

101. *Pan.* I, 2, 14; III, 2.
102. Pliny, *Pan.* 14 (the divinity of Trajan's father).
103. *Pan.* X, 14; VI, 3, 14.
104. *Ibid.*, VII, 2.
105. Hercules: *Pan.* II, 1, 2; VI, 2, 8, 11. Jupiter: VI, 12. Apollo: VII, 21, 22.
106. *Pan.* VI, 1; VII, 20; X, 26.
107. *Ibid.*, IX, 4; X, 7, 12.
108. *Ibid.*, II, 1; VI, 2; VII, 7, 8.
109. *Ibid.*, VIII, 7.
110. *Ibid.*, VII, 1.
111. *Ibid.*, III, 18. *Pietas* and *felicitas* are closely related: *Pan.* III, 6, 13, 19.
112. *Ibid.*, VII, 20.
113. *Ibid.*, VII, 14.
114. *Ibid.*, VI, 2.
115. *Ibid.*, IV, 12.
116. *Ibid.*, IX, 10.
117. *Ibid.*, IV, 2; X, 16.
118. *Ibid.*, IX, 2; X, 7 (circumstances were *varios at volubiles*), 17, 19. Pliny, *Pan.* 13: Trajan shared the inconveniences of the campaign with his soldiers.
119. *Pan.* VIII, 11.
120. *Ibid.*, IX, 9.
121. Eg., justice, generosity, prudence, moderation, courage, diligence, clemency, liberality, indulgence, leniency.

It can readily be seen that there is an intimate connection between Eusebius' view of Constantine, Constantine's view of himself, and the view of the pagan panegyricists as to the ideal ruler.

In the light of this evidence Eusebius' conception of the Christianity of Constantine is quite clear. Rather than portraying Constantine as a genuine Christian, Eusebius' message in the *Vita*, reflected in the "Eusebian Constantine" portrayed therein, is that Constantine was Christian only to the same extent that former emperors were pagan. The panegyricist predecessors of Eusebius had presented Roman emperors closely connected with divine forces primarily through their *pietas*. Being pious they expected, and received, victory as a just reward and, then, could propagandize benefits which only came with the peace that followed victory.

Eusebius, as a Christian panegyricist, does not make Constantine an exception. Being interested in divine aid, the emperor turned to the Christian God, as a protector deity and never-failing military ally, whose favor he earned through piety. The testimony of Eusebius' *Vita* sheds no more, and no less, light on the much-debated question of the genuineness of Constantine's personal Christianity.

Constantine and the Miraculous

Ramsay MacMullen

O NE DAY saw Constantine a pagan, the next a Christian, all thanks to the vision of a refulgent cross burning above him. So runs the familiar story. But told in this manner, apparently lacking precedent or preparation or context, it challenges belief. Readers of Lactantius or Eusebius, more alert than those historians themselves to the course of the events they trace, now point to many gradual steps by which the emperor actually changed his public adherence from old gods to new, bringing his empire with him. They point, moreover, to bridges of thought touching both paganism and Christianity by which men like Constantine could pass from one to the other without need violently to repudiate their earlier worships and without need of any miraculous or magical act from on high. In fact, acts of the latter sort themselves constituted a part of the bridge, and it is on them that the following pages will focus, with citation of as many authors of Constantine's whole lifetime as are pertinent. It is the spread and prevalence of ideas as much as their content that will concern us.

Constantine's cross, a model for several similar appearances later, evidently served the credulity of his times. Such a sign was to meet the Caesar Gallus at Antioch as he entered that city, "a cruciform pillar in the sky" visible to other spectators as well, and Constantius, about to engage Magnentius in battle, was not only favored with the same miracle but the citizens of Jerusalem attested its simultaneous appearance in the East stretching from the Mount of Calvary as far as the Mount of Olives. To the pious emperor it brought victory, to Magnentius' troops terror, "because they worshipped demons."[1]

---

[1] Socr. 2.28 (Gallus), with parallels afforded by Philostorgius, *HE* ed. Bidez (*GCS* 1913) 3.26, involving Constantius, and by Soz. 2.3, where Constantine's physician, his conversion not yet complete, is won over to Christianity by a vision of the cross and a voice explaining its significance as the guarantor of salvation; *cf. ibid.* 4.5, a cross 15 stadia high seen by multitudes in Jerusalem, who rush to the churches to be shriven or converted.

Constantius' reign witnessed divine intervention on another front. Persians beleaguered Nisibis where, among the Roman defenders, the holy bishop James of Antioch sent up his entreaties for aid. In response a kingly figure ablaze with crown and purple robe stood out upon the battlements, in whom the Persians recognized the Christian God; and James, himself mounting next, cursed the enemy with hordes of gnats that attacked their horses and elephants, putting them all to flight.[2] Plagues of stinging insects first fell at Moses' command on Egypt; more recent ones were known, attributed to divine anger;[3] and the efficacy of prayer in battle was to recur also, as that which Theodosius uttered against Eugenius in 393, raising a mighty wind to blow the rebels' missiles back in their faces.[4] In so many ways did the incidents at Nisibis build on themes which were the common property of Christians in that period, just as the story of Theodosius and Eugenius likewise could be counted on to remind its audience of a storm they all had heard about, the famous storm that saved the "Thundering Legion" under Marcus Aurelius when Germans and Sarmatians beset his army. For this miracle, in an altogether typical contention over events certainly historical (confirmed by Marcus Aurelius' sculptured Column as well as by his coin-issues), Christians credited their fellows, pagans turned for explanation to a wonder-worker of the time, one Julianus, or to an Egyptian magician, Arnouphis, who "had summoned by enchantment certain demons, above all, Hermes the aerial, and through them had brought on the rainstorm."[5]

But the figure of God Himself threatening Persians from the walls of Nisibis was more spectacular than these deluges and winds. Parallels are thus correspondingly rare. An early glimpse into the popular mind is offered by the *Acta Andreae* of the last quarter of the second century. It relates how the saint and his companions, "proceeding through Thrace, met a troop of armed men who made as if to fall on them. Andrew made the sign of the cross against them and prayed

---

[2] Thdrt. *HE* 2.26.

[3] *Exod.* 8.16f; *Ps.* 105.31f; *cf.* Thdrt. *Graec.affect.cur.* 10.58 (ed. P. Canivet, *Sources chrét.* 57.2 [1958] 378 n.2), on pests of mice, bats, snakes and scorpions; the last, with various stinging insects, appear often on magical amulets (S. Eitrem, *SymbOslo* 7 [1928] 70–73; *cf.* Cypr. *Ep.* 69.5). In Arnobius' day (*adv.Nat.* 1.3) plagues of locusts and mice were still blamed on Christians.

[4] Socr. 5.25, "so powerful was the emperor's prayer."

[5] Dio 72.8.4; *cf.* Euseb. *HE* 5.5.1–3, adding the detail of lightning-bolts, and E. R. Dodds, *JRS* 37 (1947) 56; full treatment in J. Guey, *RevPhil* 22 (1948) 17f.

that they might be made powerless. A bright angel touched their swords and they all fell down."[6] Eusebius later (*Vita Const.* 2.6) tells of detachments of Constantine's forces—where none really were, hence miraculous troops—marching through eastern cities on the eve of the battle with Licinius, sent "by a divine and superior power." Two other examples are found in Socrates' *Ecclesiastical History* (6.6, 7.18): "multitudes of angels . . . like armored soldiers of great stature" who vanquished Gainas; "the angels from God [who] appeared to people in Bithynia . . . [and] said they were sent as arbiters over the war." Better yet is the "demonic apparition" drawn by Eusebius from Josephus (*HE* 3.8.5; Joseph. *BJ* 290f): "before sunset in the air throughout the country chariots and regiments [were seen] flying through the clouds and encircling the cities." Among pagan writers, on the other hand, such miraculous beings play a smaller part. A woman of gigantic form turns up in Dio Cassius' pages almost as a genre-figure. Dio asserts his personal belief in her, whether in the scene of Drusus crossing the Elbe or upon the crisis of Macrinus' reign in 217.[7] Herodian (8.3.8) goes further. The occasion as he describes it is the closing in of Maximinus' legions on Aquileia in 238. To the townspeople "certain oracles were given that the deity of the region would grant them victory. They call him Belis, worship him mightily, and identify him with Apollo. His image, some of Maximinus' troops reported, often appeared in the skies fighting in defense of the city"—which returns us to Constantine.

For that susceptible emperor had *two* visions, not only of a cross but (somewhat less well known if hardly less debated by scholars) an earlier one of Apollo. It came to him on his way south from the Rhine to defeat Maximian in Marseilles. He turned aside en route to a temple of Apollo, "whom you saw, I believe, O Constantine—your Apollo accompanied by Victory holding out laurelled crowns to you each of which brought the presage of thirty years [of rule] . . . And yet why do I say, 'I believe'? You saw and you recognized him in the form to which . . . the reigns of all the world were destined" (*Paneg. vet.* 7[6].21.3–5). "You saw," presumably as others by the score had seen some deity invoked by magic or freely offering himself to them, and as, in later embroidered versions, Constantine's second vision was

<hr>

[6] M. R. James, *The Apocryphal New Testament* (Oxford 1924) 339; date (*ibid.* 228) revised upward by P. M. Peterson, *Andrew, Brother of Simon Peter* (Leiden 1958) 26.
[7] Dio 55.1.3f, 79[78].25.5; *cf.* 73.13.3, and Plin. *Ep.* 7.27 and Soz. 7.23.

explained to him personally by Christ.[8] Superhuman beings, then, who revealed themselves to their worshippers before armed conflict or whose agents or powers were exerted for the battalions of the pious were a feature of pagan as of Christian mythology in the third and fourth centuries; and no better illustration of this common ground can be found than the spiritual career of Constantine between 310 and 312.

His panegyrists noted elements throughout his rise and reign beyond mere mortal reach. Sometimes such notice was blurred and vague, for example, in the emphasis of Nazarius on Constantine's "celestial favor," the victims "divinely granted to your arms," "the divinity accustomed to forward your undertakings," and so forth—expressions shading off into ambiguities common among both pagan and Christian writers.[9] So victory comes to Valentinian *magni numinis adiumento*, Julian's armies feel confident *caelestis dei favore . . . freti*, spurred on by *salutaris quidam genius praesens*.[10] More often the notices of Constantine's protector are explicit, as in the paragraphs devoted by Eusebius (*HE* 10.8.6–9) to proving his hero God's representative on earth.

With Constantine, indeed, the sense that men, especially leaders of state, acted as servants of some supernal purpose and thus played their rôles under its direction, took firm hold on the minds of contemporaries, as was bound to come about from the ascendance of so historically oriented a religion as Christianity. The view, destined long to prevail, was new to the Roman world. It left faint traces in the Augustan History, where a favorite of pagan polemic, the emperor Marcus Aurelius, was imagined Stoically receiving news of a pretender's revolt in the certainty that *di me tuentur, dis pietas mea . . . cordi est.* "We have not so worshipped the gods nor so lived that he

---

[8] A catalogue of pagan epiphanies—of Asclepius alone—would be endless. For a selection of those sent to Christians, see Constantine's being led on the founding circuit of Constantinople by some divine being, in Philostorg. *HE* 2.9; Theodosius' vision of "the blessed Meletius," in Thdrt. *HE* 5.6; and of St John and St Philip on the eve of battle, promising him success, *ibid.* 5.24 (confirmed by a second witness); Constantius' beholding of his own guardian angel or genius, in Amm. 21.14.2; Arnobius' conversion by visions, in Hieron. *Chron.* A.D. 326/7; and the angel sent to Licinius in a dream, in Lact. *Mort.pers.* 46. For Christ appearing to Constantine, see Soz. 1.3.

[9] *Paneg.vet.* (ed. Baehrens², Leipzig 1911) 10[4].2.6, 12.1, 13.5, 16.2, 17.1, 28.1.

[10] Amm.Marc. 29.5.40, 16.12.13; *cf.* frequent references to the emperor's *numen* or *divinitas* in the *Paneg.vet.* 3 and 4 (*e.g.* 4.15.6, 4.17.1); Constantine's conversion ἀφράστῳ τινὶ δυνάμει, in Soz. 1.18. Even such loosely conceived Powers might still be thought of as actually operating on history. We see events taking place ὑπό τινος δαιμονίου τύχης, in Hdn. 1.9.4; ἐξ ἐπιπνοίας τινὸς θείας, in Dio 79[78].8.2, *cf.* 76[75].4.5; or ὥσπερ ὑπὸ πνεύματος δεινοῦ τινος, in Euseb. *HE* 4.2.2.

should overcome us."[11] On the other hand, the acts of Christian emperors were frequently hailed as approved, inspired, intended or made possible by God. God (says a writer addressing Constantine's sons) has bestowed the *imperium*, the *vexillum fidei; vobis hoc divinitas reservavit. Favore eminentis dei victores estis omnium hostium vestrorum . . . Strati sunt adversantium cunei, et rebellantia ante conspectum vestrum semper arma ceciderunt . . . Haec vobis deus summus . . . pro fide vestra reddidit praemia.* And if this be a view no doubt deeply colored by the established supremacy of Christian rulers in whom the devout would wish to see the workings of Providence, we may yet match it with the statement of an Alexandrian bishop a century earlier, for whom God "entrusted the monarchy to the most pious Valerian and Gallienus," whose reign he prays Him to uphold.[12] So late as the fourth century, moreover, vestiges survived of a belief in guardian angels set over each people, giving to them their worships, languages and separate characters and, beyond that, controlling their destiny through their own high or low position in God's favor. Angels might sometimes exert their power on the battlefield.[13]

Upon his conversion, Constantine entered into this whole heritage of beliefs—the belief that a pious people would receive divine protection, that their ruler ruled according to divine plan, and that God directly or through his angels could be expected to intercede in their behalf at crucial moments. Thus, to Maxentius' fateful collision with Constantine at the Milvian Bridge, "God Himself as with chains dragged the tyrant far away from the [safety of Rome's] gates."[14]

The question how pagans looked on the position of the Roman emperors *vis à vis* the gods has been surprisingly little studied, despite a mass of material.[15] It is fortunately tangential to our purpose. Two

---

[11] Interesting passages: SHA *Avid. Cassius* 2.2; 8.2f, 11.8, quoting Hor. *Od.* 1.17.13. I cannot recall any earlier pagan texts hinting at the existence of a divine plan for history, though it is easy to find the belief that the accession and demise of an emperor were divinely intended. See J. Béranger, *Recherches sur l'aspect idéologique du principat* (Basel 1953) 155f, 164f. In the fourth century, no doubt in a spirit of anti-Christian polemic, Eunapius (*Vit.soph.* 476) describes Julian's "conquering all [the barbarians] because he worshipped the gods"—a more explicit statement of cause and effect than fits in the earlier Empire. Cf. *infra* n.17.

[12] Firm.Mat. *Err.prof.rel.* 16.4, 20.7, 29.3; bishop Dionysius in Euseb. *HE* 7.11.8; cf. Tert. *Apol.* 33; Orig. *c.Cels.* 8.68 and 70; and, of course, Eusebius throughout the *Vita Const.*, e.g. 1.38.

[13] The basic text was *Deut.* 32.8f (and *Dan.* 10.13), with later adherence clearest in Orig. *c.Cels.* 1.24, 3.2, 4.8, 5.25, 5.30; see H. B. Kuhn, *JBL* 67 (1948) 218–31; E. Peterson, *TheolZ* 7 (1951) 81–90; and C. M. Morrison, *The Powers That Be* (London 1960) 18–23 and *passim*.

[14] Euseb. *V.Const.* 1.38.

[15] Some slight help from A. D. Nock, *JRS* 37 (1947) 112–14.

points only need be made. In the first place, the idea of national guardian angels, though familiar to writers like Celsus, Porphyry, Iamblichus and Julian,[16] did not lead to a concept of supernatural intervention in terrestrial happenings; nor (in the second place) did the concept of the ruler favored or even chosen by the gods develop further into the expectation that they would miraculously succor him in the hour of national crisis. Not until challenged by Christianity did pagans give any sharpness to their claims that their own piety could secure the safety of the state or the victorious outcome of a campaign.[17] In Constantine's lifetime, a change can be seen. In the transition to an era of far more intense and vaunting religious propaganda, the battle of the Milvian Bridge was critical. Thereafter, through the conflicts involving Licinius and Maximin and so to the historic conversion of Clovis in the following century, battle was determined, so men said, by divine judgement.

But to return to Constantine: newly converted, he advanced into Italy in 312. His decision to make war, his march, his feelings and motives, all receive a characteristic treatment at the hands of spokesmen for the Church. But they make the meaning of the march clearer by their description of his opponent, who, we are told, huddles in Rome gripped by terror, vice and superstition, dupe to countless religious charlatans, petitioner to countless vain spirits, convert to such revolting measures as the tearing of unborn babes from the womb for use in prognostic sacrifices. Though the picture of his *superstitiosa maleficia* is a compendium of commonplaces,[18] it sets the stage for the dramatic collision of the two religious worlds. This is the

[16] Julian, *adv.Gal.* 115ᴅ; Orig. *c.Cels.* 8.35; Ael.Arist. *Or.* 43.18, cited from H. Chadwick, *Origen: Contra Celsum* (Cambridge 1965) xix; Iambl. *Myst.* 5.25; Morrison, *op.cit.* (*supra* n.13) 84f; on the related idea of a supreme god with angel-agents, like the Persian king surrounded by his satraps, which was fitted into both Origen's and Neoplatonic thought, see F. Cumont, *RevHistRel* 72 (1915) 163–74.

[17] Note the references, of a new explicitness, by the Egyptian prefect Aemilianus, to "the gods that preserve their [*scil.* of Valerian and Gallienus] monarchy," or by Maximin, to the city that is "by many proofs revealed to flourish through the presence of the heavenly gods," etc., or his assertion that "by the gods the government of the state and all individuals in it have their being" (Euseb. *HE* 7.11, 9.7.5, 9.7.7f, 9.9ᴀ.6). Pagan supporters attributed Julian's spectacular success against Constantius to Julian's divine protectors (Eunap. *Vit.soph.* 476; Greg.Naz. *Or.* 4, *adv.Juln.* 1.47). For even approximate parallels to such views, one would have to go back three centuries and more to Vergil's age (R. Syme, *The Roman Revolution* [Oxford 1939] 448f).

[18] On Maxentius' desperate measures, see *Paneg.vet.* 9[12].16.5; Euseb. *V.Const.* 1.36, *HE* 8.14.5, 9.9.2; Lact. *Mort.pers.* 44; Zos. 2.15.4; for these clichés of the tyrant's last days, compare SHA *Julianus* 7.9f; Soz. 1.7; Dio 74.16.5, 80[79].11; Euseb. *V.Const.* 2.4f, *HE* 8.14.8; and Zon. 13.1.2; for the prognostic sacrifices, also Amm.Marc. 29.2.17.

significance felt by historians of the battle of the Milvian Bridge. The old world failed, whatever devices were desperately attempted; the new conquered, in the first campaign of a century's religious strife. This strife was carried on not merely by men but by supernatural forces, too. If the Sibylline books, demons, priests and the rest deceived Maxentius, it is at any rate they who fought as well as he; and their enemy was not the western emperor but the Savior's sign. The sign may then have been the *chrisma* and only in later battles the cross; more likely, at the Milvian Bridge as throughout the rest of Constantine's career, the cross.[19] Its cherished use in war, its invariable efficacy whether on armor or on the *labarum* and whether to protect emperor or humble standard-bearer, set it above all other forces;[20] yet the relation between the *labarum* and the traditional Roman *vexillum* is obvious,[21] while the painting of a declaratory or magical device on the shields of one's troops had earlier close parallels.[22] Even the tales of the defensive properties of the cross in combat are matched by the inscriptions found on pieces of military equipment from the centuries just before Constantine, reading "Luck to the bearer" or "Best and Greatest, save the corps of all our soldiers"; Mars or Victory might be depicted on armor.[23] Such evidence shows us the well-worn paths that Constantine trod when, according to the ancient arts of apotropaic magic though with a different device, he put the insignia of Christianity in the hands of his followers.

On the history of those insignia there is no need for much discussion. Their potency to tear demons from their lairs in statues, to uproot them from unhappy maniacs, to drive them forever from

[19] A. Alföldi, *Conversion of Constantine* (Oxford 1948) 17f, argues for the *chrisma*, but points out (126 n.7) the magical properties which it as well as the cross might be supposed to possess.

[20] On the power given to Constantine by use of the cross, see Socr. 1.2; Soz. 1.4, the cross venerated by soldiers and the *labarum* work miracles; *ibid.* 1.8, cross marked on weapons; Thdrt. *HE* 1.17, and Socr. 1.17, Helena sends her son nails and wood from the true cross, which he uses on his equipment and bears into battle "in order to avert the missiles of his enemies."

[21] Firm.Mat. *Err.prof.rel.* 20.7, the *labarum* called the *vexillum fidei*; and, on its warlike properties, Alföldi, *op.cit.* (*supra* n.19) 84 and n.3, coins of Constantine showing "the imperial standard with the emblem of Christ piercing with its point the snake of paganism."

[22] Thunderbolts on shields in W. F. Volbach, *Altchristliche Mosaiken* (London 1947) pl. II; E. Petersen *et al.*, *Die Marcus-Säule* (München 1896) plates 5.1, 10.1f, 11.1, 15.1, etc.; *RE* 2A (1921) 919 *s.v.* SCUTUM on Trajan's Column; for identification of units by their shields, see Tac. *Hist.* 3.23; Dio 64.14.2; Amm.Marc. 16.12.6; for Vespasian's name on his *vexilla*, Suet. *Vesp.* 6; for apotropaic animal symbols on shields, MacMullen, *ArtB* 46 (1964) 442.

[23] A. Ruhlmann, *CRAI* 1935, 67f; P. Wuilleumier, *Gallia* 8 (1950) 146f; J. M. C. Toynbee, *Art in Roman Britain* (London 1962) 168 and pl. 107.

shrines and temples to the accompaniment of their anguished howls and supplications—all this is attested in dozens of accounts of Christ's cross or name in the service of the faithful.[24] So mighty was the weapon that Constantine aimed at Maxentius' weaker gods. But Constantine extended its use. His mother Helena sent him a piece of the true cross. "When he received it, confident that the city in which it was kept would be preserved forever, he hid it in a statue of himself standing in the so-called Forum of Constantine in Constantinople, on a large porphyry column"—thereby producing the Christian equivalent of those images of the pagan gods that, both earlier and later, deflected enemies' attacks. They guarded Nero against conspiracies, Ephesus against plagues, Athens against earthquakes, Rome against sedition.[25]

Constantine's actions fitted the times. Apotropaic magic to ward off disease was on the increase. Lucky stones with mystic signs and spells on them grew more popular in the third and fourth centuries than ever before, evidently among both Christians and pagans, since the synods of Ancyra (under Constantine) and of Laodicea (between 341 and 381) spoke out against "those who foretell the future and follow the customs of the heathen, or introduce persons into their houses to find out magical remedies or to perform purifications," or against priests who "shall not be magicians or enchanters or astrologers or make so-called phylacteries [amulets] . . . and those who wear them we order to be expelled from the Church."[26]

Eusebius tells the tale of Caesarea in Palestine where once lived the woman whom Christ cured of an issue of blood. At the gates of her house stood two statues which he himself had seen, one of a woman

---

[24] For example, Cypr. *ad Demetrianum* 15; *Acta Andreae* 9; Thphl.Ant. *ad Autol.* 2.8 (Migne *PG* 6.1061f); Marc.Diac. *V.Porph.* 61; *Consultationes Zacchaei et Apollonii*, ed. G. Morin (Bonn 1935) 1.5; Greg.Nyss. *V.Greg.Thaum.* (Migne *PG* 46.916A and 949D–952D); Soz. 4.16 and 5.2; Thdrt. *HE* 3.1, 5.21; Athan. *Or. Incarn.verbi* 48 (Migne *PG* 25.181); idem, *V.Anton.* 13.23, 35, 40, 53, 63f, and 80; Lact. *Mort.pers.* 10.2f; Euseb. *c.Hierocl.* 4; Juln.Imp. *Ep.* 79 (ed. Bidez); and *Acta Xanthippae et Polyxenae* (ed. James) 17f.

[25] To the references in MacMullen, *Enemies of the Roman Order* (Cambridge [Mass.] 1966) 319, on apotropaic statues, add Suet. *Nero* 56, Philostr. *V.Apollon.* 4.10, and Dio 37.9.2; *cf.* effective apotropaic rites against the enemies of the state, SHA *Aurelian* 18.5, 20.5–7, 21.4, described with considerable emphasis to match, in pagan history, the miracles wrought by Christians. On Constantine's statue, see Socr. 1.17.

[26] J. Stevenson, tr., *A New Eusebius* (London 1957) 312, Council of Ancyra; *Concilium Laodicenum* (ed. Jonkers) 36; *cf.* Basil on medical magic resorted to by his congregation, Migne *PG* 29.417. Further, on superstition prevalent among Christians, *cf.* Stevenson 308 (Council of Elvira, A.D. 305), *infra* n.44, and esp. compare Plut. *Mor.* 356B with August. *Conf.* 8.12.29.

praying, the other of a man resembling Jesus. At the base of the latter grew a curious herb able to "cure diseases of all kinds." To this wonder we must add the power of the true cross that Helena discovered to heal the sick: thus, two illustrations of the workings of *Christus medicus*, in opposition especially to the authority enjoyed by Asclepius.[27] But it was, after all, essential for the Church to present its founder as a God of deeds equal to the performances of pagan deities, since, particularly for a mass audience, proof through miracles offered an infinitely more persuasive appeal than the type of argument carried on in written form. Simple people wanted simple proof of the superior ability of Christianity to do for them what older worships had always promised: that is, to defend them from the ills of this earth. The dreams granted at Asclepieia taught suppliants how to be healed. Could Christ or his holy men do as much? And if the answer was yes, in scores of wonders wrought especially by monks, there remained the more general affliction of epidemic disease. Throughout antiquity men attributed plagues to divine anger. A persistent conviction blamed their onset on the progress of Christianity and the resulting neglect of pagan cults.[28] It was a heavy charge variously answered; but one response as it was ultimately framed in pious myth said that even in averting disease Christians had access to a more greatly beneficent power than pagan wonderworkers.

With a few exceptions—Eusebius was one—Christians, like pagans, acknowledged the supernatural origin of plagues, as they did of other bodily ills which they could not understand. Ailments afflicting (in grotesquely disgusting descriptions) especially the intestines and genitals marked the victim as the target of a god's, or of God's, wrath; the genre is well known and meets us most often in the heated religious atmosphere of the fourth century.[29] Manic fits likewise

[27] Euseb. *HE* 7.18.1–3; Socr. 1.17; R. Arbesmann, *Traditio* 10 (1954) 3f. Note that, as Christ was lowered to a healer of bodies, pagan propaganda sought to raise Asclepius to a healer of souls, Juln.Imp. *adv.Gal.* 200B. At the same time the ability of the gods, notably Asclepius, really to heal their worshippers was persistently depreciated, *e.g.*, in Cypr. *Idol.vanit.* 6F; Tat. *Ad Graec.* 16; Tert. *Apol.* 22; Ps.-Clem. *Hom.* 9.15f; and Athan. *V.Anton.* 33. F. Dölger, *AuChr* 6 (1950) 242–54, discusses some of these and other passages.

[28] Cypr. *ad Demetr.* 2f; Arnob. *adv.Nat.* 1.1 and 3; Porphyry in Thdrt. *Graec.affect.cur.* 12.96f. For a pagan and a Christian in competition to avert plague from Rome, only the Christian successful, see Dodds, *op.cit.* (*supra* n.5) 57.

[29] Medical details meet us in Plut. *Sulla* 36, but earlier examples that he draws from Greek literature could be easily multiplied. See the full history of θεομάχοι in W. Nestle, *Griechische Studien* (Stuttgart 1948) 568f. Other roots of the genre reach into Judaism, continued by Christian writers against pagans, persecutors and heretics, and usurped for use

called more for the exorcist than the doctor, and Christians claimed to possess the requisite skills more than their opponents. Palladius and Sozomen supply an abundance of case-histories. It was the same with other mysterious catastrophes: sterility of the fields, insect-pests, hail, drought, earthquakes, storms. Great winds, said Maximin Daia, were controlled by the gods,[30] and could be turned on or off by their favor or displeasure. Jealous courtiers of Constantine accused the influential wise man Sopater of having "chained the winds" that were to bring the grain fleet to the capital; whereupon the emperor, evidently convinced that the man was actually capable of the necessary enchantments, executed him.[31]

Believing that natural phenomena, from earthquakes to the wasting of the flesh, were in fact all supernatural, people of the later Empire saw in their afflictions a working out of divine conflicts on a terrestrial plane or stage. Pagans accused Christians of causing these conflicts and their resultant sufferings. In the Apologists the echoes of such accusations—*popularia verba*, said Arnobius—are plainly heard; individual instances of persecution breaking out in the train, and because of the typical interpretation, of droughts and earthquakes are fairly often recorded. It was thought that droughts and the like might be deliberately inflicted in response to invocation or upon people hateful to the gods, though it was still more usually argued that the protectors of cities and nations had been neglected, and had for this reason departed.[32] The sum total of the later Empire's ill-fortunes could thus, to Zosimus, appear to follow from the abandonment of ancestral cults and rites. He singles out for his criticism the decision of Constantine not to hold the *ludi saeculares*, in order that he may strike a blow at that hero of the Church.[33]

---

against Christians by pagans. See *II Chron.* 21.15 and 18; *I Macc.* 6.8; *II Macc.* 9.8f; *Acts* 1.18, 12.23; Herod smitten, in Joseph. *AJ* 17.168–170, *BJ* 1.656–660, both texts familiar to Eusebius (*HE* 1.8.5f); Arius smitten in answer to bishop Alexander's prayer, in Socr. 1.38 and Thdrt. *HE* 1.13; Galerius smitten, in Lact. *Mort.pers.* 33 and Euseb. *HE* 8.16.3–5; Julian, uncle to the Apostate, smitten in Soz. 5.8, in Thdrt. *HE* 3.9, and in Philostorg. *HE* (Bidez) 7.10, adding the names of other victims of φθειρίασις; and used against Christians by Juln.Imp. *Ep.* 55 and 90 (ed. Bidez).

[30] Euseb. *HE* 9.7.10; cf. Marc.Diac. *V.Porph.* 56; Iambl. *Myst.* 5.6, and *V.Pythag.* 135; *supra* n.5. Though this evidence deals only with storms, much more could be gathered on other types of natural disaster.

[31] The poisoned source for the incident is Eunap. *Vit.soph.* 462f.

[32] Marc.Diac. *V.Porph.* 19; Cypr. *Ep.* 75.10.1f, ed. Bayard (Paris 1961).

[33] Zos. 2.7; Z. Petre, *Studii clasice* 7 (1965) 263f, noting (264 n.4) "the obviously magical nature of these games."

Here, then, is another part of the background to the battle of the Milvian Bridge: terrestrial events of a striking, public character were thought to result from supernatural intercession whether spontaneous or invoked. It was neither improper nor uncommon for Christians to give credence to happenings of this order, and it was frowned on only if it degenerated to the private practice of magic. Pagans of course enjoyed a wider latitude in superstition, without, however, any fundamentally different views.

To understand a further aspect of the collision between Maxentius and Constantine, some discussion of demons is needed. The term, in Greek or by adoption in Latin, had the broadest meaning. Pagan philosophers used it to designate, between the crass material of mankind and the etherial realm of pure intellect, the denizens of an intermediate world who served as agents and emissaries from the higher to the lower and (conducting the souls of the dead and the prayers of the living) from the lower to the higher. These denizens had ranks according to their insubstantiality and intellectuality, the purer ones sometimes called angels but often not differentiated under a separate category. They linked men to gods. Foreign as was most of this hierarchy of intermediaries to classical Greek thought, it can be seen developing in the second century and went virtually unquestioned in the later Empire. Its roots lay partly in a substratum of popular superstition, partly in Oriental religions.[34] To mention only points of interest to our present purpose: it was demons who occasioned earthquakes, pests and so forth; they again who brought oracles from the gods and cured the sick; sometimes, too, harmed men when called on with the proper enchantments. Outstanding minds of late antiquity, Porphyry and Libanius, were quite sure that magic could be enlisted in the cause of personal vendettas—though the pure in spirit were beyond the reach of demons.[35] The more evil among demons

---

[34] K. Svoboda, *La démonologie de Michel Psellos* (Brno 1927) 11–14, 31, 34f; F. Cumont, *Lux perpetua* (Paris 1949) 81–95; idem, *RevHistRel* 72 (1915) 159–74; T. Hopfner, *Griechisch-ägyptischer Offenbarungszauber* I (Leipzig 1921) 6, 8, 21f, 43f; and the sources, from the less important forerunners like Plutarch (*e.g. Mor.* 361Af), Albinus (*e.g. Epit.* 15.1), and Artemidorus (*e.g. Oneir.* 2.34), to the chief Neoplatonists, Plotinus (*Enn.* 3.5.6), Porphyry (*Ep. ad Anebo, passim*; August. *De civ.D.* 10.9.26; Procl. *In Tim.* 142c), Iamblichus (*Myst.* 1.3–9, 12, 20; 2.3; 3.16; etc.), and Proclus (*In Crat.* 122).

[35] Demons caused pests, etc., in Porph. *Abst.* 2.40 and Iambl. *Myst.* 2.6 and 56; they cure the sick, *ibid.* 3.3; bring oracles, *ibid.* 3.2 and 16; Plut. *Mor.* 362; respond to *defixiones*, in Iambl. *Myst.* 2.7, and Cumont, *RevHistRel* 72 (1915) 175; they attack men at the command of magic, Marc.Diac. *V.Porph.* 10; Liban. *Or.* 1.43, 36.1–3 (*cf.* Zon. 13.8.17f, and Amm.Marc.

longed to gorge themselves on sacrifices, to experience sexual intercourse vicariously through the bodies of the possessed, and to deceive with false revelations.[36] Sometimes demons dwelt in cult images; they would not appear in impure places and shunned a hostile presence.[37] To different ones among them different temples, even different zones or, more specifically, nations and peoples, had been assigned for oversight,[38] and they occasionally took visible human shape to meddle directly in the course of events.[39] According to a particularly common conviction, the Devil—ὁ μισόκαλος—or his agents continually worked against the progress or unity of the Church by spreading false doctrines, libels, suspicions against Christians, and the like. Infected with these diabolical errors, heretics and persecutors became mere instruments of a wickedness from beyond.[40]

Strange views, perhaps. But as a darkness of irrationality thickened over the declining centuries of the Roman empire, superstition blacked out the clearer lights of religion, wizards masqueraded as philosophers, and the fears of the masses took hold on those who passed for educated and enlightened.[41] From the same world, reflecting of necessity the same ideas because surrounded by them in all social classes, rose the leaders of the Church. Thus all of the opinions about demons (by that specific term, daemon or δαίμων) just now reviewed as representing the consensus of pagan thought also reigned as orthodoxy among Christians like Origen, Lactantius, Eusebius,

---

26.3.2)—though the pure were immune, Plot. Enn. 4.4.43; and MacMullen, op.cit. (supra n.25) 317.

[36] Svoboda, op.cit. (supra n.34) 24f, 29–31; Iambl. Myst. 2.9f.

[37] Euseb. Prep.ev. 4.23 (Porphyry); C. Bonner, Studies in Magical Amulets (Ann Arbor 1950) 15f; Dodds, op.cit. (supra n.5) 64f; Corp.Herm., ed. Nock II (Paris 1945) Asclepius 37; Macrob. Sat. 1.23.13; Porph. V.Plotin. 10; Hopfner, op.cit. (supra n.34) 1.14.

[38] Fronto, Ep. 3.9.1–2; Celsus in Orig. c.Cels. 5.25; Iambl. Myst. 1.20, 5.25; Juln.Imp. adv.Gal. 143A–B; Hopfner, Ueber die Geheimlehren von Jamblichus (Leipzig 1922) 243, adding Procl. In Tim. 142c; supra n.16.

[39] Iambl. Myst. 3.3; Dio 65.25.5, 79[78].7.4, 80[79].18.1; supra n.7. "The term [δαίμων] ordinarily indicates, in Dio Cassius, a divinity of the second rank often foreign, entrusted with functions among mortals"—J. Beaujeu, La religion romaine à l'apogée de l'empire (Paris 1955) 344 n.4.

[40] Constantine attributed stasis in the Church to the operation of "the envious daemon" (Soz. 1.19). For similar views on the deceitful activity of daemons who control events through the control of men's minds, see Athenag. pro Christ. 27; Cypr. Idol.vanit. 6f; Thphl.Ant. ad Autol. 2.8 and 28; Arnob. adv.Nat. 1.56; Greg.Naz. Or. 1.47, 39.7; Thdrt. HE 1.1c; Euseb. HE 2.14.1, 3.8.9; 4.7.1, 9, and 10; 5.14.1, 7.17.1; Justin, Apol. 1.5 and 26, 2.13; Orig. c.Cels. 3.32, 4.32, 4.92, 5.5; Tert. Apol. 27; and Lact. Mort.pers. 3.

[41] See the discussion and sources in MacMullen, op.cit. (supra n.25) ch.3–4.

Basil, Gregory and many others,[42] though with this major difference, that the intermediaries between mortal and divine were conceived of as good and bad angels, the latter being equated (under the name 'demons') with the pagan gods. It hardly occurred to Christians to deny the whole infinite list of the older deities; only as many as possible were traced back to men as heroes, according to the traditional teachings of Euhemerism, while those that could not be talked out of existence in this fashion were left to deceive men with false visions, false cures, false oracles and insidious intrusions of shameful lust. This last trial especially will be recalled by readers of Athanasius' *Vita S. Antoni*. Anthony declared himself the target of temptation by beautiful succubi some of whom, it is permissible to imagine, were simply pious peasant girls coming to venerate the saint. The mistake, at any rate, is once attested of a bishop of Constantius' time, spending the night at an inn. A woman entered in the dark, the bishop asked, "Who's there?" and hearing her voice concluded she was a demon in female form. "Straightway he called on Christ the Savior to help him."[43] The instinctive assumption that unearthly forces were at work tells us much about the spirit of the age.

Priests forbidden by the Council of Laodicea to engage in magical practices are joined by the clients of charlatans in Basil's congregation; together they and their like form the audience for one of the charges most frequently (surely, because most credibly) launched by

---

[42] Demons were seen as intermediary beings (Arnob. *adv.Nat.* 2.35; Euseb. *Prep.ev.* 4.5), formerly angels until their fall (Tat. *ad Graec.* 12; Tert. *Apol.* 22; Lact. *Div.Inst.* 2.15; Euseb. *Prep.ev.* 7.16; Athenag. *pro Christ.* 24; *Consult.Zacchaei* (*supra* n.24) 1.30f; Phot. *Bibl.* 234f= Methodius; Svoboda, *op.cit.* [*supra* n.34] 6f). What pagans called gods were either formerly mortals (Euhemerism: Arnob. *adv.Nat.* 1.37; Firm.Mat. *Err.prof.rel.* 2.3, 7.6; Cypr. *Idol. vanit.* 1; Athenag. *pro Christ.* 28) or simply demons (Tat. *ad Graec.* 22; Justin. *Apol.* 1.5; Clem.Alex. *Cohort.* 1.2.63 and 69; Tert. *Apol.* 22; Euseb. *c.Hierocl.* 25 and *Prep.ev.* 4.5 and 23; *Consult.Zacchaei* 1.5; Socr. 3.23; Soz. 2.5; Thdrt. *HE* 1.1c, 3.3). They lodged in cult statues (*Ps.* 96.5; Ps.-Clem. *Hom.* 9.15; Cypr. *Idol.vanit.* 7; Rufin., Migne *PG* 12.789B; Basil, Migne *PG* 30.532C; Firm.Mat. *Err.prof.rel.* 13.4; Athenag. *pro Christ.* 26f), delighting in the smoke and blood of sacrifices (Orig. *c.Cels.* 7.5; Tert. *Apol.* 22; Firm.Mat. *Err.prof.rel.* 13.4; Basil, Migne *PG* 30.165c and 532c), issuing deceitful oracles to pagans (Cypr. *Idol.vanit.* 6; *Consult. Zacchaei* 1.27; Svoboda, *op.cit.* [*supra* n.34] 34); they sought sexual license through possession (Ps.-Clem. *Hom.* 9.9f; [Clem.Rom.] *Recog.* 4.16; *Consult.Zacchaei* 1.30; Svoboda, *op.cit.* 31). Especially by controlling men's minds and impulses they intervened to shape historical events (Justin. *Apol.* 1.44.12; Cypr. *Idol.vanit.* 7; Euseb. *V.Const.* 1.45, 1.49, 3.12, 3.26, *HE* 3.8.5, 4.7.2, 4.11.9, 9.10.2; Greg.Naz., Migne *PG* 36.341B; Socr. 4.19; Thdrt. *HE* 1.1c). They could be called or banished by spells (Arnob. *adv.Nat.* 1.43–45), but could not hurt the pure (Lact. *Div.Inst.* 2.16). Nations and peoples were assigned to the oversight of angels (*supra* n.13; Clem.Alex. *Cohort.* 2; J. Daniélou, *Origène* [Paris 1948] 236f; *idem, Recherches de science religieuse* 38 [1951] 132–34).

[43] Thdrt. *HE* 2.7.

Christians at their fellows, heretics or schismatics or simply personal foes, namely, the charges of attempted sorcery. It is irrelevant that these were no doubt often untrue; the fact remains that they were believed.[44] They could be launched, moreover, at more ambitious targets, and used in polemics of a yet graver importance. When enemies of the Church competitively inflated the reputation of that renowned wonder-worker of the first century, Apollonius of Tyana, Christians could dismiss him, too, as a mere 'magician'; in reply, the term was turned against Christ, lowering Him to the rank of *magus*.[45] Could pagan miracles truly equal those wrought by Christ? A didactic tract pointed to his raising of the dead to life, whereas heathen wizards could only boast that *magicis carminibus non mortuorum sed daemonum spiritus evocari*.

The atmosphere of contentious comparison, the tendency to prove the superiority of one's faith by matching its miraculous powers with another's, emerged suddenly from books to the stage of real events in Constantine's lifetime. The conditions making this possible were all present. What was required was a conviction that powers accessible to men through invocation, and willing to intervene in tangible forms and happenings—moreover, powers potentially hostile to each other —filled the universe. It was necessary, too, that such a conviction should be held by the great mass of people, as was indeed the case. Our sketch so far, relying more on anecdotes than analysis, has been intended to reveal society shot through at all levels with the colors of a grosser superstition, with cruder expectations of the supernatural than one could find in the Empire at its height.

The consequences appeared first in the origins of the Great Persecution, of which Constantine, incidentally, was a witness. As Diocletian was assisting in the ceremony of *extispicium*, Christians in his retinue crossed themselves, "by which act the demons were put to flight and the ritual disturbed." The chief priest explained why the

[44] *ibid.* 1.28; Socr. 1.27; Soz. 2.25, 4.10—all recounting accusations against Athanasius; also against Eusebius of Emesa (Socr. 2.9; Soz. 3.6), Cyprian (Prudent. *Perist.* 13.21f), Constantius (Amm.Marc. 21.1.6), and various heresiarchs (Iren. *adv.Haer.* 1.13.3, and Euseb. *HE* 4.7.2 and 4.11.4, quoting Irenaeus and Justin; Tert. *De praescr.haeret.* 43; *idem, adv.Marc.* 1.18). One set of charges against a certain Syrian bishop in 444 is interestingly analyzed by E. Peterson in *Miscellanea Pio Paschini* I (Rome 1948) 95–99. The usual term of abuse was γόης and γοητεία (cf. Joseph. *AJ* 20.5.1, 20.8.5f, 20.8.10).

[45] On *Christus magus* see Lact. *Div.Inst.* 5.2, refuting Hierocles' comparison of Apollonius and Christ; *ibid.* 5.3; Athan. *Or. Incarn.verbi* 48 (Migne *PG* 25.181); and Arnob. *adv.Nat.* 1.53; cf. Athan., Migne *PG* 25.129 and 149, and *Consult.Zacchaei* 1.13, on *magica carmina*.

entrails refused to yield their prophetic message, whereupon the emperor flew into a rage at those guilty of the disturbance. The incident is well known; but not so often emphasized is the conception of demonic conflict that lay behind Lactantius' account: one superhuman power could drive away another, magic worked only in the absence of inimical forces. Evidence for those views has been gathered above.[46] After Lactantius, Church historians multiplied imitations of the story, sometimes by retrojection: for example, "The teacher and arch-priest of Egyptian magicians persuaded him [Valerian] to get rid of them [Christians], bidding him kill and drive away the pure and holy men as being enemies and preventers of his foul and disgusting spells (for they are and were able, by being present and by watching and by simply breathing on them and speaking, to scatter the plots of baneful demons)."[47] Until the end of Eusebius' century and even beyond, though with diminishing report, the noise of battle was to sound as it were contrapuntally between Christians and pagans on earth, and between their gods invisible in shrines, in the heavens, in the nether regions and in men's minds—a battle, however, in which the combatants struggled with identical weapons of attack and on the same field of ideas.

Men who controlled gods, great wonder-workers, launched their superhuman agents or allies against their rivals, in duels more fit for a Greek novella; yet they were recounted in sober prose. Witness the vision of a certain persecutor of pagan wise men, one Festus, in which he saw a former victim "throwing a noose around his [Festus'] neck and dragging him down to Hades ... As he came out [of the temple in which the vision came to him], his feet slipped from under him and he fell on his back and lay speechless there. He was borne away immediately and died, and this seemed to be an outstanding work of Providence (πρόνοια)."[48] We need change only the proportions of the story, from two individuals to two causes and armies, to have the prelude to the battle of the Milvian Bridge. On the one side is Constantine with his vision, his prayers, his divine support, his miraculous symbol borne before his troops; on the other is Maxentius busied

[46] See nn. 35, 37 and 42, and especially Porph. V.Plotini 10, with Thdrt. Graec.affect.cur. 12.96f; Arnob. adv.Nat. 2.2; Tert. Apol. 46; Orig. c.Cels. 1.60, 3.29; Euseb. HE 7.10.4, 9.3; Socr. 3.18; Soz. 5.2, 5.19; and Hopfner, op.cit. (supra n.34) I.14 (a Neoplatonist view).

[47] Euseb. V.Const. 2.50, HE 7.10.4, cf. 7.17 and 9.3; Socr. 3.18, 4.24.

[48] Eunap. Vit.soph. 481; cf. the attack repulsed by Plotinus, in MacMullen, op.cit. (supra n.25) 100f.

with "certain unspeakable invocations to demons and deterrents of war,"[49] vain, as it turns out, and powerless against the mightier arsenal of Christianity.

How much in the scene can be credited? Were our whole basis of understanding the pages of Eusebius alone, we might, like Burckhardt a hundred years ago, replace the supernatural elements with others more easily acceptable to a modern mind. Anachronistic rationalism, however, only misleads; the interpretation suggested by more recent scholars, notably Alföldi, is surely right. In the light of the beliefs surveyed in the foregoing pages, we must suppose that Constantine's contemporaries (why not himself, then?) did in truth fear antagonistic wizardry, did put their faith in supernatural aid to be exerted visibly on the very field of battle, accepted without skepticism the powers claimed both for Maxentius' sacrifices and for the symbol of the cross, and looked on the whole struggle of old against new religion as being greater than, but no different in kind from, the operation of magicians' spells and counter-spells.

YALE UNIVERSITY
October, 1967

---

[49] Euseb. *HE* 8.14.5; *supra* n.18.

Constantine The Great in the Light of the Christus Victor Concept

by

IAN GILLMAN

MODERN historiography has recognized long since that the standards by which a figure in the past is to be judged should at least reflect those of his own day. Thus we are no longer as outraged by the earthiness of Luther's dialogue as were some of our forebears. Nor do we accept without demur Weber's application of the ethics of 17th century English Puritanism or of Benjamin Franklin to the 16th century Calvinism of Geneva. Such misapplications we imagine that we have put behind us.

And yet one of history's most significant figures has suffered long from such a discredited method of assessment. Constantine the Great has had much to bear at the hands of historians up through Jacob Burckhardt[1] to C. N. Cochrane.[2] Even the efforts of Bishop Lightfoot,[3] N. H. Baynes[4] and A. H. M. Jones,[5] to cite but three in the English-speaking world, while presenting Constantine in a much more sympathetic light, have not been able to dispel the suspicion that his espousal of Christianity was but a political gamble which paid off handsomely. This has happened, the writer contends, largely because Constantine has been approached from the point of view of post-Anselmic Western soteriology, in the light of which his claims to Christianity seem fanciful. It is sobering to reflect just how fanciful that same Western soteriology would have appeared to the majority of Christians in Constantine's day.

Such an approach to and assessment of Constantine is rendered even more strange by the fact that it is now thirty-one years since Gustav Aulen redirected the attention of Western theologians and historians to a leading, if not *the* leading, soteriology of the patristic era. As distinct from the views of the Atonement propounded by Anselm (the so-called 'objective' view) and by Abelard (the so-called 'subjective' view), Aulen put forward what he called the 'classic' view, which, he claimed,

> dominates the whole of Greek patristic theology from Irenaeus to John of Damascus.[6]

In this view the

> central theme is the idea of the Atonement as a Divine conflict and victory; Christ . . . fights against and triumphs over the evil powers of this world, the "tyrants" under whom mankind is in bondage and suffering, and in Him God reconciles the world to Himself.[7]

Aulen goes on to develop it in this way:

> The work of Christ is the overcoming of death *and* sin; strictly, it is a victory over death because it is a victory over sin. And, further, the note of triumph which rings through this Greek theology depends not only on the victory of Christ over death accomplished once for all, but also on the fact that His victory is the starting-point for His present work in the world of men, where He, through His Spirit, ever triumphantly continues to break down sin's power and "deifies" man.[8]

By no means the only soteriology of patristic times, it can be shown that this view commanded many supporters from varied schools. So in the period immediately preceding and leading into the time of Constantine evidence of it can be found in the works of Origen,[9] Methodius of Olympus,[10] Arnobius,[11] Lactantius,[12] and Alexander of Alexandria.[13] Another supporter, perhaps less expected by some, is to be found in the redoubtable Athanasius, who, in one of his early works, says:

> As the demons confess Him, and His works bear Him witness day by day, it must be evident, and let none brazen it out against the truth, both that the Saviour raised His own body, and that He is the true Son of God, being from His, as from His Father, His own Word, and Wisdom, and Power, who in all ages later took a body for the salvation of all, and taught the world concerning the Father, and brought death to nought, and bestowed incorruption upon all by the promise of the Resurrection, having raised His own body as a first-fruits of this, and having displayed it by the sign of the Cross as a monument over death and its corruption.[14]

When we turn to Eusebius of Caesarea, far and away the most typical churchman of his day, we find example after example of this view of the Atonement. Here we will give only one from this bishop who was the Emperor's confidant and advisor:

> The Word of God evinced His gracious character, and proved to man His own superiority over death, recalling His mortal body to a second life, displaying an immortal triumph over death in the eyes of all, and teaching them to acknowledge the Author of such a victory to be the only true God, even in death itself.[15]

For Eusebius, Christ is the 'power (*dynamis*) of God',[16] and the cross becomes less the sign of His agony and death than 'the signal mark of His victory'.[17]

Or, to return once more to Aulen,

> The cross is the chief Christian symbol because it is a symbol of victory. It is a crucifix of triumph. Those images of the Crucified which have revelled in picturing the sufferings of martyrdom in the most gruesome manner have missed what is essential to the Christian faith: the idea of victory, and have obscured the fact that suffering love is at the same time the victorious and sovereign love.[18]

With this brief sketch of the theological background we turn now to examine some of the key events in the life of Constantine.

Whatever the natural possibilities of such a vision as that described by Constantine to Eusebius,[19] the fact remains that something did occur to cause Constantine, at very least, to adopt the Labarum sign for his army.[20] The years may well have added embellishments, but there was some basic skeleton upon which to build. And there is general agreement that it could not have been political considerations alone which caused Constantine to take such a step.[21] A realistic politician would have seen Christianity as a harried minority movement and Maxentius as secure behind Rome's walls, buttressed by recent successes and pagan seers. But Constantine chose to try where Severus, Galerius and Maximian had all failed, and he chose to try with inferior forces and under the sign of a despised minority religious cult. History is by no means marked always by the rational and explicable, but, as Baynes has pointed out, this action of the Emperor 'is more explicable if Constantine was convinced that the Christian God had assured him victory'.[22]

The smashing success at the Milvian Bridge must have done more than confirm Constantine's wisdom of choice in an *ex post facto* manner. He had long had a belief in divine providence and this was to remain with him at all times. It was to remind him not only of the favour extended to him but also of the responsibilities that were his.[23] His successes in Gaul had now been succeeded by fresh triumphs in Italy. Such letters as those to the Donatists[24] and to Alexander of Alexandria[25] show this at a later date, but this was no exotic growth. It was a deep-rooted conviction, and thus it is possible to describe Constantine's conversion as 'the conversion of a true Roman, for whom the *do ut des* principle was at the heart of religion'.[26] Now, if Constantine's decision was simply a choice between talismans of differing efficacy,[27] such a position may be tenable. But it is at this very point that Berkhof, Cochrane and others who think like them go astray. No one claims that Constantine was innocent of political acumen or of desire for the success of himself and his house, but this is at best a partial explanation, at worst a distortion.

The cross, or in this case the Labarum, was not just another talisman nor was it merely his personal standard like a royal coat of arms.[28] It is likewise misleading to make too much of the parallel afforded by Aurelian's choice of Sol Invictus as his patron deity in the previous century.[29] After all, Aurelian made his choice *after* his victory at Emesa, while Constantine made his *before* the hazardous battle with Maxentius. Whatever the nature of his vision,[30] and whatever the true value of Eusebius' report as based on Constantine's reminiscences, there is a ring of truth in the report that Constantine

> being struck with amazement at the extraordinary vision . . . sent for those who were acquainted with the mysteries of His doctrines, and enquired who that God was, and what was intended by the sign of the vision he had seen.[31]

It is here that the thesis advanced above as to the understanding of the cross in the ancient church receives fresh confirmation.[32] Eusebius reports that Constantine was told

> that the sign which had appeared was the symbol of immortality, and the trophy of that victory over death which He had gained in time past when sojourning on earth.[33]

The Emperor's advisers went on to speak of the incarnation and of the causes of the advent so that it would seem impossible to visualize Constantine as unaware of the redemptive implications in the symbol of the cross.[34] This would seem to gain extra confirmation from the inscription reported by Eusebius[35] as being engraved on the base of the statue of Constantine in Rome. Speaking of the crossed spear (proto-Labarum) held aloft by the Emperor it began 'This symbol. of salvation' (*toutōi tōi sōtēriōdei sēmeiōi*), and again we meet soteriological implications.

The cross later appeared on the coins, and became the mark of the army, as a standard and as the insignia on shields.[36] References to Constantine's attitude towards the cross appear elsewhere, in either his own purported words[37] or those of the panegyrist.[38] And so we might go on, citing example upon example from liturgy,[39] popular piety,[40] building[41] and art,[42] to show how this concept was a dominant one in the period immediately succeeding Constantine's conversion. Much of what is to be found in this evidence might smack of the quasi-magical or superstitious to present-day Western minds, but even Constantine's use of nails from the 'true cross' in helmet and horse's bit[43] takes on new significance when seen in the light in which the cross was viewed, and this after making due allowance for the use and popularity of amulets. At the very least it must be conceded that the cross was more than a talisman, more than a royal coat of arms, and certainly more than the ecclesiastical trademark which it often becomes in present-day usage. To accord to a symbol, of such emptiness for today, the significance given to the cross by Constantine and his successors may be 'beyond our ken',[44] but, as has been said, the cross was the meaningful symbol of the victory of Christ over the powers of darkness and death. It was the sign of the power of Christ still at work in the world, the symbol which caught up into itself all that theologians had struggled to express when dealing with soteriology. When Constantine referred to the cross, these are the connotations which must be kept in mind; for here were statements which imply a Christocentric commitment. To fail to approach this was a sympathetic understanding is to cut oneself off from any hope of comprehending the age fully.

As to the means by which Constantine came to the position where such a commitment could take place little definite is known. The most tenable position seems to be that which sees Constantine as prepared by his change of loyalty from the god Hercules to the old family deity Apollo Sol Invictus. The former god had been assigned to Constantine's father under the ideological reorganization of the Empire which had taken place under Diocletian. The change to Sol Invictus came during the Gallic campaigns and the older family god claimed his devotion up until the Milvian Bridge episode. In changing Constantine had strengthened his claim to the throne on the grounds of his descent from Claudius Gothicus, the heroic emperor who had also worshipped the Unconquered Sun. He also placed himself in the tradition of Aurelian, who, faced with the decline of the value and prestige of the old imperial cult, saw that

> It was essential to find a religion which would both satisfy the emotional need of the Empire and at the same time provide means for the expression of

imperial loyalty, and the widely diffused cult of the Sun offered the best chance of success.[45]

If Aurelian had found it useful there is no doubt that Constantine was convinced likewise of the value of this cult.

Now it is obvious that there are surface connections between the 'Invictus' portion of the deity's title and the 'Victor' of the *Christus Victor* concept which has been discussed. In addition we can find parallels between the 'Sol' and various titles applied to Christ in popular piety.[46] But, as Baynes points out,[47] attempts to explain Constantine's action as the natural outcome of his background lack conviction. The rapprochement between Christianity and the best of paganism and his father's policy of tolerance to a large degree cannot be overlooked either. But the pre-Milvian Bridge experience was a shattering and decisive one, after which Constantine has to ask for explanations and guidance.[48] One is reminded of Saul on the road to Damascus[49]— preparation there doubtless was, but the climactic event can hardly be seen as arising out of the past in a simple evolutionary manner. Whatever the actual means, the evidence seems to point to a definite spiritual experience for Constantine at this time,[50] out of which came a conviction of divine providence and mission.

There began then a process of education and understanding[51] which was to last throughout his life.[52] At no time would Constantine be able to lay claim to a theological status which would command admiration down through the centuries, but he cannot be called theologically ignorant. If he failed to appreciate the significance of the Arian controversy in its early stages,[53] there is no evidence to show that his emissary, Bishop Ossius of Cordova, was any wiser when he set out for Alexandria bearing the Emperor's letter demanding an end to the trouble.

At the same time Constantine was confronted by the needs and demands of the State, weakened as it was by the wars, famines and pestilences of the opening years of the fourth century. Even when, with the defeat of Licinius, he gained sole control, Constantine still had to deal with the forces of conservatism and continuity which compelled him to adopt policies at times not unfavourable to paganism. Unlike the Puritans of Massachusetts, Constantine was not given the opportunity of carving a 'new Jerusalem' out of a virgin land. Alföldi[54] has shown how the city of Rome, for example, provided a bastion for the forces of conservatism which opposed the new ideology of the State as well as any diminution of its old prestige and legal privileges. Such considerations make even more important the founding of a 'new Rome' at Byzantium, a foundation shot through with strategic, political and religious implications. The old Rome was left many of her old privileges but was also left 'as the "museum" of the great national past . . . it was inseparably connected with the deities of Olympus'.[55]

Tradition, continuity, attempted reconciliation[56] and uncommon prudence all played a part in the foundation ceremonies of Constan-

tinople, ceremonies which have been shown to be pagan.[57] Dedicated to
a Tyche, like any other city, the new foundation thus had about it the
trappings of customary popular piety.[58] And yet the city was to be a
Christian city and as such, in a real way, to stand over against Rome.
While it was not until A.D.626 that the Tyche was clearly replaced by
the Virgin Mary,[59] there are certain aspects of considerable interest in
this dedication and the consequent acts of Constantine in the city.

The first aspect is one pointed out by Frolow.[60] It appears that, as
well as the role of the Tyche paralleling that later assumed by the
Virgin Mary, the Tyche was often associated with or assimilated to
other divinities which were concerned with the bringing of victory.
Venus Genetrix et Victrix, later Fortuna Victrix, is the example cited,
and here a reminiscent note is struck. Is it no more than sheer chance
that the city dedicated to such a victory Tyche was to be the new capital
of the Emperor who had lately given his loyalty to *Christus Victor*?

It is here perhaps that is seen most sharply the confluence of two
traditions—one the *Christus Victor* tradition of the Church, the other
the mystique of victory associated with the emperor in the past. Even
before we reach Aurelian and his attachment to Sol Invictus, we meet
'invictissimus princeps', 'imperator invictus' and the victory connotations
of Mithraism.[61] That which had a long history in the Empire now finds
something in common with that which had a long history in the Church.

The Christian city is dedicated then to a Tyche with victory associations, while the dedication is accompanied by a bloodless sacrifice—
that is, the Christian Eucharist.[62] Thus we meet the victory theme again
but it does not appear here only in connection with Constantinople. For
while this was a city which was never 'polluted by altars, Grecian
temples, nor sacrifices,'[63] there was also a striking feature in the names
and order of founding of the churches in the city associated with the
name of Constantine.[64]

The first of these churches was that of St. Irene, a sort of personified
form of 'holy peace', being that condition which followed on victory.
This church served as a pro-cathedral until the second church was
completed and dedicated. This was the church of St. Sophia, the forerunner of the famous church of the same name still standing. 'It was
the church of the Divine Wisdom (*Theia Sophia*), the church of the
Word, the second Person of the Holy Trinity'.[65] As Burch sums up
the consequences:

> When the term *Sophia* was made Christological, then was started the making
> of dedicatory complements. *Hagia Sophia* demanded its companion *Hagia
> Dynamis*, since the two are inseparable names in the earliest mode of dis-
> closing the meanings of the nature and work of Jesus Christ.[66]

And in fact the church of St. Dynamis was the third to be built in close
association with the name of Constantine. If Burch is right in another
place[67] our case is even stronger, for another church attributed to
Constantine as founder was that of St. Agathonikos, which is seen by
some as the personalized form of *nikē,* which is either victory or the

power which grants victory to the Emperor. Thus, in the city churches we have expressed a conjunction of victory and attention to the second Person of the Trinity, which conjunction can be aptly summed up in the term *Christus Victor*.

In the course of this paper we have looked at usage of Church and Empire. We have drawn examples from a number of fields, examples which point to a union at this time of concepts with rich associations and long traditions amongst both Christians and pagans. Because in many ways our sources are scanty any one of the examples might be questioned. But cumulatively the effect is convincing. What may seem far from Christological to a contemporary Western observer appears in an entirely different light when seen in the perspective of the time. The conclusion seems inescapable that Constantine shared the view of the cross consistent with the *Christus Victor* concept and gave expression to this in manifold ways. He should be judged accordingly.

FOOTNOTES

1. *The Age of Constantine the Great*, trans. M. Hadas, New York, 1949.
2. *Christianity and Classical Culture*, London, 1944.
3. 'Eusebius of Caesarea', *A Dictionary of Christian Biography*, ed. W. Smith and H. Wace, vol. II, pp. 308-48.
4. 'Constantine the Great and the Christian Church', *Proceedings of the British Academy*, XV, 1929.
5. *Constantine and the Conversion of Europe*, London, 1948.
6. *Christus Victor*, trans. A. G. Hebert, London, 1950, p. 53.
7. Ibid., p. 20.
8. Ibid., p. 60.
9. *On First Principles*, III:2.1 and III:3.2-4, and *Contra Celsum*, II:38, II:47, and VI:45-46.
10. *Three Fragments from the Homily on the Passion of Christ*, trans. W. R. Clark, *Ante-Nicene Fathers*, Grand Rapids, 1951, pp. 399f.
11. *Against the Heathen*, I:42, 53 and 65.
12. *The Divine Institutes*, IV:27.
13. *Epistles on the Arian Controversy*, V:5-6.
14. *The Incarnation of the Word*, trans. A. Robertson, *Nicene and Post-Nicene Fathers*, Grand Rapids, 1953, 32:6. Cf. also ibid., 25, 31 and 53, and *Life of Antony*, 35.
15. *Oration in Praise of the Emperor Constantine*, ed. E. C. Richardson, *P.N.F.*, Grand Rapids, 1952, 15:10. Cf. also *The Proof of the Gospel*, IV:12, and *The Theophania*, III:42-45, 55-59.
16. *The Proof of the Gospel*, VI: introduction and VII:1, and *The Theophania*, I:5, III:20 and V:46.
17. *The Theophania*, V:42.
18. *The Faith of the Christian Church*, trans. E. H. Wahlstrom and G. E. Arden, Philadelphia, 1948, p. 226.
19. Eusebius, *The Life of Constantine*, I:28-31.
20. Cf. Vogt, J., 'Die Bedeutung des Jahres 312 für die Religionspolitik Konstantins des Grossen', *Zeitschrift für Kirchengeschichte*, LXI, 1942, pp. 171-190.
21. Cf. Kraft, H., *Kaiser Konstantins religiöse Entwicklung*, Tübingen, 1955, p. 6. Baynes, N. H., op. cit., p. 9, and Lot, F., *The End of the Ancient World and the Beginnings of the Middle Ages*, New York, 1953, chap. 3.
22. Baynes, ibid.
23. Cf. Eusebius, *The Life of Constantine*, I:5 and 24, II:28.
24. Ibid., II:24ff.
25. Ibid., II:64ff.
26. Berkhof, H., *Kirche und Kaiser*, trans. G. W. Locher, Zürich, 1947, p. 58.
27. Cf. Cochrane, op. cit., p. 215 and Jones, op. cit., p. 102 for such views.
28. Cf. Cochrane, op. cit., p. 209.
29. Cf. Vogelstein, M., 'Kaiseridee-Romidee und das Verhältnis von Staat und Kirche seit Konstantin', *Historische Untersuchungen*, ed. W. Kornemann, Heft 7, Breslau, 1950, p. 57.
30. Cf. Vogt, J., 'Berichte über Kreuzerscheinungen aus dem 4. Jahrhundert nach Christ', *Annuaire de l'Institut de philologie et d'histoire Orientales et Slaves*, IX, 1949, pp. 593-606, and Cyril of Jerusalem, *Letter to Constantius*, ed. W. Telfer, *Library of Christian Classics*, Philadelphia, 1955.

31. *The Life of Constantine*, I:32.
32. Cf. Gagé, J., '*Stauros nikopoios*: La victoire impériale dans l'Empire chrétien', *Revue d'histoire et de philosophie religieuses*, XIII, 1933, pp. 370-400.
33. *The Life of Constantine*, I:32.
34. But only one aspect, viz. that of victory, is seen by K. Müller, 'Konstantin der Grosse und die christliche Kirche', *Historische Zeitschrift*, CXL, 1929, p. 269. Surely this is only possible on pre-Aulenic bases.
35. *The Life of Constantine*, I:40. Cf. also II:2, *sōtēriōi . . . sēmeiōi*, and II:3, *sōtērion (sēmeion)*. Further examples could be cited.
36. Ibid., IV:21.
37. *The Oration of Constantine to the Assembly of the Saints*, ed. E. C. Richardson, *P.N.F.*, Grand Rapids, 1952. 15.
38. *Oration in Praise of the Emperor Constantine*, ed. E. C. Richardson, *P.N.F.*, Grand Rapids, 1952, 9.
39. Seston, W., 'L'opinion paienne et la conversion de Constantin', *Revue d'histoire et de philosophie religieuses*, XVI, 1936, pp. 263f., and Gagé, op. cit., pp. 379f.
40. Cf. Dölger, F. J., 'Heidnische und christliche Brotstumpel mit religiösen Zeichen', *Antike und Christentum*, I, 1929, pp. 21ff., Kantorowicz, E., *Laudes Regiae. A Study in Liturgical Acclamation and Medieval Ruler Worship*, Berkeley, 1946, pp. 21ff., and Frolow, A., *Byzantinoslavica*, XVII, 1956, pp. 98-113.
$$\overline{NI \mid KA}$$
41. Eusebius, *Oration in Praise of the Emperor Constantine*, 9 and *The Life of Constantine*, III:49.
42. Cecchelli, C., *Il Trionfo della Croce; La Croce e i Santi Segni prima e dopo Costantino*, Rome, 1954.
43. Socrates, *The Ecclesiastical History*, I:17. Cf. Also Gagé, op. cit., p. 387.
44. Cf. Rudolf Otto's concept of the 'numinous' and the Hebrews' attitude to the ark of the Covenant (2 Samuel VI:6-7). The use of the Labarum symbol of the orb under the cross on the coins, etc., is even more striking for the portrayal of the victory of the Cross, and so of Christ, over the world.
45. Parker, H. M. D., *A History of the Roman World. A.D. 138 - 337*, rev. ed., London, 1958, p. 208.
46. Cf., e.g., Dölger, F. J., 'Das Sonnengleichnis in einer Weihnachtspredigt des Bischofs Zeno von Verona', *Antike und Christentum*, VI, 1940, pp. 1ff.
47. Op. cit., p. 3.
48. Eusebius, *The Life of Constantine*, I:32.
49. A parallel made explicit by Theodoret in *The Ecclesiastical History*, I:1. The whole question of Constantine's apostolic consciousness has been reviewed by the writer in a paper read at the Third International Conference on Patristic Studies in Oxford, 1959. The paper is to be published in the volumes covering the congress.
50. Jones, op. cit., p. 102.
51. Cf. again Paul's retirement to Arabia, a luxury not open to Constantine.
52. Kraft, op. cit., p. 24.
53. Eusebius, *The Life of Constantine*, II:48 and 49.
54. *The Conversion of Constantine and Pagan Rome*, trans. H. Mattingly, Oxford, 1948, *passim*.
55. Alföldi, A., 'On the Foundation of Constantinople', *Journal of Roman Studies*, XXXVII, 1947, p. 10.
56. Ibid., p. 14.
57. Frolow, A., 'La dédicace de Constantinople dans la tradition byzantine', *Revue de l'histoire des religions*, CXXVII, 1944, pp. 61-127.
58. Cumont, F., *The Oriental Religions in Roman Paganism*, Chicago, 1911, p. 179. Note also L. R. Taylor's comment about the close association of king, city and Tyche at this time, in *The Divinity of the Roman Emperor*, Middletown, 1931, p. 32.
59. Frolow, op. cit., pp. 110f. and 126f.
60. Ibid, pp. 109f. Cf. also Alföldi, A., 'On the Foundation of Constantinople', *Journal of Roman Studies*, XXXVII, 1947, p. 15, Toynbee, J. M. C., 'Roma and Constantinopolis in Late-Antique Art', *Journal of Roman Studies*, XXXVII, 1947, pp. 135-144; and Maurice, J., *Numismatique Constantinienne*, Paris, 1908-1912, vol. I, pp. CLff., and vol. II, p. 250.
61. Gagé, J., 'La théologie de la victoire impériale', *Revue historique*, CLXX, 1933, pp. 1ff., and Rütten, F., *Die Viktorverehrung im Christlichen Altertum. Eine kultgeschichtliche und hagiographische Studie*, Paderborn, 1936, pp. 37ff., and 16ff., where the application of the title to the martyrs is discussed.
62. Lietzmann, H., *A History of the Early Church*, vol. III, trans. B. Lee Woolf, London, 1958, pp. 145f.
63. Sozomen, *The Ecclesiastical History*, trans. C. D. Hartranft, *P.N.F.*, Grand Rapids, 1952, II:3, and Eusebius, *The Life of Constantine*, III:48.
64. Janin, R., *La Géographie ecclésiastique de l'Empire byzantin*, pt. 1, vol. III, Paris, 1953, pp. 106-111 and 471ff.
65. Ibid., p. 471.

66. *Myth and Constantine the Great,* London, 1927, p. 147. One could adduce a number of references concerning these titles from the New Testament, e.g., I Corinthians i.24, and 30. Cf. also Tertullian, *Against Praxeas,* chap. 19, Origen, *On First Principles,* I:2.1 and III:3.1, Eusebius, *The Theophania,* I:32, and the citation from Athanasius in n.14 above, for its history in the Church through the centuries.
67. Op. cit., p. 150. It should be noted that this is contested by Janin, op. cit., pp. 11 and 12, and by *Bibliotheca Hagiogrphica Graeca,* ed. F. Halkin, vol. 1, 3rd ed., Brussels, 1957, p. 12. These authorities see St. Agathonikos as a local martyr.

SACERDOTIUM ET IMPERIUM: THE CONSTANTINIAN RENOVATIO ACCORDING TO THE GREEK FATHERS

MICHAEL AZKOUL

St. Louis, Missouri

MUCH HAS has been written in recent years about the Byzantine Christocracy. Byzantine studies in the West date from the seventeenth century, but the "political theology" of East Rome has not received the attention it deserves. Erik Peterson's *Der Monotheismus als politisches Problem: Beitrag zur Geschichte der politischen Theologie im Imperium Romanum* (1935) was probably the first serious attempt to understand the intellectual, religious, and political dimensions of the Byzantine political theology. Thereafter followed such works as K. M. Setton's *Christian Attitude towards the Empire in the Fourth Century* (1941) and H. Berkhof's *Kirche und Kaiser: Eine Untersuchung der Entstehung der byzantinischen und theokratischen Staatsauffassung im vierten Jahrhundert* (1947), and five years ago Francis Dvornik published his two-volume *Early Christian and Byzantine Political Philosophy* (1966). Specialized journals also began to include scholarly analysis of the subject. The conclusion of these studies has consistently been that the Constantinian *renovatio* perpetuated Hellenistic kingship and its link between monarchy and monotheism. The task of translating that kingship into Christian terms, it is said, was accomplished by Eusebius of Caesarea, while the Greek Fathers, as his disciples, merely extended his thinking.

It appears to me, however, that this conclusion is not justified by the evidence. First, modern scholarship prejudices the evidence by a restrictive and positivist method which elicits an interpretation of the "facts," excluding thereby the genuine and Christological context of the patristic political theology. Moreover, the judgment of so many historians and patrologists has been biased by various undemonstrated but predetermining assumptions, such as the ostensible dependence of the Christian *paideia* in general upon pagan thought and the supposed effort of the Fathers[1] to create a Christian philosophy à la Origen, that is, a Christian-

---

[1] The attitude of many historians and patrologists that all prominent Christian writers of the first nine centuries of Christianity deserve the title "Father" is not shared by the Eastern Orthodox and Roman Catholic Churches. Yet, to apply "Father" only to those writers with the "marks" of orthodoxy, holiness, ecclesiastical sanction, and antiquity is to exclude some of the most distinguished theologians of the early Church, e.g., Origen, Clement of Alexan-

pagan synthesis. The invariable mistake of modern scholars has been to ignore the unspoken epistemological and metaphysical dogmas of their discipline in the treatment of the Greek Fathers. Thus it is that they are led to place all Christian thought within the narrow history of Western philosophy and consequently to insist that the Fathers adopted Hellenistic political philosophy, the "facts" establishing that Eusebius took the lead.

In truth, the Greek Fathers developed no political philosophy but merely converted the Hebrew theocracy to Christian use. Accepting this premise, A. V. Kartasheff, professor at the Saint Sergius Russian Orthodox Theological Institute in Paris, in his highly suggestive *The Restoration of Holy Russia* (1946), believes that the key to the understanding of the Byzantine Christocracy is the doctrine of the Incarnation; or, more precisely, the eventual formulation of that doctrine by Chalcedon (451): "one and the same Christ, Son, Lord, Only-Begotten, recognized in two natures, without confusion, without change, without division, without separation, the distinction of natures in no way annulled by their union...."² The political embodiment of this dogma is found in Justinian's *Symphonia:*

Maxima quidem in hominibus sunt dona dei a superna collata clementia sacerdotium et imperium, illud quidem divinis ministrans, hoc autem humanis praesidens ac diligentiam exhibens; ex uno eodemque principio utraque procedentia humanam exornant vitam. Ideoque nihil sic erit studiosum imperatoribus, sicut sacerdotum honestas, cum utique et pro illis ipsis semper deo supplicent. Nam

---

dria, Eusebius of Caesarea, and Tertullian. Most, if not all, writers recognized as Fathers have erred in some way, e.g., the chiliasm of Irenaeus or the apocatastasis of Gregory of Nyssa. And why should the "patristic era" be limited to the first eight or nine centuries? Why is no "father" possible to day? See G. Florovsky, "Gregory Palamas and the Tradition of the Fathers," *Greek Orthodox Theological Review* 5 (1959-60) 123-24. Who, then, is a Father? Any Christian author whose life and literature, in their spiritual and general content, express the faith and piety of the Church. His thought must display no fundamental opposition to the orthodoxy of the Christian tradition, his life show no conflict with the corporate piety of the Church. By "orthodox" we mean adherence to the teachings of Scripture, the doctrines defined by the ecumenical councils and held in common by preceding Fathers, and the beliefs of the Church embodied in her public worship. All other Christian theologians must be called "ecclesiastical writers": Christian theologians whose writings, though not entirely heterodox and sometimes useful, are generally, in content and spirit, not accepted by the Church as her own. Thus, Origen and Eusebius of Caesarea confused the apostolic faith and the classical *paideia*. The Christian-pagan "synthesis" which such men created led the Church to admit them neither to her liturgical calendar nor to her hagiographies.

² Actio 5 (J. D. Mansi, ed., *Sacrorum conciliorum nova et amplissima collectio* 7 [Venice, 1759] 116 f.).

si hoc quidem inculpabile sit undique et apud deum fiducia plenum, imperium autem recte et competenter exornet traditam sibi rempublicam, erit consonantia (*symphōnia*) quaedam bona, omne quicquid utile est humano conferens generi.[3]

In other words, the Christian commonwealth is to be governed by two "ministries," the *imperium* and the *sacerdotium*, for there are two natures in the one person of Christ. The "primacy" belongs to the *sacerdotium* by virtue of its spiritual character and purpose.

Of even greater importance, however, was that which the *symphonia* implied, that is, the Christian vision of history. The Byzantine Christocracy was the political explication of the Incarnation, expressing the theandric synergism which the Greek Fathers said informed the whole course and nature of history. Likewise, Eusebius, denying the actual "enfleshment of God," necessarily maintained a view of history, and consequently the Christian *politeia*, different from that espoused by the Fathers. His political theology perpetuated the pagan idea of kingship and thereby brought with it a tacit return to pagan rationalism: the problem of "first principles," the metaphysical dualism which described time as cyclical, multiform, and incarcerating, and eternity as permanent, simple, and supersensible. Against his teachings, the Greek Fathers set traditional ontology and Christology: the vision that reality was analogous to the Incarnation, the union of linear time and mysterious eternity, the created and the Uncreated, the visible and the invisible.[4]

Examining the religio-political thought of the Greek Fathers from the fourth to the ninth century, therefore, we ought to come to the conclusion that any theory which considers Eusebian political theology to be patristic and the theoretical foundation of the Christian Roman Empire must be open to serious question. We suggest that this contention can be defended by comparing Eusebianism in all its ramifications with patristic ontology and Christology, the result being at every level of discourse (and necessarily at the political level) clear opposition between them. In other words, Eusebius was not the political master of the Fathers, because he was not their intellectual and religious *magister*; and since the Christological basis of the Byzantine Empire was Chalcedonian, the Fathers were the real creators of East Roman political theory and not Eusebius. His political theology depended upon assumptions which could not be reconciled with the Christian revelation.

We hope to support our argument with evidence generally not taken into account by most historians. After describing the pagan Roman idea

---

[3] *Corpus iuris civilis: Novellae* 4 (ed. R. Schoell; Berlin, 1959) col. 1, tit. 6.

[4] On the difference between Christian and classical Greek conceptions of history, see the important work by Oscar Cullmann, *Christ and Time* (Philadelphia, 1950).

of empire—upon which Eusebius constructed his own view—we will begin to trace the Christological development of the Roman *imperium christianum* inaugurated by Constantine the Great. Our study, then, in each of its sections, will seek to link that which will prove to be its unity. There will be chronological progression, to be sure, but the unity will be found primarily in the simple equation "ontology: Christology: *politeia*."

I

The Augustan reconstruction was more than a political renewal. It was a complete religio-philosophical vision, a vision of the *urbs aeterna*, the ultimate solution to the human predicament. The *pax Romana* was to be an everlasting, universal order, a cosmopolis which "marked, indeed, the rededication of the imperial city to her secular task, the realization of those ideals of human emancipation towards which the thought and aspiration of antiquity had pointed hitherto in vain."[5] As a gift from Jove, Rome was destined to bring enduring justice, unity, and peace to the anarchic multiplicity of nations which from the beginning of history had known nothing save disorder, conflict, and suffering. Augustus, then, would accomplish this end through the exercise of power and reason. He would reintegrate the ancient world, salvaging and amalgamating those elements in it which had proved most useful, beneficial, and excellent, and, by infusing them with the great ideals of the Roman people, create ecumenical happiness. It was the genius of Augustus that he could utilize the nostalgia of Cato and Cicero as well as the imagination of Caesar and Antony.

The vision of Augustus, however, had first been divined by Alexander the Great. It was Alexander, Plutarch tells us, who discovered the formula that a world state required for its success that its citizens possess not a common blood but a common mind, *homonoia*. Moreover, the ruler of this world state must be the living symbol and source of all the dreams of those he governs. He must be a father with the profoundest concern (*philanthrōpia*) for the welfare of his subjects. He must be their Savior and Benefactor (*Sōtēr kai Euergetēs*), discharging, in imitation of God, the function of an earthly providence. Thus Toynbee finds the origin of the *pax Romana* in Alexander's belief that "God is the common father of men—a truth which argues that if the divine father of the human family is left out of the reckoning, there is no possibility of forging any alternative bond of purely human texture which will avail of itself to hold mankind together. The only society that is capable of embracing the whole of mankind is a superhuman *Civitas Dei....*"[6] Alexan-

[5] C. N. Cochrane, *Christianity and Classical Culture* (New York, 1961) pp. 27-28.
[6] *A Study of History* (Somerval abridgment; Oxford, 1951) pp. 495-96.

der, therefore, linked monarchy, monotheism, and peace. Augustus put the head of Alexander on his signet ring.

The Hellenization of the Roman *imperium* was a process consciously initiated by Augustus Caesar himself. The unfolding of his "sacral kingship" was achieved through the mobilization of all those public agencies within the Empire which could transform him from a man into a demīgod. He concentrated upon himself "the yearnings of his contemporaries (which one may call almost messianic) for a deliverer, a savior, and a benefactor."[7] Through art, literature, cultus, and cunning, he strove to make the *imperium Romanum* the definitive religio-political *ordo*, with himself the veritable father of humanity. He took the title and functions of *pontifex maximus*. He was a sacred *monarchos* with a "genius"—the Greek *daimōn* and the Persian *fravashi*. Augustus was more than a constitutional *princeps*; he was the representative of Jove, the giver of every good gift and every perfect endowment. He was *hominum pater, pater orbis, praesens et conspicuus deus, lex animata*. He did not presume to be a god as Pharaoh did, but he would not refuse the various solar ascriptions of Hellenistic and Near Eastern kingship.[8] Again, he was *pater patriae* who summoned the Roman people to a rejuvenation of their ancient duties and virtues; but, of course, in terms of the new circumstances, a people who through him would bring peace to the entire world (*oikoumenē*).

Augustus had wished to use the Hellenistic monarchies as a model, but after his death the Empire was Orientalized beyond his expectations. Perhaps it was the desire for power by some of his successors, or perhaps a reaction to something within Roman society that incited the rapid growth of despotism. Already in 38 A.D., Caligula demanded the Persian *proskynēsis* from those who came into his presence. Later Nero placed his image with the Oriental nimbus on Roman coins. Domitian styled himself *dominus et deus*, and even the "good emperors" heard themselves hailed as *Hēlios, Sōtēr, Phylax, Ktisēs*. Varius Avitus Bassianus became a priest of the Syrian god Elagabal and consequently is known to history as Elagabulus. After recovering most of the Empire lost during the third century "military anarchy," Aurelian called himself *restitutor orbis* and appeared in public with the diadem of Oriental and Hellenistic kings in his crown. It was not difficult then for Diocletian to become an Oriental *despotēs*, his court replete with Persian ceremonial, eunuchs, *proskynēsis*, sacred meals, etc. He became "the friend of the

---

[7] C. G. Starr, *Civilization and the Caesars* (New York, 1956) p. 34.

[8] See E. R. Goodenough, "The Political Philosophy of Hellenistic Kingship," in *Yale Classical Studies* 1 (1928); and L. R. Taylor, *The Divinity of the Roman Caesars* (Middletown, Conn., 1931).

Logos," *theos epiphanēs, Sol invictus,* the ecktype of Jove. He confirmed the extinction of the "old order" by the removal of the imperial residence to Nicomedia and thereby prepared the way for Constantine's historic enterprise.

Constantine the Great (312-37) arrested the progress of the Roman *despotatismos* and placed the Empire under the protection of the Christian God. If we may believe Eusebius of Caesarea, a statue of the Emperor holding the cross was erected in Rome with the words "senatui populoque Romano in libertatem asserto pristinum decus nobilitatis splendoremque restitui."[9] Henceforth he would work to convert the *Romanum imperium* into a Christian commonwealth. It is true that he did not eliminate the diadem, sacred vestments, the purple mantle, *paladumentum,* the scepter with the eagle, the *proskynēsis,* the titles of solar theology and *pontifex maximus,* but as a Christian he rejected their presuppositions.[10] The city of Constantine was the dramatic symbol of the Empire's new adventure. If one believes, as I do, that he was a genuine Christian, then that adventure must have involved a revolutionary break with the religio-political traditions of pagan antiquity. He accepted neither the fiction of *aeterna Roma* nor the pretensions of Hellenistic kingship. The Edict of Milan was certainly a departure from anything found in the ancient world. Its declaration of religious liberty, the "formal and explicit abandonment of any attempt" on the part of the state "to control spiritual life," was utterly irreconcilable with the whole conception of "divine kingship."[11] His *Ad coetum sanctorum* evidences an attitude towards his role and the uniqueness of Christianity that must have been a scandal to the Hellenists and an offense to the Romans. Constantine was a Christian, and between his religion and the world he recognized a fundamental antithesis. To be sure, he could take from the world whatever truth God had deposited in history for the preservation and enlightenment of mankind, but the classical *Weltanschauung* could have no place in the life of the saints.

II

The choice of Constantine to create a Christian *politeia* probably changed the course of history. Eusebius, recognizing the cruciality of

[9] *Vita Const.* 1, 40 (*PG* 20, 995D-996A). For convenience, we will rely upon Migne almost entirely for the Greek texts of Fathers and ecclesiastical writers; the more critical editions do not affect our arguments.

[10] A natural deduction from the belief in Constantine's genuine conversion to Christianity. An interesting summary of various scholarly opinions about that "conversion" is to be found in A. A. Vasiliev, *History of the Byzantine Empire* 1 (Milwaukee, 1964) 45-54.

[11] Cf. Cochrane, *op. cit.,* pp. 179 f.

that choice and perhaps taking upon himself the role of biographer and hierophant, sought to interpret the significance of Constantine's accession.

Eusebius believed that the providence of God elevated Constantine to the dignity of emperor. He perfected the work begun by Augustus. Eusebius, like Origen, thought that "the two roots of blessing, the Roman Empire and the doctrine of Christian piety, arose together for the benefit of mankind" (*De laud. Const.* 16, 5). The triumph of each, however, was not completed until the coming of God's "good and faithful servant" Constantine, who was rewarded by his virtue (*eusebia*) "to such a degree that he alone of all the rulers pursued a continual course of conquests, unsubdued and invincible" (*Vita Const.* 1, 6–7). Moreover, with the consolidation of the Church (*ekklēsia*) and the Empire (*basileia*), God created under Constantine a Christian society. According to Eusebius, then, the Empire had a critical place in God's plan of salvation (*oikonomia theou*). Unlike Origen, who saw the Empire as merely providing the Church with a stage for the spreading of the gospel (*Contra Celsum* 2, 30), Eusebius, by confounding the Church with the destiny of the Empire, imputed to Constantine and his successors the divine right and power to conquer and evangelize. This was the Hellenistic notion which identified the kingdom and its ruler with the imperialistic ambition of their god. Neither did the Bishop of Caesarea fail to see the correspondance of such a tenet with the Christian missionary task which was to bring not only individuals to Christ but all the kingdoms of the earth.

As any good Hellenizer, Eusebius related monarchy, monotheism, and peace.[12] Thus, Constantine rendered powerless all his enemies, just as God through His Logos reduced all the evil spirits to impotence.[13] In fact, he received his sovereignty from the Logos of God, "receiving, as it were, a transcript of the divine Sovereignty" and directing "the administration of world affairs" in "imitation of God Himself." Moreover, Constantine was victor in war as he was victor in truth, having vanquished his enemies and his passions. "His character is formed after the divine Prototype, the Supreme Sovereign, and his mind reflects the radiance of God's virtues." By the mediatory instruction of God's

---

[12] See E. Peterson, *Der Monotheismus* ... (Leipzig, 1935) p. 81.

[13] *Praep. evang.* 1, 4 (*PG* 21, 37A). Compare the teaching of the Byzantine Church as expressed by the Second Tone of the Christmas Liturgy: "When Augustus became supreme ruler of the earth, the multiplicity of governments among men ceased. And when thou became human form out of the spotless Virgin, the worship of many heathen gods also ceased. The cities came under one worldly rule, and the nations believed in one divine Supremacy; but we believers were enrolled in the name of thy Divinity, O our incarnate God ... " (Kassias, *ca.* 800).

Logos—in Platonic fashion, Eusebius separated power and its source[14]—
the Emperor seeks to "recall the whole human race to the knowledge
of God, proclaiming clearly in the ears of all with a loud voice the laws of
truth and godliness to everyone who dwells on earth." "Our Emperor"
imitates "his divine Prototype by the divine philanthropy of his own
imperial acts" (De laud. Const. 1, 16). His will illuminates his subjects
"like the radiant sun . . ." (ibid. 1, 7).

By connecting monarchy and monotheism and coupling the Emperor
with the Logos and these with the Christian religion, Eusebius, Dvornik
says, "laid the foundations for the political structure and for Eastern
policies on the relationship between Church and state."[15] This judgment
may seem correct because it is so often repeated; but is it right when we
consider what the Eusebian "Rome ideology" must have implied for the
Church and her claim to revealedness? It does not seem logical that the
Fathers, who "philosophized like fishermen, not Aristotelians," as St.
Gregory the Theologian observed (Orat. 23, 12), would have followed a
man whom they condemned as a crypto-Arian and at the same time adhered to a political philosophy they knew to be pagan. And does it not
appear curious that the Fathers should turn to the classical scientia for the
principles of Christian kingship when at their disposal they had the
Davidic monarchy of the Old Testament for a model? It seems to us
that the Greek and Latin Fathers, no matter what their rhetoric suggests
for some scholars, understood as clearly as Charles Norris Cochrane that
Eusebius of Caesarea had proclaimed the Constantinian renovatio to be
nothing less than "a realization of the secular hope of men, the dream
of universal and perpetual peace which classical Rome had made her
own. . . ."[16]

Neither logic nor the facts justify the conclusion that the Byzantine
Fathers ever recognized Eusebius as their political teacher. If we may
turn to the sixth and seventh centuries, when the composition of the
Byzantine liturgies was nearly completed, the attitude of the Church
toward Constantine, though similar at first glance, will be seen to be
fundamentally different from the theory of Eusebius. Her position is
found in the Menaion of the saints for May.[17] Everywhere may be observed the reference to the Bible. The author(s) chose to compare Constantine to David and Solomon rather than pagan kings. There is also
an unexpected allusion to St. Paul. Of particular interest must be the way
in which the author(s) interpreted the idea of Isapostolos. St. Constan-

[14] Cf. Peterson, op. cit., p. 20.
[15] Early Christian and Byzantine Political Philosophy 2 (Washington, D.C., 1966) 617.
[16] Cochrane, op. cit., p. 185.
[17] Menaion of the Saints (Athens, 1961; in Greek) pp. 175–86.

tine is "equal to the apostles," because "having beheld with his own eyes the sign of thy Cross in the heavens, and like Paul having accepted thy call not from man, was given the reigning city."[18] Again, as "the pious servant of God," he "was granted the wisdom of Solomon and the meekness of David, and the orthodoxy of the apostles."[19] Like the apostles, too, Constantine "despised idols, erecting on earth a temple to the One who was crucified for our sakes."[20] He was granted the "sceptre of kingship," because he brought all nations to Christ through the Cross, which he implanted everywhere.

Constantine is the "benefactor" (euergetēs) of mankind. He is "the superior of every sovereign."[21] He is unvanquished, because he freely offered "the oikoumenē to God."[22] He was "anointed priest and king" (hiereus te christheis kai basileus), that he might "sanctify a people and a city" and because he "established with mercy the Church of God."[23] He gives the oikoumenē to God as a "dowry" (proikos). As a "priest," he "offers" his kingdom to God and "heals" the people with the truth.[24] He rules a "priestly commonwealth" (ieras politeias) as "a prize from heaven," from the "transcendent in essence Lord and Logos who anointed thee with the Spirit."[25] Thus did "David my servant" destroy "the error of idolatry and confirm the cosmos in Christ." "The King of creation . . . having foreseen the goodness of thy heart's submission" did enlighten "thy mind with the knowledge of true worship and declare thee to the cosmos to be the sun, enlightening and shining."[26]

The Byzantine liturgists connected Constantine with the victorious ist, the Lord of history. Therefore, the apparent allusions in their ʒ to Hellenistic kingship, especially "solar theology" and "sacral gship," are better understood not so much as the adoption of Hellen-ʌstic political theology as the Christian adaptation of Hebrew kingship.[27]

---

[18] Vespers: Eighth Tone, p. 179.   [22] Vespers: Second Tone, p. 176.
[19] Vespers: Fourth Tone, p. 175.   [23] Vespers: Eighth Tone, p. 179.
[20] Vespers: Fourth Tone, p. 178   [24] Vespers: Second Tone, p. 176.
[21] Vespers: Fourth Tone, p. 178.   [25] Matins: Third Tone, p. 180.
[26] Matins: Eighth Tone, p. 186.

[27] The prophets announced the epiphany of the person called Oriens, Anatolē: cf. Za 7:8; 6:12; Mal 4:2; and in the NT, Lk 1:78. The Christmas Liturgy of the Byzantine Church also includes like ascriptions, such as Christ, "the supersensual Sun of Justice" (Sixth Tone); He "has risen as the light of knowledge over the ecumene" (Fourth Tone); Christ is also called "the glorious euergetēs" (Katabasias of the Nativity); anatolē anatolōn (Exapostelarion); and the "royal Psalms" of the Christmas Hours compare Christ to the King of Israel. In the Epiphany Vespers, Christ is "our God who is Light of Light, theos epiphanēs, who has shone forth upon the cosmos" (Idiomelon). On Hebrew and Byzantine "solar theology" and the "solar character" of Christian emperors, see E. Kantorowicz, "Oriens-Augusti-Lever du Roi," Dumbarton Oaks Papers 17 (Cambridge, 1963) 117–62.

In other terms, because the Church is "the body of Christ" (Eph 1:23), the solar theology ascribed to Christ by Scripture was communicated to the Church to which the Empire was joined and of which the emperor was the "political" head. Again, there is no doubt that the emperors claimed to be the successors to the Hebrew kings and even Moses and Melchizedek.[28] Thus the "priestly character" of the Byzantine rulers was something which followed naturally from the nature of the *societas christiana* which they governed. Inasmuch as the Empire was united to the Church, the new Israel (1 Pt 2:9), the emperor, albeit a "priest," was a "lay priest," the leading member of the *basileion hierateuma.*[29] Finally, the idea of the Empire as a "dowry" given to God suggests a conjugal relationship between Christ and the commonwealth—an analogy of that relationship between ancient Israel and Jehovah, Christ and the Church (Song of Songs; Eph 5:22-32)—thus further supporting the patristic teaching of the emperor as the *mimēsis* of Christus-Homo.

If, then, we believe that the Greek Fathers were men of faith as well as men of learning, it is fair to assume that they, recognizing the portent of Eusebianism, rejected the equation of the *imperator* and God the Father. Peterson informs us that they were acquainted with the religious, political, and philosophical tradition which the political philosophy of Eusebius presupposed. He assures us, too, that those Fathers who accepted the mating of the Church and the Empire did not hesitate to employ *mutatis mutandis* the pagan arguments of one kingdom, one king,

[28] Dvornik is hard pressed to avoid calling Saul, David, and Solomon "the ideal predecessors" of the Byzantine emperors; he wants them to be the successors of the Hellenistic kings—perhaps by virtue of some political or historical bias. See his *Early Christian and Byzantine Political Philosophy* 1, 300-304. No doubt the elements of Hellenistic, Roman, and Persian kingship can be found in the Byzantine *imperium*, but its prototype is the kingship of old Israel. On the Hebrew monarchy, see especially 1 S 8; 2 S 22; 1 K 8 (Solomon's prayer at the dedication of the Temple). Note the parallel between Jerusalem and Constantinople and Justinian's exclamation at the completion of Hagia Sophia: "Glory be to God, who has deemed us worthy of this deed! Solomon, I have conquered thee!" The Troparion (First Tone) for the Feast of the Elevation of the Cross also compares the Christian Roman Empire to old Israel: "O Lord, save thy people and bless thine inheritance, granting our believing emperors victory over the barbarians and by thy Cross preserving thy *politeuma.*" On the artistic evidence which relates Hebrew leaders with the emperors, see D. J. Geanakoplos, *Byzantine East and Latin West* (New York, 1966) p. 63. That Chalcedon greeted the Emperor Marcian with the words "May your empire be eternal" (Mansi 7, 169 f.) might very well not display anything Hellenistic but Hebrew. God promised David— the Council also called Marcian "the new David"—an everlasting house (2 S 16) and a dynasty that would exist forever (3 K 2:45). See P. Heinisch, *Theology of the Old Testament* (St. Paul, 1955) pp. 28, 368 f.

[29] G. Florovsky, "Empire and the Desert: Antinomies of Christian History," *Greek Orthodox Theological Review* 3 (1957) 142 f.

one world.[30] Also, they were cognizant of Origen's teachings—Eusebius' master—with whom "Hellenism attempts to creep into the Church."[31] In this very important connection, then, it is also true that the Greek Fathers in particular were concerned with the refutation of the pagan conception of time (i.e., cyclical becoming) and eternity (i.e., the perpetual nowness to which the disembodied spirit of man escapes); for it was the metaphysical dualism which lay behind Eusebius' conception of Christian kingship. In other words, the attitude of the Fathers towards the unity of Church and state was determined precisely by their "theology" and their understanding of the relationship between God, Christ, and history. Such facts, incidentally, lead us to consider the Hellenistic appellations given to the Christian emperors as the kind of rhetoric which characterized the literature of the so-called patristic era.

III

We have seen that logic keenly suggests the conclusion that the Eusebian and Christian political theologies were opposed. They differed for very specific reasons: not only did Eusebius seek to make the Constantinian *renovatio* a quasi-Christian extension of the Augustan revolution, while the Church viewed it as a Christian version of the Hebrew theocracy, but, as we shall see, the ontological principles involved in the debate were mutually exclusive. The intellectual clarification of those differences began with the Arian heresy and would be consummated with the Church's victory over iconoclasm—and, curiously, Eusebius was "present" at the beginning and the end. The centuries of theological controversy were instrumental in pointing up divergent views of history and salvation which the variant political theories assumed.

The essential incompatibility between Eusebianism and the Fathers was clear almost at once. The association between Eusebius and Arius[32]

[30] Peterson states that in the fourth century Homer's "the rule of many is not good, let there be one dominion" and Alexander of Aphrodisias' alteration "one rule, one source, one god," the basic assumptions of Hellenistic kingship, were familiar to the Fathers. These political ideas were expostulated in the anonymous but highly influential political treatise *De mundo*, which appeared in Alexandria around 40 B.C. It is noteworthy that the Alexandrian Fathers, e.g., Sts. Timothy, Athanasius, and Cyril, had very little to say about kingship. Peterson mentions Cyril's *Contra Julianum* 4, 7 (*PG* 76, 700D-701A), but concedes that this Father discusses kingship "doch ohne monotheismus zu sprechen" (p. 147); and Dvornik (Vol. 2) cannot offer a single quotation from Cyril on the subject.

[31] V. Lossky, *The Mystical Theology of the Eastern Church* (London, 1957) p. 32.

[32] The evidence re the orthodoxy of Eusebius tends not to support it. The testimony of the Christian writers of the early Church which favors it does not generally relate to his doctrine, with the notable exception of Socrates (*Eccl. hist.* 2, 21). He was accused of Arianism by Athanasius, Epiphanius of Salamis, Jerome, Augustine, Nicetas of Remesiana,

—not an unnatural alliance, since both had Origen as their master—brought into prominence those opposing ontologies. Although Eusebius did not openly espouse all the doctrines of Arius, they were one in their political theology. They both connected monarchy and monotheism, a theory which decidedly involved an unorthodox Christology. In common they held that the Logos was "a lesser being, however close to God," and were thereby prepared "to bow to the will of the emperor, as also God's vicegerent on earth." [33] In other terms, since theology (the doctrine of God in Himself) and Christology (the doctrine of Christ) were necessarily interrelated, a difference in theology must dictate a difference in Christology. As G. H. Williams says, "two Christologies gave rise to, or at least were associated with, two main views of the Empire and the relationship of the Church to it...." [34] The dispute between the orthodox and the Arians was a clash over the nature of the Incarnation: whether it was an event which brought the transcendental, absolute God into the very course of the time which He created or whether it was the epiphany of a Christian Apollo. Had God entered history as a man or had the *deuteros theos* merely leaped from eternity to speak for the Unknown God who remained sequestered in the abyss of the *apeiron?*

The central word in the controversy between the Fathers and the Arians was *homoousios*, "equal in essence," or, as the Nicene Creed stated, *homoousios tō patri*, "equal to the Father." The Son of God, the Logos of the Father, is true God from true God. The Arians and Eusebius wanted to designate Him *homoiousios tō patri*, "like the Father in essence." The Bishop of Caesarea conceived the Son to be infinite and be-

Patriarch Nicephorus of Constantinople, the Seventh Ecumenical Council (787), and Photius in the thirteenth chapter of his *Bibliotheca*. J. Quasten, *Patrology* 3 (Westminister, Md., 1961) 309–10, and L. Duchesne, *Early History of the Christian Church* 2 (4th ed.; London, 1931) 98–152, assert that Eusebius' continual intervention in behalf of Arius, his excommunication by the Synod of Antioch (325), his ambivalent theology, and his Origenism put his orthodoxy in doubt. H. Kraft, *Kirchenväter Lexikon* (Munich, 1966) pp. 199 f., believes the accusation against Eusebius was really guilt by association. R. Seeberg, *Lehrbuch der Dogmengeschichte* 2 (2nd ed.; Leipzig, 1910) p. 30 f., calls Eusebius a subordinationist but not an Arian. The argument that Eusebius signed the declaration of Nicaea and that his post-Nicene works are orthodox (Valesius, *Annot. on Life and Writings of Eusebius Pamp.*, in *Eccles. History*, tr. S. E. Parker [Grand Rapids, 1962] pp. xxi–xxiii) is unconvincing. The *Theophania* (*PG* 24, 609–90) and *Contra Marcellum* (*PG* 24, 707–826) are as pro-Arian as they are anti-Sabellian.

[33] Introduction to *Christology of the Later Fathers* (Vol. 3 of *The Library of Christian Classics*, ed. E. R. Hardy and C. C. Richardson; Philadelphia, 1954) p. 22.

[34] "Christology and Church-State Relations in the Fourth Century," *Church History* 20 (1951) 9.

gotten of God, but not equal to Him. The Incarnation, therefore, was not the historical revelation of God in the flesh, but the apocalypse of a lesser deity. The man Jesus was not an organ, a *mousikos anēr*, a lyre of the Logos (*Dem. evangel.* 4, 13, 7). The orthodox believed Christ to be true man and true God. These teachings were converted into political terms. The Arians equated the emperor with the Father and the priesthood with the inferior Son. The Emperor was *rex et sacerdos*, head of the *imperium*, *sacerdotium*, and *ekklēsia*. On the other hand, the orthodox proclaimed the equality of the Logos and the Father, hence subordinating the *imperium* to the *sacerdotium*, having related the former with the "humanity" of Christ and the priesthood with His "divinity." Together they governed the Christian commonwealth, which was virtually identified with the *ekklēsia*. The Arians saw the Christology (and theology) of the orthodox as a threat to their political theology, a "rebellion" on the ontological level.[35]

Neither Eusebius nor the Arians were able to construe history as the vehicle of salvation. They were unprepared to make the Incarnation— the irruption of eternity into time—the center of their *oikonomia*. The Arian-Eusebian axis was a tacit return to Hellenism. The Logos was for them "the intermediate being of Neoplatonic theology, neither 'very God' nor 'very man,' but through the Spirit which in turn he was believed to engender, a 'link' between the two."[36] Like Origen, they would not refer to the Logos as *autotheos* or *anarchos archē*, but "after the Father." They permitted the Father no contact with "multiplicity." The Logos mediated the "one and the many," He who "comes between the Unbegotten and the being of things made" (Origen, *Contra Cels.* 3, 34). Origen, Eusebius, and the Arians, Hellenists as they were, sought to discover the mystery of the universe in scientific unity, compulsively reducing multiplicity to Euclidean simplicity. Occasionally, the writings of Eusebius display an attempt to break with Origenism, but he seems unable to turn the corner.

The Origenist mentality of Eusebius is nowhere more palpable than in

---

[35] Arian monotheism, says Peterson, "ist ein politische Forderung, ein Stück der Reichpolitik" (p. 95). In this connection he states that the "orthodoxe Trinitätlehre bedrohte in der Tat die politische Theologie des Imperium Romanum" (p. 96).

[36] Cochrane, *op. cit.*, p. 223. The fact that Eusebius seems not to have rejected the eternity of the Son or that perhaps he was attempting to mediate the heresies of Sabellianism (of which he thought orthodoxy a version) and Arianism and fell inadvertently into error, fails to touch our argument. Among other things, his Hellenism is manifest by his inability to think outside its categories, e.g., the Son is "after" the Father, who is "first of all"; and the Holy Spirit is "in third order" (*Dem. evang.* 4, 4, 2).

his letter to Augusta, the sister of Constantine.[37] The entire work is written in Origenist idiom. He replies to Augusta's desire to have an ikon or sacred image. He tells her that the ikon is pagan and it is wrong for a Christian to possess one. She must not think that ikons have any religious value. In any case, it is impossible for the divine to be artistically rendered in a "perishable frame." There is an infinite disparity between the reality (*ousios*) and the image (*eikōn*).[38]

It is unworthy of the divine to be depicted in "the fashion of beasts," Eusebius continues.[39] God, Christ, and the saints must be "contemplated" in "the purity of the human heart."[40] For Eusebius, then, as for Strabo, Lucian, and Plutarch, the divine, anything spiritual, could not be embodied in matter, and all art was simply a creature of the human imagination. Moreover, as the disciple of Origen, he inherited a spiritualism which demanded that one must look beyond "symbols" for "truth." Temporal and sensual things were vastly inferior to, and profoundly less interesting than, the immaterial realities. Eusebius looked upon time as something accidental and relentless, with even the Incarnation only a moment in the continuous story of divine theophanies. In other words, the Eusebian ontology, the Origenist Middle-Platonic dualism, meant the Hellenization of Christianity, something which was reflected in his political theology.

The rejoinder of the Greek Fathers to the Eusebian philosophy was to insist that the Logos-God became man and that this unity represented a *coincidentia oppositorum*. The importance of God in history was not something "philosophical" but essentially and crucially soteriological. "For man would not have been deified if he were joined to a creature or if the Son were not true God," wrote St. Athanasius. "Nor would man have been brought in to the presence of the Father unless the Deifier were His

[37] *PG* 20, 1545–49. The letter seems to have received little attention until the eighth century, during the iconoclastic controversy, when it was condemned for its Hellenism. The common idea that iconoclasm was a "Semitic objection" to "Hellenizing iconodulism" is quite erroneous. See G. Florovsky, "Origen, Eusebius and the Iconoclastic Controversy," *Church History* 19 (1950) 77–96, and G. Ladner, "Origen and the Significance of the Iconoclastic Controversy," *Medieval Studies* 2 (1940) 11–20. The Patriarch of Constantinople, Nicephorus, wrote his *Antirrhetici tres adv. Const. Cor.* (*PG* 100, 206–534) in rebuttal to the Eusebian letter, which he viewed as iconoclastic and Origenist.

[38] *Ep. ad Aug.* (*PG* 20, 1548B). Of not incidental importance was the fourth-century debate between some Arians and the Fathers over the "image of the emperor." Athansius asserted that the reverence paid to the image of the emperor passed necessarily to him, just as he who adores the Son adores the Father with whom He is coeternal (*Contra Ar.* 3, 5 [*PG* 26, 332B]). Cf. Basil the Great, *De Spir. sanc.* 45 (*PG* 32, 149C); Cyril of Jerusalem, *Catech.* 12, 5 (*PG* 33, 723A); Gregory of Nyssa, *De hom. opif.* 4 (*PG* 44, 136C); Gregory the Theologian, *Orat.* 4 (*PG* 35, 629B); John of Damascus, *Orat. imag.* (*PG* 94, 1405C).

[39] Eusebius, 1548B.   [40] Eusebius, 1546A.

natural and true Logos who had taken to Himself a body. And we would not have been delivered from sin and its course.... For the union was necessary that He might unite what is man by nature to Him who is God by nature and through deification secure our salvation."[41] In a word, if there were no human participation in the divine, man would yet be subject to sin, death, and Satan. Salvation was precisely the union of God and man (henōsis).[42] Gregory of Nyssa makes it very clear that this "union" is not figurative: "He who sustains creation is commingled in us and is being fused to our nature in order that we might become divine through our mixing (epimixia) with God. For Christ's return from death commenced the very principle by which our mortal race gains immortality."[43]

Deification is both a process and an actuality, a becoming and a being. The telos of history is already present in the process. This teaching was expressed by "the dogma of Chalcedon," which "provides a basis of the theology of history, which otherwise is liable to founder in a doctrine of endless Becoming, or to dissolve in a timeless Ideal."[44] The awareness of

[41] Contra Ar. 2, 70 (PG 26, 296D). This is a basic theme of patristic Christology, e.g., 2 Clement 14, 5; Ignatius of Antioch, Ep. ad Magn. 14, 1; Irenaeus, Contra haer. 5, praef. (PG 7, 1120); Methodius of Olympus, Conv. dec. virg. 1, 5 (PG 18, 45B); Gregory of Nazianzus, Poem. dog. 10, 5-9 (PG 37, 456 f.); Gregory of Nyssa, Orat. catech. 25 (PG 45, 65D); Maximus the Confessor, Ad Thal. 60 (PG 90, 921AB), etc. In anticipation of certain objections, it should be observed that there are essential differences between the patristic teaching on deification (theōsis) and the pagan idea of it. The differences relate to that which separated the Church from Hellenism: time, grace, and the resurrection of the body. Hellenism believed that deification meant the absorption of soul, which had escaped the prison of the body, into the divine, beyond time. The "escape" was achieved by human effort, asceticism, and special knowledge (gnōsis). For the Greek Fathers, however, deification or salvation begins in time, body and soul, through grace en Christō. The patristic gnōsis is the gift of the Holy Spirit. See Jules Gross, La divinisation du chrétien d'après les Pères grecs (Paris, 1938). Following Origen, Eusebius apparently believed "deification" to be "spiritual perfection" and not the ontological transformation of human nature. See E. Mersch, The Whole Christ (London, 1956) pp. 253 f.

[42] The Fathers employed many words to describe the union of God and man, such as koinōnia, methexis, parousia, etc.—often borrowed from Hellenic philosophy. Their use of them, however, is unlike that to which they were put by the pagans. "Union," according to the Fathers, meant the uniting of the total man with God in Christ, in the Church, in the sacraments through the Holy Spirit. "Union" is a process which begins now, a process initiated by Christ's resurrection; it was something accomplished by grace. See G. W. H. Lampe, A Patristic Greek Lexicon, fasc. 4 (Oxford, 1964) 837-38. Plato, on the other hand, attempted, by the use of such words, to describe "the relation of an Idea to its group," the Idea being the supersensible cause (aitia). Things are mirrors reflecting their original. See the discussion in F. M. Cornford, From Religion to Philosophy (New York, 1957) pp. 253-63.

[43] Orat. catech. 25 (PG 45, 65D-68A).

[44] J. Daniélou, The Lord of History (London, 1958) p. 185.

this truth led the Councils of Ephesus and Chalcedon to subdue the heresies of Nestorianism (which sundered the divine and the human in Christ) and Monophysitism (the divine absorbing the human). The first made the deification of man impossible, the latter abrogated his humanity; and, at the same time, the consequence of Nestorianism for history was to utterly secularize it, while the end of Monophysitism was to extinguish the integrity of the created order, that is to say, it was a form of pantheism.

The defenders of the traditional Christology, however, maintained a balance of the divine and the human in history. They used Aristotelian language and concepts in their refutation of the Christological extremes. The "realism" was very effective against the sporadic revival of Origenism and growing influence of Neoplatonism.[45] Both were dualist systems, while Aristotle proved compatible with the Chalcedonian doctrine of Christ, i.e., the philosophers' idea that "form" and "matter" were joined not unlike the "two natures" in Christ, the two dimensions of history. Of course, the "two natures" were not "confused" and the "divinity" of Christ was not really the "form" of His "humanity." Nevertheless, the relationship was accurately defined by Chalcedon. It was Leontius of Byzantium (485–543) who attempted to resolve the question with his idea of the *enhypostasis*—the humanity of Christ inhered in the single divine hypostasis of the Logos without a loss of identity.[46] The Fathers after Leontius, consequently, transposed his Christology into co~ terms. In the words of Dionysius the Areopagite (*ca.* 55(^ "manifest" and "demonstrable," "unspeakable" an aspects fully "intertwined."[47] Such a concept strikes Neoplatonism.[48] Following Dionysius, Maximus the (taught that not only do we see "through phenomena w.

[45] The sixth-century revival of Origenism may be related to the work of Neoplato... teachers who, after Justinian closed the Academy of Athens (529), fled to Persia, but finding themselves unwelcome there returned to the Empire (see A. von Harnack, "Neoplatonism," *Encycl. Brit.* 19 [11th ed., 1911] 377). At the same time, the use of Aristotelian language and concepts by the Fathers was a means by which to "philosophically" oppose the Platonic and Neoplatonic hypostaticization of time: Maximus the Confessor, *Ad Thal.* 65 (*PG* 90, 757D); Gregory of Nazianzus, *In theoph.* (*PG* 36, 317B); Gregory of Nyssa, *De oct.* (*PG* 44, 609B); John Chrysostom, *De comp. ad Stel.* 2, 4 (*PG* 47, 415–16), etc. On Maximus in particular, see Hans Urs von Balthasar, *Die kosmische Liturgie* (Einsiedeln, 1961).

[46] *Contra Nest. et Eutych.* (*PG* 86, 1277D–1281A).

[47] *Ep ad Tim.* 9, 1 (*PG* 3, 1105D–1108A).

[48] Dionysius is defended against the charge of Neoplatonism by Vladimir Lossky in his *Mystical Theology of the Eastern Church*, pp. 23–43, and in *The Vision of God* (Clayton, Wis., 1963) pp. 99–110. The garb may have been Neoplatonic, but the *didascalia* of Dionysius was Christian.

nomena,"[49] but the physical cosmos is intelligible through the spiritual reality which illumines and upholds it.[50] There is a unity without the confusion of its dimensions.[51] He drew this conclusion from the fact that the Church is an analogy of the "diophysitic Christ" and the cosmos an "image of the Holy Church of God."[52]

The incarnational ontology and cosmology of the post-Chalcedonian Greek Fathers were a reply to Origenism and Neoplatonism, which appear to have passed together into the next century and into the iconoclastic controversy. It is not without significance that the iconodules or advocates of "sacred art" saw their task to be "a direct refutation of Origenism."[53] Iconodulism was also a rejection of Neoplatonism, to which historians believe the Church was obliged for her iconological assumptions, that is, the *eikōn*-prototype concept.[54] But the iconodules never taught that the ikon was an earthly *mimēsis* of a heavenly archetype. The ikon was not the mirror of a timeless world. It was, in fact, a sensual form to an abiding spiritual reality, a reality which was not separate from its visible representation. Unlike the pagan Greeks, who recongized no basic connection between the transitory and the permanent, the iconographer depicted sanctified individuals as present in their ikon. The dualism between time and eternity, Bowra says, "provided Greek art with its guiding ideal,"[55] whereas the iconographer struggled to create a vessel worthy of holding "the other world."[56] Thus, in painting the saints, for example, he never portrayed them as physically and humanly beautiful but as deified.[57]

By virtue of the Chalcedonian Christology and the patristic ontological explication of it, John of Damascus likewise contended that no insuperable barrier existed between time and eternity. The supreme demonstration of this fact, he said, was the Incarnation. Therefore, the making of an ikon of God is possible. He became "truly man, living upon the earth and dwelling among men..." (*De fid. orth.* 4, 16). His arguments in *De fide orthodoxa* and *De imaginibus* were subsequently ratified by the Seventh Ecumenical Council (787).[58] This position is Chalcedonian, not Origenist or Neoplatonic or Eusebian; for it states that "honor" is directed

---

[49] *Myst.* 2 (*PG* 91, 669C). [51] *Ibid.* 24 (705B).

[50] *Ibid.* 5 (680B). [52] *Ibid.* 3 (672A).

[53] Cf. Florovsky, "Origen . . . ," p. 87.

[54] See G. B. Ladner, "The Concept of the Image in the Greek Fathers and the Byzantine Iconoclastic Controvery," *Dumbarton Oaks Papers* 7 (Cambridge, 1953) 1–55.

[55] C. M. Bowra, *The Greek Experience* (New York, 1959) p. 172.

[56] L. Ouspensky and V. Lossky, *The Meaning of Icons* (Basel, 1952) p. 35.

[57] *Ibid.*, p. 35.

[58] Cf. Actio 7 (Mansi 13, 378). See Nilus of Sinai, *Ep. ad Olymp.* (*PG* 79, 577); Theodore of Studium, *Ref.* 3, 2, 3 (*PG* 99, 417C); also the other patristic witness cited in n. 38 above.

to the prototype through the ikon, implying thereby their unity. More importantly, however, the Council was the culmination of the Fathers' effort to define the place of the Church's Greek heritage, a heritage which Origen, Eusebius, and those like them sought to give an impossible status. The Christianization of Hellenism was a triumph of the Church, a triumph of supernatural faith over natural reason.

IV

It is probably fair to say at this point that a necessary connection exists between Christology and ontology. May we say also that because patristic thought is Chalcedonian and Eusebian thought Platonic, therefore they hold opposing "political" theories? Is there anything in the way of further empirical evidence that the Greek Fathers did not follow the political theology of Eusebius? We believe there is—a matter central to the very conception of Hellenistic kingship: caesaropapism. We must consider now whether the Fathers recognized the Christian emperor as theologically and juridically the head, *kephalion*, of the *ekklēsia* and the *basileia*. Was he the God-appointed organic head of the Church (as well as the Empire) in matters pertaining to doctrine and piety? Was the Empire in any sense "divine"? Did the Fathers think of him as a successor to King David or Augustus Caesar spiritually?

Those Fathers who accepted the mating of the Christian Church and the Roman Empire did in fact reject the idea of the emperor's preternaturality. They consciously busied themselves with severing all ties between monarchy and monotheism. They did everything possible to personalize, historicize, and biblicize him and his authority. Indeed, the Fathers contrived "to hold the Emperor under specifically Christian judgment."[59] They placed him *within* the Church and declared his *kratos* (sovereignty), *kratēsis* (civil power), and *exousia* (= *imperium*) as a ruler to be "legitimate" only under that condition. His "legal status" within the commonwealth depended upon his "good standing in the Church," his orthodoxy, and his obedience to ecclesiastical canons.[60] His reign was pleasing to God, said Basil the Great, so long as it was not sinful.[61] As a member of the Church, he must submit to those means by which any man is saved.[62] The emperor may be *autokrator*, but he is also *therapōn*, a servant, an attendant of God and wholly subject to the divine truth.[63]

---

[59] G. H. Williams, *art. cit.*, p. 16.   [60] Florovsky, "Empire and Desert . . . ," p. 142.
[61] *In ps. 32,* 9 (*PG* 29, 344–45).
[62] Gregory of Nyssa, *Contra Eun.* 1 (*PG* 45, 293A).
[63] Athanasius, *Apol. ad imper. Const.* 12.

The emperor, asserted the Fathers, is neither "absolute" nor "divine." Although Christians were to obey him, their first duty was to the gospel. It is true that he was addressed as *pietas, sacratissimus, sanctissimus*, even *dominus*, but when he was unorthodox he was called *tyrannos, antichristos, christomachos*.[64] Again, the familiar phrase "quod principi placuit, legis habit vigorem" (usually taken from Justinian's *Digest* 1, 4, 1) is often lifted from its very important context: "ut postea cum lege regia, quae de imperio ejus lata est populus ei et in eum omne suum imperium et potestatem conferat."[65] This was a description of imperial power originally stated by the Roman jurist Ulpian, the friend and adviser of Emperor Septimius Severus. It was a legal dictum which clearly announced that the authority of the emperor was conferred upon him by the Roman people. Both Augustus and Constantine claimed to have restored the Republic and thereby secured the rights of the people. Justinian, too, learned that the Roman political structure carried within it the implicit right of rebellion (e.g., the Nika Revolt of 532). And in a Christian *politeia* his powers were further curtailed by ecclesiastical law, doctrine, and morality. In 491, at the coronation of Anastasius I, the emperor took a vow of obedience to the decrees of Church councils.[66] It was the first such oath in Roman history.

Again, the emperor was not a "minister of the word and sacrament," nor could he impose doctrine upon the *sacerdotium*, let alone Christian society. To be sure, he wore vestments similar to those of the bishop and had a special place in the worship of the Church, such as censing the sanctuary at the Christmas liturgy, offering the sermon during the Vespers at the beginning of Lent, and receiving Holy Communion directly from the altar as the clergy; nevertheless, he was not a priest and many Fathers disapproved of even these privileges.[67] Emperor Marcian, as we know, was hailed as priest-king at the Council of Chalcedon, but this did not give sacerdotal status to him or any Byzantine *imperator*.[68] The quasi-sacerdotal functions of the emperor were "in fact a continuation of the fiction of *privilegium* which dispensed with certain laws in favor of Julius Caesar and Octavius, and which, in later days, recognized the

---

[64] Athanasius, *Hist. Arian.* 67 (*PG* 25, 773B).

[65] On this matter see R. W. Carlyle, *A History of Medieval Political Theory in the West* 1 (New York, 1903) 64 f.

[66] Florovsky, "Empire and Desert . . . ," p. 155.

[67] Canon 69 of Quinisext permitted no "layman" but the emperor to enter the sanctuary to make an offering to God. Yet the commentator mentions that many theological writers disapproved. See *The Rudder* (or the book of the sacred canons), tr. D. Cummings (Chicago, 1957) pp. 372–73.

[68] F. Dvornik, *Early Christian and Byzantine Political Philosophy* 1, 301.

special position assigned to the Christian Emperor."[69] Yet he, as the ruler of a Christian kingdom, had the obligation to intervene in some religious matters, for the state of religion had definite political and social ramifications; conversely, the clergy in such a kingdom had the right to advise and even defy the emperor when his policies affected the spiritual welfare of Christians.

The emperor was "bishop of the outside." Constantine is supposed to have said to a group of bishops: "You are indeed bishops of all which pertains to things within the Church, but I have been appointed a bishop also, a bishop of the outside."[70] The meaning of his remark (if indeed he made it at all) has been keenly debated. According to some historians, this expression (*episkopos tōn ektos*) indicated that Constantine claimed to possess authority over the organization and administration of the Church.[71] J. Staub believes that "bishop to or of the outside" extended the emperor's competence to everything in the Church save those things bearing directly upon the soul.[72] Dvornik rejects these theories and also the idea that the emperor's words applied only to pagans and heretics (i.e., those outside the Church). He prefers to think that by "assuming the title of bishop, Constantine recognized his role in the Christianization of the state, in helping Christianity to become victorious over other religions and in enforcing Christian precepts among all his subjects."[73] This opinion has merit, but it does not clarify for us what were the limitations of the emperor's powers and responsibilities.

The evidence suggests to us that the Emperor was *epi-skopos*, "overseer" of all things within the commonwealth whether "religious" or "secular." He provided the clergy with the machinery for the evangelization of the *oikoumenē* and the *ethnē*. He also must have had the right to watch over their effort and to ensure their success by every measure available to him. His "episcopacy" was a necessary part of his *philanthrōpia* (loving concern for mankind) and must have involved more than "secular matters." East Rome was a Christian society, which means that religious doctrine, piety, and law were the business of everyone. The emperor had not only to build orphanages, hospitals, and temples, pay the missionaries, etc., but he had to create an atmosphere in which the individual might work out his salvation in fear and trembling. He must de-

[69] J. Hussey, *The Byzantine World* (New York, 1961) p. 89.

[70] *Vita Const.* 4, 24 (*PG* 20, 1172AB).

[71] P. Sherrard, *Greek East and Latin West* (London, 1955) p. 93; D. J. Geanakopolos, *Byzantine East and Latin West*, p. 64.

[72] "Kaiser Konstantin als *episkopos tōn ektos*," in *Studia patristica* 1 (Berlin, 1957) 687.

[73] *Early Christian and Byzantine* . . . 2, 753–54.

clare and disseminate the truth of Christianity and, whenever possible, enforce the decrees and discipline of the Church. Thus, he did in fact have a religious commission from God.

In his letter to Constantius, Cyril of Jerusalem exhorted him "to emulate your blessed father Constantine, who was rewarded by finding the true Cross." He must erect "the trophy of the Cross before all men" if he wishes to defeat his enemies and bring peace to his realm and happiness to his house.[74] The historians Sozomen and Socrates tell us that the emperor was commonly referred to as "Moses,"[75] whose authority in ancient Israel, as we know, was not restricted to organizational and social matters. Finally, as a "new David," the emperor must commit himself and his people to the truth, "for truth is the protection of the emperor, especially the Christian emperor. With it, he may rule in safety," Athanasius told Constantius. "As the Scriptures say, 'Mercy and truth safeguard the king, and with righteousness is his throne surrounded' (Prv 20:28). Therefore was the wise Zorobabel victorious and all the people cried: 'Great is the truth which must prevail' (3 Esd 4, 41)."[76] In other words, the Fathers understood the emperor to be not the fountain of truth but the servant of the gospel.

The truth must rule the emperor and he must rule by it. He must be *fidei defensor*. "Knowing that nothing serves the man-loving God more than that all Christians have one and the same mind towards the true and immaculate faith," Justinian proclaimed, "and that no schism injure the Holy Church of God, it is necessary for us to take the lead on every occasion to prune the scandalizers from her. They scandalize the confession of the orthodox faith, which was delivered to the saints of God's Church. It is manifest from our edict that we have sought to protect her from dissension and to protect those professing the orthodox religion by opposing the truth to the contentious and above all to pursue diligently the unity of God's people."[77] Thus, in the case of Justinian, his condemnation of the "Three Chapters" was not entirely presumptuous. Nor may his action be viewed as the intrusion of the "secular power" into spiritual matters—there was nothing "secular" in Byzantium. Yet he did arrogate to himself authority which properly did not fall within his own sphere of power: he presumed to enter the doctrinal aegis of the *sacerdotium*, the Church from the "inside." However, his error is understandable, since the line between "inside" and "outside," often obscured by circumstance, could not always be clearly seen. And indeed, Justinian and other Byzantine

[74] *Ep. ad Const. imper.* 5–7 (*PG* 33, 1172A–1173B).
[75] See Sozomen, *Hist. eccl.* 1, 19 (*PG* 67, 920); Socrates, *Hist. eccl.* 7, 42 (*PG* 67, 832).
[76] *Apol. ad imper. Const.* 11 (*PG* 25, 906A).
[77] *Conf. rect. fid.* (*PG* 86, 993CD).

emperors may have forgotten from time to time that they were not Hellenistic theocrats.

The Greek Fathers consistently rejected caesaropapism. The emperor was admonished many times that his *imperium* did not comprehend "the things of God." In his *Historia Arianorum*, Athanasius mentions the letter of Hosius of Cordova to Constantius:

> Intrude youself not into ecclesiastical matters, neither give any command to us concerning them; but learn from us. God has put into your hands the Empire, but to us He has entrusted the Church. If anyone should steal the Empire from you, he would be resisting the ordinance of God; similarly, be fearful to usurp to yourself the things which appertain to the Church and avoid that which would make you guilty of a great offense. It is written, ":Render unto Caesar the things of Caesar, but unto God the things of God" (Mt. 22:21). Therefore, as we have no right to exercise earthly rule, so you, O Emperor, have no authority to burn incense.[78]

Athanasius wrote to the same Emperor:

> For if a judgment is made by bishops, what business has the emperor with it? Or if a threat by the emperor is decisive, what need for bishops at all? When was such a thing ever heard from the beginning of the world? When did the decision of the Church receive its validity from the emperor? There have been many councils and many judgments by the Church; but the fathers never sought the consent of an emperor to make them; nor did the latter presume to meddle with the affairs of the Church.[79]

Conciliar decrees, therefore, restricted imperial power with regard to religious matters. It is clear that neither Hosius nor Athanasius believed the emperor could make dogma or canon law.[80]

John Chrysostom (344–407) had more to say about the state. His attitude may have been determined by the great stress he placed on spirituality, asceticism, and personal responsibility, but whatever the case

---

[78] In *Hist. Arian.* 44 (*PG* 25, 745D–748A). Hosius was Constantine's adviser at the Council of Nicaea.

[79] *Hist. Arian.* 52 (*PG* 25, 756C).

[80] "We find in the Fathers the consciousness that the Church has its own laws and principles," writes R. W. Carlyle, "its own administrative authority, which is not at all to be regarded as dependent upon the State, but as something which stands beside it and independent of it; that the relations between the Church and the State are those of two independent though closely related powers, relations which it becomes necessary, as time goes by, to understand and define" (*A History of Medieval Political Theory* 1, 175–76).

may be, he contributed nothing to the so-called "Rome ideology."[81] Chrysostom attached no importance to any particular government or to any ruler:

What are you saying? That every ruler is elected by God? This is not what St. Paul said. Nor am I now speaking about individual rulers, but the very idea of government. For that there should be rulers, rule, and ruled is not to be doubted. They exist to prevent confusion, the people swaying like the waves of the sea in every direction.... Hence Paul does not say "for there is no ruler but from God," but rather it is the fact of government of which he speaks and says "there is no power but from God."[82]

In another place John says that no ruler governs "his fellow servants by natural authority and therefore he often loses his authority. In a word, things which do not inhere naturally must readily admit to change and transposition."[83]

John is really saying no more than that no particular government is necessary for the realization of the divine plan, and certainly no empire is eternal. He asserts that the course of history proves that kingdoms rise and fall, each playing its part in the purpose of God. The Roman Empire, therefore, exists for the same reason. It is the last of "the four empires" mentioned by Daniel the prophet. Rome exists to "withhold" (*katechein*) the Antichrist.[84] But just as "the Medes fell before the Babylonians, the Babylonians to the Persians, the Persians to the Macedonians, and the Macedonians to the Romans," so will Rome eventually fall before the Antichrist, who will commence an era of evil and lawlessness. Consequently, John placed little trust in the Empire as a means by which universal peace and justice would come; and assuredly he found nothing about Rome which could be viewed as "holy." The Constantinian *renovatio* was a failure because it was *ab initio* misbegotten. It was foolish to unite the Church with a sick *Romanum imperium*. There should have been no alliance with a government whose malady might very well prove to be contagious. As Carter says, "the implication was [for Chrysostom] that the Roman Empire was a tyranny and the Church a true kingdom."[85]

Whatever John's appraisal of the Empire, he was not ungrateful for the

---

[81] S. Verosta, *Johannes Chrysostomus, Staatsphilosoph und Geschichtstheologe* (Graz, 1960) p. 189. Dvornik takes the opposite point of view, asserting that the political thought of Chrysostom was dependent upon the Stoics (*Early Christian and Byzantine Political Philosophy* 2, 692–99).

[82] *Ep. ad Rom.* 23 (*PG* 60, 615).   [83] *Hom. de stat.* 7, 2 (*PG* 49, 93).

[84] *Ep. 2 ad Thess.* 4, 1–2 (*PG* 62, 485–87).

[85] R. E. Carter, "Saint John Chrysostom's Rhetorical Use of the Socratic Distinction between Kingship and Tyranny," *Traditio* 14 (1958) 369.

good it did bring.[86] Since Rome was a monarchy, he saw the blessings of the kingdom as the direct result of the emperor's rule, a rule which depended upon his character. John drew from precepts of the Old Testament and the language of Stoicism so popular in his day to describe "the good emperor." He insisted that he must rule with "temperance," "justice," and for "the common good," none of which would be possible for the ruler unless he first possessed "self-control." Moreover, in matters of religion, the emperor must seek the advice of the priests and monks. In particular, the bishop "has received authority to loose sins committed against God," John said; "much more will he be able to remit those committed against man. For the sacred laws take place under his hands and even the emperor is subject to them. Hence, when there is need for a good from God, the emperor is accustomed to fly to the priest and not the priest to the emperor."[87] He defined the jurisdiction of the emperor as cities and armies in comparison to the power of the *sacerdotium* and monks over doctrine and "the inward man." The Empire chastises evildoers, while the Church, in anticipation of the kingdom of God, sanctifies all earthly life.[88]

Chrysostom seems not to have approached the question of Church and state ideologically.[89] His thinking was more practical, more pastoral. Not unlike him, Basil the Great was alarmed by the Constantinian *renovatio*. In fact, he went further than the Patriarch of Constantinople and openly repudiated it by becoming the central figure in the monastic resistance.[90] He placed the Roman Empire among the "barbarians," the pagan *ethnē*,[91] and called for an immediate withdrawal of believers from the disastrous alliance contracted by the Church. Not that Basil was not greatly concerned with the problems of social reconstruction, but he refused to permit Christianity to substitute for the bankrupt culture of Greco-Roman civilization. Hence, the attitude he wished the Church to take with regard to the Empire was a spiritual one, that is, to convert its citizens. In any case, he declared, the Church is the *oikoumenē*, the Empire only a parody of it. Ecumenicity is a spiritual and eschatological concept, not a political one.[92] The Church is the only "country" for the followers of Christ. If the world is to be converted, it must be done without the Roman *imperium* and its earthly power.

---

[86] *In Is.* 2, 2 (*PG* 56, 33).
[87] *Ad pop. Antioch.* 3, 2 (*PG* 49, 50).
[88] *Hom. in Mt 19,* 5 (*PG* 57, 388).
[89] *In. Is.* 2, 4 (*PG* 56, 72-73).
[90] Florovsky, "Empire and Desert...," p. 150.
[91] *In. ps. 68,* 2 (*PG* 29, 433BC).
[92] *In ps. 48,* 1 (*PG* 29, 433B); *Ep.* 66, 2 (*PG* 32, 425B). On Basil's attitude towards the Empire, see Dom Amand, *L'Ascèse monastique de saint Basile de Césarée* (Maredsous, 1948) pp. 13 f.; S. Giet, *Les idées et l'action sociales de saint Basile le Grand* (Paris, 1955) pp. 166 f.

The separation from the world which Basil advocated did not imply "civil disobedience," particularly not to Christian monarchs. Believers must "render unto Caesar."[93] The state exists for the "common good" and nothing ought to pervert its legitimate ends.[94] Moreover, the withdrawal for which he called did not always mean flight into the desert— Basil himself took the See of Caesarea in 370. On the occasion of the Feast of the Forty Martyrs of Sebaste, therefore, he exhorted his listeners to make the *oikoumenē* their home and to have no attachments to any city or province.[95] Writing to Amphilochius after his consecration, Basil reminds him that he is no longer a Cappadocian; he is now a bishop and "all believers in Christ are one people, a people called by God from many regions to be one in the Church; and so our former country rejoices at the economy of the Lord. . . . "[96] "Detachment," withdrawal," then, meant for Basil primarily indifference to all earthly pleasures, which alone could release the individual to pursue the glory of God.

Basil was not contemptuous of marriage, children, and domestic routine, but he was convinced that these lead to the anxiety and ambition which must inhibit spiritual perfection. That life "brings a thousand earthly cares" which make it enormously difficult to gain "detachment of the soul from the sympathies of the body." Perfection will come only when we are "cityless, homeless, vagabond, asocial, without property. . . . "[97] Therefore, he concluded that the sure path to salvation is the monastery: the monk alone is "the true and authentic Christian."[98] Basil and his followers must have been persuasive, for under his leadership cenobitic monasteries sprang up everywhere in the Empire and remained an essential characteristic of Byzantine life until the end. It is interesting, too, that the monks were the strongest opponents of the sometime imperial ambition to control the priesthood. Since most bishops were taken from the monasteries, we can understand, in part, sacerdotal resistance to the Hellenistic nostalgia of the emperors.

V

That Eusebian and patristic ontology, Christology, and political theories are irreconcilable should now be evident. But did the teachings of the Greek Fathers in fact affect the *Romanum imperium* itself? Did Byzantium indeed become Christian through those very centuries in which the theological controversies raged and the Fathers were giving intellectual form to the Church's faith?

We have observed already that in the fourth century Eusebius and the

[93] *In ps. 32,* 9 (*PG* 29, 344C).
[94] *Hexa.* 8, 4.
[95] *Quad. martyr.* 2 (*PG* 31, 509B).
[96] *Ep.* 161, 1 (*PG* 32, 629B).
[97] *Ep.* 2, 2 (*PG* 32, 225B).
[98] *Reg. fus. tract.* 35, 3 (*PG* 31, 1008A).

Arians thought to perpetuate the Hellenistic idea of empire: the idea of the *imperator* or *basileus* as *caput mundi*, the voice of God on earth, the *pontifex maximus, pater humanitatis.* They interpreted the Constantinian *renovatio* as the Christian stage of the *pax Romana.* They were as opposed to the orthodox teaching of the Trinity as they were to the orthodox doctrine that the emperor was a "layman" and subject to the law and dogma of the Church. With the triumph and spread of Arianism after the Council of Nicaea, the Eusebian "political theology" also won the day. The pagan "reaction" of Julian the Apostate was inevitable. It may or may not have been a coincidence that at the center of his religious and political convictions was "the cult of the sun" and a crude form of Platonism. He fought zealously to wipe out Christianity in the name of paganism. Yet, orthodoxy (and to some extent Arianism) persisted and after the death of Julian (363) the tide began slowly to turn. The path to a Catholic kingdom was the arduous road through "the Valens-Valentinian compromise." Valens and Valentinian I tried to straddle two worlds, but the untenability of such a position brought the Roman *imperium* to exhaustion. The enervation of the government was graphically demonstrated by the defeat of the Roman army and the death of Valens at the battle of Adrianople (378). The failure of the "reaction" and the "compromise" demanded a quick and effective solution if the Empire was to be saved. The way was open for the "Christian revolution" of Theodosius the Great (379–95).

One of Theodosius' major problems was the relationship which must exist between *imperium* and *sacerdotium.* "As the real prototype in history of the 'Christian prince,'" says Cochrane, "he was profoundly concerned to work out the logic of his position; and it is this fact, more than anything else, which determined the scope and character of his effort to bring about a radical readjustment to the existing relationship between the temporal and spiritual powers."[99] His solution was implicit in his decision to transform the *Romanum imperium* into a Christian empire, to consummate the work of Constantine. His policy to Christianize Roman law, to create "godly and righteous legislation," and to support the clergy and implement canon law began with the edict of Thessalonica (380):

We desire that all peoples who fall beneath the sway of our imperial clemency should profess the faith which we believe to have been delivered to the Romans by the Apostle Peter and maintained in its traditional form to the present day ... by the pontiff Damasus and the bishop Peter of Alexandria ... namely, that, following apostolic discipline and evangelical doctrine, we should believe in one

[99] Cochrane, *op. cit.*, p. 324.

God, the blessed Trinity of the Father, the Son and the Holy Spirit, adored with equal majesty. And we decree that those who follow this rule of faith should embrace the name of Catholic Christians, adjudging all others to be madmen and order them to be designated heretics . . . condemning them to suffer Divine punishment and, also, the vengeance of that power, in accordance with the Will of Heaven, which we shall decide to inflict.[100]

Thus, the new basis of the Roman order was Nicene-Constantinopolitan Christianity. Making the religion of Christ the legal as well as the spiritual foundation of the Empire, Theodosius necessarily subordinated the *imperium* to the *sacerdotium*. His monarchy was "sacred," but not by virtue of any direct and explicit connection with monotheism. Its "sacredness" followed from the nature of the religion which supported the whole structure of the Byzantine Empire.

The primacy of the *sacerdotium* is shown by the sensational incident which occurred in 390, the massacre of the riotous population at Thessalonica by order of Theodosius. The results of his encounter with Ambrose (333–97)[101] are an indication of how far the Emperor was willing to carry his "solution." Ambrose told him that the *imperium* was subject to the *sacerdotium* "in the cause of faith."[102] Thus he refused Theodosius Holy Communion unless, like King David, he made public penance for the death of the Thessalonians.[103] He humbled himself and was forgiven. Now, whether the posture of Ambrose was related to the political theology maintained by the Arians with whom he was struggling in Milan, we cannot say; and whether it was Ambrose who induced Theodosius' son Gratian, the Western Emperor, to discard the old imperial title, *pontifex maximus*, we are unable to determine.[104] But the coincidence of all these facts must encourage us to believe that Rome under Theodosius was indeed changing and that the teachings of the Fathers were being felt. No doubt, too, the humiliation of the Emperor made a

---

[100] In *Documents of the Christian Church*, ed. H. Bettenson (Oxford, 1947) pp. 31–32.

[101] In his attempt to extend and correct "the Setton thesis" (i.e., Ambrose best exemplifies sacerdotal defense against the imperial pretensions to control the hierarchy of the Church), G. F. Reilly (*Imperium and Sacerdotium according to St. Basil the Great* [Washington, D.C., 1945]) demonstrates that it was the powerful influence of Basil which led Ambrose to elaborate his political opinions. Thus Ambrose belongs to the Greek patristic stratum, despite his love for Cicero. The influence of Origen on his biblical exegesis, and Athanasius, Basil, Cyril of Jerusalem, Didymus the Blind, and Gregory of Nazianzus on his Christology and theology, is sufficient evidence for this contention. Among the Western writers, Ambrose used only Hippolytus of Rome, "the most Greek of them all" (Tixeront). And, of course, Ambrosian antiphonal music is Eastern (Kraft, p. 22).

[102] *Ep.* 51, 13 (*PL* 16, 1046A).   [103] *Ep.* 51, 7 (*PL* 16, 1021B).

[104] Duschesne believes the influence of Ambrose to have been very strong (*Early History . . .* 2, 498).

vivid and practical contribution to the demise of Eusebian political theory.

While Ambrose was wrestling with the problems of Milan and Italy, a new Christological storm was gathering in the East. Out of the school at Antioch came Diodore of Tarsus, whose doctrine about Christ infected Nestorius, Patriarch of Constantinople. He preached that between the humanity and divinity in Christ no intrinsic connection may be said to exist. Theodosius II (408–50) convened an ecumenical council at Ephesus (431). The Emperor sent a letter to Cyril of Alexandria and the assembled bishops:

The stability of the Commonwealth depends upon the religion by which we honor God. They are bound closely together. Indeed, their relationship is such that the growth of the one is dependent upon the other. If true piety is perfectly observed, the Commonwealth will flourish. Since, then, the reins of government have been given to us by God and, also, the means by which piety and fidelity to doctrine are to be maintained, we seek to keep undivided the association which exists between them and thereby oversee the interest of both God and man. It is for us to provide for the prosperity of the Commonwealth and, so to speak, keep a watchful eye upon all our subjects. It is our responsibility to insure orthodoxy in faith and morality by exhorting all to fulfill their calling... to the extent of their ability.... Above all, we are most anxious that such ecclesiastical conditions exist that are most pleasing to God. We desire, therefore, that unanimity and concord produce peace which eliminates religious controversy, riot and sedition; and that our holy faith be known to be above reproach everywhere; and, finally, that the priesthood be always invested with the highest dignity, without stain or blemish. [105]

The pronouncement by Theodosius II is probably the first to openly announce the separation of "powers," a separation which clearly implied their association. He asserts his intent to "oversee," to insure—for the honor of God and the stability of the Empire—domestic tranquility through the exclusion of "religious controversy, riot and sedition." He does not act by imperial fiat, but provides the bishops with the opportunity to resolve the matter at hand.

The Council of Ephesus, led by Cyril of Alexandria, responded by condemning Nestorius and adopting the "Cyrillian formulation" of the two natures in Christ. In his *Anathemas* Cyril acknowledged that the Logos is true God, who united Himself to man *kath' henōsin physikēn*. [106] In 451 the Council of Chalcedon reaffirmed the teachings of Cyril. Its

---

[105] Mansi, 4, 1112 f. Cf. the Emperor Zeno's *Henotikon* (482), especially the words "And we write this to you for your assurance, not as producing a new formula of faith" (Bettenson, pp. 125–28).

[106] In Bettenson, pp. 65–66.

famous definition taught that Jesus Christ was one person with two natures. Subsequently, Justinian convoked the Fifth Ecumenical Council (553), which, interestingly enough, condemned the Nestorian "Three Chapters" and Origen.[107] The Emperor also gave expression to "Cyrillian Christology" in his sixth Novel:

The *sacerdotium* and the *imperium* are the greatest gifts to man from God, a bestowal of His supernal *Philanthropia*. The former governs divine matters, the latter presides over and has the diligent care of men. Both proceeding from one and the same source do adorn life. Hence, nothing ought to be more zealously pursued by the Emperor than the dignity of the *sacerdotium* even as priests should make constant petition to God for him. For if the *sacerdotium* is in every way blameless, acting with full confidence before God, while the *imperium* rightly and justly adorns the *politeia* entrusted to him, there may be expected a certain good *symphonia* from which arises all that is beneficial to humanity. Consequently, we have the greatest anxiety for the truth of the dogmas of God and the honor of the *sacerdotium* which, if faithfully upheld by it, can only result in the greatest good from God. And we will secure, also, whatever more good might be added to that which we already possess. This, indeed, will ensue if the beginning of our endeavors is appropriate and pleasing to God. We believe this will occur if unconditional observance is paid to the sacred canons which the glorious and venerable Apostles, eyewitnesses and ministers of the Divine Logos, have transmitted and the Holy Fathers of the Church have preserved and explained.

Justinian did not refer to "Church" and "state"—*ekklēsia* and *basileia*—but to *imperium* and *sacerdotium*, the government and the priesthood or leaders of the churches. Two ministries direct the affairs of the commonwealth or *politeia*. They have a common origin and purpose. The priesthood governs spiritual matters and the government has "the diligent care of men." Hence, one life with two dimensions, one society with a *symphonia* or *consonantia* of powers.

Prof. Kartasheff finds in Justinian's *symphonia* a repudiation of Nestorianism and Monophysitism, both outlawed by Chalcedon. The Chalcedonian doctrine forces us, he says, to apply "the principles of Christology to sociology." Thus, the rejection of Nestorianism is likewise a rejection of any essential dichotomy between *sacerdotium* and *imperium*; and the rejection of Monophysitism is the rejection of the absorption of one power by the other. There are "two powers of one and the same organism." The "moral primacy" belongs to the *sacerdotium*, as "the spirit has necessary primacy over the flesh."[108] It may be true that

---

[107] See Justinian, *Ep. ad Theod.* (*PG* 86, 1045 f.); Dvornik, *Early Christian and Byzantine Political Philosophy* 2, 824–25.

[108] *The Restoration of Holy Russia* (Paris, 1946) pp. 53–54.

many of the Byzantine emperors behaved as if they were the religious heads of the Church, priesthood as well as the government, but caesaropapism in Byzantium was "Christologically" impossible and, in fact, cannot be proven to have existed.[109] Despite the triumph of an emperor during his lifetime, none of the heresies or errors espoused by him ever prevailed; and though he was able to manipulate the hierarchy and "pack" the councils, the orthodoxy of the Church remained an organic and unaltered continuum.

Resistance to imperial tyranny after Chalcedon came usually from the leaders of the people, the monks. Perhaps the most important monastic Fathers were Maximus the Confessor and John of Damascus. The former was the principal figure in the conflict between the *sacerdotium* and Constans II (641–88), an adherent of Monotheletism (i.e., the idea that in Christ but one will existed, the divine). According to Maximus, the imperial law exists to check the divisive and destructive tendencies in man.[110] The Catholic faith, which gives humanity the truth, alone can bring peace among men. Consequently, in doctrinal matters "it belongs to the priesthood to inquire after and define the saving dogmas of the Church." When Maximus was asked: "Are not all Christian emperors also priests?" he replied: "The emperor does not stand at the altar, nor after the consecration of bread does he raise it and cry 'Holy Things to the Holy.' Nor does he baptize or consecrate the myrrh, nor elevate bishops nor ordain presbyters and deacons. . . . "[111]

In the following century, Emperor Leo III (717–41) sided with the iconoclasts and began to persecute the iconodules. John of Damascus protested, saying: "It is not for the emperor to legislate for the Church."[112] He reminded Leo that he was a member of the Church and under obedience, in matters of faith, to the *sacerdotium*. When Leo retorted: "I am a priest," John answered that in his description of the Church St. Paul did not mention rank of "emperor" (1 Cor 12). Then he says that Christians are obedient "in those things which pertain to our daily life . . . but in those things relating to the structure of the Church we have our shepherds who speak to us the word of God and who have shaped the

[109] Kartasheff, p. 75. Against the idea of caesaropapism in Byzantium, see D. J. Geanakoplos, *Byzantine East and Latin West*, pp. 55–83; J. Hussey, *The Byzantine World*, p. 92; G. Ostrogorsky, *History of the Byzantine State*, tr. J. Hussey (New Brunswick, 1957) p. 218; H. Gregoire, "The Byzantine Church," in *Byzantium: An Introduction to East Roman Civilization*, ed. N. H. Baynes and H. St. L. B. Moss (Oxford, 1962) pp. 86–87. Such eminent scholars as Diehl, Baynes, and Runciman believe that caesaropapism was characteristic of Church-state relations in the Christian Roman Empire. It is curious that neither group maintains its position on Christological grounds.

[110] *Ep.* 10 (*PG* 91, 524A). [111] *Rel. mot.* 4 (*PG* 90, 117B).

[112] *De imag.* 2, 12 (*PG* 94, 1296C).

ecclesiastical legislation. We do not alter the eternal decrees which the Fathers have established for us, but maintain the tradition we have received...."[113] "I am not persuaded," he concludes, "that the Church is governed by imperial laws, but only the canons of the Fathers...."[114] Thus John placed the emperor within the Church and under obedience to the Bible, the Fathers, the tradition, the canon law, as well as the *sacerdotium*. He makes these remarks in the teeth of a Eusebian revival.

After the defeat of the iconoclastic emperors, their successors became more restrained and the strength of the *sacerdotium* increased. That increase of strength may be seen in the East by the greater centralization of ecceslesiastical authority in the hands of the "ecumenical" patriarch of Constantinople. He became the symbol of the unity of the episcopate. Perhaps the most important witness to the changed relationship between *sacerdotium* and *imperium* in the ninth-century document known as the *Epanagōgē*, usually attributed to the Macedonian Emperior Basil I (867–86). It states:

Titulus II, 1: The emperor (*basileus*) is a legal authority, a blessing common to all people, who neither punishes with antipathy nor rewards with partiality, but acts without prejudice in all matters which come before him. (2) The aim of the emperor is to guard and secure by his power that which belongs to his office; to recover by sleepless care those that are lost; and to draw by wisdom and justice those that yet remain outside his dominion. (3) The purpose set before the emperor is to confer benefits; hence, he is called benefactor. Yet, should he fail to be beneficent, he becomes, to use the words of the ancients, a forgery (*paracharaxis*) of the royal stamp. The emperor is expected to enforce and maintain not only what is declared in the holy Scriptures, but the dogmas established by the Seven Ecumenical Councils; and, to be sure, the Roman laws of his predecessors."

Section 5 contains a brief exposition of the Chalcedonian Christology, and Titulus II, 6 states that "the emperor must act as the law when there is none written, save that his actions do not violate the canon law." Then Titulus III, 1 announces:

The patriarch is the living and animate image of Christ by deeds and words typifying the truth. (2) The patriarch must, first, guard those whom God has put into his care, piously and soberly; then, he must bring to the unity of orthodoxy, as far as he can, all heretics; and, finally, through the awe which he inspires, through shining and admirable conduct, to lead unbelievers to follow the faith.... (5) The patriarch alone must interpret the canons passed by the Fathers and the decrees enacted by the holy councils. (6) The patriarch must explain and decide those things which have been negotiated and set in place by the early

---

[113] John of Damascus (*PG* 94, 1297C).   [114] John of Damascus (1301D).

Fathers of the ecumenical and provincial (local) councils. . . . (8) As the commonwealth consists, like man, of parts and members, the greatest and most necessary parts of it are the emperor and the patriarch. Wherefore the peace and happiness of subjects, in body and soul, is achieved when the emperor and the priesthood find agreement and concord (symphōnian) in all things. . . . (11) The supervision of all spiritual matters is reserved for the patriarch, but it is delegated to others to which he determines such authority should be given. Also, he himself and he only (or those whom he may appoint) is the arbitrator and judge of all matters concerning repentance, turning from sin, heresy. . . .[115]

Because it seemed to ignore the ecclesiology of confederated episcopal authority,[116] this document is actually subpatristic. It ascribes to the patriarch the title "living and animate image of Christ," which many emperors had previously claimed for themselves and which the Greek Fathers continuously resisted from the very inception of the Constantinian *renovatio*. The Hellenistic title was a vestige of the Empire's pagan past, a past which Eusebius was unwilling to surrender and from which many Byzantines could not entirely escape. Nevertheless, such an ascription to the patriarch does illustrate the capitulation of the *imperium* to the *ekklēsia*.

CONCLUSION

The fight against the Eusebian political theology was for the Greek Fathers in fact the struggle against Hellenism and for the Christian economy. The foundation of Hellenistic kingship was the classical ontology or metaphysics, which compelled the inferior Logos of God to mediate being and becoming, timeless simplicity and temporal multiplicity. The king, *basileus*, *imperator*, as the *mimēsis* of the Divine, ruled the earthly replica of the heavenly kingdom of God. According to this theory, the Divine sent intermediary beings, most especially the *deuteros theos*, the Logos, to instruct His creatures. Thus, with Eusebius, the *imperium Romanum christianum* merely raised the standard of Hellenized Rome, to which was added the labarum. In other words, Constantine and his successors ruled the Church established by the Son of God. The emperor, as the analogy of God the Father, is necessarily the superior of the priesthood, which represents only the inferior Logos. If Eusebius was right, the Constantinian *renovatio* implied the utter devastation of the Christian economy.

On the other hand, the Greek Fathers taught that the Incarnate Logos was true God and true man, the two natures united without confusion or change. Since Christ as God was the equal of the Father, then, politically

[115] In *Jus Graeco-Romanum* 4, ed. K. E. Zachariae von Lugenthal (Leipzig, 1852) 181 ff.

translated, this Christology meant that the Christian Roman Empire was a religio-political organism governed by a *symphōnia* or "dyarchy of powers": the spiritual and doctrinal power of the Empire the Fathers put into the hands of the *sacerdotium* representing the divinity of Christ, while they placed within the competence of the emperor, as representing His humanity, all things pertaining to the "political" and civil matters. The priesthood was superior to the *imperium* by virtue of the former's spiritual (divine) function within the Empire. Thus the Fathers snapped the link which the ancients conceived to exist between monarchy—which many Fathers considered the best form of government[116]—and monotheism. The Emperors were the Christian equivalent of the Hebrew kings. Not an unlikely comparison, since the Fathers believed the Church—to which the Empire was united as one society—to be the New Israel. Indeed, East Rome was a "holy empire" with a transcendental purpose and hope which the Hellenizers never understood—the proclamation of the abiding and redeeming presence in history of the resurrected Christus-Deus.[117]

These are the ideas we tried to support with several arguments: that the "development" of Christology was accompanied by greater definition of sacerdotal and imperial authority. We did not find it irrelevant to note that some Fathers completely rejected the mating of Church and empire. These were the most sensitive about the limitations of the *imperium* and the dignity of the *sacerdotium*—indeed, about the antithesis between the Church and the world. Again, the elaboration of Christian ontology and Christology appeared together, and both contradicted the theology

[116] According to Greek patristic ecclesiology, each bishop and his flock constitute "the Body of Christ." Each bishop "recapitulates" in himself the flock which he paternally governs. Each bishop is "the image of Christ." The unity of the churches is essentially a mystery analogous to the unity of the persons of the Trinity. They are ontologically one while empirically many. Historically, they are united by a common origin, faith, law, and love. Yet, for administrative purposes, the churches were grouped into districts or dioceses, while "primacy" belonged to the great and ancient sees of Christianity. "The first throne belongs to the bishops of Rome," wrote Theodore of Studion, "the second, to Constantinople, then, Alexandria, Antioch, and Jerusalem. This is the pentarchic authority of the Church. These compose the tribunal of divine doctrine" (*Ep.* 129 [*PG* 99, 1417BC]). Therefore, the exalted place given to the patriarch of Constantinople by such documents as the *Epanagōgē* must be explained by circumstance rather than ecclesiology. Dvornik suggests that the ascendence of Constantinople in the Byzantine Empire was the result of many things, e.g., its competition with Rome, which led some to oppose to the See of Peter the claim that St. Andrew, "the first-called," was the evangelizer of ancient Byzantium; the desire to give the capital of the Empire apostolic origin; and, probably, the Carolingian *renovatio* (*The Idea of Apostolicity in Byzantium and the Legend of the Apostle Andrew* [Cambridge, Mass., 1958]).

[117] Gregory of Nazianzus, *Theol. orat.* 2, 2 (*PG* 36, 76AB).

and ontology of Eusebius and his teacher Origen. Is it not curious, we asked, that when Origenism (i.e., Hellenized Christianity) ceased to be a serious problem to the Church, such a document as the *Epanagōgē* appeared to proclaim the patriarch of Constantinople "the living and animate law" of the *societas christiana*? Is it not also true that the victory of the patristic political Christology also meant the defeat or, more accurately, the Christianization of Hellenism? Is it not true, moreover, that the Byzantine *exousia* evolved away from the political theology of Eusebius, which had for many of the early Byzantine emperors defined the Constantinian *renovatio*? In a word, we do not think that the evidence sustains the opinion that Eusebius was the "author" of Christian Rome's political theory. There is simply no logic to the idea that the Church which feared and incessantly denounced the classical *scientia* would accept as her political theorist the philosophy of a man who was threatening to put the asp to her bosom.

THE EDICT OF MILAN (313)

A DEFENCE OF ITS TRADITIONAL AUTHORSHIP
AND DESIGNATION ([1])

This paper is intended as a refutation of the modern paradoxographers (2) who have been seduced by the temptation of trying to

(1) I am deeply indebted to the John Simon Guggenheim Foundation for indispensable support (in 1954-55 and 1966-67) of my study of Byzantine intellectual history, the *Mind of Byzantium*, of which this paper forms a part.

I acknowledge gratefully assistance from my colleague, Professor Lynn White, Jr., Director of the Center for Medieval and Renaissance Studies, UCLA, who has made a number of valuable suggestions.

The most convenient text of the Edict is to be found in Lactance, *De la mort des persécuteurs*, 48, ed. with French translation and notes by Jacques Moreau, *Sources Chrétiennes*, 39, vols. 1-2 (Paris, 1954); and in Greek in Eusebius, HE, 10, 5, 2-14, ed. Eduard Schwartz, *Die griechischen christlichen Schriftsteller der ersten drei Jahrhunderte*, 9, 2 (Berlin 1908); with English translation by J. E. L. Oulton and H. J. Lawlor, *Eusebius, the Ecclesiastical History*, 2 (Loeb Classical Library, 1932); with French translation by Gustave, Bardy, *Sources chrétiennes*, 55 (Paris, 1958). P. R. Coleman-Norton, *Roman State & Christian Church*, 1 (London, 1966), 30-35, gives an English translation of Lactantius's version of the Edict and Eusebius's variants therefrom.

Of the vast bibliography on the Edict, I cite the following works, both for their importance in the history of the subject and for their references to the older literature, which it is profitless to repeat: Mario Agnes, "Alcune considerazioni sul cosiddetto 'Editto' di Milano", *Studi romani*, 13 (1965), 424-32: does not discuss the "problem" of the Edict; Salvatore Calderone, *Costantino e il cattolicesimo*, 1 (*Pubblicazioni dell' Istituto di storia dell' Università di Messina*, 3 [Florence, 1962]); Mario Amelotti, "Da Diocleziano a Costantino, note in tema di costituzioni imperiali", *Studia et documenta historiae et iuris*, 27 (1961), 241-323; Maurilio Adriani, "La storicità dell' Editto di Milano", *Studi Romani*, 2 (1954), 18-32; Herbert Nesselhauf, "Das Toleranzgesetz des Licinius", *Historisches Jahrbuch*, 74 (1954), 44-61; Andreas Alföldi, *The conversion of Constantine* (Oxford, 1948), 37 f., 129 n. 13; J. R. Palanque, "A propos du prétendu Édit de Milan", *Byzantion*, 10 (1935), 607-16; Norman H. Baynes, *Constantine the Great and the Christian Church* (*Proceedings of the British Academy*, 15 [London, 1929]), 11, 69-74 (the lecture was delivered in 1930); Richard Laqueur, "Die beiden Fassungen des sog. Toleranzedikts von Mailand", ΕΠΙΤΥΜΒΙΟΝ *Heinrich Swoboda dargebracht* (Reichenberg, 1927), 132-41: I see no way to reconcile with texts or logic L's tortuous theory (n. b. p. 140) that Eusebius's version of the Edict included interpolations from Maximinus's rescript to Sabinus (HE, 9, 9a, 1-9), which L deems to have been issued *before* the Edict but dishonestly represented by the Constantinian party (and Eusebius) as Maximinus's reply to the Edict (HE, 9, 9, 12f.; 9, 9a, 10-12); John R. Knipfing, "Das angebliche 'Mailänder Edikt' v. J. 313 im Lichte der neueren Forschung", *Zeitschrift für Kirchengeschichte*, 40 (1922), 206-18; Émile Chénon, "Les séquences juridiques de l'Édit de Milan (313), *Nouvelle Revue historique de droit français et étranger*, 38 (1914-15), 255-63; Pierre Batiffol, *La paix constantinienne et le catholicisme*, 2d ed. (Paris, 1914), 203-67, n. b. 229 ff.; G. L. Perugi, "La fonte giuridica dell' Editto di Milano", *Roma e l'Oriente*, 6, fasc. 35-36 (1913), 13-40: chiefly of interest for detailed references to the earlier bibliography; Carlo Santucci, "L'Editto di Milano nei riguardi del diritto", *Nuovo Bullettino di Archeologia cristiana*, 19 (1913), 71-75; Joseph Wittig, "Das Toleranzreskript von Mailand 313", *Konstantin der Grosse und seine Zeit*, ed. Franz J. Dölger (Freiburg im Br., 1913), 40-65; Valerian Şesan, *Die Religionspolitik der christlich-röm. Kaiser von Konstantin d. Gr. bis Theodosius d. Gr. (313-380) (Kirche und Staat im römisch-byzantinischen Reiche*

215

prove that, despite his friendly disposition towards the Christian Church, Constantine did not issue the * Edict of Milan (313) but that Licinius, whom Eusebius condemns as a persecutor ** (HE, 10, 8, 8-9, 9; see n. 11 below), did. This is a titillating conceit, heightened by the additional paradox, that Constantine did not even participate in the Edict (Seeck, *loc. cit.* in n. 2: "diese [Urkunde] ist erstens kein Edikt, zweitens nicht in Mailand erlassen, drittens nicht von Konstantin"). But, except possibly for the second proposition in this quotation from Seeck, these elements of the modern paradoxographic tradition concerning Constantine can be justified by neither the sources nor *a priori* considerations.

On the contrary, I hope to show (I) that Constantine was one o the authors of the Edict, (II) that he must be regarded as having published it in his part of the Empire, (III) that his version of it was in essentials identical with, or very similar, to that reproduced by Eusebius in HE, 10, 5, 2-14 and by Lactantius in MP, 48, (IV) that these two texts not only constitute the Edict of Milan, but also are properly so designated, and (V) that the celebrated phrase, *instinctu*

---

seit Konstantin dem Grossen und bis zum Falle Konstantinopels, 1 [Czernowitz, 1911]), 128-237; Guglielmo Schnyder, "L'Editto di Milano, ed i recenti studi critici che lo riguardano". *Dissertazioni della Pontificia Accademia Romana di Archeologia*, S. 2, 8 (1903), 149-79; A. Crivellucci, "L'Editto di Milano", *Studi Storici*, I (1892), 239-50; *idem*, "Intorno all' Editto di Milano", *ibid.*, 4 (1895), 267-73. A. H. M. Jones, *The Later Roman Empire (284-602)*, I (Oxford, 1964), 80 f., simply describes it as an edict without discussion. Heinz Kähler, "Konstantin 313", *Jahrbuch des deutschen archäologischen Instituts*, 67, (1952). 1-30, does not deal with the Edict, but with proof that the colossal statue of Constantine. fragments of which are preserved in the Palazzo dei Conservatori, was produced ca. 313 and set up in the (western) apse of the Basilica of (Maxentius) Constantine.

(2) The *Fons et origo* of this school was Otto Seeck, "Das sogenannte Edikt von Mailand", *Zeitschrift für Kirchengeschichte*, 12 (1891), 381-86, whose thesis was taken up enthusiastically by Henri Grégoire in *Byzantion*, 7 (1932), 645-61; 10 (1935), 616-19 (see also bibliography in Moreau, SC, 39, 1, 159 f.); and then in three papers by Jacques Moreau, "Zur Religionspolitik Konstantins des Grossen", *Annales Universitatis Saraviensis, Philosophie et Lettres*, 1 (1952), 160-68 (*idem, Scripta minora*, ed. Walter Schmitthenner, *Annales U. Saraviensis, Reihe: Philosophische Fakultät*, 1 [Heidelberg, 1964], 106-13); "Les 'Litterae Licinii'", AUS, 2 (1935), 100-105 (*Scripta minora*, 99-105, n. b. 102: "Licinius, et Licinius seul, est l'auteur de l'acte de tolérance de 313"); "Vérité historique et propagande politique chez Lactance et dans la Vita Constantini", AUS, 4 (1955), 89-97 (*Scripta minora*, 135-43); and in his notes on the MP in SC, 39, 2, 456-64, n. b. 458. The most recent exponent of these views about the Edict is Joseph Vogt, *Constantin der Grosse* (see next note), 168 f., 284. Cf. n. 13 below.

Seeck and Vogt, however, were content to attack the view that Constantine was the author of the Edict or issued it in his own realm. They accept the other elements of the historical tradition about Constantine (the conversion, etc.), which Grégoire and Moreau reject.

* To which I will refer below as the Edict or, occasionally, to avoid ambiguity, as the Edict of 313.

** HE = Eusebius's *Ecclesiastical History* (ἐκκλησιαστικὴ ἱστορία).

MP = Lactantius's *De mortibus persecutorum*.

divinitatis, in the inscription on the Arch of Constantine was in all probability derived from the Edict, which the Roman senators took delight in imitating because by so doing they were enabled to pay a particularly delicate compliment to the Emperor Constantine, whom they *knew* to be its author.

In venturing to reopen these time-worn questions once again, I lay little claim to originality, and rely on only one small point, which' however, I believe to be decisive. My cardinal principle here, and in my whole approach to historical research in general, is that the ancient and mediaeval historians who were contemporaries of the events they report, especially when uncontradicted by other authorities of equal weight, deserve considerably more respect than certain scholars have in recent years been willing to accord them.

I have reference above all to Eusebius, who, after a generation of abuse at the hands of scholars of high repute, is at last being vindicated (3) against his detractors. From the first, I have agreed with Norman H. Baynes, who was the most important of the earlier champions of Eusebius, that the latter's account of the life of Constantine is not to be rejected except for the most compelling reasons, and I

(3) Of the many excellent scholars who have devoted themselves to this task, the latest is Friedhelm Winkelmann, beginning with his dissertation, *Die Vita Constantini des Eusebius, ihre Authentizität, ihre Textbezeugung* (Halle, 1959); then in *Die Textbezeugung der Vita Constantini des Eusebius von Caesarea (Texte und Untersuchungen*, 84 [Berlin, 1962]), and also in a number of articles: "Die Beurteilung des Eusebius von Cäsarea und seiner Vita Constantini im griechischen Osten, ein Beitrag zur Untersuchung der griechischen hagiographischen Vitae Constantini", *Byzantinistische Beiträge* (Berlin, 1964), 91-119; "Zur Geschichte des Authentizitätsproblems der Vita Constantini", *Klio*, 40 (1962), 187-243: an admirable and fair-minded survey of the literature; "Konstantins Religionspolitik und ihre Motive im Urteil der literarischen Quellen des iv. und v. Jahrhunderts", *Acta Antiqua Academiae Scientiarum Hungaricae*, 9 (1961), 239-56. Among his most notable predecessors *nota bene*: Joseph Vogt, "Pagans and Christians in the family of Constantine the Great", *The conflict between paganism and Christianity in the fourth century*, ed. Arnaldo Momigliano (Oxford, 1963), 38-54; *idem, Constantin der Grosse*, 2d ed. (Munich, 1960); *idem*, "Constantinus der Grosse", *Reallexikon für Antike und Christentum*, 3 (Stuttgart, 1957), 306-79; *idem*, "Die constantinische Frage", Comitato Internazionale di Scienze Storiche, *X Congresso Internazionale di Scienze Storiche* (Rome), *Relazioni*, 6 (Florence, 1955), 731-79; Kurt Aland, *Kirchengeschichtliche Entwürfe* (Gütersloh, 1960), 165-239, including a reprint of his paper, "Die religiöse Haltung Kaiser Konstantins", from *Studia Patristica (Texte und Untersuchungen*, 63 [Berlin, 1957]); Heinz Kraft, *Kaiser Konstantins religiöse Entwicklung (Beiträge zur historischen Theologie*, 20 [Tübingen, 1955]); Johannes Straub, "Konstantins Verzicht auf den Gang zum Kapitol", *Historia*, 4 (1955), 297-313; *idem, Vom Herrscherideal in der Spätantike (Forschungen zur Kirchen- und Geistesgeschichte*, 18 [Stuttgart, 1939, reprinted 1964]); Hermann Dörries, *Das Selbstzeugnis Kaiser Konstantins (Abhandlungen der Akademie der Wissenschaften in Göttingen, Philologisch-historische Klasse*, 3. F., 34 [Göttingen, 1954]); A.H.M. Jones, "Notes on the genuineness of the Constantinian documents in Eusebius's Life of Constantine", *Journal of ecclesiastical history*, 5 (1954), 196-200 (With an appendix by T.C. Skeat); A.H.M. Jones, *Constantine and the conversion of Europe* (reprinted, N.Y., 1962); Friedrich Vittinghoff, "Eusebius als Verfasser der Vita Constantini", *Rheinisches Museum*, N.F., 96 (1953), 330-73; Andrew Alföldi, *The conversion of Constantine and pagan Rome* (Oxford, 1948); Norman H. Baynes, *Constantine the Great* (n. 1 above).

rejoice that a new generation of critics has been piling up impressive evidence in support of this position.

Specifically, with regard to the Edict, I maintain that the critical passage on which the entire decision rests, is to be found in Eusebius's preface to a collection of legal texts (HE, 10, 5, 1):

Φέρε δή, λοιπὸν καὶ τῶν βασιλικῶν διατάξεων Κωνσταντίνου καὶ Λικιννίου τὰς ἐκ τῆς Ῥωμαίων φωνῆς μεταληφθείσας ἑρμηνείας παραθώμεθα.

ΑΝΤΙΓΡΑΦΟΝ ΒΑΣΙΛΙΚΩΝ ΔΙΑΤΑΞΕΩΝ ΕΚ ΡΩΜΑΙΚΗΣ ΓΑΩΤΤΗΣ ΜΕΤΑΑΗΦΘΕΙΣΩΝ.

(i. e., "Now, then, let us quote the translations that have been made from the Latin of the imperial laws of Constantine and Licinius. *Copy of the imperial laws translated from the Latin language*").

The first of these laws is the Edict, which begins (HE, 10, 5, 4), after a brief introductory paragraph as follows:

Ὁπότε εὐτυχῶς ἐγὼ Κωνσταντῖνος ὁ Αὔγουστος κἀγὼ Λικίννιος ὁ Αὔγουστος ἐν τῇ Μεδιολάνῳ ἐληλύθειμεν καὶ πάντα ὅσα πρὸς τὸ λυσιτελὲς καὶ τὸ χρήσιμον τῷ κοινῷ διέφερεν, ἐν ζητήσει ἔσχομεν, ταῦτα μεταξὺ τῶν λοιπῶν ἅτινα ἐδόκει ἐν πολλοῖς ἅπασιν ἐπωφελῆ εἶναι, μᾶλλον δὲ ἐν πρώτοις διατάξαι ἐδογματίσαμεν, οἷς ἡ πρὸς τὸ θεῖον αἰδώς τε καὶ τὸ σέβας ἐνείχετο, τοῦτ' ἔστιν, ὅπως δῶμεν καὶ τοῖς Χριστιανοῖς καὶ πᾶσιν ἐλευθέραν αἵρεσιν τοῦ ἀκολουθεῖν τῇ θρησκείᾳ ᾗ δ' ἂν βουληθῶσιν, ὅπως ὅ τί ποτέ ἐστιν θειότητος καὶ οὐρανίου πράγματος, ἡμῖν καὶ πᾶσι τοῖς ὑπὸ τὴν ἡμετέραν ἐξουσίαν διάγουσιν εὐμενὲς εἶναι δυνηθῇ.

Eusebius differs from the Latin (see below) principally in mis-'reading *omnibus* for *hominibus* and substituting a binomial expression ὅπως ὅ τί ποτέ ἐστιν θειότητος καὶ οὐρανίου πράγματος, for the simpler *quicquid < est > diuinitatis*. Then, in a reversal of technique, he reduces the Latin *placatum ac propitium* to a single adjective in Greek. In my translation, I have followed the Latin:

" When I Constantine Augustus and I Licinius Augustus (4) had met under happy auspices at Milan and discussed all questions pertaining to the general welfare and the security of the state, we decided that,

---

(4) It makes no difference to my argument whether Emperor Maximinus's name was included in the pro-oimion of the Edict, as some contend. But I doubt that it was, since none of the texts above quoted refer to it. Knipfing, ZKG, 40 (1922), 213-15, lists authorities on both sides of this question. Moreau, SC, 39, 2, 457, agrees that Maximinus was not mentioned. For the latter's defeat by Licinius on April 30, 313, near Adrianople, in the Campus Ergenus (MP, 47), erroneously called Campus Serenus by Lactantius (MP, 46, 9), see Moreau, SC, 39, 1, 130, 28 f.; Grégoire, *Byzantion*, 13 (1938), 585.

among the other things we knew would benefit the majority of men, first consideration should be given to the regulation of the affairs which affect the worship of divinity. [Hence, we resolved] to grant the Christians and all [others] the right to follow freely whatever religion they wished, so that whatever divinity there be in heaven might be favorable and propitious to us and to all of our subjects. "

In all material respects, then, Eusebius's Greek translation is a faithful and accurate rendering of the Latin text of the Edict as represented by Lactantius in his MP 48, 2-12. The fidelity of the Greek to the Latin can be illustrated by the corresponding portion of the Edict as it appears in Lactantius:

Cum feliciter tam ego [quam] Constantinus Augustus quam etiam ego Licinius Augustus apud Mediolanum conuenissemus atque uniuersa quæ ad commoda et securitatem publicam pertinerent, in tractatu haberemus, hæc inter cetera quæ uidebamus pluribus hominibus profutura, uel in primis ordinanda esse credidimus, quibus diuinitatis reuerentia continebatur, ut daremus et christianis et omnibus liberam potestatem sequendi religionem quam quisque uoluisset, quo quicquid < est > diuinitatis in sede cælesti, nobis atque omnibus qui sub potestate nostra sunt constituti, placatum ac propitium possit existere.

Despite close agreement on all essential matters, there remain enough minor discrepancies (5) (like those noted above) between Eusebius's Greek and Lactantius's Latin to demonstrate that Eusebius's source could not have been the Edict as found in MP, 48. Hence, we have at least two separate and independent witnesses to the wording of this important document, which corroborate each other most impressively on all the principal questions at issue although neither was copied or transcribed from the other. The exact relationship, however, between HE, 10, 5, 2-4, and MP, 48 cannot be precisely determined.

---

(5) For a list of these with discussion, see I.A. Heikel, *De Constantini imperatoris scriptis edendis* (Helsinki, 1916), 17-28; Wittig, *loc.cit.* (n. 1 above), 58-61; Şesan, *Kirche und Staat*, 1, 169-73, 226 f. Cf. also Moreau, *Scripta minora*, 103 f., nn. 27 f.; and *idem*, SC, 39, 2, 456 ff. Şesan, *op. cit.*, 175 ff., 189-216, concludes from the differences between the two texts, especially from the omission in MP, 48 of the preface to the Edict as given in HE, 10, 5, 2, that Eusebius had translated directly from the original Edict of Milan, not from Licinius's version thereof (as in MP, 48) or any other such copy. Somewhat similarly, J. Maurice, "Note sur le préambule placé par Eusèbe en tête de l'Édit de Milan", *Bulletin d'ancienne littérature et d'archéologie chrétiennes*, 4 (1914), 45-47, looks upon the presence of this preface in HE, 10, 5, 2 f., and its omission in MP, 48, as proof that Eusebius' text represents the *Litterae Constantini*, which Constantine had addressed to the governors of the Western provinces, as contrasted with the *Litterae Licinii*, which Licinius promulgated in his part of the Empire.

In view of the plain meaning and obvious implications of the texts quoted, it is a great disservice to historical scholarship to be little, minimize, or ignore them; and my principal service in what follows is merely to insist not only that the passages I have cited from the HE and MP mean what they say but also that they cannot be, and have not been, refuted.

I.-II. *Constantine co-author of the Edict and his promulgation of it in his own realm.*

These excerpts from Eusebius and Lactantius prove beyond all doubt (1) that the Edict was issued by both Constantine and Licinius and (2) that their versions of it (on this point see p. 26 below), as posted individually and separately by Constantine and Licinius in their respective jurisdictions, must have been identical or nearly so. Otherwise, Eusebius would not have included this text among what he calls the laws both Constantine and Licinius, nor would both emperors have stated in so many words, as they do (« I Constantine Augustus and I Licinius Augustus »), that they had actively collaborated in this project. In other words, these passages from the HE and MP make it altogether impossible to deny that Constantine was one of the authors of this ordinance, or that he published it as a law for the portion of the Empire over which he ruled. (See also notes 7 a and 10 below.)

These conclusions follow inevitably from the opening sentence of the Edict (as quoted above), in which the two emperors declare that their chief objective was to grant religious freedom to all of their subjects, in order that by so doing they might win divine favor for the Empire and all of its inhabitants. It is difficult to imagine how Constantine could have discussed these matters with Licinius in Milan and then drafted, or assented to, a law couched in these terms, as both Eusebius and Lactantius agree that he did, without enacting it in his own name for his own part of the Empire.

It is much more likely that Constantine arranged the conference in Milan, as well as the matrimonial alliance between his half-sister and Licinius, at least in part so as to win over his imperial colleague to the policy of religious toleration which he had already adopted. Whether this really was his aim or not, it is inconceivable that Constantine, the first and greatest imperial benefactor (6) of the Christian

(6) For the gifts, privileges, and immunities Constantine bestowed upon the Christian Church, see Ludwig Voelkl, *Die Kirchenstiftungen des Kaisers Konstantin im Lichte des*

Church, and in all probability its most influential patron in the early centuries, apart from its Founder, could have failed in his own realm to promulgate this great charter of Christian liberty and privilege (7),

römischen Sakralrechts (Arbeitsgemeinschaft für Forschung des Landes Nordrhein-Westfalen, Geisteswissenschaften, 117 [Cologne-Opladen, 1964]); Clémence Dupont, "Les donations dans les constitutions de Constantin", *Revue internationale des droits de l'antiquité*, S. 3, 9 (1962), 291-324, n. b. 319 ff.; Biondo Biondi, *Il diritto romano cristiano*, 1 (Milan, 1952), 21-30, 358, 361 f.; Jean Gaudemet, "La législation religieuse de Constantin", *Revue d'histoire de l'Église de France*, 33 (1947), 25-61.

On Constantine as a lawgiver in general, see Gudrun Stühff, *Vulgarrecht im Kaiserrecht unter besonderer Berücksichtigung der Gesetzgebung Konstantins des Grossen (Forschungen zum römischen Recht*, 21 [Weimar, 1966]); Clémence Dupont, "Les successions dans les constitutions de Constantin", *Ivra*, 15 (1964), 57-116; four volumes by *eadem*, published in Lille: *La réglementation économique dans les constitutions de Constantin* (1963); *Le droit criminel dans les constitutions de Constantin, Les infractions* (1953); *Les peines* (1955); *Les constitutions de Constantin et le droit privé au début du IVe siècle* (1937); Arnold Ehrhardt, "Constantin d. Gr. Religions-politik und Gesetzgebung", *Zeitschrift der Savigny-Stiftung für Rechtsgeschichte, Romanistische Abteilung*, 72 (1955), 154-90; Joseph Vogt, "Zur Frage des christlichen Einflusses auf die Gesetzgebung Konstantins des Grossen", *Münchener Beiträge zur Papyrusforschung und antiken Rechtsgeschichte*, 35, *Festschrift für Leopold Wenger*, 2 (Munich, 1945), 118-48. Cf. E. Volterra, "Quelques remarques sur le style des Constitutions de Constantin", *Droits de l'antiquité et de sociologie juridique, Mélanges Henri Lévy-Bruhl (Publications de l'Institut de droit romain de l'Université de Paris*, 17 [Paris, 1959]), 325-34; Manlio Sargenti, *Il diritto privato nella legislazione di Costantino; persone e famiglia (Pubblicazioni dell' Istituto di diritto romano dei diritti dell' Oriente mediterraneo e di storia del diritto*, 3 [Milan, 1938]).

The vast literature on the *episcopalis audientia* is summarized by Max Kaser, *Das römische Zivilprozessrecht* (Iwan von Müller, Walter Otto, Hermann Bengtson, edd., *Handbuch der Altertumswissenschaft*, 10, 3, 4 [Munich, 1966]), 527-29; see also J. N. Bakhuizen van den Brink, "Episcopalis audientia", *Mededelingen der koninklijke Nederlandse Akademie van Wetenschappen, Afdeling Letterkunde, Nieuwe Reeks*, 19, 8 (Amsterdam, 1956), 245-301.

(7) Émile Chénon, « Les conséquences juridiques de l'édit de Milan, » *Nouvelle Revue historique de droit français et étranger*, 38 (1914-15), 255-63, suggests that the Edict has great significance because it constitutes the first formal recognition of the Christian Church as a legal corporation authorized to receive, hold, and administer property. It is possible that it should be so regarded since Constantine's order to Anulinus (HE, 10, 5, 15-17) is limited in scope (see section 4 below) and does not connect the grant of these rights with freedom of worship. But this is not altogether certain, nor have scholars been able to explain satisfactorily the legal basis or origin of the system by which the Christian communities acquired and held real estate and other property during the first three centuries of their existence.

In view of these uncertainties, I refrain from pressing this argument, despite its appeal. On the legal status implied by Constantine's Edict to Anulinus, see Ehrhardt, *loc. cit.* (in previous n.), 172 f., who takes (τὸ δίκαιον) here as the equivalent of *corpus* or σῶμα (corporation), though it is nevertheless interesting, and surely significant, that Eusebius uses this term in preference to σῶμα, which occurs in his translation of the Edict (HE, 10, 5, 10-12). See note 48 below.

On this topic see the following (with references to the older literature): Giannetto Longo, "Sul diritto sepolcrale romano", *Ivra*, 15 (1964), 137-58; *idem*, "Communità cristiane primitive e 'res religiosae'," *Bullettino dell' Istituto di diritto romano*, N.S., 18-19 = 59-60 (1956), 237-57; W. W. Buckland, *A text-book of Roman Law from Augustus to Justinian*, 3rd ed. by Peter Stein (Cambridge, England, 1963), 177-79; Charles Saumagne, "Corpus Christianorum," *Revue internationale des droits de l'antiquité*, S. 3, 7 (1960), 437-78; S. 3, 8 (1961), 257-79; Max Kaser, *Das römische Privatrecht* (Iwan von Müller, etc., edd., *Handbuch der Altertumswissenschaft*, 10, 3, 3, 2 [Munich, 1959]), 105, nn. 17-22, 106, 348, n. 21; Arnold Ehrhardt, "Das Corpus Christi und die Korporationen im spät-römischen Recht," *Zeitschrift der Savigny-Stiftung für Rechtsgeschichte, Romanistische Abteilung*, 70 (1953), 299-

which explicitly and systematically enacted into law the principles of which he was the most notable exponent.

If this reasoning be sound, as I believe it is, we are compelled to assume that Constantine would have taken action by means of a separate Edict of his own, specifically addressed to the people or to an official of his own portion of the Empire. This he would have had to do because, as it has been proved conclusively, in the years during which Constantine and Licinius were co-emperors (and also from 338 to 468), a law like Licinius's edition of the Edict (MP, 48), published as it was Nicomedia (MP, 48, 1), was valid only for the jurisdiction of the emperor who issued it, i.e., for Licinius and in his own *pars imperii*. It had no validity outside of his domain, and would not have taken effect in the regions ruled by Constantine. For in legal documents of this kind, the names of other emperors often listed in the preface or at other points in the text did not signify that the law applied to the entire Empire (7a).

In each case, the place of emission recorded in a constitution indicates the sphere in which it was intended to operate. Hence, if it was posted in the Eastern half of the Empire (like MP, 48), it had binding effect only there and not in the West as well. Only very rarely, and under the most unusual circumstances, which do not affect the general

347; 71 (1954), 25-40; Alexander Philipsborn, "Der Begriff der juristischen Person im römischen Recht", *ibid.*, 71 (1954), 41-70; Hans-Rudolf Hagemann, *Die Stellung der Piae Causae nach justinianischem Rechte* (*Basler Studien zur Rechtswissenschaft*, 37 [Basel, 1953]); Maurizio Borda, "Collegia funeraticia", *Enciclopedia Cattolica*, 3 (1949), 1950-52; Giuseppe Bovini, *La proprietà ecclesiastica e la condizione giuridica della chiesa in età precostantiniana* (Milan, 1949); *idem*, s.v. Chiesa, A, VI, "Posizione giuridica della Chiesa fino a Giustiniano," *Enciclopedia Cattolica*, 3 (1949), 1504-6, who gives the bibliography of the subject and a summary of the leading theories up to his time; Gerda Krüger, *Die Rechtsstellung der vorkonstantinischen Kirchen* (*Kirchenrechtliche Abhandlungen*, 115-16 [Stuttgart, 1935]), 234-42; J. P. Waltzing, "Collegia," DACL, 3, 2 (1914), 2107-40; Carlo Carassai, "La politica religiosa di Costantino il Grande e la proprietà della Chiesa," *Archivio della R. Società Romana di Storia Patria*, 24 (1901), 95-157. Cf. also Fernand de Visscher, *Le droit des tombeaux romains* (Milan, 1963), 261-76.

(7a) Against the older view that the constitutions of every emperor applied automatically to the entire Empire, without specific enactment in each part thereof, it has now been proved that imperial legislation (from 338 on) was valid only for the jurisdiction of the emperor who issued it, i. e., in his own *pars imperii*. This principle was established by M. Antonio de Dominicis, « Il problema dei rapporti burocratico-legislativi tra 'occidente ed oriente' nel basso impero romano alla luce delle inscriptiones e subscripticnes delle costituzioni imperiali », *Istituto Lombardo di scienze e lettere, Rendiconti, Classe di lettere e Scienze Morali e Storiche*, S. 3, 18=87 (1954), 329-487. Similar conclusions were reached independently by Jean Gaudemet, « Le partage législatif au Bas-Empire d'après un ouvrage récent », SDHI, 21(1955), 319-31; *idem*, « Le partage législatif dans la seconde moitié du ivᵉ siècle », *Studi in onore di Pietro de Francisci*, 2 (Milan, 1956), 317-54 (with particular attention to the years 364-95); *idem*, *La formation du droit séculier et du droit de l'Église au IVᵉ et Vᵉ siècles*, (*Institut de droit romain de l'Université de Paris*, 15 [Paris, 1957]), 17-26; *idem*, « Orthodoxie et interpolations (à propos de CTh. xvi, 1, 4 et xvi, 4, 1) », *Mélanges en l'honneur de*

rule under consideration, did an emperor of one *pars imperii* address a law to an official in another. Similarly, if two emperors wished to enact the same regulation, they would and did promulgate separate laws for this purpose, each in his own territory, as Licinius did in his Edict (MP, 48) and Constantine inevitably would have done in his.

Less important than this basic matter of Constantine's direct personal connection with the Edict are two subsidiary questions which unfortunately cannot be answered categorically.

(1) The first of these concerns the date and place of promulgation of Constantine's own copy of the Edict, as distinguished. from that which Licinius, as we learn from MP, 48, 1, posted in Nicomedia on June 13, 313 (8) in Constantine's name and his own. None of the extant sources gives any precise information on these matters. But it seems logical to assume that Constantine must have issued his version of the Edict in Rome some time after his victory over Maxentius on October 28, 312, either (*a*) late in 312 (9) and prior to his

---

S. E. le Cardinal André Jullien, Revue de droit canonique, 10, 3-4; 11, 1 (1960-61), 163 f.; *idem, Institutions de l'antiquité* (Paris, 1967), 673; Giovanni Gualandi, « Privilegi imperiali e dualità legislativa nel Basso Impero alla luce di alcuni testi di Libanio », *Archivio giuridico « Filippo Serafini »*, s. 6, 25=156 (1959), 5-34; Ernst Levy, « West-östliches Vulgarrecht und Justinian », ZSS, RA, 76 (1959), 2-5.

(8) Moreau in his translation, SC, 39, 1, 131 f., translates *die Iduum Iuniarum* by *le quinze juin*, momentarily forgetting the school-boy rule that the Ides fall on the thirteenth, except in March, May, July, and October, although he subsequently gives the date correctly, SC, 39, 2, 464.

The terminus *a quo* is October 28, 312, the day of Constantine's victory over Maxentius. This traditional date, called into question by Patrick Bruun, "The Battle of the Milvian Bridge," *Hermes*, 88 (1960), 361-65; *idem, Studies in Constantinian chronology (Numismatic Notes and Monographs*, 146 [New York, 1961]), 7, who pushes it back one year to October 28, 311, has, however, been vindicated by Roberto Andreotti, "Recenti contributi alla cronologia costantiniana," *Latomus*, 23 [(1964), 537-42; Maria R. Alföldi, *Die constantinische Goldprägung* (Mainz, 1963), 32; *eadem* and Dietmar Kienast, "Zu P. Bruuns Datierung der Schlacht an der Milvischen Brücke," *Jahrbuch für Numismatik und Geldgeschichte*, 11 (1961), 33-41.

(9) Calderone, *Costantino* (n. 1 above), 157-64; Şesan, *Kirche und Staat*, 1, 216-21, 358 f. (published by Constantine and Licinius). See also Nesselhauf, n. 13 below. Karl Bihlmeyer, "Das angebliche Toleranzedikt Konstantins von 312. Mit Beiträgen zur Mailänder Konstitution (313)," *Theologische Quartalschrift*, 96 (1914), 65-100, 198-224, denies that Constantine issued any such a law in 312 either before the Battle of the Milvian Bridge or thereafter. Knipfing, ZKG, 40 (1922), 209 f., agrees with Bihlmeyer and lists the modern authorities on both sides of this question.

Theoretically conceivable but hardly worthy of consideration is a third possibility, that Constantine might have held back his own Edict until after June 13. Such a delay on his part is extremely improbable because, unlike Licinius (see note 16 below), he exercised full dominion in his territories as early as October 28-29, 312. The uprising in Gaul with which he had to contend in the spring and summer of 313 affected only a small area and did not loosen his grip on Italy and North Africa, in which he legislated freely and without hindrince. For his legislation in the early months of 313, see T. Mommsen, *op. cit.* in note 10 below, vol. 1, 1, p. ccix; Seeck, *op. cit.* in note 15 below, 160 f. The insurrection in Gaul is mentioned by Ernest Stein, *Histoire du Bas-Empire*, 1, 1 (1959), 92; 1, 2, 459, n. 145; *Panegyrici latini*, XII (IX), 21, 5-23, 4, ed. Mynors (see n. 51 below), 286-88; IX (12), ed. Galletier,

meeting with Licinius in Milan, or (b) shortly thereafter, but presumably before June 13, 313, the day on which the Licinian draft of the Edict was made public. On the former supposition, Constantine would have drawn up the Edict himself very much in its present form and then persuaded Licinius to join him in sponsoring it.

In view of Constantine's attitude towards the Christians as demonstrated throughout his career from October 28, 312 on (see n. 7 above), alternative (a) seems more likely than (b), though neither is capable of proof, and both are legally (10) defensible since the emperor of one part of the Empire could, as we have seen (note 7a above), publish a law independently of his imperial colleague, who would not be bound thereby unless he wished to adopt it by a separate enactment of his own.

Both hypotheses (a) and (b), it should be emphasized, are consistent with the unambiguous statements of Eusebius (HE, 9, 9, 12; 10. 5, 1 et 4) and Lactantius (MP, 48, 2), quoted on pp. 16-17, that Constantine and Licinius were jointly responsible for the Edict. The language used in these passages goes far beyond the normal heading of an ordinary law (as, e.g., *Codex Theodosianus*, 10.19.10 of August 29, 382 : *Imperatores Gratianus, Valentinianus et Theodosius Augusti Floro Praefecto Praetorio... Dat. iiii Kal. Sept. Constantinopoli...*, which concerned Theodosius's part of the Empire alone, as can be seen from reference to Constantinople as the place of emission: see note 7a), and proves that both emperors actively took part in the issuance of the Edict.

¶ Nevertheless, whichever of these two alternatives may appear

---

v. 2, p. 106, 140 ff.; Zosimus, *Historia nova*, 17, 2 f., ed. L. Mendelssohn (Leipzig, 1887), 74.15 ff. Cf. *Excerpta Valesiana*, 13, ed. Jacques Moreau (Leipzig, 1961), 4.17 f.; Camille Jullian, *Histoire de la Gaule*, 7 (reprinted Brussels, 1964 without date of original edition). 111. Of course, there was nothing to prevent an emperor from legislating even in unsettled times.

(10) H. F. Jolowicz, *Historical introduction to the study of Roman law*, 2d ed. (Cambridge, England, 1952), 438, 481. See also *Codex Theodosianus*, 1. 1. 5; *Leges Novellae Theodosii II*. 1, 5; 2 pr.; *Leges Novellae Valentiniani III*, 26 (Haenel 25), ed. T. Mommsen & P. M. Meyer, *Theodosiani libri xvi... et Leges Novellae ad Theodosianum pertinentes*, 1, 2 (reprinted. Berlin, 1954), 29, 4-10; 2 (*ibid.*), 4f., 6, 121 f., Cf. for Zeno Biondo Biondi, "La L. 12 cod. de aed. priv. 8, 10 e la questione delle relazioni legislative tra le due parti dell' impero," *Bullettino dell' Istituto di diritto romano*, 44 (1936-37), 363-84; M. A. von Bethmann-Hollweg. *Der Civilprozess des gemeinen Rechts*, 3, *Der römische 'Civilprozess* (Bonn, 1866), 215 f. Fritz von Schwind, *Zur Frage der Publikation im römischen Recht (Münchener Beiträge zur Papyrusforschung und antiken Rechtsgeschichte*, 31 [1940]), 157 ff. (on the *Publikation der kaiserlichen Edikte*), provides no information on publication during the Dominate. The view held by Jolowicz and von Bethmann-Hollweg, *loc. cit.*, that the system of promulgation discussed in the text was a later development and did not obtain ca. 313 is erroneous. See note 7a above.

the more plausible, (a) is greatly to be preferred to the hypothesis recklessly advanced (11) without proof that the initiative for the Edict somehow lay with Licinius, who ended his days, Eusebius charges, as a persecutor of the Church. Whether this accusation be altogether just or not, there is not the slightest evidence which indicates that Licinius ever of his own accord took any action of any kind that was favorable to the Christians.

(2) Secondly, commentators do not agree on the identification of the "most perfect and fully detailed law on behalf of the Christians", which, Eusebius says (HE, 9, 9, 12; cf. 9, 9a, 12) "Constantine himself and Licinius with him... with one will and purpose together drew up" (Καὶ δὴ ἐπὶ τούτοις αὐτός τε Κωνσταντῖνος καὶ σὺν αὐτῷ βασιλεὺς Λικίννιος, ...ἄμφω μιᾷ βουλῇ καὶ γνώμῃ νόμον ὑπὲρ Χριστιανῶν τελεώτατον πληρέστατα διατυποῦνται...).

Although Eusebius does not further identify this "most perfect law", he does say (HE, 9, 9, 9-12) that Constantine and Licinius issued it soon after (ἐπὶ τούτοις) Constantine's victory over Maxentius on October 28, 312. This description of the circumstances makes it probable that he was referring thereby to the Edict, which is the

---

(11) Moreau, *Scripta minora*, 102 f.; Seeck, ZKG, 12 (1891), n.b. 381, 386. *Contra*, see *inter alios* Joseph Vogt, *Constantin der Grosse*, 168 f., 284; Calderone, *Costantino*, 164 f.; Dörries, *Selbstzeugnis* (n. 1 above), 229 ff.; J. R. Palanque, « A propos du prétendu Édit de Milan. » *Byzantion*, 10 (1935), 612 ff.; André Piganiol. *L'empereur Constantin* (Paris, 1932), 92-97; Pierre Batiffol, *La paix constantinienne et le catholicisme*, 2d ed. (Paris, 1914), 231.

See also Marcello Fortina, "La politica religiosa dell' imperatore Licinio," *Rivista di studi classici*, 7 (1959), 245-65; 8 (1960), 3-23. On the almost hopeless task of attempting to determine whether some of the legal texts now attributed to Constantine had originally been issued by Licinius, see Roberto Andreotti, "L'imperatore Licinio ed alcuni problemi della legislazione costantiniana," *Studi in onore di Emilio Betti*, 3 (Milan, 1962), 41-63; Mario Amelotti, *SDHI*, 27 (1961), 300-23; Jean Gaudemet, "Constantin, restaurateur de l'ordre," *Studi in onore di Siro Solazzi nel cinquantesimo anniversario del suo insegnamento universitario (1899-1948)* (Naples, 1948), 652-74, who analyzes the Constantinian legislation which he believes annulled and replaced the laws enacted by Maxentius and Licinius.

On Licinius as persecutor, see Eusebius, HE, 10, 8, 8-9, 9, etc., with discussion by Calderone, *Costantino*, 205-30, who, however, is too eager to explain away all the data Eusebius presents on Licinius's harshness towards the Church. From what Eusebius says, it appears that, though Licinius did not persecute the Christians in the manner of the earlier pagan emperors, he was unsympathetic towards them and enacted a number of measures which were designed to harass them. The best recent study of the whole career of Licinius is that by Roberto Andreotti, s.v., in the *Dizionario epigrafico di antichità romane*, 4, fasc. 31-33 (Rome, 1958-59), 979-1041, n.b. 994-97 on the Edict.

It cannot be proved that Constantine was the first to terminate active persecution of the Christians. He seems to have done so ca. 306-7, but apparently no sooner and no more completely than did his rival, Maxentius, who may once have outstripped him in the positive encouragement of Christianity. See HE, 8, 14, 1 and Hans von Schoenebeck, *Beiträge zur Religionspolitik des Maxentius und Constantin*, Klio, Beiheft 43 (1939, reprinted Aalen, 1962), 4-27; Alberto Pincherle, "La politica ecclesiastica di Massenzio," in *idem, Cristianesimo antico e moderno* (Rome, 1956), 38-50.

only joint declaration of these two emperors on religious liberty that he quotes. Likewise, this same text (HE, 9, 9, 9-12) makes it obvious that Eusebius could not possibly have been thinking here(a), as some have rashly supposed (12), of Galerius's Edict of 311, which preceded by over a year the above-mentioned defeat of Maxentius. This fatal objection to the proposed identification of the "most perfect law" with Galerius's Edict is fully borne out by internal evidence (to be discussed below, 5 (a)-(e)).

Likewise to be rejected (b) is the possibility that Eusebius had in mind the non-existing law which many believe (see (1) (a) above) Constantine issued on his own initiative, without reference to Licinius, late in 312 or early in 313, since Eusebius would never have confused such an enactment with one promulgated, as he says, by both of the emperors. Calderone argues (see n. 9) that Constantine acted in this instance by himself, on his own authority as senior Augustus, without consulting Licinius, but that, in accordance with the normal procedure (see n. 10), he then inserted Licinius's name pro forma in the text which he made public.

According to a somewhat similar theory (13), Eusebius deliberately added Licinius's name to HE, 9, 9, 12 as co-author with Constantine of the "most perfect law" in order to ingratiate himself with Licinius under whose jurisdiction he was residing at the time he was writing this portion of his HE. It is not clear why Licinius should have been pleased by a back-handed compliment of this kind. However that may be, both of these guesses fall wide of the mark because of Eusebius's express statement, as above quoted, that Licinius acted jointly in this matter with Constantine (Κωνσταντῖνος καὶ σὺν αὐτῷ βασιλεὺς Λικίννιος) and that they both had agreed to publish the legislation in question (ἄμφω μιᾷ βουλῇ καὶ γνώμῃ νόμον... διατυποῦνται). Eusebius would never have used such specific language if Licinius had not

(12) E.g., Moreau, Scripta minora, 102 f., without proof and relying on Grégoire, Byzantion, 7 (1932), 649, who guesses that Eusebius did not reproduce the text of this "most perfect law" since it was nothing but Galerius's Edict of 311. So universal is the respect and admiration for the erudition of the effervescent Henri Grégoire and his faithful disciple that their error about the Edict of Galerius has not previously been refuted.

(13) Nesselhauf, HJ, 74 (1954), 51 f., 54. Many authorities, e.g., Calderone, Costantino, 163-204, Nesselhauf, loc. cit., Ehrhardt, ZSS, RA, 71 (1954), 38, & 72 (1955), 171 f., and Jochen Martin, "Toleranzedikt v. Mailand," Lexikon für Theologie und Kirche, 2d ed., 10 (Freiburg im Br., 1965), 246, believe that Constantine issued a law in 312 which served as the model for the Edict (attributed to Licinius by all four).

A curiosity worthy of mention is Eusebius's remark (HE, 9, 10, 6) that Maximinus, whom he denounces elsewhere as a stubborn enemy of the Church, legislated for the Christians "in the fullest and most perfect manner" (τελεώτατα καὶ πληρέστατα διαταξάμενος).

actively participated in the formulation of this law, at least to the extent postulated in I (a) above.

Nor (c) could there have been an earlier and now no longer surviving "most perfect law". For there is no known reason why the two emperors, after turning out one "most perfect law" (at the earliest late in 312, subsequent to Constantine's victory over Maxentius; see HE, 9, 9, 12), should only a few months later have deemed it necessary to frame a revised version thereof, i. e., our extant Edict of 313. Surely, if such a putative previous "most perfect law" had ever existed or had been "more perfect" than other such legislation, Eusebius would have wished to quote it, alongside of, or in preference to, the Edict of 313. Obviously, he would have preferred to transcribe the truly "most perfect law" and actually, I conclude, did so--in the text of the extant Edict of 313.

Such uncertainty as there is on this point arises from the fact that, by some accident in the transmission of the original manuscripts, the Edict (and a number of other legal documents), which should logically have followed closely upon Eusebius's reference to the "most perfect law", have been shifted to their present position (HE, 10, 5-7). Attempts (14) have been made to determine how and why this displacement came about, but none of the theories that

(14) Henri Grégoire, *Byzantion*, 7 (1932), 649, and Jacques Moreau, *Scripta minora*, 102 f., make much of the fact that some MSS omit HE, 10, 5, 1-7, 2 (which contains the Edict and a number of laws issued by Constantine alone). But these omissions by no means prove that the Edict is not fully attested since, of course, it still remains in MP, 48 and five out of nine MSS and versions of the HE.

Hugh J. Lawlor, *Eusebiana, essays on the Ecclesiastical History of Eusebius, Bishop of Caesarea* (Oxford, 1912), 243-54, holds that there was only one edition of HE, 10, but that some MSS are defective. His argument is directed against Eduard Schwartz, RE, 6, 1 (Stuttgart, 1907), 1405 f., and *idem, Die griechischen christlichen Schriftsteller*, 9, 3 (Leipzig, 1909), xlviii-l, who maintains that the passages in question were eliminated by Eusebius in the fourth and last edition of the HE, so as to remove all references favorable to Licinius, whose name would have been obnoxious to Constantine after the war of 324. ¶ But Schwartz's argument is unconvincing since, apart from the ¦Edict ¦itself HE (10, 5, 2-14), the portion of the HE that is missing in some of the MSS consists entirely of decrees of various kinds (HE, 10, 5, 15-7, 2) by which Constantine conferred on the Church special benefits of which he would have been proud (restoration of confiscated property, convocation of ecclesiastical synods, grants of money, immunity of the clergy from public offices). Hence, it seems better to suppose, with Lawlor, that the omissions in the defective MSS are to be attributed to accident rather than design. Even if Schwartz's theory were tenable, however, the text of the Edict (in HE, 10, 5, 1-14) cannot be impugned, as he himself concedes (GCS, 9, 3, xlviii-l). ¶ Cf. Richard Laqueur, *Eusebius als Historiker seiner Zeit* (*Arbeiten zur Kirchengeschichte*, 11 [Berlin-Leipzig, 1929]), 201 ff., 207 f., who argues, quite implausibly, that the Edict was omitted in the last edition of the HE, not because of the *damnatio memoriae* of Licinius, but because ca. 324 (his date for the last edition of the HE) these laws on Christian freedom of worship were taken for granted and no longer seemed vital or relevant. For a brief summary see Gustave Bardy, *Sources Chrétiennes*, 55 (Paris, 1958), 104-13; 73 (1960), 129-32.

have been propounded has won unanimous acceptance. Nor does any of them affect the reliability or authenticity of the crucial texts from Eusebius cited above.

Hence, the principal thesis of this paper, that Constantine was directly connected with the Edict and published a version of it in his own territories, stands, whatever the time and place of its promulgation and whatever the identity of the "most perfect and fully detailed law".

III.-IV. The Edict of Milan: Constantinian and Licinian texts identical.

As we learn from both Eusebius (HE, 10, 5, 4) and Lactantius (MP, 48, 2), the Edict was based upon conversations between Constantine and his co-emperor Licinius that took place in Milan (15), sometime early in 313, if not in the latter part of 312, as some believe. The exact date cannot be ascertained, although it has been thought that Constantine would presumably have been present in Rome on January 1, 313, the day on which he assumed his third consulship. But this is by no means certain; and he might well have left the capital long before this, just as his predecessor, Diocletian, had absented himself therefrom (MP, 17, 2) at the beginning of the year (304) in which he became consul for the ninth time. Similarly, there is no necessity for assuming that Constantine must have been in Rome as late as January 18, 313 simply because one of his constitutions ad populum, of which two fragments have been preserved, was published (proposita) in Rome on that day (CT, 10. 10. 1; CJ, 11. 58. 1 = CT, 13. 10. 1). For it was not essential that the emperor be at hand when his laws were publicly posted.

Actually, the sources do not provide sufficient information for an accurate chronology of Constantine's travels at this period. There is no doubt, however, that Constantine and Licinius did meet in Milan, either late in the year 312 or more probably early in 313 (16), in order to celebrate the marriage of the latter to the former's half-

---

(15) The date is fully discussed by Calderone, *Costantino*, 158-63. Otto Seeck, *Regesten der Kaiser und Päpste für die Jahre 311 bis 476 n. Chr.* (Stuttgart, 1919), 50, 35 ff., contends that the texts cited indicate that Constantine was in Rome on January 18, 313. On posting, etc., see *idem*, 8 ff.

(16) The long delay between the sessions in Milan (which were held in January, 313, or possibly even as late as February or March) and June 13, on which Licinius's Edict appeared, is best to be explained as; the interval Licinius needed to bring Maximinus's part of the Empire under his effective control. See Calderone, *Costantino*, 182 ff.

sister, Constantia (17). At the same time, they took advantage of the opportunity thus afforded them to discuss the general situation and, above all, the status of religion in the Empire. (See the texts quoted above, pp. 16-17).

It has been argued (18) that Eusebius's version of the Edict should be regarded as the Greek translation of the original Edict which was promulgated by Constantine at Milan early in 313. But this conclusion is far from inevitable, and there is in fact no surviving document which can be *proved* without question to have been the Edict of Milan.

Nevertheless, this traditional title for our Edict is not inappropriate if by it is understood the joint imperial Edict of toleration which, as a consequence of the understandings reached in Milan by Constantine and Licinius, became effective throughout the Empire upon promulgation by each of the emperors separately in his own realm. So much at the very least is undeniable.

But the traditional designation can, and probably should, be vindicated even more completely. This possibility of vindication arises because, as it should be obvious after reflection upon the normal procedures followed by lawyers and lawmakers, the results of the Milanese conversations between Constantine and Licinius must have been put into writing (19) before the parties separated. For two Roman emperors intent upon establishing a new imperial policy to be sanctioned by a law could never have been satisfied with anything less than a written and carefully worded record of the points on which they had agreed. This would hardly have been less than a formal text of the law that was soon to be proclaimed.

Hence, we are entitled to conjecture, each of the two emperors, or their respective legal secretaries, carried away from Milan a copy

(17) *Excerpta Valesiana*, 4, 13, ed. Jacques Moreau (Leipzig, 1961), 4, 12-18; Zosimus, *Historia nova*, 2, 17, 2, ed. L. Mendelssohn (Leipzig, 1887), 74, 15 ff.; *Epitome de Caesaribus*, 41, 1, edd. F. Pichlmayr and R. Gruendel, with Sextus Aurelius Victor (Leipzig, 1961), 166, 12 ff. Constantia is not mentioned by name in MP, 43, 2 or 45, 1 f. Constantia, the daughter of Constantius Chlorus and Theodora, is not to be confused with Constantine's daughter of the same name: Adolf Lippold, s.v. Constantia, *Der Kleine Pauly*, edd. K. Ziegler & W. Sontheimer, 1 (Stuttgart, 1964), 1283 f.

(18) By Şesan, *Kirche und Staat*, 1, 181-207, 207 ff., n. b. 190-92. See n. 5 above. Wittig, *loc. cit.* (n. 1 above), agrees with Şesan except that he prefers to describe this law as a rescript rather than an edict, and ascribes it to Licinius rather than to Constantine.

(19) So *inter alios* J. Maurice "Note sur le préambule placé par Eusèbe en tête de l'Édit de Milan'", *Bulletin d'ancienne littérature et d'archéologie chrétiennes*, 4 (1914), 45. So also Hermann Dörries, *Wort und Stunde*, 1 (Göttingen, 1966), 20 n. 35, who goes almost as far as I do when he says (*ibid.*, 23) "Der herkömmliche Name 'Mailänder Edikt' ist zwar formal unrichtig, sachlich aber völlig zutreffend."

of an officially prepared text, which was then in all probability reproduced practically verbatim not only by Licinius in the Edict as we
know it from MP, 48 but also by Constantine in his own no longer
extant version thereof. These two promulgations, having been transcribed from the articles of agreement drawn up at Milan, would as a
matter of course have been all but identical. Consequently, since
our Edict (HE, 10, 5, 2-14; MP, 48) must have been a transcript of
the meticulously articulated and officially approved memorandum
worked out by the emperors in Milan, it deserves to be recognized
as the "Edict of Milan", although it was not promulgated in this
city.

Of course, there is no formal proof that the Edict actually took
shape in this way. But the logic of the situation and the clear implication of the Edict, both as quoted above (HE, 10, 5, 4; MP, 48, 2)
and as analyzed below with respect to *placuisse nobis* and its specific
provisions, which are too detailed and too circumstantial to have
been transmitted orally (pp. 31-32 below), lead inevitably to this
conclusion.

On the other hand, it is not surprising that there are minor but not
substantial discrepancies (see n. 5 above) between the Eusebian and
Lactantian texts of the Edict, just as there undoubtedly must have
been between the Licinian and Constantinian forms thereof. Absolute
identity in such texts is all but unattainable, as anyone knows who
has ever revised even an ordinary typescript, and then tried to incorporate all the final changes and *retouches* into all the carbon copies.

Some have argued (1) that this law of 313 was not an edict *(edictum)*
but a rescript (20) *(rescriptum)* or a *mandatum* (21). Others hold (2)
that it was nothing more than a statement of principle without
legal consequences (22), or (3) that it was intended solely for Licinius's part of the Empire (23), or that Constantine would not have
taken the trouble to promulgate the Edict himself (24), which would

(20) Vogt, *Constantin*, 170.
(21) Ernest Stein and J. R. Palanque, *Histoire du Bas-Empire*, 1, 2 (n. p., 1959), 458,
n. 143; Moreau, *Scripta minora*, 103.
(22) So Vogt, *Constantin*, 169, who concludes of Constantine and Licinius at Milan:
"dass sie auf die Abfassung eines Edikts verzichteten und sich damit begnügten, die Grundli-
nien einer künftigen Politik zu umreissen."
(23) Moreau, *Scripta minora*, 101-103; SC, 39, 2, 458.
* It is usually so described, though Eusebius (HE, 10, 5, 15) calls it a διάταξις (= constitutio), and it probably merits the designation edict as much as the Edict of 313. See notes
28-33 below and Ehrhardt, *loc. cit.* (n. 6 above), 171.
(24) Baynes, *Constantine the Great*, 11, 74 f.; Moreau, *Scripta minora*, 102.

have been pointless and repetitious for him, since he had anticipated it (4) in the rescript* addressed to Anulinus (HE, 10, 5, 15-17), and above all (5) in the Edict of Sardica (25) of 311, to which his name had been attached, along with those of Galerius (the senior Emperor, its principal sponsor) and Licinius (26). Moreover, some critics maintain (6) (27), this Galerian law of 311 was still in force in Africa in 314 (or rather, 315; see n. 43) and could not, therefore, have been superseded by the Edict, which, according to them, was for this reason devoid of legal significance.

Of course, as its advocates seem not to realize, point (5) above could equally well be used to support the impossible proposition, favored by no one, that Licinius himself, having already legislated sufficiently on this subject by joining Galerius and Constantine in promulgating the Edict of 311, would merely have extended this Edict to apply to his newly-conquered lands, as they argue Constantine had done, and would not subsequently have published the Edict of 313, from which no one has ever thought of dissociating him. Nor do they explain why Constantine could not have issued more than one law on religious toleration especially if the successive enactments were drafted in different terms or were designed to meet special requirements, as even the most radical critics concede he did, since no one denies that he was responsible for both the Edict to Anulinus (312-313) and that of 311 (on which his name appears along with those of Galerius and Licinius; see n. 26 above).

This logical flaw is characteristic of all six of these objections, not one of which can withstand critical examination. (1) In the first place, according to the usage of the Later Empire, such an

---

(25) Moreau, *Scripta minora*, 101-3; Seeck, ZKG, 12 (1891), 381-86.

(26) Eusebius, HE, 8, 17, 3-5. Some of the MSS (see GCS and LCL editions) omit Licinius's name.

(27) Erich Caspar, *Geschichte des Papsttums*, 1 (Tübingen, 1930), 581, followed by Jacques Moreau, *Scripta minora*, 101, who does not attempt to deal with J. R. Palanque's ingenious refutation of Caspar's theory in *Byzantion*, 10 (1935), 607-16; but see n. 44 below. Vogt, *Constantin der Grosse*, 2d ed. (Munich, 1960), 169, 284, accepts Caspar's conclusion without discussion, although he *cites* Palanque.

In BZ, 32 (1932), 117 f., Ernest Stein accepts Caspar's argument that the Edict of Galerius was being cited in Africa in 314 (as we now know 315: see n. 43 below). But he interprets this circumstance as proof that the Edict of 313 was then actually in effect. According to him, since the *actorum rescissio* operated to expunge all the legislation of a tyrant (in this case, Maxentius), Galerius's Edict could not have been re-instated after the death of Maxentius except by a law of Constantine, i.e., by the Edict of 313. This is a complex notion, and it is difficult to follow Stein's argument that Constantine's Edict of 313 re-instated Galerius's Edict, which it simultaneously replaced. On the *rescissio*, see Calderone, *Costantino*, 152-55; Theodor Mommsen, *Römisches Staatsrecht*, 2, 2, 3rd ed. (reprinted, Graz, 1952, with no reference to the original date), 1129-32.

enactment would have been regarded as an edict. The opposition to this term in the present context rests mainly upon the theory (28) that it should be restricted to documents which begin *Imperator Caesar... dicit* (i.e., "the Emperor... says"). On this account, some have thought, *mandatum* (29) would be a more accurate term than edict. But this suggestion overlooks the fact that by this time (30) *mandata* had become quite rare, and did not re-enter popular usage until the reign of Justinian. Furthermore, since the *mandatum* was the medium for transmitting administrative instructions to provincial magistrates, it would have been unsuitable for a formal pronouncement like the Edict of 313, which applied to the Empire as a whole. It may also be relevant that, by a terminological accident, the *mandatum* was never described as a *constitutio* (imperial enactment) by a Roman writer, whereas the Edict is defined by Eusebius (HE, 10, 5, 1) as a διάταξις, i.e., as a *constitutio*.

Likewise, it is not likely that the legal provisions arising out of the conference of Constantine and Licinius in Milan would have been set forth in a rescript (31), which was the form customarily used by the emperors to reply to queries from officials or petitions from private persons.

These proposals of alternative and putatively preferable designations for the Edict look back primarily to the practice of the earlier Empire (32), in which several types of laws (*edicta, decreta, rescripta,* etc.) had been distinguished. In later times, however, the difference between one form and another became less significant, and after the reign of Diocletian (284-305) the principal distinction was between laws of general application (the *leges generales*) (33), which were promulgated for the Empire as a whole, and those which were granted

(28) On this definition of the imperial edict, see Leopold Wenger, *Die Quellen des römischen Rechts (Oesterreichische Akademie der Wissenschaften, Denkschriften der Gesamtakademie,* 2 [Vienna, 1953]), 425, n. 2.

(29) So, e.g., Seeck, ZKG, 12 (1891), 381-86. For the *mandatum,* see Wenger, *op. cit.,* 425 f.

(30) Jolowicz, *op. cit.* (n. 10 above), 376, 380 f., 480; Jean Gaudemet, *La formation du droit séculier et du droit de l'église aux IVᵉ et Vᵉ siècles (Institut de droit romain de l'Université de Paris,* 15 [1957]), 26 f.; *idem, Institutions de l'antiquité* (Paris, 1967), 481, 585, 733.

(31) On rescripts, see Wenger, *op. cit.,* 427-32; Jolowicz, *op. cit.,* 378-80, 479; Adolf Berger, *Encyclopedic dictionary of Roman law (Transactions of the American Philosophical Society,* N.S. 43, 2 [Philadelphia, 1953]), 574, 680.

(32) Jolowicz, *op. cit.,* 479, cf. 376 ff.; Kipp, s.v. Edictum, RE, 5, 2 (Stuttgart, 1905), 1947. 64 ff.

(33) Jolowicz, *op. cit.,* 478 f.; Wenger, *op. cit.,* 433 f. F. Martroye, "A propos de 'l'édit de Milan,' " *Bulletin d'ancienne littérature et d'archéologie chrétiennes,* 4 (1914), 48 f., inexplicably denies that the Edict "s'agit... d'une déclaration de droits s'adressant à la population tout entière. "

ad hoc to bestow a favor or to deal with some extraordinary situation, but were not intended to serve as legal precedents that would be regularly applicable in the future.

A *lex generalis* could be issued in various ways, and if it was specifically so designated or promulgated as a law of general application, it had the force of an edict. This definition was laid down in a constitution of 426 (CJ, 1.14.3), which provided: *Sed et si generalis lex vocata est vel ad omnes iussa est pertinere, vim obtineat edicti*. These conditions were clearly fulfilled by the Edict of 313 since it prescribed rules that were directed to all the inhabitants of the Empire, to whom it specifically referred (as *omnibus* ["all"] twice in MP, 48, 2, and as *quisque* ["each"] thrice: MP, 48, 2, 4, 6), etc., and was therefore indubitably *ad omnes iussa est pertinere*.

(2) Actually, whether or not this definition is relevant for the fourth century, as it probably is, there is no need to quibble about terminology, since, under the Dominate (i.e., from the time of Diocletian) and even before, the legal channel by which the emperor chose to proceed was of little consequence and could not affect the final result. For no one could challenge his authority; and whatever method he preferred or the moment seemed to demand — whether he chose to take action through an edict or some other legal device — his decision as thus expressed became without question (34) the law of the Empire. This principle, which is traceable to Gaius and Ulpian, is set forth twice in the *Corpus Iuris Civilis*, in the *Institutes* (1.2.6) and in the *Digest* (1.4.1), and is almost too well-known to quote: *Quod principi placuit legis habet vigorem* ("What the emperor ordains (35) has the force of law").

It is significant, therefore, that the emperors used this technical term (in this instance, *placuisse nobis*: MP, 48, 4) to introduce the

---

(34) On this text, see Fritz Schulz, "Bracton on kingship", *L'Europa e il diritto romano, Studi in memoria di Paolo Koschaker*, 1 (Milan, 1954), 44 ff.; Pietro de Francisci, *Arcana imperii*, 3, 2 (Milan, 1948), 203-23.

(35) It is hardly necessary to warn the reader that *Quod principi placuit* is not to be translated crudely and unidiomatically, "What has *pleased* the king," as many of even the most erudite scholars persist in rendering it. The impersonal *placet* here is used in the technical meaning of *rule, determine, decide, ordain*, etc.; and the clause as a whole means: "What the emperor rules," i.e., what he has determined in his judicial capacity as lawgiver, presumably after consultation with his legal advisers (CJ, 1. 14. 2) or at least after due reflection on juridical matters. The full text is of great importance: *Institutiones*, 1. 2. 6: Sed et quod principi placuit legis habet vigorem, cum lege regia, quae de imperio eius lata est, populus ei et in eum omne suum imperium et potestatem concessit. Quodcumque igitur imperator per epistulam constituit vel cognoscens decrevit vel edicto praecepit, legem esse constat: haec sunt quae constitutiones appellantur. The parallel text, *Digest*, 1. 4. 1, differs in only a few minor particulars.

principal subject of their Edict (vid., that the restrictions on the Christians were to be removed). For, as any bureaucrat or educated man of the fourth century would have recognized at once, these two words (whose legal significance has been ignored by nearly (36) all of the modern commentators on the Edict) invest the text under consideration with full legal authority as a law. This would have been obvious to any Romanist, not only from the use of the wholly unambiguous *terminus technicus* just cited, but also from the form of the preface, the stress on its universal application, and a number of other legal tags (37). ¶ There is, of course, it should be added to conclude this phase of the argument, no reason to object that what we have been describing as the Edict cannot be accepted as such because it is otherwise unattested. For, as every student of Roman history knows, there is a huge corpus (38) of materials which by one accident or another were never taken up into any of the existing codes of law, and are known only from inscriptions, papyri, or the works of historians, whose authority, as in this instance, cannot be questioned.

(3) Thirdly, although the Edict was, according to Lactantius (MP, 48, 1), addressed to the governor of Bithynia, it is not reasonable to infer that it was on this account restricted to Licinius's portion of the Empire. If any such limitation had been envisaged, Eusebius would hardly have failed to draw attention to it. But he does not even mention the addressee designated by Lactantius. Besides, even in the Lactantian text (MP, 48, 2), both Constantine and Licinius are named as the authors of the Edict (tam ego Constantinus Augustus quam etiam ego Licinius Augustus... ordinanda esse credidimus), in a manner which proves that this was not a purely formal listing of the reigning monarchs but an official statement of actual collaboration and joint sponsorship. (See also HE, 10, 5, 1, quoted at the beginning of this article and p. 16 above.)

(36) An exception is Amelotti, SDHI, 27 (1961), 288-95, n. b. 292, n. 142, 308 (who ascribes it to Licinius alone, but admits it to have been an edict); Adriani, SR, 2 (1954), 24 ff., accepts it as an edict, as does Ehrhardt, ZSS, RA, 72 (1955), 171. Even Moreau, who argues that this document cannot be described as an edict, himself (SC, 39, 2, 459, on 1, 15), refers to it as *l'édit*, and fails to comment on either CJ, 1. 14. 2 f. or *placuisse nobis*, which provide the key to its legal character.

A detailed study of the phraseology of the Edict and its use of legal terminology would be rewarding.

(37) Nesselhauf, HJ, 74 (1954), 46 f.

(38) See Gustav Haenel, *Corpus legum ab imperatoribus romanis ante Iustinianum latarum quae extra constitutionum codices supersunt*, 2 vols. (Leipzig, 1857, repr. Aalen, 1965); 1, 187 ff.

(4) Fourthly, the letter (HE, 10, 5, 15-17) to Anulinus (39), proconsul of Africa, which some (see n. 24 f. above) deem to have been sufficient expression of Constantine's official attitude on toleration to have precluded his active collaboration in the Edict of 313, cannot be dated with certainty. Though Eusebius, our sole source for this document, quotes it *after* the Edict (HE, 10, 5, 15-17), logically, it would appear to be prior thereto, since it deals *ad hoc* with only one of the problems with which the Edict was concerned (i.e., with nothing but the restoration of Christian properties that had been seized by the State during the persecutions) and would in all likelihood have been unnecessary thereafter. ¶ Moreover, it lacks two of the most characteristic and indispensable elements of the Edict, (a) the promise of indemnification for pagans whose interests were damaged by the execution of this measure, and (b) the unequivocal declaration of the principle of absolute equality in the law to all religions. It was this last provision, which went far beyond the mere toleration already accorded by Galerius and Maxentius, that makes the Edict one of the most memorable monuments in the history of human freedom. No one in the fourth century, therefore, for which egalitarian ideas were, it need hardly be said, incomparably more revolutionary than they are in the twentieth, could ever have supposed that Constantine's simple instructions on a single point of law constituted an adequate substitute for the Edict.

In addition, the proponents of (4) overlook the fact that, as the emperors explain (HE, 10, 5, 2 f.; MP, 48, 4), the Edict was needed in order to remove certain *condiciones* in a previous enactment of theirs which had denied freedom of worship to many Christians. Thus, the emperors would have felt obliged to issue the Edict, even if the letter to Anulinus had been far more satisfactory a pronouncement on the religious question than it really was.

There is some dispute as to what these vexatious *condiciones* (40)

---

(39) On this document, see, Calderone, *Costantino*, 144 f.; Ehrhardt, ZSS, RA, 72 (1955), 171-73; Baynes, *Constantine the Great and the Christian Church*, 10, 68 f.; Kraft, *Kaiser Konstantins religiöse Entwicklung*, 160 f.; Dörries, *Selbstzeugnis*, 16.

(40) According to Knipfing, ZKG, 40 (1922), 211, the letter stated by Eusebius to have required correction is the one Sabinus sent at Maximinus's behest to replace the Edict of Galerius (HE, 9, 1-6). But I fail to see why Constantine and Licinius would have assumed responsibility for this document, with which they had had no connection.

Salvatore Calderone, "ΑΙΡΕΣΙΣ — 'condicio' nelle *Litterae Licinii*," *Helikon*, 1 (1961), 283-94, suggests that the word *condiciones* (in MP, 48, 4), which Eusebius translates by αἱρέσεις (HE, 10, 5, 6), in this context means, not *condition, stipulation, proviso*, etc., as it usually does, but something like *social condition* and, hence, *heretical sect*. This exegesis requires us to suppose that the law to which the emperors refer (said by C. to have been

were. But the most reasonable explanation seems to be that the clauses to which the emperors objected were contained in the special instructions (§e in the section immediately following) Galerius (41) sent his governors to supplement the Edict of 311.

(5) The same objections that have been urged against (4) in the preceding paragraphs apply *a fortiori* against the contention that Constantine was content merely to reinstate Galerius's Edict of 311 (42) and felt no necessity to issue the Edict of 313. This hypothesis, though confidently asserted, is purely an assumption, rests on no ancient or mediaeval evidence, and completely ignores the fact, which is obvious on even a casual examination, that the Edict of 313 is fuller, more decisive, and more advanced (in terms of the relations between Christianity and the State) than any of the previous constitutions which had dealt with this problem. None of the critics explains why Constantine should have preferred the inadequate measure grudgingly yielded to the Christians by one of the most ruthless persecutors of the Church to the much more humane document (the Edict of 313) which bears his own name (HE, 10, 5, 2-14; MP, 48).

Indisputably, Constantine would have found Galerius's Edict

that promulgated by Constantine alone in 312) put limitations on freedom of worship because it listed certain Christian sects which were to be tolerated but did not, and could not, include them all. The notion then arose, C. theorizes, that only the groups named were to be free. Accordingly, the clause, *amotis omnibus omnino condicionibus* (ἐξαιρεθεισῶν παντελῶς τῶν αἱρέσεων), means that the Edict eliminated this catalogue and thereby extended the scope of the religious privileges which it granted.

This is an ingenious hypothesis. But it is unnecessarily complicated, and assumes that Eusebius, or his translator, on coming upon *condicio* in the Latin original, took it to be the equivalent of *secta*. No one, it may be said categorically, would ever arrive at such a translation automatically, or without protest, even after the lexicographical analysis that has been mustered in its behalf.

Somewhat similarly, Ch. Saumagne, "Du mot αἱρεσις dans l'édit licinien de l'année 313," *Theologische Zeitschrift*, 10 (1954), 376-87, maintains that Lactantius saw *amotis omnibus omnino sectis* in the text of the Edict which he was transcribing but could not understand it and therefore corrected *sectis* to *condicionibus*.

My view is that the latter word stood in the original Edict and that αἱρέσεων in Eusebius's translation is to be understood as *restriction*, *condition*, etc., a sense which the word can, and does occasionally, bear (see Saumagne, *loc. cit.*, 382). But it must be admitted that αἱρεσις does not normally have this connotation. Perhaps, Eusebius, or his Latinist, simply made a mistake.

(41) Against this assumption, Knipfing, ZKG, 40 (1922), 210 f., argues, *inter alia*, that Galerius died too soon after issuing his Edict to have had an opportunity to circulate the letters in question. It seems more probable, however, that Galerius had these special instructions in mind from the very beginning and sent them out simultaneously with the Edict.

(42) For the text see HE, 8, 17, 3-11; MP, 34, with textual notes in Moreau, SC, 39, 1, 117; Haenel, *Corpus legum*, 1, 185. The latest study is Hans U. Instinsky, *Die alte Kirche und das Heil des Staates* (Munich, 1963). Karl Bihlmeyer, "Das Toleranzedikt des Galerius von 311," *Theologische Quartalschrift*, 94 (1912), 411-27, 527-89, still merits attention.

intolerable and in need of emendation for several reasons. (*a*) It granted the Christians nothing for their own sake and was, as Galerius frankly admitted, nothing but a last desperate attempt on his part to win over the Christians in the hope that they might then pray for his recovery from a foul disease. (*b*) It contained harsh language on the stubbornness and folly of the Christians in abandoning the [heathen] religion of their ancestors (HE, 8, 17, 6 f., 9; MP, 34, 1f., 4). (*c*) In a manner that could only have been offensive, it authorized them to "resume being Christians and build their meeting-places, on condition that they refrain from disorderly conduct" (HE, 8, 17, 9; MP, 34, 4: *ut denuo sint christiani et conuenticula sua componant, ita ut ne quid contra disciplinam agant*). (*d*) It ignored the problem of the restoration of the property which the Christians had forfeited to the government in previous years. (*e*) It tied the new privileges now vouchsafed to other, but unspecified and no longer extant, requirements, which Galerius said he would communicate to his governors (HE, 8, 17, 9; MP, 34, 5: *Per aliam autem epistulam iudicibus significaturi sumus quid debeant obseruare*).

These imperfections are so numerous and so glaring that Eusebius could not possibly have pronounced the document embracing them to be "the most perfect and fully articulated law" promulgated by Constantine and Licinius in behalf of the Christians (HE, 9, 9, 12; cf. 9a, 9, 12). The scholars who have propounded this unfortunate theory did not compare the two texts and, still worse, detached Eusebius's sentence on the most perfect law from the paragraph in which Eusebius makes it clear (see p. 23 above) that the "most perfect law" appeared some one and a half years later than Galerius's Edict.

Indeed, the very existence of the Edict of 311, bearing his name as one of its imperial sponsors, would have been enough to persuade Constantine of the necessity for superseding it with one that would be more expressive of his own sentiments. He had joined Galerius in the pronouncement of 311 *bon gré mal gré*, when, as a junior Augustus, he had no alternative but to accede to the senior Emperor's demands. But after he had won his way to the rank of senior Augustus as a result of his victory over Maxentius (MP, 44, 11), he would surely have wished to assert himself in the spirit of his overwhelming spiritual experience on the eve of October 28, 312.

Notwithstanding all the compelling reasons Constantine would have had for preparing new legislation of his own on religious freedom, it has been argued that he never did so, that Galerius's edict of 311 was still in force as late as 315 (n. 27 above), and that it had not been superseded by Constantine's Edict of 313, which, accordingly, it is said, never had the force of law. Proof of these propositions is found in the proceedings of a trial held in 315 before a certain Aelian, who was proconsul in Carthage and is quoted as having said (43): *Constantinus Maximus semper Augustus et Licinius Caesares ita pietatem christianis exhibere dignantur, ut disciplinam corrumpi nolint, sed potius obseruari relegionem (sic) istam et coli uelint.*

These words have been taken to be a citation of the Edict of Galerius *(ita ut ne quid contra disciplinam agant)*. Even if this interpretation be correct, however, and even if Aelian was not merely giving his own exegesis of the Edict of 313 (which, like any other new law, overthrew certain regulations without abolishing the legal system as a whole), it has been shown (44), he was not citing the Edict of Galerius as his authority on religious toleration (since this was not at issue) but only as his justification for requiring the Christians, like all others, to obey the ordinary civil law.

In this case, a certain Ingentius, a Donatist who had forged a letter libelling Bishop Felix of Aptungi as a *traditor* (i.e., one who had "handed over" the Scriptures to imperial officials in order to escape persecution), pleaded that he was a Christian in order to avoid confessing the crime of which he had been guilty. To this defence Aelian replied (45): *Noli itaque tibi blandiri, quod cum mihi dicas dei cultorem te esse, [ac delendum] propterea non possis torqueri. Torqueris, ne mentiaris, quod alienum christianis esse uidetur. Et ideo dic simpliciter, ne torquearis.* ("Don't deceive yourself that, since you tell me you are a worshipper of God, you are for this reason exempt from torture. The rack is to prevent lies, which, I hear, the

---

(43) *Acta purgationis Felicis*, ed. C. Ziwsa, *S. Optati Milevitani libri vii (Corpus Scriptorum Ecclesiasticorum Latinorum*, 26 [1893]), 203, 5 ff. On the identity of Ingentius, Bishop Felix of Aptungi, etc., see Ernst L. Grasmück, *Coercitio, Staat und Kirche im Donatistenstreit (Bonner historische Forschungen*, 22 [Bonn, 1964]), 65 ff., 68 ff., and passim, who puts this episode in 315 rather than 314 (p. 68, n. 300); W. H. Frend, *The Donatist Church* (Oxford, 1952), 150 ff.

(44) By J. R. Palanque, in a masterly article, "A propos du prétendu Édit de Milan," *Byzantion*, 10 (1935), 607-16. In *Histoire de l'Église*, 3, edd. A. Fliche & V. Martin, *De la paix Constantinienne à la mort de Théodose* (Paris, 1935), 23 f., however, he abandons his former position, which was sound, and attributes the Edict to Licinius. But Ernest Stein, *Histoire du Bas-Empire*, 1, *De l'État romain à l'État byzantin (284-476)* ([Bruges], 1959), 92, 458, edited by Palanque, still clings "à la réalité de la décision de tolérance de Milan," which he ascribes to both Constantine and Licinius, although he prefers to call it a *mandatum* rather than an edict.

(45) CSEL, 26, 203, 8 ff.

Christians abhor. So, tell the truth, and you will not be tortured.")
Ergo, this allusion to the Edict of Galerius (if that is what it really
be), does not by any means prove that Aelian was unaware of the
Edict of 313, but only that, as a competent magistrate, he knew
what precedents to cite on the precise question that was being adju-
dicated.

Since we have disposed of all possible objections, there can be
no doubt that in 313 Constantine and Licinius issued an Edict which
clarified and restated in new terms the principle of religious freedom
as set forth by Galerius in 311. What the two emperors now did was
to put the Christians on a plane of complete equality with the pagans
in all matters of religion and worship (HE, 10, 5, 4-8; MP, 48, 2-6).
At the same time, the restrictions previously imposed upon the
Christians were lifted, and immediate restitution was ordered of
all the property which had been confiscated from the churches (HE,
10, 5, 9-11; MP, 48, 7-11). Pagans who suffered financial loss as a
result of complying with this regulation were to be indemnified by
the State (HE, 10, 5, 10f., MP, 48, 8f.).

Nothing was said about making similar amends to individual
Christians (46). But the Christian communities as a whole gained
immeasurably more than this in now being accorded by both emperors
the status of legal corporations (47) (corpus, σῶμα in Greek: HE, 10
5, 10-12; MP, 48, 8-10). It has been argued (48) that Constantine had
granted this right to the Christians of Africa somewhat earlier, in his
Edict to Anulinus (HE, 10, 5, 15-17). But there are objections to this
view, and the Edict the first document that indubitably recognizes
both the corporate legal capacity of the Church and the principle of
freedom of worship.

At the same time, the new privilege of religious liberty granted
the Christians was specifically extended to all others (HE, 10, 5, 4 f.,
8; MP, 48), so that no one might feel any restraint in the free exercise
of his predilections with regard to belief or cultus. On the contrary,

(46) It was not until a few years later, ca. 319, that Constantine ordered that indemnification be made to private individuals: *Vita Constantini*, 1, 41, 3; 2, 20, 2, ed. Ivar A. Heikel,
Eusebius Werke, 1 (*Die griechischen christlichen Schriftsteller der ersten drei Jahrhunderte*,
7 [Leipzig, 1902]), 27, 10 ff., 49, 13 ff., discussed by Arnold Ehrhardt, ZSS, RA, 72 (1955),
171-75.

(47) See literature cited in n. 7 above.

(48) So Ehrhardt, ZSS, RA, 72 (1955), 172 f. Ludwig Schnorr von Carolsfeld, *Geschichte
der juristischen Person*, 1 (Munich, 1933), 206 f., denies that τὸ δίκαιον in HE, 10, 5, 15-17
can be equated with *corpus* and σῶμα in the sense of a legal corporation, as does Artur Stein-
wenter, "Die Rechtsstellung der Kirchen und Klöster nach den Papyri", ZSS, KA, 19
(1930), 31-35.

the emperors expressed the hope (HE, 10, 5, 4f., 13; MP, 48, 2f., 11, quoted above) that in this way they might placate for themselves and their subjects every form of divinity that there might be, and thus hold the favor of the highest divinity, to which, they averred without naming it, they paid homage without reserve *(summa diui-nitas, cuius religioni liberis mentibus obsequimur)*. Eusebius omits the last relative clause and the adjective *summa*, but he shares with Lactantius the abstract noun *diuinitas*, which he translates simply by τὸ θεῖον.

Although the Edict guaranteed freedom to all religions, the emphasis throughout is on the Christians, who had never before been granted this privilege so unreservedly. The studied ambiguity in the references to the Godhead, on the other hand (HE, 10, 5, 4 & 5; Greek quoted above; MP, 48, 2: *quicquid est diuinitatis in sede caelesti; ibid.*, 3: *summa diuinitas)*, as many have remarked, was both acceptable to the Christians, whom it was the primary purpose of the Edict to conciliate, and also at the same time inoffensive to the pagans, who were too numerous (49) to alienate. Since the latter constituted the majority throughout the Empire, especially in his portion of it, Constantine, despite the sincerity of his conversion to Christianity, would have made a special effort (as in the choice of an innocuous substitute for the divine name in this Edict) to avoid alarming them or goading them into rebellion under the banner of the ancient gods. Similar considerations would have weighed heavily also with Licinius, in whose part of the Empire the Christians, though more numerous than in the West, were nevertheless outnumbered by the pagans.

V. *Imitation of the Edict on the Arch of Constantine.*

Under these circumstances, it was inevitable that Constantine's panegyrists and others who wished to honor him (like the designers of the Arch of Constantine [dedicated in 315]) (50) would have imitated

(49) The best and most detailed treatment of the size of the Christian population remains Adolf von Harnack, *Mission und Ausbreitung des Christentums in den ersten drei Jahrhunderten*, 4th ed. (Leipzig, 1924), 2, 946-58. For later surveys, see B. Kötting, "Christentum I (Ausbreitung)," *Reallexikon für Antike und Christentum*, 2 (Stuttgart, 1954), 1138-59; Kenneth S. Latourette, *A history of the expansion of Christianity*, 1 (New York, 1937), 158-60 and passim.

(50) Hans P. L'Orange and Armin von Gerkan, *Der spätantike Bildschmuck des Konstantinsbogens* (*Studien zur spätantiken Kunstgeschichte*, 10 [Berlin, 1939]), 4-28; Antonio Giuliano, *Arco di Costantino* (Milan, 1955). Alföldi, *The conversion of Constantine*, 69 ff., comes close to enunciating my theory of the connection between Constantine's Edict and the Arch.

the terminology which the Edict had by its example established as proper for reference to the imperial tutelary deity. In other words, there can be little doubt that the Edict was the obvious, but so far as I can see hitherto unrecognized, source for the new caution in the use of religious language which now came into style.

Thus, in an oration delivered soon after the Edict, in the summer or fall of 313, an unknown panegyrist (51), addressing Constantine directly, asks what god or favoring divinity it was which inspired him to make his daring assault upon Rome [in October, 312], against the advice of his advisers and soothsayers:

> Quisnam te deus, quae tam praesens hortata
> [est?] maiestas ut... contra consilia hominum,
> contra haruspicum monita ipse per temet
> liberandae urbis tempus uenisse sentires (2,4).

Later, the orator touches upon the *diuina praecepta* (4, 4) to which Constantine hearkened, and the divine guidance which directed him *(11, 4: diuino monitus instinctu)*. Likewise in the spirit of the Edict, at the end of this discourse, there is an apostrophe (26) to the lord of the universe, who is described as either some divine force or intellect or a power exalted above the heavens, in whom the highest goodness dwells. Several years later, in 321, the panegyrist Nazarius (52) took over the same terminology: *illa diuinitas* (13, 5), *diuinitus* (14,1), *uis diuinitatis* (27, 5).

The influence of the Edict upon these vague and circumlocutory expressions can be illustrated by comparison with two other panegyrics, both anonymous, which were pronounced in 310 and 312, respectively. In the former of these (53), the unknown author, while cele-

---

(51) *XII panegyrici latini,* ed. R.A.B. Mynors (Oxford, 1964), no. XII (IX), p. 271 ff.; *Panégyriques latins,* ed. with French translation, by Édouard Galletier, 2 (Paris, 1952), no. IX (12), p. 103 ff. (with essay on the date, etc., 105 ff.). The passage summarized in the text (26, 1) runs: Quamobrem te, summe rerum sator, cuius tot nomina sunt quot gentium linguas esse uoluisti (quem enim te ipse dici uelis, scire non possumus), siue tute quaedam uis mensque diuina es, ... siue aliqua supra omne caelum potestas es quae hoc opus tuum ex altiore Naturae arce despicias... Et certe summa in te bonitas est et potestas (26, 3).

On the emperor as deus, etc., see François Burdeau, "L'empereur d'après les panégyriques latins," *Aspects de l'empire romain (Travaux et recherches de la faculté de droit et des sciences économiques de Paris, Sciences historiques,* 1 [Paris, 1964]), 1-60, n. b. 10 ff.; and on the panegyrists in general, besides the introductions in Galletier's edition, cf. René Pichon, *Les derniers écrivains profanes* (Paris, 1906), 97 f., 101 f., 103-8. On the passages cited in notes 50-55, see also Johannes Straub, *Vom Herrscherideal in der Spätantike* (n. 3 above), 99 ff.

(52) Mynors, IV (x), p. 145 ff.; Galletier, X (4), v. 2, 147 ff.

(53) Mynors, VI (vii), p. 186 ff.; Galletier, VII (6), v. 2, p. 31 ff.

brating Constantine's virtues, catalogues his divine sponsors without reticence and lists, among others, Jupiter (7, 3; 8, 5; cf. 15, 6), the *di boni* (8, 2; 9, 4), Iris (8, 5), Ceres (9, 2), Liber, i.e., Bacchus (9, 2 & 4), Mercury (9, 4), Apollo (21, 4 & 7; 22, 1), the *di immortales* (22, 1), and so on. In the second of these, the anonymous *Gratiarum Actio Constantino Augusto* (54), mention is made of the *di immortales* (7, 6; 13, 1), the "statues of all our gods" (8, 4: *omnium deorum nostrorum simulacra*), and Jupiter (13, 6).

The new restraint and meticulous avoidance of the names of the pagan divinities which characterizes the oration of 313 are inexplicable except as an acknowledgement of Constantine's momentous experience on the eve of October 28, 312, and, more particularly, as a sign of deference to his terminological approach to divinity in the Edict.

Even more striking is the celebrated inscription on the Arch of Constantine (55), which copied the ambiguous and neutral language of the Edict of 313 in declaring that Constantine had won his victory over Maxentius at the Milvian Bridge (on October 28, 312) *instinctu divinitatis* ("under the guidance [or inspiration] of divinity "). Obviously, these ambivalent words were chosen deliberately in order to express gratitude for supernatural intervention without indicating a preference for either the Christian God or any of the pagan divinities. This is exactly the kind of appeal to unnamed divine powers which Constantine and Licinius had made in the Edict.

The reappearance of *divinitas* in this inscription is doubly significant, since the Roman Senate was predominantly pagan (56). Hence, their adoption of this equivocal term proves that the senators, like the anonymous panegyrist of 313, had been informed about Constantine's religious experience on the eve of October 28, 312. In addition, and more specifically, they showed thereby that they were consciously following the Constantinian religious policy and deferring to his method of referring to God as set forth in the Edict. For this reason, in order not to offend the Emperor or violate the terms and spirit of the Edict, they scrupulously refrained from naming his former divine champion (*Sol Invictus* (the unconquered, i.e., unconquerable Sun), whom they would presumably have found congenial. At the

(54) Mynors, V (viii), p. 174 ff.; Galletier, VIII (5), v. 2, p. 76 ff.
(55) For the text of the inscription, see Hermann[us] Dessau, *Inscriptiones latinae selectae*, 3rd ed. (repr. Berlin, 1962, original date unfortunately not given), no. 694.
(56) On the paganism of the Senate, see Alföldi, *The conversion of Constantine*, 61-73.

same time, they also abstained from mentioning the Emperor's new God, and no doubt were pleased to be able to cloak their own religious feelings under the ambiguity of the colorless *divinitas*, which Constantine had invested with imperial sanction in the Edict.

It is therefore improper to interpret the inscription on the Arch as if it were connected with the solar iconography (57) of the fourth century. The attempt to read elements of a Neoplatonized solar mysticism into *instinctu divinitatis* has been popular in recent years. But this interpretation ignores both the political consequences of Constantine's conversion on the night of October 27-28, 312, and the true significance of the Edict. The solar and lunar sculptural elements in the decoration of the Arch were from Constantine's point of view purely adventitious, like most of the sculptures on this famous monument, which, as L'Orange and von Gerkan have demonstrated, were taken from other imperial structures of various kinds.

Therefore, the panegyric of 313 and the inscription of 315 prove not only that Constantine's subjects in the West were aware of the revolutionary change that had taken place in his religious beliefs in 312, but also that they realized that he was the author of the Edict.

University of California.
Los Angeles.   Milton V. ANASTOS.

---

(57) E. g., L'Orange and von Gerkan, *op. cit.* (n. 50 above), 5 f., 174 ff.; Franz Altheim *Aus Spätantike und Christentum* (Tübingen, 1951), 49 ff. Bernard Berenson, *The Arch of Constantine, or the decline of form* (London, 1954), who concerns himself with style rather than iconography, is unsympathetic to the art of the fourth century.

A STUDY OF THE CATECHUMENATE

LAWRENCE D. FOLKEMER
Lansdowne, Md.

A fresh study of early catechetical procedures, and an explanation of the instructions and techniques used in adult baptism in the early Church, are always welcome. Comparatively speaking, little has been done on the subject.[1] This article makes no pretension of being a detailed study of the subject, but is only a partial treatment of it, with special emphasis upon the contributions of St. Augustine. Occasionally, references are drawn from Church canons and other early Church writings on the catechetical practice of the time.

THE STAGES OF THE CATECHUMENATE

In the earliest days of the Church the preparation for baptism was comparatively simple in method. However,

as early as the end of the second century the increasing number of Christian candidates rendered it necessary to systematize this preparation, to lay down definite rules for its performance, and to determine the period of probation. Hence arose the discipline of the catechumenate.[2]

The third and fourth centuries were the age in which the catechumenate flourished in its full form. It was only when Christianity finally triumphed over paganism, when the Church gained its footing in the Empire, and when the majority of children were born into Christian homes and brought into the Church through infant baptism, that the reasons for retaining the catechumenate became less urgent.

At first, i. e., in the second century, the instruction of the catechumens was more practical than doctrinal. The *Didache*, for example, devotes the first six chapters to Christian conduct and life. The *Apostolic Constitutions* dwells on the character and practices of the believers.[3] Justin Martyr enjoins the catechumen to enter into a life of prayer and fasting in order that

---

1 Some study has been made both of the Western and Eastern Church. Cf. Duchesne, Louis, *Christian Worship, Its Origin and Evolution* (London, 1912), particularly 292-341; *Catholic Encyclopedia, Encyclopedia of Religious Knowledge, Encyclopoedia of Religion and Ethics*, etc.
2 Duchesne, *Christian Worship*, 292.
3 *Ante-Nicene Christian Library* (Edinburgh, 1868-1871), VII, 20-27.

he may receive the remission of sins.[4] The inference is not that the matters of doctrine were ignored but rather that the fullest development of dogmatic instruction came later.

As the Church became organized, there evolved three orders of members; the clergy, the believers, and the catechumens. Some divided the clergy into bishops, presbyters, and deacons. The believers were strictly the laity who had been baptized.[5]

In addition to the clergy and believers was the group of catechumens. Though they were not strictly members, they were in some measure considered within the pale of the Church and reckoned as one of the orders. They were part of the Christian community and were regarded as Christians. With the insufflation, exorcism, the signing of the cross, and the administering of salt, they became catechumens.[6] The Council of Elvira gives them expressly the name of Christians.[7] Augustine thinks of the catechumens as members of the household of faith but as yet only servants:

Et quod signum crucis habent in fronte catechumeni, iam de domo magna sunt; sed fiant ex servis filii. Non enim nihil sunt qui iam ad domum magnam pertinent.[8]

In another place he indicates that the catechumen is entitled to be called a Christian though he is not looked upon as one of the "faithful";

Interroga hominem, Christianus es? Respondet tibi, non sum, si Paganus est aut Iudaeus. Si autem dixerit, Sum; adhuc quaeris ab eo, Catechumenus, an fidelis? Si responderit, Catechumenus; inunctus est, nondum lotus. Sed unde inunctus? Quaere et respondet; quaere ab illo in quem credat: eo ipso quo Catechumenus est, dicit, in Christum. Ecce modo loquor et fidelibus et catechumenis.[9]

There has been much discussion concerning the number of stages in the catechumenate, but modern scholarship both Roman and Protestant has accepted only two classifications.

4 Ibid., "First Apology," LXI.
5 Bingham, J., Antiquities of the Christian Church (London, 1843), I, 34f, gives a list of the names common to the believers: "Photidsomenoi," or "Illuminati," "The Initiati," "The Teleoi," "Cari Dei," "Filii Dei," "Hagioi," "Fideles," etc.
6 Duchesne, Christian Worship, 292-297; cf. also Augustine, De Catechizandis Rudibus, XXVI.
7 Mansi, Johannes D., Sacrorum Conciliorum Nova, et Amplissima Collectio (Paris and Leipzig, 1901), Concilium Eliberitanum, can. XXXIX.
8 Migne, J. P., Patrologiae Cursus Completus, Series Latina: Opera Omnia Sancti Aurelii Augustini (Parisiis, 1887), "Tractatus XI in Joannis Evangelium," cap. 4.
9 Ibid., Tractatus XLIV, cap. 2.

Church canons, East and West, have used various names to describe the catechumens but seem to agree on the number. For example, one Greek canon divides them into "hearers" and "illuminate";[10] another into "hearers" and "kneelers." So reads the Council of Neocaesarea:

Catechumenus si in dominicum ingrediens, in catechumenorum ordine steterit, is autem peccat: si genu quidem flectens, audiat, non amplius peccans. Sin autem etiam audiens adhuc peccet, extrudatur.[11]

Some Greek expositors of the canons, according to Bingham, term them "imperfect" and "perfect."[12]

Bingham himself, however, is of the opinion that there were at least four classes of catechumens. He lists them as:

1. Those privately instructed outside the Church
2. Hearers
3. Kneelers
4. *Competentes* or immediate candidates for baptism.[13]

He bases his first group on the canon of Neocaesarea, quoted above, and declares that when the canon states that they were to be cast out of the Church, that means only that they were to be reduced to the state of instruction outside the Church or private instruction. For the group of "hearers" he finds his support in the *Apostolic Constitutions* and the Council of Nicaea (can. XIV). Scholars generally agree to this classification. His third class, "kneelers," he finds in the same canon of Neocaesarea (can. V) and in others. To substantiate his fourth group, he quotes Cyril of Jerusalem, Augustine, and others.

It may very well be that in some parts of the Church and during certain periods these distinctions may have been understood even though they were not officially recognized. Bingham's references, however, do not really support his views.

According to the canons of Hippolytus,[14] the *Apostolic Constitutions*,[15] various church canons, Augustine, and secondary authorities,[16] catechumens were divided into two main classifications; namely, (1) a lower class of catechumens, "pure

10 *Concilium Nicaeum*, can. XIV. The reference is found in Bright, W., *The Canons of the First Four General Councils* (Oxford, 1892), 55, notes.
11 Mansi, *Concilium Neocaesarense*, can. V.
12 Bingham, *Antiquities*, III, 269f., "atelesteroi" and "teleioteroi."
13 *Ibid.*, 270-274.
14 *Canones S. Hippolyti, Arbice e Codicibus Romanis*, XIX, XXX, De Haneberg, ed., (Monachii, 1870).
15 Book VII, 30-45.
16 *Catholic Encyclopedia*, "Catechumenate."

and simple," sometimes known specifically as catechumens, and (2) the higher class or those who have submitted their names for baptism and were ready to enter upon a definite course of instruction. These latter were known by various names, such as *illuminati*,[17] *electi, competentes*,[18] etc.

One gathers from Roman authority that there was a distinction between "inquirers" and "catechumens," much as is the practice in some mission fields today, and that an inquirer did not become a catechumen until he had indicated his intention and showed that he was in earnest by thought and conduct. He was then signed on the forehead and received the imposition of hands with suitable prayers. It was only then that he was considered among the body of Christians.[19] Augustine testifies to that practice when he writes, *"solemniter signandus est et ecclesiae more tractandus."*[20] Eusebius, in his life of Constantine, mentions that the Emperor, at the close of his life, knelt on the pavement of the Church and received the imposition of hands with prayer.[21]

Having received the imposition of hands, the inquirer joined the first group of catechumens. He was given general instruction in the Christian faith and life and when he had proved himself worthy of advancement, he was given specialized, intensified training preparatory to the baptismal rite. So Augustine indicates:

Quid autem aliud agit totum tempus quo catechumenorum locum et nomen tenent, nisi ut audiant, quae fides et qualis vita debeat esse Christiani, ut, cum se ipsos probaverint, tunc de mensa domini manducent et de calice bibant? Quoniam 'qui manducat et bibit indigne, iudicium sibi manducat et bibit'. Quod autem fit per omne tempus, quo in ecclesia salubriter constitutum est, ut ad nomen Christi accedentes catechumenorum gradus excipiat, hoc fit multo diligentius et instantius his diebus, quibus competentes vocantur, cum ad percipiendum baptismum sua nomina iam dederunt.[22]

There was no fixed period of time for the first stage of the catechumen. Generally, it lasted long enough to test thoroughly the sincerity and character of the candidate. The

17 Signified both those already baptized and those about to be baptized.
18 ''Competentes'' refers to the handing in of their names; ''electi'' to their acceptance by the bishop for baptismal instruction. Augustine also uses ''baptizandus,'' ''one about to be baptized''—*De Fide et Operibus, passim.*
19 *Catholic Encyclopedia*, ''Catechumenate.''
20 *De Cat. Rud.*, XXVI, XIV; cf. also *Confessions*, I, 11.
21 Thus becoming a catechumen. Eusebius, *The Life of the Blessed Emperor Constantine* (London, 1845), Bk. IV.
22 *Corpus Scriptorum Ecclesiasticorum Latinorum*—S. Aurelii Augustini (Vindobonae, Lipsiae, etc., 1900). *De Fide et Operibus*, VI, 9.

Council of Elvira, in the instance of a pagan priest who desires to become a catechumen, prescribes a period of three years[23] and in the case of a worthy candidate coming to the faith for the first time suggests the practice of two years.[24] Civil laws for a time fixed it at this.[25] The *Apostolic Constitutions* reads, "Let him who is to be a catechumen be a catechumen for three years"; but then qualifies the statement by adding, "but if any one be diligent, and has a good will to his business, let him be admitted: for it is not the length of time, but the course of life that is judged."[26] Later canons and practices of the Church shortened the period. The duration depended entirely on the wish and the moral progress of the catechumen· in question. He might either be reduced by ecclesiastical censure to the ranks of the inquirers for his misbehavior[27] or he might choose to put off his baptism for a long time,[28] even to his deathbed.[29]

The policy of the early Church was somewhat similar to that followed in certain congregations of the Lutheran Church today in regard to confirmation. Children of the first year are given general instruction in the Christian faith and life and then, if they merit advancement, are promoted to the second group where they are taught the Catechism and the practices of the Church. The period of time may or may not be fixed depending on the individual child.

When the catechumen had completed his first stage of preparation and testing, he was admitted to the group of advanced catechumens, or *Competentes*.[30] As one of the *Competentes,* his name was handed in for the bishop's examination and approval. It he was accepted, he began his specialized training, usually at the beginning of Lent, and was baptized at Easter or Pentecost.[31]

23. Can. IV.
24 Can. XLII.
25 *Cath. Encycl.,* "Justinian Novel," CXLIV.
26 Bk. VIII, 32.
27 *Concilium Neocaesarense,* can. V; *Concilium Nicaeum,* can. XIV; Migne, *Apost. Const.,* VIII, 8.
28 e.g. Augustine, Ambrose, Basil, Chrysostom, etc.
29 Constantine the Great. There was an intense fear of post-baptismal sin among many of the ancients.
30 cf. other names, Greek and Latin, used to designate this group of catechumens— footnote 5.
31 If at Easter the competent had not had sufficient time for probation, his baptism was postponed, sometimes to Pentecost. That was the latest time in the Western Church. It came later to be regarded as a second baptismal festival. In the East, Epiphany was often the season of baptism. Duchesne, *Christian Worship,* 293.

INSTRUCTIONS PREPARATORY TO BAPTISM

It appears that a longer period of time was spent in the first class of catechumens than in the second. By that means the Church could more effectively safeguard itself against the admission into its fellowship of undesirable and insincere members. During the first period, the catechumen was constantly under the observation and instruction of the Church and had virtually proved himself when he was admitted to the *Competentes*. One may safely say, then, that the preliminary stage was one of testing the motives and directing the course of personal development of the catechumen.

When, however, the catechumen became a competent, he was carefully scrutinized, indoctrinated, and disciplined. The period of time was shorter but the preparation was more intense and specialized. It was necessary that he learn the specific doctrines of the Church, measure up to rigid moral and ascetic requirements, and undergo a series of liturgical purifications. A brief explanation is here given of each of these three types of instruction.

1. *Doctrinal and Moral*

The preparation for baptism consisted of a series of instructions and exercises during the season of Lent, called "scrutinies." They were designed as periodic tests of the progress of the candidates to be baptized. Usually at the first scrutiny their names were registered and they were examined on what they had learned or assimilated during the first stage of their catechumenate. By the seventh century the number of those scrutinies amounted to seven.[32] Every morning during Lent the *Competentes* were summoned to the Church and listened to expositions on the Scriptures either by the bishop or someone appointed by him.

Actually, the only formal collection of catechetical instructions in existence is that of Cyril of Jerusalem. No western or Roman collection is extant.[33] In his lectures, Cyril gives us some idea of the nature and form of the teaching preparatory to baptism. At the beginning of the Lenten season, the candi-

---

32 Duchesne, *Christian Worship*, 298.
33 "The Catechetical Lectures of St. Cyril, Archbishop of Jerusalem," translated in the *Oxford Library of the Fathers* (London, 1845). The sermons of Augustine "ad competentes" (56-59, 112-116) are considered as representative of Western practice. These sermons will be dealt with under "Augustine's Contribution."

dates are instructed in the glory of their baptism and the joy with which they should anticipate it.

Great indeed is the Baptism which is offered you. It is a ransom to captives; the remission of offences; the death of sin; the regeneration of the soul; the garment of light; the holy seal indissoluble; the chariot to heaven; the luxury of paradise; a procuring of the kingdom; the gift of adoption.[34]

Such a gift as baptism calls for a new heart and new spirit on the part of the recipient, a mind filled with humility, repentance, and confession and a life committed to righteousness and ascetic exercises.[35] Having been taught proper attitudes for baptism, the *Competentes* receive instruction in Christian doctrine along with the daily expositions of choice passages in the Old and New Testaments.[36] Various articles of faith are expounded and the Apostles' Creed is presented to them for the first time with complete explanation. Such subjects as Faith, the Unity of God, the Sovereignty of God, the Incarnation, the Crucifixion, Resurrection, Ascension and Exaltation of Christ, the Second Coming, the Last Judgment, the Holy Ghost, the Catholic Church, and Life Everlasting, are taught to the candidates.

The third of the scrutinies during Lent possessed a special importance. It was on this day that the competents received the formal *"traditio Evangelii, traditio Symboli, traditio* of the *Pater Noster."*[37] On this day they remained after the gradual and heard the reading of a chapter with an exposition of each of the Gospels after which the Creed was read and expounded by the priest. The candidates were taught the words of the Creed which they were obliged to learn by heart in order to repeat it before the bishop at the last scrutiny before baptism. In some churches this was done twenty days before the initiation.[38] The Council of Agde in France, however, appoints it for Palm Sunday.

Symbolum etiam placuit ab omnibus ecclesiis una die, id est ante octo dies dominicae resurrectionis, publice in ecclesia competentibus tradi.[39]

34 *Ibid.*, Introductory Lecture, 16.
35 *Ibid.*, I, II.
36 Usually the historical and moral books. Cf. Augustine, *De Cat. Rud.*
37 Duchesne, *Christian Worship*, 300-303. Augustine reserves the traditio of the Pater Noster until eight days after that of the Symboli—*Sermones ad Competentes*, LVIII, LIX. He does not include the traditio Evangelii at all. Some feel that each traditio may have been delivered on a separate occasion.
38 Bingham, *Antiquities*, III, 283.
39 Mansi, *Concilium Agathense*, can. XIII.

At any rate there was a certain day appointed for the candidates to give an account of the Creed.

When they had learned the Creed, they were also taught the Lord's Prayer and the significance of each of the petitions. This was not usually allowed the *Competentes* until immediately before their baptism, for it was known as the *"oratio fidelium."*[40] No one could pray "Our Father" until he had been made a son of God by regeneration in baptism. To address God as Father without receiving the gift of adoption was presumptuous. Consequently, the teaching of the Lord's Prayer to the candidates was reserved until the very last, when by anticipation they were permitted to say the *Pater Noster*. This occurred eight days before their baptism as Augustine indicates.[41]

Doctrinal instruction also had its moral implications. The acceptance of Christ in the Creed meant also the rejection of the devil. That rejection was not merely liturgical in the act of renunciation at baptism. During the entire period of their catechetical instruction they were carefully examined and scrutinized concerning their moral life, and particularly during the period when they were candidates. So reads the *Apostolic Constitutions* in the directions given to the priests:

And when it remains that the catechumen is to be baptized, let him learn what concerns the renunciation of the devil, and the joining of himself with Christ. . . . He must beforehand purify his heart from all wickedness of disposition, from all spot and wrinkle, and then partake of the holy things; for as the skilfullest husbandman does first purge his ground of the thorns which are grown up therein, and does then sow his wheat, so ought you also to take away all impiety from them, and then to sow the seeds of piety in them, and vouchsafe them baptism.[42]

Such things as honest repentance, self-denial, examination of motives, self-renunciation, are necessary to one who would be a member of the community of the faithful. Cyril says:

For the course of godliness is made up of these two; pious doctrines and good works: neither are the doctrines without good works acceptable to God; nor are works allowable works done apart from pious doctrines. For what boots it, to know excellently the doctrines concerning God, and

---

40 i.e., Augustine's phrase. *Sermones ad Competentes, passim.*
41 *Sermo ad Competentes*, LVIII, 1.
42 *Ante-Nic. Chr. Lib., Apostolic Constitutions*, VII, 40 et passim. Throughout the entire eight books there is constant emphasis upon moral life.

to commit vile fornication? or what again avails it to possess an excellent self-command, and to blaspheme impiously.[43]

Tertullian, earlier, had stressed the importance of prayer and moral vigilance in the preparation for the reception of baptism. Personal conduct and habits both before and after baptism had to be of the highest quality.[44]

Augustine is very emphatic in his insistence on the good life in preparation for baptism. The crux of his *De Fide et Operibus* is about that very matter. There were those who were willing to make a profession of faith in Christ through the Creed and yet unwilling to renounce pagan practices and immoral life. They impudently pretended to demand baptism of the Church—even pleading Scripture for their support—notwithstanding their incorrigible behavior. They felt that adulterers, harlots, stage-players, frequenters of the games, etc., should indiscriminately be admitted to baptism, regardless of their practices. Their word of acceptance of Christ was alone necessary.[45] Augustine, however, condemns that profession of faith that ignores the moral demands of the Christian life. It is a dead faith. Neither by logic nor Scripture can that incongruous position of theirs be supported. The Bible as well as the tradition of the Church speak against it. Augustine is in line with the teachings of the Fathers and the canons and practices of the Church when he insists on the moral implications of doctrinal instruction.[46]

2. Ascetical

The ascetical preparation for baptism during Lent was especially severe. As far as was possible, the *Competentes* were exhorted to keep silence:

> Be still, and know that I am God, saith the Scripture. Give over talking many idle words, neither backbite, nor lend a willing ear to backbiters, rather be prompt to prayer.[47]

If they were married, they were asked to observe continence. So Augustine writes:

> . . . quo sine dubio non admitterentur, si per ipsos dies, quibus eandem gratiam percepturi suis nominibus datis abstinentia, ieiuniis exorcismisque purgantur, cum suis legitimis et veris uxoribus se concubituros profiteren-

---

43 *Cat. Lect.,* IV, 2.
44 *Ante-Nic. Chr. Lib., On Baptism,* XX.
45 *De Fide et Operibus,* XV, XVII, XVIII *et passim.*
46 *Ibid.,* VI, 9.
47 Cyril, *Cat. Lect.,* I.

tur atque huius rei, quamvis alio tempore licitae, paucis ipsis sollemnibus diebus nullam continentiam servaturos.[48]

Fasting and daily prayers were encouraged. Justin Martyr says:

> As many as are persuaded and believe that what we teach and say is true, and undertake to be able to live accordingly, are instructed to pray and to entreat God with fasting, for the remission of their sins that are past, we praying and fasting with them.[49]

Tertullian writes:

> They who are about to enter baptism ought to pray with repeated prayers, fasts and bendings of the knee and vigils all the night through.[50]

Cyril pauses in his exposition of *Ten Points of Faith* to speak concerning fasting:

> For we fast, abstaining from wine and flesh, not because we abhor them as abominations, but because we look for the reward; that scorning things sensible [used in the literal sense] we may enjoy the spiritual and invisible table. . . . For thy soul's sake, at no time eat ought of the things offered to idols.[51]

The *Constitutions* give some specific directions concerning fasting:

> But let not your fasts be with the hypocrites; for they fast on the second and fifth days of the week. But do you either fast the entire five days, or on the fourth day of the week and on the day of the preparation [i.e. for baptism, Good Friday], because on the fourth day the condemnation went out against the Lord, Judas then promising to betray Him for money; and you must fast on the day of preparation, because on that day the Lord suffered the death of the cross under Pontius Pilate.[52]

They also prescribe certain prayers for the *Competentes* and enjoin them to pray three times a day.[53] The Fourth Council of Carthage has a canon dealing with the immediate preparation of the candidates. They are to be exercised for a long time with abstinence from wine and flesh, with imposition of hands and frequent examination.[54] In like manner Augustine puts abstinence, fastings, and exorcism together.[55]

48 *De Fide et Operibus*, VI, 7.
49 *Ante-Nicene Christian Library*, "The First Apology," LXI.
50 *Ibid.*, "On Baptism," XX.
51 Cyril, *Cat. Lect.*, IV, 27, 28.
52 *Apost. Const.*, VII, 23.
53 *Ibid.*, 24, 25.
54 *Concilium Carthagense*, IV, can. LXXV.
55 *De Fide et Operibus*, VI, 7.

Frequent confession was also required during Lent. So Tertullian writes:

They were baptized, saith [the Scripture] confessing their own sins. To us it is matter for thankfulness if we do now publicly confess our iniquities or our own turpitudes: for we do at the same time both make satisfaction for our former sins, by mortification of our flesh and spirit, and lay beforehand the foundation of defences against the temptations which will closely follow.[56]

Cyril enjoins his candidates to confess their sins:

The present [i.e. Lent] is the season of confession: confess therefore what thou hast done, whether in word, or in deed; whether in the day, or in the night; confess in a time accepted, and in the day of salvation receive the heavenly treasure.[57]

The doctrinal ascetical preparation of the *Competentes* was intense and somewhat severe. It was the purpose of the Church to elevate the standards for baptism in order to preserve itself from various abuses. Now a word about the third form of preparation.

3. *Liturgical*

Because exorcism properly comes under liturgical exercises, it is given attention here. It is not within the scope of this work to give a detailed account of exorcism and its vagaries in ethnic religions and even in sections of Christendom, but rather to present an explanation of its place in the sacrament of Christian baptism in the early Church.

In the early centuries, as in later times, the usual form of exorcism was a simple and authoritative adjuration addressed to the demon within the person in the name of God and particularly in the name of Christ crucified. It was given by some of the Fathers as a strong argument for the supremacy and divinity of the Christian faith. So Minucius Felix writes:

Since they themselves [i.e. the demons] are the witnesses that they are demons, believe them when they confess the truth of themselves; for when adjured by the only and true God, unwillingly the wretched beings shudder in their bodies, and either at once leap forth, or vanish by degrees, as the faith of the sufferer assists or the grace of the healer inspires.[58]

56 "On Baptism," XX.
57 Cyril, *Cat. Lect.*, I, 5.
58 *Ante-Nicene Christian Library*, "The Octavius," XXVII.

Justin Martyr, speaking of the power of the name of Christ, says:

> For numberless demoniacs throughout the whole world, and in your city, many of our Christian men exorcising them in the Name of Jesus Christ, who was crucified under Pontius Pilate, have healed and do heal, rendering helpless and driving the possessing devils out of the men, though they could not be cured by all the other exorcists, and those who used incantations and drugs.[59]

Now it is not implied that the candidates were considered to be obsessed, like demoniacs, but only that in consequence of original sin and of personal sins, they were subject more or less to the power of the devil. It was for that reason that in the service of renunciation, the candidate was asked to "renounce Satan, and his works, and his pomps, and his worship, and his angels, and his inventions, and all things that are under him."[60] The form was not always that long. In the Arabic Canons of Hippolytus it reads, *"Abrenuncio tibi o Satana cum omni pompa tua."*[61]

Exorcism in this connection symbolically anticipated the principal effect of baptism. It was looked upon as a cleansing formula, and with the use of water, salt, and oil the *Competentes* were thus cleansed every day during Lent. This may be inferred from the Fourth Council of Carthage when it prescribes the daily imposition of hands by the exorcist.[62] Duchesne, in writing of the seventh or last scrutiny immediately before baptism [i.e., on Saturday before Easter], quotes the form of exorcism used, which was pronounced by the priest himself instead of one of the inferior clergy.[63] The symbolical meaning at this last exorcism was that the crucial battle with Satan had arrived.[64] The candidates were now prepared to throw off the power of the devil in their final renunciation and be bound to Christ. Other symbolic acts of exorcism were the *"exsufflatio,"* the out-breathing of the devil, the *"insufflatio,"* the in-breathing of the Holy Spirit by the priest, the purifying anointment with oil, the imposition of hands, and the signing of the Cross.

59 *Ibid.*, "The Second Apology," VI; cf. also Tertullian, *Apologeticus*, 22, 23.
60 *Apost. Const.*, VII, 41.
61 Hippolytus, *Canones*, XIX, 9. The Service of Adult Baptism in the Lutheran Church today reads; "Dost thou renounce the devil, and all his works and all his ways?" The answer, "Yes, I renounce."
62 *Conc. Carth.*, IV, can. XC.
63 *Christian Worship*, 303.
64 *Ibid.*, 304.

REQUIREMENTS AND PRIVILEGES OF BAPTISM

For the *Competentes,* now about to receive baptism, three things were indispensably required. First, they must make their sincere, formal, and solemn renunciation of the devil. That was, in a measure, required of them before, but now they were to make a solemn profession of it before the congregation. The form and content of that renunciation is gathered from Cyril's post-baptismal lectures.[65]

They were to stand facing the West, the region of darkness, and renounce the dark and gloomy potentate.[66] They were to renounce everything that pertained to the devil, namely, "all deeds and thoughts which are against better judgment."[67]

In addition to the devil "and his works," they were commanded to renounce "all his pomp." By pomp was understood the affairs at the circus, the games, the theatre, dancing, the hunts, intemperance, pagan festivals, etc.[68] In the directions given to the bishops, presbyters, and deacons, the *Constitutions* draws up a specific list of all those who are to be refused baptism unless they abandon their practices.[69] When, therefore, Augustine launches out in his *De Fide et Operibus* against those who would ignore at baptism disgraceful conduct and habits, he is in step with the sentiment of the Church.

Having made their renunciation of the devil, the *Competentes* promised to live in obedience to Christ and the laws and rules of the Christian faith. The Greeks referred to this act of obedience as "giving themselves up to the government and conduct of Christ."[70] Bingham refers to passages in several of the Greek Fathers that substantiate the fact.[71] The Latins refer to this step as *"promissum, pactum, et votum."*[72] Augustine calls it "A profession made in the court of angels; and the names

65 It was the feeling among the Fathers that the mysteries of the Christian faith should be presented only in a covert way before baptism. Consequently, more thorough and elucidative lectures were given on the sacraments after baptism. They were considered more fit, then, to receive them.
66 Cyril, *Cat. Lect.,* XIX, 4.
67 *Ibid.,* 5.
68 *Ibid.,* 6, 7.
69 *Apost. Const.,* VIII, 32.
70 Bingham, *Antiq.,* III, 538. The Greek form is "suntassomai soi, Christe".
71 *Ibid.,* 540f.
72 *Ibid.,* 541.

of the professors are written in the Book of life, not by any man, but by the heavenly powers."[73]

The third requirement was to face the East, the region of light, and make profession of their faith in the Creed that had been taught to them by the catechist a little before the day of baptism. The Creed was never written because some who were not *Competentes* might be able to read it. The candidates were directed to let their "memory be their record-roll."[74] They were encouraged to recite the Creed every day and have it firmly planted in their minds.

Some in Augustine's day were of the opinion that the Creed should be reduced to a single article, "I believe Jesus Christ to be the Son of God." They used as their argument the example of Philip baptizing the eunuch. Augustine's reply was to the effect that for brevity's sake the other points of doctrine, e.g., the Holy Ghost, the Church, the Incarnation, Resurrection, etc., were omitted from the Scripture text but understood in the conversation.[75] The Church never omitted any of the Articles of the Creed, not even in clinical baptism. If the candidates were not able to memorize the Creed, they were still questioned in every particular.[76] By one means or another the whole Creed was repeated and assented to.[77]

A word has yet to be said concerning the rewards or privileges of the baptized. That there were special privileges beyond those granted to them as *Competentes* is clear in Augustine and elsewhere. It was the very anticipation of those good things and the psychology of withholding them from those to be baptized that was a cause for increase in membership.

A fuller explanation of the meaning of baptism itself was one of the special privileges. Though the candidates were prepared for baptism, it was not until after their initiation that they were instructed in the deeper meaning of the mystery. So Cyril in his post-baptismal lectures explains to the neophytes the significance of the various acts of the baptismal liturgy; the meaning of 'putting off the garment', the anointing with exorcised oil over the entire body, entering the pool of baptism and

73 Quoted from Bingham, III, 542.
74 *A Select Library of the Nicene and Post-Nicene Fathers of the Christian Church* (Buffalo, 1886), Augustine, "On the Creed," I.
75 *De Fide et Operibus*, IX.
76 Bingham, *Antiquities*, 544.
77 The formal liturgy of baptism has been thoroughly treated by Duchesne and others and will not be treated here.

the symbolism of the service there and the administration of the holy chrism to parts of the body.[78] These explanations were reserved for the octave of Easter and could not be imparted sooner. So reads the *Pilgrimage of Etheria*:

> But the teachings of the deeper mystery, that is, of Baptism itself, you cannot hear, being as yet catechumens [i.e. competentes]. But, lest you should think that anything is done without good reason, these, when you have been baptized in the Name of God, you shall hear in the Anastasis, during the eight Paschal days, after the Dismissal from the Church has been made. You, being as yet catechumens, cannot be told the more secret mysteries of God.[79]

Of course, the greatest privilege was that of receiving the sacrament of the Body and Blood of Christ for the remission of sins and the strengthening of faith. It must be remembered, of course, that the unbaptized as long as they remained so were living in mortal sin. They received no forgiveness. As long as they were catechumens so long did they carry the guilt of all their sins. Consequently, their baptism brought them the greatest of all blessings, the complete remission of their sins. Sins committed after baptism were venial and remediable by prayer, or penance in serious cases. Immediately upon their baptism, at the Easter service, they participated in the communion and every day during the Octave they received the sacrament. When the faithful were about to receive the elements, the deacon would proclaim *"hagia hagiois,"* "holy things for holy men."[80] Yet the deeper mystery of the Eucharist was not explained until after the baptismal service. The neophytes were instructed more carefully concerning the meaning of the bread and wine and the various parts of the liturgy in the communion service, e.g., the spiritual kiss, the *sursum corde,* the thanksgiving, the *sanctus,* etc.[81]

The use of the Lord's Prayer also was a privilege of the neophytes even though in anticipation they were taught the words and meaning of the prayer immediately preceding their baptism. Still it was considered the prayer of the faithful, *oratio fidelium,* and not to be used except by those who had become "sons of God" by regeneration. There were other prayers also that were denied the catechumens because they spoke of the

78 Cyril, *Cat. Lect.,* XX-XXI.
79 Quoted from Duchesne, *Christian Worship,* Appendix, 575.
80 Bingham, *Antiquities,* I, 36.
81 Cyril, *Cat. Lect.,* XXII-XXIII; cf. also Augustine, *Sermo ad Competentes,* LVII, 7.

divine mysteries but which were entered into by the neophytes and the faithful.[82]

In addition to the above, it must be assumed that the normal privileges of Church membership were open to the baptized, such as the administration of Church matters and full participation in all the affairs of the Church.

AUGUSTINE'S CONTRIBUTION

No one in the early eastern or western Church has contributed more to the development of the catechetical system or has kept more clearly in mind the great group of inquirers and catechumens than Augustine. The difficulties involved in his own personal pilgrimage to Christianity and his varied experience, intellectual and moral, provided an excellent background for an understanding of the catechumens' problems and needs. He was also in a position to advise intelligently the catechists regarding the proper psychological approaches, the content and method of instruction. Catholic and Protestant catechetics alike through the centuries have been indebted to him. For that reason we give attention to his contribution now.

Chief among his catechetical writings and specifically for the use of catechists is the *De Catechizandis Rudibus*. It is addressed to one Deogratias, a deacon of Carthage, who apparently had been known as a popular catechist but who had repeated difficulties in finding satisfactory techniques or vehicles for the presentation of his material. His discourses often became languid and profitless to the teacher and learners alike.[83] With those facts in mind, Augustine wrote his treatise.

This work, like most of his other writings, is intensely practical and indicates that he himself devoted careful attention to the business of instructing those who wished to learn the rudiments of the Faith. It indicates that he also had experienced the tediousness and even monotony of the task and had given careful consideration to the best methods of dealing with the various classes of converts.

It is a model on the art of catechising and an actual demonstration of instructing the unlearned and the learned. The work is neatly arranged into the following outline:

1. Practical methods of instruction (I-VII)

82 e.g., the communion prayers were not used in the presence of the unbaptized.
83 *Corp. Script. Eccl. Lat.*, De Cat. Rud., 1. Because of its distinctive and exemplary character, this work will be treated at some length.

2. Dealing with the learned (VIII, IX)
3. Causes of weariness and remedies (X-XV)
4. A typical demonstration lesson (XVI-XXVII)

To the teacher who is dissatisfied with his discourses and fears that the hearers are receiving very little that is worthwhile, Augustine remarks that the teacher must not judge the value of his lessons by the effect upon himself but by the effect upon the hearers. The lecture may not be so frigid as it seems. The very fact that the catechumens come with regularity is one indication that it is not displeasing to them.[84] Above all the catechist himself must have a deep interest in his work:

And in reality we are listened to with much greater satisfaction, indeed, when we ourselves also have pleasure in the same work; for the thread of our address is affected by the very joy of which we ourselves are sensible, and it proceeds from us with greater ease and with more acceptance.[85]

The successful instructor is one who has learned the art of putting himself constantly in the position of the hearer and acting as if he were telling something always new. A bright and cheerful[86] manner is one of the qualifications of the teacher. Another is the contagiousness of his whole personality in teaching.

. . . Whatever you narrate, narrate it in such a manner that he to whom you are discoursing on hearing may believe, on believing may hope, on hoping may love.[87]

Augustine displays a certain wisdom of pedagogical method in his directions regarding the examination into the motives of inquirers. Recognizing that some will come out of faulty motives, desiring only personal advantages, he indicates how the instructor may use the false motive as a point of departure in his teaching of the unlearned:

Nevertheless, the very untruth which he utters should be made the point from which we start. This should not be done, however, with the (open) intention of confuting his falsehood, as if that were a settled matter with you; but taking it for granted that he has professed to have come with a purpose which is really worthy of approbation . . . it should rather be our aim to commend and praise such a purpose as that with which, in his reply, he has declared himself to have come; so that we may make him feel it is a pleasure to be the kind of man actually that he wishes to seem to be.[88]

84 *Ibid.*, 3, 4.
85 *Ibid.*, 4.
86 "hilaritas."
87 *Ibid.*, 8.
88 *Ibid.*, 9.

In every instance it is important to ascertain their frame of mind and motives. More than usual kindness, gentleness, and patience should be exercised lest the ignorant inquirer be confused and disturbed from the start. Augustine then proceeds to outline the content and manner of relating Christian truth to this class of the ignorant, beginning with the story of creation and continuing on to the present period of the Church, not in the greatest detail but in a somewhat cursory manner.[89] It is of utmost importance to indicate the relationship between the Old and New Testaments showing that "in the Old Testament there is a veiling of the New, and in the New Testament there is a revealing of the Old."

Dealing with the well-educated and those already acquainted with the Scriptures and other Christian writings requires a briefer period of instruction. Very little time should be spent on the things they already learned previously. Recognition should be given of their knowledge of the Faith and enquiries ought to be made into the causes which have led them to Christianity, particularly, what books have influenced them. The major emphasis will be placed, therefore, not on the body of doctrine, but on the mysteries.[90]

Regarding the method to be used with grammarians and rhetoricians, Augustine is especially skillfull and is obviously speaking out of his own experience. Having been one of the learned himself, and a rhetorician, he could well understand the approach to be used. They must be taught to "clothe themselves with Christian humility" and not be so presumptuous as to compare purity of heart with a practiced tongue.[91]

The section on the causes of weariness and its remedies from the standpoint of catechetics, is the most practical and valuable part of the work. For those who grow weary from constantly having to come down to the level of the hearers and sacrificing the joys of superior knowledge, Augustine draws the example of Christ who humbled himself, taking the form of a servant and suffering the death of the cross. When the constant repetition of the same material causes weariness, the instructor must vary the presentation of the subjects and increase in earnestness of mind. He must remember that though the instruction is not up to his ideal and to his delight, it may be exact-

89 *Ibid.*, 6, 7.
90 *Ibid.*, 8.
91 *Ibid.*, 9.

ly suited to the listener and completely fresh and new to him. When the hearer makes little progress and seems to be un-moved so that it causes weariness to the instructor, he should be questioned concerning the material, personally examined and kindly exhorted and if his sluggishness is the result of practical difficulties or inconveniences[92] they should be remedied. If weariness is the result of having to give up some preferred employment to train catechumens, the catechist must ever remember that it is a matter of duty and of performing the will of God regardless of one's own wishes.[93]

Having given a somewhat detailed, theoretical, and psychological bit of advice, Augustine turns to the very practical, and gives a demonstration lesson to be taught to a group of ordinary inquirers, neither grossly ignorant nor highly intelligent. In his discourse he dwells upon the importance of right motives for baptism, introduces gradually key passages in Old and New Testament literature, a sketchy summary of Christ's life, death and resurrection with their meanings, the cardinal doctrines of the Church, the sanctity of the sacraments, and a subtle introduction of the significance of the Creed. From first to last, Augustine is careful to weave the doctrinal and moral together in the thread of his discourse. The hearer is not left in doubt about what kind of life is expected of him and at the concluding lecture is asked whether he is willing to renounce pagan practices before he is signed as a catechumen.[94]

It was said above that no one in the early eastern or western Church kept more clearly in mind the group of inquirers and catechumens than Augustine. One needs only to select at random sermons of Augustine to discover that he had them constantly in view. He looked upon the sermon as a means primarily of teaching, and never tired—though sometimes he tired his hearers—of presenting to them Christian doctrine and its inevitable moral implications. Even in an obviously doctrinal presentation of the Creed to the *Competentes,* Augustine concludes with the words:

> When ye have been baptized, hold fast a good life in the commandments of God, that ye may guard your Baptism even unto the end. . . . Do

92 The reference here is to the practice of making the hearers stand during the instruction. When the period of teaching was lengthy, it became a great inconvenience and made instructing difficult. Augustine urged the abolition of that practice wherever possible and advocated sitting during the lessons.
93 *Ibid.,* 10-15.
94 *Ibid.,* 16-27.

not commit those things for which ye must needs be separated from Christ's body: which be far from you![95]

Often in a sermon primarily addressed to the faithful, he would leave off to address himself to catechumens regarding their personal preparation for baptism, which at the same time served as an injunction to the believers.

There are extant a few sermons preached specifically to the *Competentes* on the Lord's Prayer and the Creed, probably delivered within the last two weeks before baptism.[96] In those discourses on the Prayer, Augustine takes each petition separately, analyses it simply, that all may understand, and then makes the application. The following passage will illustrate his method:

Quae et dicitis, in cordibus vestris dicite. Sit orantis affectus, et erit exaudientis effectus. 'Sanctificetur nomen tuum.' Quid rogas ut sanctificetur nomen Dei? Sanctum est. Quid rogas, quod iam sanctum est? Deinde cum rogas ut sanctificetur nomen ipsis, nonne quasi pro illo illum rogas, et non pro te? Intellige, et pro te rogas. Hoc enim rogas, ut quod semper sanctum est in se sanctificetur in te. Quid est, sanctificetur? Sanctum habeatur, non contemnatur. Ergo vides quia cum optas, tibi bonum optas. Tibi enim malum est si contempseris nomen Dei, non Deo.[97]

Again, let it be said that Augustine's emphasis is always simultaneously doctrinal and moral, faith and the good life. For example, in the somewhat lengthy passage on the petition, "forgive us our trespasses as we forgive those who trespass against us," he says:

Et hoc orare, sentinare est. Non tantum autem debemus orare, sed et eleemosynam facere; quia quando sentinatur ne navis mergatur, et vocibus agitur et manibus[98]. . . Nihil mali faciat manus; non currat pes ad aliquid mali; non dirigatur oculus in lasciviam; non auris libenter pateat turpitudine; non moveatur lingua ad id quod non decet.[99]

The candidate for baptism may learn to pray "Thy Kingdom come," but if he shall remain a moral reprobate, that Kingdom will come to others but not to him.[100] To qualify for baptism he must establish a right relationship with his fellowmen, put away all sin and lust and avarice and learn to conquer himself.[101] The

95 "On the Creed," 15.
96 Migne, *Pat. Lat.*, *Sermones*, LVI-LIX, CCXII-CCXVI.
97 *Sermo* LVI, 5. There is a startling similarity between Augustine's words and approach and Luther's in his *Small Catechism*.
98 *Ibid.*, 11.
99 *Ibid.*, 12.
100 *Sermo* LVII, 5.
101 *Ibid.*, 8-13.

Christian must always abound in the doing of good works, in the forgiving of wrong-doers, in the giving of alms, both from the heart and out of his substance, in the control of his tongue and conduct.[102] A person who has found that he has a Father in heaven ought to live that he may be worthy of the inheritance.[103] In a remarkable passage on the Creed, Augustine encourages the *Competentes* to repeat the symbol daily until it becomes part of them:

. . . quotdie dicit; quando surgitis, quando vos ad somnum collocatis, reddite Symbolum vestrum, repetere. Bona est enim repetitio, ne subrepat oblivio.

Commemora fidem tuam, inspice te: sit tanquam speculum tibi Symbolum tuum. Ibi te vide, si credis omnia quae te credere confiteris, et gaude quotidie in fide tua. Sint divitae tuae, sint quotadiana ista quodam modo indumenta mentis tuae. Numquid non quando surgis vestis te? Sic et commemorando Symbolum tuum vesti animam tuam, ne fórte eam nudet oblivio, et remaneas nudus.[104]

In his sermons specifically on the delivery of the Creed to the *Competentes,* though Augustine speaks considerably more in theological terms as may be expected in any treatment of the unity of the Godhead, the mystery of the Trinity, and the significance of the Cross and Resurrection, still he endeavors to make clear to the *Competentes* what is expected of one who makes such a declaration of faith. This is most clearly brought out in a sermon on the *"Redditio Symboli"*[105] and a separate discourse on the significance of the renunciation of the world and the devil and the meaning and implications of regeneration.[106]

A decade before his death, Augustine wrote a book on *De Fide, Spe, Charitate* in which he summarized for a certain Laurentius[107] the various articles of the Christian faith under the headings of the Creed, the Lord's Prayer, and Christian love. This work was not meant to be specifically a catechetical treatise, but a kind of handbook or *Enchiridion.* Yet by the very fact that it was written simply and for the laymen indicates that Augustine meant it for instructive purposes. As a handbook, it could easily be carried and perused by the individual and serve as a facile source of reference for the believer's own benefit as well as for the catechist in his teaching. One notes immediately

102 *Sermo* LVII, 10, 11.
103 *Ibid.*, 2.
104 *Ibid.*, 13.
105 *Sermo* CCXV.
106 *Sermo* CCXVI.
107 Nothing other is known of the man; probably a layman. P. Schaff.

upon reading it that its style and language is fitted for popular instruction and by its development is intended to present briefly and compactly the whole scope of Christian teaching and its moral demands on the believer. A disproportionate space is given to an explanation of the matters of faith (I-CXIII) and virtually nothing to the Prayer (CXIV-CXVI) and the discourse on Christian love (CXVII-CXXII). What a person should believe and how he should live are thoroughly discussed. Little is said of the hidden meanings of the sacraments disclosed only to the faithful.[108]

Just a few words must be said concerning the *De Fide et Operibus* as it relates to Augustine's contribution to catechetical literature and practice. It has been customary to consider this work as one of the moral treatises in that it arose out of social perversions prevalent in parts of the Church whereby some were admitted to baptism who were living profligately. In that sense it is a moral treatise and Augustine condemns the practices with the ardor of a social reformer. Bardenhewer, on the other hand, includes the work among the dogmatic writings of Augustine in that he develops the truth, which is soundly biblical, that faith and works are inseparable and must be united through love.[109] In that sense it is a dogmatic treatise and Augustine speaks as a sound theologian. Yet in a still larger sense, the *De Fide et Operibus* takes into view the whole system of catechetical instruction and is written for the direct benefit of catechists to guide them in their selection of catechumens and their course of teaching, and for the benefit of catechumens who desire baptism and are uninformed or misinformed about the requirements. From first to last, Augustine is concerned with baptism and the worthiness of the candidates to receive it. This work is part of the unique contribution of Augustine to catechetical literature and is a complement to his *De Catechizandis Rudibus,* his *Sermones,* particularly to the *Competentes,* and his *Enchiridion.*

108 This would seem to be in keeping with the practice of the catechumenate.
109 Bardenhewer, O., *Patrology—The Lives and Works of the Fathers of the Church* (St. Louis, Mo., 1908).
1908).

AUX ORIGINES DU CATÉCHUMÉNAT

Alors qu'il y a encore une trentaine d'années on ne parlait guère de catéchuménat avant le IIIe ou le IVe siècle, diverses études se sont attachées depuis à retrouver, sinon un catéchuménat primitif, du moins les premiers éléments de l'organisation de la catéchèse baptismale, les premiers jalons de cette institution (1). On essaiera dans cet article de faire le point de la question, non sans souligner dès l'abord que, en dépit de bien des affirmations solides, il reste beaucoup d'incertitudes qu'on a parfois tendance à résoudre trop systématiquement.

1. L'enseignement aux chrétiens.

« Ceux qui accueillirent sa parole (le discours kérygmatique de Pierre qui précède) furent baptisés, et, ce jour-là, trois mille personnes environ se joignirent aux disciples. Ils se montraient assidus aux instructions (τῇ διδαχῇ) des Apôtres, fidèles à la communion fraternelle, à la fraction du pain et aux prières » (*Act.* 2, 41-42).

Ce texte situe bien notre point de départ. Il y a ici successivement proposition du kérygme, conversion et foi, baptême, développement de la foi dans la vie chrétienne en ses trois temps forts : enseignement, vie de charité, vie liturgique. « L'enseignement des Apôtres », dans ce contexte, c'est l'enseignement donné aux

---

(1) Depuis l'article classique de dom B. Capelle, *L'introduction du catéchuménat à Rome*, dans *Rech. Théol. anc. méd.*, (1933) pp. 129-154, les ouvrages récents donnent toute la bibliographie désirable. Notons, parmi les plus récents : R. F. Refoulé, *Introduction au « De Baptismo » de Tertullien* (Sources chrétiennes 35), Paris 1952 ; A. Stenzel, *Le Baptême, Étude génétique de la liturgie baptismale* (= *Die Taufe*, Innsbruck 1958) ; M. Dujarier, *Le parrainage des adultes aux trois premiers siècles*, Paris 1962 ; A. Turck, *Évangélisation et Catéchèse aux deux premiers siècles*, Paris 1962 ; dom Th. Maertens, *Histoire et Pastorale du rituel du catéchuménat et du baptême*, Saint André-de-Bruges 1962.

chrétiens (2) ; ce n'est plus l'Évangile aux païens ; ce n'est pas une instruction aux postulants. C'est, à l'usage des nouveaux baptisés qui se joignent aux Apôtres, une vraie *catéchèse* qui déploie pour les auditeurs les dimensions et les exigences de leur existence renouvelée par le baptême.

Cet enseignement n'est pas laissé au caprice de chacun ; il est d'abord διδαχὴ τῶν 'Αποστόλων.. Puis, de nombreux textes du N. T. témoignent également de l'existence des *docteurs* (διδάσκαλοι). En *Act.* 13, 1, les docteurs sont situés à côté des prophètes ; en *1 Cor.* 12, 28-29, à côté des apôtres et des prophètes, et même des thaumaturges et des glossolales. Leur fonction (ou mieux ici : leur charisme) est « d'exposer les vérités élémentaires du christianisme : l'enseignement élémentaire sur le Christ d'*Heb.* 6, 1 » (3). Ces *didaskaloi* sont donc « les chrétiens instruits chargés dans chaque église de l'enseignement régulier et ordinaire » (4). En *Eph.* 4, 11, on trouve, après les apôtres et les prophètes : les évangélistes, les pasteurs et les docteurs. Il y manque les diacres, qu'on trouve en particulier en *Rom.* 12, 6-8 *(diakonia)*. Certes, presbytres et épiscopes doivent être capables d'enseigner (*1 Tim.* 3, 2. 5, 17) ; l'épiscope doit avoir « à cœur de donner un enseignement sûr (littér. « fidèle à la doctrine »), pour être capable à la fois d'exhorter dans la saine doctrine et de réfuter les contradicteurs » (*Tite* 1, 9). Mais d'autres que les presbytres et les épiscopes peuvent être docteurs ; et en revanche presbytres et épiscopes n'ont pas pour unique tâche d'enseigner ; ils sont plutôt le collège autour des Apôtres, qui prend en charge l'administration et la surveillance des premières communautés (5).

Il est, dès lors, tout naturel que les docteurs, ces responsables de l'enseignement dans la communauté chrétienne, prennent aussitôt en charge ceux qui ont adhéré à l'Évangile par la conversion et la foi et qui ont reçu le baptême. Nous avons appelé *catéchèse* cet enseignement ; ce terme serait impropre ici s'il désignait toujours et strictement la *préparation* au baptême. Mais il désigne aussi, un peu plus largement, l'instruction et l'initiation *liées* au baptême :

(2) P. Benoit, *Les « sommaires » des Actes*, dans *Exégèse et Théologie* II, Paris 1961, p. 185 ; J. Dupont, *Bible de Jérus.*, note sur *Act.* 6, 4.

(3) E. Osty, *Bible de Jérus.*, note sur *1 Cor.* 12, 8 (le λόγος γνώσεως). Le renvoi de E. Osty à *Heb.* 6, 1 est fort intéressant pour notre propos. Cf. A. Turck, *op. cit.*, pp. 144-150. Contre la distinction de E. Osty entre « parole de sagesse » et « parole de science », voir R. Bultmann, γνῶσις, dans *TWNT* (Kittel), I, 707.

(4) E. Allo, *Iʳᵉ Épître aux Corinthiens*, Paris 1934, p. 325, cité par E. Osty, *ibid.* Sur ces « docteurs », cf. A. Harnack, *Die Mission und Ausbreitung des Christentums*, 2ᵉ éd., Leipzig 1906, tome 1, pp. 298-307.

(5) Voir note sur *Tite* 1, 5 dans *Bible de Jérus.*, et J. Colson, *Le Collège apostolique et l'évangélisation primitive*, dans *Mission sans frontières*, Paris 1960, pp. 75-82.

la catéchèse, c'est toujours, d'une façon ou d'une autre, la catéchèse *baptismale*. On ne peut donc refuser ce terme à l'enseignement des tout premiers convertis ; ils sont tous néophytes ! Et c'est à partir de ces catéchèses aux premiers chrétiens que va peu à peu s'organiser, se structurer, la catéchèse au sens strict, l'enseignement aux postulants, très tôt appelés catéchumènes (6). Mais nous n'en sommes pas encore là.

2. Le baptême « accordé facilement et sans délai ».

« Ceux qui accueillirent sa parole furent baptisés, et, ce jour-là, trois mille personnes environ se joignirent aux disciples » (*Act.* 2, 41).

Sur la catéchèse stricto sensu nous avons commencé comme chacun par lire l'article classique et remarquable de dom Capelle sur « l'introduction du catéchuménat à Rome ». Or le début de cet article va à l'encontre de plusieurs thèses actuelles. Il commence ainsi : « Nous nous proposons, après avoir rappelé brièvement ce qu'on sait de la préparation au baptême à Rome jusqu'à S. Justin, etc. » (7). En fait ce « rappel bref » est totalement inexistant : il y a une page pour citer les textes kérygmatiques des Actes, mais rien de spécifiquement catéchétique. Et il continue avec les explications suivantes, qui sont capitales : « c'est donc la foi qui est la condition principale du baptême et c'est dans l'enseignement de la foi que consiste la préparation essentielle au sacrement. Les dispositions morales sont le plus souvent sous-entendues. On mentionne comme évident et sans y insister le repentir préalable. Le baptême est accordé facilement et sans délai. C'est de lui plus que des dispositions du cœur que le candidat attend le renouvellement profond de son âme » (8). Puis, sans transition, on passe à S. Justin.

Il faut souligner les mots « facilement et sans délai », ainsi que la dernière phrase citée de dom Capelle. Ne sont-ils pas la preuve que, pour l'auteur, il n'y a pas de catéchèse *préalable* au baptême au début de l'Église ? A l'encontre de ce point de vue, L. Villette a écrit plus récemment : le baptême ne se donne « qu'après une instruction doctrinale destinée à parfaire et contrôler la foi du postulant ». Mais bon nombre des textes des *Actes* qu'il cite à l'appui renvoient à l'annonce kérygmatique plutôt qu'à l'instruction doctrinale ; et le baptême suit immédiatement la conversion et la foi (9).

---

(6) Sur les questions de vocabulaire, voir A. Turck, *Catéchein et Catéchèsis chez les premiers Pères*, dans *Rev. Sc. ph. th.*, 47 (1963) pp. 361-372.

(7) *Art. cit.* à la note 1, p. 130.

(8) *Art. cit.*, p. 131.

(9) L. Villette, *Foi et Sacrement*, Paris 1959, p. 111 et note ; cf. *Act.* 2, 37-41, 47. 4, 4. 8, 12-16. 16, 29-33, etc.

« Paul aussi fut baptisé sans délai » écrit Tertullien. Certes il souligne que c'est parce que « la faveur de Dieu d'avance a donné des signes du choix qu'elle a fait » (10). Mais comment croire que Tertullien, si strict par ailleurs et déplorant si fort le relâchement de la préparation au baptême, n'aurait pas saisi l'occasion de développer ses exigences s'il les avait trouvées en germe dans le cas de S. Paul (11) ? Et de même dans le commentaire qu'il fait du baptême de l'eunuque (*Act.* 8) (12).

Certains textes des *Actes Apocryphes* vont dans le même sens. Ainsi dans *Actes de Barnabé* 13 : « nous croyons au Dieu vivant et vrai que tu annonces. — Alors il les emmena à la source, et il les baptisa » : il y a ici kérygme (κηρύττεις) — foi (πιστεύομεν) — baptême. De même dans *Actes de Thaddée* 4 : « ayant instruit (κατηχήσας) des multitudes, il les baptisa... », l'emploi populaire de κατηχεῖν fait penser aux grands discours kérygmatiques des *Actes des Apôtres*, et également la présence des foules (πολλὰ πλήθη) (13).

Or ces baptêmes rapides ne reflètent pas seulement une pratique de l'Église primitive ; certains écrits se sont essayés à les justifier théologiquement, témoin ce texte d'*Homélie Clémentine* 8, 23 :

« Empressez-vous de vous dépouiller tout d'abord de vos sales préoccupations, qui sont un esprit impur et un vêtement souillé. Or vous ne pouvez vous en dépouiller qu'en vous faisant préalablement baptiser en vue d'accomplir de bonnes actions » (14).

Soulignons encore le « préalablement » : le baptême est la source et le point de départ des actions bonnes, car Dieu seul, et par le rite baptismal, dépouille du péché ; il n'y a pas à vouloir essayer

---

(10) *De Baptismo* 18, 3 ; R. F. REFOULÉ, p. 92.

(11) Point de vue différent chez Th. MAERTENS, *op. cit.*, pp. 49-51 ; M. DUJARIER, *op. cit.*, p. 130.

(12) Cf. A. TURCK, *Évangélisation et catéchèse*, pp. 64-67. Pour l'exégèse et l'apparat critique d'*Act* 8, 36-38, voir F. JACKSON and K. LAKE, *The beginnings of Christianity, the Acts of the Apostles*, éd. 1933, vol. III, pp. 82-83 ; et pour le commentaire, vol. IV, note sur *Act.* 8, 36. On ne peut guère forcer la portée de ce passage des Actes. Certes, le v. 37 du *textus receptus* est cité par IRÉNÉE, *Adv. Haer.* III, 12, 8 (trad. SAGNARD, Sources chrétiennes 34, p. 231) ; mais il est le témoin du kérygme primitif, et peut-être surtout d'un dialogue de type liturgique (MAERTENS, *op. cit.* p. 43, DUJARIER, *op. cit.* pp. 126-127) plutôt que de l'absence d'une catéchèse autre que celle sur le Christ Jésus. Que ce verset soit interpolé ne prouve pas qu'il n'ait une « provenance très ancienne », qu'il ne nous « renvoie aux temps les plus reculés de l'Église » : O. CULLMANN, *Les traces d'une vieille formule baptismale dans le N. T.*, dans *Le Baptême des enfants*, Neuchâtel-Paris 1948, pp. 63-69. Mais il n'est pas comme tel le signe que la catéchèse, au temps d'Irénée, est réduite à la seule affirmation christologique.

(13) Ceci nuance l'affirmation de M. DUJARIER, *op. cit.* p. 298 : « les récits (des Actes Apocryphes) laissent apercevoir distinctement l'étape de conversion et l'étape d'enseignement ».

(14) SIOUVILLE p. 218.

de s'en dépouiller par soi-même préalablement : « Si vous ne renaissez pas par l'eau vive au nom du Père, du Fils et du Saint-Esprit, vous n'entrerez pas dans le Royaume des Cieux » (15). L'Église, en opposition à tous les rites de purification juifs, se sait et s'affirme la vraie Communauté de l'Alliance, le Peuple eschatologique ; en ce sens, elle n'a et ne peut avoir « ni postulat ni noviciat, parce qu'elle inaugure l'ère de l'Esprit et que la conversion à l'Évangile est d'abord grâce » (16).

Certes ce n'est là qu'un des courants dans l'Église primitive, on le verra par la suite ; et « il serait (...) faux d'arguer de la rapidité des premiers baptêmes pour prétendre justifier une administration trop hâtive du sacrement » (17). Mais il le serait également d'arguer de la présence de certaines conditions au baptême, posées dans certains cas, pour étendre ces conditions à tous les cas. Bardy, après Tertullien, pense qu'il y eut des baptêmes trop hâtifs (18) et qu'il a fallu y remédier en organisant une catéchèse préalable et institutionnelle.

3. Une catéchèse préalable.

Dès l'époque apostolique, la prédication revêtit toutes les formes offertes par les circonstances : annonce (kérygmatique) et instruction (didactique), en public et en privé, s'adressant aux Juifs et aux Grecs, ayant pour objet Dieu et Jésus-Christ (19). Ces diverses formes sont parfaitement exposées par S. Paul lui-même, en deux textes :

« Je n'ai rien omis de ce qui pouvait vous être utile, vous prêchant et vous instruisant, en public et chez vous, adjurant Juifs et Grecs... » (*Act.* 20, 20-21).

« Paul demeura deux années entières dans un logement qu'il avait loué. Il y recevait tous ceux qui venaient le trouver, prêchant le Royaume de Dieu et enseignant ce qui concerne le Seigneur Jésus-Christ » (*Act.* 28, 30).

Il n'y a donc pas toujours eu, à l'origine, une distinction très claire entre annonce et instruction, kérygme et catéchèse. Avec A. Seeberg, on peut penser que parallèlement aux discours missionnaires sur la place publique — qui sont typiquement le kérygme —

---

(15) *Hom. Clem.* 11, 26 ; Siouville p. 256.
(16) J. Schmitt, cité dans M. Dujarier, pp. 113-114.
(17) M. Dujarier, *op. cit.*, p. 118.
(18) G. Bardy, *La conversion au Christianisme durant les premiers siècles*, Paris 1947, p. 300.
(19) Cf. J. Dupont, *Le discours de Milet*, Paris 1962, pp. 80-83.

il y eut couramment aussi la « mission à domicile » (Hausmission), plus proche de l'enseignement (20).

Or cette catéchèse ou évangélisation à domicile est un des traits marquants des Actes Apocryphes. En voici un bon exemple :

«... Thècle entra donc avec elle et se reposa huit jours dans sa maison, lui enseignant (κατηχήσασα) la parole de Dieu ; aussi crut-elle, ainsi que la plupart des servantes » (21).

Ici l'enseignement mène à la foi ; les deux étapes ne sont guère distinguées : l'Évangile du Salut semble être donné d'emblée sous forme d'enseignement. Et bien d'autres textes de ces Actes Apocryphes témoignent de l'existence d'une instruction avant le baptême. Par exemple :

« (Jean) le catéchisa, lui expliqua les règles (κανόνας) (de la vie chrétienne) et le renvoya chez lui » (22).

« L'Apôtre (Philippe) commença à leur enseigner à partir des Écritures ce qui touche le Fils de Dieu (...) Ils lui répondirent : tout ce que tu nous as dit, nous le faisons, et nous croyons en Notre-Seigneur Jésus-Christ (...) Alors il les baptisa » (23).

Cette catéchèse préalable au baptême vise donc la foi et la vie (ποιοῦμεν καὶ πιστεύομεν).

« Il commença donc à leur enseigner (διδάσκειν) ce qui touche la foi et le Fils de Dieu, et les ayant catéchisés (κατηχήσας), eux et tous ceux de la maison, il les baptisa. »

« Tous crurent à Notre Seigneur Jésus-Christ ; alors, dès l'aurore, Philippe commença à les catéchiser (κατηχεῖν) et à les baptiser... » (24).

Ici la catéchèse s'inscrit bien entre la conversion et le baptême ; elle semble être l'ultime préparation au baptême. Dernier exemple, dans les *Actes de Pierre* 5 : l'Apôtre, embarqué de la Palestine vers Rome, a fait connaissance de Théon :

« Chaque jour il lui communiquait la parole de Dieu. Et à le voir, il se rendit compte, par ses entretiens, qu'il partageait sa foi et serait un digne serviteur (de Dieu) ; et comme un calme plat arrêta le navire dans l'Adriatique, Théon le fit remarquer à Pierre

---

(20) A. Seeberg, *Die Didache des Judentums und die Urchristenheit*, Leipzig 1908, pp. 86-87. Rengstorf, *TWNT* (Kittel), II, 141-150, a bien expliqué la diversité des sens de διδάσκω dans le NT.

(21) *Actes de Paul et Thècle* 39 ; L. Vouaux, p. 222.

(22) *Actes de Jean* 57 ; trad. F. Amiot, *Les Évangiles Apocryphes*, Paris 1952, p. 169.

(23) *Actes de Philippe* 35-36 ; éd. Lipsius-Bonnet, Leipzig 1898-1903.

(24) *Actes de Philippe* 63. 85-86.

et lui dit : « Si tu veux bien me juger digne d'être baptisé dans le
signe du Seigneur, voilà l'occasion. » En effet tous les passagers,
ivres, s'étaient endormis. Pierre, descendant à l'aide d'une corde,
baptisa Théon au nom du Père et du Fils et du Saint-Esprit.
Et Théon sortit de l'eau, joyeux d'une grande joie ; Pierre lui-même
devint plus heureux de ce que Dieu avait rendu Théon digne de
son nom » (25).

Ici l'Apôtre prend son temps : il attend de *se rendre compte* que
Théon a bien la foi et qu'il sera *digne* du baptême — ou mieux :
qu'il sera *capable* de vivre selon son baptême. Et c'est Théon qui
demande à être baptisé. Enfin l'on souligne que c'est Dieu qui rend
digne de son nom : cela ne s'acquiert pas par les forces humaines.
Tous ces traits, malgré le caractère insolite de la célébration,
révèlent certainement une pratique assez courante vers le milieu
du IIe siècle.

Résumons : les exigences de foi-conversion et d'aptitude que
révèlent ces textes ne s'accompagnent pas d'exigence de durée.
On baptise en général assez rapidement ; la catéchèse vise à donner
les « premiers éléments de la doctrine de vérité » (26). Dès que
l'Apôtre « se rend compte » que le converti vit selon sa foi, il accède
à sa demande de baptême. Est-ce que « la rapidité des cérémonies
baptismales », « la participation de la communauté (...) réduite »
sont dues, comme le pense M. Dujarier, aux « circonstances excep-
tionnelles de ces romans » (27) ? Ne peut-on pas penser plutôt
que ces romans populaires décrivent bien la vie courante d'une
Église dont la pratique est encore peu et mal institutionalisée ?
Cela semble évident si l'on se reporte maintenant à S. Justin :

« Nous vous exposerons (...), dit-il, comment, renouvelés par
le Christ, nous nous consacrons à Dieu » (28).

Et voici les différents points qu'il signale :

— d'abord foi en la doctrine et assurance qu'on est capable de
vivre selon cette doctrine.

— puis prière et jeûne

— enfin la régénération dans l'eau.

Ici encore dom Capelle commente : « la préparation véritable
avait lieu auparavant » (29). Certainement ; mais comme on

---

(25) L. Vouaux, p. 259.
(26) *Hom. Clem.* 1, 13 : τοῦ ἀληθοῦς λόγου βραχέα κατηχήσας με. Siouville,
p. 99, traduit très exactement. On baptise « rapidement » (*Act. Thomas,* 139), après
une « catéchèse » qui dure « peu de jours » (*Hom. Clem.* 7, 4-5).
(27) M. Dujarier, *op. cit.,* pp. 310-311.
(28) *1 Apol* 61 ; L. Pautigny pp. 126-129 ; M. Dujarier, p. 189.
(29) *Art. cit.* p. 132.

regrette que Justin dise si peu de chose, alors qu'il va ensuite développer longuement les liturgies baptismale et eucharistique ! N'est-ce pas justement le signe que la catéchèse n'est pas encore au niveau de la liturgie ? Celle-ci est communautaire, mais l'enseignement est souvent individuel, comme l'apostolat ; en tous cas, il n'a pas encore de caractère officiel, institutionnel. Et c'est pourquoi, en bonne partie, la formation chrétienne, tant doctrinale que morale, demeure généralement insuffisante (30).

4. Vers l'institution catéchuménale.

Quand on parle de catéchuménat, il faut entendre une institution bien précise : institution d'Église, qui vise à préparer au baptême en commun ceux que, justement, l'on appelle catéchumènes, tout d'abord par un enseignement structuré appelé catéchèse, mais aussi par tout un ensemble de disciplines et de rites (31).

On a vu plus haut que, chez S. Justin, la catéchèse paraît encore peu organisée et individuelle. Mais dans le cadre de la liturgie baptismale, la préparation immédiate au baptême comporte le jeûne et la prière, dans une ambiance très communautaire, fidèles et catéchumènes restant ensemble (32). Or la mention du jeûne comme rite préparatoire revient fréquemment dans les récits populaires, témoins de la pratique courante, que sont les Actes Apocryphes et les *Homélies Clémentines*. Voici, par exemple, dans la *Passio Pauli* 19 *(Actes de Paul)* :

« ... imponentes eis mox manus et dantes signaculum sanctificationis perpetuae, sicque jejunio usque ad vesperam percurrente, baptizati sunt in nomine Domini nostri Jesu Christi. »

Et dans les *Homélies* :

« Vous tous qui désirez être baptisés, commencez à jeûner à partir de demain, recevez chaque jour l'imposition des mains et posez toutes les questions que vous voudrez. »

---

(30) R. F. REFOULÉ, *op. cit.*, p. 30. Cf. M. DUJARIER, *op. cit.*, p. 181. Quant au contenu doctrinal et moral de la catéchèse primitive, nous avons essayé de le présenter dans *Evangélisation et Catéchèse aux deux premiers siècles*. Il n'y a pas à y revenir ici.

(31) Cf. entre autres P. DE PUNIET, art. *Catéchuménat*, dans DACL, col. 2579-2621. Notons donc que, si le terme « catéchèse » a parfois un sens plus large, les termes « catéchumène » et « catéchuménat » sont toujours à prendre au sens strict.

(32) Cf. M. DUJARIER, *op. cit.*, p. 191. Et sur l'ensemble de cette question, J. LEBRETON, *Le développement des institutions ecclésiastiques à la fin du second siècle*, dans *Rech. Sc. rel.*, 24 (1934) pp. 129-164. Et Ph. OPPENHEIM, *Sacramentum regenerationis christianae*, Rome 1947.

Ici le baptême a lieu trois jours après (33). Plus loin :

« Trois mois s'étant ainsi passés, Pierre m'ordonna de jeûner pendant quelques jours ; puis, m'ayant conduit aux sources voisines de la mer, il m'y baptisa » (34).

Il ne s'agit pas de trois mois de catéchèse, car dans les pages précédentes Pierre a sans cesse prêché aux païens la nécessité absolue du baptême pour être sauvé, à quoi correspond parfois dans ces écrits — on l'a vu — l'absence d'une catéchèse préalable au baptême. Sans doute s'agit-il plutôt ici d'un temps de probation qui se termine, les derniers jours, par le jeûne préalable et le rite de l'imposition des mains. Ce jeûne semble obligatoire : si, en effet l'aptitude au baptême est excellente, il durera « au moins un jour (...) ; autrement (...) pendant de longs jours » (35).

Au terme de cette évolution, nous arrivons au récit suivant :

« Puisque j'ai décidé de passer trois mois avec vous, si quelqu'un d'entre vous le désire, qu'il soit baptisé (...) Qu'il s'approche donc de Zachée (l'évêque ordonné par Pierre) celui qui le veut, qu'il lui donne son nom et qu'il entende de lui les mystères du Royaume des cieux. Qu'il s'applique à des pénitences fréquentes et qu'il s'éprouve en toutes choses, afin que, ces trois mois accomplis, il puisse être baptisé... » (36).

Inscription du Nom, trois mois de catéchèse sur les mystères du Royaume, jeûnes et pénitences en signe de probation, puis le baptême : l'institution catéchuménale a pris corps.

Mais la coutume du jeûne comme rite de préparation et l'association prière-jeûne sont très anciennes et débordent largement le cadre du catéchuménat (37). Elles ne sont pas sans rappeler les rites de la communauté de Qumrân, le climat de pénitence du baptême de Jean, les quarante jours de Jésus au désert *après* son baptême, etc. Et c'est sans doute très tôt que ces pratiques se sont introduites dans l'Église : ainsi, lorsque Paul aura adhéré au kérygme et se sera converti, bien que son baptême suive « sans délai » c'est-à-dire sans catéchèse préalable, il restera cependant « trois jours » à jeûner et prier, comme signe de sa conversion intérieure (*Act.* 9, 9-19). De même pour Corneille (*Act.* 10) : sa vie antérieure (à la différence de celle de Saul), toute de prières et

---

(33) *Hom. Clem.* 3, 73 ; Siouville p. 161.

(34) *Hom. Clem.* 11, 35 ; Siouville p. 260.

(35) *Hom. Clem.* 13, 9.

(36) *Rec. Clem.* 3, 67. D'après M. Dujarier, *op. cit.*, p. 321, ce texte indique bien le terme d'une évolution, car il est plus récent.

(37) Classiques dans l'AT, elles sont dans le NT un « trait caractéristique de Luc ». J. Dupont, *Le discours de Milet*, p. 367, note 1.

d'aumônes au dire même de la communauté juive, semble lui tenir lieu de rites préparatoires au baptême ; la préparation immédiate est encore la prière (et le jeûne, selon la variante d'*Act.* 10, 30), trois jours avant, ou pendant trois jours (38). Tout porte à croire que l'on rattache à ces conversions célèbres des usages assez courants où toute la communauté chrétienne prend en charge le baptisand et va se mettre avec lui en prière et en pénitence (39).

Nous en arrivons ainsi à une autre pratique et à une autre justification théologique que celle du baptême « sans délai ». Ainsi Tertullien insiste pour ne pas baptiser prématurément. Il faut, dès le début, que l'Église exerce son discernement ; et, puisqu'on ne doit pas jeter « les choses saintes aux chiens » (*De Bapt.* 18, 1), des membres de la communauté devront juger les candidats — non pas tellement d'ailleurs sur la catéchèse elle-même que sur la conversion de leurs mœurs. En effet

« nous ne sommes pas plongés dans l'eau pour mettre fin à nos péchés ; mais parce que nous y avons mis fin, déjà nous sommes moralement lavés » (40).

On insiste donc ici sur la conversion morale *préalable* au baptême. La dernière semaine, dans la dernière phase du catéchuménat, nous retrouverons, comme en « une sorte de retraite », les prières, jeûnes et veilles (41).

La durée du catéchuménat pour Tertullien est encore variable mais l'institutionalisation est pratiquement achevée. Cela ne tient, certes, pas seulement au tempérament sévère de l'auteur, car on retrouve partout cette évolution (que nous n'avons pas à détailler ici, spécialement d'après la *Tradition Apostolique* d'Hippolyte et d'après Clément et Origène pour Alexandrie). Cela tient surtout à toute une série de causes conjuguées ; affaiblissement de la ferveur initiale, apostasie de certains, offensive toujours active du paganisme, influence des hérésies (42). Mais cela tient aussi au fait que les églises sont maintenant parvenues à « adapter leur caractère eschatologique à leur situation de peuple encore inséré

---

(38) Sur Corneille, Th. Maertens, *op. cit.*, pp. 49-51 ; M. Dujarier, *op. cit.*, pp. 139-155. Quant au contenu même de la catéchèse, le cas de Corneille est typique du passage de la catéchèse juive à la catéchèse chrétienne, avec ses deux aspects complémentaires de continuité et de nouveauté radicale. Voir A. Turck, *op. cit.*, pp. 114-115.

(39) Cf. *Didachè* 7, 2-4 (passage interpolé ?) : jeûne préalable d'un jour ou deux, que fait non seulement le baptisand mais le baptiseur avec toute la communauté. Th. Maertens, *op. cit.*, pp. 59-60 ; M. Dujarier, *op. cit.*, pp. 292-296.

(40) *De Paen.* 6, 17. Cf. R. F. Refoulé, *op. cit.*, p. 31.

(41) *De Bapt.* 20, 1 ; R. F. Refoulé, *op. cit.*, pp. 34-36. Cf. M. Dujarier, *op. cit.*, pp. 220-237. Et. D. Grasso, dans *Parole et Mission*, 6 (1963) pp. 360-361.

(42) B. Capelle, *art. cit.*, p. 150 ; Ph. Oppenheim, *op. cit.*, p. 11.

dans l'histoire » (43). Et c'est maintenant seulement qu'elles peuvent, sans préjudice pour la radicale nouveauté de la foi chrétienne, récupérer quelques-unes des structures du « postulat », du « noviciat » essénien, et du judaïsme en général.

Il y a donc, autour de l'an 200, un catéchuménat organisé. Les docteurs représentent une fonction officielle, instituée par l'évêque (44) ; parfois même on les appelle les « catéchètes » (45). Les catéchumènes forment un groupe à part des fidèles (46). Le catéchuménat est intimement lié à la liturgie baptismale, au point que dans l'ultime semaine préparatoire ceux qui sont « élus » pour le baptême font un groupe spécial et que par les exorcismes Dieu sanctionne le discernement de l'Église. La solennité que l'Église semble avoir très vite donnée à l'initiation sacramentelle — même lorsqu'on accordait le baptême « rapidement et sans délai » — reflue maintenant sur l'institution catéchuménale elle-même. L'Évêque était de droit le célébrant de la liturgie (47) ; il est clair qu'il est de droit le responsable du catéchuménat, le docteur par excellence. Par tout son côté rituel, le catéchuménat est pris en charge par la liturgie, ou plus exactement il correspond à une prise en charge des catéchumènes par la liturgie officielle de l'Église. Sous son aspect de catéchèse, le catéchuménat vient à la fois du kérygme aux païens et de l'enseignement aux chrétiens, et il s'insère entre les deux comme une étape transitoire mais indispensable.

*
* *

Le christianisme, à ses débuts, ne s'est pas développé d'une façon rectiligne mais le fonds commun a donné des formes diverses. Ces formes nous paraissent se ramener finalement à deux grands courants qui parfois s'interpénètrent, l'un en continuité très nette avec le judaïsme (catéchèse et rites), un autre plus marqué par la rupture avec le passé et la nouveauté absolue de la foi chrétienne

---

(43) M. Dujarier, op. cit., p. 114. Cf. supra, note 16.

(44) Ainsi fait le pape Victor à Rome, selon G. Bardy, Les écoles romaines au second siècle, dans Rev. Hist. eccl., 28 (1932) pp. 501-532. Ainsi Démétrius à Alexandrie : Eusebe, Hist. Eccl. VI, 3, 3, et note de G. Bardy, Sources chrétiennes, p. 98. Cf. Aux origines de l'école d'Alexandrie, dans Rech. Sc. rel., 27 (1937) pp. 65-90, etc.

(45) Ep. Clem. ad Jac. 13-14 ; Siouville, pp. 84-85. Hom. Clem. 3, 71 ; Siouville p. 160.

(46) Hippolyte, Trad. Apost. 18 ; Tertullien, De praescr. 41, 4 ; Origène, In Jeremiam hom. 14, 4. 18, 8 ; etc.

(47) Voir dès l'époque apostolique, par ex. Act. 8, 12-17 ; puis, Ignace, Smyrn. 8, 2 ; Tertullien, De Bapt. 17, 1-2.

(baptême sans délai) (48). L'étude historique de la naissance du catéchuménat rejoint par là l'étude du contenu de la catéchèse primitive. La conclusion de cette dernière recherche était, à gros traits, celle-ci : la catéchèse primitive se présente en différents schémas. L'un, l'enseignement moral, du type des « deux voies », vient du judaïsme : tout juif est supposé l'avoir reçu. Il suffit donc d'adhérer au Credo nouveau (soit sous forme de kérygme, soit sous forme de catéchèse doctrinale) pour pouvoir être baptisé. D'autres schémas sont plus christianisés, plus typiques par exemple des épîtres de Paul et de Pierre, et développent les implications de l'adhésion au Christ dans la vie renouvelée (49)

Diversité des formes catéchétiques, diversité des « techniques » d'agrégation à l'Église. Disons plutôt : l'Église, société humaine animée par l'Esprit, n'a pris que peu à peu conscience des richesses de sa foi, de son rattachement unique au Christ ressuscité et de son rattachement historique à Israël, des différentes façons de se présenter au monde et d'accueillir en son sein Juifs et Païens, en foules et individuellement. Elle a ainsi rencontré d'emblée, par sa vie et son dynamisme missionnaire avant d'y réfléchir en théologienne, la première question que pose toute pastorale : quels sont les critères d'admission au baptême. Question qui reste de la plus authentique actualité.

A. TURCK.

(48) Cf. notre recension de l'étude de M. DUJARIER, dans *Parole et Mission*, 6 (1963) pp. 518-520.

(49) A. TURCK, *op. cit.*, pp. 140-143.

La Catéchèse
dans la Tradition patristique

par *Jean DANIÉLOU, S.J.*

La catéchèse est la tradition vivante du dépôt de la foi aux nouveaux membres que l'Eglise s'agrège. Elle constitue ainsi un aspect particulier de l'exercice du Magistère. Elle se distingue d'une part du Kérygme, qui est l'annonce de la bonne nouvelle de la Résurrection aux païens, et d'autre part de l'Homélie, qui est l'enseignement donné aux membres de la communauté chrétienne. Ceci implique un double caractère. Par opposition au Kérygme, elle présente un caractère complet : elle doit instruire le candidat au baptême de tout ce qu'un chrétien doit croire. Mais par opposition à l'Homélie, elle a un caractère élémentaire. Elle va aux points essentiels, en laissant de côté les approfondissements spirituels ou spéculatifs.

Il serait intéressant de retracer l'histoire de la catéchèse depuis les origines. Elle est aussi ancienne que l'Eglise. Nous en saisissons la structure à travers les plus antiques formes du Symbole. Nous en entrevoyons le contenu à travers des œuvres comme la *Démonstration de la prédication apostolique* de Saint Irénée, le *Traité du Baptême* de Tertullien ou les *Testimonia* de Saint Cyprien. Nous la voyons s'institutionnaliser au III° siècle avec la *Tradition Apostolique* d'Hippolyte de Rome. Mais son âge d'or est le IV° siècle. Elle atteint alors un développement exceptionnel et inégalé par sa place dans la vie de l'Eglise, liée au nombre considérable des baptêmes d'adultes que connaît cette époque. Les formes qui se fixent alors sont encore celles qui régissent notre catéchuménat actuel. C'est donc

21

avant tout de la catéchèse telle que la présente cette époque que nous parlerons.

Nous avons de plus la chance de posséder sur la catéchèse du IVᵉ siècle un ensemble de documents, qui nous viennent en partie des plus grands esprits du temps. Ceci nous donne une documentation exceptionnelle et constitue une raison de plus de nous attacher à cette période. Les principaux de ces documents sont les *Catéchèses* de Saint Cyrille de Jérusalem (1), les *Homélies catéchétiques* de Théodore de Mopsueste (2), les *Catéchèses baptismales* de Saint Jean Chrysostome (3), les *Traités sur les sacrements et sur les mystères* de Saint Ambroise (4), le *Discours catéchétique* de Saint Grégoire de Nysse (5), le *De catechizandis rudibus* de Saint Augustin (6). Ces ouvrages qui sont tous des chefs-d'œuvre chacun dans leur genre donnent accès à la tradition catéchétique des Pères de façon incomparable.

Avant d'aborder le contenu de la catéchèse, nous devons parler de sa structure. La question a aussi l'intérêt de nous montrer la catéchèse dans la richesse de ses aspects. Non seulement comme instruction, mais comme initiation aux mœurs chrétiennes et comme agrégation à la communauté ecclésiale : la catéchèse est une pastorale complète de l'entrée dans l'existence chrétienne. Vue du côté de l'Eglise et non plus du côté des catéchumènes, elle nous aide à voir l'importance dans la vie de l'Eglise de la fonction catéchétique, puisque nous constatons la place qu'elle tient dans l'activité des évêques, l'influence qu'elle exerce sur la structure de l'année liturgique. Tout ceci montre l'importance exceptionnelle attachée par l'Eglise à la formation des nouveaux chrétiens.

Dans l'Eglise du IVᵉ siècle, le catéchuménat comprend quatre

---

(1) *P.G.* XXXIII, vol. 332-1228.

(2) Texte syriaque et traduction française par R. Tonneau, Cité du Vatican, 1949.

(3) Texte grec et traduction française par A. Wenger, « Sources chrétiennes », 50, Paris, le Cerf 1957.

(4) Texte latin et traduction française par Dom Botte, « Sources chrétiennes », Paris, Le Cerf 1950.

(5) Texte grec et traduction française par L. Méridier, Paris, Picard 1908.

(6) Texte latin et traduction française par G. Combès et A. Farges, Paris, Desclée 1949.

22

stades nettement distincts. Le premier est celui des candidats ou *accedentes*. Il nous met en présence de païens et d'hérétiques. Augustin les désigne par le terme de *rudes*, c'est-à-dire ceux qui sont encore totalement incultes en ce qui concerne la foi et la vie chrétienne. Durant ce stade, ces personnes, encore entièrement étrangères à l'Eglise, se renseignaient sur elle. Quand elles étaient décidées à se préparer au baptême, elles devaient se présenter devant celui qui était chargé de leur examen. Celui-ci était à Carthage un diacre nommé Deogratias. Il leur faisait alors un exposé de l'essentiel de la foi. C'est de cet exposé qu'il est question dans le *De catechizandis rudibus* de Saint Augustin. Si la sincérité de leurs dispositions était reconnue, elles étaient admises au catéchuménat. Cette introduction comportait en Afrique la *signatio* sur le front, l'imposition des mains et le sel. Pour les enfants de famille chrétienne cette première initiation était assurée par la famille et l'enfant était considéré comme catéchumène.

Le second stade est le catéchuménat proprement dit. La *Tradition Apostolique* prescrivait au III° siècle que ce temps de probation devait durer au moins trois ans. Ceci était une réaction contre des baptêmes prématurés, qui correspond bien aux tendances rigoristes de l'auteur de la *Tradition*. Au IV° siècle le problème est inverse. Les évêques doivent réagir contre la tendance à prolonger indéfiniment ce temps du catéchuménat. Chaque année, à l'époque de l'Epiphanie, l'évêque adressait aux catéchumènes un appel à se faire inscrire pour la préparation immédiate au baptême. Les catéchumènes sont appelés κατηχούμενοι en Orient, *auditores* en Occident. Leur instruction est confiée à des catéchistes. Ainsi, à Alexandrie, nous voyons Origène chargé de l'école catéchétique au début du III° siècle. Les catéchumènes avaient certains droits, en particulier celui d'assister à l'avant-messe. C'est souvent à eux que s'adressent les évêques et les prédicateurs, ce qui montre qu'ils constituaient une partie notable de leur auditoire (7).

La troisième étape est constituée par la préparation immédiate au baptême. C'est celle sur laquelle nous sommes le plus renseignés. La veille du premier dimanche de Carême, les catéchumènes qui désiraient être baptisés donnaient leur nom au prêtre chargé de cette mission. Le lendemain avait lieu la céré-

---

(7) Voir V. Monacchino, *La Cura pastorale a Minalo Cartagine e Roma nel secolo IV*, Rome 1947, pp. 31-36 ; 165-171 ; 336-337.

23

monie solennelle de l'inscription. Nous en avons la description détaillée pour Jérusalem dans le *Journal* d'Ethérie (45). En présence de l'évêque et du presbyterium, les candidats se présentaient l'un après l'autre, les hommes accompagnés de leur parrain, les femmes de leur marraine. L'évêque interrogeait la communauté pour savoir s'ils étaient dignes d'être admis au baptême. Si la réponse était favorable, l'évêque les inscrivait de sa main sur le registre. Ils étaient désormais en grec des « φωτιζόμενοι », en latin des *electi* ou des *competentes*. L'évêque prononçait alors l'homélie intitulée *Pro-catéchèse*. Les rites de cette cérémonie solennelle présentaient des variantes. Ils sont commentés par de nombreux écrivains (8).

La préparation immédiate commençait alors. Elle comportait trois aspects. D'une part elle était un enseignement. Il y avait chaque matin, sauf les jours festifs, une assemblée présidée par l'évêque. Pendant les premières semaines, celui-ci commentait l'Ecriture. Ces instructions pouvaient avoir des formes variées. Nous en avons des exemples caractéristiques dans plusieurs traités de Saint Ambroise, *l'Hexaméron* en particulier. Puis le IV° dimanche de carême (le VI° en Orient où le carême avait huit semaines) commençait la catéchèse doctrinale proprement dite. Elle débutait par la *Traditio Symboli*. L'évêque communiquait aux *electi* le contenu du Symbole, qui est le schéma de la catéchèse. Cet acte solennel constitue vraiment la tradition en acte, la transmission officielle de la foi par l'Eglise à ses nouveaux membres. Pendant les deux semaines suivantes, l'évêque commentait les divers articles. Ce sont ces commentaires que nous avons conservés dans les dix-huit catéchèses de Cyrille de Jérusalem et les *Homélies catéchétiques* de Théodore de Mopsueste. Au terme de ces deux semaines avait lieu la *Redditio Symboli*.

A côté de l'aspect doctrinal, la préparation au baptême comportait un aspect spirituel. C'est un temps de rupture avec les mœurs païennes et d'initiation aux mœurs chrétiennes. Nous avons conservé une *Homélie* de Cyrille de Jérusalem sur la conversion, prêchée l'un des premiers dimanches de carême. Les *Homélies quadragésimales* d'Ambroise ont un caractère principalement moral. Ceci s'accompagnait chez le candidat au baptême d'une vie plus pénitente. Le carême est un temps de

---

(8) Voir Jean Daniélou, *Bible et Liturgie*, p. 39 sqq.

24

retraite. Et la communauté tout entière y était associée. L'initiation à la prière y tenait aussi une part. Les *Homélies caté-chétiques* de Théodore de Mopsueste comportent un commentaire du *Pater*. A Carthage il y avait une *traditio* de l'Oraison dominicale suivie d'une *redditio* pendant la Semaine Sainte.

Il y a enfin l'aspect rituel. Ces semaines de préparation sont un temps d'épreuve où le démon essaie de garder en son pouvoir celui qui est sur le point de lui échapper. Le candidat au baptême doit être aidé dans ce combat contre le Prince de ce monde. C'est à cet aspect que correspondent les exorcismes ou *scrutini* (9), qui avaient lieu à Rome les III°, IV° et V° dimanches de carême. Cet aspect du catéchuménat comme combat spirituel relève d'une tradition tout à fait primitive. D'après les plus anciens documents catéchétiques, la *Didachè* et *l'Epître de Barnabé,* la catéchèse se présente en effet sous l'aspect de la doctrine des deux voies, celle du Christ et celle de Satan. Ce schéma peut correspondre à un schéma juif anté-rieur, que nous trouvons dans les Manuscrits de Qumran. Le choix de l'évangile de la Tentation du Christ pour le premier dimanche de carême s'inspire également de cette perspective. La renonciation à Satan et l'adhésion au Christ marqueront au seuil du baptême le terme de ce combat.

Restera enfin une dernière étape de la catéchèse. Dans la tradition ancienne, l'explication des sacrements n'est pas donnée avant le baptême. Elle constitue l'objet des catéchèses mystagogiques. Celles-ci sont faites par l'évêque durant la semaine de Pâques, la semaine *in Albis*. Nous avons sans doute une première ébauche de cette catéchèse mystagogique dans la *Première Epître de Pierre,* qui fournit encore son leit-motiv au dimanche de Quasimodo. Cette catéchèse s'adresse aux *neophyti*. Nous avons conservé des documents éminents de cette catéchèse sacramentaire dans les *Catéchèses mystagogiques* de Cyrille de Jérusalem et de Théodore de Mopsueste, le *De Sacramentis* et le *De Mysteriis* de Saint Ambroise. Ces catéchèses comportent à la fois une explication du symbolisme des rites, un exposé des figures bibliques des sacrements, une exhortation à vivre dans le Christ. Ces divers éléments peuvent prendre plus ou moins de place. Les *Homélies baptismales* de Saint Jean Chry-sostome sont consacrées essentiellement au dernier de ces éléments.

---

(9) Voir A. Chavasse, R S R, 35 (1948), pp. 325-381.

25

*
**

On voit à travers ces diverses étapes la richesse des éléments qui constituent la catéchèse. On voit aussi la liberté laissée au catéchète dans l'organisation de ces éléments. Il reste toutefois que certaines lignes générales se dégagent. L'enseignement catéchétique comporte trois grands ensembles qui se présentent toujours dans le même ordre : une catéchèse biblique, qui remplit les premières étapes ; une catéchèse dogmatique, dont le cadre est le Symbole ; une catéchèse sacramentaire, qui constitue l'achèvement. Mais surtout à travers ces diverses étapes et sous ces différents aspects, la catéchèse garde toujours certains caractères communs qu'il est possible de dégager. Ceci nous permettra de pénétrer plus profondément dans le contenu même de la catéchèse patristique et d'en tirer les enseignements.

La catéchèse est d'abord une explication. Elle est présentation du donné de la foi et elle a pour objet de faire comprendre ce donné. Elle a en ce sens un caractère extrêmement concret. Le catéchumène est mis en présence d'un certain nombre d'éléments : les événements de l'histoire sainte, les articles du Symbole, les rites des sacrements Mais ces réalités demandent à être bien comprises. Elles sont par essence mystérieuses. Elles s'expriment à travers des mots, des images, des gestes qui sont empruntés à la vie ordinaire. Mais elles ont un contenu divin. C'est ce contenu qu'il s'agit de faire saisir. Ceci ne relève pas seulement de la connaissance discursive. C'est d'une éducation de la foi qu'il s'agit. La catéchèse est une éducation des vertus théologales. Saint Augustin l'a admirablement dit : « Tout ce que vous racontez, racontez-le de telle manière que votre auditeur croie en écoutant, espère en croyant, aime en espérant » (*Catech.* IV, 8).

Donnons de ceci des exemples précis. D'abord en matière de catéchèse biblique. Augustin le montre dans un remarquable passage. Il faut présenter la totalité de l'histoire sainte, de la création du monde aux « temps présents » de l'Eglise. Il ne faut pas se perdre dans le détail. Il faut retenir, parmi les *mirabilia Dei,* qui sont le contenu de l'histoire sainte, les *mirabiliora,* les articulations essentielles. Et ces événements, il faut s'y arrêter, les déployer (*expandere*), dégager de l'anecdote extérieure le contenu divin, le *mirabile,* de façon à susciter l'*admiratio,* à éveiller dans l'âme de l'auditeur le sentiment du sacré, à susciter la foi. La tâche du catéchète est ici admirablement

26

définie. Il ne s'agit pas seulement d'exposer la suite des faits de l'histoire sainte, d'accabler la mémoire avec des listes de rois de Juda ou d'Israël. Il faut aller à l'essentiel, aux articulations de l'histoire du salut et en dégager le contenu théologique. Augustin en donnera des exemples : le Déluge, la Sortie d'Egypte, la construction du Temple, la Maternité virginale de Marie, la Résurrection, la Pentecôte.

La catéchèse dogmatique présente quelque chose d'analogue. Ici ce ne sont pas les événements, mais les catégories fondamentales dont il faut faire saisir le sens exact. Cyrille de Jérusalem donne de ceci des exemples remarquables. La *Catéchèse X.* sur le Christ, commence par un traité des noms et titres du Christ dans le Nouveau Testament. Ce traité paraît d'ailleurs faire partie de la catéchèse traditionnelle. On le trouve dans le *Dialogue* de Justin, dans le *Commentaire sur Jean,* d'Origène. Il constitue une sorte d'inventaire concret des divers aspects du Christ, précédant toute systématisation. Mais il est aussi une élucidation du sens authentique d'expressions comme Christ, Fils de l'Homme, Sauveur, ou de symboles comme Agneau, Pierre, Porte. Il est remarquable de voir un exégète moderne, comme Vincent Taylor, refaire ce traité dans son livre *The Names of Jesus.* De même chez Cyrille la catéchèse sur le Saint Esprit commence par un traité sur les divers sens du mot « *pneuma* », qui dissipe les équivoques dont le mot *esprit* reste chargé pour nous. Que de confusions subsistent dans la pensée de beaucoup de chrétiens du seul fait que le sens biblique du mot *esprit* et sa radicale distinction du sens hellénique n'aient pas été clairement exposés.

La même méthode se retrouve dans la catéchèse sacramentaire. Elle est conçue essentiellement comme une leçon de choses. Elle part des rites des sacrements. Et elle a d'abord pour objet d'expliquer le symbolisme authentique de ces rites. Ici encore la catéchèse patristique est d'une étonnante actualité. Elle dégage les symboles sacramentaires des analogies plus ou moins fantaisistes qu'ils suscitent dans l'esprit des hommes de notre temps. Si les symboles bien compris sont une des voies les plus fécondes de la pédagogie divine, les symboles mal compris sont un des poisons les plus dangereux pour la foi. Ils constituent un bazar hétéroclite où voisinent la pomme d'Eve, le doux agneau et la tendre tourterelle, les lys du Cantique et le lavage baptismal — et dans lequel la sentimentalité le dispute à la vulgarité. La catéchèse patristique restitue aux ailes de la colombe leur signification de souffle créateur, à l'eau baptis-

27

male son symbolisme de puissance de destruction et de puissance de vivification, au fruit de l'arbre de vie sa valeur eucharistique, à l'Agneau immolé son contenu rédempteur.

La catéchèse est donc d'abord explication élémentaire du donné de la foi, qu'il s'agisse des événements, des dogmes ou des rites. Elle est en second lieu démonstration, *apodeixis,* selon le mot de Saint Irénée. Elle a pour but d'apporter à l'acte de foi sa justification. Cette justification n'est pas étrangère à la foi elle-même. L'apologétique, les préliminaires de la foi relèvent du Kérygme, de la présentation aux païens. La démonstration de la foi est l'analogie de la foi. C'est-à-dire que ce qui fonde l'adhésion à tel aspect particulier, c'est qu'il se réfère à d'autres aspects, en sorte qu'il apparaisse ainsi comme l'expression d'une réalité permanente. La démonstration de la foi consiste à dégager les lois de la foi, à ramener le particulier au général, comme la démonstration scientifique consiste à dégager les lois de la nature, à rattacher le particulier au général. Elle est donc essentiellement l'établissement des correspondances entre les manières d'agir de Dieu aux différentes étapes de l'histoire du salut.

Cette démonstration consiste avant tout dans la relation établie entre le Nouveau Testament et l'Ancien Testament. Cette relation présente plusieurs aspects. Dans la catéchèse dogmatique, elle est principalement prophétique. Cet aspect de la catéchèse remonte aux temps apostoliques et, au-delà, au Christ lui-même. C'est celle du Christ montrant aux disciples d'Emmaüs que les événements de la Passion et de la Résurrection ont été annoncés par tout l'Ancien Testament, en partant de la loi et des Prophètes. C'est celle de Paul, écrivant aux Corinthiens que le Christ est ressuscité « conformément aux Écritures ». Dès les origines se constituent pour les catéchètes des recueils de *Testimonia,* de textes de l'Ancien Testament, en relation avec les divers dogmes chrétiens. Nous possédons un de ces recueils, dû à Saint Cyprien. Il contient tous les textes qui aujourd'hui encore sont fondamentaux. Chacune des catéchèses de Cyrille de Jérusalem comporte ainsi les prophéties qui se rapportent à l'article du symbole correspondant. Ainsi pour la Passion : « Venons-en à la démonstration à partir des prophètes » (XIII, 23). Cet argument prophétique garde toute sa valeur s'il est compris non comme la maigre réalisation de quelques prédictions souvent discutables, mais comme l'accomplissement massif dans le Christ des événements eschatologiques annoncés par tous les prophètes.

28

La démonstration sacramentaire est essentiellement typologique. Elle consiste à montrer l'analogie des actions de Dieu dans l'Ancien Testament, le Nouveau Testament, les sacrements de l'Eglise. Ceci est une des évidences les plus massives que nous présentent les catéchèses patristiques. Cette typologie sacramentaire a son point de départ dans le Nouveau Testament. La relation entre la manne du désert et l'Eucharistie est johannique, celle de la traversée de la Mer Rouge et du baptême est paulinienne. Tertullien dans son *De Baptismo* présente d'abord les grandes figures baptismales de l'Ancien Testament, puis celles du Nouveau : les noces de Cana, la piscine de Béthesda. Ce sont exactement celles qu'un exégète moderne comme Cullmann reconnaît à son tour (10). On est étonné de la place considérable que cette étude des figures tient dans les catéchèses mystagogiques du IV° siècle, chez Cyrille de Jérusalem, chez Ambroise, chez Chrysostome. Elles ont une valeur considérable. Elles montrent dans les sacrements la continuation dans le temps de l'Eglise des *magnalia Dei*, alliance, libération, demeure, etc..., de l'Ancien et du Nouveau Testament (11).

Après l'*explicatio* et la *demonstratio*, vient enfin, dans nos catéchèses, un dernier élément qui est l'*exhortatio*. C'est par elle que Saint Augustin termine le *De catechizandis rudibus*. Il met en garde le catéchumène contre les illusions qu'il pourrait avoir. Une fois baptisé, il sera encore exposé à la tentation. Plus encore il risque de rencontrer des chrétiens qui lui donnent de mauvais exemples. Ainsi le problème si délicat de la persévérance des néophytes et de la nécessité de les intégrer dans une communauté vivante est déjà souligné. De son côté, Cyrille de Jérusalem, à propos de chacun des articles du Symbole qu'il explique, ne manque pas de montrer les conséquences pratiques que chacun d'entre eux entraîne pour la vie du chrétien. La catéchèse sur le Dieu créateur se termine par un appel à l'admiration devant les œuvres de Dieu, celle sur la Résurrection par une promesse de la résurrection du catéchumène dans le baptême.

Le point important pour nous est que cette catéchèse morale n'apparaît pas au IV° siècle comme faisant l'objet d'un enseignement particulier. Elle est mise en relation avec l'enseignement dogmatique dont elle constitue l'application pratique.

---

(10) *Les sacrements dans l'évangile johannique*, passim.

(11) Voir Jean Daniélou, *Bible et Liturgie*, passim.

29

Aussi la trouve-t-on aux différents stades de la catéchèse. Nous l'avons rencontrée chez Augustin dans l'instruction aux *accedentes*. Elle tient une place considérable chez Saint Ambroise dans les catéchèses bibliques du début du carême. Les sermons sur Abraham, sur Isaac, sur David, sont en grande partie des exhortations morales. Saint Jean Chrysostome lui consacre la plus grande partie de ses exhortations aux néophytes durant la semaine de Pâques. On voit ainsi que ses références sont diverses. Saint Ambroise présente en exemple les saints de l'Ancien Testament. Saint Jean Chrysostome décrit la vie du baptisé comme un revêtement des mœurs du Christ.

Ceci vient confirmer la conclusion à laquelle nous étions amenés dans notre étude du cadre de la catéchèse. L'enseignement moral n'apparaît pas séparé de l'enseignement doctrinal. Mais c'est la catéchèse tout entière qui est à la fois doctrinale et pratique. Il ne s'agit pas seulement d'instruire, il s'agit de convertir. Le but du catéchète est de faire l'éducation du futur baptisé sous tous ses aspects, de l'introduire dans l'existence chrétienne. Ainsi la catéchèse morale pourra aussi bien prendre son point de départ dans l'Ecriture, dans le symbole, dans les sacrements. Elle accompagnera la catéchèse dans tout son développement, depuis le début de la conversion jusqu'à l'épanouissement de la vie baptismale. Elle marquera l'incidence pratique des vérités par ailleurs enseignées.

*
**

Nous avons parlé du cadre et du contenu de la catéchèse. Il reste une dernière question qui est celle de sa présentation. Après l'aspect liturgique et l'aspect dogmatique, il y a l'aspect psychologique. Le contenu de la catéchèse est la tradition de la foi ; et ce contenu est immuable. Mais cette foi doit être annoncée aux hommes d'un temps et d'un milieu donné. C'est dans ce domaine de l'adaptation au milieu que se situe proprement la recherche catéchétique. Celle-ci relève de la pastorale et non de la théologie. Le catéchète n'a pas à faire de recherche théologique. Ceci est l'objet de la théologie spéculative. Il doit enseigner la doctrine commune de l'Eglise. Mais cette doctrine commune, il doit la rendre accessible aux âmes. C'est là où la psychologie en général, la psychologie de la foi, la sociologie religieuse, la pédagogie catéchétique jouent leur rôle important.

Ces préoccupations, qui sont si modernes, sont aussi celles

30

des Pères de l'Eglise. Elles inspirent en particulier ce chef-d'œuvre de pastorale catéchétique qu'est le *De catechizandis rudibus*. En dehors des exposés proprement dits, que nous avons déjà utilisés, celui-ci contient de nombreuses indications concernant la question qui nous occupe. On peut les ranger sous deux chefs. Le premier est celui de la diversité des milieux. Augustin l'aborde d'abord de façon générale. Il expose qu'il faut tenir compte du fait qu'on a affaire à des savants ou à des ignorants, à des ouvriers ou à des paysans, à des garçons ou à des filles, à des adultes ou à des enfants. Organisée, la catéchèse doit être en même temps assez souple pour s'adapter aux situations particulières.

Ceci dit, Augustin examine quelques cas particuliers. S'il s'agit d'un homme ordinaire, sans instruction, Augustin demande d'abord qu'on s'assure des raisons qui le poussent à désirer se faire chrétien. Il faut voir en effet si ce n'est pas pour des avantages humains. Il peut y avoir des raisons politiques, ce qui est le cas dans une société chrétienne. Il peut y avoir aussi l'idée de s'assurer la protection de Dieu en vue d'une réussite terrestre. Cyrille de Jérusalem prévoit le cas du baptême demandé par un païen en vue d'épouser une jeune fille chrétienne. Il ne l'écarte pas a priori. Ce motif peut être l'occasion d'une authentique conversion. Mais il faut que cette conversion se fasse. Augustin recommande ensuite de souligner l'incertitude des biens terrestres et la nécessité de chercher les vrais biens (XVI-XVII, 24-28).

A propos des hommes cultivés, Augustin observe qu'il ne faut pas avoir l'air de vouloir tout leur apprendre, car généralement, s'ils désirent se convertir, c'est après avoir étudié la question. Il faut les interroger sur leurs lectures et prendre occasion de cela pour corriger une erreur, pour compléter une lacune. Il faut voir où sont leurs difficultés. C'est cette nécessité d'une catéchèse particulière pour les intellectuels qui avait amené Origène, chargé de l'école catéchétique d'Alexandrie, à fonder, à côté de celle-ci, le Didascalée. Nous avons par ailleurs un remarquable exemple de catéchèse adaptée aux intellectuels dans le *Discours Catéchétique* de Grégoire de Nysse, qui suit le plan du Symbole, mais aborde, à propos de chaque dogme, les problèmes philosophiques qu'il pose.

Augustin distingue enfin un dernier groupe, celui des hommes qui ne sont ni illettrés, ni très instruits. Ce sont les plus prétentieux. Ils sont imbus de ce qu'ils savent et seraient

31

portés à se moquer de la simplicité des récits de l'Ecriture. Ceci reste encore aujourd'hui caractéristique de cette catégorie, avec la différence que la culture était plus littéraire au temps d'Augustin, plus scientiste aujourd'hui. De même sont-ils portés à mépriser leur catéchète si celui-ci fait des fautes de langage. Il faut leur apprendre que la sainteté est plus importante que l'éloquence. Mais par ailleurs il faut faire quelques concessions à leurs prétentions, montrer qu'on connait aussi la littérature en y faisant quelque allusion. Toutes choses qui agaceraient un homme vraiment cultivé, mais qui flattent les prétentions des demi-lettrés. Mais il faut surtout leur apprendre à dépasser le plan superficiel où ils se meuvent et leur faire découvrir l'humilité.

Nous observerons que ces problèmes d'adaptation concernent principalement les premières étapes de la catéchèse. Celles-ci ont un caractère assez individuel, selon les milieux originaires des candidats au baptême. De même qu'ils doivent se dépouiller de leurs mœurs anciennes pour revêtir les mœurs de Jésus-Christ, ils doivent se dépouiller de leur mentalité ancienne pour entrer dans la simplicité de la foi. Une fois ce premier travail réalisé — qui concerne essentiellement le catéchète — le catéchumène pourra recevoir l'enseignement officiel, donné par l'évêque, et qui rassemble alors la totalité des candidats. Sous cet aspect, le développement de la catéchèse apparaît comme une intégration progressive, dans l'unité de la communauté locale présidée par l'évêque, d'éléments humainement disparates. Et son but est d'amener à dépasser progressivement les différences humaines de classe, de culture, de milieu, considérées comme superficielles par rapport à l'unité dans le Christ. La « spécialisation » ne saurait jamais être que secondaire et doit toujours tendre à être dépassée.

A côté de l'adaptation, la présentation du message demande aussi ce qu'Augustin appelle l' « hilaritas », c'est-à-dire la préoccupation de rendre la catéchèse vivante. C'est à cette préoccupation que répond principalement le traité d'Augustin. Et les pages qu'il y consacre, nourries d'expérience pastorale, restent inégalées à la fois par leur pénétration psychologique et leur profondeur spirituelle. Nous ne pouvons que noter quelques traits. Il peut arriver que le catéchète soit au-dessus de son auditoire. Il est obligé de se faire plus simple, d'expliquer des choses élémentaires. Il préférerait parler de ce qui l'intéresse, alors qu'il doit s'attarder à des choses qui lui paraissent évi-

32

dentes. Il doit imiter en cela les abaissements du Christ, qui s'est fait petit avec les petits. En soi, il n'y a pas d'attrait à balbutier des choses que l'on pourrait exprimer mieux. Mais l'amour y fait trouver de l'intérêt.

Il peut arriver d'autre part que le catéchète heurte son auditoire. Ceci peut provenir de trois causes. Ou bien il a employé des expressions maladroites : que ce soit une occasion de rappeler que le fond importe plus que la forme. Ou bien il a dit quelque chose d'inexact, il a été confus : qu'il profite d'une catéchèse ultérieure pour revenir sur le même sujet et l'exposer plus clairement. Il peut arriver enfin que ce soient les vérités mêmes que nous enseignons qui heurtent. Mais ceci alors est le scandale même de la Croix : « Consolons-nous par l'exemple du Seigneur. Des hommes, scandalisés par ses paroles, s'éloignèrent sous prétexte qu'elles étaient dures » (XI, 16). Aussi ne devons-nous rien minimiser de l'enseignement du Christ. La catéchèse doit être intégrale. Ce serait une fausse conception de l'adaptation que taire ce qui est vrai pour ne pas heurter. Du moins ne devons-nous pas ajouter au scandale essentiel de la Croix celui qui viendrait de notre négligence à présenter comme il le faut le message.

Augustin passe ensuite à l'absence de réaction dans l'auditoire. Il note qu'elle peut venir de ce que le catéchète est trop intimidant, de ce que l'auditoire ne comprend pas, de l'indifférence à ce qui est dit. A chacune de ces difficultés il apporte le remède. Il montre ensuite qu'il faut tenir compte de la fatigue de l'auditoire, savoir le détendre, animer l'exposé par une discussion. Le catéchète enfin peut être préoccupé par d'autres tâches. Il faut qu'il se rappelle qu'aucune n'est plus importante que la catéchèse. Et, si ce sont ses péchés qui lui enlèvent son élan, il faut qu'il se souvienne que la meilleure manière de s'en purifier est l'acte même de charité que représente la catéchèse. C'est toute une spiritualité du catéchète qui se dégage ainsi de ces remarques, toutes pratiques.

*
**

Il était difficile en quelques pages de donner une idée de la richesse étonnante des documents catéchétiques que nous a légués la tradition patristique. Ce que nous avons dit doit du

33

moins montrer l'intérêt qu'il y a pour la catéchèse contemporaine à être en contact avec ces sources. A peu près rien n'y
parait vieilli. On y trouve l'écho de la foi de l'Eglise dans ses
données essentielles. On y trouve les problèmes pastoraux qui
restent les mêmes à travers les transformations historiques. Ce
qui aussi, il faut le dire, fait la valeur de ces catéchèses, c'est
qu'elles sont l'œuvre des plus éminents des grands Docteurs du
IV° siècle. Il est remarquable qu'ils aient consacré à la catéchèse une part si importante de leur activité pastorale. C'est
dire l'importance qu'elle revêt à leurs yeux. Et ceci aussi est
une leçon que nous pouvons tirer d'eux.

Jean DANIELOU, s. j.

34

L'INITIATION CHRÉTIENNE ET SES REFLETS DANS L'ART PALÉOCHRÉTIEN

Selon la division devenue traditionnelle, l'«initiation chrétienne» comportait les trois rites essentiels du Baptême, de la Confirmation et de l'Eucharistie. Le triptyque que je me propose d'ouvrir ici présente une variante et réunit sous ce même titre d'« initiation » : la Foi, le Baptême et l'Eucharistie. Le premier de ces groupements s'inspire de l'examen des sources littéraires ; l'autre est imposé par l'analyse des monuments. Leur divergence pourra surprendre à première vue, mais elle est un fait que l'histoire du culte aurait tort de laisser échapper ultérieurement, car elle est de nature à imprimer de nouvelles orientations à la recherche et à enrichir le trésor d'inspirations que l'antiquité chrétienne offre à nos générations modernes.

A y regarder de plus près, cependant, pareille divergence est plus apparente que réelle. Si nos manuels de liturgie, en effet, s'en tiennent à la première présentation, ils sont obligés cependant de rattacher au Baptême la longue préparation qui le précédait pendant la période du cathéchuménat (1). Et si, d'autre part, les monuments figurés ne semblent retenir des trois sacrements en question que le Baptême et l'Eucharistie, l'iconologue n'en est pas moins obligé de reconnaître que les évocations artistiques du Baptême se rapportent en même temps à la Confirmation (2). Ainsi donc, de part et d'autre, ce sont, au fond, quatre entités qui font l'objet du triptyque, mais l'une d'entre elles est tenue, en quelque sorte, en

---

(1) Voir par exemple, le dernier en date : A. G. Martimort, *L'Eglise en prière. Introduction à la Liturgie* (Paris-Tournai-Rome-New York 1961) 514-528, au chapitre : « L'Initiation chrétienne », signé par R. Béraudy.

(2) J'ai développé longuement mon opinion à ce sujet dans *L'Imposition des mains dans l'art chrétien ancien : Rivista di archeologia cristiana,* 20 (1943) 212-247.

sourdine. Au fait, dans les deux systèmes, toute l'initiation chrétienne est présente.

Quoi qu'il en soit, une différence subsiste. D'accord entre elles pour l'importance qu'elles donnent au Baptême et l'Eucharistie, la première conception met en évidence la Confirmation ; la seconde, au contraire, la Foi. L'unique raison de cet écart se trouve, je pense, dans une différence des points de vue. Les théologiens et les historiens des rites primitifs ont voulu définir l'initiation chrétienne dans les trois sacrements qu'elle comporte, tandis que la communauté plus modeste, et les artistes qui sont son organe, la considéraient plutôt sous l'angle de son efficacité comme moyen du salut. La forte impression, aussi, que leur avait laissée la préparation au Baptême, ainsi que la transformation totale qu'avait opérée en eux l'acceptation de la « bonne nouvelle », ne durent pas être étrangères à la haute idée qu'ils s'en faisaient. C'est donc bien plutôt d'un déplacement d'accent qu'il s'agit ici, que d'une divergence dans les concepts de base.

La vue d'ensemble dont je me propose de tracer les grandes lignes, ne date pas d'aujourd'hui. Je la conçus, il y a quelque vingt-cinq ans, le jour où je tentai de voir clair dans le répertoire iconographique paléochrétien considéré, non point par bribes et morceaux, mais, pour autant que faire se peut, dans la totalité de ses thèmes. Il s'agissait simplement d'en reconnaître les divers secteurs en groupant les monuments selon leurs affinités les plus apparentes : scènes et cycles de l'Ancien Testament, thèmes christologiques, miracles du Christ, compositions représentatives, évocation de l'au-delà, figures isolées, etc. La vue panoramique, simple et claire, que ce travail de classement amena comme résultat, fut simplement révélatrice. Elle me plaça d'emblée, en même temps que devant les riches nuances qu'avait parcourues l'idée chrétienne à ses origines, en présence d'une unité des concepts fondamentaux si limpide et si persistante, que pendant tout le reste de ma carrière scientifique je ne me suis jamais vu obligé de modifier en quoi que ce soit ma vision première.

Voici, en peu de mots, ce que ce panorama révèle. Autour des deux figures centrales, celle du Sauveur et celle du Sauvé, se développe l'illustration de l'œuvre même du salut. Œuvre du salut qui est préfigurée ou préparée dans l'Ancien Testament, élaborée dans le Nouveau Testament, continuée dans l'Eglise et couronnée au Paradis. Dans tout le répertoire symbolique de l'art des catacombes, il n'y a pas une scène, pas un cycle de scènes, pas une figure isolée qui ne trouve sa place naturelle dans cet ensemble. C'est ainsi que tous les motifs, se rapportant à la doctrine ou à la Foi s'inscrivent exactement dans la troisième de ces sections.

Si j'évoque ces souvenirs en cette occasion, c'est tout simplement pour souligner que la trilogie : Foi, Baptême, Eucharistie, illustrant l'initiation chrétienne dans le domaine monumental, n'a pas été imaginée pour obéir à un plan préconçu, ni pour démontrer une thèse, mais s'est offerte, pour ainsi dire, d'elle-même, autant dans son ensemble que dans chacun de ses composants. Dans son ensemble, elle se dégage par une simple démarcation des groupes iconographiques immédiatement reconnaissables ; considérée dans ses parties, elle se révèle automatiquement par un triple triage des matériaux qui l'illustrent. Du point de vue méthodologique, on ne saurait désirer, nous semble-t-il, meilleure garantie d'objectivité.

LA FOI

Par ce qui précède, on aura déjà deviné que le terme « Foi » a ici comme arrière-fond tout ce qui faisait l'objet et la finalité de la discipline prébaptismale et qui, effectivement, trouvait son accomplissement dans le Baptême. J'ai préféré ce terme de « Foi » à ceux de « doctrine » ou de « catéchèse » parce que le fait iconographique qu'il s'agit de mettre en lumière ici c'est l'insistance de l'art, non pas tant sur la doctrine elle-même, que sur l'adhésion personnelle du fidèle à cette doctrine.

L'art chrétien, bien sûr, n'ignore pas la « foi chrétienne » entendue comme ensemble des vérités qui en font l'objet matériel et que tout chrétien est obligé d'admettre. Bien au contraire, la presque totalité de son répertoire ne fait que rappeler et illustrer ce contenu de la foi. C'est d'ailleurs l'aspect que les publications iconographiques sur « la Foi dans l'art » (3) n'ont cessé d'examiner jusqu'à nos jours, au point que, après les avoir parcourues, on finit par avoir l'impression que le relevé de la documentation artistique du

---

(3) Citons parmi les exemples les plus récents : G. WILPERT, *La Fede delle Chiesa nascente secondo i monumenti dell'arte funeraria antica* = *Collezione « Amici delle Catacombe »*, 9 (Città del Vaticano 1938); G. BELVEDERI et G. BOVINI, *La Catechesi di S. Pietro e il « Credo » della Chiesa antica nell'arte paleochristiana* = *Collezione « Amici delle Catacombe »*, 13 (Roma 1951).

dépôt de la foi constituait à peu près tout ce que la recherche iconologique pouvait atteindre dans ce domaine.

Mais il y a aussi la foi considérée en elle-même ; la foi, vertu
théologale qui nous fait connaître Dieu et nous unit à Lui, racine de
toute justification et fondement de toute la vie chrétienne ; celle que
saint Paul visait dans son texte : « Le juste vit de la foi » (4) et que
les Pères mettent à l'origine de l'initiation chrétienne. Infusée dans
l'âme avec la grâce sanctifiante, elle incline le chrétien à adhérer
avec fermeté, à cause de la véracité de Dieu, à toutes les vérités
que Dieu a révélées et que son Eglise propose à notre croyance.

Elle est à la fois vertu, lumière, adhésion, prise de position, en-
gagement sous la mouvance du Saint-Esprit. Le croyant c'est l'initié,
l'homme nouveau, l'enfant de Dieu. Croire, c'est avoir la foi et
vivre par elle la vie de citoyens dans la cité de Dieu.

Bien qu'on ne puisse séparer la foi de son objet, puisque, comme
l'a très bien dit Guardini, « la foi est son contenu » (5), c'est dans
cette perspective que nous l'envisagerons ici. Nous voudrions donc
relever, dans les monuments de l'art chrétien ancien, le témoignage
direct et éloquent que les premières générations chrétiennes y lais-
sèrent de leur attachement à ce don de Dieu et de la valeur incom-
mensurable que représentait pour eux sa possession aussi bien que
sa profession.

Dans sa fameuse épitaphe, à laquelle nous aurons à revenir,
l'évêque Abercius, « disciple d'un saint Pasteur » qui lui «a enseigné
les écritures dignes de foi », nous raconte qu'après être allé à Rome
« contempler la maison royale et voir une reine aux vêtements d'or »,
il fut guidé partout, dans ses pérégrinations ultérieures, par la
Foi (6).

---

(4) *Rom.* 1,17 ; *Hebr.* 10,38.
(5) Romano Guardini, *Vie de la Foi = Foi vivante* (Paris, Editions du
Cerf 1958) 23 s.
(6) Pour l'inscription d'Abercius, voir : J. Wilpert, *Fractio panis. Die
älteste Darstellung des Eucharistischen Opfers in der «Cappella Greca»*
(Freiburg i. Br. 1895) 103-127 ; A. Greiff, *Zum Verständnis der Aberkiosinschrift : Theologie u. Glaube*, 18 (1926) 78-88; Id., *Zur Aberkiosinschrift :*
ΙΧΘΥC, 1 (1928) 8-11 ; 454-507 ; A. Ferrua, *Nuove osservazioni sull'epi-
Theologische Quartalschrift*, 110 (1929) 242-261 ; 447-474 ; F.J. Doelger,
taffio di Abercio : Rivista di archeologia cristiana, 20 (1943) 279-305 (avec
bibliographie antérieure) ; H. Strathmann-Th. Klauser, dans : *Reallexikon für Antike u. Christentum*, 1 (1950) 12 ss.; M. Burzachechi, *La* ΠΗΓΗ
e la ΠΑΡΘΕΝΟΣ ΑΓΝΗ *dell'iscrizione di Abercio : Rivista di archeologia
cristiana*, 31 (1955) 261-267.

C'est dans l'atmosphère qui baigne ces hexamètres qu'il nous faut aborder les tout premiers monuments chrétiens mis à jour par les fouilles, puisque c'est bien à la même époque, ou peu s'en faut, qu'ils nous ramènent.

*
* *

A peine descend-on dans les plus anciennes régions des catacombes romaines, qu'un phénomène étrange nous y surprend. Parmi tant de motifs et de compositions immédiatement reconnaissables, et souvent en marge de ceux-ci, se trouvent distribuées des figures d'hommes, la plupart debout, dont le moins qu'on puisse dire est qu'elles ne semblent plus correspondre à nos façons de voir, puisque nous avons toute la peine du monde pour leur trouver un nom.

Qu'on entre dans le double cubicule XY de la région de Lucine, à Saint-Calliste. Le Baptême du Christ et la composition eucharistique, dont nous parlerons tout à l'heure, le Bon Pasteur, l'Orante, Daniel entre les lions, le reste d'un cycle de Jonas, tout cela nous paraît aussez connu. L'insolite et le mystérieux réside bien plutôt dans ces figures isolées d'hommes qu'on découvre parsemées un peu partout, aux places secondaires. Il devait y en avoir quatre sur la première voûte, comme il y avait quatre orantes entourant le Bon Pasteur central (7). Deux autres sont encore conservées, en partie du moins, sur la paroi d'entrée de la seconde chambre. Il y en a encore une sur la paroi de fond de la première chambre, à droite de la porte intermédiaire (8). D'autres encore se laissent présumer comme pendants aux endroits abîmés. Leur habillement, pour autant que la mauvaise conservation permet de l'identifier, peut différer légèrement ; ce qui les caractérise toutes, c'est le geste de la parole.

Qu'on descende ensuite, à quelques pas de là, aux « chapelles des Sacrements » (9), des constatations identiques nous y attendent,

---

(7) G. WILPERT, *Le pitture delle catacombe romane*, cité : WP (Roma 1903) pl. 24,1.

(8) WP pl. 24,2.

(9) Pour l'ensemble de ces chambres, souvent citées, voir G. B. DE ROSSI, *Roma sotterranea*, 2 (1867) 328-348 ; J. WILPERT, *Die Malereien der Sacramentskapellen in der Katakombe des hl. Callistus* (Freiburg i. Br. 1897) ; ID., *Pitture, passim* ; L. v. SYBEL, *Christliche Antike*, 1 (Marburg 1906) 117 ss., 293 ss.; O. WULFF, *Altchristliche u. byzantinische Kunst* (Berlin 1914) 74 ss. ; P. STYGER, *Die altchristliche Grabeskunst* (München 1927) 16 ss., 43 ; W. ELLIGER, *Zur Entstehung u. frühen Entwicklung der altchristlichen Bildkunst* (Leipzig 1934) 77-80 ; 240-254.

mais cette fois-ci encore plus éloquentes (10). Au geste de la parole, s'ajoute l'habillement du philosophe : le pallium porté à l'exomide, en même temps que, parfois, le « volumen » ou rouleau tenu dans la main gauche (11). Particulièrement suggestif le « philosophe » assis, sur la paroi de fond de la chambre A₂, dont le pendant fut malheureusement détruit avec le stuc (12). Ici même, plusieurs de ces figures ont disparu, mais la loi des correspondances symétriques permet de reconstituer sans trop de difficulté leur distribution originale.

Pareils motifs, surtout à une époque où les méthodes d'investigation avaient besoin de perfectionnement, étaient tout indiquées pour être le cauchemar des interprètes. Limitant souvent l'examen à l'une seule d'entre elles, alors que de toute évidence elles doivent s'éclairer mutuellement, on les identifia au « docteur » qui aurait guidé le décorateur de ces chambres (13), au propriétaire qui donne ses instructions pour l'aménagement de sa chambre mortuaire (14), aux Saints avocats intercédant auprès du Christ juge en faveur du défunt (15), au « Pédagogue divin » (16), dans le sens de Clément d'Alexandrie. Une seule opinion, timidement avancée mais imparfaitement formulée, mettait ces figures de docteurs en relation avec les lectures de l'Ancien Testament qui accompagnaient l'administration du Baptême et de la Communion eucharistique (17).

---

(10) WP pl. 39,2 ; 40,1.

(11) A rappeler aussi, que dans ce même ensemble de chambres c'est encore le costume du philosophe que le peintre a prêté au Christ dans son colloque avec la Samaritaine (WP pl. 29,2) et au personnage qui bénit pains et poisson sur la table trépied (*ibid.*, pl. 41,1). Dans les deux peintures, l'artiste invite le spectateur à se souvenir du discours qui accompagne le fait évoqué.

(12) WP pl. 39, 2.

(13) G. B. DE ROSSI, *Roma sotterranea* 2, 346.

(14) V. SCHULTZE, *Archäologische Studien über altchristliche Monumente* (Wien 1880) 57, 95 ; P. STYGER, *Op. cit.*, 17.

(15) J. WILPERT, *Sacramentskapellen* cité, 13 s. ; *Pitture*, 375. Ces figures s'appellent des « saints » tout court chez C. M. KAUFMANN, *Handbuch der christlichen Archäologie* (Paderborn 1922 ³) 262.

(16) Ainsi, du moins pour le philosophe assis de la chambre A3 à Saint-Calliste, O. WULFF, *Op. cit.*, 75. J. KOLLWITZ, *Christusbild* : RAC, III,7, l'appelle une image du Christ docteur, alors qu'il voit dans WP pl. 40,3 plutôt un « Schüler » du Christ.

(17) V. DE BUCK, *Le cimetière de Saint-Callixte et les travaux de MM. de Rossi* : *Etudes religieuses, historiques et littéraires par les pères de la Compagnie de Jésus*, 2 (1868) 300.

C'était la seule qui s'approchait de la vérité, avec une vision pénétrante pour l'époque : sauf chez M. Kraus (18), elle trouva peu de crédit chez les autres érudits de l'époque (19).

Si, au lieu de s'arrêter à un seul monument, les savants se fussent donné la peine de faire un tour d'horizon général sur l'art paléochrétien, pour examiner de plus près les cas analogues, on peut espérer qu'ils auraient été mieux éclairés. Qu'on passe, par exemple, de la via Appia à la via Salaria, à la soi-disant « cappella greca » du cimetière de Priscille : les quatre figures masculines dont on trouve des restes sur la seconde voûte, parmi les rinceaux de vigne, peuvent très bien avoir été, non pas des « orants », comme Mgr Wilpert a reconstitué deux d'entre elles (20), mais des « docteurs ». Fort significative, à cet égard, une note marginale de sa main, dans son exemplaire personnel de la « Fractio » : « Aujourd'hui (8-2-35), je donnerais à cette figure de Saint (sic) un rouleau dans la main ».

Il ne faut pas tarder de beaucoup, pour voir réapparaître nos mystérieuses figures dans d'autres ensembles encore, et à d'autres endroits. Deux parmi elles, habillées de tunique et de pallium et tenant le rouleau des deux mains, nous les retrouvons au cimetière de Domitille, où elles encadrent une scène des trois Hébreux dans la Fournaise (21). Nous sommes dans une chambre dont le décorateur nous fournira bientôt une preuve éclatante (22) de l'importance qu'avait pour lui la parole du Seigneur. Contentons-nous, pour le moment, de nous demander ce que ces figures se trouveraient à faire, dans cette combinaison, au cas où il faudrait y reconnaître des Saints, ou s'il y a la moindre chance de pouvoir les identifier avec les inspirateurs de cette décoration...

Au cimetière de la « Nunziatella », c'est-à-dire, à une distance de sept kilomètres de Rome sur la voie Ardéatine, un plafond (23) réunit, une fois de plus, quatre de nos figures caractérisées par le

---

(18) F. X. KRAUS, *Geschichte der christlichen Kunst* (Freiburg i. Br. 1896) 163.

(19) J. WILPERT, *Sacramentskapellen* cité, 9.

(20) J. WILPERT, *Fractio* cité, 7 et fig. 2.

(21) WP pl. 54,1.

(22) Voir *infra*, p. 36.

(23) WP pl. 75.

rouleau et le geste de la parole (24) autour (notons-le bien) du Christ enseignant (25), tout en les faisant alterner avec quatre figures d'Orants encadrées des brebis du Bon Pasteur.

On remarquera les affinités de cet ensemble avec la première voûte dans la double chambre de la région de Lucine (26). L'art est en évolution : le Bon Pasteur est remplacé par le Christ docteur ; ses brebis perpétuent cependant son souvenir en restant dans la compagnie des orants. Il n'y a que nos quatre « docteurs » qui sont restés eux-mêmes, mais eux aussi se trouvent intimement associés aux orants, puisqu'ils sont compris dans la même zone décorative. Ceux de mes lecteurs qui connaissent l'importance qu'a eue pour l'antiquité chrétienne le « binôme » ποιμήν διδάσκαλος (27) sauront évaluer toute la signification de l'entremêlement de ces deux sphères, du Bon Pasteur et du Christ docteur, que des monuments de cette espèce nous révèlent avoir remué les artistes. Mais, pour revenir à l'hypogée de la Nunziatella et à la question qui nous occupe, ce qui semble déjà hors de doute, dès maintenant, c'est que ces figures de « docteurs », qui ne sont pas des portraits, qui se laissent multiplier et distribuer selon les nécessités purement techniques de la décoration, ne peuvent d'aucune façon être prises

---

(24) Pour être plus exact, deux de ces figures font le geste oratoire ; une semble tenir la droite enveloppée dans le pallium ; la quatrième est détruite.

(25) Il est notoire que Mgr Wilpert (*Pitture*, 372 s.) reconnut dans cet ensemble une scène de jugement de l'âme, exemple typique de la facilité avec laquelle on force le vocabulaire et la syntaxe figurative choisis par l'artiste. Non seulement il manque dans cet ensemble tout trait caractéristique d'un jugement (le *suggestus* du juge p. ex.), mais nous pouvons rapprocher cette voûte d'une autre qui en est presque une réplique au « coemeterium maius » (WP pl. 168 et texte p. 377 s.) où le Christ central, outre à tenir son *volumen* entr'ouvert, comme ici (allusion manifeste au contenu qu'il est en train de commenter), est accosté des deux côtés des *capsae* contenant d'autres rouleaux. Ces *capsae*, attribut constant de la doctrine, comme nous verrons bientôt, il faut les restituer, sans aucun doute, des deux côtés (abîmés) de notre Christ enseignant de la Nunziatella.

(26) Une autre affinité se trouve dans le fait qu'ici, comme à Saint-Calliste, ces figures au rouleau se retrouvent sur la paroi d'entrée de la même chambre (WP pl. 40,1).

(27) Voir à ce propos Th. KEMPF, *Christus der Hirt, Ursprung und Deutung einer altchristlichen Symbolgestalt* (Roma 1942) 36. Cf. F. SAXL, *Frühes Christentum und spätes Heidentum in ihren künstlerischen Ausdrucksformen : Wiener Jhb. f. Kunstgeschichte* 2 (16) (1923) tiré à part (1925) 90 ; J. KOLLWITZ, *l. c.* 6.

pour des figures individuelles, concrètes, mais doivent être interprétées comme des images conventionnelles, abstraites, d'une portée purement symbolique (28). Elles n'ont de sens que comme symboles. Acceptées comme telles, elles se concrétisent — gestes et attributs nous le prouvent — comme des allusions à une doctrine, qui ne saurait être que celle du Christ. Par elles, à travers elles, le souvenir de l'initiation chrétienne est partout présent. On ne saurait les appeler des « personnifications » de la Foi ; elles sont simplement destinées à la rappeler. Dans des monuments comme celui-ci, on ne saurait plus mettre en doute qu'elles incarnent un concept qui tient le milieu entre la parole divine en action, au centre de la composition, et le résultat final de ce ministère de la parole : la béatitude céleste symbolisée dans les orants. Or, ce concept intermédiaire, c'est celui de la doctrine et de la foi qui y correspond.

Cette interprétation, que l'examen progressif des monuments nous suggère, est indirectement confirmée par le décor de l'hypogée des Aurelii, au Viale Manzoni (29). Quoique l'opinion courante le tienne pour hérétique, l'analyse de cet ensemble et de son langage iconographique offre des éléments utiles pour l'interprétation des ensembles orthodoxes. Les figures isolées qu'on y trouve disséminées un peu partout, sur les voûtes, sur les parois, dans les niches, toujours à des endroits secondaires, rappellent singulièrement bien celles que nous avons rencontrées dans les catacombes examinées jusqu'ici. Identiques leur costume et le rôle qui leur est assigné dans l'ensemble décoratif, identique aussi l'un de leurs attributs : le *volumen*. Mais elles en reçoivent un second : la baguette, qui semble interchangeable avec le premier, ou qu'elles peuvent aussi tenir à la main ensemble avec celui-ci. *Volumen* et baguette, voilà les deux instruments qui se trouvent mis en vedette avec une insistance, qui a de quoi surprendre, et qui ont une relation indiscutable avec les

---

(28) Tenu compte de l'âge de cette fresque (IIIe s.), il serait prématuré de penser à des figures d'Apôtres. Mais si la chronologie eût permis pareille identification, l'idée de la propagation de la parole du Christ ne s'en serait trouvée nullement compromise.

(29) Voir pour cet ensemble : G. BENDINELLI, *Il monumento sepolcrale degli Aurelii = Monumenti antichi*, publiés par l'Académie des Lincei 28 (1922-23) 290-514 ; G. WILPERT, *Le pitture dell'ipogeo di Aurelio Felicissimo presso il Viale Manzoni in Roma = Memorie della Pont. Accademia romana di Archeologia*, I,2 (1924) 1-42 ; J. CARCOPINO, *De Pythagore aux Apôtres* (Paris 1956) 83-221.

attributs apparaissant dans une des compositions principales (30). Faut-il y reconnaître l'allusion à une mystique et une magie, ou est-ce que les deux n'en font qu'un, en ce sens qu'ils caractérisent tous les deux le docteur ou l'enseignant ? La discussion est encore ouverte et le contexte présent ne permet pas d'en explorer les méandres. Mais une chose est certaine : c'est que personne, en ce cas, n'a osé parler de figures de « Saints ». Selon toute vraisemblance, il s'agit de nouveau d'évocations d'une prose et d'une δύναμις que seuls les initiés pouvaient se rappeler. Il y a même plus : maintes fois ces figures reposent sur un piédestal végétal plus ou moins stylisé, comme si elles faisaient partie intégrante du décor, ce qui souligne encore mieux leur caractère abstrait (31), par quoi elles vont rejoindre leurs correspondants dans les ensembles cémétériaux déjà rencontrés.

Lorsque des monuments d'une même époque, qui d'abord ne paraissaient être que des *disiecta membra* sans affinité apparente entre eux, commencent à s'aligner ainsi dans la même perspective, grâce à un concept fondamental commun, l'interprète a d'excellentes indications d'être sur la bonne voie. Tout se simplifie, tout rentre dans l'unité, et les reflets mêmes par lesquels ils s'éclairent réciproquement deviennent une preuve de la justesse de la vision qui découvre leur parenté.

C'est sans doute dans la même perspective qu'il faut placer la figure imposante du Cimetière de Domitille, dans laquelle Wilpert reconnut, une fois de plus, le Christ juge (32), et que von Sybel baptisa : « der aufrufende Herr », le Seigneur qui appelle tous à son Evangile, gage de félicité éternelle (33). Si l'on interprète sa longue

---

(30) Nous faisons allusion ici à la Triade qui occupe le centre de la voûte dans la chambre souterraine du sud : WILPERT, *op. cit.* pl. III ; BENDINELLI, *op. cit.* pl. XIV ; CARCOPINO, *op. cit.* pl. VI,2.

(31) Voilà ce qui semble avoir échappé aussi bien à Wilpert, qui y reconnaît le Christ des Naasséniens (*op. cit.*, p. 20), qu'à M. Carcopino, qui en fait des effigies du Christ gnostique (*op. cit.*, pp. 118, 124 s., 136). Il s'agit cependant d'une loi générale appliquée souvent par l'iconographie paléochrétienne.

(32) WP pl. 40,2 ; texte p. 375.

(33) L. v. SYBEL, *Der Herr der Seligkeit* (Marbourg in Hessen 1913) frontispice et p. 8 s., ID., *Frühchristliche Kunst, Leitfaden ihrer Entwicklung* (München 1920) frontispice et p. 16 s.

chevelure et sa barbe, ainsi que le rouleau tenu ouvert à la première page, comme des accentuations intentionnelles — tout à fait traditionnelles, du reste — de son caractère « philosophique », cette figure rentre parfaitement bien dans le rang de celles que nous avons rencontrées jusqu'ici.

Récemment d'ailleurs, les fouilles de la Commission pontificale d'Archéologie sacrée au Coemeterium Maius ont amené la découverte d'une peinture analogue, qu'on peut dater vers la moitié du iiie siècle (34). Presque identique à la précédente pour ce qui concerne la conception générale de la figure et sa caractérisation selon le type du philosophe cynique, elle n'en diffère que dans l'attitude de la main droite qui, au lieu d'être complètement ouverte ne tient que deux doigts étendus, et dans le fait que la figure, au lieu d'être debout, cette fois-ci est assise. Mais ce sont là des détails qui n'effacent pas la signification fondamentale. L'on y note, du reste, la présence du *scrinium* rempli de rouleaux.

On peut être certain, que si cette fresque eût été découverte quelque cinquante ans plus tôt, l'on y aurait reconnu tout de suite une figure du Christ. Ce nous a été une satisfaction de constater que le P. Fasola l'appelle une figuration de l'enseignant et la met en relation directe avec la catéchèse, telle qu'elle est souvent évoquée sur les sarcophages.

Au risque de prolonger outre mesure l'énumération des monuments, nous ne pouvons omettre une découverte encore plus récente et pas moins instructive. Il s'agit de l'hypogée de la Voie Latine, qui vient d'être publié par le P. Ferrua (35), où c'est surtout la salle I qui nous attire, parce qu'on pourrait vraiment l'appeler « la salle des docteurs ». Plusieurs bustes de « docteurs », le plus souvent en pallium philosophique, se partagent le centre et les principaux panneaux de la voûte hexagonale, les *volumina* ou les *codices* les accompagnant comme attributs (36), tandis que les panneaux secon-

---

(34) U. M. Fasola, *Nuove scoperte nel « Coemeterium Maius »* : *L'Osservatore romano* (25 déc. 1954) 3 ; Id., *Le recenti scoperte agiografiche nel Coemeterium Maius : Atti della Pont. Accademia romana di Archeologia,* Serie III. *Rendiconti,* 28 (1956) 81, fig. 4.

(35) A. Ferrua, *Le pitture della nuova catacomba di Via Latina* (Città del Vaticano 1960) 33 s., 67-71 ; Cf. *La Civiltà cattolica,* 107,2 (1956) 118-131 ; *Etudes* (juin 1956) 396-403.

(36) A. Ferrua, *Le pitture della nuova catacomba di Via Latina,* pl. 55 ; 56,1 ; 57,1 ; 59.

daires encore conservés contiennent comme unique motif central,
une fois le *codex* ouvert, une autre fois, la *capsa* remplie de rouleaux (37). La porte d'entrée est pour ainsi dire gardée par deux
personnages, barbus et debout, vêtus de tunique et pallium tenant
le rouleau fermé des deux mains ; deux autres, mais jeunes cette
fois-ci, se trouvent postés dans la même attitude des deux côtés
de la porte de sortie (38). Mais ce qui est beaucoup plus important
pour la question qui nous occupe, c'est que l'architecte et le décorateur de cet ensemble, par un arrangement des plus ingénieux des
espaces rayonnants, obligent en quelque sorte le visiteur à découvrir
les compositions principales au fond même des deux arcosalia symé-
triquement disposés. A gauche, le groupe monumental du Christ
enseignant entre les Apôtres Pierre et Paul ; à droite, comme pendant, le dialogue entre un philosophe et ses compagnons ou disciples (39). Ce philosophe (car c'est bien ainsi qu'il est caractérisé
par le pallium exomide et le type cynique) constitue avec les personnages assis à ses côtés un groupe de sept ; l'un de ceux-ci touche,
avec une verge longue et fine, le corps d'un personnage nu étendu
par terre et le ventre ouvert par une plaie béante. D'autres personnages d'importance secondaire se trouvent derrière le groupe
principal.

On sait les discussions que cette peinture, à peine découverte,
a déjà soulevées (40). Nous nous contenterons de signaler ici notre
opinion personnelle, que nous espérons pouvoir démontrer bientôt
ailleurs. Il s'agit, pensons-nous, d'un dialogue entre Socrate et son
école sur le sens de la mort. Ce qui nous importe en ce moment
est le rapprochement entre le grand philosophe et le Christ enseignant (41). Quels que puissent avoir été les propriétaires de cet

---

(37) *Ibid.*, pl. 55.

(38) *Ibid.*, pl. 60 et 106 ; 61 et 62. — On ne saurait pas ne pas être
frappé de la ressemblance qu'offre cette salle I avec l'hypogée des Auréliens, cité tout à l'heure, quant à l'insistance sur les figures «philosophiques».
C'est, sous une forme plus archaïque ou moins « ecclésiastique », la même
insistance que celle qu'on remarque dans un sarcophage d'Arles (J. WILPERT,
I sarcofagi = cité : WS, pl. 34,3), où le Christ docteur, les Apôtres, les
quatre Evangélistes et d'autres disciples ou lecteurs sont présentés avec une
abondance presque excessive.

(39) A. FERRUA, *Op. cit.*, pl. 108 et 107.

(40) *Ibid.*, p. 70, note 1.

(41) Voir pour ce rapprochement : M. A. HANFMANN, *Socrates and
Christ—Harvard Studies in classical Philology*, 60 (1951) 205-233.

hypogée, on ne pourra plus révoquer en doute l'importance qu'ils attachaient à la doctrine dont ils se proclament les disciples avec une insistance pareille. Et du même coup — cela nous suffit pour le moment — cet ensemble monumental vient confirmer tout ce que nous savons déjà par l'analyse des monuments picturaux du IIIᵉ siècle, et nous sommes conduits par l'analogie à y reconnaître la même spéculation que celle qui, dans les catacombes, établissait des liens intimes entre le fondateur d'une doctrine et les évocations plusieurs fois répétées de celle-ci, sous forme de personnages y faisant allusion.

Nous n'avons examiné jusqu'ici que les peintures. Puisque la méthode saine et intégrale nous interdit de négliger la sculpture, autre domaine majeur où l'âme chrétienne s'est manifestée avec clarté, c'est vers elle qu'il nous fait maintenant diriger nos démarches.

Par une curieuse coïncidence, l'un des thèmes principaux qui ont été choisis pour l'ornementation des plus anciens sarcophages chrétiens, se trouve être de nouveau en relation directe avec le livre sacré, la doctrine, la foi. Depuis l'étude excellente que M. Marrou leur dédia (42), les sarcophages ornés d'une scène de doctrine, ou d'autres motifs « philosophiques », sont bien connus ; nous pouvons donc nous dispenser d'en reprendre en détail une description qui allongerait trop ce texte et nous limiter à quelques remarques supplémentaires, qui paraissent indispensables (43).

Et d'abord, ce qui caractérise avant tout les exemplaires chrétiens, c'est l'introduction, dans l'ensemble philosophique, des deux figures centrales du répertoire chrétien primitif : le Bon Pasteur et l'Orante (44); trait caractéristique qui associe les premiers sarco

---

(42) H. I. MARROU, *MOYCIKOC ANHP. Etudes sur les scènes de la vie intellectuelle figurant sur les monuments funéraires romains* (Grenoble 1938).

(43) Pour le concept de la « vraie philosophie » du christianisme, voir : J. KOLLWITZ, *Christus als Lehrer und die Gesetzübergabe an Petrus in der konstantinischen Kunst Roms : Römische Quartalschrift*, 44 (1936) 49 s.; Id. *Das Christusbild des 3. Jahrhunderts = Orbis antiquus*, 9 (Münster i. W. 1953) 13 11.

(44) Bon Pasteur et Orante se rencontrent sur les sarcophages de la Gayolle (WS pl. 1,3), de la Via Salaria (WS pl. 1,1), de Sainte-Marie-Antique (WS pl. 1,2), du Palazzo Sanseverino (WS pl. 2,3), de Velletri (WS pl. 4,3), etc.

phages aux premières peintures (45). Parfois même, par le truchement de contaminations ingénieuses, le sculpteur établit un lien
intime et mystique entre ces diverses figures. Sur le fameux sarcophage de la Via Salaria (46), trois motifs se disposent d'une manière
nettement symétrique. Un groupe de lecture à gauche ; un autre
semblable à droite ; le Bon Pasteur au milieu : optiquement parlant,
un vrai triptyque. Mais attention ! A y regarder de plus près, cette
symétrie a été légèrement dérangée par une contamination aussi sub-
tile qu'éloquente.

L'Orante, traditionnellement une figure indépendante, a été ici
obtenue par voie de transformation d'une des auditrices de la scène
de lecture. Non seulement cela, mais tout en continuant à faire partie intégrante de son groupe original, une nouvelle contamination
lui fait tourner la tête du côté opposé, vers le Bon Pasteur, qui la
regarde à son tour. Du point de vue conceptuel, trois choses sont
à remarquer ici. De par son appartenance au groupe de lecture (46 bis), cette figure féminine se proclame adhérer à une doc-

---

(45) Voir *supra*, p. 31 et 34.

(46) WS pl. 1,1

(46 bis) Contrairement à la tendance de plusieurs auteurs, parmi lesquels il faut compter aussi MM. Marrou et Kollwitz, nous pensons qu'on
fait fausse route en voulant trop préciser la personnalité de chacun des
personnages composant ces groupes de lecture ou de doctrine (maître ou
disciple ?, père ou fils ? mari et épouse ? Christ et disciple ? etc.) L'intention des sculpteurs, qui préparaient la plupart du temps leurs sarcophages
à l'avance, sans même en connaître les destinataires, n'était pas là. Sans
doute tenaient-ils compte de la tendance contemporaine d'y introduire des
portraits individuels, mais le fait même que de sarcophage en sarcophage ces
masques individuels voyagent d'un personnage à l'autre prouve que le symbolisme visé était confié au groupe dans son ensemble, et non point à l'un de
ses composants. En d'autres termes, l'allusion à la doctrine selon les besoins
compositionnels des ensembles, pouvait se faire soit par des personnages
isolés, comme nous verrons, soit par des groupes de personnages combinés
en scène, comme dans le cas présent. Et quand on voulait concentrer le
symbolisme sur un ou deux défunts déterminés, on pouvait toujours les faire
figurer, soit comme « docteurs », soit comme disciples, puisqu'il suffisait
d'être du groupe pour proclamer sa propre adhérence à la doctrine évoquée.
C'est exactement la même démarche d'esprit que celle qui présida aux combinaisons iconographiques adoptées pour les « orants ». Admettre cette opinion, qu'il serait trop long prouver dans le détail, c'est voir disparaître
toutes les difficultés que les érudits rencontrent dans l'effort désespéré
d'identification des divers personnages. Ajoutons, pour finir, que dans des
ensembles symétriques, comme l'exemple cité, les deux groupes ont exactement le même rôle symbolique à remplir.

trine ; l'adhésion à cette doctrine fait d'elle une disciple fidèle du Bon Pasteur, ce qui prouve que la doctrine elle-même remonte à Celui-ci ; et enfin, la béatitude céleste symbolisée par son attitude d'orante (47) est présentée comme le résultat final de l'adhésion fidèle à cette doctrine divine.

Nous voilà d'emblée, grâce à cette sculpture, en présence d'indices positifs, bien clairs et bien nets. Dans son commentaire du matériel chrétien, M. Marrou remarque à juste titre : « Dans ces monuments, il y a plus qu'une allusion à la première initiation reçue par le catéchumène : c'est une étude approfondie, quotidienne, continue qu'on veut évoquer ici. Ces défunts veulent nous faire savoir qu'ils ont, leur vie durant, poursuivi avec ardeur, possédé avec amour la science sacrée » (48). Ce n'est pas seulement leur foi qu'ils proclament, c'est en même temps tout le prix qu'ils y attachaient. Ajoutons même qu'ils la considèrent, non seulement comme le commencement d'une existence nouvelle, mais aussi comme gage certain du salut éternel.

Il se produit par la suite, dans la plastique chrétienne, un phénomène curieux, que nous ne pouvons esquisser que très brièvement. Dès que, sur d'autres types de sarcophages, l'Orante se sépare du Bon Pasteur, dès qu'elle quitte cette ambiance des groupes doctrinaux, non seulement les arbres qui caractérisaient le paradis du Pasteur la suivent, pour l'encadrer à son tour (49), mais même les attributs de la doctrine sacrée, les *volumina* ou les *capsae* qui les contiennent, l'accompagnent comme un accessoire à peu près inséparable (50). Le fait a été peu souligné. Il est cependant d'une impor-

---

(47) Dans une communication à l'Académie pontificale romaine d'Archéologie (*Rendiconti*, 23, 1960, 7), que nous espérons pouvoir compléter et publier dans un avenir non lointain, nous avons cherché, en effet, à établir que le sens fondamental de l'Orant(e) est la félicité dans la paix éternelle.

(48) H.-I. MARROU, *Op. cit.*, 278.

(49) WS pl. 19,1-2 ; 19,6 ; 61,3 ; 92,1 (palmiers) ; 99,5 ; 113,1 (palmiers); 119,2 ; 217,1 ; 245,3 ; 246,2 ; 249,1 ; 249,10 (palmiers); 250,2 ; 246,3 (palmiers); 278,6.

(50) WS pl. 19,1 et 62,1; 45,4; 59,2; 59,4; 63,3; 81,2; 81,3; 92,1; 114,3; 117,1; 118,4; 119,1; 133,1; 133,2; 158,1; 159,2; 217,1; 220,2; 228,3; 228,7; 233,4; 245, 1-2; 246, 1-2; 246,5; 248,2; 249,3; 268,1 ; 285,1-2; Texte III, fig. 216, à p. 33.

tance capitale. Pour peu qu'on connaisse les lois de l'art paléochrétien, il nous prouve que pour nos sculpteurs ce jeu de rappels était le moyen simple et efficace de garder frais auprès de l'Orant(e), le souvenir de la doctrine à laquelle elle devait son état, aussi bien que du Pasteur auquel elle devait la doctrine. Il leur fournissait le moyen de rappeler que le sort heureux du défunt trouvait une garantie certaine dans la foi qu'il avait professée.

L'évolution ultérieure des détails iconographiques ne fait que confirmer cette interprétation. Tout à fait anonymes au début, du moins pour qui ne se doute pas de leur provenance, ces livres, par une progression lente et insensible, se définissent toujours plus explicitement comme textes sacrés contenant les Saintes-Ecritures, dans la suite. Nous assistons ici à un phénomène qui est propre à toute la production artistique d'après la paix de l'Eglise. Etant donné que cette évolution se produit selon une ligne continue, sans heurt ni interruption, il paraît tout à fait légitime d'arguer du plus clair, mais plus récent, au plus ancien, mais voilé davantage.

Nous pensons, par exemple, aux sarcophages qui présentent l'Orante acclamée par deux Apôtres (51). Comment saurait-on encore douter du caractère chrétien des livres qui l'accompagnent, lorsque les deux Saints qui l'acclament partagent avec elle le même attribut ? (52). Et comment pourrait-on rester sceptique sur l'action salutaire de ces livres — conditionnée par la foi du défunt, bien entendu —, lorsque sur l'un des sarcophages, conservé à Saint-Calliste (53), l'Orante, déjà acclamée par les Apôtres, est couronnée en même temps par l'aigle de l'Apothéose ?

Ou si l'on veut des témoignages encore plus explicites, citons les cas où le monogramme du Christ, ajouté à l'ensemble, détermine sans équivoque le caractère divin de la doctrine qui a inspiré, sa vie durant, le chrétien dont on perpétue le souvenir (54). Parfois même, de menus fragments, émouvants dans leur simplicité, comme celui de deux mains serrant contre une poitrine un codex contresigné de

---

(51) WS pl. 31,7; 60,5; 159,2; 244, 1-4; 245, 1-3; 246, 2-3.

(52) On remarquera que sur certains sarcophages ils acclament l'Orante comme sur d'autres ils acclament le Christ (voir p. ex. WS pl. 37). Parfois même le Christ et les défunts ensemble sont acclamés (*ibid.*, nn. 4 et 5 et pl. 244,2). Les attributs du Christ, des Apôtres, de l'Orante sont les mêmes. Voir encore *ibid.*, pl. 41.

(53) WS pl. 159,2.

(54) WS pl. 246,1. Cf. pl. 27,3.

la marque du Christ (55), ne sont rien moins qu'une profession de foi pétrifiée.

Ils nous apprennent, mieux que jamais, que le christianisme ne consistait pas seulement dans l'admission de la doctrine du Seigneur comme conviction ou comme règle de vie, mais bien plutôt dans l'unification avec lui, par l'Esprit, dans le plus intime de l'être.

Dans le domaine de la peinture cémétériale aussi on trouve des reflets des mêmes spéculations, qui ne manquent pas de clarté. Lorsque, au cimetière de Domitille, sainte Pétronille introduit la défunte Vénéranda au Paradis (56), et qu'elle indique en même temps de la main gauche une *capsa* remplie de volumes, au-dessus de laquelle on voit aussi un *codex* ouvert, on pourra discuter si celui-ci n'indiquerait pas le livre de la vie (57), mais on ne pourra mettre en doute que la Sainte établit ainsi une relation intime entre la foi de Vénéranda et son heureuse entrée au Paradis.

Et quand à Naples, aux catacombes de Saint-Janvier, et au terme d'une longue évolution, les rouleaux primitifs sont devenus les volumes mêmes des quatre évangiles, contresignés par leur noms et assurant à la chrétienne VITALIA la paix éternelle (58), qui oserait encore nous contester le droit de reconnaître dans les rouleaux de nos premiers « docteurs », dans l'attribut fidèle de nos Orants, dans les livres de nos scènes de lecture le livre même de la révélation divine, et dans l'importance qu'on ne cesse de lui donner un véritable acte de Foi ?

Arrivés à ce point, nous pourrions nous arrêter dans l'examen des figures isolées, idéales ou individualisées, puisque désormais une certitude nous est acquise sur leur véritable signification. Mais leur série, déjà si riche, n'est pas close ; d'autres encore, qui offrent avec les précédentes une affinité à l'abri de toute contestation, ont été conçues d'un point de vue légèrement différent et contiennent d'autres indices, tout aussi probants, des spéculations symboliques dont nous avons cherché à percer le secret. Force nous est donc, si nous ne voulons pas nous cantonner dans une vision incomplète

---

(55) WS II, pl. 359, fig. 221; cf. pl. 108,2.

(56) WP pl. 213.

(57) Dans la tautologie apparente des livres dans cette composition se cache probablement l'intention d'insister sur le fait que la doctrine du Christ était devenue pour la défunte un principe de vie.

(58) H. ACHELIS, *Die Katakomben von Neapel* (Leipzig 1936) pl. 28.

de la symbolique de la Foi, de prendre en considération les deux dernières séries d'images isolées, dont, par ailleurs, les archéologues ne se sont guère préoccupés : celles des « lecteurs » seuls et celles des personnages qui indiquent du doigt le livre qu'ils tiennent ouvert.

Dans une des fresques les plus précieuses à cet égard, mais malheureusement abîmée par des mains vandales et restituée d'après mémoire par Mgr Wilpert (59), un lecteur assis, vu de face, tenait un *volumen* largement ouvert. Qu'on n'ait pas hésité, dans le passé, à y reconnaître le Christ, ne doit pas trop nous étonner. Aujourd'hui, à la lumière d'autres exemples, il semble indiqué de le faire entrer dans la lignée des figures idéales destinées à évoquer la doctrine et la foi chrétiennes.

Aux catacombes des Saints-Marcellin-et-Pierre, trois autres figures de « lecteurs » réclament notre attention. L'une, debout, identifiée par erreur au Christ guérissant le paralytique (60), tient le rouleau ouvert des deux mains et s'abîme dans sa lecture. L'autre (61) nous offre un jeune homme assis presque de profil tenant le volume de la même façon. A quelques mètres de là, dans une chambre donnant sur la même galerie, la troisième figure, barbue cette fois-ci, se présente dans une attitude identique que la précédente (62). S'il n'est pas exclu qu'il faille voir dans ces deux derniers exemplaires, une fois le Christ lui-même et une fois saint Pierre (63), il n'en reste pas moins que l'acte dans lequel ils se trouvent représentés, celui de la *praelectio,* est avant tout une allusion directe à la parole du Christ. On se rappellera, à ce propos, la figure du Christ dans le colloque avec la Samaritaine, dans une des chambres « des sacrements » à Saint-Calliste (64).

Ici de nouveau, passant aux sarcophages, de précieux parallèles s'offrent tout de suite à la recherche. Un premier exemple de lecteur assis et vu de profil, que personne ne prendra pour le Christ,

---

(59) WP pl. 49. La fresque se trouve aux catacombes de Prétextat. Voir *op. cit.,* p. 216, note 4.

(60) WP pl. 68,2; texte, p. 201.

(61) G. P. KIRSCH, *Un gruppo di cripte dipinte inedite del Cimitero dei SS. Pietro e Marcellino : Rivista di archeologia cristiana,* 7 (1930) 209 et fig. 3.

(62) WP pl. 94.

(63) L. DE BRUYNE, *Les « lois » de l'art paléochrétien comme instrument herméneutique : Rivista di archeologia cristiana,* 35 (1959) 157.

(64) WP pl. 29,2.

se trouve sur le fameux sarcophage de Velletri (65), presque comme un rappel tardif des scènes de doctrine antérieures. Une lectrice debout se rencontre dans un fragment de couvercle de sarcophage à Saint-Sébastien hors-les-murs (66) : on y reconnaît, en effet, une jeune femme, vue de trois quarts, placée entre deux arbres et absorbée dans la lecture du *volumen* qu'elle tient ouvert des deux mains. Un autre couvercle conservé au Musée de Latran (67) en offre presque une réplique, mais la désigne de son nom, cette fois-ci, CRISPINA et la place, non plus entre deux arbres mal définis, mais entre deux palmiers (68) ; il marque, au surplus, une page du livre du monogramme du Christ. Ceci nous mène, une fois de plus, au signe explicite, qui caractérise l'origine divine du contenu de ce livre. Et de fait, le même monogramme se retrouve au-dessus d'un lecteur assis, conçu tout à fait comme dans les fresques déjà citées, dans le relief d'un sarcophage au Musée du Camposanto Teutonico, à Rome (69).

Et comment ne pas rapprocher de tous ces exemples la composition qui représente même saint Pierre comme lecteur d'un *volumen* ouvert, en présence des soldats venus pour l'arrêter ? L'exemplaire qui mérite d'être mis ici en vedette est celui du Musée d'Art Chrétien, en Arles, où le livre de l'Apôtre, une fois encore, est nettement marqué du christogramme (70).

On voudra bien remarquer, dans l'entre-temps, que l'attribut du livre, tout aussi bien que les caractéristiques qui en spécifient la nature, appartiennent en commun aux figures idéales, aux figures individualisées et à celle du premier apôtre du Christ.

Non moins éloquentes sont les figures qui montrent ostensiblement la page d'un livre ouvert. On en trouve une, masculine, dans une voûte d'arcosolium au cimetière des Saints-Marcellin-et-Pierre,

(65) WS pl. 4,3 ; Marrou, *Op. cit.* p. 73, N. 64.

(66) WS pl. 141,4. — Vu l'identité formelle de cette image avec celle qui se trouve sur un sarcophage d'Arles (WS pl. 195,4 ; cf. pl. 196,1 et 197,4), on pourrait être tenté de la rapporter à Susanne. Il faut se détromper, car il manque ici toute allusion aux deux vieillards.

(67) WS pl. 249,11.

(68) On connaît le rôle du palmier comme arbre paradisiaque.

(69) WS pl. 27,3.

(70) WS pl. 152,1 ; 153,2 et texte III, 61, fig. 292. — E. Stommel, *Beiträge zur Ikonographie der konstantinischen Sarkophagplastik = Theophaneia*, 10 (1954) 110 s. conjecture que le motif ait pu se développer de l'ancienne scène de lecture philosophique. Cela ne semble pas impossible.

où elle reçut comme pendant une femme au rouleau fermé (71). Le caractère abstrait des deux se trouve rehaussé du fait, que dans l'arcosolium d'en face le même jeu des pendants se répète entre une figure d'homme au rouleau fermé et une orante. Il y a manifestement une liaison intentionnelle entre ces trois formules du rouleau fermé, de l'écriture indiquée du doigt et de l'attitude d'orant. Plus typique encore, sous cet aspect, l'ensemble qui décore un autre arcosolium au même cimetière (72), où l'œil du visiteur est conduit spontanément de l'homme au livre ouvert, qu'il désigne de l'index, à l'orant qui lui correspond du côté opposé, et à la chaire du refrigerium céleste survolée par la colombe de la paix, au beau milieu de l'ensemble. Tous ces détails parlent de par eux-mêmes et n'ont pas besoin de commentaire. Au centre d'une frise continue de scènes bibliques, le sarcophage n. 193 du Musée de Latran (73) place une figure de femme voilée, qui elle aussi semble feuilleter, pour en faire voir une page, le *codex* qu'elle tient à la gauche, tout en esquissant des deux doigts étendus un geste de commentaire.

Et pour finir cette série, est-ce la personnification de l'Eglise, est-ce la défunte, ou est-ce la figure idéale de la Foi, cette femme voilée que deux Apôtres acclament sur la pierre votive de la Collection Wilshere (74) ? Je laisse la réponse à mes lecteurs. Toujours est-il, que la relation entre les *volumina* qui accompagnent les Apôtres et le livre tenu par la femme regarde directement la prédication apostolique et la foi des fidèles.

Quand on sait toute l'importance que le christianisme primitif attacha aux prophéties messianiques et l'insistance avec laquelle il souligna leur accomplissement dans le Christ Notre-Seigneur, il ne

---

(71) G. P. KIRSCH, *l. c.* 7 (1930) 214-222, fig. 7-8 et 10-11. L'A. souligne à juste titre qu'on ne saurait bien interpréter l'un de ces arcosolia sans l'autre. Leurs décorations semblent en effet se compléter mutuellement.

(72) G. P. KIRSCH, *Pitture inedite di un arcosolio del cimitero dei SS. Pietro e Marcellino : Rivista di archeologia cristiana*, 7 (1930) 31-46.

(73) WS pl. 186,2.

(74) G. B. DE ROSSI, dans *Bullettino di archeologia cristiana*, 2,3 (1872) 36-40, pl. 1; R. GARRUCCI, *Storia dell'arte cristiana*, 4 (Prato 1877) 11, pl. 411, 4; WS pl. 31, 7 et texte I, 36.

faut pas s'étonner que l'art chrétien ancien, même dans l'ombre des cimetières, ne se laissa pas échapper l'occasion de souligner par elles le bien-fondé de la Foi qu'il célébra de toute part. Aussi pouvons-nous être brefs à leur sujet.

A de rares exceptions près, elles ont été évoquées à nouveau par des figures isolées, debout, indiquant d'une main levée une étoile (ou monogramme) apparue dans le haut (75). La composition la plus fameuse est celle des Catacombes de Priscille (76), où l'étoile surplombe la Madonne avec l'Enfant ; d'autres identifications proposées par Mgr Wilpert sont plus sujettes à caution. De quels prophètes s'agit-il ? d'Isaïe, de Balaam, de Michée ? La question a fait couler déjà beaucoup d'encre. Récemment encore, le P. Kirschbaum (77) a proposé d'y reconnaître presque partout le prophète Balaam. Je me garderai bien de vouloir ici dérimer cette question (78). Je désire seulement faire remarquer que, selon toute vraisemblance, d'après l'habitude adoptée pour tant d'autres figures, nos peintres ne voulaient point du tout représenter Isaïe, Balaam ou Michée, mais simplement la prophétie (79), tout comme, il y a un instant, nous avons vu qu'ils évoquaient la doctrine ou la Foi par une figure de docteur. Mais qu'importe, le principal pour eux c'était de rappeler la ligne continue de développement historique qui reliait leur présent avec le passé lointain.

Nous ne pouvons pas quitter nos prophètes sans signaler la découverte d'un nouvel exemplaire dans la Catacombe de la Voie Latine (80) et sans leur associer la figure isolée indiquant du doigt non plus une étoile, mais une croix, dans l'hypogée des Auré-

(75) WP pl. 22; 159,3 ; 158,2; 165; (241). Cf. pl. 229.
(76) WP pl. 22.
(77) E. KIRSCHBAUM, *Der Prophet Balaam und die Anbetung der Weisen : Römische Quartalschrift,* 49 (1954) 129-171.
(78) Comme je l'ai souligné ailleurs (*Rivista di archeologia cristiana* 35, 1959, 114), il faut, en effet, que l'interprète, qui n'est que l'intermédiaire entre celui qui parle et celui qui écoute (ou regarde), donne exactement l'équivalent, ni plus ni moins, du message à transmettre, et ne cherche pas à spécifier davantage que l'artiste, quand celui-ci parle en termes génériques.
(79) Voir, dans le même sens, O. CASEL, *Ältere Kunst und Christusmysterium : Jahrbuch für Liturgiewissenschaft,* 12 (1934) 54, qui tire l'attention, comme l'avait déjà fait avant lui WILPERT, *Pittura* 174, sur le fait que Justin martyr I Apol. 32 fusionna déjà la prophétie de Balaam (Num. 24,17) avec le texte d'Isaïe (11,1; 10).
(80) A. FERRUA, *Op. cit.* p. 83, pl. 86,1.

liens (81). Il n'est pas exclu, en effet, que cette association, suggérée par l'identité du schéma figuratif, ne la fasse jouir, un jour, d'une meilleure explication que celles qu'on lui a données jusqu'ici.

*
**

Dans la grande rénovation qui se produit dans l'art chrétien vers l'an 300, où les voiles symboliques des premiers temps doivent céder devant des expressions plus explicitement chrétiennes, une figure s'impose plus qu'aucune autre : celle de saint Pierre. Mais ce qu'il y a d'étonnant, c'est que le cycle qu'on lui dédie débute par un motif qui rappelle d'une façon fort transparente son triple reniement du Christ (82). Et ce qui paraît plus grave encore, c'est l'importance qu'on semble y attacher, comme si c'était un titre de gloire (83). Ceci résulte avec une évidence inéluctable, non pas tellement de la fréquence de cette scène, au cours du IVe siècle, mais beaucoup plus d'un fait généralement peu connu, qui est celui-ci. Dès qu'on essaie de classer en ordre chronologique les sarcophages constantiniens, qu'ils soient décorés de strigiles ou d'une frise de scènes ou à colonnade, on est surpris de constater que les scènes bibliques qui dorénavant viennent occuper l'espace central de la composition sont : le soi-disant « Reniement de Pierre » (84), la Multiplication des pains (85), et l'Entrée de Jésus à Jérusalem (86).

---

(81) Voir G. WILPERT, *Le pitture dell'ipogeo di Aurelio Felicissimo*, cité, pl. X, A ; J. CARCOPINO, *Op. cit.*, pl. 5,2 et p. 113 ss. Cet A. y reconnaît non un homme mais une femme, qu'il identifia avec la Sophie des Valentiniens.

(82) Voir pour cette scène E. STOMMEL, *Beiträge zur Ikonographie der konstantinischen Sarkophagplastik = Theophaneia*, 10 (Bonn 1954) 93-101 ; 103-117 ; 121-129. Cf. WILPERT, *Pitture*, p. 302, ss., L. v. SYBEL, *Christliche Antike*, 1, 274.

(83) Aux catacombes de Sainte-Cyriaque, il y a même une fresque (WP pl. 242,1) où le peintre donna à l'apôtre une taille notablement supérieure à celle du Christ qui lui parle. Un second exemplaire de ce motif a été découvert récemment : A. FERRUA, *Scoperta di una nuova regione della catacomba di Domitilla : Rivista di archeologia cristiana*, 34 (1958) 20, fig 16.

(84) « Reniement » central : WS pl. 109,4 ; 109,6 ; 120,2 ; 214,2 ; 226,2 (sarcophages à strigiles) ; pl. 112,3 ; 128,1 ; 206, 5-7 ; 225,3 (sarcophages à scènes bibliques) ; pl. 124, 2-3 ; 116, 1-2 ; 122,1 ; 180,2 (sarcophages à colonnes ou à arbres).

(85) « Multiplication » centrale : WS pl. 158,3 ; 182,1 ; 203,2 ; 214,8 ; 232,3 ; 232,5 ; 266,4.

(86) « Entrée à Jérusalem » centrale : WS pl. 212,2 ; 235,7. Tout ceci sans compter les fragments qui pourraient appartenir à une composition centrale.

Le phénomène continue par après. Cela signifie que ce soi-disant « Reniement de Pierre » avait toutes les qualités pour occuper la place réservée jusqu'ici au Bon Pasteur ou à l'Orante. Une constatation pareille qui, certes, ne dit pas grand'chose au profane, est révélatrice pour l'iconologue, parce qu'à elle seule elle le rassure que ce motif ne fut pas et ne pouvait pas être choisi par l'art chrétien pour mettre en relief la défection de l'Apôtre, mais bien au contraire pour rappeler à l'esprit la triple profession de foi que l'Evangile même et les écrits des Pères (87) mettent en contraste transparent avec elle (Jo. 21, 15-17). Le P. Lagrange (88) note à ce propos : « Tout le monde reconnaît dans la triple question de Jésus et dans la triple réponse de Pierre une compensation éclatante du reniement ».

Ce qui me confirme dans l'interprétation de cette « felix culpa », c'est d'abord le beau sarcophage du Louvre (89) où notre scène figure au milieu de quatre autres sur lesquelles flotte une ombre de péché lointain : Abel et Caïn, Sem et Japhet bénis par Noé, la Samaritaine et la Cananéenne, la première païenne convertie (90). C'est ensuite le rapprochement fréquent que l'art établit entre notre motif et la guérison de l'aveugle-né, qui ensemble avec la lumière des yeux trouve celle de l'âme, rapprochement dont le plus bel exemple nous est fourni par le sarcophage 104 du Musée de Latran (91), où l'aveugle, en plus, figure à côté de l'Epiphanie de Celui qui descendit sur terre, sous le signe de l'étoile, comme étant la vraie Lumière. Soit dit entre parenthèses : ce sarcophage offre déjà une synthèse de notre triptyque (92). Ce qui me rassure encore, c'est que sur les sarcophages de la période qui suit celle de Constantin, notre scène partage l'honneur du centre de composition avec les premières représentations solennelles du Christ enseignant. Et c'est finalement un sarcophage découvert dans les fouilles sous Saint-Pierre (93), où le rouleau tenu par le Christ comme emblème de son enseignement est marqué de son monogramme, tout

---

(87) Voir les références données par E. STOMMEL, *Op. cit.*, 96 s.
(88) J. M. LAGRANGE, *L'Evangile de Saint Jean* (1927 ³) 528.
(89) WS pl. 116,1.
(90) Voir L. DE BRUYNE, *L'Imposition des mains dans l'art chrétien ancien : Rivista di archeologia cristiana*, 20 (1943) 10-12.
(91) WS pl. 96. — Cf. L. DE BRUYNE, *Op. cit.*, 77.
(92) L. DE BRUYNE, *Op. cit.* 76-79.
(93) E. STOMMEL, *Op. cit.*, pl. 1-3.

comme celui de l'Apôtre, à l'autre bout de la frise, et comme le couvercle même du sarcophage. Il n'y avait guère moyen d'exprimer plus clairement la relation entre la Foi professée par le chrétien, la Foi de l'Apôtre dans les paroles du Christ et leur propagation par l'Eglise. *Per os Petri Christus locutus est.*

*
**

Il me faudrait prendre encore en considération les compositions où le Seigneur lui-même, d'une manière plus solennelle, prend la place des anciens « docteurs », des fidèles, de son Apôtre, comme ceux du Sermon sur la Montagne (94), du Christ enseignant au milieu des Evangélistes (95) ou des Apôtres (96), de la « Traditio Legis » (97), mais je me trouve débordé par la documentation et l'espace disponible ne le permet plus.

Il faut se limiter à souligner que l'idée du Christ « docteur » ne s'est jamais perdue, depuis son apparition sous les apparences d'un philosophe dans certaines scènes bibliques jusqu'aux évocations les plus grandioses du Conseil apostolique réuni autour du Christ enseignant, pas plus que n'a jamais été perdu de vue le concept du *magister-pastor* (98), tel que nous le trouvons typiquement représenté par des chrétiens probablement hétérodoxes, dans l'hypogée des Auréliens (99).

Tout au contraire : « Plus que jamais l'élément doctrinal du christianisme est mis en évidence ; mais ce n'est plus de la même façon. On réalise davantage son caractère divin, on ressent davantage l'humilité qui doit pénétrer l'âme humaine en face de la révélation. *Fides ex auditu...* lisions-nous dans saint Paul : « la foi vient de la prédication entendue, et la prédication se fait par la parole du Christ », *per verbum Christi,* διὰ ῥήματος Χριστοῦ. C'est sur le second terme qu'on insiste maintenant » (100).

---

(94) Voir p. ex. WS pl. 220,1.

(95) WP pl. 162,2; WS pl. 162,2. Cf. pl. 31; 34,3; 37, 2-3.

(96) WP pl. 96; 126; 148; 152; 155; 170; 177, 1-2; 193; 225,1: *Rivista,* 5 (1928) 193, fig. 19 ; A. FERRUA, *Via Latina,* pl. XI; WS pl. 34,1; 34,2; 34,3; 43,5; 187,2.

(97) Une liste des monuments chez J. SAUER, *Das Aufkommen des bärtigen Christustypus in der frühchristlichen Kunst : Strena Buliciana* (Zagreb-Split 1924) 317. Pour la bibliographie relative à ce thème, voir *infra,* n.

(98) F. J. DÖLGER, IXΘYC 2, 466-469.

(99) BENDINELLI, *l. c.,* pl. IX ; WILPERT, *l. c.,* pl. XII-XIII; CARCOPINO, *l. c.,* pl. XI 1 et pp. 142, 151.

(100) H-I. MARROU, *Op. cit.,* 283.

Quant à la « Traditio Legis » (101), dont le moins qu'on puisse dire est qu'elle est l'ordre solennel lancé par le Christ de propager la Loi que lui-même avait prêchée, point n'est besoin d'y insister longtemps dans ce contexte. Etudiée maintes fois, continuellement citée dans les ouvrages généraux, on peut la supposer assez connue. Tel un second Moïse, comme le suggère très efficacement un sarcophage de Tarragone (102) en donnant à Saint Pierre la pose de Moïse et au volumen le monogramme du Christ. Pierre y reçoit le livre de la « Loi » divine. Malgré la variété des formules qui marquent la composition, c'est le DOMINUS LEGEM DAT qui prévaut largement : le fragment d'une coupe de verre du Vatican appelle le rouleau directement LEX DOMINI (103). Or tout le monde est d'accord pour reconnaître dans cette « loi » l'ensemble de la doctrine et des préceptes du Seigneur : ce qu'il faut croire et ce qu'il faut pratiquer pour Lui être « fidèle ».

La relation directe entre cette cérémonie idéale et le fidèle est manifeste. Les exemples qui y associent les fidèles rendant hommage au Maître ne manquent d'ailleurs pas. Et comment auraient-ils pu manquer si l'on réfléchit à l'origine vraisemblablement baptismale du motif ? (104). Mgr Duchesne, avec l'intuition géniale qui était sienne, ne craignait pas d'établir un rapport entre cette scène célèbre du Don de la Loi et le rite solennel de la *Traditio Symboli* : « je n'oserais assurer, écrit-il (105), que cette scène ait été composée expressément d'après le rituel de la *Traditio legis christianae* ; mais il y a entre ces deux choses un rapport trop évident pour qu'il n'ait point été remarqué. Beaucoup de fidèles en jetant les yeux sur les

(101) Pour la « Traditio Legis » voir J. Kollwitz, *Christus als Lehrer und die Gesetzübergabe an Petrus in der konstantinischen Kunst Roms : Römische Quartalschrift*, 44 (1936) 45-46; E. Weigand, *Die spätantike Sarkophagskulptur im Lichte neuerer Forschungen : Byzantinische Zeitschrift*, 41 (1941) 108 s. ; K. Wessel, *Das Haupt der Kirche: Archäologischer Anzeiger* (1950-51) 298-323 ; E. Stommel, *Op. cit.*, (1954) 123-133; W. N. Schumacher, « *Dominus legem dat* »: *Römische Quartalschrift*, 54 (1959) 1-39 ; Cf. *ibid*. 137-202.
(102) WS II, 199 et fig. 117 ; 358.
(103) WS III, 61 et fig. 291. Pour νόμος, voir E. Peterson, *Der Monotheismus als politisches Problem* (1935) 62 et n. 115.
(104) L. De Bruyne, *La décoration des baptistères paléochrétiens : Actes du Vᵉ Congrès d'Archéologie chrétienne* (Cité du Vatican — Paris 1957) 346-348.
(105) L. Duchesne, *Origines du culte chrétien* (Paris 1925) 320.

peintures qui ornaient le fond de leur église (lisons : leur baptistère), devaient se rappeler une des plus belles cérémonies de leur initiation ».

Il n'est alors pas étonnant que les autres rites de l'Initiation : le Baptême et l'Eucharistie devaient venir spontanément, par voie d'association, à l'esprit de l'un ou l'autre artiste. Un sarcophage de Marseille (106) en fournit une éclatante épreuve. Alors qu'une « Traditio Legis » s'y développe solennellement sur la face principale, le couvercle est orné de deux dauphins nageant vers le monogramme du Christ, au centre, tandis que de part et d'autre se trouvent disposés : les cerfs buvant à la quadruple source jaillissant de la montagne de l'Agneau, le Miracle de Cana et les Explorateurs rentrant avec une énorme grappe de raisin.

Pour conclure. — Nous avons vu que l'iconographie, depuis qu'elle existe comme science, ne s'est guère rendu compte de l'empreinte profonde qu'avait laissée dans la communauté chrétienne primitive l'accès à la foi, préparé dans la première phase de l'initiation chrétienne. Telle une petite fourmi qui voit la brique d'une façade mais ne voit pas la façade elle-même, l'iconographie dormait tranquillement sur ses lauriers, dès qu'elle avait identifié, dans les monuments figurés, une partie ou l'ensemble du contenu de la foi. Mais pour ce qui est de la Foi elle-même, en tant que vie de l'esprit et du cœur, elle ne se doutait pas le moins du monde qu'elle ait pu faire l'objet d'une attention continue de la part des artistes chrétiens. Or, c'était là l'essentiel.

Continuellement, et avec une persistance qui étonne sous le changement des formules iconographiques, l'art évoque et réévoque cette source de l'existence chrétienne, gage de la vie définitive dans l'au-delà. A travers les siècles, la même voix continue à se faire entendre : « soyez rassurés sur le sort de vos frères, puisqu'ils étaient fidèles à une Foi qui donne la vie éternelle ». Verbum veritatis ⚌ Evangelium salutis (Eph. 1, 13). Que ce fût par le truchement des figures de philosophes qui invitaient à réfléchir à la « vraie philosophie » ; de lecteurs de livres dont on était invité à définir de par soi-même le caractère sacré, d'abord voilé et puis nettement défini ; des prophètes qui avaient prédit la bonne nouvelle ; de rappels du discours sur la Montagne ; de la *felix culpa* du pre-

---

(106) WS pl. 17,2.

mier des Apôtres, des interventions solennelles du Christ enseignant ou de la mission des Apôtres, le livre qui en fait la constante iconographie, ainsi que le geste de la parole qui l'accompagne, constituaient le trait d'union permanent et inchangé des diverses démarches entreprises par l'art pour évoquer le même concept.

Le volume, métaphoriquement la doctrine, la foi comme dépôt, tenu dans la main, montré du doigt, serré contre la poitrine, traduit une valeur affective qui ne peut échapper à notre attention. Le placer comme attribut à côté d'une figure, c'est établir entre lui et le salut de celle-ci, un rapport de cause à effet.

Peut-être s'étonnera-t-on de la simplicté avec laquelle cette enquête, tout en en frôlant d'autres, résout tant de problèmes. Pour ma part, je vois justement dans cette simplicité de la solution un signe de sa justesse. Quand la simplicité s'obtient, non point en esquivant les difficultés, mais en les résolvant, on peut être sûr de se trouver sur une voie qui mène à Dieu. « Je vois, disait un jour Rodin, je vois pourquoi cela est si beau. Parce que c'est si simple que plus rien n'y accroche la curiosité ».

Parmi les monuments qui ont été ici présentés, il n'y en a peut-être aucun qu'on ne connaissait déjà ; plusieurs parmi eux ont été discutés à plusieurs reprises..., seule la ligne de parenté qui les reliait tous attendait le grand jour. Une fois qu'on l'a découverte, qu'on s'en est pénétré, il descend dans l'esprit du chercheur, et dans tout un secteur de l'art chrétien, un calme, une paix, semblables à ceux-là mêmes que procurait au fidèle son accès à la foi. Car la science, quand elle est sur la bonne voie, devient, quelque peu comme la Foi, une lumière de la raison et une paix de l'âme.

LE BAPTÊME

Parmi les reflets que l'initiation chrétienne a laissés dans l'art chrétien des origines, le moins sujet à être mis en doute est bien celui qui regarde le Baptême. Les figurations qui s'en inspirent sont généralement reconnaissables à première vue ; leur présence dans le répertoire iconographique est un fait que personne n'oserait mettre en doute ; leur rôle même dans ce répertoire ne saurait soulever, je pense, des discussions sérieuses. Aussi pourrons-nous être plus bref à leur sujet. Il n'entre d'ailleurs pas dans nos intentions de traiter ici ce sujet d'une façon exhaustive. Les monuments anciens relatifs au Baptême ont fait l'objet d'innombrables analyses

et des quelques points en discussion il y en a peu qui nous intéressent directement. Nous nous attacherons avant tout à ce qui
relève des intentions qui guidèrent les artistes dans le choix de ce
thème et dans la combinaison des éléments qui devaient l'évoquer.
Nous ne perdrons pas de vue non plus les contextes figurés dans
lesquels les figurations du Baptême ont été insérées, puisque ce
rapprochement est des plus aptes à nous révéler l'unité des concepts
qui préside à la composition de notre triptyque.

Nous venons de parler de la Foi considérée par nos artisans
comme une partie intégrante de l'économie du salut dont ils avaient
fait le sujet de leurs décorations. Or, « dans les lettres de l'apôtre
Paul, la foi est souvent rapprochée du baptême, au point que les
deux semblent presque confondus. Il y a, semble-t-il, identité entre
« être baptisé » et « croire ». Ou bien le baptême se présente comme
l'implantation du germe, dont l'effet immédiat serait la foi. Que
signifie le baptême ? Ce n'est pas seulement l'incorporation de
l'individu dans la communauté, ni la consécration de son appartenance à celle-ci, ni la prise en charge du néophyte par la communauté. Dans le baptême, il se passe quelque chose de tout autrement profond : un germe de vie se forme. Dans l'homme qui jusqu'ici vivait au cœur d'une perspective profane, Dieu dépose le
germe d'une structure nouvelle et d'une activité nouvelle. Une existence nouvelle s'éveille en lui, ayant son sens propre, sa loi propre
et son propre pouvoir de réalisation... Cela s'effectue par le Christ.
En lui l'homme renaît, par le Saint-Esprit, pour participer à la vie
humaine et divine du Christ » (107).

C'est bien cela. « C'est pourquoi saint Paul peut dire : "je vis,
non ce n'est plus moi qui vis: c'est le Christ qui vit en moi" (Gal. 2.20).
La vie du chrétien est donc vie du Christ. Tout le salut consiste en
ce que le vieil homme, le moi, meurt et que se lève le nouvel homme.
Il s'ensuit que le Christ se trouve au centre de tout l'être et de
toute la pensée du chrétien, non seulement comme l'idée, autour
de laquelle tout gravite, ou comme la personne qu'on veut imiter,
mais comme le plus intime et en même temps objectif principe de
vie. ,Pour moi, la vie c'est le Christ' (Ph. 1,21) » (108).

---

(107) R. Guardini, *Vie de la Foi = Foi vivante* (Paris 1958) 117 s.
(108) O. Casel, *Aelteste christliche Kunst und Christusmysterium :
Jahrbuch für Liturgiewissenschaft*, 12 (1934) 21.

Tout cela, Tertullien, se rapportant directement au Baptême, l'avait déjà résumé aux environs de 200, dans sa fameuse phrase tout imprégnée du symbolisme de l'époque : « Nos pisciculi secundum IXΘYN nostrum Jesum Christum in acqua nascimur, nec aliter quam in acqua permanendo salvi sumus » (109).

C'est donc dans le Baptême que le chrétien naît à la vie divine du Christ ; et c'est grâce à cette nouvelle naissance qu'il acquiert la garantie de la résurrection et de la vie éternelle. « Nisi quis renatus fuerit ex acqua, et Spiritu sancto, non potest introire in regnum Dei » (*Jo*, 3, 3-5). Déjà le *Pasteur* d'Hermas commente : « ils (les Apôtres et les Prophètes) devaient nécessairement remonter par l'eau pour obtenir la vie ; car ils ne pouvaient pas entrer autrement dans le règne de Dieu qu'en déposant la mortalité de la vie... Car avant que l'homme ne porte le nom du Fils de Dieu, il est mort ; mais dès qu'il a reçu le sceau, il dépose la mortalité et accepte la vie. Mais le sceau c'est l'eau ; dans l'eau ils sont immergés comme morts et en émergent comme vivants » (110). Saint Irénée (111) reprendra la formule en appelant le baptême le « bain de l'immortalité ».

A la lumière de ces textes, on comprend mieux comment le Baptême, apparemment un thème sans caractère sépulcral, ait pu être incorporé dès le début dans l'imagerie des catacombes. S'il ne figure pas, pas plus que l'Eucharistie, dans les prières antiques qu'on aime rapprocher du répertoire iconographique sépulcral (112), cela ne fait que mieux ressortir que nos peintres et nos sculpteurs s'inspiraient d'une certitude personnelle, optimiste et sans mélange : le Baptême, notamment, tout comme par ailleurs la Foi et l'Eucharistie, constituait à leurs yeux une garantie pour le sort des chrétiens dont ils ornaient les tombes. Ils se rendaient compte qu'après avoir eu recours aux paradigmes de l'Ancien Testament, aux miracles et à la vie du Christ, c'eût été une lacune dans leur symbolisme,

---

(109) *De bapt.* 1. - Cf. Clément d'Alex., Pédagogue III, 52,2 et 59,2.
(110) *Simil.* 9,16.
(111) *Contra haer.* III,17,2.
(112) K. Michel, *Gebet und Bild in frühchristlicher Zeit* = *Studien über christliche Denkmäler* N.S., 1 (Leipzig 1902) *passim*. — On pourrait faire cependant une exception pour le baptême du Christ, mentionné dans la version éthiopienne des prières pseudo-cypriennes : voir *ibid.* p. 19. L'A. ne la mentionne pas dans sa tabelle à p. 58.

que de ne pas insister aussi sur ce que le chrétien devait à sa propre existence, comme chrétien, au sein de l'Eglise.

Aussi bien, n'ont-ils pas hésité à réserver à ce thème, dès les débuts, une place d'honneur en rapport étroit avec le Bon Pasteur et l'Orant, avec les évocations de la doctrine ou de la Foi, avec l'autre sacrement de l'Initiation : l'Eucharistie. Devant traiter chacun de ces thèmes séparément, nous risquons de perdre de vue les liens qui les unissent ; il faut donc, au fur et à mesure qu'on procède dans l'analyse des monuments, replacer sans cesse les détails rencontrés dans la perspective convergente voulue par les artistes.

Nombreux sont les thèmes que l'exégèse ou la typologie a mis en rapport avec le Baptême et l'iconologie symboliste moderne n'a certes pas cherché à en diminuer le nombre. Un chapitre de Mgr Wilpert (113) énumère dans ce sens : la source de Moïse, le baptême de Corneille, la Samaritaine au puits de Jacob, le Baptême de Jésus, celui du catéchumène, le pêcheur, le paralytique de la piscine probatique, les cerfs buvant à la source, saint Philippe et le baptême de l'eunuque, et l'on pourrait en ajouter d'autres.

Il va de soi qu'il n'entre pas dans les intentions de cette communication de reprendre l'examen de tous ces motifs iconographiques ; force nous est de nous en tenir aux évocations directes de ce sacrement de l'Initiation. Tout au plus, pouvons-nous nous arrêter un instant au motif symbolique du pêcheur à la ligne, qui compte parmi les toutes premières évocations du baptême, quittes à nous contenter de quelque brève allusion aux autres thèmes là où le contexte iconographique le demande.

Le pêcheur à la ligne, motif fort connu dans le monde gréco-romain qui aimait l'idylle bucolique-maritime (114), se rencontre

---

(113) *La fede della Chiesa nascente secondo i monumenti dell'arte funeraria antica* = *Collezione « Amici delle Catacombe »* (Città del Vaticano 1938) 67-92.

(114) Voir H. Dütschke, *Ravennatische Studien* (Leipzig 1909) 165. Cf. H. U. v. Schoenebeck, *Die christlichen Paradeisossarkophage : Rivista di archeologia cristiana,* 14 (1937) 291 ss. — Pour la symbolique du pêcheur dans l'antiquité, ainsi que pour celle du pasteur, voir R. Eisler, *Orpheus the Fischer* (London 1921) 171 ss. ; Id., dans : *Vorträge der Bibliothek Warburg,* 2 (1925) 52 ss., 107 s. et 118 s. M. Vloberg, *L'Eucharistie dans l'art,* 1 (Paris 1946) 16 en fait un symbole eucharistique. J. Kollwitz, *Christusbild :* RAC, III,9 compte le pêcheur parmi les images du Christ.

déjà, on le sait, dans l'hypogée des Flaviens, au cimetière de Domitille (115). Malgré la présence de motifs nettement chrétiens dans ce monument, on ne saurait pas trop en vouloir, à la rigueur, à l'interprète qui se refuserait de reconnaître dans ce pêcheur isolé une image symbolique du Baptême. Mais quand on passe aux « chapelles des sacrements » (116), où on le rencontre à deux reprises, la situation change. Il n'est plus isolé ici, comme un morceau de genre idyllique, décoratif. Il se trouve directement associé, sans séparation aucune, une fois à l'image du Baptême, une autre fois à celle de la Source miraculeuse (117), au point que c'est la même eau qui sert aux trois compositions (118). On ne peut pas non plus lui refuser toute valeur symbolique chrétienne, comme d'aucuns ont prétendu (119), en y voyant une simple personnification de l'eau courante. Non seulement pareille interprétation est en flagrant conflit avec les coutumes de ces décorateurs lorsqu'ils juxtaposent des motifs chargés de sens mystique (120), mais elle a reçu un coup de grâce d'importance par la découverte du petit mausolée des

(115) WP pl. 7,1.

(116) Voir *supra*, n. 9.

(117) WP pl. 27,2 (chambre A2, paroi gauche) ; pl. 27,3 (chambre A3, paroi gauche).

(118) Pour les diverses opinions au sujet du miracle de la Source, voir G. STUHLFAUTH, *Die apokryphen Petrusgeschichten in der altchristlichen Kunst* (Berlin 1925) 54-57 ; P. STYGER, *Die altchristliche Grabeskunst* (München 1927) 69 s. ; E. WEIGAND, *Die spätantike Sarkophagskulptur im Lichte neuerer Forschungen : Byzantinische Zeitschrift*, 41 (1941) 29 s. —M. v. SCHOENEBECK, *l. c.* 324, note très judicieusement : « Wenn Quellwunder und Taufe wechseln können, so deutet dies bereits auf einen überhistorischen, allegorischen Gehalt der Bilder und auf eine innere Gleichwertigkeit beider Themen ». Voir aussi l'excellent commentaire de E. STOMMEL, *Beiträge zur Ikonographie der konstantinischen Sarkophagplastik = Theophaneia*, 10 (1954) 84-87.

(119) Comme p. ex. C. M. KAUFMANN, *Handbuch der christlichen Archäologie* (Paderborn 1922 ³) 347 ; P. STYGER, *Die altchristliche Grabeskunst* (München 1927) 43 ; cf. 60 ; ID., *Die römischen Katakomben* (Berlin 1933) 59 ; W. ELLIGER, *Zur Entstehung und frühen Entwicklung der altchristlichen Bildkunst = Studien über altchristliche Denkmäler* N.S. 23 (Leipzig 1934) 78 ; cf. A. STUIBER, *Refrigerium inferim, Die Vorstellungen vom Zwischenzustand und die frühchristliche Grabeskunst = Theophaneia*, 11 (Bonn 1957) 152.

(120) Remarquons, en outre, qu'une indication supplémentaire de l'eau était absolument superflue dans ces ensembles, même du point de vue purement réaliste ou décoratif.

Julii, sous les cryptes Vaticanes (121). Là, en effet, un monumental pêcheur à la ligne occupe, à lui seul, juste la paroi du fond de la chambre (121). Puisque le mosaïste lui réserva toute une paroi, tout comme il fit pour le Bon Pasteur, à gauche, et pour la scène de Jonas, à droite (122), il sera difficile désormais de reconnaître dans nos pêcheurs à la ligne, soit des motifs purement idylliques, soit des compléments personnifiant l'eau. Cette découverte pourra en même temps conseiller une certaine prudence aux commentateurs des premiers sarcophages, puisque là aussi le pêcheur et la pêche sont associés parfois (123) à d'autres thèmes chrétiens.

A propos du pêcheur, une dernière remarque s'impose. On a la tendance, s'inspirant de certains textes littéraires, de lui donner un nom individuel, l'identifiant notamment soit avec le Christ (124), soit avec l'apôtre saint Pierre (125), soit avec le simple fidèle (126). La présence d'une barbe, chez le pêcheur joue parfois elle aussi son rôle dans l'interprétation. Cette tendance ne date pas d'aujourd'hui. Comme pour d'autres figures originellement abstraites, l'orante et le docteur par exemple, même les anciens avaient ce goût de l'individualisation. Il y a peu d'années, M. Feuille trouva, aux Thermes d'Antonin à Carthage, une belle coupe de verre gravé représentant deux pêcheurs armés l'un d'une ligne, l'autre d'un filet, poursuivant divers poissons entre des rochers et accompagnés de l'inscription *Apostoli Petrus et Johannes* (127). Remarquons cependant que cette

---

(121) *Esplorazioni* (Città del Vaticano 1951) pl. XII, a ; O. PERLER, *Die Mosaiken der Juliergruft* (Freiburg i. Schw. 1953) pl. IV, a et pp. 8-12 ; E. KIRSCHBAUM, *Die Gräber der Apostelfuersten* (Frankfurt a/M 1959) 33-35, fig. 4.

(122) C'est donc à tort que M. STUIBER, *Op. cit.*, 152, n. 5, pense que dans ce monument le pêcheur à la ligne doive être mis en rapport avec l'eau de la scène de Jonas.

(123) Voir citations et analyses chez H. DÜTSCHKE, *Op. cit.*, 143 ss.

(124) O. WULFF, *Altchristliche und byzantinische Kunst*, 1 (Berlin 1914) 75, 103 ; *Nachtrag*, 10. L. RÉAU, *Iconographie de l'art chrétien*, 2 (Paris 1957) 31 classe, lui aussi, le pêcheur parmi les symboles anthropomorphiques du Christ.

(125) G. WILPERT, *Sarcofagi* 1, 156, ss. a tout un chapitre sur saint Pierre pêcheur d'âmes.

(126) G. WILPERT, *Pitture* 243 voit dans le pêcheur à la ligne le baptisant et dans le poisson le néophyte.

(127) G. PICARD, *Vase gravé de Carthage : Fasti archaeologici*, 4 (1949 [1951]) 530, n. 5031 ; J. VILLETTE, *Une coupe chrétienne en verre gravé, trouvée à Carthage : Fondation E. Piot, Monuments et mémoires*, 46 (Paris 1952) 131-151.

coupe ne semble pas antérieure au IVe siècle. Mais, il s'agit là d'un monument tout à fait exceptionnel. En règle générale, là où les artistes se contentent de figures anonymes, il ne paraît pas justifié de leur attribuer des spéculations de ce genre. Le problème est analogue à celui qui s'est posé tout à l'heure à propos des docteurs et des prophètes (128); on peut le poser également à propos des « pasteurs » et des orants, à propos des baptisants et des convives au banquet des sept. Il est pour le moins vraisemblable — et l'analogie qui joue entre les thèmes cités le prouve — que nos premiers artistes n'entendaient pas appliquer l'image du pêcheur à tel ou tel personnage en particulier, mais simplement évoquer par elle, de façon générique, la pêche des âmes. Ce qui n'empêche évidemment pas que des assimilations familières à la pensée du temps aient pu contribuer à l'introduction de ce motif générique et plus abstrait dans le répertoire figuratif. Ainsi comprise, l'image se prêtait à merveille à de multiples applications : seule, elle symbolise directement le Baptême ; associée au Baptême, elle en souligne l'aspect fondamental ; mise en rapport avec la Source miraculeuse, elle en spécifie le sens baptismal.

*
* *

Si nous en venons maintenant aux images du Baptême, celles notamment qui s'inspirent directement du rite baptismal, nous voyons que les idées fondamentales esquissées au début de ce chapitre sont encore celles qui ont inspiré le choix de ce thème.

A peine entre-t-on dans le cubiculum duplex XY aux « cryptes » de Lucine qu'on est frappé — nous l'avons déjà dit — de trouver placées dans la même perspective les figurations du Baptême et de l'Eucharistie, la première au beau milieu de la paroi intermédiaire au-dessus de la porte (129), la seconde sur la paroi de fond (130). Comme on le pense, cet arrangement n'est pas dû au hasard : le Baptême d'abord, l'Eucharistie ensuite. A vrai dire, il s'agit du Baptême du Christ au Jourdain, le peintre s'étant directement inspiré du texte de l'Evangile. Cette façon plus ou moins réaliste de combiner l'image ne se rencontrera plus qu'une fois dans la

---

(128) Voir *supra*, p. 46 ss.
(129) WP pl. 29,1.
(130) WP pl. 27,1.

peinture cémétériale (131) ; on lui préférera une combinaison plus adhérente au symbolisme de l'image.

Dans cette liaison que le peintre établit entre les deux sacrements, nous saisissons sur le fait l'équivalence symbolique qu'avaient pour lui le Baptême du Christ et celui du simple fidèle. Il ne trouve aucune difficulté à se servir du premier pour faire allusion à l'autre. Et ceci est bien dans l'esprit de l'époque. Comme je l'ai fait remarquer ailleurs (132), il s'agissait là de deux thèmes interchangeables, puisque l'un était universellement reconnu, et non seulement en Orient, comme type de l'autre (133). Aussi bien ne suivrons-nous pas, dans cette analyse, l'exemple des nombreux savants qui ont perdu un temps précieux en recherchant les critères permettant une distinction entre ces deux baptêmes (134). Comme nous venons de le remarquer pour la figure du pêcheur, il semble bien que l'art veut indiquer, symboliser en quelque sorte la notion de baptême plutôt que représenter ou décrire tel ou tel baptême réel.

Le fait, d'ailleurs, que pour représenter le Baptême du Jourdain, les artistes aient eu recours au geste de l'imposition de la main, qui n'est documenté par aucun des quatre Evangélistes, mais apparaissait par contre comme le plus expressif dans le rite de l'initiation des simples fidèles, prouve bien que ce fut le rite baptismal qui se trouva à l'avant-plan de leurs spéculations. En d'autres termes, car il importe de bien préciser, à l'époque où l'art chrétien chercha le moyen terme compréhensible pour tout chrétien et apte à traduire le concept « baptême », il ne trouva rien de mieux que la combinaison suivante : une personne nue et debout dans l'eau, à laquelle une autre personne impose la main. Et ce schéma vaudra aussi bien pour les « baptêmes » du Christ que pour celui des néophytes.

Ceci apparaît d'une façon incontestable dès qu'on pénètre dans les « chapelles des sacrements ». Dès maintenant c'est l'imposition de la main qui est utilisée comme acte baptismal. L'iconographie qui

---

(131) Sur le plafond du cubiculum III aux catacombes des Saint Marcellin-et-Pierre (WP. pl. 73). On y remarquera, cependant, l'absence de la colombe.

(132) L. DE BRUYNE, *L'Imposition des mains dans l'art chrétien ancien : Rivista di archeologia cristiana*, 20 (1943) 101 ; 122 ; 246.

(133) Voir p. ex. F. SÜHLING, *Die Taube als religiöses Symbol im Christlichen Altertum* (Freiburg 1930) 134 ss.; O. CASEL, *l. c.*, 55.

(134) Voir entre autres : WILPERT, *Pitture*, 239. Cf. W. ELLIGER, *Op. cit.*, 75 s.; L. DE BRUYNE, *l. c.*, 101.

est adoptée ici deviendra de règle, aussi bien dans le domaine de la sculpture que dans celui de la peinture, à ce point que les rares monuments, où le baptême est administré selon le rite de l'infusion au moyen d'une coupe (135), se révèlent être, en réalité, des falsifications, puisque ce geste y a été introduit par des restaurations modernes.

Dans la chambre A_3, en effet (136), où il semble bien s'agir du Baptême du Christ, puisque le baptisant porte comme seul vêtement le perizoma, l'acte du baptême s'exprime par la droite imposée sur la tête du baptisé. Il ne pourrait s'agir ici de l'imposition de la main accompagnant, dans la liturgie, la triple profession de foi et la triple immersion, puisque la nappe d'eau dans laquelle se trouve le baptisé arrive à peine un peu plus haut que les chevilles.

Dans la chambre A_2 (137), au contraire, le baptisant revêt la tunique et le pallium, et la colombe symbole du Saint-Esprit, présente dans la scène précédente, n'apparaît plus. Dès maintenant, l'imposition des mains devient un élément constant dans les fresques (138), ainsi que dans presque toutes les sculptures de sarcophages des IIIe et IVe siècles (139). Mais, tandis que la peinture ancienne, dans toute son évolution ultérieure, et la sculpture, jusqu'à la fin du IIIe siècle, ne connaissent plus aucune allusion au bain

---

(135) Le sarcophage n° 183 du Musée de Latran (WS pl. 8,4) ; coupole du baptistère des Orthodoxes, à Ravenne : C. Ricci, *Battistero della cattedrale = Tavole storiche dei mosaici di Ravenna* (Rome 1932) pl. D et XI ; M. van Berchem et E. Clouzot, *Mosaïques chrétiennes du ive au xe siècle* (Genève 1924)) 100, fig. 112. Pour l'une des cuillers émaillées d'Aquilée, voir L. De Bruyne, *l. c.* 223.

(136) WP pl. 27,3.

(137) (WP pl. 39,2). Cette fois-ci, la scène du baptême se trouve au beau milieu de la paroi de fond de la chambre.

(138) Saints-Marcellin-et-Pierre, crypte double, arcosolium de droite : WP pl. 57 et 58,1. — *Ibid.*, voûte de la chambre 54 : J. Wilpert, *Ein Cyclus christologischer Gemälde* (Freiburg i. Br. 1891) pl. I-IV. — *Ibid.*, Voûte de la chambre au fond de la galerie Y : J. Wilpert, *Mosaiken und Malereien* 1 (1916) 198, fig. 60 ; G. P. Kirsch, dans : *Rivista di archeologia cristiana*, 9 (1932) 29-32, fig. 8. — Domitille, voûte de l'arcosolium 15 : WP pl. 240,1. — *Ibid.*, voûte de l'arcosolium 29: WP pl. 228,2. — Saint-Hermès: WP p. 206, pl. 246, motif que l'A. interprète comme guérison du possédé.

(139) IIIe siècle : WS pl. 1,2 et 3,1 ; 8,2 ; 19,3. Cas spécial, sans eau : *ibid.* pl. 65,5; voir L. De Bruyne, *l. c.*, 236-239. — IVe siècle : WS pl. 8,1; 11,2 ; 20,1 (imposition de la main gauche) ; 13.

baptismal autre que l'eau horizontale dans laquelle plongent les pieds ou les jambes du baptisé, la sculpture du iv⁰ siècle associe à l'imposition de la main et à la nappe d'eau horizontale une chute d'eau verticale, semblable à celle qu'on rencontre dans la source miraculeuse de Moïse ou de Pierre. Parfois, on y ajoute les rayons de lumière qui partent de la colombe pour descendre sur le baptisé (140). Dans des cas très rares, enfin, remontant à l'époque constantinienne, la main du baptisant s'étend en avant sans toutefois reposer sur le chef du baptisé (141). Les monuments postérieurs (142), qui ne nous intéressent guère dans ce contexte, conserveront l'imposition de la main presque sans aucune exception.

L'insistance de l'art sur ce rite mérite donc une attention toute spéciale, parce qu'elle jette une vive lumière sur les conceptions archaïques au sujet du Baptême. Comme je l'ai développé dans *L'imposition de la main* (143), on a beau rapprocher des monuments tout ce que nous savons par les textes scripturaires, liturgiques ou patristiques, la seule imposition de la main qui ait pour se présenter à l'esprit des artistes dans le choix de ce signe semble avoir été le rite post-baptismal du Saint-Esprit. Ceci revient à dire que les créateurs de cette composition figurative ont voulu réunir en un seul ensemble, d'une façon peut-être surprenante pour nous, mais tout à fait naturelle à leur époque, les deux rites du Baptême proprement dit et de la Confirmation. Et ceci est confirmé par l'histoire, puisque « l'habitude de considérer indistinctement les deux sacrements persévéra dans l'Eglise jusqu'au début du troisième

---

(140) J. WILPERT, *Mosaiken und Malereien*, 198, fig. 60 ; WS pl. 13.
(141) WS pl. 19,4, où la main dépasse la tête ; 11,1; 14,3.
(142) Voir pour ceux-ci J. STRZYGOWSKI, *Iconographie der Taufe Christi* (München 1885). Signalons toutefois, à cause de l'importance qu'ils pourraient avoir ici, un fragment de verre gravé, au Musée sacré du Vatican : G. B. DE ROSSI, dans : *Bullettino di archeologia cristiana*, 3,1 (1876) 7-15, pl. 1 (facsimilé) ; R. GARUCCI, *Storia dell'arte cristiana* 6 (1880) pl. 464,1; A. PROFUMO, dans : *Studi romani*, 1 (1913) pl. 14,1 ; FR. SÜHLING, *Die Taube als religiöses Symbol im christlichen Altertum* (Freiburg i. Br. 1930) 140, s. et pl. 3,3 ; ainsi qu'une épitaphe d'Aquilée : voir : *Bullettino di archeologia cristiana* 3,1 (1876) pl. 1 ; R. GARUCCI, *Storia* 6 (1880)) pl. 487, 26 ; J. WILPERT, dans : *Ephemeris Salonitana* (1894) 39, fig. 1 ; FR. SÜHLING, *Op. cit.*, 139, pl. 3,1 ; C. CECCHELLI, dans : *I Sacramenti*, a cura di A. PIOLANTI (Roma 1960), tiré à part, p. 169-185.
(143) L. DE BRUYNE, *l. c.*, 215-244.

siècle » (144). Ainsi donc, nos peintres et nos sculpteurs n'ont pas voulu séparer ce qui constituait, certes, deux rites distincts, mais se trouvait, dans la réalité, intimement uni dans un ensemble complexe. Auraient-ils voulu représenter aussi le sacrement de la Confirmation (145) ? On restera plus près de la réalité historique, je pense, en répondant, dans le sens paulinien, qu'ils ont voulu évoquer de toute façon le baptême dans l'eau et dans l'Esprit Saint (146). Voilà pourquoi, dans notre introduction, nous avons indiqué, en passant, qu'en réalité la Confirmation faisait partie de notre triptyque.

Tout ceci ne devient que plus évident par une analyse plus serrée de la syntaxe figurative mise en œuvre par nos artistes. Si nous évitons, en effet, de parler de « représentations » du Baptême, ce n'est pas sans raison. Dans tout le répertoire cémétérial, il n'y a pas une seule reproduction réaliste de ce rite de l'Initiation. Sans doute, les éléments qui composent l'image sont empruntés à la réalité, comme d'ailleurs tous les signes dont l'art se sert pour se faire comprendre. Mais, d'abord, l'art se contente de choisir dans les rites réels les détails qui en feront souvenir le mieux et, ensuite, il les combine entre eux d'une façon qui n'a plus rien à voir avec la réalité et est purement conventionnelle (147). Ceci relève directement

---

(144) J. Coppens, *L'Imposition des mains et les rites connexes dans le Nouveau Testament et dans l'Eglise ancienne* (Wetteren 1925) 397 ; 257-283. Cf. J. Behm, *Die Handauflegung im Urchristentum nach Verwendung, Herkunft und Bedeutung in religionsgeschichtlichem Zusammenhang untersucht* (Leipzig 1911) 166 s.; F. J. Dölger, *Das Sakrament der Firmung historisch-dogmatisch dargestellt* (Wien 1906) 1-55; B. Welte, *Die postbaptismale Salbung* (Freiburg i. Br. 1939) 4 s., et tant d'autres. Voir cependant aussi, tout récemment J. Daniélou, *Les symboles chrétiens primitifs* (Paris 1961) 49-63.

(145) Question que M. Dölger s'est posée dans son étude : *Die Firmung in den Denkmälern des christlichen Altertums : Römische Quartalschrift* 19 (1905).

(146) Pendant des siècles, le terme « baptiser » ne signifia pas seulement le rite du bain baptismal, mais en même temps l'imposition de la main qui le suivait. Voir c. a. P. de Puniet, dans *Dict. d'Archéol. et de Liturgie*, III 2, col. 2516.

(147) Des événements successifs sont présentés comme simultanés : des détails caractéristiques d'un thème (imposition de la main, colombe...) servent à en caractériser un autre; des traits réalistes fusionnent avec des signes symboliques; ce qui paraîtrait absurde sur le plan réaliste est présenté comme naturel. Que penser, par exemple, du bain baptismal d'une jeune fille habillée, en présence d'un Saint nimbé et d'une colombe avec un rameau d'olivier dans son bec (verre gravé du Vatican) ?

du caractère symbolique du langage figuratif, qui ne veut pas « représenter » mais rappeler à l'esprit, évoquer des souvenirs et des idées.

Pour l'art, deux choses étaient essentielles : le bain baptismal et la collation de l'Esprit Saint. Le bain baptismal est évoqué par l'eau et par la nudité de l'initié, mais de ces deux éléments l'un peut manquer pourvu que l'autre y soit ; quant à l'Esprit Saint, sa communication est évoquée soit par l'imposition de la main, soit par le symbole de la colombe, qui reçoit parfois un complément dans le rayon qu'elle envoie, mais ici de nouveau, la première peut manquer pourvu que l'autre y soit et inversement. Et c'est par la voie d'une simple juxtaposition, ou peu s'en faut, de ces signes, qu'est née l'image du Baptême.

D'avoir perdu de vue la nature intime de cette imagerie, que de discussions sont nées et se sont prolongées pendant des siècles ! Par contre, une fois ceci admis, toutes les difficultés que l'interprétation du Baptême dans l'art rencontra sur son chemin se trouvent aplanies. Il sera difficile de découvrir de nouvelles figurations de ce thème, qui ne trouvent, de par ces critères. une prompte explication.

Mais alors, si telles étaient les visées des décorateurs des tombes chrétiennes, qui ne voit pas que seule l'initiation chrétienne considérée comme garantie de salut pouvait les amener à insérer ce thème, à côté de celui de la Foi, dans un répertoire entièrement consacré à ce concept fondamental ? L'initiation chrétienne, la naissance à la vie nouvelle par la mort au vieil homme et la communication de l'Esprit était un « argument » qui ne pouvait manquer dans le chant de triomphe de la certitude chrétienne.

Et de fait, le contexte des ensembles figuratifs, où le motif du Baptême pénètre, jette sur ces visées sotériologiques une lumière assez vive. Ces contextes sont multiples et nous ne saurions pas les passer tous en revue. Quelques exemples pourront d'ailleurs suffire au but que nous nous proposons.

Nous avons déjà parlé des chambres de Lucine et de Saint-Calliste à propos de la Foi et du Baptême (148), et nous devrons encore y retourner à propos de l'Eucharistie. Ceci est déjà assez significatif en soi, puisque nos trois thèmes réunis s'y révèlent

---

(148) Voir *supra*, p. 29 et 53.

former le contour prédominant autour de l'image centrale du Sauveur-Pasteur. Si nous jetons maintenant un coup d'œil sur les sculptures les plus anciennes et sur d'autres contextes iconographiques empruntés à la peinture, nous ne tardons pas à y découvrir des rapprochements de thèmes non moins instructifs. Sur le sarcophage de Sainte-Marie-Antique (149), le Baptême fait pendant avec la scène de Jonas en repos, des deux côtés de l'Orante centrale et du Lecteur. Une évocation de la pêche encadre le tout, aux deux extrémités. Le sarcophage de la Lungara (150), dont il importe de bien remarquer que l'Orante y est le motif central, le Baptême semble accompagner, sur le petit côté gauche, la figure du pêcheur à la ligne, tout comme le groupe de brebis sur le petit côté droit semble se rapporter à la figure du Pasteur. Nous sommes toujours, on le voit, dans la même atmosphère qu'avec les premiers monuments picturaux. A Mas-d'Aire (151), où les scènes bibliques se sont multipliées, le Baptême fait pendant à une Résurrection de Lazare et s'insère dans un ensemble où figurent le Bon Pasteur, le paradigme de Daniel entre les lions et le rappel de la chute d'Adam et Ève.

Avec le fragment d'un couvercle de sarcophage au Musée de Latran (152), nous nous trouvons à nouveau en présence d'un rapprochement entre le Baptême et l'Eucharistie, symbolisée par un banquet où figurent les (sept) corbeilles remplies de pains. Plus tard encore, dans la gracieuse série de scènes allégoriques du sarcophage de Junnis Bassus (153), c'est une fois de plus, le Baptême et la Multiplication des pains qui se trouvent les plus rapprochés de la niche centrale. La sculpture théodosienne, enfin, aimera mettre en pendants sur les petits côtés des sarcophages le Baptême et la Source « d'eau vive » (154).

Quant à la peinture ultérieure, citons un premier exemple dans un arcosolium du cimetière des Saints-Marcellin-et-Pierre (155), où l'Orante, image idéale de la paix éternelle, se trouve placée entre

----

(149) WS pl. 1,2 et 3,1.
(150) WS pl. 19,3.
(151) WS pl. 65,5.
(152) WS pl. 8,2.
(153) WS pl. 13 ; F. GERKE, *Der Sarkophag des Iunius Bassus* (Berlin 1936) pl. 44 s.
(154) WS pl. 11,2 — 3 ; 12, 1-2.
(155) WP pl. 57 et 58,1.

le Baptême et sa préfiguration par la Source miraculeuse, alors que,
dans le fond de cet arcosolium se déploie le banquet de Cana, un
des symboles eucharistiques. Une très belle voûte au même cimetière (156) entoure le Bon Pasteur central d'une couronne de motifs
où les trois paradigmes de salut paléotestamentaires : Abraham,
Daniel et Noé trouvent comme seul complément emprunté au Nouveau Testament une évocation du Baptême. Un arcosolium des catacombes de Domitille (157) est encore plus suggestif : au milieu de
sa voûte, une Multiplication des pains, symbole eucharistique ;
à gauche, le péché originel évoqué dans les figures d'Adam et Ève,
et, à droite, la régénération de l'homme concrétisée dans le motif
du Baptême (158). On remarquera, une fois de plus, le rapprochement des deux sacrements compris dans notre triptyque. Dans
le fond de cet arcosolium, la fête des guirlandes de fleurs souligne
bien le ton optimiste que le décorateur entend donner à l'ensemble.
Un autre arcosolium du même cimetière (159) réunit dans sa voûte,
au-dessus d'un canthare survolé par des colombes (symbole du
refrigerium dans l'au-delà, le bel ensemble que voici : au milieu, le
Sauveur sous les apparences du Bon Pasteur ; à gauche, le Baptême
et, à droite, la Multiplication des pains. Voici donc les deux rites
essentiels de l'initiation chrétienne qui se font pendant. Tout l'ensemble prend plus de relief encore par la présence de l'Orante sur
le front antérieur du monument. Ajoutons que dans un autre arcosolium de la même région (160), dû probablement au même pinceau,
le peintre, pour éviter une redite, tout en voulant garder une
combinaison significative, rapprocha comme pendants, des deux
côtés d'un buste du Christ cette fois-ci, la même Multiplication des
pains, nourriture donnant l'immortalité, et la Résurrection de Lazare (161). Dans la lunette de cet arcosolium on découvre le Christ
entouré de ses disciples. De cette façon, compte tenu notamment de

---

(156) WP pl. 73.
(157) WP pl. 240,1.
(158) Cette antithèse avec le Péché originel acquiert une importance de
poids quand on se rappelle que la Chute des protoplastes se trouve déjà
insérée dans le tableau du Bon Pasteur à Doura Europos. Rappelons-
nous, au surplus, qu'elle figure aussi sur le sarcophage de Mas d'Aire (WS
pl. 65,5, déjà cité).
(159) WP pl. 228,2.
(160) WP pl. 228, 3-4.
(161) Se rappeler à ce propos le sarcophage 104 du Musée de Latran :
voir L. DE BRUYNE, L'Imposition des mains, cité, 76-79.

ces deux ensembles, le Baptême et l'Eucharistie, ainsi que la doctrine du Christ se trouvent mis en rapport direct avec la foi en la résurrection.

Si nous voulons résumer le choix des motifs que l'art a rapprochés du Baptême dans les ensembles jusqu'ici rencontrés (162), nous y relevons d'abord le symbole du pêcheur à la ligne, ainsi que la source d'eau vive que Moïse fit jaillir du rocher du désert. Nous découvrons ensuite une liaison assez fréquente avec le souvenir du Péché originel, d'un côté, et la Résurrection de Lazare, de l'autre côté. Qu'est-ce à dire, sinon que le sacrement de la régénération était considéré comme le point vital, où s'insère, pour le chrétien, la victoire définitive sur la mort par le péché ? Enfin, ce qui est remarquable, c'est que les motifs de loin les plus fréquents que nous trouvons rapprochés de celui du Baptême, sont justement ceux qui ont trait à la Foi (ou la doctrine) et à l'Eucharistie (163).

L'EUCHARISTIE

Puisque l'examen des figurations du Baptême amène sous nos regards, sans le vouloir, les évocations de l'Eucharistie, passons sans plus à l'analyse de ce thème.

Je dis bien « évocations », car pendant longtemps la recherche iconologique a suscité à leur sujet les mêmes difficultés que pour le Baptême, en prêtant au langage des artistes un réalisme qu'il n'avait pas, ou une syntaxe qui n'était pas la sienne. Ainsi que nous l'avons fait remarquer à propos du Baptême, dans tout le domaine de l'art sépulcral il n'y a aucune représentation réaliste de l'Eucharistie (164). En d'autres termes, ni la dernière Cène, ni le sacrifice eucharistique, ni la sainte Communion ne s'y trouvent directement

---

(162) D'autres ont été réservés pour notre conclusion. Voir *infra* p. 81.

(163) Plus rarement associés au Bâptême sont les motifs de Noé, du sacrifice d'Abraham, de Jonas et de Daniel. Nous pouvons ne pas en tenir compte ici, puisque leur présence occasionnelle dans l'entourage du Bâptême est due au fait qu'ils rentrent dans le cadre plus général du symbolisme sotériologique.

(164) Même Mgr Wilpert l'a reconnu, non sans un soupçon de réserve toutefois : « se del Battesimo vedemmo immagini che ne rappresentano svelatamente l'atto, invece per le rappresentazioni eucaristiche predomina l'elemento simbolico in tal grado, che fra di esse non se ne ha una che sia *esclusivamente realistica* » (*Pitture*, 261 s.). Mais ce sera justement ce degré de réalisme, qu'il semble quand même admettre, qui le conduira — nous le verrons bientôt — à des identifications inadmissibles.

représentés. Et ce serait donc vain que de vouloir reconnaître dans les figurants de ces « scènes » soit le célébrant, soit le plus commun des fidèles. La tournure d'esprit qui présida à la création de ces motifs n'était pas la nôtre. Ou mieux, elle était plus délicate que la nôtre. Se rendant bien compte qu'il fallait un minimum de points d'attache, sans quoi le langage métaphorique aurait manqué son but, elle orienta bien plus l'attention vers des « signes » éloquents, que vers des concrétisations qui risquaient de faire dévier la compréhension des visiteurs. Devant un « mystère » si délicat à reproduire (165), l'art avait le choix entre les signes symboliques, la typologie inspirée des textes sacrés et les rapprochements iconographiques suggestifs des contextes figuratifs. Voilà justement le triple chemin qu'il a suivi.

Retournons, pour la troisième fois, aux cryptes de Lucine. Après avoir été frappé par le Baptême du Christ, au milieu de la paroi face à l'entrée ; après avoir identifié les allusions à la Foi, aux endroits secondaires, le regard est porté, comme dans une même perspective, sur la paroi de fond, au milieu de laquelle on découvre une évocation ingénieusement mystique de l'Eucharistie (166). Au centre, il y avait probablement un festin, aujourd'hui disparu (167) ; il est accosté, de part et d'autre, d'un résumé symbolique des mets qui faisaient les délices des convives : deux grands poissons symétriques ayant derrière eux une corbeille remplie de pains et d'un gros verre de vin que les claies laissent transparaître (168). Faut-il encore

---

(165) Remarquons que les premières évocations figurées du Baptême et de l'Eucharistie coïncident juste avec le moment où la discipline de l'arcane semble s'être imposée davantage. Voir P. BATIFFOL, La discipline de l'Arcane : Etudes d'histoire et de théologie positive, (Paris, 1926[7]) ; E. VACANDARD, dans Dict. d'histoire et de géographie 3, 1497-1513.

(166) WP pl. 27,1.

(167) G. WILPERT, Pitture 266. — La présence d'un banquet en cet endroit ne semble pouvoir être mise en doute. Une confrontation avec les ensembles décoratifs des « chapelles des sacrements », tout proches et presque contemporaines, en est garante. Manifestement, les deux paniers dont il s'agit ici tiennent lieu des rangées de corbeilles accompagnant les festins là-bas. Notre analyse ultérieure le montrera.

(168) WP pl. 28, 1-2. — P. STYGER, Die altchristliche Grabeskunst (München 1927) 47 s. refuse audience à ces identifications: « Die Behauptung, dass die rote Farbe in dem durchbrochenen Flechtwerk der Körbe ein mit Rotwein angefüllter Glasbecher sei, bleibt noch unbewiesen, solange die andere Möglichkeit des eingeflochtenen Stoffmusters nicht ausgeschlossen ist ». Seulement, il y aussi l'indication bien nette des deux verres et les corbeilles ne sont point du tout « durchbrochen », comme il n'y a point de trace non plus d'une « Einflechtung ». Pour d'autres, le rouge serait

s'arrêter à l'assertion de certains auteurs qui cherchèrent à réduire ces motifs au rang de simples natures mortes, tout au plus allusives aux repas funéraires célébrés auprès des sépulcres ? (169). Franchement, dans des milieux où tout respire le symbolisme mystique, était-ce bien l'endroit de s'adonner à un réalisme de cet aloi ? Et la liaison transparente avec le Baptême, que nous venons de souligner, compterait-elle pour si peu de chose ? Et a-t-on le droit de séparer ces paniers, comme un *membrum disjectum,* de ceux que nous allons bientôt rencontrer dans d'autres ensembles ? Certes, on ne saurait mettre en doute que dans tout repas romain il entrait du poisson, du pain et du vin, mais n'est-ce pas également sûr, et une gloire pour lui, que le christianisme a su puiser ses symboles les plus profonds dans les choses les plus humbles, les plus communes et journalières ?

Relisons Abercius (170), à peu près contemporain : « Partout elle (la Foi) m'a donné en nourriture un poisson de la source, très grand et très pur, pêché une vierge pure. Elle le donnait sans cesse à manger aux amis, versant un vin délicieux, donnant du vin mélangé d'eau ensemble avec du pain » (171).

Ecoutons aussi Pectorius d'Autun, dans son fameux épigramme : « Race divine (ou fils divin) du céleste Poisson, conserve pure ton âme, car tu as reçu parmi les mortels la source immortelle de l'eau divine. Ami, réjouis ton âme par l'eau éternellement jaillissante de sagesse qui donne des trésors. Reçois du Sauveur des saints cet aliment doux comme le miel. Mange avec délices, tenant dans tes mains le poisson » (172).

---

simplement une tache accidentelle. Nous leur demandons : « Accidentelle, deux fois de suite ? ».

(169) P. Styger, *Op cit.,* 47.

(170) Pour la bibliographie relative, voir *supra* (note 6). Y ajouter : G. Grabka, *Eucharistic Belief manifest in the Epitaphs of Abercius and Pectorius : The American Ecclesiastical Review,* 131 (1954) 245-255.

(171) F. J. Dölger, IXθYC, 2 (Münster i. W. 1922) 492 souligne très bien : « Fisch = Wein und Brot ». Mais tout ce paragraphe est à lire : « Das Fischmysterium der Aberkiosinschrift als Symbol der Eucharistie » (pp. 486-507).

(172) F. J. Dölger, *Op. cit.,* 1 (1929) 12 ss.; 177 ss.; 2 (1922) 507-515 : « Der Fisch als Sinnbild der Eucharistie in der Pektoriusinschrift ». Autre bibliographie chez P. Testini, *Archeologia cristiana,* 1 (Roma 1958) 422. Voir aussi O. Perler, *Glosen zur Pektoriusinschrift : Miscellanea Giulio Belvederi* (Città del Vaticano 1954-1955) 109-208, qui interprète la nutrition par le poisson dans le sens de l'union avec le Seigneur dans l'au-delà.

Ne semble-t-il pas que nos peintures répondent comme des échos fidèles à ces textes ? Et cela d'autant plus que dans ces derniers on retrouve sans difficulté les reflets de trois parties de l'Initiation qui font l'objet de cette étude. Mais ne nous fions pas trop facilement à ce qui pourrait n'être qu'une simple coïncidence entre textes épigraphiques et monuments figuratifs, ou relever uniquement de notre façon d'interpréter ces textes. Suivons attentivement les démarches de l'art.

Ce que nous avons entrevu à propos des deux paniers de la région de Lucine, se vérifie en effet dès que nous reprenons, comme précédemment, notre visite des « chapelles des sacrements ». Nous les retrouvons, en effet, multipliés et alignés, associés de diverses façons aux festins qui reviennent plusieurs fois dans cette série de chambres (173). Leur nombre peut varier entre sept, huit ou douze ; la place qu'ils occupent dans la composition peut changer : soit devant, soit des deux côtés du banquet ; ce qui ne change pas c'est leur présence dans l'ensemble (174). Ceci vaut également pour le banquet de la « cappella greca » que Mgr Wilpert appela la « fractio panis » (175), et pour une fresque aujourd'hui perdue, sous la Vigne Massimi (176).

Or, c'est justement le retour inopiné et insistant de ces paniers qui doit éveiller l'attention de l'interprète, beaucoup plus, par

---

(173) Voir G. WILPERT, *Pitture*, pl. 15,2; 41,3; 41,4. A pl. 27,2 on trouve un banquet généralement interprété comme le repas des sept au bord du Lac de Tibériade.

(174) P. STYGER, *Op. cit.*, 15 ss. dédie tout un chapitre : « Die Bilderfolge » au prétendu manque de cohésion de ces premiers cycles de peintures. Particulièrement pour les chambres de Saint-Calliste, il est d'avis que leur décoration était une sorte de collection d'échantillons destinée à provoquer des commandes analogues de la part des visiteurs (p. 17), ce qui ne l'empêche pas de faire remarquer, à la page suivante, que des dix images énumérées dans la chambre A 3 sept étaient déjà présentes dans A 2. Il insiste : « Wenn man bedenkt, dass diese Cubicula ziemlich rasch nacheinander entstanden sind und dass sie, an einem gemeinsamen Gang liegend, lange Zeit zugleich besucht waren, so kann man sich des Eindrucks einer gewissen armseligen Eintönigkeit nicht leicht erwehren ». D'où il ressort que ces peintres devaient être de bien mauvais commerçants !

(175) J. WILPERT, *Fractio Panis. Die älteste Darstellung des eucharistischen Opfers in der « Cappella Greca »* (Freiburg i. Br. 1895).

(176) Voir J. WILPERT, *Die Katakombengemälde und ihre alten Kopien* (Freiburg i. Br. 1891) 29 et pl. XV. — On y comptait sept cistes.

exemple, qu'une analyse détaillée des convives ou des mets qu'ils consomment (177). Car, par leur insistance sur ces accessoires, nos artistes nous signifient l'importance qu'ils leur attribuent et nous laissent entrevoir qu'ils ont recours ici à la loi des « rappels » intentionnels, que j'ai developpée ailleurs (178). Mais, pour peu qu'on se familiarise avec cette « loi », on a vite fait de se rendre compte qu'elle est appliquée surtout là où l'art quitte le terrain réaliste pour ne plus retenir que des allusions symboliques. Et ceci nous fournit une première indication — encore assez vague, certes, mais qui se précisera dans la suite — du sens qu'il faudra donner à cet attribut.

Un autre signe nous est donné par le nombre extraordinaire de ces paniers dans chaque exemplaire. Alors que les convives sont sept, les corbeilles peuvent atteindre — nous l'avons dit — à huit ou à douze. Si l'on rapproche, toutefois, les scènes de banquet des autres représentations que nous allons bientôt rencontrer, le nombre de sept semble avoir été préféré. Quoi qu'il en soit, un nombre si important de paniers auprès d'un banquet ne laisse pas de surprendre, si l'on se place sur le plan réaliste. La peine que se sont donnée, pour contourner cet obstacle, ceux qui considèrent ces banquets comme purement funèbres (179) en fournit bien la preuve (180). Car, en somme, s'il est indéniable que dans certains banquets païens l'on compte autant de pains sur la table qu'il y a

---

(177) Dans le passé, en effet, on prêta à ces détails, à mon avis, une attention presque excessive, menant la recherche dans des impasses dont elle a encore aujourd'hui beaucoup de peine à sortir. On s'est mépris, semble-t-il, sur ce qui avait le plus d'importance pour les artistes. Bien sûr, le choix des aliments représentés (poisson, pain, vin) peut fournir des critères d'interprétation symbolique, mais jusqu'à un certain point seulement.

(178) L. DE BRUYNE, Les « lois » de l'art paléochrétien comme instrument herméneutique : Rivista di archeologia cristiana, 35 (1959) 160-172; pour les images « eucharistiques » en particulier, voir pp. 167-171.

(179) A la suite surtout de F. J. DÖLGER, Op. cit., 5 (1940) 391-394; 451-462; 503-527 (surtout p. 523 ss.). On ose même affirmer que : « Alle angeblichen Kriterien für die eucharistische Deutung sind hinfällig geworden, seitdem aus einer besseren Kenntnis der antiken Umwelt die Gemeinsamkeiten zwischen neutral-heidnischen und christlichen Lebensgewohnheiten offenbar geworden sind » : A. STUIBER, Refrigerium interim. Die Vorstellungen vom Zwischenzustand und der frühchristlichen Grabeskunst = Theophaneia 11 (Bonn 1957) 134.

(180) Voir à ce propos nos quelques remarques dans : Rivista di archeologia cristiana, 34 (1958) 110.

de convives (181), il faut tout de même reconnaître qu'ici le cas est quelque peu différent, puisqu'il ne s'agit plus d'un pain par convive, mais d'un panier tout plein, ce qui dépasse notablement la mesure (182). On a beau chercher une explication à ce fait étrange, dans le domaine réel on n'en trouve aucune qui résiste à un examen sérieux.

Mais on a pensé aussi au domaine historique et, notamment, à la restauration des foules dans le désert (183). Effectivement, c'est bien dans cette direction que l'art lui-même, toujours par la « loi des rappels », semble aiguiller la recherche sur la provenance de ces corbeilles (184). Encore s'agit-tl de bien établir de quelle façon.

Nous devons compter ici avec une double possibilité. Ou cette formule (juxtaposition du banquet des sept et d'une rangée d'un minimum de sept paniers) a été imaginée pour reproduire le fait historique narré dans les Evangiles (185), et dans ce cas les artistes

---

(181) F. J. DöLGER, *Op. cit.*, 5, 461, et surtout, 524 s.

(182) TH. KLAUSER, *Die Cathedra im Totenkult der heidnischen und christlichen Antike* (Münster i. W. 1927) 140, n. 151 s'était déjà demandé si le grand nombre de paniers remplis ne devait pas s'expliquer comme une allusion aux distributions de pain aux pauvres, à l'occasion des repas funèbres. M. DöLGER, *Op. cit.*, 5, 526 appelle cette conjecture « echt beachtungswert ». Mais on se demande en vain ce qui aurait pu amener peintres et sculpteurs à rappeler pareil usage dans leurs créations figuratives, surtout si l'on tient compte des solutions parfois peu esthétiques que cet alignement de cistes leur imposait. Souvenons-nous, par exemple, de la table tripode entre septs corbeilles, disposées assymétriquement (3 + 4) de part et d'autre.

(183) Mt. 14,20; 15,37; Mc. 6,43; 8,8; Lc. 9,17; Jo. 6,13.

(184) Par « provenance » nous n'entendons pas la dérivation iconographique, qui serait évidemment en contraste avec la chronologie des monuments, mais bien la source d'inspiration. — Nous disons aussi « restauration des foules » et non point « multiplication des pains », car à l'époque de nos peintures (fin IIe et premières décennies du IIIe s.) l'attention se concentre encore beaucoup plus sur la nourriture de vie, sur le repas mystique, que sur le miracle comme tel. Ce qui, par ailleurs, est parfaitement conforme à la tradition contemporaine, comme le souligne fort bien L. CERFAUX, *La multiplication des pains dans la liturgie de la Didachè* (Did. IX, 4) dans : *Studia biblica et Orientalia*, 2 = *Analecta biblica*, 11 (Roma 1959) 375-390.

(185) Cette façon d'évoquer une foule rassasiée ne doit pas surprendre a priori, puisque, aux yeux des anciens, le concept « manger » s'exprimait fort bien par un groupe de personnes installées sur le sigma autour d'une table. Remarquons cependant qu'elle s'exprimait encore mieux par plusieurs sigmas et groupes ainsi conçus.

auraient pu y voir, à la rigueur (186), un simple paradigme évangélique. Ou bien la formule obéit à une spéculation symbolique tout en empruntant au miracle du désert le signe des corbeilles remplies de pain, et alors elle peut très bien relever de la symbolique de l'Initiation et se rapporter directement à l'Eucharistie.

La question n'est pas aussi simple qu'elle puisse paraître à première vue et n'a pas encore fini de diviser les interprètes en plusieurs camps. Pour bien la résoudre il faut admettre les distinctions nécessaires et conduire progressivement l'examen des monuments.

Effectivement, l'art des catacombes a produit des compositions de ce genre qui semblent se rapporter directement à la narration évangélique. Nous n'en voulons comme première preuve que les reliefs du Musée national des Thermes (186 bis) déjà rencontrés à propos de la Foi (186 ter). La présence du Seigneur et d'un de ses disciples dans ce groupe de huit personnages ajoute à la composition un trait trop réaliste pour ne pas lui reconnaître un caractère « historique ». Nous citerons aussi la représentation fort développée sur l'attique de l'hypogée de Clodius Hermès *ad catacumbas* (187), où le groupe central du Christ entouré de ses disciples et la multiplication des groupes de convives donnent à l'ensemble la même tonalité « historique ». Citons enfin la composition grandiose d'un hypogée anonyme de la Voie Latine (188), où au banquet des douze commensaux étendus autour du sigma fut ajoutée la figure de Notre Seigneur opérant le miracle de la multiplication. Bien que pour la plupart détruits par un loculus, les paniers n'y manquaient pas plus que dans les deux compositions précédentes.

---

(186) Nous verrons bientôt ce qu'il convient de penser de cette hypothèse.

(186 bis) WS pl. 220.

(186 ter) Voir *supra*, p. 50. — Notons que dans ce banquet le nombre des paniers à été réduit à six (autant qu'il y des convives) et que la présence d'un sigma y est douteuse.

(187) G. MANCINI, *Notizie degli scavi*, 20 (1923) pl. X, 1; H. LIETZMANN, *Petrus und Paulus in Rom* (Berlin-Leipzig 1927 2) 301-303 et pl. 9; F. J. DÖLGER, IXΘYC, 5, 514, J. FINK, *Gemälde im Grab der Nasonier : Mitteilungen des Deutschen Archäologischen Instituts,* 6 (1953) 67, n. 46 ; J. CARCOPINO, *De Pythagore aux Apôtres* (Paris 1956) 361-364, pl. XII ; A. STUIBER, *Op. cit.,* 131 s., n. 35 ; 154.

(188) O. MARUCCHI, *Nuovo bullettino di archeologia cristiana,* (1901) 303 ss. ; WP p. 492 ss., pl. 265, 267,1.

Ici toutefois une remarque importante s'impose. A y regarder de plus près, dans chacune de ces compositions se découvrent des détails qui ne trouvent plus aussi facilement leur justification dans le récit évangélique. *Ad catacumbas*, on note à deux reprises un grand calice placé devant les convives ; à la Voie Latine, la figure d'une orante se trouve associée au banquet, tout en faisant pendant avec le Christ qui opère le miracle ; au Musée des Thermes, un des convives boit d'un calice, le pain que reçoit son voisin est marqué du monogramme du Christ (189), le Christ lui-même ne tient pas seulement le rouleau à la main, mais il porte aussi le pallium philosophique (190) et, finalement, il impose la main droite juste sur la tête de celui qui reçoit le pain (191).

Or, voici que cette même imposition de la main donnée en rapport direct avec la nourriture et effectuée par un « docteur » analogue, se rencontre déjà dans la chapelle A₃ « des sacrements » à Saint-Calliste, à côté, justement, d'un banquet des sept (192). La bénédiction n'est pas donnée directement à un convive, cette fois-ci, mais au pains et au poisson placés sur une petite table à trois pieds (193). L'effet produit par cette nourriture bénie est concrétisé dans l'image de la félicité éternelle : l'Orante (194), placée de l'autre côté de la table (195). La combinaison iconographique de

---

(189) G. WILPERT, *I due frammenti di scultura policrome del Museo delle Terme: Römische Quartalschrift*, 35 (1927) 279 s. Cf. *Sarcofagi*, 2 343 et A. PROFUMO, *Studi romani* 1 (1913) 97 s. Voir aussi F.J. DÖLGER, IXΘYC 5, 535 s. et *Antike und Christentum*, 1 (1929) 17-20, avec pl. 9.

(190) Ce détail devait indiquer que l'événement représenté est en rapport avec un discours ou une doctrine supposés fort connus. Rappelons que le miracle du désert servit d'introduction au discours du Christ sur l'Eucharistie : Jo 6.

(191) Notons en outre que dans ce bas-relief, la scène se trouve insérée entre deux guérisons de paralytiques, tout comme nous avons vu le discours sur la montagne encadré par deux guérisons d'aveugles.

(192) WP pl. 41,1. — Voir L. DE BRUYNE, *L'Imposition des mains dans l'art paléochrétien : Rivista di archeologia cristiana*, 20 (1943) 200 et fig. 22.

(193) Dans les deux cas, l'imposition de la main souligne plutôt les grâces spirituelles qui descendent dans celui auquel cette nourriture mystique est destinée.

(194) Pour la vraie signification de l'Orante, voir *supra*, p. 40.

(195) Plutôt que d'examiner les multiples interprétations qui ont été données de cette image, nous préférons nous en tenir au sens littéral des éléments qui la composent, tel qu'il nous est fourni par d'autres contextes iconographiques. C'est là, pensons-nous, le meilleur moyen d'éviter tout subjectivisme exégétique.

cette image, unique en son genre, est d'une importance capitale pour la compréhension exacte de toute l'iconographie qui nous occupe en ce moment. Les trois « signes » extraordinaires par où elle s'apparente aussi bien au relief du Musée des Thermes qu'à la fresque de la Voie Latine, formant même avec celle-ci un parallèle en raccourci (196), sont les suivants : l'habillement en philosophe, signe du docteur ; l'imposition de la main, signe d'une bénédiction conférant un don surnatural ; l'orante, signe symbolique de la béatitude céleste (197). Leur choix judicieux nous révèle que même les représentations soi-disant « historiques » de la restauration des foules dans le désert obéissaient à des visées symboliques de la part des artistes, et devaient signifier autre chose encore qu'un simple événement miraculeux. Mais alors, à plus forte raison, les autres banquets caractérisés par un minimum de sept paniers, et qui ne peuvent même pas se vanter de la présence du Seigneur opérant le miracle, doivent nécessairement se ranger dans la même série de motifs symboliques. C'est ce qu'ont méconnu tous ceux qui les identifiaient avec des représentations de la restauration des foules dans le désert.

Il n'en faut pas davantage pour conférer à nos séries de corbeilles remplies de pain, que toutes ces représentations ont en commun, non seulement une origine évangélique, mais aussi une valeur nettement symbolique. Dès maintenant aussi, nous saisissons mieux le parallélisme qui court entre les combinaisons iconographiques relatives à la Foi, au Baptême et à l'Eucharistie. Ce que le livre était pour les évocations de la doctrine et de la Foi, ce que l'eau baptismale et l'imposition de la main étaient pour les illustrations du Baptême, nos paniers le sont pour les évocations de l'Eucharistie : le moyen terme, notamment, pour porter l'esprit, au delà

---

(196) Voie Latine : Orante — Banquet — Christ opérant le miracle. Chambre A 3 à Saint-Calliste (mais en sens inverse): Orante — Mets sur la table — Docteur imposant la main.

(197) En 1934, W. ELLIGER, *Zur Entstehung und frühen Entwicklung der altchristlichen Bildkunst* (Leipzig 1934) 78 était d'avis qu'on n'était pas encore parvenu à « déchiffrer littéralement » cette image. Avait-on seulement une notion exacte de chacun de ses composants et de la syntaxe suivie par le peintre ? A. B. SCHUCHERT, *Die römischen Katakombenmalerei im Wandel der Kunstkritik : Römische Quartalschrift*, 39, (1931) 14 appelle la composition un « Beispiel fast unüberwindlicher Schwierigkeiten ». Comment pouvait-il en être autrement à une époque où l'on établissait un lien réaliste entre les deux figures et que l'on voyait dans l'Orante, et jusque dans ses « gespreizten Finger », une expression du « Notgebet » ?

de l'événement historique auquel ils doivent leur origine, au souvenir d'une nourriture qui donne la vie éternelle.

Tout ceci ne nous fait encore qu'entrevoir l'éclaircissement du
mystère ; d'autres images et d'autres combinaisons d'images nous
confirmeront dans nos premières impressions.

Nous retrouvons d'abord nos sept corbeilles dans une petite
composition, une espèce de nature morte, devenue célèbre beaucoup
plus par les discussions qu'elle a soulevées que par l'exacte compréhension de sa teneur symbolique (198). Elle se trouve — notons-
le bien — dans la chambre A_2, à côté de celle qui nous offrait
tout à l'heure le petit groupe autour de la table tripode (199). Elle
se présente comme suit : la même petite table, au milieu, garnie
probablement de pains et de poisson ; à gauche, par terre, trois
corbeilles remplies de pains, à droite, quatre autres de ces corbeilles. Combinaison assez étrange, comme on le voit, et où le peintre
a même renoncé à résoudre un tout petit problème de symétrie. De
toute évidence le nombre de sept était sacré pour lui. M. Styger a
affirmé (200) — et d'autres l'ont suivi — que ces sept corbeilles
« appartenaient en réalité au banquet funèbre ». Il ne nous a pas
dit comment il pouvait prouver cela, pas plus qu'il ne nous a expliqué pourquoi un motif aussi secondaire aurait évincé de sa place
naturelle — ce en quoi il se trompe — une des scènes du cycle de
Jonas, qui remplit, avec notre motif, les quatre lunettes de la
voûte (201). A la lumière de ce qui précède, par contre, cette composition symbolique reprend toute son importance et l'on comprend
mieux pourquoi le peintre l'a placée dans l'axe de l'entrée, juste
au-dessus de la figuration du Baptême qui occupe le centre de la
paroi de fond. On aura remarqué, en effet, qu'il ne procéda pas
diversement que le décorateur du cubiculum duplex en la région
de Lucine (202).

Nous devrions ensuite citer les nombreux exemples de la Multiplication des pains et des poissons, où l'art fait intervenir comme

(198) WP pl. 38.
(199) WP pl. 41,1 ; voir L. DE BRUYNE, *l. c.* 200 et fig. 22.
(200) P. STYGER, *Op. cit.*, 17.
(201) La soi-disant scène de Jonas jeté à la mer, que M. Styger suppose avoir été déplacée du plafond sur la paroi de fond pour faire place
à notre composition, n'est autre que la fameuse scène de la barque dans la
tempête (WP pl. 39,2). A cette époque, les artistes n'utilisent pas
encore le cycle de Jonas en quatre scènes.
(202) Voir *supra,* p. 34 et 59.

thaumaturge le Christ en personne. Nous en avons traité assez longuement dans des études antérieures (203) et pouvons donc nous dispenser d'y revenir dans le détail. Contentons-nous d'en souligner quelques aspects qui intéressent plus particulièrement ce contexte. Remarquons d'abord que parmi les diverses formules auxquelles on eut recours pour évoquer ce miracle, il y en a une dont le schéma correspond parfaitement à celui du Miracle de Cana : le Christ y touche de la « virga thaumaturga » les paniers posés par terre, à ses pieds (204), exactement comme il fait avec les urnes de Cana (205). Le parallélisme entre les deux conceptions est frappant. Nous avons des difficultés à croire que les artistes s'en sont servis uniquement à des fins d'ordre technique ou artistique (206). Même si cette identité de formule devait leur fournir le moyen de rapprocher ces deux miracles entre eux, la recherche même de ce rapprochement cache une raison d'être d'un ordre supérieur. Elle prouve, en effet, que nos imagiers voulaient marquer par là que la multiplication des pains et le changement de l'eau en vin allaient de pair. Et s'ils allaient de pair, ce ne put être qu'à raison de rapport sympolique qu'ils avaient tous les deux avec l'Eucharistie.

L'analyse des monuments ultérieurs en donne des preuves éclatantes. Quand, par exemple, les deux miracles se placent en série, l'un à côté de l'autre, cette juxtaposition mène à la Résurrection de Lazare. C'est le cas, entre autres, du sarcophage 104 du Musée de Latran (207) et cela se vérifie encore dans un des panneaux de la porte en bois de Saint-Sabine (208). Pareille trilogie correspond à

----

(203) Voir *Rivista di archeologia cristiana* 16 (1939) 256-258, 268 ; 20 (1943) 195-204.

(204) Citons comme exemples, parmi les fresques : WP pl. 45,1; 54,2; 74,2; 115; 120,1; 186,1 etc.; ainsi que les découvertes récentes : *Rivista di archeologia cristiana,* 9 (1932) fig. 10; A. FERRUA, *Le pitture della nuova catacomba di Via Latina* (Città del Vaticano 1960) pl. 89,2 et *Rivista,* 34 (1958) 35, fig. 28. Parmi les sculptures : WS pl. 29,3 ; 104,6 ; 127,2; 129,1; 218,1; *Rivista,* 16 (1939) 255.

(205) WP pl. 57, 168,1; WS pl. 86,3; 92,2; 96; 98,1; 111,1; 112,3; 113, 2-3, etc.

(206) Et cela d'autant plus qu'ils avaient à leur disposition d'autres formules pour la Multiplication des pains. Voir *supra,* n. 203. Ajoutons qu'ils ont même eu recours parfois à des contaminations entre les deux motifs (WS pl. 11,1 219,3).

(207) WS pl. 96. — Cf. WS pl. 61,3 (à intégrer sans doute avec une Résurrection de Lazare); 115,2; 158,1.

(208) Voir une belle reproduction chez W. F. VOLBACH et M. HIRMER, *Arte paleocristiana* (Firenze 1958) pl. 103. Bibliographie relative à p. 78.

Jo VI, 55 « Qui manducat meam carnem et bibit meum sanguinem habet vitam aeternam et ego resuscitabo eum in novissimo die », et cette portée mystique ne prend que plus de relief quand on se rappelle que le sarcophage de Latran lui donne comme contraste, dans les scènes d'Adam et Eve, les paroles de la Gen. II, 17 « in quocumque enim die comederis ex ea morte morieris ».

Plus tard encore, sur le couvercle du reliquaire de Saint-Nazaire à Milan les deux miracles, évoqués par leurs attributs, sont posés aux pieds du Christ enseignant comme indiquant l'objet de son discours (209).

Quand, par contre, on les dispose d'une façon symétrique, c'est l'Orante, symbole de la félicité dans la paix éternelle, qui se place au milieu (210). Autre façon de notifier, que l'un et l'autre de ces deux miracles, ou les attributs qui les remplacent (211), sont considérés comme symboles de la nourriture de vie, gage d'immortalité.

Et quand, enfin, le pendant est une autre scène biblique, le choix tombe facilement, encore une fois, sur la Résurrection de Lazare (212). On remarquera l'analogie avec la formule, Baptême — Résurrection de Lazare, citée plus haut (213).

Nous n'avons pas encore avec cela épuisé le trésor d'indications que l'art nous livre sur ses propres intentions. J'ai étudié ailleurs toute une série de figurines mystérieuses qui pénètrent, d'une façon fort significative, justement dans les trois compositions de la Multiplication des pains, du Miracle de Cana et de la Résurrection de Lazare (214). Si l'on voulait leur donner un nom, il faudrait les appeler « les symboles des immortalisés ». Il s'agit de figurines des deux sexes, tantôt nues, tantôt habillées, qui se trouvent directement associées aux trois miracles, sans qu'on puisse leur trouver une justification plausible sur le plan historique ou réaliste. Je n'en

---

(209) *Op. cit.*, pl. 111 ; bibliographie à p. 80.
(210) WS pl. 113,2; 127, 1-2; 227, 1-2; (278,5). Cf. WS pl. 8,3, duquel est à rapprocher le couvercle à pl. 17,2.
(211) WP pl. 92,1. On y voit la figure d'une défunte, à gauche de laquelle il y a sept paniers ; ils faisaient probablement pendant avec les urnes de Cana. Ces attributs rappellent à l'esprit le groupement de sept paniers et de deux amphores au Coemeterium Maius (WP p. 280). Il faut y reconnaître des raccourcis des représentations des deux miracles.
(212) WP pl. 45,1; 228, 3-4.
(213) Voir *supra*, p. 66.
(214) L. DE BRUYNE, *L'Imposition des mains* 204-212.

citerai ici que quelques exemples, tout en soulignant l'importance que revêtent, dans leur ensemble, tant l'imposition de la main que la nudité d'aucunes d'entre elles.

Sur le sarcophage 191 du Musée de Latran (215) on remarque une petite figure de femme agenouillée, les mains jointes, à laquelle un apôtre barbu, émergeant de l'arrière-plan, impose la main sur la tête. Elle est associée directement au groupe central du Christ bénissant les pains et les poissons présentés par des disciples. Le sarcophage 455 du Musée national des Thermes (216) présente comme motif central l'Orante entre les Miracles de la Multiplication des pains et du Changement de l'eau en vin. Or, dans ce dernier, nous trouvons, de la façon la plus inattendue, un petit bonhomme nu, debout à côté de Notre-Seigneur. Alors que la main droite du Christ abaisse la baguette pour toucher les urnes placées à ses pieds, sa gauche se pose sur la tête du petit garçon ; celui-ci à son tour avance les deux mains pour toucher la baguette. L'association de la figurine au miracle ici évoqué ne saurait être plus intime, puisque la main qui sert d'instrument à l'infusion de la puissance divine dans la matière inerte trouve son équivalente dans celle qui infuse quelque don d'orde spirituel dans l'être animé. Par ailleurs, le seul point d'attache satisfaisant que l'iconologue peut trouver pour la nudité de la figurine est donné par les ressuscités de la Vision d'Ezéchiel (217). Cette façon de voir est heureusement confirmée par au moins trois sarcophages (218), ou le « nu » est ajouté à une Résurrection de Lazare. D'où il ressort que les scènes de résurrection, telles que la Vision d'Ezéchiel et la Résurrection de Lazare, d'un côté, et les représentations du Miracle de Cana et de la Multiplication des pains, de l'autre côté, sont liées entre elles par une connexion intime, dont il serait difficile de ne pas s'apercevoir. Et les artistes, étant donné les tournures d'esprit caractérisant l'époque, n'auraient su trouver de « signe » plus éloquent pour mettre l'accent sur l'efficacité de la nourriture mystique que ces miracles du Christ étaient chargés d'évoquer.

---

(215) WS pl. 184,1.

(216) WS pl. 127,2.

(217) Voir pour ce thème WS p. 269 s. et pl, 112,2; 123,3; 156,; 184,1; 194,4; 194,9; 204,7; 215,7; 219,1.

(218) WS pl. 233,3 ; 235,7 et une photographie en possession de l'A.

Les peintres, de leur côté, savaient eux aussi se servir du jeu des rapprochements significatifs. A la chambre III des catacombes de Domitille (219), le Christ multipliant les pains au moyen de la baguette occupe le centre de la paroi de fond. De part et d'autre, ont été disposées les deux parties d'un Colloque avec la Samaritaine : à gauche, la femme au puits de Jacob ; à droite, le Christ qui lui parle, mais qui tient en même temps quelques pains dans les plis de son pallium (220). Allusion manifeste, tant à l'eau jaillissante en vie éternelle (Jo 6) qu'au pain de vie évoqué par le Christ lui-même à l'occasion de la multiplication des pains dans le désert (Jo 6, 48 ss.). A Saint-Calliste, dans la lunette de l'arcosolium dit de la Madonne (221), une figure de femme à l'attitude suppliante, qu'on pourrait très bien rapprocher des génies de l'immortalité cités toute à l'heure, s'approche du Seigneur opérant le miracle des pains. Elle rappelle en même temps à la mémoire l'orante à côté de la table tripode mentionnée précédemment. Aux catacombes de Saint-Hermès, toujours en rapport étroit avec la Multiplication des pains (222), c'est une énorme colombe perchée sur une colonne qui a été introduite dans la composition. A la lumière de ce qui précède on n'aura pas de difficulté à y reconnaître un symbole de l'âme qui trouve ses équivalents dans les autres figures rencontrées dans cette analyse et qui, comme elles, signifie les destinataires privilégiés de cette nourriture mystique.

Ainsi donc, d'anneau en anneau, notre enquête nous a menés des symboles primitifs, encore assez voilés, à des images dont le sens mystique s'affirma progressivement. Des poissons « eucharistiques »

---

(219) A. Bosio, *Roma sotterranea* (Roma 1622) 245; R. Garrucci, *Storia dell'arte cristiana*, 2 (Prato 1873) pl. 26,2 ; WP pl. 54,2 ; texte p. 144, 270, 382 ss.; L. v. Sybel, *Christliche Antike*, 1 (Marburg 1906) 232 s.; P. Styger, *Op. cit.*, 48; H. Achelis, *Römische Katakombenbilder in Catania* (Berlin, Leipzig 1932) 11 s., pl. 3-4; O. Casel, *Älteste christliche Kunst und Christusmysterium: Jahrbuch für Liturgiewissenschaft*, 12 (1934) 55 s.

(220) M. Styger, *l. c.*, avait mis en doute l'authenticité de ces pains dans le dessin de Bosio, mais la découverte des originaux, malgré les retouches modernes, a rendu vain tout scepticisme à cet égard.

(221) WP pl. 143,1; 144,2; cf. p. 272.

(222) WP pl. 115 ; cf. p. 272 ; F. Sühling, *Die Taube als religiöses Symbol im christlichen Altertum* (Freiburg i. Br. 1930) 85 s. propose un rapprochement de cette colombe avec le pneuma de l'épiclèse eucharistique. Nous ne saurions souscrire pareille opinion.

aux corbeilles remplies de pains, des corbeilles aux banquets mystérieux, de la table tripode à l'imposition de la main, du geste de
bénédiction à l'orante, de l'orante aux symboles de l'Immortalité et
de la résurrection, des événements évoqués à la parole du Maître
qui les commente, à travers tout un réseau d'interférences de
vocables figuratifs et de symboles constants, se dessine une ligne de
continuitr mystique telle que seule l'Eucharistie, visée comme
garantie de vie éternelle, réussit à l'expliquer.

A travers les images, nous touchons du doigt toute la confiance
que nos premières générations avaient placée en l'efficacité du saint
sacrement de l'Eucharistie. Depuis que le Seigneur avait affirmé :
« Cest moi qui suis le pain de la vie » (Jo 6, 48) et avait solennellement promis que « si quelqu'un mange de ce pain, il vivra éternellement » (Jo 6, 51, cfr. 58), ce mystère, à côté de celui de la
Foi et de l'eau vive, était devenu pour tous une garantie de survie
et de salut éternel. Point n'est besoin de multiplier ici les textes ;
d'autres avant nous en ont réuni un choix très riche (223). Mais,
que ce soit saint Ignace (224), Clément d'Alexandrie (225), saint
Irénée (226) ou d'autres, sans relâche ils nous rappellent que cette
nourriture sacrée est un antidote contre la mort, une médecine
d'immortalité, le viatique pour la vie éternelle (227). Un reflet de
cette foi si vive ne pouvait manquer sur les tombes de ceux qui
avaient commencé leur existence terrestre en s'incorporant dans le
Christ et en laissant le Christ s'incorporer en eux.

Je voudrais terminer cet exposé par l'analyse rapide de trois
monuments qui réalisent des synthèses éloquentes du triple mystère
jusqu'ici contemplé. Ce qui, dans les ramifications de la recherche,
aurait pu paraître quelque peu dispars, s'y trouve ramené à une
unité d'ensemble qui semble bien nous forcer à nous rendre à
l'évidence.

---

(223) Voir e.a. G. WILPERT, *Fractio Panis*, 73; *Pitture*, 260 ss.; F. J.
DÖLGER, IXΘYC, 2 569 ss.
(224) *Ad Ephes.* 20,2.
(225) *Strom.* 1,1
(226) *Contra haer.* 4,18.
(227) « Vie éternelle et Eucharistie sont deux concepts inséparables »
note très bien Mgr WILPERT (*Fractio* 73). « La tradition chrétienne des
trois premiers siècles interprétait de cette manière la multiplication des
pains. Elle y voyait déjà l'eucharistie, réalisée et présente pour le monde
païen dans les douze paniers de restes », souligne Mgr CERFAUX, *l. c.* 381 s.

Le premier de ces monuments est encore assez mal connu, puisque sa découverte ne date que d'il y a peu d'années et il n'a pas été publié d'une façon systématique. Il s'agit des fresques qui ornent une des chambres du Coemeterium Maius (228). Dans le fond d'un arcosolium, le regard est tout de suite arrêté par la figure imposante du « docteur » assis, que nous avons déjà rencontré. Il lève la droite dans un large geste oratoire et serre de sa gauche un *volumen* ouvert à la première page. A sa droite, la *capsa* contient d'autres rouleaux. Après tout ce qui précède, on n'aura plus de difficultés à y reconnaître le docteur anonyme qui explique les saintes écritures, et dans son geste et ses attributs des allusions à la doctrine et la Foi. Dans un arcosolium voisin, nous assistons à l'une des combinaisons les plus ingénieuses que l'art chrétien a imaginées comme reflets de sa mystique, tellement ingénieuse qu'il suffit d'en donner une description littérale pour en saisir immédiatement le caractère symbolique. Sept personnages, vêtus de simple tunique, assistent à un festin. Les pains qu'ils y dégusteront, ils vont les prendre dans les sept paniers énormes rangés en file à gauche du sigma. Tout cela se passe dans le voisinage immédiat, au bord même d'une nappe d'eau qu'on voit au premier plan. Et dans cette eau nagent cinq énormes poissons.

Pareille disposition, au risque même de devenir peu esthétique, ne trouve sa justification que dans la volonté décidée de rapprocher entre eux les symboles du Baptême et de l'Eucharistie. Ensemble avec celui de la Foi, ils composent la trilogie complète de l'Initiation. Comme images complémentaires de cet ensemble on y note, encore une fois, les figures d'orantes et le rapprochement du Miracle de la Source et de la Résurrection de Lazare. L'évocation de l'atmosphère de vie est au complet.

Cet ensemble, conçu entièrement dans l'esprit du IIIe siècle, trouve son correspondant dans un autre, postérieur de quelques décennies et combiné d'après une iconographie un peu plus évoluée. Il s'agit de la voûte d'une chambre aux catacombes « ad duas lauros ». Mgr Kirsch, qui l'a publiée (229), a bien souligné, le sens fondamental qui fait la trame de cet ensemble pictural : « L'allu-

(228) U. M. Fasola, *Nuove scoperte nel « Coemeterium Maius »* : *L'Osservatore romano* (25 déc. 1954) 3 ; Id., *Le recenti scoperte agiografiche nel Coemeterium Maius* : *Rendiconti della Pont. Accademia romana di Archeologia* III,28 (1956) 81, fig. 4.

(229) G. P. Kirsch, *Cubicoli dipiniti del cimitero dei SS. Pietro e Marcellino sulla Via Labicana* : *Rivista di archeologia cristiana*, 9 (1932) 27-36.

sione all'iniziazione solenne dei cristiani in tutto questo gruppo è evidente : Cristo, il Maestro divino della Fede ; il battesimo rappresentato nel battesimo del Salvatore e nel tipo del miracolo della fonte, l'Eucharistia simboleggiata dalla moltiplicazione dei pani e dei pesci nel deserto » (230). Il oublia seulement d'ajouter que l'autre scène complémentaire, aujourd'hui disparue, ne pouvait être — tout l'indique — que la Résurrection de Lazare, qui était devenue désormais le pendant naturel du Miracle de la source d'eau vive. On remarquera l'équivalence symbolique entre ce monument et le précédent. Une fois de plus, rien ne manque au triptyque : Foi, Baptême et Eucharistie, considérés comme moyens de salut.

Et pour finir, c'est encore dans la perspective de nos trois moyens du salut que se résout probablement la difficulté que présenta jusqu'ici le décor de la « cripta delle pecorelle », à Saint-Calliste (231). Nous entrons dans une niche destinée à abriter un sarcophage. A notre droite nous découvrons deux fois la figure de Moïse : jeune et imberbe, d'abord, il se délie les sandales pendant que du haut la main de Dieu lui « parle » ; barbu et à la chevelure abondante, ensuite, il frappe le rocher pour en faire jaillir l'eau vive. M. de Rossi s'efforça d'expliquer la différence des deux physionomies en opposant la figure historique du législateur à la figure symbolique de Moïse, type de Saint Pierre. Mgr Wilpert, par contre, tout en reconnaissant dans le miracle de la Source le symbole du Baptême, voit dans le jeune Moïse devant le buisson ardent la figure du chrétien apparaissant devant Dieu après sa mort. Il ne serait pas difficile d'émettre à ce sujet encore d'autres hypothèses. J'ai l'impression que la piste qui nous est offerte par notre trilogie pourrait bien nous conduire à l'exégèse la plus obvie.

En effet, ce n'est pas chercher bien loin que de reconnaître dans la vocation du futur législateur (Ex 3, 1-4, 18) un symbole de la vocation du fidèle à la Foi. Il suffit de relire le texte sacré, pour se convaincre de l'insistance avec laquelle il revient sur le pour et le contre de l'acceptation du message divin. Certes, l'iconographie paléochrétienne préférera à ce motif celui de la Tradition de la Loi à Moïse, mais nous avons affaire ici, me semble-t-il, à un

---

(230) *Ibid.*, p. 33.
(231) G. B. DE ROSSI, *Roma sotterranea*, 2 (Roma) 1867) pl. A-B et pp. 349-351 ; pl. IX (vol. 3) ; J. WILPERT, *Die Malereien der Sakramentskapellen*, 38-46 ; *Pitture*, pl. 236-237.

modèle qui réunissait en une seule page les deux images présentes. Ce n'est pas forcer non plus l'exégèse, nous l'avons vu déjà plusieurs fois, que de reconnaître dans la Source miraculeuse un symbole du Baptême. Quant à la troisième composition, la Bénédiction des pains et des poissons, nous la retrouvons, à notre gauche, sur la paroi opposée, ce qui nous place en présence d'un des symboles traditionnels de l'Eucharistie.

Tout ceci se trouve confirmé par la grandiose composition qui occupe la paroi de fond. On y voit, en effet, le Bon Pasteur entouré de ses brebis (232). Mais un détail important a été ajouté au schéma habituel : de part et d'autre du Pastaur, deux sources versent leurs eaux abondantes et deux figures d'hommes habillés de tunique et de pallium s'y désaltèrent. Dans ces sources d'eau vive (233) jaillies au milieu du paradis du Pasteur (234), nous sommes obligés de reconnaître le refrigerium sans fin. C'est dans leurs eaux éternelles que confluent les grâces de la Foi, du Baptême et de l'Eucharistie.

Conclusion

Nous ne saurions mieux conclure notre exposé qu'en reproduisant ici une page que M. Martimort dédia à *L'Iconographie des Catacombes et la catéchèse antique*.

« On s'étonnera sans doute que nous inclinions vers une telle interprétation pour des peintures qui décorent un lieu dont la destination exclusivement cimétériale ne fait plus de doute pour personne. Pourquoi rappeler la vocation, la foi, le baptême, l'eucharistie, devant la tombe des défunts qui attendent la résurrection et non pas la naissance, qui doivent jouir de la vision au lieu de participer aux mystères ? C'est que précisément l'espérance du chrétien se fonde sur la vocation, la foi, le baptême et l'eucharistie. „ Ceux que Dieu a prévenus et appelés, il les glorifiera", écrit saint Paul [Rm 8, 30] ; „celui qui croira et sera baptisé sera sauvé, dit Jésus [Mc 16, 16] ; „celui qui mange du pain que je lui donnerai vivra éternellement" [Jo 6, 12] ». Puis il cite les inscriptions d'Abercius et de Pectorius et continue : « C'est bien l'espé-

---

(232) WP pl. 236.

(233) « Ego sitienti dabo de fonte aquae vitae » : Apoc. 21,6 ; cf. 22,1 et 27.

(234) Le « lieu de pâturage » dont parle le psaume 22.

rance du chrétien que proclament les murs des catacombes. Mais cette espérance s'appuie sur les arrhes déjà reçus ici-bas. L'espérance des fidèles de Rome est la même que celle d'Abercius, la même que celle de Pectorius. Lorsque le Chrétien venait prier sur la tombe de ses morts, au bord de la Voie Appienne et de la Salaria Nova, il était ramené, par les décorations qu'il voyait dans les hypogées, aux jours fervents de son catéchuménat et de son initiation. L'Ancien et le Nouveau Testament ne lui apparaissait pas comme matière à anecdotes et à tableaux : il y retrouvait l'explication des mystères auxquels il prenait part, et ces mystères, à leur tour, étaient pour lui le gage de la vie qui ne finit pas (235).

L. De Bruyne.

Professeur au Pontificio Istituto di
Archeologia cristiana de Rome (Italie)

---

(235) A. G. Martimort, *L'Iconographie des catacombes et la catéchèse antique : Rivista di archeologia cristiana* 25 (1949) 113 s.

Baptismal Motifs in the Ancient Church*

Everett Ferguson

The design of this paper will be to lay out some of the important doctrinal conceptions associated with baptism in the early centuries of the church. An examination will be made to determine which motifs can be traced back to the New Testament. We are thus presented with an opportunity to test the validity of using the practices and teaching of the early church as a tool in the interpretation of New Testament texts. Then, how the doctrinal conceptions found expression in the baptismal ceremony will be shown. Our grouping of the motifs is largely arbitrary, but in general they relate to the preparation, performance, and effects of baptism.

MOTIFS OF CONVERSION: FAITH AND REPENTANCE

The catechetical instruction given candidates for baptism was an essential part of the preparation for the rite.[1] Justin states that baptism is for "as many as are persuaded and believe that what we teach and say is true, and undertake to be able to live accordingly."[2]

Faith was the essential subjective condition of pardon. Regeneration according to Justin was through "water, faith, and wood."[3] Gregory of Nyssa writing *On the Holy Spirit* states concerning baptism that "belief in our Lord must precede." Baptism as an act of faith is seen in the accompanying verbal confession. "When we

---

*The substance of this paper was read at the Biblical Forum at Abilene Christian College, February 1964.

Since the first draft of this paper was prepared, I have received and read J. Ysebaert, *Greek Baptismal Terminology* (Dekker & Van de Vegt: Nijmegen, 1962). This work will now be a standard reference work in its field. Compare this writer's review of this work in this issue of the *Restoration Quarterly*. In general his linguistic analysis supports conclusions I have reached from a motif approach —for a notable example the separation of *palingenesia* from the rebirth concept (pp. 130ff). I would register a strong dissent to his separation of the "gift of the Holy Spirit" from baptism (pp. 252ff). Some account of Ysebaert's notable contributions will be taken in the footnotes.

[1]*Didache* 1-6 may represent a model for pre-baptismal catechesis. A clear description is found in Hippolytus' *Apostolic Tradition* 16-19 and documents dependent upon it such as the *Canons of Hippolytus* and the *Apostolic Constitutions*. The catechetical lectures of Cyril of Jerusalem (or, in part, his successor John), John Chrysostom, and Augustine, among others, have come down to us. The earliest catechetical instruction appears to have been moral in content; the lectures of the later men are also doctrinal.

[2]*Apology*, 61.
[3]*Dialogue*, 138.

202

have entered the water, we make profession of the Christian faith in the words of its rule."[4] "Ye were led to the holy pool of divine baptism . . . and each of you was asked, whether he believed in the name of the Father and of the Son and of the Holy Spirit, and ye made that saving confession."[5]

The close connection of faith and baptism in the New Testament is apparent in Galatians 3:26f; Colossians 2:12. In Hebrews 10: 19-22 we have the same grouping of faith, water, and the blood (of the cross) as in Justin. The confession with the mouth of the faith in the heart is expressed in Romans 10:9f. This profession of faith may be the "word" which accompanies the water in Ephesians 5:19.[6] "Calling upon the name of the Lord" (as in Acts 22:16) may be a reference to the baptismal confession and the basis for speaking of baptism as "in the name of Christ."

Baptism was also viewed as an act of repentance. Justin describes the one being baptized as him who "chooses to be reborn and repents of his sins."[7] Thus Hermas speaks of the "repentance . . . which takes place when we descended into the water."[8] Benoit has developed the relationship of repentance and baptism in the apostolic fathers—Hermas, Barnabas, 1 and 2 Clement.[9] The last three of these writers view the Christian life as a life of penitence, so that baptism is not only a result of repentance but an act committing one to a penitent life. Even as baptism is an act of repentance, so the life it inaugurates is one of faith and repentance.[10] Later Cyril of

---

[4]Tertullian, *De Spectaculis*, 4.

[5]Cyril Jerus., *Mystagogical Catechesis* ii.4. When infant baptism was practiced, sponsors made the confession on behalf of the child, for example in the *Barberini Euchologion* of the Byzantine Rite, written c. 790, translated by E. C. Whitaker, *Documents of the Baptismal Liturgy* (SPCK: London, 1960), p. 68. Cf. Tert., *De Baptismo* 18.

[6]Cf. B. F. Westcott, *St. Paul's Epistle to the Ephesians* (Wm. B. Eerdmans: Grand Rapids, 1952), *in loc.* for this interpretation. This view brings the passage into relation with other passages where the value of baptism is connected with the moral response of the convert —Acts 2:38; Gal. 3:26f; Col. 2:12; 1 Peter 3:21. The other interpretation for which there is support in the baptismal ceremony of the early church, that the "word" is the formula, finds no support in the New Testament. It would be consistent with other New Testament passages to refer this "word" to the preached Gospel, but this finds no support in patristic exegesis.

[7]Justin, *Apol.* 61.

[8]Hermas, *Mandate* IV.3.

[9]André Benoit, *Le Baptême Chrétien au Second Siècle* (Paris, 1953).

[10]In Hermas and, as Benoit argues, in some passages in Justin and Irenaeus a different view of repentance is taken—an act rather than an attitude, a temporary rather than an enduring state. Here baptism commits you not to a life of penitence but to a life without sin. "This notion certainly differs from that of the Synoptics where *metanoia* is a dynamic notion, an attitude, which has its origin in a precise act but characterizes the whole life of believing"—Benoit,

203

Jerusalem can speak of believing in the "one baptism of repentance."[11] The same writer applies the terminology of putting off the old and putting on the new to baptismal repentance:

> Thou hast a penitence of forty (days); thou hast full time to put off, and to wash thee, to put on, and to enter in. But if thou abide in thy evil purpose . . . thou must not look for grace: for though the water shall receive thee, the Spirit will not accept thee.[12]

> At the holy laver of regeneration God has wiped away every tear from off all faces. For thou shalt no more mourn, now that thou hast put off the old man; thou shalt keep holy-day, clothed in the garment of salvation, even Jesus Christ.[13]

In the New Testament John's baptism was a "baptism of repentance" (Mark 1:4), and the command of Peter was "repent and be baptized" (Acts 2:38). The "putting off and putting on" of Colossians 2 and 3 continues the baptismal imagery of 2:12 and may be considered an elucidation of performing "deeds worthy of repentance" (Acts 26:20).

The repentance, as a renunciation of the devil, and the profession of faith, as an adherence to Christ, were viewed as a pledge of allegiance, a promise, a contract. Justin (*Apology* 61) describes baptism as "the manner in which we dedicated ourselves to God." Tertullian, *De Baptismo* 18, indicates that the confession of faith was a promise.[14] But Theodore of Mopsuestia's *Sermons on the Lord's Prayer and the Sacraments* 2 and 3 give the fullest discussion of the baptismal ceremony as a contract with God to live in harmony with his commands.[15] This understanding of the baptismal rite, and especially of the profession of faith, as marking a new loyalty may provide the proper explanation of the "answer of a good conscience" in 1 Peter 3:21. Bo Reicke has shown that *eperōtēma* often means an "agreement," "undertaking," or "contract," and so would

---

p. 156. The thought of Hermas was the starting point for the sacrament of penance, a second "baptism" bringing forgiveness of postbaptismal sins. The view that repentance inaugurates a life offers a different solution to the problem of sins committed after baptism: the continuing effects of baptism, as of the death of Christ, means that one appropriates the pardon continually by the same things that give baptism its initial value, namely, faith and repentance.

[11]Cyril Jerus., *Mys. Cat.*, i.9.

[12]*Procatechesis* 4.

[13]*Mys. Cat.* i.10.

[14]*In Ad Martyras* 3 Tertullian compares the profession of faith to the taking of an oath as a soldier does on entering military service. For baptism as a contract see *De Bapt.* 6.

[15]Chrysostom, *Cat. Bapt.* II:17, 21, 22 speaks of the renunciation and adherence as an "agreement." In the Byzantine rite they are called a "contract" (Whitaker, *ibid.*, p. 62). May Pliny's description (*Ep.* X.96) that "it was their habit on a fixed day to assemble before daylight and recite by turns a form of words to Christ as a god; and that they bound themselves with an oath. . ." refer to a baptismal instead of a communion service?

204

translate "an agreement about," or "an undertaking to" a good conscience (genitive of content).[16]

Thus the profession of faith marks a new allegiance, a change of relationship, and so is the counterpart on the human side of the triadic formula by which the divine "name is called upon"[17] the one being baptized. From the earliest post-apostolic times in *Didache* 7[18] the consistent testimony is to baptism administered "in the name of the Father, Son, and Holy Spirit."[19] By baptism believers are brought under the authority or control of God; by imposing his name upon the person God lays a claim to his life.[20] The formula expressed God's ownership.[21] One now wore Christ's name. "May you then enjoy the fragrant waters which bear Christ: may you then receive Christ's name and the efficacious power of divine things."[22]

The origin of triple immersion is obscure, but its widespread practice from at least the end of the second century is a good illustration of how the doctrine of baptism was made explicit in the ritual. To the verbal confession was added the bodily confession, each immersion expressing the faith in one divine person: Our earliest full account reads as follows:

---

[16]Bo Reicke, *The Disobedient Spirits and Christian Baptism* (Copenhagen, 1946), pp. 182ff. This is the best treatment of 1 Peter 3:17-22 in print.

[17]Justin, *Apol.* 61.

[18]Benoit, *op. cit.*, pp. 7ff says the triadic expression here is the baptismal formula, whereas "name of the Lord" in 9:5 is a summary statement of the character of the baptism (Christian baptism in contrast to other kinds). This is a distinction which would seem to hold true generally.

[19]Matt. 28:19 is the only verbal formula attested for use at baptism in the earliest literature—Irenaeus, *Demonstration* 3; the baptisms in the *Acts of Judas Thomas; History of John Son of Zebedee; Acts of Xanthippe and Polyxena* 2 and 21; *Didascalia* 16; *Apos. Const.* VII.44.1; *Can. Hipp.* 133, to mention but a few of the references.

[20]Cullen I. K. Story, "Justin's Apology I.62-64: Its Importance for the Author's Treatment of Christian Baptism," *Vigiliae Christianae* XVI (1962), pp. 172-78. The author calls attention to Justin's triple repetition of *onoma*; the name of each divine person is imposed upon the baptizand.

[21]Cf. J. H. Moulton and George Milligan, *The Vocabulary of the Greek Testament* (Hodder and Stoughton: London, 1930), p. 451. Ysebaert, *op. cit.*, pp. 48-51, treats *eis to onoma* and *en to onoma* as both telic, "with a view to." He notes the Rabbinic phrase used in such a way that one now has the name of that "into the name of which" he was baptized.

[22]Cyril, *Procat.* 15. On the other hand, in the *Mys. Cat.* iii.1 disciples are said properly to be called "Christs" because they are anointed with oil. The name "Christian" is also derived from the practice of anointing in *Apos. Const.* III.16. Cf. Tert., *De Bapt.* 7. Since anointings preceded baptism, the name "Christians" came to be applied to the catechumens awaiting baptism—Augustine, *Tract. in St. Jno.* 44:2.

205

> Let him who baptizes lay hand on him saying thus:
> Dost thou believe in God the Father Almighty?
> And he who is being baptized shall say:
> I believe.
> Let him forthwith baptize him once. . . .
> And after this let him say:
> Dost thou believe in Christ Jesus, the Son of God . . . ?
> And when he says: I believe, let him baptize him the second time.
> And again let him say:
> Dost thou believe in the Holy Spirit . . . ?
> And he who is being baptized shall say: I believe.
> And so let him baptize him the third time.[23]

Tertullian states, "And indeed it is not once only but three times that we are baptized at each separate name into each separate person."[24] Ambrose brings the baptizing into close relation with the confession: "Thou wast baptized in the name of the Trinity, thou didst confess the Father—remember what thou didst—thou didst confess the Son, thou didst confess the Holy Spirit."[25]

Preceding the baptismal confession of faith there was a verbal renunciation of the devil.[26] The wording varies, but "I renounce thee, Satan, and all thy service and all thy works"[27] is typical. This was followed by "I adhere to thee, O Christ" in some rites.[28] One faced west for the renunciation and turned east for the adherence and so enacted repentance.[29] The renunciation was connected with the removal of the clothing for baptism. "Ye put off your garment; and this was an image of putting off the old man with his deeds."[30]

MOTIF OF CLEANSING: WASHING

Water was prominent in the ceremonial cleansings of the Old Testament and in the purification ceremonies of pagan antiquity.[31] And the early church spoke of baptism as a washing.[32] Justin explains, "For in the name of God, the Father and Lord of the uni-

---

[23]*Apos. Trad.* 21.
[24]*Adv. Praxean* 26. In *De Corona* 3 Tertullian writes, "We are thrice immersed, replying somewhat more fully than the Lord has appointed in the Gospel." Does Tertullian mean the triple immersion (Matt. 28:19) or the triple confession (Matt. 10:32) is fuller than the Gospel requires?
[25]Ambrose, *De Mysteriis* 21. Cf. 28 and *De Sacramentis* II:20. It should be noted that some writers refer the trine immersion to the three days burial of Christ—Cyril, *Mys. Cat.* ii.4; Narsai, *Hom.* 21; Gregory Nyssa, *On the Baptism of Christ.*
[26]*Apos. Trad.* 21:9; Tert., *De Spec.* 4; *De Cor.* 3; Cyril, *Mys. Cat.* i.2-8; Serapion, *Prayer* 9; Ambrose, *De Sac.* I:4f; *De Mys.* 5, 7.
[27]*Apos. Trad.* 21:9.
[28]*Apos. Const.* VII:40f; Chrysostom, *Cat. Bapt.* II:18, 20.
[29]Cyril, *Mys. Cat.* i.9; Narsai, *Hom.* 22.
[30]Cyril, *Mys. Cat.* ii.2.
[31]For a survey of the terminology, Ysebaert, *op. cit.*, pp. 12-39.
[32]Ambrose, *De Sac.* I:9 and *De Mys.* 21; Serapion, *Prayer* 10 and 15; *Acts of Xanthippe and Polyxena* 2, 21; the "Baptism of the priests of Artemis" in *History of John Son of Zebedee.*

verse, and of our Saviour Jesus Christ, and of the Holy Spirit, they then receive the washing with water.[33]

Christians made clear that their cleansing was not external. Tertullian puts the idea succinctly, "The flesh indeed is washed, in order that the soul may be cleansed."[34] The favorite way of describing the moral value of baptism was in terms of a remission or forgiveness of sins.[35] Irenaeus states, "The faith above all teaches us that we have received baptism for the forgiveness of sins."[36] The phrase "baptism for (unto) the remission of sins" is fairly common.[37] *Barnabas* expressly contrasts this feature with the deficiency of the Jewish washings.[38]

The cleansing, purifying effect of baptism is attributed, not to the water, but to the Holy Spirit. Cyprian declares, "For water alone is not able to cleanse away sins, and to sanctify a man, unless he have also the Holy Spirit."[39] Gregory of Nyssa asks the following:

> Is that life-giving power in the water itself . . . ? Or is it not rather clear to every one that this element . . . of itself contributes nothing towards the sanctification unless it be first transformed itself by the sanctification and that what gives life to the baptized is the Spirit.[40]

Tertullian describes pagan cleansings as "widowed waters."[41] Also common is the attributing of the efficacy of the water to the invocation of the triune name.[42]

The New Testament often employs the cleansing motif. In Ephesians 5:26 the church is saved "by the washing of water," and in Titus 3:5 salvation is the "washing of regeneration." "Our bodies washed with pure water" of Hebrews 19:22 is phrased on the model of Old Testament washings. "Not the putting away of the filth of the flesh" in 1 Peter 3:21 contrasts the bodily purification with the purpose of Christian baptism. The Holy Spirit as the active agent

---

[33]*Apology*, 61; cf. chap. 65.

[34]*De R. Carn.* 8.

[35]For example, Hermas, *Mand.* IV.3; Justin, *Apol.* 61; Theophilus, *Ad Autolycum* II.16; Tert., *De Bapt.*, 18; *Apos. Trad.* 22:1; Cyril, *Procat.* 9, 15; Narsai, *Hom.* 21.

[36]*Dem.* 3; cf. also chap. 41.

[37]*Clem. Hom.* XI.27; Clement Alexandria, *Paedagogus* I.vi (note in the same chapter, the "washing by which we cleanse away our sins"). Other references in Ysebaert, *op. cit.*, p. 69.

[38]*Barn.*, 11.

[39]*Ep.* 73:5; cf. Iren., *Adv. Haer.* III:17:2. See further the references in footnote 63.

[40]*On the Holy Spirit.* For the sanctification of the waters by the invocation of the Holy Spirit, see footnotes 45 and 63.

[41]*De Bapt.* 5.

[42]Narsai, *Hom.*, 21, "The defilement of men he cleanses with water; yet not by water, but by the power of the Name of the Divinity. . . . The names give forgiveness of iniquity." Note the claim in the re-baptism controversy of the 3rd century that the baptismal formula gave baptism its efficacy—Cyp., *Epp.*, 72-74.

207

in baptism is implied in several passages (John 3:5; Titus 3:5; 1 Corinthians 12:13).

The act of baptism itself, of course, suggested the ideas of bathing, cleansing, and purifying. In the later ritual the idea of cleansing was reinforced by the clothing of the newly baptized in white garments for their entrance into the assembly.[43]

THE CHRISTIAN VICTORY: DEATH AND THE DEVIL

The strongest expression for conversion, the turning from evil, is in the figure of dying. This was a favorite conception with the compiler of the *Apostolic Constitutions*:

> This baptism therefore is given into the death of Jesus: the water is instead of the burial. . . the descent into the water the dying together with Christ: the ascent out of the water the rising again with him.[44]
> "Look down from heaven and sanctify this water and give it grace and power, that so he that is baptized, according to the command of thy Christ, may be crucified with him, and may die with him, and may be buried with him, and may rise with him to the adoption which is in him, that he may be dead to sin and live to righteousness.[45]

This figure of dying with Christ and being raised with him, obviously drawn from Romans 6:3f., was noticeably absent from second century literature.[46]

There is more to the conception than a symbolism of individual psychological experience. A real community with Christ is established, for Christ is present and his death is actualized in baptism.[47] One of the favorite descriptions of the benefits of baptism (as we have seen) was pardon or the forgiveness of sins.[48] This was also the achievement of the Cross.[49] *Barnabas* is our earliest post-apostolic writer to bring the two ideas into rapport: baptism as the subjective appropriation of the remission of sins objectively accomplished by the death on the cross.

> Let us further inquire whether the Lord took any care to foreshadow the water and the cross. . . . Blessed are those who, placing their trust in the cross, have gone down into the water.[50]

---

[43]*History of John Son of Zebedee;* Theod. Mops., *Serm.* 4 *On the Lord's Prayer and the Sacraments;* Ambrose, *De Mys.,* 34.
[44]III.17.
[45]VII.43.5.
[46]Benoit, *op. cit.,* p. 227. Was this the avoidance of a common pagan conception?
[47]Per Lundberg, *La Typologie Baptismale dans l'Ancienne Eglise* (Uppsala, 1942), pp. 209-215.
[48]See the references in note 35. Benoit suggests that "to receive remission of sins" may be a technical term for baptism—Acts 10:43; *Barnabas,* 16:8; Hermas, *Mand.* III.3.1; Justin, *Dial.* 111:4; 141:2— *op. cit.,* pp. 148ff.
[49]Justin, *Dial.* 54:1; 1 Clement 7:4.
[50]Barnabas 11:1, 8.

208

Justin, as pointed out above—in agreement with Hebrews 10, connects baptism on one side with the blood of Christ as the divine work of purification and on the other with faith, which concerns the manner by which man is prepared to receive it.[51] A later writer states, "Giving thanks that he undertook to die for all men by the cross, the type of which he has appointed to be the baptism of regeneration.[52] Baptism therefore was regarded as more than one's dying to sin in repentance—it brought one into saving contact with the death on the cross.

In the New Testament baptism is "for the remission of sins" (Acts 2:38) as also is the shedding of Christ's blood (Matt. 26:28). Baptism and the death of Christ are in close relation also in 1 John 5:6-8; Ephesians 5:25f; and Hebrews 10:19-22. The designation of baptism as a "death" may be based on the very words of Jesus about his own death—Mark 10:38; Luke 12:50.[53]

Underlying this identification of death and baptism was yet another conception. In ancient mythology the sea was the kingdom of the dead and to die was to go down into the waters of death.[54] Thus the connection between the baptism of Jesus and his death on the cross was a natural one. Recent scholars have called attention to the baptism of Jesus as an announcement of the Passion.[55] And the convert's immersion was a passing through the realm of death.

But death is especially the domain of the devil. In the early church Christ's death and resurrection were a victory over the demonic forces of evil. Serapion, *Prayer* 16, "By which cross Satan and every opposing power was routed and triumphed over," is in a baptismal context|[56] Colossians 2:15 (once more a baptismal context—v. 12) is the classic New Testament text for this idea. Christ's

---

[51]Benoit, *op. cit.*, p. 153, with reference to *Dial.* 13-14 and 138 ("water, faith, and wood"). Gregory Nyssa, *Vita Moysis* (Migne, XLIV, 361 D) on the crossing of the Red Sea develops the same grouping with the addition of the Holy Spirit: "The water, by virtue of the rod of faith and of the luminous cloud, became the vivifying principle for those who sought there a refuge." The rod of Moses is a type of the Cross and the cloud of the Holy Spirit. The grouping of water, blood, and Spirit in patristic thought is well brought out in A. A. Maguire's monograph *Blood and Water: The Wounded Side of Christ in Early Christian Literature* (Catholic University of America Studies in Sacred Theology. Catholic University of America Press: Washington, 1958), esp. pp. 2, 11, and 24f.

[52]*Apos. Const.* VII.43.3.

[53]Ysebaert calls attention to the connotation of "perishing" which *baptizō* had in the classical profane usage, a feature which he thinks led the apologists writing for non-Christians to avoid the use of this word and to adopt substitutes wherever possible (*op. cit.*, pp. 13, 66f). This connotation of perishing may have aided the identification of the motif of death with baptism.

[54]Lundberg, *op. cit.*, pp. 64-72.

[55]E.g., Oscar Cullmann, *Baptism in the New Testament* (SCM Press: London, 1950), pp. 13-22.

[56]Cf. also Cyril, *Mys. Cat.* ii.2.

209

baptism too was thought of as a victory over the demonic forces dwelling in the waters (the symbol of death).[57] Even so in the Christian's baptism "liberty is restored" from the "evil one who had brought them into the slavery" of sin.[58] In *Barnabas* 16:8 the soul is a house of demons until the forgiveness of sins makes one a new creature. The baptismal formula of the divine name was considered efficacious in dispelling demons.[59]

A New Testament reflection of this type of thinking may be found in 1 Peter 3:18ff. According to this viewpoint there would be no digression, but a logical progression, in Peter's moving from a descent of Christ into the underworld to a description of Christian baptism, the symbolism of the waters of death providing the transition.[60] It is not hard to find baptismal allusions in Luke 11:24-26, and the passage becomes very meaningful in the framework of ideas we have been considering.

Baptism as a death required no special elaboration in the ceremony, for the action of immersion amply suggested the idea.[61]

Baptism as a deliverance from the power of Satan may be seen in two ceremonies. An elaborate series of exorcisms preceded the baptism itself.[62] And the power of God was evoked in blessing and purifying the water in which the baptism was to take place.[63] These rites supplanted mention of baptism itself expelling demons in most texts. Nevertheless, the prominence, frequency of notice, and im-

---

[57]Cyril, *Cat.* III:10, "Since, therefore, it was necessary to break the heads of the dragon in pieces, He went down and bound the strong one in the waters, that we might receive power to tread upon serpents and scorpions."

[58]Narsai, *Hom.* 22; cf. also the *Excerpta ex Theodoto* 76:2; Iren., *Adv. Haer.* III:8:2.

[59]Narsi, *Hom.* 21 and 22; Armenian baptismal rite (Whitaker, *op. cit.*, p. 54).

[60]Reicke, *op. cit.*, pp. 245-47.

[61]Cf. Cyril, *Mys. Cat.* ii.4; Ambrose, *De Sac,* II:20; III:1.

[62]*Apos. Trad.* 20:8, "And laying his hand on them he shall exorcise every evil spirit to flee away from them and never to return." 21:7ff, "And he shall take other oil and exorcise over it, and it is called the Oil of Exorcism. . . . And when he has said this (renunciation of Satan) let him anoint him with the Oil of Exorcism, saying: 'Let all evil spirits depart far from thee.'" *Can Hipp.* 108, 120; Cyril, *Procat.* 9; *Mys. Cat.* ii.3; Theodore Mops., *Sermon* 2 and 3 *On the Lord's Prayer and the Sacraments;* Ambrose, *De Sac.* I:2f.

[63]Tert., *De Bapt.* 4; *Apos. Trad.* 21:1; *Apos. Const.* VII.43; Theodore Mops., *Sermon* 4 *On the Lord's Prayer and the Sacraments;* Ambrose *De Sac.* I:18; II:14. Serapion, *Prayer* 7 is typical: "Look down now from heaven and behold these waters and fill them with Holy Spirit. Let thine ineffable Word come to be in them and transform their energy and cause them to be productive. . . . And as thy only begotten Word coming down upon the waters of the Jordan rendered them holy, so now also may he descend on these and make them holy and spiritual." See J. D. C. Fisher, "The Consecration of Water in the Early Rite of Baptism," *Studia Patristica* (Berlin, 1958), Vol. II, pp. 41-46.

210

portance given to these rites show how real was the fear of demons and how closely their power was associated with water in the early days of the church. The victory won by Christ in their own element gave a basis for the Christian hope of life through water.

MOTIFS OF THE NEW LIFE: RESURRECTION AND REBIRTH

The concept of newness, a new beginning, is quite prominent in early Christianity.

Completing the imagery of baptism as a death was the baptismal resurrection. The earlier cited passages are applicable here, to which we may add Narsai's statement that in baptism the resurrection is preached.[64]

Much more frequent, indeed one of the favorite baptismal conceptions, is the idea of the new birth. John 3:5 was the favorite text on baptism in the second century,[65] and Benoit states that it is the best commentary on Irenaeus' baptismal theology.[66] The *History of John Son of Zebedee* speaks of the one baptized as a "firstling" and later as one who has "become a youth." Cyril describes him as "true born," as receiving the "life giving baptism," in the "laver of regeneration," and receiving the new name "Christian" at the new birth.[67] In the *Apostolic Constitutions* VII.45 the newly baptized signifies his new sonship by reciting the "Our Father." Theodore of Mopsuestia speaks of the "water of second birth" and calls the water a "womb."[68] These are but some of the more striking statements which show the unanimous understanding of the ancient church about John 3:5. And this verse is but another bringing together of the ideas of sonship and the gift of the Holy Spirit with baptism also to be seen in the baptism of Jesus (Matt. 3:16ff).[69]

The word for "regeneration" in Titus 3:5 is not related to the new birth concept, but to the idea of a new creation; it is baptism that brings one into the new age.[70]

---

[64]*Hom.* 21.

[65]*E.g.*, Justin, *Apol.* 61; Irenaeus, *Adv. Haer.* III:17:1f; Theophilus, *Ad Autolycum* II:16; Tertullian, *De Bapt.* 12; Clement Alex., *Strom.* IV.25. Cf. Ysebaert, *op. cit.*, pp. 149-152.

[66]*Op. cit.*, p. 222.

[67]*Mys. Cat.* i.1, 10; iii.5.

[68]*Sermon 4 On the Lord's Prayer and the Sacraments*. This motif may offer the explanation for the baptizand ordinarily being represented as child-sized in early Christian art. Cf. C. F. Rogers, "Baptism and Christian Archaeology," *Studia Biblica et Ecclesiastica*, Vol. V (1903), pp. 244f.

[69]Cf. Ysebaert, *op. cit.*, p. 151, for passages connecting the Holy Spirit with the rebirth.

[70]On the basis of the common association of *palingenesia* with the theme of the new creation I had been led to question the usual identification of it with the rebirth concept (as in Benoit, *op. cit.*, p. 40, and *passim*). Now Ysebaert has given linguistic confirmation for a distinction (*op. cit.*, pp. 130ff). He finds in the Latin translation *regeneratio* for *palingenesia* the basis for the confusion (pp. 134, 148).

211

Once more the symbolism of the resurrection was implicit in the act and required no additional ceremonial expression. The new birth motif may be found in certain other actions. The removal of the clothes was identified with the stripping off of sin (as seen above), but proceeding from the water unclothed could suggest a birth. Narsai, who also employs the penitence motif, says, "As a babe from the midst of the womb he looks forth from the water; and instead of garments the priest receives him and embraces him."[71] The practice of giving milk and honey (the food of infants) to the newly baptized at their first Eucharist may also be seen as carrying out the new birth motif. Tertullian explains, "When we are taken up as new-born children, we taste first of all a mixture of milk and honey."[72] The milk and honey also remind one of entering the land of promise (*Barnabas* 6:13), and that may be the idea behind this liturgical practice.[73]

MOTIFS ASSOCIATED WITH THE HOLY SPIRIT:

THE SEAL AND ILLUMINATION

If baptism is the driving out of the evil spirits or demons, something positive must be put into the life. Moreover, the Holy Spirit is the power of renewal in the motifs of the new life. Many writers connect the bestowing of the Holy Spirit with baptism.[74] The phrase "baptism of the Holy Spirit" is used for water baptism at which time the Holy Spirit is conferred.[75] The Holy Spirit is the distinctive gift of Christian baptism distinguishing it from other washings.[76] The Holy Spirit as the gift of baptism (Acts 2:38) or as the agent of the renewing power of baptism (John 3:5; Titus 3:5) is clearly the New Testament teaching also.

Especially related to the gift of the Holy Spirit in baptism is the terminology of the "seal." "The seal then is the water" in Hermas, *Similitude* 9:16:4, is perhaps the first allusion to this concept.[77] But it is especially in 2 Clement that *sphragis* ("seal") is synonymous

---

[71]*Hom.* 22 for the penitence motif; the quotation is from *Hom.* 21.
[72]*De Corona* 3.
[73]The *Barnabas* passage, however, goes on to mention milk and honey as the food of infants. Similarly, *Can. Hipp.* 144 says that the milk and honey remind the new converts that they are little children, but 148 regards the custom as a symbol of the future life in the promised land. For the suggestion that a pagan practice has been borrowed, see W. R. Halliday, *The Pagan Background of Early Christianity* (1925), ch. X.
[74]Irenaeus, *Dem.* 3;7;42; Novatian, *De Trinitate* 29; Cyprian, *Ep.* 62:8; Athanasius, *Ad Serapion* I:4; Jerome, *Dial. c. Lucif.* 6; 9.
[75]Justin, *Dial.*, 29:1; Iren., *Dem.* 42.
[76]Cyril, *Mys. Cat.* ii.6.
[77]Benoit, *op. cit.*, p. 131. *Barnabas* 4:8 is a probable allusion to baptism. Hermas, *Similitude* 9:17, makes the reception of the seal follow upon the hearing and believing in the name of the Son God. See A. Hamman, "La signification de *sphragis* dans le Pasteur d' Hermas," *Studia Patristica*, IV (1961), pp. 286ff.

212

with baptism.[78] Benoit concludes that by "seal" 2 Clement simply means baptism in all of its implications, not one notion such as the Holy Spirit alone.[79] But more often the baptismal "seal" refers to the gift of the Holy Spirit.[80]

After Tertullian identified the bestowal of the Holy Spirit with the post-baptismal imposition of hands[81] rather than with the baptism itself, the seal became especially the word for the signing with oil.[82] From this separation of baptism from the gift of the Holy Spirit came the separate sacrament of confirmation.

In the New Testament the "seal" is the Holy Spirit (Eph. 4:30; 1:13f; 2 Cor. 1:22); but, since the Holy Spirit was given in baptism, there was a close connection accounting for the application of the term later to the baptismal ceremony. The association with the Holy Spirit seems to have been fairly constant. As long as the gift of the Holy Spirit was still connected with baptism, that rite was called the "seal," and, when the gift of the Spirit was separated from baptism, the anointing became the "seal."

The seal and illumination are united in the phrase from the *Epistle of the Apostles*, "the light of the seal."[83] Whereas the "seal" was popular with the common people, the terminology of "illumination" is found mainly in more educated circles.[84]

Illumination, or enlightenment, is especially the work of the Holy

---

[78]Cf. 6:9 with 7:6 and 8:6. Other passages using "seal" of baptism include the *Acts of Paul* 25; Iren., *Dem.* 63; Tert., *Repent.* 6; Clem. Alex., *Quis Dives* 42; Origen, *Jer.* 2, 3. Clement's conception of baptism as a seal has received special study in Harry A. Echle's *The Terminology of the Sacrament of Regeneration According to Clement of Alexandria* (Catholic University of America Studies in Sacred Theology. Catholic University of America Press: Washington, 1949).

[79]*Op. cit.*, pp. 97-100. F. J. Dölger has found the following different acceptations in the usage of *sphragis*: (1) Seal of the preaching (1 Cor. 9:2; Hermas, *Sim.* 9:16:5) or of faith (Tert. *Repent.* 6) and so of the baptismal confession or oath; (2) distinctive mark on a slave or beast, so a mark imprinted by God marking his property and a sign identifying Christians; (3) God's protection given to his property; (4) the baptismal formula which invokes the name of the divine person on the baptized and signifies the entrance into the souls of the neophyte of a new principle of life; (5) Christ himself who is imprinted as a new impression on man at the moment of baptism; (6) a seal authenticates a document and in religious language the seal authenticates eternal life, hence the expression "seal of life eternal." *Sphragis: Eine altchristliche Taufbezeichnung* (Studien zur Geschichte und Kultur des Altertums. V:3/4. Paderborn, 1911). Ysebaert, *op. cit.*, pp. 374-421, should also be consulted.

[80]Cf. Serapion, *Prayer* 16; Amb. *De Mys.* 42.

[81]*De Bapt.* 6, 7. Cf. Cyril, *Mys. Cat.* iii.1ff.

[82]*Apos. Trad.* 22; Theod. Mops., *Sermons* 3 and 4 *On the Lord's Prayer and the Sacraments*; cf. Ambrose, *De Sac.* III:8 and *De Mys.* 41f.

[83]Chap. 41. Cf. Clem. Alex., *Strom.* VI:12, "gleaming seal of righteousness."

[84]Ysebaert, *op. cit.*, 176 and 395.

213

Spirit. On the basis of association of ideas Benoit finds the motif of illumination in 1 Clement, 2 Clement, and Hermas.[85] The knowledge of God by faith and eternal life are prominent in the complex of ideas dominated by "light." However, it is in Justin that we meet for the first time *phōtismos* ("illumination") as a designation for baptism.[86] But he uses it as a traditional term equivalent to baptism. Justin explains it as a rational, intellectual illumination. According to this explanation the illumination would seem to be produced by the catechumenate and would be applied to baptism as that which summarizes, confirms, and manifests what has taken place in the catechumenate. A second possibility (and the two ideas are not mutually exclusive) is the gift of the Spirit. The vision of God is a grace made possible by the illumination of the Holy Spirit.[87] The concept of spiritual illumination prevails over that of intellectual illumination. Tertullian says that the soul is "enlightened by the Holy Spirit."[88] Thus I see in this terminology the light of God which now fills one's life and prepares for the eschatological vision of God.

The normal reference of illumination to baptism makes probable a similar reference in Hebrews 10:32 and 6:4f. It is to be noted that the grouping of spiritual blessings in 6:4, 5 are benefits of the Holy Spirit. The enlightenment motif may also be present in the healing of the blind man in John 9, a story otherwise full of baptismal allusions and a favorite in the symbolism of baptism in early Christian art.[89]

The conception of the giving of the Holy Spirit was made concrete in the ceremony of anointing with oil, a traditional symbol of the Holy Spirit even in Biblical times. "The oil instead of the Holy Spirit"[90] is one writer's description of the outward action for the spiritual reality.

Not only was the term "sealing" applied to the anointing or signing with oil,[91] but it was also used of the invocation of the triune

---

[85]With reference to 1 Clem. 35, 36; 2 Clem. opening chapters; Hermas, *Sim.* 9:18:1; 16:3.

[86]*Apol.* 61, 65.

[87]Benoit, *op. cit.*, pp. 165-67.

[88]*De R. Carn.* 8. For baptism as an illumination see also *Acts of Judas Thomas* "Baptism of Siphor" (Greek version); Cyril, *Procat.* 1; Clem. Alex. *Paed.* I:25 (and often, for this is his favorite term).

[89]Oscar Cullmann, *Early Christian Worship* (SCM Press: London, 1953), pp. 102-105. F. van der Meer and C. Mohrmann, *Atlas of the Early Christian World* (Nelson: London, 1958), p. 127.

[90]*Apos. Const.* III:17. For this as the explanation of the name "Christian," see footnote 22. Ysebaert, *op. cit.*, pp. 340-367, has a large number of references, not all of which do I think are correctly interpreted.

[91]See note 81.

214

name at baptism.[92] Since the "seal" was a mark of ownership[93] and the baptismal formula signified the same thing, there was a mingling of motifs, a phenomenon not at all unusual.

The illumination was made vivid in the ceremony by leading the newly baptized out of the darkened baptismal chamber into a room filled with lights.[94]

CONCLUSION

The most frequent conceptions of the earlier second century—remission of sins and the bestowal of the Holy Spirit[95]—may fairly be considered the main themes of the New Testament in connection with baptismal blessings.[96] In time the new birth and the dying and rising with Christ assume the largest roles—perhaps because of a superficial similarity with the pagan mysteries. Remission of sins became explained in reference to original sin after the spread of infant baptism.[97] This practice also relegated the ideas of faith and repentance to a purely formal connection with baptism. The victory over Satan became attached to the pre-baptismal exorcisms and the bestowal of the Holy Spirit was attached to the post-baptismal rites of confirmation. Of the less common motifs the "seal" found its future in the sacrament of confirmation and other signings with oil, and "illumination" had its future as a theme in Christian mysticism.[98]

The use of early church literature in interpreting New Testament teaching has the danger of reading later concepts back into the New Testament. There is often the possibility that a writer is quoting a passage to support a later interpretation or practice without preserving the original meaning or framework or thought. Nonetheless, when used with discretion and critical skill the literature of the early church offers a valuable aid in New Testament interpretation and gives perspective to its total teaching. At the same time the New Testament balance may show the shifting emphases of later times and thus alert believers to the necessity of maintaining not only scriptural conceptions but also the scriptural relationships and proportions in regard to these conceptions.

---

[92]Perhaps in Ignatius, *Mag.* 5; Iren., *Dem.* 100; and Clem. Alex., *Strom.* V:12; more explicitly in Epiphanius, *Haer.* 76.20.12 and Tert., *De Bapt.* 6. Cf. Ysebaert, *op. cit.*, pp. 379ff. Revelation 14:1 and 22:4 compared with 7:2 may afford a New Testament indication of the "naming" at baptism as a "seal."

[93]Ysebaert, *op. cit.*, pp. 390-421.

[94]Perhaps the first indication of this practice is in the baptism of Gundaphorus in the *Acts of Judas Thomas.*

[95]Benoit, *op. cit.*, pp. 223f.

[96]Cf. Acts 2:38. This negative and positive treatment of conversion may also be seen as underlying the discussion in Romans and Colossians.

[97]J. N. D. Kelly, *Early Christian Doctrines* (Adam and Charles Black: London, 1960), p. 430.

[98]Jean Daniélou, *Platonisme et Théologie Mystique* (Seconde Edition, 1953), pp. 23-35. From the illumination motif the episode of the Burning Bush became a baptismal text.

215

It is seldom clear which came first—a ritual action (which came to be connected with a doctrine) or the doctrine (which was taught through the ceremony). Tertullian's embarrassment over the multiplication of rites in connection with baptism seems to be behind his separating the bestowal of the Holy Spirit from the remission of sins so as to give a doctrinal explanation to the existing rites of anointing and imposition of hands. An anointing was part of the regular bathing procedure. Also the taking off and putting on of clothes may be regarded as necessary parts of the rite to which doctrinal explanation was given. On the other hand, the giving of milk and honey may have been added to carry out a theme. Exorcism and blessing the water were extensions of ideas connected with the efficacy of baptism. The general course of religious history is that actions precede doctrines, and it may just be lack of information that prevents our seeing this sequence in each instance. Yet it is not unknown that ritual prescriptions were adopted as teaching devices; indeed much the same thinking is involved in giving doctrinal content to previously existing or necessary actions.

216

ARTICLE

CREEDS AND BAPTISMAL RITES IN THE FIRST FOUR CENTURIES

THE Western creed is by right of many centuries of usage correctly described as a baptismal creed. For a period which is but little shorter the Nicene Creed has been used throughout the Eastern churches as a baptismal confession and is probably based as a whole or in part on earlier confessions which were similarly used. This constant and deeply rooted connexion of the creeds with baptism during the most luminous period of their history has naturally led scholars to approach the question of the use and development of these formulae in the ante-Nicene period with assumptions derived from the later practice. The fact that the creeds are based on the threefold Name and that the baptizand from New Testament times onwards was required to make a confession of faith has seemed to justify these assumptions. The purpose of this article is to argue that our knowledge of the way in which credal forms were used in the baptismal rites of the earlier period is extremely limited, and that in fact the evidence tells against the presupposition that the usage established in the fourth century was operative in the second or even in the early third century. It will also be suggested how this result may affect our reading of the early evidence for the development of credal forms.

At the outset of our inquiry, one general consideration should be noticed. Few aspects of the life of the Church escaped significant change in the fourth century. In the new conditions of that period, ecclesiastical organization, the formulation of doctrine, the manner of dealing with heresy, and the development of liturgical forms all entered on a new phase. The tendency to uniformity and fixity both of doctrinal expression and of liturgical rites became marked throughout the Church. In looking back from this period to the earlier centuries it would be highly unscientific to fail to make due allowance for the special characteristics of post-Nicene Church life and practice. This would now be generally recognized in the sphere of the history of doctrine; it is coming to be recognized also in the history of the liturgy.[1] A similar principle ought to exercise a cautionary restraint when light is sought on the early development and use of credal forms from what is known of these subjects in the fourth century and later.

The evidence of this later period is clear on the points with which

---

[1] cf. E. C. Ratcliff in *The Study of Theology*, pp. 430-8.

B

we are mainly concerned. At Rome it was the established custom for candidates for baptism to recite the creed publicly before the congregation. Both Rufinus[1] and Augustine[2] make special reference to the public character of the recitation at Rome, and imply that the presence of the general congregation at this ceremony was a feature peculiar in their day to the custom of that church. Rufinus thinks that the vigilance of these large audiences has helped to preserve the Roman creed from changes in its wording, whereas in other churches, where the formal statement of faith was recited less publicly, additions had been made to the formula. This recitation or *redditio*[3] of the creed implies the existence of an exactly worded formula which was previously imparted to the candidate with some care in the ceremony which was probably already, and certainly later, known as the *traditio symboli*. It was essential that the formula should be recited exactly. The Roman liturgical books which describe in detail the pre-baptismal and baptismal liturgy of the succeeding centuries show the important place which the *traditio* and *redditio symboli* had come to hold. These ceremonies concerning the creed may have been less elaborate in the fourth century, but from the evidence of Rufinus and Augustine it is clear that they were established in essentials.

Nor were these customs a Roman peculiarity. They are implied (except for the public character of the *redditio*) for his own church of Aquileia by Rufinus. In the African church Augustine refers to a similar usage.[4] Ambrose mentions the *traditio* on the Sunday before Easter, and the later Gallican service books and writers of Spain and Gaul refer both to this and to the *redditio*, which took place on the Thursday in Holy week.[5] We are entitled to conclude that the practice of the *traditio* and *redditio symboli* was general in the West by the end of the fourth century.

In the East a similar practice prevailed in a number of churches.[6] The Catechetical Lectures of Cyril of Jerusalem constitute a *traditio* of the creed with detailed comments. The creed is to be learned by heart; it must not be written down, and catechumens must not overhear it.[7] He does not, however, refer to a formal *redditio*. The account of the rites and ceremonies of the Jerusalem church written by the pilgrim Etheria later in this century describes both ceremonies

---

[1] Rufinus, *Comment. in Symb. Apost.* 3.

[2] Augustine, *Confessions*, viii. 2. Distinguished converts could, however, be excused the ordeal of public recitation.

[3] Augustine, loc. cit., already uses *reddere* as a technical term.

[4] See, e.g., *de Symbolo Sermo ad Catechum.* 1.

[5] Duchesne, *Origines*, pp. 337 ff.

[6] But not in Egypt. The practice is unknown in the Coptic rites; cf. Kattenbusch, i, p. 330, note.

[7] *Cat.* v. 12.

in some detail.¹ The Council of Laodicea² (in Phrygia) prescribes that the φωτιζόμενοι shall learn the creed by heart (τὴν πίστιν ἐκμανθάνειν) and render it (ἀπαγγέλλειν) to the bishop or the presbyters on the fifth day of the week.³ What we know of Antiochene usage may be held to imply a similar practice. In the *Apostolic Constitutions*, vii. 41, a long creed is put into the mouth of the candidate immediately after the renunciation of Satan, and Cassian and Nestorius refer to the Antiochene creed and quote it in a way which implies that candidates for baptism had learnt it formally.⁴

This impartation of the creed to baptizands was hedged about with circumstances of solemnity and injunctions against writing it down and uttering it in the presence of the uninitiated, and all this laid emphasis on the sacred character of the formula. Its doctrinal contents were public property to anyone who cared to read Christian books or hear sermons, but the formula as a whole was to be the possession only of the baptized. It was the exact wording which was therefore sacred, and this was carefully preserved in each church.⁵

The liturgical *traditio symboli*, with all its implications, is such a widespread practice in the fourth century that its origin can hardly lie entirely in that century. But insufficient attention seems to have been given to points in the earlier evidence which warn us not to carry back the fourth-century practice very far. In the first place, the *traditio* and *redditio*, when we have clear evidence about them, form part of the preparation for baptism rather than of the baptismal rite itself. They are the culminating points of the instruction, and the *redditio* takes place either at an earlier hour on the day of baptism or some days before this. Though evidence about the early catechumenate is scanty, it is clear that in this century its whole organization reached a stage of elaboration which was quite unknown in the second, and only beginning to develop in the third century. If the *traditio* and *redditio* formed part of the preparation for baptism we may expect these practices to have grown up with the developing organization of the catechumenate as a whole. Further, it is to be noted that even in the fourth century the essential and effective confession of the baptizand is not the *redditio*, but the answers to the

¹ *Peregrinatio S. Silviae, C.S.E.L.*, vol. xxxix, c. 46. The candidates came one by one to the bishop sitting in his cathedra and ' rendered' the creed.
² Canon XLVI.
³ Probably Maundy Thursday, Duchesne, op. cit., p. 339.
⁴ The relevant passages are quoted in Lietzmann, *Symbole* (1931), pp. 22, 23.
⁵ In the West the title *symbolum apostolorum*, together with the legend of apostolic composition, helped towards the end of the fourth century to reinforce the sanctity ascribed to the words of the creed. In the East the sanctity of the formula rested on the fact that it was a summary of Scripture; cf. Cyril, *Cat.* v. 12.

interrogations[1] at the moment of baptism. We ought to approach the evidence of the earlier centuries with the possibility in mind that the *traditio* and *redditio* will be either altogether absent or only at a rudimentary stage.

Two passages of Dionysius of Alexandria first call for comment. He accuses[2] Novatian of having 'set at nought the holy washing, and the faith and confession which precede it' (τήν τε πρὸ αὐτοῦ πίστιν καὶ ὁμολογίαν). Kattenbusch and de Puniet[3] think this means that a creed was recited by the candidate before the act of baptism, and they find this confirmed by the short creed which is interpolated into the Egyptian versions of the *Apostolic Tradition* of Hippolytus immediately before the baptismal interrogations. If they are right, it must be noted that this creed as it stands is not the *redditio* of a formula which the candidate has previously learned, but is repeated by him after the minister.[4] Later Egyptian rites show no knowledge of the *traditio* and *redditio*.[5] Dionysius, however, may refer only to the question and response made before each of the three immersions. In another passage[6] he refers explicitly to these ἐπερωτήσεις καὶ ἀποκρίσεις as the point at which one of the congregation present at a baptism detected that his own baptism had been defective. When these points are considered together with the evidence of later Egyptian practice, Dionysius gives us no ground for assuming that in his day at Alexandria the baptizand formally recited a carefully rehearsed formula of belief.

In his denunciation of Novatianist baptism Cyprian[7] refers to the identity of the rite used by the schismatics with that of the Catholics, and rejects the argument that this makes their baptism valid. The fact that they are outside the church destroys any argument which might be drawn from the fact that they 'baptize with the same symbol' (*eodem symbolo quo et nos baptizare*) and 'appear not to differ in the interrogation' (*quod videatur interrogatione baptismi a nobis non discrepare*). A similar contention is put forward by Firmilian[8] of Cappadocia in a letter to Cyprian, which quotes the case of a mad woman who baptized using the 'symbol of the Trinity' and 'the lawful ecclesiastical interrogation' (*cui nec symbolum trinitatis nec*

---

[1] cf. de Puniet, art. 'Baptême', *D.A.L.C.*, col. 315 f. on Augustine's evidence. Cyril, *Cat.* xx. 4 describes the answers to the interrogations in the baptismal water as the σωτήριον ὁμολογίαν.

[2] apud Euseb. *H.E.* vii. 8.

[3] Kattenbusch, i, pp. 326 ff. and de Puniet, op. cit., col. 264.

[4] cf. Dix, *The Apostolic Tradition*, p. 35, c. xxi. 11 b. Dix, however, thinks in his note ad loc. that this interpolated creed was originally interrogative in form.

[5] Kattenbusch, i, p. 330.

[6] apud Euseb. *H.E.* vii. 9.

[7] *Ep.* lxix. 7.

[8] Cyprian, *Ep.* lxxv. 11.

interrogatio legitima et ecclesiastica defuit). The *symbolum* here might appear to refer to a creed recited by the candidate. Cyprian goes on, indeed, to quote from the baptismal confession, but it is part of the interrogation which he quotes and not a section of a declaratory creed. I have attempted in the JOURNAL[1] to interpret *symbolum* in these passages, and if that interpretation is correct the declaratory creed is not mentioned at all. The word refers to the baptismal act as a whole, interrogations, responses, and triple immersion or affusion, as the pledge of the covenant into which the baptizand enters with the Trinity. But even if that interpretation be rejected, and *symbolum* be taken to mean a credal form, it would be more natural to suppose that the reference is to the interrogations which occurred at the moment of baptism rather than to a declaration by the candidate before the ceremony, for which the expression *symbolo baptizare* would be a strange phrase.[2]

African evidence of a few decades earlier certainly strengthens our negative interpretation of that of Cyprian.[3] Tertullian's references to baptism are particularly frequent, and he has given us the one ante-Nicene treatise on the general significance of the rite. Kattenbusch, who has examined Tertullian's references with his usual meticulous care, expresses surprise[4] that he does not mention the *traditio* and *redditio symboli*. Since Kattenbusch is disposed to find evidence for these practices at this period, and expects to find it in Tertullian, it may be sufficient to quote his conclusions.

'It is remarkable that Tertullian fails to mention either the act of the *traditio* or that of the *redditio*. It is, however, probable that he knows at least the former. The *lex*, the *sacramentum*, and its definite *verba* must naturally be exactly imparted and imprinted, if they have the importance for faith which we have already observed above. From *de Spectac.* i we learn that a very exact instruction was envisaged, in which the *status fidei*, the *ratio veritatis*, together with the *praecepta disciplinae* were transmitted and elucidated. We may without more ado insert at this point also a solemn act of the *traditio symboli*. In view of Tertullian's silence it is doubtful whether there

---

[1] xliii. 1–11.

[2] *Symb. trinitatis* in Firmilian's letter is interpreted by both Kattenbusch, ii, p. 189 and de Puniet, op. cit., col. 293, as the triple immersion which is a token of the Trinity.

[3] The *de Rebaptismate* (probably African and contemporary with Cyprian) discusses (c. 10) the question of a true faith as affecting the validity of baptism and refers only to the interrogations and answers, not to a declaratory creed. 'Mysterium fidei tradant' (ibid.) does not refer to the *traditio symboli* but to the baptismal act; cf. ibid. 5 *mysterium fidei* (= baptism, as the context shows) and ibid. 10 *baptisma tradere*.

[4] Kattenbusch, ii, pp. 60–2.

was a definite liturgical act of the *redditio symboli*. The whole event of the positive confession seems to have been enacted in the water, in the form of the response to the questions.'[1] With regard to these interrogations, Kattenbusch concludes (a little reluctantly) that in view of expressions like *in sacramenti verba* (not *verbis*) *respondere* and *in legis verba profiteri*, it is likely that the minister recited the formula while the baptizand replied merely with a repeated simple *credo*.[2]

There is nothing to add to Kattenbusch's just conclusion on the absence of any *redditio symboli*. With regard to his assumed *traditio*, it is strange that one so legally minded as Tertullian does not mention this act if it was at all formal and usual. He does not even imply that the candidate was instructed in a formula to be learnt by heart. The 'exact instruction' of *de Spectac.* i, no doubt, means the instruction of catechumens, but not necessarily in a formula, and as to the *lex*, *sacramentum*, and *verba* of baptism, we learn what they are in de Baptismo xiii : *Lex enim tinguendi imposita est et forma praescripta. Ite inquit, docete nationes, tinguentes eas in nomen Patris et Filii et Spiritus Sancti.* Unless we are determined to find the *traditio* and *redditio* in Tertullian, his evidence would lead us to conclude that he knew of neither.

This radical conclusion is supported by the one full baptismal order preserved from the ante-Nicene period, namely, that in the *Apostolic Tradition* of Hippolytus.[3] This document gives a full account of the catechumenate (cc. xvi–xx), followed by the actual baptismal rite (c. xxi). The instruction of catechumens, which is to last three years, is described only in general terms, but from the point at which the candidates for baptism have been selected the description of the ceremonies becomes detailed (c. xx). There is no word which can be interpreted as referring to a *traditio* and *redditio symboli*. The baptismal rite itself is described in great detail and the words of the interrogation are given in full.[4] To each of the three sections of these the candidate answers with a simple *credo*, and after each response he is baptized once. The rite exactly corresponds with Tertullian's descriptions. In the Arabic, Ethiopic, and Sahidic versions of the *Apostolic Tradition*, immediately before the interrogations, there is inserted a creed which, as it stands, is a confusion of a declaratory and an interrogatory formula. Whatever its original form,

---

[1] Kattenbusch, ii, p. 62.

[2] cf. also *de Cor. Mil.* 3, 'dehinc ter mergitamur amplius aliquid respondentes quam dominus in evangelio determinavit'; *adv. Prax.* 26, 'nec semel sed ter, ad singula nomina, in personas singulas tinguimur'.

[3] ed. G. Dix, 1937.

[4] For the reconstruction of the Greek text of the interrogations see Connolly, *J.T.S.* xxv. 131–9.

it is an interpolation into the text of Hippolytus.[1] Similarly, the text as preserved in the *Testamentum Domini* and in the *Canons of Hippolytus* has interpolations of a short declaration by the candidate of belief in Father, Son, and Holy Ghost (c. xxi, 10a and 11a). It is clear that in the original text the candidate makes no detailed declaration of faith in his own words but simply assents to the interrogations made in detail by the minister.

The theology of Hippolytus was not representative of Roman Christianity in his day, and some of the language in the prayers of the *Apostolic Tradition* certainly expresses his own characteristic teaching,[2] but Dix[3] has given good reasons for supposing that the liturgical usage described in this treatise is a conservative account of that of the contemporary Roman church. The baptismal interrogations themselves differ by only a few words from what we know in the fourth century as the declaratory Roman baptismal creed.

In the case of Tertullian and Hippolytus, the argument from silence is strong enough to be held conclusive. The two principal churches of the West knew nothing of a *traditio* and *redditio symboli* in the first quarter of the third century. The question of the Roman usage is of particular importance, since Kattenbusch holds that 'the custom of the *traditio symboli* is bound up with R [the old Roman creed] which has its special character only in conjunction with this custom'.[4]

Second-century authors do not offer evidence to modify our conclusions. When Irenaeus speaks of the κανὼν τῆς ἀληθείας . . . ὃν διὰ τοῦ βαπτίσματος εἴληφε[5] he refers to the preparation for baptism in which the catechumen was instructed in Christian truth[6] (whether Scripture or unwritten 'tradition'). A body of teaching is implied but not a set form of words.[7]

In the light of our investigation it may fairly be questioned whether the assumption that the practices of the *traditio* and *redditio symboli* were established in the second and third centuries, is any more than an unjustifiable reading back of fourth-century custom into a period when it did not yet obtain. I propose to suggest how in general the raising of this question might bear on the study of the early history and development of credal forms.

The classical investigators of the history of the creed, Zahn,

---

[1] cf. Dix, ad loc. and p. lxii.
[3] op. cit., pp. xxxviii ff.
[4] Kattenbusch, ii, p. 961, note 4.
[2] Ratcliff, op. cit., pp. 422 ff.

[5] *adv. Haer.* i. 9, 4.
[6] For a conclusive treatment of the meaning of the κανὼν τῆς ἀληθείας and related expressions in Irenaeus see Ammundsen, *J.T.S.* xiii. 574 ff.

[7] In Clement and Origen Kattenbusch finds only very uncertain traces of the *traditio*, ii, pp. 116 and 155.

Harnack, Kattenbusch, and, in England, Burn, held that at least some churches in the West, and particularly Rome, had an official baptismal creed, certainly in the third century, and in the case of Rome for a great part of the second century also. This creed was an exactly worded formula which was carefully imparted to candidates for baptism as the proper form in which they must confess their faith at, or as a prerequisite to, baptism. It may be said that this conclusion was reached along three apparently converging lines of evidence: first, the actual quotation of the formulae in the fourth century and the known usage with regard to them at that period; secondly, the echoes of the formulae and apparent references to this usage in significant passages of the writers of the earlier centuries; thirdly, the character of the formulae themselves. The question we have raised in this article bears directly upon the first two points. We have seen that the fourth-century use of the creed in baptism may, on general grounds, be a later development, and further that such evidence as exists of earlier usage tells against the assumption that it coincided with the later. These doubts in turn affect our reading of the significance of the passages in the earlier authors which appear to echo (perhaps in a deliberately inexact manner) the fixed baptismal creed of the local church. If we are not entitled to assume that every church handed over to its baptizands a carefully guarded credal formula, we must go further and ask whether such an official formula existed. We may feel bound to consider seriously other possible explanations of the creed-like passages in the earlier authors than that adopted by the classical investigators mentioned above. More recent investigation has called attention to the great variety of such passages even in a single author, such as Irenaeus. If we do not confine our attention solely to passages which are of the type of the later Western creed, we find in fact a variety of *types* of summaries of belief.[1] Even in those statements which have the structure of the later formula, the wording varies, not only from author to author but in the same author, in a way which may be explicable as deliberate concealment if we presuppose a fixed baptismal creed, but which may be capable of other explanations apart from that presupposition. It is at any rate safe to say that no one could with any plausibility reconstruct the exact baptismal creed of any church from the writings of these authors, without the guidance of the later complete and exact forms.

We may have to test the hypothesis that for a period lasting well into the third century, there were current in the same locality a number of more or less stereotyped forms of summaries of the faith, outlines rather than formulae, which were used as the basis of instruc-

[1] Lietzmann, *Z.N.W.*, Bd. xxii (1923), *Symbolstudien*, x–xii.

tion, but not regarded as sacred formulae to be imparted to and retained by the catechumen with verbal exactness. This hypothesis explains the utterances of writers such as Irenaeus and Tertullian at least as satisfactorily as the more usual view that they are loosely referring to a fixed formula, which custom forbids them to quote exactly.[1] It is beyond doubt that stereotyped summaries of faith existed in the second and early third centuries; it is quite another thing to assume that one fixed and exclusive formula was recognized in each local church as the baptismal confession. Even with this re-orientation of approach to the history of the creeds, it remains possible to take the fourth-century formulae and argue to their date of composition from the evidence of their internal character. But when this can be done with any result,[2] we are still not entitled to assume that from the date of its composition this creed held an exclusive place in the church of its origin.

One point in the evidence we have examined earlier in this article may appear to destroy the cogency of these considerations. In the *Apostolic Tradition* of Hippolytus the baptismal interrogations differ but little in length, content, and wording from the Old Roman creed as we have it exactly quoted in the fourth century. In *Ep.* lxix. 7 and lxx. 2, Cyprian quotes a section of the African interrogations, *credis in remissionem peccatorum et vitam aeternam per sanctam ecclesiam?*[3] We do not know the extent of the earlier sections of the African interrogations, but since the passage just quoted shows that some additions had been made to the threefold Name, the earlier sections were probably more ample than the bare mention of the Three.[4] If the interrogations both in Rome and Africa had at this period reached this fullness of form, is it not probable that these churches had an equally full and precise declaratory creed, which was learnt by the baptizand before he responded to the interrogations? This is an important point, but should not be allowed without further

[1] Kattenbusch, ii, p. 101, concludes that the general *disciplina arcani* is unknown to Tertullian, but that he refrains from quoting the creed exactly in deference to the Christian feeling that it must not be written down. But where is the evidence for this feeling in any writer as early as Tertullian? Irenaeus, iii. 4, 1 (Katt. ii, p. 45) refers only to the *gentes barbarorum* who have no scriptures in their own tongue, but retain the true tradition written on their hearts by the Spirit. This is not evidence of a feeling against the writing of the creed but merely a proof that some Christians can and do hold the pure faith independently of the written tradition (the Scriptures).

[2] When this method is applied to the Old Roman Creed which alone seems to offer any substantial basis for it, the result is less precise and certain than has generally been supposed; cp. *J.T.S.* xl. 31 ff.

[3] In *Ep.* lxx. 2 the order of *remiss. peccat.* and *vit. aet.* is reversed.

[4] cf. Tertullian, *de Cor. Mil.* 3, 'amplius aliquid respondentes quam dominus in evangelio determinavit'.

consideration to outweigh the main result of our investigation. The interrogations mention points of teaching which must have been imparted to the catechumen in his instruction more fully and are here conveniently summarized. For his confession to be real and explicit it was not necessary for him to know the precise words in which it was to be formulated to him at the moment of baptism. The interrogations were the liturgical utterance of the minister of baptism and to judge from the analogy of other liturgical forms may have been beginning in the third century to assume a more stereotyped phraseology.[1] In baptism, however, the outlines of the formula were fixed by Matt. xxviii. 19. It was the threefold Name which mattered; the rest was added by way of explanation and amplification; and the minister may have felt free within the divinely commanded framework to vary the wording of his questions.[2] This is at least more in accordance with the liturgical spirit and practice of the second century than any contrary assumption.[3] There may well have been interaction between the form of the interrogations and current catechetical formulae, just as there was between these formulae and the language of liturgical prayer, but later variations between the interrogations and the contemporary creed forbid us to assume that the two forms have a completely parallel history. Thus at Rome, Milan, and Turin[4] for a century and more after the baptismal creed had come to be regarded as a fixed apostolic formula, the contemporary interrogations differed from it considerably. What we should naturally expect is that, like other liturgical words, the amplifications of the threefold Name which formed the interrogations were in the third century becoming more fixed in the local churches. The evidence of Cyprian here supports what would otherwise be a probability of analogy. Certainly in his time there was a *legitima et ecclesiastica interrogatio*, with the *usitata et legitima verba*,[5] which provided the candidate with the opportunity of formally confessing the faith in which he was baptized. The movement towards fixity was in progress.

At some point in the same century there arose the practice of instructing the candidate verbally in a confession of faith which he

---

[1] cf. Hippolytus, *Apostolic Trad.* x. 3–5, on extempore Eucharistic prayer.

[2] Thus Canon VIII of the Council of Arles (314) orders that, if a heretic desires to come into the Church, they are to 'put the baptismal interrogations to him' (*interrogent eum symbolum*). If he acknowledges the threefold Name, he is to be regarded as already baptized.

[3] cf. Connolly, *J.T.S.* xxv. 137. 'At the beginning of the third century the Roman creed was probably not so rigid in its formulation but that the personal element may still have had some play.'

[4] cf. the formulae quoted by Kattenbusch, i, p. 51; p. 100, note 17; and p. 101, note 1.

[5] *Ep.* lxxv. 10, 11.

was required to repeat exactly as a condition of baptiśm. The interrogations were not in consequence superseded in their function, nor
necessarily altered in their customary wording, except perhaps in the
direction of greater fixity and exactness. As regards the question
where the practice of the *traditio symboli* originated, it is possible
here only to express an opinion that the fourth-century evidence
points to the West rather than the East, and in the West to Rome.
The date can hardly be later than the second half of the third century
and may even fall in its second quarter.[1]

In his recent series of *Symbolstudien*[2] Lietzmann has examined
afresh the evidence for the early history of the creeds. Although he
has not discussed the particular question of the use of the creed with
which this article has been mainly concerned, it may be said that the
suggestions for a fresh approach to the early evidence which we have
been led to put forward as a result of inquiry on this particular point
are substantially supported by his independent examination of the
evidence in detail. Briefly, Lietzmann finds the second century
prolific in summaries of the faith, some Christological, some based
on the threefold Name, and some having yet other structural forms.
Within the similar forms the details and emphasis varied. No writer
down to and including Tertullian can be quoted as showing exclusive
attachment to one structural form of summary, much less to one
exact formula. Gradually, however, certain forms and finally a certain
formula attained exclusive predominance locally. To this general
picture drawn by Lietzmann we can now add the point that the
local victory of the particular formula was completed and rendered
permanent by the establishment at some time in the third century of
the practice of the *traditio* and *redditio symboli*; first, perhaps, in
Rome, then in other Western churches and in the East.[3]

H. J. CARPENTER

[1] *The Apostolic Tradition* was probably written about A.D. 217 or shortly
before. See Dix, op. cit., p. xxxv. The composition of R and the institution
of the *traditio* do not necessarily coincide in date. R may have existed before
it attained the exclusive place which the *traditio* gave it.

[2] H. Lietzmann, *Symbolstudien*, i–xiv, in *Z.N.W.* Bd. xxi, xxii, xxvi. See
esp. Bd. xxvi, pp. 84–95. The general results are given in the second volume
of his recent history of the early Church, *Ecclesia Catholica*, c. 4.

[3] The 'baptismal formula' in the more modern sense of the term ('I baptize
thee, &c.') has not been brought into our discussion, since there is no evidence
for its use in the early centuries. See de Puniet, loc. cit., cols. 340–4. The
interrogations were the baptismal formula.

The History of the Baptismal Formula

by E. C. WHITAKER

Vicar of Kirkby-in-Furness, Lancashire

1. Types of baptismal formula.

Among the many forms which were used by the early Church to accompany the baptismal washing we may certainly count those forms which are at present in use in the eastern and western Church. At a later stage in this study we shall examine their origin and ancestry. First it is necessary to draw attention to certain other forms which are attested by the Fathers in their writings and liturgical remains, and which appear to have been invested at one time with the same importance and to have fulfilled the same purpose as the formula which is universally used to-day.

The lost work of Hippolytus known as *The Apostolic Tradition* is the first document in point of time to furnish a detailed account of the Church's baptismal rites. The text of this work has been reconstructed by Dom Gregory Dix,[1] and although its origins and background remain uncertain, especially since J. M. Hanssens's study[2] of it, we need not doubt the substantial accuracy of Dix's reconstruction, at least as far as concerns the baptismal rite and the forms which surround the act of the baptismal washing. The *Apostolic Tradition* attests a situation in which the candidate for baptism is asked, as he stands in the water, 'Dost thou believe in God the Father Almighty?' He replies, 'I believe', and his head is then immersed in the water by the deacon who accompanies him. Two further questions follow, relating to the second and third Persons of the Trinity, and each question is followed by the answer, 'I believe', and by a second and third immersion. No other spoken words accompany the baptismal washing, and we must draw the inference that these credal questions, together with their answer, constitute for Hippolytus the decisive form in the sacrament, since it is they above all else which indicate the Christian character of the act which is performed. Apart from varying credal details an identical practice is indicated in the *Testamentum Domini*,[3] which is an edition of the *Apostolic Tradition*, by St. Ambrose,[4] and in the *Gelasian Sacramentary*.[5]

A variant of this form is possibly attested by the *Tractates concerning*

[1] *The Treatise on the Apostolic Tradition*, London 1937.
[2] *La Liturgie d'Hippolyte*, Rome 1959.
[3] Cooper and Maclean, *The Testament of our Lord*, Edinburgh 1902, 226.
[4] *De Sacramentis*, ii. 7. 20.
[5] H. A. Wilson, *The Gelasian Sacramentary*, Oxford 1894, 116 f.

I

Baptism ascribed to Maximus of Turin, but probably[1] written by some other North Italian bishop c. 550. In this case the three questions are asked of the candidate and their answer is received before the candidate goes down into the water. This is the reasonable interpretation which J. H. Crehan[2] has placed upon the words: '*In hoc ergo fonte antequam vos toto corpore tingeremus, interrogavimus: Credis . . .?*', which are followed later in the same tractate by the sentence: '*Haec autem quae hucusque diximus, postquam vos credere promisistis, tertio corpora vestra in sacro fonte demersimus*'.[3] The same practice is most probably indicated in the relevant passage in the paschal liturgy of the *Gelasian Sacramentary*. The passage runs: '*Inde benedicto fonte baptizas unumquemque in ordine suo, sub has interrogationes:*

> *Credis in Deum Patrem Omnipotentem?*
> *Resp. Credo.*
> *Credis et in Jesum Christum, etc?*
> *Resp. Credo.*
> *Credis et in Spiritum Sanctum, etc?*
> *Resp. Credo.*

Deinde per singulas vices mergis eum tertio in aqua'.[4]

The interpretation of this passage appears to depend on the meaning which we assign to the word *deinde* and to the phrase *per singulas vices*. If *per singulas vices* is to be translated 'each in his turn', as Crehan would have it,[5] *deinde* will take its natural meaning 'then', and we infer that the triple interrogation came first and was followed by the triple washing. But if *per singulas vices* means 'at each interrogation', the implication is that question and answer alternate with the washings. One difficulty of this is that it leaves the word *deinde* without any meaning: another is that it implies a triple washing after each question. It seems better, therefore, to conclude that Crehan is right when he argues that the triple interrogation preceded the triple washing in this case. Such a practice might have developed from that attested by Hippolytus on practical grounds, because it was found more convenient where large numbers of candidates were involved, or it might have had an independent origin of equal antiquity.

It appears that a similar practice of credal question and answer was followed by the Church in Africa. Thus the first 'canon' of the Council of Carthage (c. 342) includes the following passage: 'I ask your holinesses to consider whether a man who has gone down into the water and has been interrogated about the Trinity (*interrogatum in Trinitate*) according to the faith of the gospel and the apostles' doctrine, and has confessed a good confession towards God concerning the resurrection of Jesus Christ— whether he may be questioned again about the same faith and be immersed again in the water'.[6] There are indications, however, that the

---

[1] *Revue Bénédictine*, xlv (1933), 108 f.
[2] *Early Christian Baptism and the Creed*, London 1950, 122.
[3] P.L., lvii, 775–8. [4] Op. cit., 86. [5] Op. cit., 83n.
[6] F. Lauchert, *Die Kanones der wichtigsten altkirchlichen Concilien*, Leipzig 1896, 152. See also Cyprian, *Ep.* lxix, 2, 7; Tert., *De Spect.*, 4.

2

practice in Africa and elsewhere may have involved some variation in detail upon the practice represented in the *Apostolic Tradition* or in the *Gelasian Sacramentary*. Thus, when Tertullian says: 'We are thrice immersed, replying somewhat more fully than the Lord has appointed in the gospel',[1] we may wonder whether the questions and answers, and particularly the answers, followed quite the same course as they did elsewhere when the answer was a simple *Credo*. Similarly, the anonymous *De Rebaptismate* poses the problem of ignorant or unlettered bishops 'who may not have spoken clearly or honestly (*integre*), or even have spoken otherwise than is fit in the tradition of the sacrament, or at least may have asked anything, or asking may have heard from them that answered what ought by no means to be so asked or answered'.[2] If the candidate's only reply were a simple *Credo* it would not allow him much room for improper answers. A similar uncertainty about the character of the responses is raised by the eighth canon of the Council of Arles, which reads: 'With regard to the Africans, forasmuch as they practise rebaptism according to their own regulations, it is decided that if anyone comes to the church out of heresy they should address to him the symbol questions (*interrogent ei symbolum*). If they perceive that he has been baptised in the Father and the Son and the Holy Spirit, it will only be necessary for a hand to be laid upon him so that he may receive the Holy Spirit. But if on being questioned he does not answer with this Trinity (*non responderit hanc Trinitatem*), he should be baptised'.[3] These passages suggest that the responses to the credal interrogations may sometimes have been a recitation of the creed in its declaratory form.

The 'Egyptian Church Order'[4] provides evidence of yet another practice whereby the formularies of faith were employed in baptism. According to the Ethiopic version (the others do not vary significantly), the candidate stood in the water and was instructed in the words of an affirmative creed[5]: 'I believe in one God, etc.'. To this the candidate was to reply: 'I believe', and then three times, after each immersion, he was again to say: 'I believe'. At this point his baptism was presumably complete, but before he came up from the water a credal interrogation was addressed to the candidate, who replied: 'Yea, I believe in this'.

Another Egyptian work which demands a brief notice is the *Canons of Hippolytus*.[6] This attests the same practice as the *Apostolic Tradition* of which it is a derivative, that is to say, it prescribes an interrogation, reply, and immersion, thrice repeated, but with a significant difference. The canon directs the officiant to say after each immersion: 'I baptise thee in the name of the Father and of the Son and of the Holy Spirit'. There can be no doubt that this formula is an interpolation into the primitive text,

---

[1] *De Cor. Mil.*, iii.
[2] P.L., iii, 1194, c. 10.
[3] Mansi, ii, 472.
[4] *The Statutes of the Apostles*, ed. G. Horner, London 1904, 153, 254, 317.
[5] But in the Arabic version the creed is interrogative.
[6] Achelis, *Die Canones Hippolyti*, Leipzig 1891 (*Texte und Untersuchungen*, vi, 4), 97.

3

for it is clear that it represents a development upon the original practice described in the *Apostolic Tradition*.

This survey has revealed some variety in detail in the forms which the Church has employed to accompany the baptismal washing. The important feature, which all have in common, is that invariably the triple washing of baptism was accompanied by credal forms to which the candidate gave his assent and which vindicated the Christian character of the sacrament. The view that for many parts of the Church these credal forms and their answer constituted the essential baptismal formula was first propounded by Dom Pierre de Puniet,[1] and has won wide acceptance. Johannes Brinktrine[2] and J. H. Crehan[3] have sought to deny this opinion, but their arguments proceed ultimately from the assumption that the forms which the Church uses today are of universal obligation as being the only ones which have dominical sanction. It is a fact, however, that the literature of the Latin Church provides no clear and incontestable reference to our modern *forma* earlier than the *De Cognitione Baptismi*[4] of Hildephonsus of Toledo, which was written at some date before his death in 667; and that the earliest Roman reference is in a letter[5] written by pope Gregory II in the year 726. On the other hand, whenever the Fathers of earlier centuries make reference to the core and heart of the rite, mention is invariably made of the interrogations and their answers, but never of any other formulary.[6] Again, the absence of the modern formula from the *Gelasian Sacramentary* and, apparently, from the *Apostolic Tradition* must indicate simply that it was not known, or at least that it was not used, by their compilers. There is no other satisfactory explanation. To explain their absence by reference to the *disciplina arcani* is to mistake the character of the *Apostolic Tradition*, for Hippolytus does not hesitate to set out a model eucharistic prayer and the formularies of consignation, and to forget that the *disciplina arcani* had ceased to have any meaning when the *Gelasian Sacramentary* was compiled. We may think, also, that it invests the *disciplina arcani* with more significance than it deserves. There is, in any case, a passage[7] in the second *Tractatus de Baptismo* ascribed to Maximus of Turin which we may think decisive in the matter. It reads: 'And so, before we immersed your whole body in this font, we asked: Dost thou believe in God the Father Almighty? You answered: I believe. Again we asked: and dost thou believe in Jesus Christ . . .? One by one you replied: I believe. Again we asked: and dost thou believe in the Holy Ghost? You replied likewise: I believe. This we did in accor-

---

[1] *D.A.C.L.*, ii, pt. I, col. 336 f.
[2] *Ephemerides Liturgicae*, xxxvi (1922), 328–37.
[3] *Early Christian Baptism and the Creed*, 72 f., 118 f.
[4] P.L., xcvi, 158. [5] P.L., lxxxv, 525.
[6] It is true that there are a number of passages in the *De Rebaptismate* which speak of 'baptism in the name of Jesus Christ', but Dom Gregory Dix argued convincingly that the reference in these passages is to the formula which in the Hippolytean rite accompanied the post-baptismal administration of oil, viz. 'I anoint thee with holy oil in the name of Jesus Christ'. See G. Dix, *The Theology of Confirmation in Relation to Baptism*, London 1946. [7] P.L., lvii, 775.

4

dance with the command (*iuxta imperium*) of our Lord Jesus Christ, who gave commandment saying: "Go and baptise all nations in the name of the Father and of the Son and of the Holy Ghost"'. Here we have the plainest imaginable statement that the writer regards the interrogations and their answers as the fulfilment of the dominical command in the Great Commission, and that when an individual had descended into the water and answered the Trinitarian interrogations, he had indeed been baptised in the name of the Father and of the Son and of the Holy Ghost.[1]

In setting out the antecedents of the particular *forma baptismi* which the Church uses to-day it will be convenient to start from three courses of catechetical addresses which were all written in Syria at very much the same date. St. John Chrysostom, in a course of Lenten lectures delivered at Antioch in the year 390 or thereabouts, refers to the form 'Such an one is baptised in the name of the Father and of the Son and of the Holy Ghost', and goes on to comment upon it in the following words: 'He does not say "I baptise such an one", but "Such an one is baptised", showing that he is only the minister of grace . . . He who accomplishes everything is the Father and the Son and the Holy Ghost'.[2] St. John Chrysostom's contemporary, Theodore of Mopsuestia, makes exactly the same point,[3] and offers the same reason, and so a few decades later does Narsai.[4] All three writers specifically attest both of those forms which today we call eastern and western. Although, as we shall see, there are earlier attestations of the formula in its active 'western' form, these three writers are the first to make reference to the passive form. Crehan may, therefore, possibly be right when he detects in these passages an anxiety to justify a practice which was felt to be a novelty.[5]

It is not, however, to be assumed without proof that the copious references in the early Syrian literature to baptism 'in the name of the Father and of the Son and of the Holy Ghost' such as we find in the *Didache*,[6] St. Matthew's Gospel,[7] and many other sources, must necessarily imply the use of either of these forms. The possibility must not be ignored that the reference in such passages may be theological rather than liturgical, and has regard to the Trinitarian character of the sacrament rather than to its liturgical forms. Nevertheless, the proof exists that the formula as we have it today existed at an early date in Syria, and in its active, so-called western form. Thus the *Acts of Xanthippe and Polyxena*,[8] which was written in the middle of the third century, contains the passage: 'And Paul said, "We baptise thee in the name of the Father and of the Son and of the Holy Ghost"'. Similarly, in the *Acts of Paul and Thecla*,[9] written in

---

[1] See, however, Crehan, op. cit., 122.
[2] A. Wenger, *Huit catéchèses baptismales* (Source Chrétiennes, 1, 147).
[3] A Mingana, *Woodbrooke Studies*, vi, 59 f.
[4] *Texts and Studies*, viii, pt. I; R. H. Connolly, *The Liturgical Homilies of Narsai*, 51.
[5] Op. cit., 79.   [6] *Didache*, vii.   [7] Mt. xxviii, 19.
[8] *Texts and Studies*, ii, 3; M. R. James, *Apocrypha Anecdota*, 73.
[9] Lipsius and Bonnet, *Acta Apostolorum Apocrypha*, i, 260.

5

the middle of the second century, Thecla is represented as baptising herself and saying, 'In the name of Jesus Christ do I baptise myself for the last day'. If we may assume that we have here a case of a formula in ordinary use adapted to extraordinary circumstances, then it appears that the formula in ordinary use must have been 'I baptise thee in the name of Jesus Christ'. This not only brings our evidence for a baptismal formula of this type to a very early date; it also strengthens the view, suggested in the *Acts of the Apostles*, that an invocation of Jesus Christ had a place in the baptismal practice of the early Church. These two passages alone provide clear evidence that the modern *forma baptismi* existed in Syria from a very early date; and they justify the conclusion that the many other references to 'baptism in the name of the Father and of the Son and of the Holy Ghost' in the literature of the Syrian Church must be understood not only as theological but also as liturgical statements.[1]

2. Geographical distribution.

Hitherto our survey has brought to light a variety of forms which the early Church used in the performance of the baptismal washing, and it appears clearly that they divide themselves into two main types. There is the type which alone survives to this day in the East and West, the Trinitarian formula pronounced by the officiant alone. We will venture to call this the Syrian type of formula, since we have seen that its history is connected with the Syrian Church from a very early date. The other type involved the use of fuller and more specifically credal formularies which called for the spoken assent of the candidate. These credal formularies appear generally to have been of an interrogative kind, although we have observed one instance in which a creed was used in an affirmative manner. We shall call this the Western type of formula and shall show evidence that it was universally used outside Syria. We may suppose that it is of equal antiquity with the Syrian formula, for it is difficult to imagine that if the Syrian type was used by the earliest church communities anywhere else it would have been supplanted by the more complex type of formula. It is necessary, therefore, to complete our survey in order to set out the evidence that the Western type which is now obsolete was once in general use throughout the whole Church with the solitary exception of Syria.

St. Cyril of Jerusalem attests the use of an interrogatory form in the closest connexion with the baptismal washing. He says: 'After this then ye were led to the holy pool of divine baptism . . . and each of you was asked whether he believed in the name of the Father and of the Son and of the Holy Ghost, and ye made that saving confession and descended three times into the water and ascended again'.[2] From Caesarea in Cappadocia Firmilian, in a letter to Cyprian, speaks of a possessed woman who 'baptised many, arrogating to her own use the customary and legitimate

---

[1] For a fuller study of the Syrian formula, see E. C. Whitaker, 'The Baptismal Formula in the Syrian rite', *C.Q.R.*, clxi (1960), 346–52.
[2] *Cat. Myst.*, ii, 4.

6

words of interrogation, so that she appeared not to depart from the ecclesiastical rule'.[1] For North Italy we have already quoted the evidence of the *Tractate concerning Baptism* ascribed to Maximus of Turin and referred to a passage of Ambrose, both of which clearly attest the use of the interrogatory form. We have also observed evidence that the African Church made use of a similar form. The use of the Western type of formula in the Gallican Church is indicated by the eighth canon of the Council of Arles (314), which we have already quoted. At a much later date (c. 800) the *Stowe Missal*,[2] which is a composition from Roman and Gallican sources, does not include the Syrian formula, though it reproduces the same interrogations which we have already quoted from the *Gelasian Sacramentary*. From this we may infer that the Gallican source of the *Stowe Missal*, which appears to have been a document of some antiquity, did not include the formula. The *Missale Gothicum*, which was written about the year 700, provides one of the earlier Western attestations of the Syrian formula, but it is preceded by a rubric which seems to preserve a trace of the more ancient custom of interrogating the candidate in the water. It reads: '*Dum baptizas interrogas ei et dicis baptizo te illum in nomine Patris et Filii et Spiritus Sancti in remissionem peccatorum ut habeas vitam eternam*'.[3]

Spain provides no evidence of a baptismal formula of the Western type, and none of the Syrian type before the sixth century at the earliest.

There is sufficient evidence to demonstrate the use of the interrogatory formula at Alexandria without resorting to the *Apostolic Tradition*. Most notable is a passage in the *Ecclesiastical History* of Rufinus in which he describes an incident in the youth of Athanasius.[4] As a boy, Athanasius had been 'playing at baptism' with some other boys and in the course of their play had baptised some catechumens. The bishop instituted an inquiry to determine whether in fact the catechumens had been baptised. Rufinus says that the bishop 'carefully examined those who were said to be baptised, asking them what questions they had been asked and what replies they had made: and at the same time he questioned him who had put the questions. When he saw that everything was in accordance with the rites of our religion, he is said to have conferred with a council of clergy and to have pronounced that baptism should not be repeated upon those over whom water had been poured out with perfect questions and answers, but that only those things should be repeated which are customarily done by bishops (*sacerdotibus*)'. We could have no clearer statement than this that the credal questions and answers were regarded as the valid and effective form in baptism. An earlier example of the practice of Alexandria is supplied in a letter written about 250 by Dionysius of Alexandria to pope Xystus. He wrote: 'One who is reckoned faithful among the brethren ... had been present at a recent baptism and heard

---

[1] *Ep.*, lxxv of the Cyprianic corpus.
[2] G. F. Warner, *The Stowe Missal* (H.B.S., xxxii), London 1915, 31.
[3] H. M. Bannister, *Missale Gothicum* (H.B.S., lii), London 1917, item 260.
[4] P.L., xxi, 487.

7

the questions and answers at that service. He came to me weeping . . . and protesting that the baptism he had received among heretics was not this nor had anything in common with it'.[1]

The evidence of the *Gelasian Sacramentary* is sufficient to show that the Roman Church employed the interrogatory form until a relatively late date: no earlier Roman evidence exists except that of Justin Martyr, and that is too imprecise to support any firm conclusions.

3. The expression 'forma baptismi'.

Although several passages may be cited from the early patristic writings in which the expression *forma baptismi* or *forma baptismatis* is used, it does not follow that it had the same technical connotation then that it has to-day. Thus, when St. Ambrose wrote: '*Non sanat aqua nisi Spiritus descenderit et aquam illam consecraverit, sicut legisti quod, cum Dominus noster Jesus Christus formam baptismatis daret, venit ad Iohannem . . .*',[2] we may best translate the phrase *forma baptismatis* as 'pattern of baptism': in any case it is clear that it does not refer to the baptismal formula as we understand it to-day. St. Ambrose used the same expression in yet another sense in the same work when he wrote: '*Descendit Christus, descendit et Spiritus Sanctus. Quare prior Christus descendit, postea Spiritus Sanctus, cum forma baptismatis et usus hoc habeat tu ante fons consecretur et tunc descendat qui baptizandus est?*',[3] for here he plainly meant what we mean to-day when we speak of the Order of Baptism, referring to the rite as a whole. Similarly, pope Leo wrote: '*Nam hi qui baptismum ab hereticis acceperunt, cum antea baptizati non fuissent, sola invocatione Spiritus Sancti per impositionem manuum confirmandi sunt, quia formam tantum baptismi sine sanctificationis virtute sumpserunt*',[4] and clearly referred to the sacrament in all its exterior aspects.[5]

Amidst this variety of use it is not impossible that some writers might by chance have used the expression in something approaching its modern technical sense, to denote the spoken words regarded as essential to the sacrament. In fact, there exist at least two passages in which the word *forma* is used in approximately this sense. Thus Tertullian wrote: '*Lex enim tinguendi inposita est et forma praescripta. Ite inquit docete nationes tinguentes eas in nomine Patris et Filii et Spiritus Sancti*'.[6] At first sight this passage might seem to suggest that Tertullian was accustomed to the formula 'I baptise thee in the name of the Father and of the Son and of the Holy Ghost', and that this was the *forma praescripta*. In the light of our other knowledge of Western and African practice, however, this seems most improbable: a more reasonable interpretation of the passage is that it was the Trinitarian scheme of the interrogations which Tertullian had in mind and regarded as the form prescribed in the gospels. The second passage which may be cited in this connexion is Canon 110 of the African

[1] Eusebius, *H.E.*, vii, 9. See also Origen, *In Numeros Homilia*, v, i: P.G., xii, 603.
[2] *De Sacr.*, i. 5. 15. [3] Ibid., i. 5. 18.
[4] *Ep.*, clix, 7: P.L., liv, 1138 f.
[5] See also Augustine, *De Pecc. Mer. et Rem.*, xxxiv, 63: P.L., xliv, 146.
[6] *De Bapt.*, xiii.

8

Codex, *Quod parvuli in peccatorum remissionem baptizentur*.[1] It reads: '*Item placuit ut quicumque parvulos recentes ab uteris matrum baptizandos negat, aut dicit in remissionem quidem peccatorum eos baptizari, sed nihil ex Adam trahere originalis peccati, quod lavacro regenerationis expietur, unde fit consequens, ut in eis forma baptismatis in remissionem peccatorum non vera sed falsa intelligatur: anathema sit*'. The words *in remissionem peccatorum*, as they appear in this canon, are known to be an exact quotation from the customary interrogations in Africa, as we learn from the letters of Cyprian. Writing of heretical baptism, Cyprian says: '*Nam cum dicunt, "credis in remissionem peccatorum et vitam eternam per sanctum ecclesiam?", mentiuntur in interrogatione, quando non habeant ecclesiam*'.[2] It is difficult to avoid the conclusion that when the canon uses the expression *forma baptismatis* it does so to refer to the customary interrogations, the verbal part of the sacrament.

The medieval analysis of a sacrament into its *materia* and *forma* corresponds, no doubt, to a reality which has existed from the beginning. But it would be an anachronism to suppose that the phrase *forma baptismi* was generally accepted by the Church in the third century as a technical expression with the same connotation that it has to-day. The examples of its use which we have quoted show that when it was used in its modern sense it was a coincidence.

4. *The spread of the Syrian formula in the West.*

It is reasonable to regard the adoption of the Syrian formula in Rome as the token of its establishment in the West, although, in fact, the Stowe Missal[3] shows that in at least one remote corner of Christendom the ancient form of the West survived until the beginning of the ninth century. Evidence of the use of the Syrian formula in Rome is first attested by a letter of pope Gregory II to Boniface in the following passage: '*Enimvero quosdam absque interrogatione Symboli ab adulteris et indignis presbyteris fassus es baptizatos. In his tua dilectio teneat antiquum morem ecclesiae, quia quisquis in nomine Patris et Filii et Spiritus Sancti baptizatus est, rebaptizari eum minime licet. Non enim in nomine baptizantis, sed in nomine Trinitatis, huius gratiae donum percipitur*'.[4] The date of this letter is 726, and so we may infer that the Syrian formula had been adopted at Rome at some time before then, but not so long ago that Boniface was not troubled at the absence of the interrogations. The *Bobbio Missal*, the *Missale Gothicum*, and the *Missale Gallicanum Vetus* all show that the Syrian formula was in use in the Gallican Church by the year 700, which is the approximate date when they were written. The form in the *Bobbio Missal* reads: '*Baptizo te in nomine Patris et Filii et Spiritus Sancti unam abentem (habentium?) substantiam ut habeas vitam eternam parte cum sanctis*';[5] in the *Missale Gothicum*: '*Baptizo te illum in nomine Patris et Filii et Spiritus Sancti in remissionem peccatorum ut habeas vitam*

---

[1] Bruns, *Canones Apostolorum et Conciliorum*, Berlin 1839, i, 188.
[2] *Ep.*, lxix, 7. [3] G. F. Warner, ed. cit., 31.
[4] P.L., lxxxix, 525.
[5] E. A. Lowe, *The Bobbio Missal* (H.B.S., lviii), item 248.

9

eternam';[1] and in the *Missale Gallicanum Vetus*: *'Baptizo te credentem in nomine Patris et Filii et Spiritus Sancti'*.[2] From these forms we note that local churches in the West felt free to decorate the basic form with their own additions, as was also done in the East. The opposition to Arianism which is implied in the form from the *Bobbio Missal* may suggest a date appreciably earlier than 700. According to M. Andrieu,[3] the phrase *ut habeas vitam eternam*, which appears in the *Bobbio Missal* and the *Missale Gothicum*, is a sign of Spanish influence: it is certainly true that this phrase in this context is attested by Hildephonsus of Toledo some fifty years earlier. The testimony of Hildephonsus[4] to the use of the Syrian formula at Toledo is perfectly clear and we may regard his evidence as valid for about the year 650.

There is room for the opinion that the Syrian formula was in use in the Spanish peninsula at a much earlier date in at least some places. Thus, in the letter *De Trina Mersione*,[5] written by St. Martin of Braga in 579, St. Martin defends his own practice in the performance of the sacrament by claiming that the same practice was observed at Constantinople by legates from Braga one Easter, and there can be no doubt that what the legates heard at Constantinople would be the Syrian formula. There are certain obscure and enigmatic passages in St. Martin's letter which call for special study. Here it must be sufficient to suggest that the explanation of them may well be found in the statement of Alcuin[6] that some of the Spanish exponents of triple washing were accustomed to repeat the entire Syrian formula three times, once with each washing. Independent evidence of such a practice, in a rubric which is plainly designed to correct it, is to be seen in the supplement to the *Gregorian Sacramentary*.[7] It seems very probable from the terms of St. Martin's letter that the practice was already known in his day as a matter of controversy. Martin also quotes in support of his own practice the letter[8] which pope Vigilius had written in 538 to his predecessor Profuturus. The second paragraph of this letter appears to relate to the baptismal formula. Vigilius quotes the example of heretics who add to the Psalms the ascription *'Gloria Patri et Filio, Spiritui Sancto'*. Against them he adduces the text of the Great Commission in St. Matthew's gospel, and concludes: *'Ergo, cum non dixerit: In nomine Patris et Filii, Spiritus Sancti, sed aequalibus distinctionibus Patrem et Filium et Spiritum Sanctum jusserit nominari, constat illos omnino a doctrina dominica deviare, qui aliquid huic voluerint confessioni derogare. Qui si in errore permanserint, socii nobis esse non possunt'*. Now this paragraph of Vigilius's letter is written specifically in answer to some question about baptism, although

---

[1] E. A. Lowe, op. cit., item 260.
[2] P.L., lxxii, 369.
[3] M. Andrieu, *Les Ordines Romani du haut moyen-age*, iii, Louvain 1948, 89.
[4] *De Cognitione Baptismi*, c. 112: P.L., xcvi, 158.
[5] C. W. Barlow, *Martini Ep. Brac. opera omnia*, Yale 1950, 251f.
[6] P.L., c, 342.
[7] Ed. H. A. Wilson (H.B.S., xlix, London 1915), 163.
[8] P.L., lxix, 15.

10

it is not clear what the question was. But it seems impossible to interpret it except on this assumption: that some Spanish heretics, who are described in the clause *qui aliquid huic voluerint confessioni derogare*, had been baptising with a perversion of the Syrian formula, using the words '*In nomine Patris et Filii, Spiritus Sancti*'. If this is correct we may conclude that since heretics in Spain were using the Syrian formula, albeit in a perverted form, no doubt the Catholics may have been using it also, and at a date not later than 538.

It seems that Alexandria provided the bridge by which the Syrian formula made its way from East to West. We have already examined the evidence which shows that the original practice of Alexandria was to use the credal interrogations as their formula in baptism. Evidence for a change in practice comes earlier from Alexandria than from anywhere else. A clear notice of the Syrian formula, in its Western, active form, is provided by an Alexandrian priest, Ammonius, in a fragment which survives from his *Commentary on the Acts of the Apostles*. The passage in question compares the baptism of John with Christian baptism and reads: 'When John baptised, he said "I baptise thee into him that cometh after me . . ."., But he that baptised in the Faith says: "I baptise thee in the name of the Father and of the Son and of the Holy Ghost"'.[1] Varying estimates of when Ammonius lived assign this evidence to the period 450–550. Another piece of Alexandrian evidence is provided in the *Canonical Responses* of Timothy of Alexandria. The thirty-eighth response[2] enjoins the use, on appropriate occasions, of the conditional formula: 'If thou hast not been baptised, I baptise thee in the name . . . etc.'. If it was certain that this response was the genuine work of Timothy it would bring our earliest evidence for this formula, outside Syria, to approximately the year 380: but, in fact, we cannot confidently assign it to a date earlier than the late fifth century.[3]

There remains one strong reason for supposing that the Syrian formula made its way into Alexandrian use not later than the middle of the fifth century. We have noted that the Alexandrian attestations are of the personal, active, form. We noted earlier that, as early as 390, St. John Chrysostom expressed his disapproval of this form and that his contemporaries followed him, and in fact later Syrian literature provides no evidence of the active form. We may, therefore, reasonably suppose that if the Syrian formula had been adopted in Alexandria any later than about 450 it would have been in its Eastern, impersonal, form.

5. The reasons for the abandonment of the ancient western formula.

The credal interrogations never lost their place in the baptismal rites of the Western Church, where they continued in their position immediately

[1] P.G., lxxxv, 1594.
[2] I. B. Pitra, *Iuris Ecclesiastici Graecorum Historia et Monumenta*, Rome 1864, 635.
[3] Bardenhewer, *Geschichte der altkirchlichen Literatur*, iii, 104; F. E. Brightman, *J.T.S.*, i (1899), 248n.

I I

before the sacramental washing—until archbishop Cranmer disfigured the Anglican rite by moving them to a different position. Nevertheless, the letter of Gregory II, which we have already quoted, suggests that as early as his day they had ceased to be regarded as the *forma* in baptism, and in this respect their place had been taken by the form which had made its way from Syria throughout the Western Church. The reason why the West should thus abandon her ancient form is a matter for pure speculation, since history is silent upon the point. One possibility is that the simpler form from Syria was found to be more suitable for infant baptism. So long as adults were commonly baptised, for whom their baptism was a notable and decisive occasion, no doubt the solemnity of the credal interrogations was valued: when infant baptism became the norm, the ancient form which demanded the assent of the candidate may have come to seem clumsy, inappropriate and inconvenient. Another possibility is suggested by the fact that the Syrian form lends itself to adjustment for the purpose of conditional baptism, which the interrogatory form does not. Possibly it is no accident that one of our earliest notices of the Syrian form in the West, in the *Canonical Responses* of Timothy of Alexandria, is in its conditional sense.

INSCRIPTIONS AND
THE ORIGIN OF INFANT BAPTISM

JOACHIM JEREMIAS gave considerable attention to the inscriptional evidence in presenting his history of infant baptism in the early church.[1] K. Aland's reply to Jeremias showed that the inscriptions add nothing to what is known from literary sources concerning the time when infant baptism began. Christian inscriptions commence in the third century and by that time infant baptism is already attested.[2] Aland appears to have confirmed the judgement of early twentieth-century critical scholars that there is no certain evidence for the practice of infant baptism before the late second century.[3]

Aland argued that the introduction of infant baptism is to be attributed to a belief in original sin. A change in attitude toward children from regarding them as innocent to regarding them as tainted with sinfulness can be seen in Origen and Cyprian.[4] This change combined with a decline in eschatological expectations that the Lord would return before children passed from an age of innocence made baptism a necessity.[5]

Aland's theological explanation of the origin of infant baptism, however, has not held up as well as his historical arguments. Why the retreating eschatological expectation did not affect the practice of baptism until late in the second century is not clear. The eschatological outlook was the strongest in North Africa where infant baptism had its earliest and most widespread acceptance.[6] More significantly, the eschatological atmosphere could be argued as working in the opposite direction. Jeremias suggested that it was the understanding of baptism as an eschatological sacrament which made it plausible for children as

---

[1] *Die Kindertaufe in den ersten vier Jahrhunderten* (Göttingen, 1958), pp. 49 f., 59 f., 88–95, 100 f., 105–7; English translation, *Infant Baptism in the First Four Centuries* (London, 1960), pp. 41 f., 55 f., 75–80, 85, 89 f. Some points are reaffirmed more briefly in *Nochmals: Die Anfänge der Kindertaufe* (München, 1962), pp. 42–6; English translation, *Origins of Infant Baptism* (Studies in Historical Theology, London, 1963), pp. 49–53.

[2] *Die Säuglingstaufe im Neuen Testament und in der Alten Kirche*, Theologische Existenz Heute, 86 (München, 1961), pp. 48–53; English translation, *Did the Early Church Baptize Infants?* (London, 1963), pp. 75–9.

[3] Jeremias acknowledges that there is no *provable* evidence before Tertullian—*Nochmals*, p. 5 (= *Origins*, pp. 9 f.).

[4] *Säuglingstaufe*, p. 75 (= *Did the Early Church*, pp. 103 f.).

[5] Ibid. pp. 77 f. (106); *Taufe und Kindertaufe* (Gütersloh, 1971), pp. 37–9.

[6] W. H. C. Frend, *Martyrdom and Persecution* (Oxford, 1965), p. 418.

[Journal of Theological Studies, N.S., Vol. XXX, Pt. 1, April 1979]

well as their parents to receive this sign of salvation before the imminent overthrow of the present world order.[1]

The relationship between infant baptism and original sin appears, as Jeremias noted, to be the reverse of that stated by Aland.[2] The practice of infant baptism was an argument for infant sinfulness rather than infant guilt being the basis for infant baptism (at least in the early sources). The argument of Augustine in this regard is well known. The practice of baptizing infants was by his time general and was one of his strongest points against the Pelagians.

> The inevitable conclusion from these truths is this, that, as nothing else is effected when infants are baptized except that they are incorporated into the church, in other words, that they are united with the body and members of Christ, unless this benefit has been bestowed upon them, they are manifestly in danger of damnation. Damned, however, they could not be if they really had no sin. Now, since their tender age could not possibly have contracted sin in its own life, it remains for us, even if we are as yet unable to understand, at least to believe that infants inherit original sin.[3]

Cyprian and Origen introduced the idea of a stain or pollution attaching to birth and did so in the context of a consideration of infant baptism. Cyprian speaking for the North African bishops in favour of conferring baptism immediately after birth and not waiting until the eighth day says:

> If forgiveness of sins is granted, when they afterwards come to believe, even to the worst transgressors and to those who have previously sinned much against God, and if no one is held back from baptism and grace; how much less ought an infant to be held back, who having been born recently has not sinned, except in that being born physically according to Adam, he has contracted the contagion of the ancient death by his first birth. He approaches that much more easily to the reception of the forgiveness of sins because the sins remittted to him are not his own, but those of another. (*Ep.* lxiv [lviii]. 5)

The line of argument is that if baptism is not denied to the worst of sinners, it should not be denied (or delayed) to the new born. Cyprian recognizes that they have no sins of their own; therefore, he can only refer the forgiveness to the sins of Adam. By his birth the infant contracts the death which Adam's sins brought into the world, and so in a

---

[1] *Kindertaufe*, p. 28 (= *Infant Baptism*, p. 23); *Nochmals*, pp. 69–72 (= *Origins*, pp. 83 f.).

[2] *Nochmals*, p. 62 (= *Origins*, pp. 73 f.).

[3] *De pecc. mer. et rem., et de bapt. parv.* III. 39; cf. I. 23, 28, and 39; III. 2; *C. Julian. Pel.* III. 5. 11; *De gratia Chr. et de pecc. orig.* II. 2–4.

sense the infant is in touch with Adam's sins.[1] Origen more explicitly indicates that the idea of baptizing infants raised the question, 'For the forgiveness of whose sins?' His answer does not move much beyond the idea of a ceremonial or physical impurity associated with birth.

I take this occasion to discuss something which our brothers often inquire about. Infants are baptized for the remission of sins. Of what kinds? Or when did they sin? But since 'No one is exempt from stain,' one removes the stain by the mystery of baptism. For this reason infants also are baptized. For 'Unless one is born of water and the Spirit he cannot enter the kingdom of heaven.'[2]

The movement is clearly from the existing practice to the doctrine and not from the doctrine to the practice.[3] Whatever influence the doctrine of original sin had in establishing a fairly uniform practice after Augustine's time, it seems not to have been the reason for the introduction of infant baptism.

If we are convinced by Aland that there is no sure evidence for infant baptism before Tertullian, and if we agree with Jeremias that original sin was not the explanation for its origin, then we are obligated to offer an alternative explanation. One who is not willing to use theology to fill in the blanks left by history will not be satisfied to stop where the researches of Jeremias and Aland have left us.

It is here that the inscriptions may offer assistance. Although most of the inscriptions are difficult to date and those which carry dates are later than the time for which there is literary testimony to the practice of infant baptism, they do reveal the popular Christian religious sentiments. They indicate the motives operative in infant baptism. They give a specificity and scope of evidence which the surviving literary records do not provide.

The collection by E. Diehl affords an excellent instrument by which to study the Latin evidence.[4] The Greek Christian inscriptions do not yet have a comparable corpus, so the same comprehensiveness is not possible in studying them.[5] A consideration of the inscriptions as a

---

[1] J. Pelikan, *Development of Christian Doctrine* (New Haven, 1969), pp. 79–87. It is usually assumed that Cyprian is talking about normal practice, but in view of the evidence presented below one may raise a question whether this is a discussion only about the age for emergency baptism.

[2] *Hom. Luc.* XIV. 5. Cf. *Hom. Lev.* VIII. 3 with reference to Job xiv. 4 and Ps. li. 5 and *Comm. Rom.* V. 9 with reference to Lev. xii. 8 and Ps. li. 5 in justification for baptizing infants for the remission of sins.

[3] N. P. Williams, *The Ideas of the Fall and of Original Sin* (London, 1927), pp. 220–6.

[4] *Inscriptiones latinae christianae veteres* (2nd edn., Berlin, 1961). Numbers will be to this edition unless otherwise stated.

[5] See the collections on this subject by J. C. Didier, *Le Baptême des enfants*

whole leaves some unmistakable impressions. Moreover, they suggest a specific setting in which infant baptism took its rise and which is consistent with the surviving literary evidence.

Only those inscriptions which undeniably refer to baptism and state when it was conferred permit definite conclusions. Inscriptions employing the terms 'in peace', 'innocent', and 'believer' have not been found especially helpful in themselves for determining the age of baptism. *In pace* has often been appealed to as an indication that the person was baptized and so died 'in the peace' of the church. There are many cases where this is likely,[1] but if one assumes the sinlessness or innocence of children, there is no reason why *in pace* would not be used of children apart from baptism. That there was no necessary connection between dying or resting 'in peace' and baptism may be seen from Diehl no. 1509B: 'Boniface, a hearer in peace, who lived 1 year and 4 months.' The child evidently had been enrolled as a catechumen, died unbaptized, but 'in peace'.

The word 'innocent' (*innocentia*) had no necessary suggestion of sinlessness. As well as being used of children from infancy on,[2] it is even used of quite elderly persons: 'more or less 50 years' (no. 3444, A.D. 397), 36 years old (no. 461), and even 80 years old (no. 2932). Did these persons die recently baptized? More likely the meaning is 'blameless', 'upright'.

'Believer' or 'faithful' (*fidelis*, πιστός) means 'baptized' and is used of persons of varying ages: an infant (no. 3160), 4 year old (1334), 8 year old (1349), 33 year old (1347), etc.[3] Unless specifically stated, no firm conclusions can be drawn as to when the person became a 'believer'. The wording of an inscription like 1366 (near Aquileia) makes one think of an emergency baptism, but this is not explicit:

To the divine dead. For the well-deserving son Covoideonus who lived 9 years, 2 months, 7 days. Buried December 28. He departed a believer in peace. His grieving parents made this according to a vow.

No doubt attaches to the important 1549, now in the Louvre and dated *c.* A.D. 314:

dans la tradition de l'église, Monumenta Christiana Selecta VII (Tournai, 1959) and H. Kraft, *Texte zur Geschichte der Taufe, besonders der Kindertaufe in der alten Kirche* (2nd edn., Berlin, 1969).

[1] Notably is this the case where a *fidelis* is said to have lived in peace (*vixit in pace*) for a given period of time—nos. 1346, 1348, 1349, 1349A, 1351, 1372, 1381A, *et al.* Fidelis in pace was characteristic of North Africa (LeBlant, *Rev. Arch.*, 1881, p. 240).

[2] No. 3489 has a brother 11 years old and a sister 2 years old whose 'innocent souls deservedly went to God, assured of eternal life'.

[3] The word 'Christian' is rarer than 'believer' and I have not found it applied to children.

Her parents set this up for Julia Florentina, their dearest and most innocent infant who was made a believer. She was born a pagan on the day before the nones of March before dawn when Zoilus was censor of the province. She lived eighteen months and twenty-two days and was made a believer in the eighth hour of the night, almost drawing her last breath. She survived four more hours so that she entered again on the customary things. She died at Hybla in the first hour of the day on September 25. . . .[1]

Little Julia was baptized clearly because she was on the point of death, and that accords with the information in a great many inscriptions.

The word baptism is rare, but the ceremony is referred to by such expressions as 'made a believer' (*fidelis facta*, as in no. 1549 above), 'received grace', and neophyte. One of the earliest dated inscriptions to allude to baptism is quite typical of the later inscriptions: no. 3315, dated A.D. 268, from the catacomb of Callistus.

Pastor, Titiana, Marciana, and Chreste made this for Marcianus, a well-deserving son in Christ the Lord. He lived 12 years, 2 months, and . . . days. He received grace [*crat(iam)* (*sic*) *accepit*] on September 20 when the consuls were Marinianus and Paternus the second time. He gave up (his soul) on September 21. May you live among the saints in eternity.

From Diehl's numbers 1523–43 the following are pertinent:

1523 (Salona, late 4th century)—For Flavia, dearest infant, who with sound mind obtained the grace [*gratiam consecuta*] of the glorious font on Easter day and survived after holy baptism five months. She lived 3 years, 10 months, 7 days. The parents, Flavian and Archelais, for their pious daughter. Burial on the 18th of August.

1524 (Rome, early 4th century)—*IXΘYC N(εοφωτιστων?)* Postumius Eutenion, a believer, who obtained holy grace the day before his birth day at a very late hour and died. He lived six years and was buried on the 11th of July on the day of Jupiter on which he was born. His soul is with the saints in peace. Felicissimus, Eutheria, and Festa his grandmother, for their worthy son Postumius.

1525 (Capua, A.D. 371)—Here is laid Fortunia, who lived more or less 4 years. The parents set this up for their dearest daughter. She obtained (grace) on July 27 . . . and died on July 25 [*sic*, evidently the workman exchanged the dates]. Gratian for the second time and Probus were the consuls.

1527 (Rome)—The boy Maurus, age five years and three months, was buried on the nones of August. He obtained grace at two or three.

---

[1] See observations by Christine Mohrmann, 'Encore une fois: *paganus*', *Vigiliae Christianae* 6 (1952), pp. 113 f.

1528 (North Africa)—. . . obtained (the grace) of God on December 5 and lived in this world after the day of obtaining until December 7 and died. . . .

1529 (Rome)—For the well-deserving Antonia Cyriaceti who lived 19 years, 2 months, 26 days. Received (the grace) of God and died a virgin on the fourth day. Julius Benedictus her father set this up for his sweet and incomparable daughter. November 20.

1530 (Rome—Blessed Crescentine, my dear sweet wife, who lived 33 years, 2 months. She received (grace) on June 29 and was buried on October 27. Well-deserving.

1531 (Rome, Catacomb of Priscilla, third century)—Sweet Tyche lived one year, 10 months, 15 days. Received (grace) on the 8th day before the Kalends. . . . Gave up (her soul) on the same day.

1532 (Rome, Catacomb of Priscilla, third century)—Irene who lived with her parents 10 months and 6 days received (grace) on April 7 and gave up (her soul) on April 13.

1535 (Rome)—To the divine dead. For Euphrosune, dear wife of Kampano, who lived with him 12 full years, 2 months, 5 days. She passed away in her 35th year. After the day of her receiving (grace) she lived 57 days.

1536a—For the well-deserving Simplicius who lived 51 years and after his reception (of grace) 27 days. Buried on February 1 in peace.

1539 (Rome, Catacomb of Domitilla, A.D. 338)—In the consulship of Ursus and Polemius the girl named Felite, more or less 30 years old, obtained (grace) on March 26 and died in peace after April 29 on the day of Mercury at the 9th hour.

1540—Euphronia, daughter of Euphronius and her mother, killed in a shipwreck. Born November 1, obtained (grace) April 11, died May 1.

Diehl's numbers 1477–1507, as well as many others, use the word 'neophyte' ('newly baptized') for the deceased. Where ages are given they are mostly young. A few examples may be cited:

1477 (Rome, St. Agnes outside the walls, A.D. 348)—Flavius Aurelius, son of Leo, marvellously endowed with the innocence of generous goodness and industry, who lived 6 years, 8 months, 11 days. A neophyte, he rested (in peace) on July 2 in the consulship of Julius Philip and Sallias. . . .

1478 (Rome, A.D. 370)—For the well-deserving Perpetuus in peace, who lived more or less 30 years. . . . Buried April 13, died a neophyte. . . .

1478A (Rome, A.D. 371)—For Romanus, well-deserving neophyte, who lived 9 years, 15 days. May he rest in the Lord's peace. Flavius Gratian Augustus for the second time and Petronius Probus consuls.

1480 (Rome, A.D. 385)—In the consulship of Flavius Arcadius and Baudone on the 22nd of June died Leontius a neophyte who lived more or less 28 years, 5 months, 15 days. Well-deserving, in peace.

1481 (Rome, A.D. 389)—Aristo, an innocent child, who lived 8 months, a neophyte, departed on June 4, Timasius and Promotus being consuls.

1484 (Rome, Catacomb of Callistus)—Innocentius a neophyte lived 23 years.

1484B (Rome, Cemetery Cyriacae)—For Paulinus, a neophyte, in peace, who lived 8 years.

1484C (Ravenna)—For Proiectus, an infant neophyte, who lived 2 years, 7 months.

1485A (Rome, Catacomb of Pontianus)—For Domitian, innocent neophyte, who lived 3 years, 30 days. Buried May 24.

1485B (Rome, Catacomb of Praetextatus)—Mercury a neophyte is buried here. He lived 42 years, 2 months, 15 days. Eugenia while she lived made this.

1485C (Rome, Catacomb of Praetextatus)—Pisentus, an innocent soul, who lived 1 year, 8 months, 13 days, a neophyte, buried on September 13 in peace.

1485D (Rome, Capitoline Museum)—For the dear son Casiacinus who lived six years and 3 days, a neophyte, buried on May 5. Well-deserving, in peace.

1487—For Zosimus, who lived 5 years, 8 months, 13 days, neophyte in Christ. Donatus his father and Justa his mother for their well-deserving son.

1488B (Naples)—For the well-deserving Eugenia of happy memory who lived not 19 years, a neophyte.

2764 (Rome, Catacomb of Callistus)—For Felix, a well-deserving son, who lived 23 years, 10 days. He departed a virgin with reference to the world and a neophyte in peace. His parents made this. Buried August 2.

Neophytes could come in all ages: from 24 days (no. 1497) or 80 days (4462B) to 42 years (1483) or 59 years (3352).

A few of the deceased are described as catechumens instead of neophytes. Diehl's no. 1508 (dated A.D. 397) is a 60-year-old catechumen. No. 1509A from Rome reads, 'Lucilianus for his son Bacius Valerius who lived 9 years, 8 months, 22 days, a catechumen'. Note 1509B quoted above about a 'hearer' who died in peace.

The Greek inscriptions which have been brought into the discussion yield the same picture.

CIG IV. 9810—Achillia, a neophyte, fell asleep in her first year, fifth month, on February 24.

CIG IV. 9855—Here lies Macaria, daughter of John of the village Nikeratos. She lived 3 years, 3 months, 16 days. She died a believer on the 24th of the month Sandikou in the 11th consulship of Honorius Augustus and 2nd of Constantius.[1]

It is noteworthy that all of the inscriptions which mention a time of baptism place this near the time of death. The explicit inscriptional evidence is not an argument for infant baptism as the normal practice. Rather, the evidence points to the opposite conclusion. The inscriptions do not tell the whole story, but as far as they go they provide an argument that in the third and fourth centuries infant baptism was abnormal. All of the above cited examples may be considered cases of 'emergency baptism'. Death was near, and the person received baptism 'on his death-bed' as it were. Jeremias has pointed to the practice of the delay of baptism in the fourth century,[2] but the third century inscriptions show the same practice. Why is baptism not mentioned except when it was administered near death? Any effort to argue from silence will be subjective. Instead of trying to fill in the silence in the archaeological record with conjectures (as has been done with the literary record), we should listen to what the existing evidence is saying. The newborn were not routinely baptized in the period of our early inscriptions. Baptism was administered before death, at whatever age. This fact offers the most plausible explanation of the origin of infant baptism. One early inscription says it explicitly:

Sacred to the divine dead. Florentius made this monument for his well-deserving son Appronianus, who lived one year, nine months, and five days. Since he was dearly loved by his grandmother, and she saw that he was going to die, she asked from the church that he might depart from the world a believer. (Diehl, no. 1343, from the Catacomb of Priscilla, third century.)

The discussion centring on the likelihood that the father was a pagan and the bearing of this on the baptism has diverted attention from the most important thing which this inscription has to say, namely the desire that the child die a 'believer', i.e. 'baptized'. Why was there this

---

[1] The other Greek inscriptions introduced by Jeremias do not help: the Zosimus inscription (*Kindertaufe*, p. 59 [= *Infant Baptism*, p. 56]) actually gives no information on the time of baptism, and the Dionysius inscription (*Kindertaufe*, p. 90 [= *Infant Baptism*, p. 77]) gives no indication of baptism.

[2] *Kindertaufe*, pp. 102–7 [= *Infant Baptism*, pp. 87–91]. Jeremias argues that the third century examples (nos. 1611C, 1343, 3891C, 1531, 1532, 3315) are children of non-Christians. This seems unlikely: why then were they baptized and buried in a Christian cemetery? At least the parents would have been catechumens. We may leave this question aside as we look for the motivation.

strong desire, reflected in all the 'emergency baptisms' above, even though baptism was not administered earlier?

Since the inscriptions are epitaphs, reception of baptism must have been considered an important preparation for the after-life. As the inscriptions indicate, the approach of death was the occasion for the baptism. Many children must have died unbaptized, and so the urge for baptism soon after birth became strong. I would suggest that John iii. 5 (cited by Origen above) supplied the biblical basis for the Christian concern about children in the after-life. This logion was the favourite baptismal text of the second century.[1] John Chrysostom continued to defend infant baptism in terms of its positive benefits while rejecting a doctrine of original sin.

You have seen how numerous are the gifts of baptism. Although many men think that the only gift it confers is the remission of sins, we have counted its honors to the number of ten. It is on this account that we baptize even infants, although they are sinless, that they may be given the further gifts of sanctification, righteousness, filial adoption, and inheritance, that they may be brothers and members of Christ, and become dwelling places for the Spirit.[2]

John iii. 5 has remained a proof-text for infant baptism in the Catholic tradition. The universal understanding of baptism as for the remission of sins gave impetus to the doctrine of original sin which then in turn became the theological basis for infant baptism.

John iii. 5 could be thought as debarring any unbaptized person from heaven. Baptism was the rite which assured a blessed hereafter. The request from parents (or a grandparent, as above) for baptism for a gravely sick child would be natural and would be hard to refuse. Even an opponent of infant baptism like Tertullian appears to allow for emergency baptism as a regular practice.

It follows that deferment of baptism is more profitable, in accordance with each person's character and attitude, and even age; and especially so as regards children. For what need is there, if there really is no need, for even their sponsors to be brought into peril. (*De bapt.* 18.4)

Tertullian stood at the point where there was pressure from some to extend the emergency measure to other circumstances. It is not uncommon for emergency procedures to become regular practice. That is, I submit, what happened here. If baptism was a necessary precaution

---

[1] Hermas, *Sim.* IX. xvi. 3; Justin, *Apol.* I, 61; Theophilus, *Ad Autol.* II. xvi; Irenaeus, *Adv. Haer.* III. xvii. 1 f.; Clement of Alexandria, *Strom.* IV. xxv; Tertullian, *De bapt.* 12.

[2] *Bapt. Lect.* III. 6. Cf. Gregory Nazianzus, *Carmina* I. i. 9, lines 87–92.

before death, it would be easy to make the precautionary measure normal, especially as it gained the support of powerful theological reasons. The initiative in infant baptism, therefore, lay with parents of sick children who asked of the church that they might not die unbaptized. These parents then gratefully recorded the fact of the baptism at the burial site.

The practice of baptism before death exerted an influence in two directions. The association of baptism with the time of death might cause baptism to be put off until the end of life, so that its saving benefits could be applied to the entire life. Thus occurred the delay of baptism which became a problem in the fourth century. Baptism in adult years when there was no immediate threat of death, to be observed in the lives of several prominent church leaders in the fourth century, however, was not the same thing as the death-bed baptism of Constantine and others. On the other hand, the desire to die baptized, or to have one's children die baptized, could exert an influence in the opposite direction. The high mortality rate of infants in the ancient world, to which the Christian inscriptions are a powerful if mournful witness, would encourage the practice of giving baptism soon after birth as insurance no matter what might happen. The inscriptions say that it was in such natural, human feelings that we are to find the real origin of a practice which later acquired such significant theological support.

EVERETT FERGUSON

UNE ADAPTATION DE LA LITURGIE BAPTISMALE
AU BAPTÊME DES ENFANTS
DANS L'ÉGLISE ANCIENNE

Dans une communication sur « L'initiation à Rome dans l'antiquité et le Haut Moyen Age » donnée au Centre de Pastorale liturgique et parue dans le cadre d'un volume de la collection « Lex orandi [1] », M. le Pr A. Chavasse a signalé brièvement l'adaptation des rites baptismaux que rendait nécessaire la généralisation du baptême des enfants. Il note en particulier l'évolution de la discipline des scrutins et la substitution de la formule baptismale actuelle aux anciennes interrogations sur la foi, substitution qui est chose acquise, à Rome, au VIIe siècle.

C'est un fait : le rituel baptismal s'est constitué originellement en fonction des seuls adultes et son évolution en vue de l'adapter aux tout-petits jusqu'à la pratique actuelle s'avère longue et complexe ; elle s'est manifestée à toutes les étapes de la liturgie baptismale et elle n'a pas manqué de tâtonnements et de gaucheries.

Ainsi, par exemple, on sait qu'à Arles, au temps de l'évêque saint Césaire (+ 542), les parents devaient amener leurs bébés aux *vigiliae* préparatoires au baptême et se plier en leur lieu et place à toutes les obligations du catéchuménat, le jeûne entre autres : *qui filios suos baptizari desiderant, jejunent, ad vigilias suas frequentius veniant* [2].... Ces exigences se situaient d'elles-mêmes dans la logique de la thèse augustinienne de « la foi des autres », substitut de la profession personnelle de foi dont l'enfant était incapable. Mais naturellement bien des parents ne témoignaient pas d'un grand enthousiasme pour ces démarches qui, malgré leur caractère traditionnel, ne répondaient plus à grand' chose dans le présent, et ils s'en dispensaient facilement. D'où les véhéments reproches de leur évêque à l'égard surtout, des mères négligentes ou peu scrupuleuses [3]. Les enfants ne risquent-ils pas, quand on les présentera plus ou moins subrepticement au baptême, de n'avoir pas reçu les rites du catéchuménat et d'être baptisés irrégulièrement [4] ? Au XIIe siècle encore, les *Sententie divine pagine* éprouveront le besoin de mettre au point cette question en précisant que les rites préparatoires au baptême ne lui sont pas essentiels [5].

1. (Symposium), *Communion solennelle et profession de foi* (« Lex Orandi », 1.), Paris, 1952, pp. 13-32 ; voir encore : Histoire de l'initiation chrétienne des enfants de l'antiquité à nos jours, *La Maison-Dieu*, nº 28, 1951, pp. 26-44.
2. *Serm.* 225, 6 (édit. MORIN, I, 2, p. 846). Cf. notre dossier du *Baptême des enfants dans la Tradition de l'Église* (désormais cité « Dossier »), Tournai-Paris, 1959, p. 130.
3. *Serm.* 84, 6 (édit. MORIN, I, 1, p. 333). Cf. Dossier, p. 129.
4. *Serm.* 229, 6 (édit. MORIN, 1, 2, p. 865).
5. « Cum autem quedam observantie et quedam proparationes fiant in baptismo, ut quod infans catekizatur, post adiuratur, post inducitur ad ecclesiam, queritur

Un Théodulfe d'Orléans, en 812, tout en maintenant le catéchuménat pour les tout-petits au nom des anciens usages, se rendait bien compte qu'il fallait autre chose [1]. La solution à intervenir se trouvait, d'une part, dans une simplification des rites ou du moins dans leur condensation en une seule cérémonie ; d'autre part et surtout dans l'organisation d'un enseignement religieux qui attendît l'âge où s'éveille la conscience, pour s'adresser aux enfants baptisés.

On sait combien « la première moitié de l'époque carolingienne est marquée, dans l'Église franque, par un effort énergique pour propager l'instruction religieuse. Sous l'influence de Charlemagne, les évêques se préoccupent de répandre les connaissances qui, de nos jours, sont contenues dans le catéchisme ; de nombreux textes des capitulaires, des conciles et des statuts diocésains attestent cette tendance [2] ». C'était vouloir répondre en grande partie à la situation nouvelle créée par un pédobaptisme généralisé. Que cet enseignement, au reste, ne se soit pas instauré sans peine, le concile de Paris de 829 nous le laisse clairement entendre en son sixième canon : « Aux origines de la sainte Église de Dieu, nul n'était admis à recevoir le saint baptême s'il n'avait été au préalable instruit du mystère de la foi et du baptême.... Mais parce que la foi chrétienne est partout en honneur et que les petits enfants nés de parents chrétiens reçoivent les sacrements du baptême avant d'atteindre l'âge de raison, il faut que cet âge de raison s'empresse d'apprendre ce dont le bas âge était incapable. Le fait qu'il s'éloigne de la pratique de la religion chrétienne par l'incurie de certains, on ne peut assez dire quelle négligence et quel péril il représente [3] ».

Beaucoup d'autres observations seraient à noter, du point de vue liturgique, sur le baptême des enfants. Si, comme nous l'avons dit plus haut, le rituel baptismal s'est constitué, à l'origine, en fonction des adultes, très tôt cependant on jugea bon, par exemple, de ne pas faire attendre les enfants et de leur donner un tour de faveur : au début du IIIe siècle, Hippolyte les fait passer avant les adultes [4].

an sine istis sit baptismus. Dicunt quidam quod non est, et hoc volunt habere ex verbis ipsius Christi dicentis : Ite, docete baptizantes eos ; non simpliciter dixit, baptizantes, sed prius iubet docere, per quod volunt habere illas preparationes. Nesciunt enim omnes, quod ille preparationes non sunt necessarie ad baptismum, sed sola invocatio Trinitatis dicendo : Baptizo te in nomine Patris et Filii et Spiritus Sancti, sed sunt ad ornatum ecclesie et decorem domus ». (F. BLIEMETZRIEDER, *Anselmus von Laon systematische Sentenzen*, Munster i-W., 1919, p. 44 ; cf. Dossier, p. 130, note *a*).

1. « Infantes ergo et audientes et catechumeni fiunt, non quo in eadem aetate et instrui et doceri possint, sed ut antiquus mos servetur.... Quia ergo parvuli, necdum ratione utentes, haec minime capere possunt, oportet ut cum ad intelligibilem aetatem pervenerint doceantur.... » *De ordine baptismi* 1 *et* 7 (*P. L.*, **105**, 224 ; Dossier, p. 140).

2. Paul FOURNIER, Notions sur trois collections canoniques inédites de l'époque carolingienne, *Revue des sciences religieuses*, 1926, p. 514.

3. « Monumenta Germaniae Historica », *Concilia* II, 2, p. 614 ; Dossier, pp. 147-148.

4. *Tradition apostolique*, 21 (Coll. : « Sources chrétiennes », p. 46 ; Dossier, p. 19).

L'on pourrait s'attarder aussi à décrire la lenteur et les tâtonnements qui caractérisèrent le passage de l'immersion à l'ablution [1] ou l'évolution des piscines qui, de dimensions disproportionnées à l'enfance [2], se réduisirent à n'être plus que de petites cuves, peu symboliques, hélas, du mystère de l'eau vive. Plusieurs points encore pourraient nous retenir : la date du baptême et l'avènement du « quamprimum [3] », la conception nouvelle du parrainage [4], la réorganisation des scrutins [5]. Nous choisirons de nous arrêter, ici, à la seule profession de foi baptismale.

Cette profession de foi était exigée de tout candidat au baptême. Situées au cœur même du rite, trois interrogations portant sur la foi trinitaire lui étaient posées, auxquelles il répondait lui-même par un triple acte de foi et c'était dans cet acte de foi, démarche éminemment personnelle, qu'il était baptisé. Le baptême était vraiment et dans tout son relief le « sacrement de la foi ». Comment la passivité du bébé n'aurait-elle pas fait problème ?

Déjà la Tradition apostolique de saint Hippolyte s'en préoccupe, stipulant que si les enfants présentés au baptême ne pouvaient pas répondre par eux-mêmes, il appartenait à leurs parents ou à quelqu'un de leur famille de répondre à leur place [6]. Dans la pratique un tel avertissement est assez clair, il suffit, et les Pères ne se font pas faute de le monnayer [7]. Mais d'abord ne peut-on pas déterminer de façon plus précise l'âge auquel, en droit, l'enfant sera censé capable de donner personnellement une réponse valable ?

1. Corrélativement à la substitution de l'ablution à l'immersion, il faut noter aussi l'abandon progressif, et assez différent d'une Église à l'autre, de cette nudité à laquelle les anciens Pères attribuaient une telle portée symbolique.
2. En 383, un enfant, échappant à son parrain, risqua de se noyer dans la piscine baptismale (BARONIUS, ad an. 383 ; cf. Dict. d'archéol. chrét. et de liturgie, s. v. « Baptistères », col. 395, n. 2).
3. Voir Pierre-M. GY, Quamprimum. Note sur le baptême des enfants, La Maison-Dieu, n° 32 (1952), pp. 124-128).
4. On peut distinguer ici une double question. D'une part la « garantie » apportée par le parrain ne concerne plus le passé mais l'avenir (quant au présent, il y a transposition du rôle du parrain, comme nous le verrons plus loin) ; d'autre part cette « garantie », l'Église l'a plus d'une fois demandée, dans l'antiquité, aux parents eux-mêmes, contrairement à l'usage actuel mais non sans logique (ainsi Trad. apost., 21 ; Testam. D. N. J. C., II, 8 ; Peregr. Aether., 45, 2-4 ; S. AUGUSTIN, Épist. 98, 7 : s. CÉSAIRE, Serm. 12, 3) et peut-être fut-ce là l'usage primitif ? Cf. notre article : Le pédobaptisme au ive siècle, Mélanges de science religieuse, 1949, pp. 243-244.
5. Sur ce point, voir A. CHAVASSE, Le carême romain et les scrutins prébaptismaux avant le ixe siècle, Recherches de science religieuse, 1947, pp. 325-381 et les deux rituels romain et gaulois de l'admission au catéchuménat que renferme le sacramentaire gélasien, dans Mélanges Vaganay, Lyon 1948, pp. 79-98. Voir en outre les références données ci-dessus, n. 1.
6. Il va de soi que la littérature qui s'apparente à la Tradition apostolique (Testam. D. N. J. C., II, 8 : édit. Quastm., p. 258 ; Can. Hipp., 113 : édit. L. DUCHESNE, p. 539) reproduit le même avertissement. Cf. Ps.-DENYS, Hier. eccl., VII, 11 (P. G., 3, 565-568).
7. Ainsi saint AUGUSTIN, De baptismo, IV, 31 (P. II., 43, 175 ; Dossier, p. 60).

Un Grégoire de Nazianze [1] pensait, quant à lui, qu'aux environs de la troisième année l'enfant pourrait comprendre quelque chose de son baptême et déjà prendre une part active à sa liturgie en répondant par lui-même aux questions rituelles. C'est peut-être un peu tôt s'il s'agit de donner aux réponses la portée d'un démarche consciente et raisonnée. Saint Augustin parle de sept ans comme de l'âge où l'enfant est normalement à même de discerner le vrai du faux et de s'engager par conséquent dans un acte personnel de foi ; où par conséquent l'Église, en fait, lui demandera sa participation active lors de son baptême [2]. On ne peut manquer, ici, de songer que c'est la septième année qui s'est imposée dans le droit de l'Église comme étant officiellement « l'âge de raison ».

Mais dans le cas traité par la *Tradition apostolique*, d'un tout petit qui est proprement « *infans* », comment légitimer les interrogations du rituel baptismal ? Elles apparaissent tellement vaines, comme l'a bien noté notre éminent collègue, M. Chavasse [3], qu'une autre formule dut s'y substituer, un jour, pour exprimer la foi trinitaire — une formule affirmative, cette fois, et prononcée par le ministre du baptême, celle que nous considérons à présent comme la « forme » du sacrement : *Ego te baptizo in nomine Patris et Filii et Spiritus Sancti.*

On ne s'étonnera pas, cependant, surtout après ce que nous avons dit plus haut, que ce changement ait passé par certains tâtonnements à l'intérieur même de la solution préconisée par la *Tradition apostolique*, avant d'atteindre à l'adaptation adéquate et de se stabiliser définitivement. C'est l'un de ces tâtonnements inscrit dans certains rituels baptismaux que nous voulons précisément signaler.

Pour résoudre la difficulté de l'acte de foi chez l'*infans*, on avait bien, parfois, essayé d'interpréter ses vagissements et ses pleurs comme une supplication [4]. Mais l'essai, pour être empreint d'un mysticisme touchant, n'en était pas moins fragile et inconsistant. La *Tradition apostolique* avait raison : la seule solution était, assurément, de se rabattre sur « la foi des autres ». C'est bien ce que fit saint Augustin lors de la controverse antipélagienne, justifiant en raison l'attitude de l'Église :

[L'enfant] est guéri par le fait des paroles d'un autre, comme il est blessé par le fait du péché d'un autre. « Croit-il en Jésus-Christ », demande-t-on ; et la réponse est : « Il croit ». La réponse est faite pour [cet enfant] qui ne

---

1. *Oratio 40*, 28 (*P. G.*, **36**, 400 ; Dossier, p. 35). Cf. Un cas typique de développement du dogme. A propos du baptême des enfants, *Mélanges de science religieuse*, 1952, pp. 206-207.
2. « Illius aetatis pueri et mentiri et verum loqui et negare jam possunt. Et ideo, cum baptizantur, jam et symbolum reddunt et ipsi pro se ad interrogata respondent » (*De anima et illius origine*, I, 10, 12, et III, 9, 12 : *P. L* ; **44**, 481 et 517 ; Dossier, p. 61, note *b*).
3. Voir ci-dessus, note 1.
4. Voir s. Cyprien, *Epist. 64*, 6 (Édit. BAYARD, t. 2, p. 216 ; Dossier, p. 25) ; s. AUGUSTIN : *Serm. 293*, 11 ; *294*, 12 et 17 (*P. L.*, **38**, 1334, 1342, 1346 ; Dossier, pp. 84, 88, 90).

parle pas, qui se tait, qui pleure et qui prie en quelque sorte par ses pleurs, et elle est valable.... Il croit à travers un autre, parce qu'il a péché à travers un autre [1]....

A bien des reprises, saint Augustin est revenu sur « la foi des autres », mais ce qui rend particulièrement intéressant le texte que nous citons, c'est qu'il argumente à partir du rituel baptismal. Il en ressort qu'à Hippone, les interrogations sur la foi trinitaire qui s'incorporaient à la liturgie du baptême et constituaient alors la vraie « forme » sacramentelle, s'adressant à ceux qui présentaient l'enfant, étaient posées non pas à la deuxième personne mais à la troisième. La chose peut bien nous paraître à présent surprenante, elle n'en est pas moins incontestable.

Sans doute saint Augustin avalise-t-il, en la mettant au point, une affirmation de Pélage selon laquelle les tout-petits doivent être baptisés selon le même rituel, avec les mêmes formules sacramentelles, que les adultes [2]. Mais ceci ne s'oppose nullement à une adaptation de la forme littéraire au cas des bébés, car le problème qui met aux prises Augustin et Pélage est beaucoup plus foncier, comme l'évêque d'Hippone s'en explique plus loin. Et d'autre part nous voyons l'évêque Boniface apporter sa caution, dans une lettre à saint Augustin à la forme des interrogations que nous signalons [3].

Si je te présente un bébé et que je te demande s'il sera chaste quand il sera grand, ou s'il ne deviendra pas voleur, tu répondras sans aucun doute : « Je l'ignore » ; et s'il a quelque idée du bien ou du mal dans le même bas âge où il se trouve, tu diras : « je l'ignore ». Si donc tu n'oses rien avancer de certain concernant sa conduite future et sa pensée actuelle, comment se fait-il que, quand on les présente au baptême, leurs parents, en tant que leurs garants, répondent pour eux et disent qu'ils font ce dont leur âge ne peut avoir l'idée ou s'il le peut, ce qui nous est caché ? Nous interrogeons en effet ceux par

1. « Ad verba aliena sanatur, quia ad factum alienum vulneratur. *Credit in Jesum Christum* ? fit interrogatio ; respondetur : *credit*. Pro non loquente, pro silente, pro flente et flendo quodam modo orante, respondetur et valet ... Credit in altero quia peccavit in altero... » (*Serm. 294*, 12 : *P. L.*, **38**, 1342 ; Dossier, p. 88).
2. « Nempe ipsi a Pelagio vos praesente scripsistis audisse, recitante vobis de libello suo quem etiam Romam se misisse asserebat, quod iisdem sacramenti verbis dicant debere baptizari infantes quibus et majores » (*De gratia Christi et de peccato originali*, II, 1 : *P. L.*, **44**, 385 ; Dossier, p. 107. Cf. II, xxi, 24 : *P. L.*, **44**, 397).
3. « Si constituam (...) ante te parvulum et interrogem utrum, cum creverit, futurus sit castus vel fur non sit futurus, sine dubio respondebis : Nescio, et utrum in eadem parvula aetate constitutus cogitet aliquid boni vel mali, dices : nescio. Si itaque de moribus ejus futuris nihil audes certi promittere et de ejus praesenti cogitatione, quid est illud quod, quando ad baptismum offeruntur, pro eis parentes tamquam fidedictores respondent et dicunt illos facere quod illa aetas cogitare non potest aut, si potest, occultum est ? Interrogamus enim eos a quibus offeruntur et dicimus : *Credit in Deum* ? De illa aetate quae, utrum sit Deus, ignorat ; respondent : *Credit* ; et ad cetera sic respondetur singula quae geruntur. Unde miror parentes in istis rebus tam fidenter pro parvulo respondere, ut dicant eum facere tanta bona quae, ad horam qua baptizatur, baptizator interrogat ; tamen eadem hora si subjiciam : Erit castus, qui baptizatur, aut non erit fur ? nescio utrum audet aliquis dicere, aliquid horum erit aut non erit, sicut mihi sine dubitatione respondet quod credat in Deum et quod se convertat ad Deum » (S. Augustin, *Epist. 98*, 7 ı *P. L.*, **33**, 363 ; Dossier, pp. 66-67).

qui ils sont présentés et, de cet âge qui ignore si Dieu existe, nous disons : « *Croit-il en Dieu* ? » ; on répond : « *Il croit* » ; et telle est la réponse à chacune des autres questions qui sont posées. Sur quoi je m'étonne qu'en ces choses les parents répondent pour leur enfant avec tant d'assurance au point de dire qu'il accomplit tous les actes bons, objets des questions que le ministre pose au moment où il le baptise ; cependant, si j'ajoutais par la même occasion : « Celui qui est baptisé sera-t-il chaste ou ne deviendra-t-il pas voleur ? », je ne sais si quelqu'un oserait dire qu'il réalisera ou non l'une de ces choses, avec autant de certitude qu'il me répond sur sa foi en Dieu et sa conversion à Dieu ?

Boniface n'avait pas, tant s'en faut, l'envergure intellectuelle d'Augustin mais il était, au dire de ce dernier, d'une exceptionnelle droiture : la difficulté qu'il soumettait à son collègue d'Hippone le montre assez. La façon de poser les interrogations liturgiques à la troisième personne, qui se manifeste dans sa lettre et qui s'y trouve confirmée péremptoirement par le contraste du double : « je l'ignore » qui précède, devait plaire à cet évêque par le fait qu'elle écartait toute fiction dans l'administration du sacrement : les questions ne s'adressaient pas directement aux bébés incapables de les entendre mais à leurs répondants ; et ceux-ci les engageaient par leurs réponses mais, en disant : « il croit » et non « je crois », ils ne se substituaient pas à eux.

Cette particularité liturgique du baptême des enfants n'est pas le propre de saint Augustin puisque l'évêque Boniface la fait sienne également. C'est une pratique africaine, qu'elle soit exclusive ou non, qui vaut au moins pour le début du ve siècle. Mais elle déborde ce lieu et ce temps, comme il est facile de le constater.

Nous avons eu, en effet, l'occasion voici déjà bien des années, d'attirer l'attention sur certaines homélies qui venaient d'être rendues à leur auteur Astérius le Sophiste, pour l'intérêt qu'elles présentaient en faveur du pédobaptisme [1]. L'un de ces textes [2] nous dit ceci :

Lorsque quelqu'un présente au baptême un nourrisson, le prêtre exige aussitôt de cet âge fragile des engagements et des assentiments ; il prend le parrain comme répondant de cette jeunesse et il lui demande : « Renonce-t-il à Satan ? ». Or il ne dit pas : « [Renoncera-t-il à Satan] pour la fin [de sa vie] ? ou « s'engagera-t-il envers le Christ pour la fin [de sa vie] ? » Mais c'est immédiatement, pour le commencement de la vie, qu'il exige ces renonciations et ces engagements.

Astérius nous transporte d'emblée en Asie Mineure environ trois quarts de siècle avant les témoignages que nous venons de citer de l'Afrique [3]. Dans la rareté des témoignages orientaux concernant le

---

1. Le pédobaptisme au ive siècle, Documents nouveaux, *Mélanges de science religieuse*, 1949, pp. 233-246.
2. *In ps. XIV homil. 2*, 2 (édit. M. RICHARD, Oslo, 1956, p. 215 ; Dossier, p. 30 ; *Mél. sc. rel.*, 1949, pp. 245-246).
3. Le *Sermon 294* de saint AUGUSTIN a été prêché en juin 413 ; la *Lettre 98* fut écrite entre 408 et 412 ; le traité *De gratia Christi* date de l'année 418. Astérius disparaît après 347.

baptême des enfants, et vu l'époque où il se situe, un document comme celui-ci, même si l'on ignore combien d'Églises (et quelles Églises) il engage, prend un relief saisissant. En fait, dans les débuts du VIe siècle, le Pseudo-Aréopagite recoupe curieusement la donnée d'Astérius en faisant état de certaines critiques visant l'usage qu'a l'Église de faire prononcer par d'autres, au moment du baptême des enfants, « les abjurations rituelles et les promesses sacrées ». Or, répond Denys, « le parrain ne dit pas qu'il abjure ou qu'il s'engage saintement à la place de l'enfant, mais bien que c'est l'enfant lui-même qui abjure et qui promet » [1]. Pour la bonne intelligence de cette mise au point, l'on doit normalement supposer que, dans son Église, Denys lisait les interrogations baptismales à la troisième personne.

Mais revenons en Occident. La victoire de saint Augustin contre Pélage, l'influence de sa doctrine, ont généralisé de plus en plus le baptême des enfants. Les rites baptismaux s'en ressentent de plus en plus. On pourrait s'attendre, en conséquence, à ce que les interrogations baptismales à la troisième personne se généralisent également. Eh bien, non ; et l'on pourra se demander pourquoi. Les liturgies wisigothique et gallicane vont toutefois nous offrir les derniers témoignages de l'usage en question.

En ce qui regarde la liturgie wisigothique, le *Liber Ordinum* que Dom Férotin a édité [2] nous offre un *Ordo baptismi celebrandus quolibet tempore* qui, de toute évidence, a été spécialement — sinon exclusivement — rédigé pour les baptêmes d'enfants (les rubriques qu'il comporte le disent amplement, mais le titre seul — *quolibet tempore* — le suggérerait déjà, compte tenu de l'époque dont il est le témoin).

Or cet *ordo baptismi* possède un double série d'interrogations dont la particularité n'a pas retenu l'attention d'un Mgr Duchesne [3] ou d'aucun autre liturgiste mais qui nous intéressent ici de très près. Nous trouvons, en effet, des interrogations sur le symbole situées avant la bénédiction des fonts et qui sont rédigées à la troisième personne. Le manuscrit qui a servi de base à l'édition de Dom Férotin ne contient, il est vrai, que la question suivante : *Credit* ille *in Deum* ? Mais la rubrique qui s'y ajoute (*usque in finem*) est indicative à souhait ; en outre, le manuscrit de 1039, appelé en référence [4], nous transmet l'ensemble des interrogations.

Credit ille *in Dominum Patrem omnipotentem* ?
Et in Ihesum Christum ? usque in finem.
Credit in Sanctum Spiritum ? *Sanctam Ecclesiam catholicam* ?

Immédiatement avant l'immersion, prend place une nouvelle série de questions rituelles portant sur la renonciation au démon et la foi

1. Ps-DENYS, *Hier. eccl.*, VII, 11 (trad. GANDILLAC, p. 325).
2. Dans les *Monumenta ecclesiae liturgica*, t. 5, Paris, 1904.
3. *Les origines du culte chrétien*, 5e édit., Paris, 1909, p. 332.
4. *Liber Ordinum*, col. 28, n. 1 ; Dossier, p. 135.

trinitaire. Formulées à la deuxième personne dans le texte de base, elles le sont, par contre, à la troisième personne dans le manuscrit de 1039 et celui de Madrid cités l'un et l'autre en note [1], et qui reflètent, à n'en pas douter l'usage primitif :

Abrenuntiat hic famulus Dei diabolo et angelis ejus ?
— Respondetur a ministris : *Abrenuntiat.*
Operibus ejus ? — Resp. : *Abrenuntiat.*
Imperiis ejus ? — Resp. : *Abrenuntiat.*
Quis vocatur ? Ille.
Credis [2], ille, *in Dominum Patrem omnipotentem ?* — *Credit.*
Et in Ihesum etc... ? — Resp. *Credit.*
Et in Spiritum Sanctum ? — Resp. *Credit.*
Et ego eum baptizo in nomine Patris et Filii et Spiritus Sancti ut habeat vitam aeternam. Amen.

La liturgie gallicane, pour sa part, nous présente le missel de Bobbio, dont le rituel du baptême [3] comporte des interrogations à la troisième personne [4], comme le *liber ordinum* wisigothique :

Interrogas nomen ejus, dicens : *Quis dicitur ?* — *Ille.*
Abrenuntias [5] *satanae etc... ?* — *Abrenuntiat.* Hoc ter dices.
Interrogas nomen ejus : *Quis dicitur ?* — Ille.
Credit in Deum, Patrem omnipotentem etc... ? — *Credat.*
Credit et in Jesum Christum etc... ? — *Credat.*
Credit in Spiritum Sanctum etc... ? — *Credat.*
Baptizas eum et dicis : *Baptizo te in nomine Patris et Filii et Spiritus Sancti, unam habentem substantiam, ut habeas vitam aeternam, partem cum sanctis.*

A la lumière de ces documents liturgiques, certains textes anciens prennent un relief nouveau et méritent d'être considérés comme des témoignages positifs en faveur de cette adaptation du rituel que nous signalons, quand ils nous disent que les répondants de l'enfant « parlent à sa place ». Non pas tous les textes qui disent cela, bien sûr, car c'est encore se substituer à l'enfant que de répondre à sa place *abrenuntio* et *credo* comme *abrenuntiat* et *credit.* C'est donc le rituel baptismal en usage qui donne sa portée aux textes patristiques en question.

En conséquence, puisque aucun texte liturgique d'origine romaine ne nous laisse supposer une adaptation du rituel baptismal au cas des *par-*

---

1. *Liber Ordinum*, col. 32, n. 1 ; Dossier, pp. 135-136.
2. Ce *credis* ne peut que représenter une erreur du copiste du xie siècle, influencé par un autre usage désormais généralisé à son époque, si l'on en juge non seulement par la réponse qui suit immédiatement (*credit*) mais encore par l'ensemble des autres questions et réponses et surtout, peut-être, par la formule de l'immersion (*eum baptizo*).
3. MARTÈNE, *De antiquis Ecclesiae ritibus*, Rouen, 1700, I, p. 171 ; *P. L.*, **72**, 502.
4. Dom DE PUNIET eut le mérite de le remarquer (art. « Baptême », dans *DACL*, II, col. 328), mais sans aller plus loin.
5. Nous devons faire sur cet *abrenuntias* une remarque analogue à celle que mérite le *credis* du rituel wisigothique (voir ci-dessus, n. 2). Il ne peut s'expliquer que comme un lapsus du copiste et, loin d'être primitif, il témoigne plutôt, d'un temps où l'usage romain commençait à supplanter l'usage gallican.

vuli quant aux interrogations qui leur sont faites, nous n'avons le droit d'interpréter dans ce sens ni la remarque de la *Tradition apostolique* d'Hippolyte ni quelqu'autre document romain postérieur. Ainsi lorsque le Diacre Jean, dans sa *Lettre à Sénarius*, insiste sur le fait que les rites du baptême sont les mêmes pour des *parvuli* qui n'y comprennent rien que pour les adultes et signale que le salut de ces tout-petits dépend de la profession de foi des autres [1], il ne peut être question que d'interrogations à la deuxième personne.

Par contre, dans les Églises d'Afrique, d'Espagne et de Gaule, nous pouvons lire sans hésitation dans ce sens les témoignages patristiques sur le rôle des répondants. Il serait fastidieux de reproduire toutes les affirmations de saint Augustin sur ce sujet [2]. Que si nous passons en Gaule, nous trouvons les mêmes assertions chez Gennade de Marseille [3] vers la fin du ve siècle, et chez saint Césaire d'Arles [4] dans la première moitié du vi[e]. Il en est de même en Espagne au viie siècle avec saint Isidore de Séville [5] et saint Ildefonse de Tolède [6]. Tous ces textes des ve-viie siècles auxquels nous faisons allusion, doivent incontestablement s'entendre dans le cadre d'un liturgie baptismale où les interrogations rituelles étaient posées à la troisième personne lorsqu'il s'agissait de *parvuli* et s'adressaient directement à leurs répondants (parrains ou parents).

Le missel de Bobbio nous situe au viie siècle. L'*ordo baptismi* wisigothique n'est certainement pas d'une date plus tardive mais a pu être observé plus longtemps. Ce sont, comme nous l'avons dit, les derniers témoins liturgiques de l'usage signalé et ils manifestent eux-mêmes, déjà, les traces d'une certaine influence de la liturgie romaine qui ira s'accentuant au point de s'imposer rapidement et, pour ainsi dire, totalement. L'*ordo* romain ne connaissait pas cette façon de poser les questions rituelles dans le cas d'un baptême d'enfant : l'usage africain, gallican, wisigothique, disparut.

1. *Epist. ad Senarium*, 7 (*P. L.*, **59, 403** ; Dossier, pp. 128-129).
2. Voir Dossier, pp. 55-116 (qui, du reste, n'offre qu'un choix de textes).
3. *Liber seu diffinitio ecclesiasticorum dogmatum*, 52 (*P. L.*, **58**, 993 ; Dossier, p. 126) = Si vero parvuli sunt vel hebetes, qui doctrinam non capiant, respondeant pro illis qui eos offerunt juxta morem baptizandi. — Ce texte sera repris littéralement par un concile de Rouen de la fin du viie siècle. c. 5 (MANSI, X, 1201).
4. *Serm. 12*, 3 (édit. MORIN, Maredsous, 1937, I, p. 58 ; Dossier, p. 129) : « Quia infantes per se minime profiteri non possunt, parentes ipsorum pro eis fidejussores existunt ». — *Serm. 200* (édit, MORIN, V, p. 769(: « Agnoscant [parentes] se fidejussores esse ipsorum [parvulorum] : pro ipsis enim respondent quod abrenuntient diabolo, pompis et operibus ejus ».
5. *De eccl. officiis*, II, 21, 3 (*P. L.*, **83**, 815) : « Quod quia parvuli per se renuntiare non possunt, per corda et ora gestantium adimpletur » — Cf. *ibid.*, II, 25, 7 (*P. L.*, **83**, 822 ; Dossier, p. 134) : « Parvuli alio profitente baptizantur quia adhuc loqui vel credere nesciunt, sicut etiam aegri, muti vel surdi, quorum vice alius profitetur, ut pro eis respondeat dum baptizantur ».
6. *De cognitione Baptismi*, 114 (*P. L.*, **96**, 159) : « [Fidejussores] pro ipsis [parvulis] respondent quod abrenuntient diabolo, angelis et operibus ejus, affirmantes credere eos in nomine Trinitatis ».

Il disparut mais non pas au point d'être aussitôt oublié. L'archevêque de Lyon Leidrade (+ 816) éprouve en effet le besoin de le désavouer, au cours de son livre *De sacramento baptismi* :

Selon l'usage et l'enseignement traditionnels de l'Église, nous célébrons les mystères du baptême avec les mêmes paroles sacramentelles pour les enfants que pour les adultes. De là vient que le prêtre, quand il accomplit ces sacrements, ne questionne pas l'un pour l'autre, autrement dit l'adulte pour le petit, sur la renonciation au diable ou la foi en Dieu ; mais il interroge celui-là même qu'il va baptiser, en disant : « Renonces-tu ? ou « Crois-tu ? ». Et le parrain ne répond pas à sa place en disant : « Il renonce » ou « Il croit » mais « Je renonce » ou « Je crois ». Et il en est ainsi pour que les tout-petits puissent être dits pénitents et fidèles. A ceux qui nient cela, voici la réponse qui est fournie par les Pères : Si l'on ne doit pas considérer ces enfants comme des pénitents, parce qu'ils n'ont pas présentement conscience de se repentir, de même il ne faut pas voir en eux des fidèles, car ils n'ont pas non plus présentement conscience de croire. Mais si, à juste titre, on les dit fidèles parce qu'ils professent en quelque sorte leur foi par la bouche de ceux qui les portent, pourquoi ne seraient-ils pas aussi et d'abord considérés comme des pénitents, alors que, par la voix de ceux qui les portent, ils renoncent clairement au diable et à ce siècle ? Tout cela se fait en espérance, par l'action du sacrement et de la grâce divine que le Seigneur a donnée à l'Église, lors de leur baptême, du fait de la vertu et de la célébration d'un si grand sacrement, encore qu'ils n'accomplissent ni de cœur ni de bouche ce qui concerne cette foi et cette confession. Pourtant ils sont comptés au nombre des croyants [1].

Tout, dans ce texte, porte à croire que Leidrade, en cherchant à légitimer en raison l'usage romain qui venait de s'imposer à la Gaule par la grâce des Carolingiens, connaissait encore une certaine persistance de l'autre usage, ne serait-ce que par le fait de ses missions à travers les pays de rite wisigothique.

Quoi qu'il en soit, dans la première moitié du XIIe siècle, si les théologiens sont amenés à discuter du bien-fondé des paroles du rituel baptismal — et l'occasion leur en est donnée avec la polémique néocathare — il n'est plus question que du rituel romain et de ses interrogations à la deuxième personne. Ainsi chez Maître Herman [2] :

On a coutume de se demander de qui sont ces paroles : de l'enfant ou du parrain ? Mais qu'elles soient prêtées à qui l'on voudra, il semble bien qu'elles sont un mensonge de la part de qui répond. Si, en effet, le parrain répond en son nom : « Je veux être baptisé », il ment car il n'a pas dans l'esprit de vouloir l'être. Si, de même, il parle au nom de l'enfant, il ne peut absolument pas échapper au reproche de mentir, car il sait indubitablement que celui-ci ne le veut pas, étant incapable d'un acte de volonté. Qu'il ne le veuille pas, dis-je, il est facile de le déduire du fait qu'il se débat de toutes ses forces.

---

1. Leidrade, *Liber de sacramento baptismi*, 10 (*P. L.*, **99**, 868 ; Dossier, pp. 138-139).
2. *Sentences* (= *Epitome theologiae christianae*) : *P. L.*, **178**, 1739-1740 ; Dossier, pp. 170-171.

Telle est l'objection que faisaient couramment les hérétiques [1]. Le disciple d'Abélard y répond :

Le parrain parle en son propre nom. Mais quand il dit : « Je crois », c'est comme s'il disait : « J'ai cette foi par laquelle celui-ci peut être sauvé. De même quand il répond : « Je veux être baptisé », le sens est : « Je veux que cet [enfant] soit baptisé dans ma foi ». Cependant on prête ces paroles à l'enfant lui-même pour que l'identité des paroles de l'enfant fasse voir l'identité du parrain avec lui.

Citons encore un autre théologien, Robert Pull, contemporain d'Herman [2]. Il commente le rituel :

C'est donc aux parrains qu'on s'adresse. Mais parce qu'il s'agit de l'enfant, on parle comme si l'on s'adressait à l'enfant. Quant vous entendez le prêtre interroger ainsi : « Enfant, crois-tu en Dieu ? Renonces-tu au diable ? », cela veut assurément dire : « Parrains, promettez-vous au nom de l'enfant qu'il renoncera au diable durant sa vie ? ». Augustin, cependant, explique ainsi la réponse des parrains : « Je crois », c'est-à-dire « Je reçois le sacrement de la foi ». Aussi, quand vous entendez la question : « Enfant, crois-tu en Dieu ? » et la réponse : « Je crois », vous la comprendrez évidemment ainsi : « Parrains, par les bons soins de qui cet enfant est présenté à Dieu, recevra-t-il le sacrement de la foi ? — Il le recevra.

Nous n'avons pas à discuter ici de la valeur ou de la faiblesse des arguments apportés (on doit honnêtement reconnaître que si les objections au baptême des enfants sont, en soi, très fortes, les réponses, elles, sont passablement tâtonnantes et dissonantes). Ce que l'on retiendra, c'est l'effort de la théologie pour légitimer en raison un fait traditionnel qu'il faut accepter avec soumission : nous voulons dire le pédobaptisme et, à l'intérieur de ce fait primordial, la pratique rituelle des Églises. Or les théologiens ne connaissent plus d'autre forme d'interrogation que *credo* et *abrenuntio*.

Cette même constatation, nous pouvons la faire, en terminant, chez saint Thomas d'Aquin [3] :

Celui qui répond pour l'enfant baptisé : « Je crois », ne prédit pas que l'enfant croira une fois arrivé à l'âge adulte ; autrement, il dirait : « Il croira ». Mais il professe au nom de l'enfant la foi de l'Église, foi à laquelle celui-ci est associé, dont le sacrement lui est conféré, et à laquelle il s'engage par un autre. Car il n'y a pas d'inconvénient à ce qu'on soit engagé par un autre en ce qui est nécessaire au salut....

La question a vraiment été dominée de très haut et l'argumentation est excellente. La méthode reste la même que chez ses prédécesseurs et le point de départ est le *credo* du rituel en usage. Même le *credet* (saint

---

1. Voir nos lignes à ce sujet dans : La question du baptême des enfants chez saint Bernard et ses contemporains (*Analecta sacri ordinis cisterciensis*, IX, 1953, fasc. 3-4, p. 195).
2. *Sentences*, V, 20 (*P. L.*, **186**, 845 ; Dossier, p. 170).
3. *S. Th.*, 3a, q. 71, a. 1, *ad* 3 (Dossier, p. 182) ; cf. 3a, q. 68, a. 9, *ad* 3 (Dossier, pp. 177 et 179). Traduction P. Th. CAMELOT, Paris, 1956.

Thomas ne dit pas *credit*) reste une supposition théorique. L'ancienne pratique d'interroger à la troisième personne est définitivement ignorée.

Il n'est jamais oiseux de s'attarder aux moindres détails de ce qui est ou a été l'usage des Églises et surtout leur usage liturgique.

Mais particulièrement en un moment de la vie de l'Église où la réforme liturgique est en cours et où, au sein de celle-ci, le rituel du baptême des enfants semble pouvoir être révisé, il peut ne pas être inutile d'attirer l'attention sur le petit point de l'histoire de nos rites que nous venons d'étudier.

J.-Ch. Didier.

Montréal-Lille.

UNTERSUCHUNGEN

Der Ketzertaufstreit zwischen Karthago und Rom und seine Konsequenzen für die Frage nach den Grenzen der Kirche[1]

Von Hubert Kirchner

I.

Im Jahre 1962, kurz vor der Eröffnung des II. Vatikanischen Konzils, erschien fast wie ein evangelischer Beitrag zu den Vorüberlegungen zu diesem Konzil die systematisch-theologische Dissertation von *Wolfgang Dietzfelbinger:* „Die Grenzen der Kirche nach römisch-katholischer Lehre".[2] Diese Arbeit versteht sich „als ein Versuch, für das interkonfessionelle Gespräch mit der römisch-katholischen Kirche die kirchlichen Positionen des evangelischen Partners . . . zu klären",[3] und vermag diese selbstgestellte Aufgabe durch die ausführliche Aufarbeitung einer Fülle von Material wohl zu erfüllen. Die Ergebnisse des II. Vatikanischen Konzils haben jedoch diese Positionen gründlich verschoben und damit praktisch jene Überlegungen sehr schnell überholt. Besonders das Dekret über den Ökumenismus, dessen Voraussetzungen aber schon in der Konstitution über die Kirche gelegt werden, hat eine ganze Reihe von Bewegungen ausgelöst und Tendenzen erkennen lassen, die zu neuer gründlicher Prüfung aufrufen.

Das Dekret beginnt mit der Feststellung: „Die Einheit unter allen Christen wiederherstellen zu helfen ist eine der Hauptaufgaben des Heiligen Ökumenischen II. Vatikanischen Konzils".[4] Damit steht es nicht nur äußerlich in der Mitte der beschlossenen Dokumente. Es stellt sich auch sachlich als ein Kernstück der Beschlüsse dar, die jenen Zielen dienen sollen. Es soll, wie es heißt, „allen Katholiken die Mittel und Wege nennen und die Weise aufzeigen, wie sie selber dem göttlichen Ruf" zur Einheit und der „Gnade Gottes", die in der aufgebrochenen Sehnsucht nach Einheit zu spüren ist,

---

[1] Überarbeitete Fassung der Probevorlesung zur Habilitation, gehalten am 16. Januar 1969 an der Universität Greifswald.
[2] W. Dietzfelbinger, Die Grenzen der Kirche nach römisch-katholischer Lehre = Forschungen zur systematischen und ökumenischen Theologie 10 (Göttingen 1962).
[3] Ib., Vorwort.
[4] Die Beschlüsse des Konzils. Der vollständige Text der vom II. Vatikanischen Konzil beschlossenen Dokumente in deutscher Übersetzung, hrsg. v. W. Becker (Leipzig 1967) 238.

„entsprechen können".[5] Es hat darüber hinaus die Aufgabe, die grundsätzlichen Voraussetzungen aufzuweisen, unter denen eine Bewegung der Gläubigen überhaupt erst möglich erscheint.

Sogleich am Anfang wird festgestellt, daß die Schuld der Trennung unter den Christen nicht den Menschen angelastet werden dürfe, die in den verschiedenen christlichen Gemeinschaften geboren wurden. „Die katholische Kirche betrachtet sie als Brüder in Verehrung und Liebe," heißt es. Und es folgt die grundlegende These: „Wer an Christus glaubt und in der rechten Weise die Taufe empfangen hat, steht dadurch in einer gewissen, wenn auch nicht vollkommenen Gemeinschaft mit der katholischen Kirche."[6] Das scheint der wichtigste Satz in dem ganzen Zusammenhang. Damit wird behauptet, daß es für die nicht-römischen kirchlichen Gemeinschaften wie für die römische Kirche selbst eine gemeinsame Basis gibt. (Dem entspricht die Terminologie des Dekrets bzw. der Konzilsdokumente überhaupt: Man spricht von den „von der Gemeinschaft mit dem apostolischen Stuhle" getrennten Brüdern[7] und enthält den christlichen Gemeinschaften außerhalb der eigenen Grenzen nicht länger die Bezeichnung „Kirche" vor, obwohl es dabei immerhin noch deutliche Nuancen gibt). Und es wird sogleich auch umschrieben, worin diese gemeinsame Basis besteht: Im Glauben an Jesus Christus und im rechten Empfang der Taufe.

Es ist klar, daß seitens der protestantischen Kirchen gerade dies mit dem größten Interesse und gespannter Aufmerksamkeit aufgenommen wurde.[8] Es bedeutet doch einen ganz erheblichen Fortschritt gegenüber dem bisherigen Status der gegenseitigen offiziellen Beziehungen, die ein so ganz anderes Gesicht trugen und doch im Grunde auf den gleichen grundsätzlichen Voraussetzungen beruhten. Denn auf dieser so von Rom selbst bezeichneten Basis hätte man sich schon lange finden können. Ja, es ist vielleicht nicht ganz müßig, weiter zu fragen, ob nicht bei Ernstnehmen dieser gemeinsamen Basis in der Vergangenheit vieles hätte vermieden werden können, nicht nur das abendländische Schisma.

So erwächst nicht von ungefähr die Aufgabe, stärker und gezielter, als es die Arbeit von Dietzfelbinger (der übrigens dann zu den evangelischen Konzilsbeobachtern gehörte) noch tun konnte, die einzelnen Elemente jener Basis einmal näher zu untersuchen. Sie sind nicht neu, nicht einmal in dieser Zusammenstellung, und enthalten doch Momente, die ihnen heute einen besonderen Akzent verleihen. Gerade das zeigt auch ein Vergleich mit den Ergebnissen Dietzfelbingers. Das betrifft vor allem die überaus betonte Hervorhebung der Taufe als Moment der Verbundenheit der nicht-römischen Christen mit der römischen Kirche. Sie wird mehrfach herausgestellt, schon in der

---

[5] Ebenda.
[6] Ebenda 240 f.
[7] Ebenda 53 in der Erklärung zur Kalenderreform als Anhang an die Konstitution über die heilige Liturgie.
[8] Vgl. z. B. U. Kühn, Die Ergebnisse des II. Vatikanischen Konzils (Berlin 1967) 109 u. ö.

1*

Konstitution über die Kirche[9] und dann vor allem in jener Basis des Ökumenismus-Dekrets. Das in sachlichem Anschluß daran 1967 promulgierte Ökumenische Direktorium, die „Durchführungsbestimmungen über das ökumenische Anliegen",[10] spricht es sogar noch deutlicher aus, „daß die Taufe das sakramentale Band der Einheit, ja sogar das Fundament der Gemeinschaft unter allen Christen ist".[11] Ähnlich äußerte sich Papst Paul VI. in seiner Ansprache bei der Audienz für die Mitglieder des Sekretariats zur Förderung der Einheit der Christen im November 1968.[12]

Es lohnt sich also, gerade diesen einen Punkt einmal näher ins Auge zu fassen und nach den geschichtlichen Grundlagen dieser Sätze zurückzufragen, nicht der Meinung, die Entwicklung damit zurückdrehen zu können, aber doch der Meinung, aus den Erkenntnissen der Geschichte heraus einen Maßstab gewinnen zu können, der für die Orientierung innerhalb der späteren Entwicklung einschließlich der gegenwärtigen und zukünftigen Entscheidungen von Wichtigkeit sein dürfte.

Damit ist das Thema unserer Untersuchung festgelegt. Wir stehen vor den Entscheidungen des sog. Ketzertaufstreites zwischen Karthago und Rom um die Mitte des dritten nachchristlichen Jahrhunderts.

II.

Als Ketzertaufstreit wird die Auseinandersetzung vornehmlich zwischen Cyprian von Karthago und Stephanus von Rom in den Jahren 255 und 256 über die Gültigkeit der nicht in der offiziellen Kirche gespendeten christlichen Taufe bezeichnet. Dabei sind freilich von vornherein Vorbehalte geboten: Es ging dabei 1. nicht nur um diese partielle Frage. Es knüpfte sich daran weit mehr, und man ist versucht zu sagen: weit entscheidenderes. Es ging dabei unbedingt auch um die Gültigkeit der Ordination und schließlich um die Kirche in ihrem Selbstverständnis gegenüber den anderen Gruppen überhaupt. Und das ist ja das Thema dieser Vorlesung. — Beteiligt waren daran 2. auch nicht nur diese beiden Personen. Die Auseinandersetzung ergriff weitere Kreise, nicht nur auf Seiten Cyprians, der sich nicht darauf beschränkte, den Klerus seines unmittelbaren nordafrikanischen Einflußgebietes zu aktivieren, sondern sich auch um Unterstützung nach dem Osten wendete, von wo er nach altem Herkommen in dieser Frage am ehesten Beifall erhoffen konnte und tatsächlich auch erhielt. — Und schließlich – 3. – erfaßt auch die zeitliche Fixierung auf die beiden Jahre nicht alles. Das Thema war schon länger aktuell, mindestens seit Tertullians Schrift „De baptismo", die schon

---

[9] Becker 70 f.
[10] Umdruck S. 1 Nr. 1.
[11] Ebenda S. 5 Nr. 11.
[12] „Wir kölnnen nicht schließen, ohne ein herzliches und ehrerbietiges Gedenken an alle unsere christlichen Brüder zu richten, die noch von uns getrennt, aber uns doch schon mit so vielen geistigen Banden vereint sind: Durch die Taufe vor allem und durch den Glauben an den einen und lebendigen, dreifaltigen Gott und durch den Glauben an Jesus Christus, unseren Herrn und Erlöser." Nach Hedwigsblatt 15 (1968) Nr. 48.

vor mehr als 50 Jahren den Häretikern jede Möglichkeit zu taufen abgespro-
chen hatte (eine noch weiter zurückliegende ausführlichere griechische Schrift
speziell zu diesem Thema, die Tertullian in diesem Zusammenhang erwähnt, ist
nicht überliefert). Und es war auch über jene beiden Jahre hinaus aktuell. Meh-
rere Synoden befaßten sich damit und konnten ihrer Entscheidung doch nicht
sofortigen Eingang in die universale kirchliche Praxis verschaffen. Andererseits dürfte, soll der Begriff des Streites nicht an Gewicht verlieren, eigentlich
nur das Jahr 256 ins Auge gefaßt werden, wenn anders zu einem Streit wirkliche Äußerungen beider Seiten gehören. Die primäre Begrenzung des Themas
auf diese spezielle Frage, den kleinen Kreis agierender Hauptpersonen und
die wenigen Jahre folgt lediglich seiner durch diese drei Komponenten be-
stimmten besonderen Kristallisation.

Schon eine oberflächliche Einschätzung der Quellensituation beleuchtet das
zur Genüge: Was vor und nach diesen Jahren außerhalb des Einflußgebietes
dieser beiden Männer zum Thema beigetragen wurde, bleibt an Umfang und
Bedeutung – abgesehen lediglich von den konziliaren Beschlüssen – wesentlich hinter dem zurück, was innerhalb dieser räumlichen und zeitlichen Grenzen geleistet wurde: 6 teilweise bereits traktatgewichtige Schreiben Cyprians
und eines an ihn sowie die erhaltenen Sentenzen der 87 zum Septemberkonzil
256 in Karthago versammelten Bischöfe einerseits und die anonyme Schrift
De rebaptismate andererseits sind erhalten. Es ist damit zu rechnen, daß ein
Großteil der überaus wichtigen Korrespondenz dieser unmittelbar beteiligten
Personen verloren gegangen ist, was umso schmerzlicher ist, als sich hierin
der eigentliche Streit abspielte und sich doch nicht alles aus dem Erhaltenen
rekonstruieren läßt

Das Problem, um das der Streit entbrannte, war folgendes: Die Heraus-
bildung sich christlich nennender und fühlender Gruppen neben der offiziellen Kirche stellte diese vor die zunächst ganz neue Frage nach ihrem Verhältnis zu jenen. Ließ diese sich in den Anfängen noch relativ leicht dadurch be-
wältigen, daß man jegliche Gemeinschaft von vornherein ablehnte und einen
scharfen Schnitt zwischen sich und den von der Wahrheit Abgefallenen zog,
so komplizierte sich auf die Dauer doch das Problem dadurch, daß unter
jenen bald auch Neubekehrte anzutreffen waren, die zuvor noch nicht schon
Glieder der Kirche gewesen waren, und zumal dadurch, daß der Fall eintrat,
daß von solchen die Aufnahme in die katholische Kirche begehrt wurde.
Standen die Gruppen, aus denen sie kamen, der Kirche verhältnismäßig fern
in Lehre und Disziplin, so lag eine Antwort im Sinne Tertullians durchaus
nahe. Entsprechend verfuhr man im Orient, und eine nordafrikanische
Synode unter Agrippinus von Karthago entschied ca. 220 ebenso. Wie sollte
man sich jedoch verhalten in dem Falle, daß die Grenze zwischen ihnen und
der Kirche lehrmäßig überhaupt nicht mehr zu erfassen war, sondern es nur
noch um Disziplinfragen ging, wie also erst jüngst in dem novatianischen
Streit um die Wiederaufnahme der während der Verfolgung schwach gewordenen Gemeindeglieder, welcher zu einem weiteren Schisma geführt hatte?
Waren auch sie wie Heiden zu betrachten und also beim Übertritt wie diese
erst einmal zu taufen? Oder war nicht vielmehr von der Tatsache auszuge-

hen, daß sie ja eigentlich denselben Glauben bekannten und schon eine gültige Taufe erfahren hatten? Die Frage war diffizil. Es waren weder hinreichend Autoritäten für die eine oder andere Meinung beizubringen, noch konnte man sich auf eine entscheidende Tradition zurückziehen. Es gab höchstens Ansätze von örtlichen Traditionen, welche aber ebenfalls noch nicht, wie sich im Verlaufe des Streites zeigte, im Feuer der Kritik einer prinzipiellen theologischen Klärung der Sachverhältnisse bewährt waren. Insofern konnten sich die Vertreter jeder der beiden Meinungen – sofern nicht schon in den Grundlagen entscheidende Irrtümer geschahen, die über Recht oder Unrecht der Folgerungen entschieden – wirklich auf dem Boden der Kirche stehend wissen. Dem entsprach, daß die verschiedenen Praktiken jahrzehntelang offenbar unangefochten nebeneinander geübt worden waren. Zu einer Krisis kam es erst, als man unter dem Druck der seit dem novatianischen Schisma besonders brennend gewordenen Situation die Isolierung verließ und mit der beiden Seiten eigenen Überzeugung die andere ansprach.

Es war wohl Cyprian, um den sich alles drehte. Offenbar gab es im nordafrikanischen Episkopat Unklarheiten über die rechtmäßige Praxis, ausgelöst vielleicht durch die auseinandergehenden Übungen in Mauretanien und Numidien.[13] Jedenfalls gab es Anfragen an Cyprian, ob man die Taufe der Abgefallenen anerkennen könne oder nicht,[14] welche dieser unter Hinweis auf die Synode von Karthago von ca. 220 negativ beschied.[15] Die auf dem Maikonzil von 255 in Karthago versammelten 32 Bischöfe[16] faßten einen dahingehenden Beschluß, der eine neue Rechtsgrundlage schuf.[17] Offenbar reichte diese jedoch nicht aus. Denn ein Jahr später, im Frühjahr 256, versammelte sich noch einmal ein mit diesmal 71 anwesenden Bischöfen[18] ungleich besser beschicktes Konzil in Karthago über diese Frage und wendete sich an Stephanus in Rom,[19] um, wie man schrieb, ihm diese Dinge um ihrer

---

[13] Die Anfragen an Cyprian kamen, zumindest teilweise, aus Mauretanien. Sicher ist das von der des Quintus, dem Cyprian mit ep. 71 antwortete, vgl. ep. 72, 1, CSEL 3, 2, 776, 10, ferner v. Soden, Der Streit zwischen Rom und Karthago über die Ketzertaufe = Quellen und Forschungen aus italienischen Archiven und Bibliotheken 12 (1909) 10 f., sowie zur kirchlichen Einteilung Afrikas im fraglichen Zeitraum ders., Die Prosopographie des afrikanischen Episkopats zur Zeit Cyprians. In: Ib. 247–270, bes. 250 f.

[14] Magnus an Cyprian. Der Brief ist verloren, die Anfrage folgt aber aus der Antwort Cyprians an Magnus, ep. 69, 1, CSEL 3, 2, 749, 5 ff. Damit soll die umstrittene Datierung von ep. 96 nicht präjudiziert werden. Auch wenn sie nicht an den Anfang der Korrespondenz über den Ketzertaufstreit gesetzt werden kann, ist sie doch ein gutes Beispiel für die eingehenden Anfragen. Und insofern steht sie hier. Vgl. auch ep. 70, 1 ib. 766, 15 ff. (das Präskript bietet eine Liste der Anfragenden, immerhin 18 Personen); 71, 1 ib. 771, 3 ff. und 73, 1 ib. 778, 11 ff.

[15] Der erste Konzilsbeschluß, Cyprian ep. 70, 1, erwähnt nur allgemein eine „sententia . . . iam pridem ab antecessoribus nostris statuta" CSEL 3, 2, 767, 1–6. Ep. 71, 4 beruft sich auf Agrippinus, ib. 774, 12 ff., ebenso ep. 73, 3 ib. 780, 14.

[16] Zur Anzahl der im Präskript genannten Namen s. v. Soden, Ketzertaufstreit 9 und Anm. 2.

[17] Cyprian ep. 70 CSEL 3, 2, 766–770.

[18] Siehe ep. 73, 1 ib. 779, 4.

[19] Cyprian ep. 72 ib. 775–778. Auf die Kontroverse zwischen den Forschern, wel-

besonderen Gewichtigkeit willen mitzuteilen und mit ihm zu besprechen.[20] Das war der eigentliche Beginn des Streites. Es muß zwar dahingestellt bleiben, ob mit diesem Schreiben tatsächlich der Fehdehandschuh geworfen werden sollte. Denn es ist auch durchaus nicht klar, wer in den bisherigen Schreiben auf die Anfragen hin das eigentliche Gegenüber war, ob noch immer gültige, von der karthagischen Linie abweichende lokale Überlieferungen, vielleicht besonders in Mauretanien,[21] oder unausgesprochen doch schon Rom, das sich hinter diesen vielleicht doch schon verbarg nicht nur in der Pflege übereinstimmender Traditionen, sondern auch mit entsprechender Unterstützung.[22] Jedenfalls beginnt jetzt erst der Streit insofern, als wir erst jetzt von direkten Gegenäußerungen aus Rom etwas hören. Alles Frühere muß nicht, trotz sachlicher Übereinstimmung, von dort stammen, wie vor allem v. Soden in seinen Untersuchungen über den Ketzertaufstreit herausarbeiten wollte. Stephan antwortete nämlich auf jenes Synodalschreiben. Er schrieb einen Brief an Cyprian,[23] der freilich auch nicht erhalten ist. Aus einem Brief Cyprians an seinen Kollegen Pompeius bald darauf erfahren wir aber ziemlich genau seinen Inhalt. Stephan widersprach nicht nur den Afrikanern in allen Stücken. Er befahl ihnen auch, ihre Praxis aufzugeben und beim alten Herkommen zu bleiben, d. h. dem Herkommen, so wie Rom es verstand. Und er drohte wohl sogar bereits jetzt mit der Exkommunikation für den Fall, daß diese seine Aufforderung keinen entsprechenden Erfolg haben sollte.[24] Die folgende sich fast überschlagende Entwicklung ist nun allerdings nicht ganz durchsichtig. Um jetzt nämlich auch in den Einzelheiten ganz sicher zu gehen, um z. B. die Frage sicher beantworten zu können, ob Stephan seine Drohung tatsächlich wahrgemacht hat, müßten wir wirklich im Besitz aller in dieser Zeit gewechselten Schriftstücke sein und darüberhinaus nicht nur wissen, wann sie abgesendet wurden, sondern auch, wann sie beim Adressaten eingingen. Inzwischen tagte nämlich, wohl im September 256, in Kar-

---

chem Konzil dieser Brief zuzuteilen ist, dem vom Frühjahr oder dem vom Herbst 256 (s. u.), soll hier nicht noch einmal eingegangen werden. Vgl. G. Rauschen, Der Ketzertaufstreit zur Zeit des hl. Cyprian. In: Theologie und Glaube 8 (1916) 629–638, bes. 631 f.

[20] „de eo uel maxime tibi scribendum et cum tua grauitate ac sapientia conferendum fuit quod magis pertineat et ad sacerdotalem auctoritatem et ad ecclesiae catholicae unitatem pariter ac dignitatem de diuinae dispositionis ordinatione uenientem . . ." Ib. 775, 6–10.

[21] Vgl. o. Anm. 13.

[22] Vgl. die Annahme eines Schreibens von Stephanus an Jubajan wohl in Mauretanisch bei verschiedenen Forschern – vgl. die gewichtigen Untersuchungen von J. Ernst, Papst Stephan I. und der Ketzertaufstreit = Forschungen zur christl. Literatur- und Dogmengesch. 5, 4 (Mainz 1905), die Zusammenstellung der verschiedenen Meinungen bei Rauschen (s. o. Anm. 19) 637 f. – sowie eines weiteren noch früheren Briefes, den Harnack, Geschichte der altchristlichen Literatur 2, 3, 359 aus ep. 71, 2.3 folgern will. Vgl. auch die Interpretation des ganzen Streites bei v. Soden, der den Gegensatz Karthago–Rom besonders scharf heraushebt.

[23] Vgl. Cyprian an Pompeius, ep. 74, 1 CSEL 3, 2, 799, 9 ff.

[24] Vgl. ep. 74, 8 ib 805, 12–16. Freilich kann die Stelle auch anders verstanden werden, s. v. Soden, Ketzertaufstreit 20.

thago ein neues Konzil, das dritte in dieser Sache, diesmal mit 87 Bischöfen beschickt, das sich ausschließlich der Ketzertaufe widmete und dessen Protokoll noch vorhanden ist.[25] Ihm lag dieses Schreiben Stephans offenbar noch nicht vor.[26] Einstimmig bestätigten die Bischöfe in namentlicher Votierung die karthagische Praxis. Eine eindrücklichere Demonstration war kaum denkbar. Was sich nun aber weiter ereignete, erfahren wir nur aus einem Brief, den Bischof Firmilian von Caesarea in Kappadozien einige Monate später, wohl Ende des Jahres 256 an Cyprian sendete, damit ein verlorenes Schreiben Cyprians beantwortend.[27] Dieser Brief zeigt zuerst die Weite des Streites. Er zeigt, daß er nicht nur als eine begrenzte Angelegenheit zwischen Rom und Karthago, und d. h. zwischen Nordafrika und Italien und damit also des lateinischen Westens abgetan werden kann. Es war quasi doch die ganze Kirche mit eingespannt. Und er zeigt auch, in welcher Weise das geschehen war: das mit der karthagischen Praxis übereinstimmende Vorgehen im Osten in Sachen der Gültigkeit bzw. Ungültigkeit der Ketzertaufe wurde schon einmal erwähnt. Man wußte im Westen offenbar sehr genau darüber Bescheid, und nicht nur in Karthago, sondern auch in Rom. Denn offenbar – das folgt ebenfalls aus diesem Brief – hatte Stephan nicht nur nach Karthago geschrieben. Er hatte sich auch nach dem Osten gewendet – der konkrete Anlaß dafür ist uns unbekannt – und hatte zumal wohl nach beiden Seiten hin das wahrgemacht, was sein Brief an Cyprian vielleicht nur angedroht hatte: er hatte die Exkommunikation ausgesprochen. Damit nähern wir uns dem Höhepunkt, zugleich aber auch dem Ausgang des Streites.

Nun ist es freilich wegen der außerordentlich schmalen Quellenbasis[28] bis heute umstritten, ob Stephan diesen äußersten Schritt tatsächlich vollzogen hat oder nicht. Eine Übersicht über die dazu abgegebenen Stimmen benötigt die ganze Breite der Skala aller möglichen Urteile, wobei der konfessionelle Standpunkt der Urteilenden nicht unbedingt ins Gewicht fällt, wie J. Ernst es noch in seiner speziellen Untersuchung über diese Frage[29] anzunehmen geneigt war. Augustin hat den Donatisten gegenüber immer wieder betont, daß Cyprian die Einheit der Kirche bewahrt habe. Einen ähnlichen Standpunkt vertreten unter den Modernen am entschiedensten Hefele in seiner Konziliengeschichte,[30] dazu das LThK (2. Aufl.)[31] sowie auch die RGG (3.

---

[25] bei Augustin, de baptismo contra Donatistas 6–7, CSEL 51 Augustinus 7, 1, sowie separat als Sententiae episcoporum numero LXXXVII de haereticis baptizandis, bei Cyprian, op. I, CSEL 3, 1, 435–461.
[26] Siehe Rauschen 632 f.
[27] Cyprian ep. 75, CSEL 3, 2, 810–827.
[28] Zu dem Brief Firmilians an Cyprian und hier bes. die §§ 6.24 und 25, deren Echtheit hier vorausgesetzt werden soll, ohne die Diskussion darüber noch einmal zu referieren, kommt lediglich noch eine knappe Notiz bei Euseb, eccl. 7, 5, 4, GCS 9, 2 Euseb 2, 2, 640 über den Abbruch der Beziehungen mit dem Osten.
[29] J. Ernst, War der heilige Cyprian excommuniciert? In: Zeitschrift für kath. Theologie 18 (1894) 473–499.
[30] Bd. 1, 121: „Gewiß ist nur, daß die Kirchengemeinschaft zwischen beiden nicht abgebrochen wurde."
[31] Bd. 6, 132 Art. „Ketzertaufe" von J. Finkenzeller: „Ein eigentliches Schisma wurde vermieden."

Aufl.).[32] Dagegen spricht Seebergs Dogmengeschichte von der Aufhebung der Kirchengemeinschaft mit den afrikanischen und kleinasiatischen Kirchen seitens Stephan[33] und findet darin bei Lietzmann,[34] aber auch bei Baus im neuen katholischen Handbuch der Kirchengeschichte[35] Unterstützung, um beiderseits nur die Entschiedensten zu nennen. Andere Urteile bleiben vorsichtig unentschieden.

Es geht einfach darum, welches Gewicht man einigen Stellen aus dem Brief Firmilians an Cyprian beimißt. Hier heißt es immerhin, Stephan habe Frieden und Einheit der Kirche zu brechen gewagt.[36] In direkter Anrede hält Firmilian Stephan vor, in Wirklichkeit habe er sich selbst getrennt, denn der sei ein „schismaticus, qui se a communione ecclesiasticae unitatis apostatum fecerit".[37] Vor allem aber kommt es darauf an, wie die Szene zu deuten ist, über die Firmilian in dem dann folgenden Abschnitt berichtet: Eine Bischofsdelegation aus Afrika, welche in dieser Sache mit Rom verhandeln sollte, wurde nicht nur von Stephan nicht empfangen. Ihr wurde darüber hinaus jegliche Aufnahme und Gastfreundschaft verweigert.[38] Über den Zeitpunkt dieser Gesandschaft läßt sich nichts Endgültiges feststellen. Sie gehört sicher in die 2. Hälfte des Jahres 256, wie es auch sicher scheint, daß ihre Rückkehr nicht vor Abfassung des Briefes 74 anzusetzen sein wird. Näheres aber bleibt dunkel.

Mir scheint doch, daß dieser Vorgang die praktische Aufhebung der Kirchengemeinschaft zwischen Karthago und Rom seitens Rom genügend beweist. In welcher Form die Gemeinschaft aufgekündigt wurde,[39] ist demgegenüber zweitrangig. Die Spaltung war da. Und daran ändert nichts, ob sie durch eine peremptorische Exkommunikation zustande kam oder solenn ausgesprochen wurde. Ferner bleibt dabei zu bedenken: daß wir von einer ausdrücklichen Erklärung Stephans nichts wissen, besagt noch nicht, daß sie nicht erfolgte. Manche Forscher sind geneigt, ein entsprechendes formales Schreiben Stephans anzunehmen.[40] Und weiter: es geht nicht an, in jener Zeit Formen vorauszusetzen, welche sich erst im Laufe der Kirchengeschichte langsam herausbildeten. Von Exkommunicatio maior und minor wußte man damals noch nichts. Und außerdem ist das Beispiel geeignet, noch einmal zu unterstreichen, wie wenig Stephan schon imstande war, wirklich päpstlich im

---

[32] Bd. 3, 1257 Art. „Ketzertaufstreit" von H. Karpp: „Der Tod Stephans und Cyprians verhinderte die Kirchenspaltung" und: „Stephan drohte mit dem Abbruch der Kirchengemeinschaft". Von einer Ausführung der Drohung wird nicht gesprochen.
[33] Bd. 1 (Basel [4]1953) 622.
[34] Geschichte der alten Kirche (Berlin [2]1953) 241.
[35] Handbuch der Kirchengeschichte, hrsg. v. H. Jedin, 1, Von der Urgemeinde zur frühchristlichen Großkirche, v. K. Baus (Freiburg–Basel–Wien 1963) 405 ff.: „Bruch", „Spaltung".
[36] CSEL 3, 2, 813, 27 ff.
[37] Ebenda 825, 17 f.
[38] Ep. 75, 25, CSEL 3, 2, 826, 7–12.
[39] Darauf legt vor allem die Untersuchung von Ernst großes Gewicht, s. o. Anm. 22.
[40] Z. B. Harnack, Chronologie 2, 2, 359.

Sinne der Gesamtkirche zu handeln. Alles, was er tun konnte, war, seiner-
seits die Kirchengemeinschaft aufzukündigen. Das bedeutete aber keineswegs,
daß der davon Betroffene deshalb auch schon von der Gesamtkirche getrennt
war.[41]

Der endliche Ausgang des Streites ist schnell berichtet. Beide Gegner,
Cyprian und Stephanus, wurden fast gleichzeitig im nächsten Jahr schon
ihren Wirkungskreisen entrissen. Stephan war das erste Opfer der neuen Verfolgung unter Valerian. Er starb am 2. August 257 den Märtyrertod. Cyprian
wurde zunächst (Ende August) nur verbannt, ein Jahr später aber, am 14.
September 258 erlangte auch er die Märtyrerkrone. Zuvor jedoch war bereits
der Verkehr mit Rom wieder normalisiert. Es ist offenbar der Intervention
des Dionys von Alexandrien, worüber Euseb berichtet,[42] zuzuschreiben, daß
der Nachfolger Stephans auf dem Bischofsstuhl in Rom, Sixtus II., den Verkehr wieder aufnahm. Damit war jedoch keine Bereinigung der Angelegenheit in sachlicher Hinsicht verbunden. Beide Seiten blieben offenbar bei ihrer
Überzeugung. Augustins spätere Meldung von einem Widerruf Cyprians, die
auch in der Geschichtsschreibung zuweilen Anerkennung gefunden hat, dürfte
nicht den Tatsachen entsprechen.[43] Die sachlichen Fronten blieben noch jahrzehntelang bestehen. Doch wurden sie wie schon vordem nicht mehr für
kirchentrennend erachtet. Erst das Konzil von Arles 314 setzte speziell für
die Afrikaner definitiv fest, daß eine Taufe, sofern sie auf die Trinität er-
folgt sei, nicht wiederholt werden dürfe. Lediglich die Handauflegung habe
zu erfolgen, damit der Heilige Geist vermittelt würde.[44]

III.

Kommen wir nun zum Sachlich-Inhaltlichen und betrachten zunächst die
Position Cyprians. Ausschlaggebend für ihn ist nicht die Frage nach dem
Sakrament, sondern die nach der Kirche. In zwei Briefen, die hierher gehören, stehen z. B. die so berühmt gewordenen Sätze: „ut habere qui possit
Deum patrem, habeat ante ecclesiam matrem".[45] Und: „salus extra ecclesiam
non est".[46] Schon Hans v. Soden hat auf diesen Aspekt aufmerksam gemacht.[47] Ich meine, er ist noch bedeutend stärker in den Vordergrund zu
rücken, weil die schließlich herbeigeführten Entscheidungen hier sogleich zum
Tragen kommen.

Fragen wir also nach der Kirche, so ist damit freilich für Cyprian ein gan-

---

[41] Vgl. auch v. Soden, Ketzertaufstreit 33.
[42] Hist. eccl. 5, 7.
[43] Siehe vor allem J. Ernst, Der angebliche Widerruf Cyprians in der Ketzer-
tauffrage. In: Zeitschrift f. kath. Theologie 19 (1895) 234–272.
[44] Siehe Mansi 2, 472 A; Denzinger 53 sowie auch Hefele, Konziliengeschichte
1, 209.
[45] Ep. 74, 7, CSEL 3, 2, 804, 23 f.
[46] Ep. 73, 21, ib. 795, 3 f.
[47] v. Soden, Ketzertaufstreit 38: „Ganz mit Recht sagt Cyprian wieder und
wieder, daß man mit der Taufe den Häretikern auch eine Art von Kirche zuge-
steht."

zer Problemkreis angeschnitten, der hier auch nicht im entferntesten in seinem ganzen Ausmaß abgeschritten werden kann. Zur Frage nach der Kirche in der Theologie Cyprians gehört vor allem das Thema, ob und wie weit es für ihn eine päpstliche Gewalt gegeben hat, die sich im Bischof von Rom manifestiert und als solche die Einheit der Kirche garantiert. Da sich seine Bestreitung der Gültigkeit der Ketzertaufe gerade gegen Stephan von Rom richtete, ist dieses Thema natürlich auch hier nicht auszuklammern. Es lassen sich aus den Äußerungen und dem Verhalten Cyprians in der Auseinandersetzung mit Stephan gewisse Rückschlüsse zur Beantwortung auch jener Frage ziehen. Dies soll aber dennoch hier am Rande stehen bleiben, weil das eigentliche Thema eben ein anderes war. Dieses möchte ich so formulieren: Grundlage der Stellungnahmen Cyprians gegen die Gültigkeit der Ketzertaufe ist seine These: Nur die bischöflich verfaßte Kirche ist wirkliche Kirche. Sie hat ihre Einheit in der Einheit und gegenseitigen Anerkennung der einzelnen Bischöfe und findet ihren Grund in der Jurisdiktion der einzelnen Bischöfe. Wer sich aus dieser Einheit löst oder aus diesen Grenzen ausbricht, trennt sich damit auch von Christus und seinem Heil.

Besonders aufschlußreich ist dafür gleich das zeitlich früheste Dokument im Streite, die ep. 69 ad Magnum, welche auf die Frage antwortet, „ob man unter den übrigen Ketzern auch die von Novatianus kommenden nach seinem unheiligen Bade (das meint die dort gespendete Taufe) in der katholischen Kirche mit der gesetzmäßigen und wahren und einzigen kirchlichen Taufe versehen und heiligen müsse".[48] Aufschlußreich ist diese Frage insofern, als sie nicht durch Ausweitung auf alle möglichen Ketzereien verwischt wurde. Diese blieben im Verlauf der Erörterung keineswegs ausgeschlossen. Cyprian gibt mehrfach regelrechte Ketzerlisten, auch schon in diesem Brief,[49] die alle mit bedacht werden müßten. Aber in dem mit Novatian angesprochenen Falle ging es eben nur um eine disziplinäre Entscheidung, nicht um Lehrgegensätze. Cyprians Antwort ist ein Loblied auf die eine Kirche. Es gibt nur eine Kirche. Diese war, betrachtet man den Fall nach seiner Genese, vertreten in dem rechtmäßig eingesetzten und dann mit dem Martyrium ausgezeichneten Bischof Cornelius, der als einziger legitim dem Bischof Fabian folgte.[50] Novation hingegen ist nicht eingesetzt, sondern hat sich selber zum Bischof gemacht, sagt Cyprian. Er ist nicht Nachfolger irgendeines anderen[51] und steht insofern außerhalb der Kirche. Er hat sich selber ausgeschlossen.[52] Damit hatte Cyprian seinem Kirchenbegriff entsprechend praktisch schon alles gesagt.

1. Es gibt – betrachten wir die Kirche – ein ganz scharf auseinander zu haltendes Drinnen und Draußen, das sich also gerade hierin entscheidet. Weil Novation den rechtmäßigen Bischof Cornelius nicht anerkannte, sondern sich

[48] Ep. 69, 1, CSEL 3, 2, 749, 6–9, Übersetzung nach der Bibliothek der Kirchenväter 60, Cyprian 2 (München 1928) 306.
[49] Siehe ep. 69, 8; 73, 4; 74, 2.7.
[50] Ep. 69,3 (752, 10 ff.).
[51] Ib. (752, 13 ff.); 69, 5 (753, 20 ff.).
[52] Ep. 69, 4 (753, 12 ff.).

selber zum Bischof gemacht hat, steht er nun draußen und hat nichts, aber auch gar nichts mehr gemein mit denen, die drinnen sind. Die eine Kirche ist nicht zugleich drinnen und draußen.[53] Denn drinnen heißt das, wo der rechtmäßige Bischof ist.

Von dieser Grundentscheidung ist alles, was Cyprian im Verlauf des Streites zu sagen hatte, abgeleitet. Der Begriff „foris" – „draußen" ist die alles beherrschende Vokabel, die überall und immer wiederholt wird.[54] Dazu gebrauchte Cyprian sehr aufschlußreiche Bilder. Die Kirche ist, nach Hohel. 4, 12 ein verschlossener Garten und eine versiegelte Quelle,[55] oder noch stärker: die Kirche nimmt die Stelle des Paradieses ein, das mit Mauern umgeben ist und fruchttragende Bäume in sich schließt, welche durch vier Ströme gewässert werden. Wer sich aber außerhalb dieser Mauern befindet, muß verdursten.[56] Die diesem Bilde zugrunde liegende Stelle Gen. 2, 8 ff. sagt nichts von solchen Mauern. Das Zitat zeigt, worauf es Cyprian ankam: auf feste Grenzen, auf eine deutliche Unterscheidung. Dasselbe unterstrich Cyprian mehrfach in eindrucksvollen Vergleichen: „Es gibt keine Gemeinschaft von Lüge und Wahrheit, Tod und Unsterblichkeit, von Antichrist und Christus."[57]

2. Infolgedessen ist Cyprian nicht bereit, zwischen den Draußenstehenden irgendwie zu differenzieren, also z. B. in seiner Antwort auf die Frage des Magnus nach Novatian und seinen Anhängern disziplinäre und lehrmäßige Unterschiede auseinander zu halten. Die Gegner sind sämtlich haeretici;[58] schismatici,[59] adversarii,[60] antichristi,[61] blasphemantes,[62] inimici,[63] hostes,[64] rebelles,[65] alieni,[66] profani,[67] peruersi[68] und was Cyprian sonst noch an Begriffen zu Gebote stand. Dabei machte er durchaus keinerlei Unterschiede. Vor allem unterschied er nicht zwischen Häretikern und Schismatikern. Denn der Effekt ihres Tuns – und auf den kam es Cyprian ausschließlich an – ist in jedem Falle derselbe: ob Häretiker oder Schismatiker, alle sind Antichristen.[69] Auch Schismatiker sind den Heiden gleichzuachten.[70]

---

[53] Ep. 69, 3 (752, 9).
[54] Ep. 69, 4 (752, 18); 5 (754, 20); 11 (760, 5); 71, 1 (775, 10); 73, 1 (778, 13); 74, 8 (805, 19) u. ö.
[55] Ep. 69, 2 (751, 2); 74, 11 (808, 24).
[56] Ep. 73, 10 (785, 16 ff.), vgl. Gen. 2, 8 f.
[57] Ep. 71, 2 (773, 5–7), ähnlich ep. 74, 4 (802, 10–13) oder noch weiter ausgeführt 74, 8 (806, 5–8).
[58] Ep. 69, 1. 10. 11. 16; 70, 1. 2. 3; 71, 1 usw.
[59] Ep. 69, 1.6. 7. 9. 11; 70, 1. 3; 71, 1 usw
[60] Ep. 69, 1. 11. 16; 70, 2. 3; 71, 1; 73, 14 u. ö.
[61] Ep. 69, 1.10. 11. 16; 73, 14; 74, 2.
[62] Ep. 74, 7. 8.
[63] Ep. 69, 1. 5.
[64] Ep. 69, 1; 71, 1. 2; 73, 2. 10. 15.
[65] Ep. 69, 1; 73, 2. 10.
[66] Ep. 69, 2. 5.
[67] Ebenda.
[68] Ep. 74, 2.
[69] Vgl. ep. 69, 1.
[70] Ep. 69, 6: „ostendit (Christus), schismaticos gentilibus adaequari." CSEL 3, 2, 756, 4 f. ähnlich 70, 3 (770, 15–17).

3. Es ist auch ein Trugschluß anzunehmen, daß, wie im Falle Novatians, der Glaube in der Kirche und bei ihm ein und derselbe sei und in Bezug auf die Tauflehre doch kein Unterschied bestehe. Denn wenn z. B. bei der Taufe auch der Novatianer die Frage gestellt werde: „Glaubst du an die Vergebung der Sünden und an das ewige Leben durch die heilige Kirche?", so sei schon in dieser Frage eine Lüge enthalten, denn eine Kirche gäbe es ja eben dort gar nicht.[71] Die Rotte Korah sei ein gutes Beispiel dafür, daß ein übereinstimmendes Bekenntnis nicht das Vergehen angemaßter Amtsbefugnisse aufwiege.[72] Deshalb gilt: weder Gott den Vater noch Christus seinen Sohn noch den Heiligen Geist, weder den Glauben noch die Kirche haben wir mit den Ketzern gemeinsam.[73]

4. Wer nicht in der Kirche ist, hat nicht den Heiligen Geist. Wer aber den Heiligen Geist nicht hat, vermag keine geistlichen Güter mitzuteilen.[74] Wer nicht in der Kirche ist, ist unter die Toten zu rechnen. Wer aber tot ist, vermag nicht wieder Leben zu spenden.[75] Wer den Heiligen Geist nicht hat, vermag keine Sünden zu vergeben[76] und kein Taufwasser zu heiligen,[77] kein Öl zu weihen zur Salbung und keine Eucharistie zu spenden.[78] Folglich vermag er auch überhaupt nicht zu taufen.[79] Folglich kann keine Rede davon sein, daß die zur Kirche Übertretenden „wiedergetauft" würden. Denn sie sind noch nicht getauft,[80] sondern lediglich mit Wasser begossen,[81] ja besudelt worden.[82] Nichts, was draußen geschieht, kann gebilligt werden. Alles ist leer und falsch.[83] Deshalb muß auch gesagt werden, daß die Draußenstehenden ohne jede Hoffnung sind und sich selber in das größte Verderben stürzen.[84]

5. Worum es Cyprian ging, erhellt vor allen Dingen aus den Stellen seiner Briefe, wo er den Standpunkt seiner Gegner näher ins Auge fassend Konsequenzen zu ziehen versucht: „Nicht um ein kleines und unbedeutendes Zugeständnis an die Ketzer handelt es sich," sagte er,[85] „wenn wir ihre Taufe als gültig hinnehmen; hier nimmt ja doch der ganze Ursprung des Glaubens und der heilbringende Zugang zur Hoffnung des ewigen Lebens und die göttliche Gnade zur Reinigung und Belebung der Diener Gottes ihren Anfang. Denn wenn einer bei den Ketzern die Taufe empfangen könnte, so könnte er sicher-

---

[71] Ep. 69, 7 (756, 6 ff.); 70, 2 (768, 6 ff.).
[72] Ep. 69, 8 (756, 19 ff.).
[73] Ep. 73, 21 (795, 7–9); vgl. auch die Erwägungen zu Marcion ib. 4 f. (781 f.).
[74] Ep. 70, 2 (769, 4–6).
[75] Ep. 71, 1 (772, 11–13).
[76] Ep. 69, 11 (759, 11–13. 18–20); 73, 7 (783, 22–784, 2).
[77] Ep. 70, 1 (767, 14 f. 20–768, 2).
[78] Ep. 70, 2 (768, 13–20).
[79] Ep. 69, 10 (759, 6–10).
[80] Ep. 71, 1 (771, 17–772, 2), ähnlich 73, 1 (779, 6–8).
[81] Ep. 71, 1 (771, 9; 772, 7 f.).
[82] Ep. 69, 16 (765, 13–15); 72, 1 (775, 10 f.), ähnlich 73, 21 (795, 4–7). Vgl. auch 73, 6 (782, 21), sowie „aqua mendax et perfida" ib. (783, 4 f.) und 74, 2 (800, 6 f.).
[83] Ep. 70, 3 (769, 20–770, 1).
[84] Ep. 69, 6 (754, 15–17).
[85] Ep. 73, 12 (786 f.), die Übersetzung folgt wiederum der Bibliothek der Kirchenväter, s. o. Anm. 48.

lich auch die Vergebung der Sünden erlangen. Hat er die Vergebung der
Sünden erlangt, so ist er geheiligt; ist er geheiligt, so ist er ein Tempel Gottes
geworden . . . " Damit wird aber auf einmal Weiß und Schwarz nebeneinander gestellt und Dinge werden miteinander vereinigt, welche nicht zu verein-
baren sind. Die Folge davon ist, daß bei den Ketzern und besonders deren
Anhängern der Annahme Vorschub geleistet wird, „auch die Kirche und ihre
ewigen Gaben auf gültige und rechtmäßige Weise zu besitzen".[86] Und damit
gerät mehr als das Missionswerk der Kirche an ihnen ins Wanken. Praktisch
fängt alles an zu wackeln! Die Taufe der Ketzer verteidigen heißt, den Glauben und die Wahrheit preisgeben![87] „Dann laßt uns die Waffen wegwerfen,
dann wollen wir uns freiwillig gefangen geben, dann wollen wir die Anord-
nung des Evangeliums, die Verfügung Christi, die Majestät Gottes dem Teu-
fel überantworten, dann mag man den Fahneneid des göttlichen Kriegsdien-
stes brechen und die Feldzeichen des himmlischen Heerlagers ausliefern, dann
mag unterliegen und weichen die Kirche den Ketzern, das Licht der Finster-
nis, der Glaube dem Unglauben, die Hoffnung der Verzweiflung, die Ver-
nunft dem Irrtum, die Unsterblichkeit dem Tode, die Liebe dem Haß, die
Wahrheit der Lüge, Christus dem Antichrist."[88] Soweit Cyprian.

Daß er trotz dieser so emphatisch vorgetragenen Entschiedenheit dennoch
mehrfach betonte, niemanden von seiner persönlichen Meinung und Praxis
abbringen, niemandem Vorschriften machen zu wollen,[89] ehrt zwar seine
Friedensliebe, ist aber trotzdem sachlich wenig verständlich und schwächte
deshalb auch entschieden seine Position.

IV.

Betrachten wir nun die Gegenseite, so müssen wir zunächst festhalten, daß
sie weit weniger eindeutig zu bezeichnen ist, nämlich deswegen, weil sie, wie
schon festgestellt, auch weit weniger Eloquenz entwickelte als Cyprian in diesem Falle; zum anderen aus dem Grunde, daß sich nicht einmal dieses Wenige
mehr erhalten hat, sondern sich in nur wenigen Leitsätzen lediglich aus den
Äußerungen der Gegner rekonstruieren läßt. Nur an einer einzigen Stelle
tritt die Cyprian gegenüberstehende Front unmittelbar in Erscheinung, in
einer kleinen separaten Schrift, dem „Liber de rebaptismate", der aber auch
wiederum noch im Halbdunkel bleibt dadurch, daß er anonym überliefert ist
und sich nur mit Wahrscheinlichkeitsgründen zeitlich etwa im Jahre 256 und
räumlich – vielleicht! – in Mauretanien unterbringen läßt.[90] Schließlich jedoch
wird eine genaue Fixierung der Gegenseite noch dadurch erschwert, daß zwi-

---

[86] Ep. 73, 24 (797, 5 f.).

[87] Ep. 74, 8 (806, 13).

[88] Ebenda (806, 2–8). Vgl. auch die dem entsprechenden Ausfälle gegen die Ver-
teidiger der Ketzertaufe. Diese sind für Cyprian u. a. „praevaricatores fidei atque
ecclesiae proditores" ep. 69, 10 (759, 3 f.).

[89] Vgl. ep. 69, 17; 72, 3; 73, 26.

[90] Siehe J. Ernst, Wann und wo wurde der Liber de rebaptismate verfaßt? In:
Zeitschrift f. kath. Theologie 20 (1896) 193–255; L. Nelke, Die Chronologie der
Korrespondenz Cyprians und der pseudocyprianischen Schriften Ad Novatianum

schen den bei Cyprian und Firmilian überlieferten Äußerungen Stephans und
dem Traktat de rebaptismate keineswegs Lehreinheit besteht,[91] und die Dif-
ferenzen gerade den Punkt betreffen, der in unserem Zusammenhang von
wesentlicher Bedeutung ist. Denn vertrat der Anonymus des liber de rebaptismate auch die Gültigkeit der bei den Ketzern geübten Taufe, trat er damit
also neben Stephan in einer Front gegen Cyprian an, so doch nur insofern,
als er scharf zwischen der Geisttaufe und der Wassertaufe unterschied. Nur
die Geisttaufe bewirke das Heil, während die Wassertaufe, und zwar auch
die in der Kirche geübte, nur eine Anwartschaft verleihe. In der Kirche zwar
verlaufen beide Akte in der Regel parallel, weil der Taufende der Bischof ist
und die Handauflegung des Bischofs den Geist vermittelt. Bei den Ketzern
aber wird nur die Wassertaufe gespendet, denn dort ist selbstverständlich
der Geist nicht.[92]

Diese Anschauung bildete natürlich keinen echten Gegensatz zu der Position Cyprians, sondern schuf gänzlich neue Fronten, indem sie nämlich nun
wirklich die Taufe als Thema in den Mittelpunkt stellte durch die Vorlage
einer ganz neuen Interpretation derselben. Ein weiterer Blick auf die wenigen von Stephan überlieferten Fragmente zeigt, daß an der Taufe als solcher
auch von Seiten Stephans überhaupt nichts fraglich war. Über Ritus und Bedeutung der Taufe qua Wassertaufe waren sich Stephan und Cyprian durchaus einig.[93] Zur Debatte stand einzig und allein die Frage, wer diese gültig
zu spenden vermag, und d. h. also: die Frage nach der Kirche.

Denn von Stephan heißt es nun immerhin nach dem Zeugnis Firmilians,
der die meisten der fraglichen Stellen überliefert, „die Vergebung der Sünden
und die zweite Geburt könne bei der Taufe der Ketzer erfolgen".[94] Stephan
räume den Ketzern „nicht etwa nur eine geringe, sondern die höchste Gewalt
der Gnade ein, indem er behauptet und versichert, sie vermöchten durch das
Sakrament der Taufe den Schmutz des alten Menschen abzuwaschen, die
alten Totsünden zu vergeben, durch die himmliche Wiedergeburt Kinder

---

und Liber de rebaptismate (Thorn 1902) 171–203; H. Koch, Zeit und Heimat des
liber de rebaptismate. In: ZNW 8 (1907) 190–221; v. Soden, Ketzertaufstreit
29–33. Auf die Frage, ob Cyprian den liber gekannt, benutzt und gegen ihn ge-
stritten hat, bzw. der Verfasser des liber umgekehrt die Briefe Cyprians, muß hier
dahingestellt bleiben. Sicherheit ist weder in der einen noch der anderen Frage zu
erhalten.

[91] Siehe Ernst ib. 217–219, auch Koch ib. trotz seiner von der Ernsts abweichen-
den Deutung der Tauflehre des liber de rebaptismate, s. die folgende Anm.

[92] Siehe J. Ernst, Die Lehre des liber de rebaptismate von der Taufe. In: Zeitschrift f. kath. Theologie 24 (1900) 425–462 sowie H. Koch, Die Tauflehre des Liber
de rebaptismate = Vorlesungsverzeichnis Braunsberg 1907, der sich von Ernst insofern unterscheidet, als er den Anonymus des liber „hinsichtlich der Wirksamkeit
der kirchlichen Taufe im großen und ganzen auf kirchlichem Standpunkt" stehen
läßt. In dieser werden schon „die Sünden nachgelassen, die Seelen gereinigt, die
Erlösungsgnade dem einzelnen zugewandt, das Heil des Menschen begründet" (59).

[93] Auf die Debatte über die Taufformel, ob Stephan eine Taufe nur auf den
Namen Jesu anerkannte und sich Cyprians Protest dagegen gerichtet habe, kann
hier nicht näher eingegangen werden, vgl. J. Ernst (s. o. Anm. 22) 93–116.

[94] Ep. 75, 8 (815, 10 f.).

Gottes zu schaffen und durch die Heiligung des göttlichen Bades zum ewigen Leben zu erneuern".[95] D. h. die Taufe auch bei den Ketzern ist eine nicht nur formal, sondern auch inhaltlich vollgültige Taufe, die keiner Ergänzung mehr bedarf.[96]

Der Grund dafür liegt in der Tatsache, daß in der Taufe etwas geschieht, was unabhängig ist von dem, der da tauft.[97] Konkreter und positiv: die Taufe auch bei den Ketzern hat ihre volle Gültigkeit vermöge der Tatsache, daß in ihr der Name Jesu Christi angerufen wird. Dieses Argument begegnet mehrfach. Es war offenbar nicht erst im (zweiten?) Schreiben Stephans nach Afrika enthalten, wovon Cyprian in ep. 74 an Pompeius berichtet,[98] sondern ganz analog dazu schon in dem Schreiben an Jubaian, welches jener Cyprian übersandte und von diesem in ep. 73 beantwortet wurde.[99] Selbstverständlich begegnet es dann auch in dem Schreiben Firmilians an Cyprian.[100] Hier heißt es in der Form eines regelrechten Zitates: „Der Name Christi trägt viel zum Glauben und zur Heiligung der Taufe bei, so daß jeder, der irgendwo im Namen Christi getauft wird, sofort die Gnade Christi erlangt."[101] Wie das gemeint ist, erhellt schon aus ep. 69: „Novation beobachte ja das heilige Gesetz wie die katholische Kirche, er taufe unter der gleichen Glaubensformel wie wir, er erkenne den gleichen Gott Vater, den gleichen Christus, Gottes Sohn, den gleichen Heiligen Geist an, und deshalb könne er die Gewalt zu taufen für sich in Anspruch nehmen, weil er offenbar in der Fragestellung bei der Taufe von uns gar nicht abweiche".[102] Auf das Glaubensbekenntnis also kommt es an, so daß Stephan auch sagen konnte: „Man darf nicht fragen, wer getauft habe, denn der Getaufte habe aufgrund seines Glaubens Vergebung der Sünden empfangen können."[103] Mit Nachdruck wird dasselbe dann auch von dem Anonymus des liber de rebaptismate vertreten.[104] Die Fragmente Stephans erfahren gerade in dem Punkte von hier eine wichtige Ergänzung. Hier geht es vor allem darum, die virtus des Namens Jesu herauszustellen. Darauf beruhe im Grunde genommen die ganze Kraft der Taufe und könne sich durchsetzen auch da, wo gar kein Glaube vorhanden sei. Wo und von wem der Name Christi angerufen wird, ist gleichgültig. Es kommt darauf an, daß es geschieht, dann kann es nämlich nicht leer und umsonst sein. Dann wird vielmehr eine Beziehung zwischen dem, über dem der Name ausgerufen wird, und Christus hergestellt, die von

---

[95] Ep. 75, 17 (821, 27–31), vgl. auch ep. 74, 7 (805, 2–7).

[96] Vgl. ep. 74, 2: „Omnium haereticorum baptismata iusta esse et legitima iudicauit (scil. Stephanus)" (799, 20 f.).

[97] Ep. 73, 4: „Quaerendum non sit quis baptizauerit, quando is qui baptizatus sit accipere remissam peccatorum potuerit secundum quod credidit" (781, 2–4), ähnlich ep. 75, 9 (815, 26–29).

[98] Ep. 74, 5 (802, 22–803, 1). 7 (805, 2–7).

[99] Ep. 73, 4 (781,5–8) und 16 (789, 22–790, 1).

[100] Ep. 75, 9 (815, 26–29) und 18 (822, 7–9).

[101] Ep. 75, 18.

[102] Ep. 69, 7 (756, 6–11).

[103] Ep. 73, 4 (781, 2–4).

[104] Vgl. vor allem die Kap. 6 und 7, CSEL 3, 3, 75 ff.

den äußeren Umständen unabhängig ist und respektiert werden muß. Folglich ist die Taufe, die jemand außerhalb der Kirche empfangen hat, nicht noch einmal zu wiederholen, vorzunehmen ist lediglich die Handauflegung, aber zur Rekonziliation,[105] nicht zur Taufergänzung, also zum Empfang des Hl. Geistes nach dem liber de rebaptismate.

Es ist eine zweite Frage, ob dieses Argument wirklich ausreicht, die eigene Position zu begründen. Harnack und auch Seeberg ist wohl Recht zu geben, wenn sie in dem Zusammenhang von „einer zauberhaften Kraft, die dem Namen Christi einwohnt" sprechen[106] und besonders auf jene Stellen des liber de rebaptismate hinweisen, welche betonen, daß auch von Fernstehenden und sogar von Übeltätern durch den Namen des Herrn Wundertaten vollbracht werden könnten.[107] Cyprian und seine Gesinnungsgenossen bedienten sich dieses modernen – ich möchte sagen „protestantischen" – Argumentes natürlich nicht. Für sie war eine solche Auffassung einfach ein absurdum[108] und ridiculum.[109] Und Cyprian unterscheidet in seiner Entgegnung darauf einmal mehr: „Es ist etwas anderes, wenn diejenigen, die drinnen in der Kirche sind, von dem Namen Christi sprechen, als wenn solche, die draußen stehen und gegen die Kirche handeln, im Namen Christi taufen."[110] Die letzte Instanz ist für ihn also auch in diesem Falle wieder die Grenze der Kirche. Außerhalb ihrer hat auch der Name Christi, die Anrufung Gottes, keine Kraft.

V.

Damit dürften die Anliegen der beiden einander gegenüberstehenden Fronten hinlänglich deutlich sein. Zu vereinigen waren sie kaum. Sich gegenseitig anzuerkennen als eine Möglichkeit, wie es vordem mehr oder weniger unbewußt geschehen war und auch nach dem Streite wieder geschah, war schon höchste Form der Askese, ohne jedoch Verheißung für die Zukunft zu haben. Denn die Meinungen schlossen einander aus. Welche weiteren Gründe mit dafür verantwortlich zu machen sein könnten, daß sich, wie dargestellt,[111] schließlich der Standpunkt Roms durchsetzte, bleibe hier unerörtert. Ohne Zweifel war er der realere von beiden und lag ganz auf der Linie der sich herausbildenden katholischen Sakramentslehre, so wenig formuliert eine solche damals auch noch war.

Was hier an den schließlichen Entscheidungen interessiert, ist eben ihr Ausschlag in Sachen jener von Cyprian so scharf gezogenen Grenzen der Kirche.

---

[105] Ep. 74, 1: „Si qui ergo a quacumque haeresi uenient ad uos, nihil innouetur nisi quod traditum est, ut manus illis inponatur in paenitentiam" (799, 15–17). Ob dazu die Bestimmung der Synode von Arles stimmt, s. o. bei Anm. 44, ist zweifelhaft, vgl. Hefele, Konziliengeschichte 1, 209.
[106] E. Seeberg, Dogmengeschichte 1, 621, vgl. Harnack, Dogmengeschichte 1, 475.
[107] Cap. 7, CSEL 3, 3, 78, 10 f. 17–19.
[108] Ep. 75, 9 (815, 26).
[109] Ib. (816, 7).
[110] Ep. 73, 14 (788, 19–22).
[111] S. o. bei Anm. 44.

„Außerhalb der Kirche gibt es kein Heil". Dieser Satz stand für Cyprian unerschütterlich fest. Daß sich ein ähnlicher Satz in den überlieferten Äußerungen der Gegenseite nicht findet, muß nicht besagen, daß er dort nicht auch möglich war. Sicher wurde auch von Rom und seinen Anhängern nicht das genaue Gegenteil vertreten. Aber wenn der Anonymus des liber de rebaptismate von der Anwartschaft auf das Heil sprach, welches die Wassertaufe vermittelt, und das war sicher auch im Sinne Stephans nicht zu viel, so war jene Grenze Cyprians doch zumindest den Gruppen gegenüber, welche sich in ihrem Glaubensstande von der Catholica nicht allzu weit entfernten, und vor allem den Novatianern gegenüber stark durchlässig gemacht. Dann war damit anerkannt, daß auch dort – um einen Ausdruck v. Sodens wieder aufzunehmen – „eine Art von Kirche" statt hat,[112] in welcher gültige, nur nicht endgültige Beziehungen zu Christus hergestellt werden können. Dann war damit de facto doch jener exklusive Standpunkt Cyprians zugunsten eines „ökumenischen" – wenn dieses moderne Wort einmal gebraucht werden darf – aufgegeben. Dann war damit der Weg freigekämpft für den späteren Einsatz Augustins, auch diejenigen als Brüder zu lieben, welche zwar mit der Kirche dasselbe Haupt bekennen, aber doch vom Leibe getrennt sind (womit nun Augustin freilich nicht zu einem Vater der modernen ökumenischen Bewegung erhoben werden soll, das würde auch seiner Tauflehre wenig entsprechen[113]).[114] Dann war im Grunde doch damals schon das Prinzip gewonnen, das – und damit kehren wir nun zu unserer ursprünglichen Fragestellung zurück und fassen dabei wohlgemerkt nur den Standpunkt Roms ins Auge – trotz Arles und Augustin eigentlich doch erst in der Moderne seiner Verwirklichung entgegen zu gehen scheint. Denn die Anerkennung anderer kirchlicher Gemeinschaften als Brüder und Kirche aufgrund der gemeinsamen Taufe ist eben – wiederum: trotz Augustin – das Neue, was das II. Vatikanum brachte. Zwischen Karthago und Rom war es damals um die Frage der Wiederaufnahme zur Kirche Zurückkehrender gegangen. Es geht Rom praktisch heute noch nur darum, wenn man dort von den „getrennten Brüdern" spricht. Das wird auch im Dekret „De oecumenismo" deutlich genug ausgesprochen, um protestantischerseits keine zu großen Illusionen darüber aufkommen zu lassen.[115] Entschieden aber wurde schon damals mehr, wesentlich mehr. Entschieden, und zwar positiv entschieden wurde nicht nur die Frage einer möglichen Koexistenz, sondern zumindest im Prinzip die Frage eines wirklichen Zusammenlebens und Zusammengehens, einer wirklichen Gemeinschaft, wovon heute die Konzilsdokumente sprechen. Denn wer die Taufe des anderen als gültig und wirkungskräftig anerkennt, wer zugibt, mit dem anderen unter dem gleichen Gesetz des Glaubens anzutreten, wer den anderen Bruder nennt, und das aus ehrlichem Herzen, der kann eigentlich nicht so freigebig sein in der Verteilung von Ketzerhüten, wie man sich trotz-

---

[112] S. o. Anm. 47.
[113] Vgl. W. Jetter, Die Taufe beim jungen Luther = Beiträge zur hist. Theologie 18 (Tübingen 1954) 1–32.
[114] Augustin, Ennar. in psalmos 32, 2, 2, 29, CChL 38, 272 f.
[115] Becker 242 f.

dem zeigte, der kann nicht interessiert daran sein, so unüberschreitbare Grenzen zu ziehen, wie Cyprian es versuchte und nach ihm die Kirche durch viele Jahrhunderte hindurch, seinen Standpunkt gleichsam durch die Praxis noch rechtfertigend.

Die protestantischen Kirchen, die die Ergebnisse des II. Vatikanischen Konzils mit Aufmerksamkeit prüfen, werden sich also nicht nur ihrer freuen können, so unübersehbar der Fortschritt im einzelnen auch sein mag. Sie werden auch mit ihrer Kritik nicht sparen dürfen. Und diese sollte sich wiederum nicht allein auf das Geltendmachen ihrer eigenen Wünsche und Standpunkte zu den jeweiligen Fragen beschränken. Oskar Cullmann hat mit Recht darauf aufmerksam gemacht, daß bei keinem Urteil, vor allem protestantischerseits vergessen werden darf, daß es ein katholisches Konzil war und die Kirche bei ihrem Neuaufbruch diesen doch als katholische Kirche tut.[116] Gerade dem soll auch hier Rechnung getragen werden. Wir haben hier ja nur einen Aspekt eines Teils jener Basis ins Auge gefaßt. Der zweite, der gemeinsame Glaube an Jesus Christus, mußte ganz ausgeklammert bleiben. Er birgt wahrlich nicht weniger Probleme als der vom rechten Gebrauch der Taufe, welcher ja auch noch mehr Probleme in sich schließt als hier verhandelt. Erinnert sei hier nur noch einmal an das im Anschluß an das Konzil intern kirchlich ergangene ökumenische Direktorium. Die protestantischen Kirchen sollten gerade im Herausarbeiten sachlicher Gesichtspunkte versuchen, den römisch-katholischen Brüdern zu helfen, ihren eigenen Standpunkt zu finden, und ihnen Mut zu machen, konsequent zu sein und damit, wie dargestellt, auch Desiderata zu erfüllen, die schon lange anstehen, nicht um eines Programms der Vergangenheit willen, sondern um der Gegenwart gerecht zu werden und um Wege zu finden, die wirklich in die Zukunft weisen.

---

[116] O. Cullmann, Die Reformbestrebungen des 2. Vatikanischen Konzils im Lichte der Geschichte der katholischen Kirche. In: ThLZ 92 (1967) 1–22.

2*

Acknowledgments

Nock, A.D. "The Spread of Christianity as a Social Phenomenon." In his *Conversion* (Oxford: Clarendon Press, 1933): 187–211. Courtesy of Yale University Sterling Memorial Library.

MacMullen, Ramsay. "Two Types of Conversion to Early Christianity." *Vigiliae Christianae* 37 (1983): 174–92. Reprinted with the permission of E.J. Brill. Courtesy of Yale University Seeley G. Mudd Library.

Skarsaune, Oskar. "The Conversion of Justin Martyr." *Studia Theologica* 30 (1976): 53–73. Reprinted with the permission of *Studia Theologica*. Courtesy of Yale University Divinity Library.

Daly, Lawrence J. "Psychohistory and St. Augustine's Conversion Process." *Augustiniana* 28 (1978): 231–54. Reprinted with the permission of Augustijns Historisch Instituut. Courtesy of Yale University Seeley G. Mudd Library.

Frend, W.H.C. "The Winning of the Countryside." *Journal of Ecclesiastical History* 18 (1967): 1–14. Reprinted with the permission of Cambridge University Press. Courtesy of Yale University Seeley G. Mudd Library.

Case, Shirley Jackson. "The Acceptance of Christianity by the Roman Emperors." *American Society of Church History, Papers*, Second Series, 8 (1928): 45–64. Courtesy of Yale University Seeley G. Mudd Library.

Ehrhardt, Arnold. "The Adoption of Christianity in the Roman Empire." *Bulletin of the John Rylands Library* 45 (1962): 97–114. Reprinted with the permission of the John Rylands University Library of Manchester. Courtesy of the John Rylands University Library.

Storch, Rudolph H. "The 'Eusebian Constantine.'" *Church History* 40 (1971): 145–55. Reprinted with the permission of the American Society of Church History. Courtesy of Yale University Seeley G. Mudd Library.

MacMullen, Ramsay. "Constantine and the Miraculous." *Greek, Roman, and Byzantine Studies* 9 (1968): 81–96. Reprinted with the permission of Duke University Press. Courtesy of *Greek, Roman, and Byzantine Studies.*

Gillman, Ian. "Constantine the Great in the Light of the Christus Victor Concept." *Journal of Religious History* 1 (1961): 197–205. Reprinted with the permission of the Association for the Journal of Religious History. Courtesy of *Journal of Religious History.*

Azkoul, Michael. "Sacerdotium et Imperium: The Constantinian Renovatio According to the Greek Fathers." *Theological Studies* 32 (1971): 431–64. Reprinted with the permission of *Theological Studies*, Georgetown University. Courtesy of *Theological Studies.*

Anastos, Milton V. "The Edict of Milan (313): A Defence of its Traditional Authorship and Designation." *Revue des études Byzantines* 25 (1967): 13–41. Reprinted with the permission of Association de l'Institut. Courtesy of Yale University Sterling Memorial Library.

Folkemer, Lawrence D. "A Study of the Catechumenate." *Church History* 15 (1946):286–307. Reprinted with the permission of the American Society of Church History. Courtesy of Yale University Seeley G. Mudd Library.

Turck, A. "Aux origines du catéchuménat." *Revue des sciences philosophiques et théologiques* 48 (1964): 20–31. Reprinted with the permission of Librarie Philosophique J. Vrin. Courtesy of Yale University Seeley G. Mudd Library.

Daniélou, Jean. "La Catéchèse dans la tradition patristique." *Catéchèse* 1 (1960): 21–34. Reprinted with the permission of *Catéchèse.* Courtesy of *Catéchèse.*

De Bruyne, L. "L'Initiation chrétienne et ses reflets dans l'art paléochrétien." *Revue des Sciences Religieuses* 36 (1962): 27–85. Reprinted with the permission of the Université de Strasbourg. Courtesy of Yale University Seeley G. Mudd Library.

Ferguson, Everett. "Baptismal Motifs in the Ancient Church." *Restoration Quarterly* 7 (1963): 202–16. Reprinted with the permission of Restoration Quarterly Corp. Courtesy of *Restoration Quarterly*.

Carpenter, H.J. "Creeds and Baptismal Rites in the First Four Centuries." *Journal of Theological Studies* 44 (1943): 1–11. Reprinted with the permission of Oxford University Press. Courtesy of Yale University Seeley G. Mudd Library.

Whitaker, E.C. "The History of the Baptismal Formula." *Journal of Ecclesiastical History* 16 (1965): 1–12. Reprinted with the permission of Cambridge University Press. Courtesy of Yale University Seeley G. Mudd Library.

Ferguson, Everett. "Inscriptions and the Origin of Infant Baptism." *Journal of Theological Studies*, n.s. 30 (1979): 37–46. Reprinted with the permission of Oxford University Press. Courtesy of Yale University Seeley G. Mudd Library.

Didier, J.-Ch. "Une adaptation de la liturgie baptismale au baptême des enfants dans l'Église ancienne." *Mélanges de science religieuse* 22 (1965): 79–90. Courtesy of Yale University Divinity Library.

Kirchner, Hubert. "Der Ketzertaufstreit zwischen Karthago und Rom und seine Konsequenzen für die Frage nach den Grenzen der Kirche." *Zeitschrift für Kirchengeschichte* 81 (1970): 290–307. Courtesy of *Zeitschrift für Kirchengeschichte*.